THE ROMAN EMPIRE F
TO CONSTAN1

The third century AD in the Roman Empire began and ended with Emperors who are recognised today as being strong and dynamic – Septimius Severus, Diocletian and Constantine. Yet the intervening years have traditionally been seen as a period of crisis. Beating off rivals and coping with immediate emergencies occupied a rapid succession of rulers. The 260s saw the nadir of imperial fortunes, with every frontier threatened or overrun, the senior Emperor imprisoned by the Persians, and Gaul and Palmyra breaking away from central control. It might have been thought that the Empire should have collapsed – yet it did not.

Pat Southern shows how this was possible by providing a chronological history of the Empire from the end of the second century to the beginning of the fourth; the emergence and devastating activities of the Germanic tribes and the Persian Empire are analysed, and a conclusion details the economic, military and social aspects of the third century 'crisis'.

She shows that many of the rulers of the third century – in particular Gallienus, whose reign has been called the lowest point in imperial history – have been significantly underrated. Far from being responsible for the problems of the era, it was thanks to their determination to consolidate that the Empire survived and was able to transform itself into the sacrosanct, absolutist, dynastic regime of the fourth century.

Lucidly written, fully illustrated and incorporating the latest scholarly findings, this work makes a fascinating but little-known period of imperial history accessible to both students and the general reader.

Pat Southern studied Ancient History and Archaeology at the Universities of London and Newcastle upon Tyne. She is the author of numerous books on Roman history, including *The Roman Cavalry* (with Karen Dixon, Routledge 1997), *The Late Roman Army* (with Karen Dixon, Routledge 2000), *Domitian – Tragic Tyrant* (Routledge 1997) and *Augustus* (Routledge 1998, paperback 2001).

THE ROMAN EMPIRE FROM SEVERUS TO CONSTANTINE

Pat Southern

London and New York

First published 2001
by Routledge
11 New Fetter Lane, London EC4P 4EE

Simultaneously published in the USA and Canada
by Routledge
29 West 35th Street, New York, NY 10001

Routledge is an imprint of the Taylor & Francis Group

© 2001 Pat Southern

Typeset in Garamond by Wearset, Boldon, Tyne and Wear
Printed and bound in Great Britain by
Biddles Ltd, Guildford and King's Lynn

British Library Cataloguing in Publication Data
A catalogue record for this book is available from the British Library

Library of Congress Cataloging in Publication Data
Southern, Pat
The Roman Empire from Severus to Constantine/Pat Southern.
p. cm.
Includes bibliographical references and index.
1. Rome–History–Severus, 193–235. 2. Rome–History–Period of military
anarchy, 235–284. 3. Rome–History–Diocletian, 284–305. 4.
Rome–History–Constantine I, the Great, 306–337.

DG298.S67 2001
937'.06–dc21
2001019483

ISBN 0–415–23943–5 (hbk)
ISBN 0–415–23944–3 (pbk)

CONTENTS

ILLUSTRATIONS

INTRODUCTION AND
ACKNOWLEDGEMENTS

This book attempts to document the changes in the Roman Empire between the end of the second century and the beginning of the fourth. The Roman world was an organic entity that evolved and changed all the time, but at varying rates and in different aspects; in the third century, changes accelerated, affecting many if not all areas of life in many if not all parts of the Empire, including areas beyond its frontiers.

The Empire of Severus already displayed several differences from that of the Julio-Claudians, but the Empire of Diocletian and Constantine shared hardly anything with its first-century counterpart – not surprising perhaps, given the timescale between the first and the fourth centuries. The events of this time-span can be compared to the evolving state mechanisms and social transformations that took place, for instance, in Britain between the Angevins and the Tudors, or in France between the Valois and the Bourbons. Time alone would have produced changes in the Roman world, without the particular catalysts that affected the Empire of the third century. Foremost among these catalysts was the relentless pressure on the northern frontiers and the efforts of the Roman government to contain it. The Rhine suffered badly until the frontier died; the Danube was brought back from ruin, rebuilt and strengthened, and it survived in an altered form. The pressure from the new and vigorous Persian Empire was great, but not as damaging, and though resources of men and money were continually marshalled to combat this threat, the choice was more often than not Rome's, for she was often the aggressor. As a broad generalisation, in the east, Rome attacked to pre-empt attacks; in the west and on the Danube, Rome reacted to attacks.

It is impossible to document all the changes in all the provinces and work the details into a continuous narrative, not least because the available information has alarming gaps. Compared to the previous two centuries the sources are meagre. There is no contemporary history beyond the first four decades of the third century, so the written sources fail as the Empire is most threatened. Many of the gaps in our knowledge have been filled in recent years by studies emanating from scholars all over the world, whose work has remedied the lack of interest in the period. An accumulation of details has been assembled, illuminating, sometimes at great depth, the Roman experience in the third century. A great deal of work has been devoted to the difficult chronology of third-century events, aided and supported by numismatic studies. There is an abundance of new and interesting work incorporating archaeological and climatic studies on the so-called barbarian societies that threatened the Empire, giving a clearer understanding of the interactions between the two cultures, Roman and tribal. The world of the tribesmen was changing too in the third century, and their contact with Rome was not always on a war footing. Without the tribal societies as fertile recruiting grounds, the Romans may not have been able to stem the tide of incursions and hit-and-run raids.

Though there is already a vast bibliography on the third century, there will always be a need for further studies on the period; as new facts emerge and new opinions are formed the history of the crucial period between the last of the Severans and the first of the Byzantines will be revised. This book should be regarded as an interim assemblage.

I am grateful (not an adequate term to express thanks) to Graeme Stobbs for producing the maps and plans, and to Trish Boyle for drawing the coins and sculptures. The photographs are reproduced courtesy of the Ny Carlsberg Glyptotek.

ABBREVIATIONS

AE	*Année Epigraphique*
Ant. Afr.	*Antiquités Africaines*
Ant. J.	*Antiquaries Journal*
ANRW	*Aufstieg und Niedergang der Römischen Welt*, Berlin: de Gruyter
AT	*Antiquité Tardive*
BAR	British Archaeological Reports
BG	*Bellum Gallicum* = Caesar *Gallic War*
BGU	*Berliner Griechische Urkunden (Aegyptische Urkunden aus den Königlichen Staatlichen Museen Berlin)*
BJ	*Bonner Jahrbücher*
BMC	*Coins of the Roman Empire in the British Museum*
BRGK	*Bericht der Römisch-Germanisch Kommission*
BSNAF	*Bulletin de la Société Nationale des Antiquaires de France*
CAH	*Cambridge Ancient History*
CIL	*Corpus Inscriptionum Latinarum*
CIS	*Corpus Inscriptionen Semiticarum*
CJ	*Codex Justiniani*
Class. Jnl.	*Classical Journal*
Cod. Th.	*Codex Theodosianus* = *The Theodosian Code and Novels and the Sirmondian Constitutions*, trans. by C. Pharr, New York: Greenwood Press
CQ	*Classical Quarterly*
EHR	*English Historical Review*
Ep. Stud.	*Epigraphische Studien*
FGrH	*Fragmente der Griechische Historiker*, ed. F. Jacoby, Berlin
FHG	*Fragmenta Historicorum Graecorum*, ed. C. Müller, Paris
HA	*Historia Augusta* = *Scriptores Historiae Augustae*
HAC	*Historia Augusta Colloquium*
HSCPh	*Harvard Studies in Classical Philology*
IGR	*Inscriptiones Graecae ad Res Romanas Pertinentes*
ILS	*Inscriptiones Latinae Selectae*, ed. H. Dessau, Berlin, 3 vols
JEA	*Journal of Egyptian Archaeology*

JRA	*Journal of Roman Archaeology*
JRGZM	*Jahrbuch des Römisch-Germanischen Zentralmuseums Mainz*
JRMES	*Journal of Roman Military Equipment Studies*
JRS	*Journal of Roman Studies*
JS	*Journal des Savants*
MEFRA	*Mélanges de l'Ecole Française de Rome* (*Antiquité*)
Migné	J.P. Migné (ed.) *Patrologia Latina*, Belgium, 221 vols
NC	*Numismatic Chronicle*
OCD	*Oxford Classical Dictionary* eds. S. Hornblower and A. Spawforth, Oxford University Press, 3rd ed., 1996
OGIS	*Orientis Graeci Inscriptiones Selectae*, ed. W. Dittenberger, Leipzig 1903–5, 2 vols
Origo	*Origo Constantini Imperatoris* = *Excerpta Valesiani*, ed. J. Moreau, Leipzig: Teubner, 1961
P. Dur.	*Excavations at Dura-Europos: final report V part I: the parchments and papyri*, eds C.G. Welles, R.O. Fink and J.F. Gilliam, New Haven: Yale University Press, 1959
P. Grenfell	*New Classical Fragments and other Greek and Latin Papyri*, eds B.P. Grenfell and A.S. Hunt, Oxford, 1897
P. Lond.	*Greek Papyri in the British Museum*, eds F.G. Kenyon and H.I. Bell, London, 1893–
P. Mich.	*Papyri in the University of Michigan Colection*, eds C.C. Edgar *et al.*, Ann Arbor: University of Michigan Press, 1931–date
P. Oxy.	*The Oxyrhynchus Papyri*, eds B.P. Grenfell *et al.* London 1898–date
P. Ryl.	*Catalogue of the Greek Papyri in the John Rylands Library, Manchester*, eds A.S. Hunt *et al.*, Manchester, 1911–52
P. Strassb.	*Griechische Papyrus der Kaiserlichen Universitäts- und Landesbibliotek zu Strassburg* (1912–)
PIR2	*Prosopographia Imperii Romani saec. I. II. III*, Berlin, 1932–
PLRE	*Prosopography of the Later Roman Empire*, Cambridge, 1971
REA	*Revue des Études Anciennes*
RIC	*Roman Imperial Coinage* (1923–)
RIU	*Die Römische Inschriften Ungarns*, Vols 1–4, Budapest: Akadémiai Kiado; Vol. 5, Bonn: Rudolf Habelt
RN	*Revue Numismatique*
SDHI	*Studia et Documenta Historiae et Iuris*
TAPhA	*Transactions of the American Philological Association*
ZPE	*Zeitschrift für Papyrologie und Epigrafik*
ZSS	*Zeitschrift der Savigny-Stiftung für Rechgeschichte* (*Romanische Abteilung*)

1

THE THIRD CENTURY
The nature of the problem

The third century opened and closed with the emergence of strong, vigorous Emperors victorious in civil war, each of whom survived long enough to consolidate his power and reorganise the state. Septimius Severus defeated his last rival and embarked on sole rule in 197. Diocletian's turn came nearly a hundred years after Severus in 284. Both made determined efforts to secure the succession, each in his own way, and not entirely successfully in the longer term. Both developed an autocratic style of government, and both relied upon a fabricated divinity and sacrosanctity of the Imperial household to bolster up their absolutist regimes. Both strengthened the frontiers and built or rebuilt fortifications. Finally, both reorganised the army in accordance with their own immediate needs and those of the state. Constantine took the work of his predecessors to its conclusion, creating a sacrosanct, absolutist, dynastic regime, but the changes that he crystallised had already begun under Diocletian.

The similarities between the upheavals of the 190s and the 280s, and the parallel responses of the reforming Emperors, are very beguiling, giving rise to the immediate impression that the Diocletianic reformation was inevitable if not preordained a century earlier. The superficial resemblance between Severus and Diocletian tends to overshadow the important developments of the century that separated them. The problem is that the considerable contributions made by other Emperors from 211 to 284 suffer from a comparative lack of self-advertisement. In many cases there was and is a complete dearth of reliable information, either because none existed at the time or what did exist has been lost, and on occasion the extant information has been subjected to deliberate falsification by contemporary or later authors. Even where some information is available it has been manipulated for ease of use, with the result that the emphasis has sometimes shifted or been distorted. The artificiality of modern chronological divisions in Imperial history imbues certain episodes with more weight than they perhaps deserve. Aurelius Victor pinpointed the assassination of Severus Alexander in 235 as a deeply significant event, before which all was reasonably well and after which things were irretrievably damaged. Following his lead, 235 is

1

still seen as a turning point, but in reality changes were never so sudden nor so starkly defined; they had longer histories and continuing developments that are somewhat masked by the acceptance of the single date used as a dividing line. It is true that the rapid turnover of Emperors after the reign of Severus Alexander compromised the Empire; continuity was shattered, and there was no time for the establishment of consistent or constructive policies. Beating off rivals, plugging gaps, and general emergency fire-fighting occupied much of each successive Emperor's time. These internal upheavals can be traced to several causes, all firmly established in the past. Not all of them were self-generated. Events outside the Empire stretched Roman ingenuity and resources to breaking point, with the consequence that the pressures on the population and army engendered dissensions of increasing magnitude. But other dates apart from 235 could be advocated as portents of change. The response of Marcus Aurelius to the Marcomannic wars led to changes in the military command structure and in social mobility; the elevation of the first equestrian Emperor, Macrinus in 217, was a tremendous departure from the normal routine. In the search for significant turning points in Roman history, it is often only the internal events that are utilised, but the Roman Empire did not exist in isolation, and was subject to external influences as well as internal ones. The most important external developments, with the most far-reaching consequences, were on the one hand the rise of the vigorous and aggressive Persian Empire after the change of dynasty in the early years of the third century, and on the other hand the expansion of power bases and the growth of the great tribal federations among the northern tribes beyond the Rhine and Danube. Rome had no control whatsoever over these factors, and could only respond to each attack or perceived threat, without being allowed the luxury of negotiation from a permanent and all-pervading position of superior strength. Gains in one sector were offset by loses in another.[1]

The 260s saw the nadir of the Empire's fortunes, with all the frontiers threatened or overrun, the senior Emperor a prisoner of the Persians, and Gaul and Palmyra breaking away from Rome under independent rulers of different status. Yet the Roman Empire did not collapse and die at that point. It survived because determined Emperors such as Gallienus, Aurelian and Probus threw their energies into reconstituting it. The first of these, the Emperor Gallienus, received a very bad press from the ancient authors, perhaps even from contemporaries, or those who followed immediately after him. He was not only blamed for causing the misfortunes of the Empire but also condemned for failing to pull it all back together. This was far from being the case, since Gallienus did make considerable efforts to prevent the Empire from falling apart any further, but there was no immediately obvious success that could be directly attributed to these efforts. Successive Emperors benefited from his work, without which it is likely that Aurelian and Probus would have faced a much more uphill struggle than they

2

actually did. The achievements of Gallienus are tremendously underrated, largely because of the overwhelmingly hostile sources which are not balanced by any remotely moderate information. Gallienus' modern champions cannot bring hard evidence to bear in his defence, but can put together inferences and nuances to attempt a reconsideration. Some of the changes that eventually transformed the Empire can be detected in their nascent forms in his reign, in the adaptations that he made to the army and the government, which he made out of necessity. Gallienus was forced to improvise because he was denied access to the full resources of the Empire and was threatened on several fronts at once. He adapted what was available, and in doing so he pointed the way to some of the solutions that Diocletian proposed, less than two decades later. Thus at the beginning, the middle, and the end of the third century, three separate Emperors set in motion political, military and social changes in response to a series of problems, and though their measures were dissimilar when examined in great detail, in broad general outline it could be said that first Gallienus and then Diocletian continued what Severus had begun, leaving Constantine to complete the whole. This simplistic statement demands qualification. It should not be taken to imply that from 197 onwards the Emperors of Rome moved unerringly in a direct line to their goal of absolutism, each making preconceived adjustments on the way, consciously striving towards what has been termed the new Empire of Diocletian and Constantine. The Empire had a limited repertoire of responses to the dangers it faced, and every adaptation or change was firmly rooted in the customs of the past. Though there was considerable continuity of government thanks to the maturing civil service of the Empire, long-term planning did not feature largely in Roman life, and it was not a luxury that was granted to the government of the third century. In many instances, rapid and decisive reactions were needed, leaving no time for consideration of the possible long-term consequences. Modern historians, with the benefit of hindsight, identify certain turning points where, for better or worse, fundamental changes became irrevocable. The blame for detrimental developments is sometimes attributed to unavoidable circumstances, and sometimes to the overweening ambition of tyrannical Emperors. Economic factors have been advocated as a reason for crisis and decline, along with stagnation of technique, the inevitable decline of a slave-owning society. Single factors such as these are highly unlikely to have led directly to decline, nor is any one fault likely to have led to changes in every sector of Imperial government and social life, since human existence consists of multiple, inextricably linked and mutually dependent aspects, some of which can shore up deficiencies in other areas. A decline in Roman living standards has been detected in the second or even in the first century, and it has been inferred that the crisis of the mid-third century was an inevitable consequence. It remains largely a matter of opinion, involving speculation as to whether things could have turned out any other way, if only a different

Emperor had ruled or a different response had been made to a given set of circumstances.[2]

The events of the third century are generally catalogued under the all-embracing heading of crisis, though the hyperbole implicit in this term has been challenged in favour of less emotionally charged descriptions such as 'transformation' or the more simplistic expression 'change'. This viewpoint should not be interpreted as a denial that the third-century crisis existed, along with all the attendant destruction, damage, pain and suffering. On the one hand, crisis does not necessarily embody disaster, and on the other, change is not necessarily a peaceful, anodyne process even if the end results are benign. Indeed, crisis as defined in the dictionary implies a turning point of some kind, as in a patient with a high fever, which reaches a critical point and then subsides, leaving the patient on the road to recovery. Crises are part of the natural process; it could be said that the Roman Empire simply lurched from crisis to crisis as part of its natural evolution. The argument becomes one of semantics rather than a historical discussion. It is the historian's task to decide whether the third-century crisis was more serious, longer in duration, or engendered more changes than any other crisis before or after.[3]

Considered individually, the various troubles which afflicted the Empire in the third century were not new, nor did they cease once the century ended. Military disasters, folk migrations, hit-and-run raids across the frontiers, external and internal rebellions, civil wars, bankruptcy, famines and plagues, were recurrent and familiar events in the history of Rome. One has only to utter the names of Crassus, who met defeat at Carrhae, or Varus, who lost three legions in Germany, and Fuscus, who lost troops on the Danube, to recall the fact that Roman armies did not always prevail over their adversaries. Folk migration, peaceful or belligerent, was not a new phenomenon engendered by the events of the third century. The invasions of Italy by the Celtic Cimbri and Teutones at the end of the second century BC were averted only after the energetic Gaius Marius had campaigned for six unrelenting years to prevent the devastation of the whole peninsula and even of Rome itself. If that was not the aim of the Celtic tribes, the Romans can be excused for thinking that it was, and were entitled to defend themselves. In other cases it is possible that the aggressive wars of the Romans precipitated folk movement. In the midst of his Gallic campaigns, Gaius Julius Caesar had to deal with a wholesale migration of the Helvetii, who burned their homes and looked for lands on which to resettle.[4]

These threats from external sources were encountered wherever Rome extended her influence. Contact with new peoples was not always smooth. Occasionally, perceived threats from neighbouring peoples were used as excuses for aggressive expansion, but the establishment of Roman rule was often prolonged, involving periods of bitter fighting. An enumeration of the names of some of the tribal leaders who rebelled against Rome, such as

Jugurtha, Vercingetorix, Civilis, Arminius, Tacfarinas, and Viriathus, serves to illustrate the constant need for vigilance and occasional adaptation on the part of the Roman state. Some of the revolts were led by men who had served in Roman armies, so these men were able to put their acquired knowledge to good use in fighting against Rome. As Rome evolved, so did the peoples with whom she came into contact; a mutual symbiosis and exchange of ideas ensured that Roman armies were not always at the foremost cutting edge of military science. Spectacular advances were offset by stagnation or reverses on both sides, in the third century as in any other period.[5]

Even within the Roman state, from the earliest times of the Republic, all was not harmonious and peaceful. The Social War of 90 BC, when the Italian allies of Rome at last demanded fair treatment instead of exploitation, and the revolt of Spartacus twenty years later, revealed that allies and slaves alike were capable of unified, active and effective dissent. There were self-generated internal threats as well, mostly in pursuit of personal gain or power; at all times the Romans themselves were prone to creating their own disruption and disaster. The civil wars between Caesar and Pompey, Octavian and Antony, and those of AD 69 and AD 192–3, were all waged for the mastery of the Roman world, and from each of them one man emerged victorious, able at last to turn to the repair of the internal and external damage that had resulted from the wars. Not infrequently, attacks from beyond the confines of the Roman world erupted while the high command was preoccupied with the civil wars. Sometimes it was the inability of the Emperor to deal with external troubles that precipitated the civil wars. The distinction is important in historical terms, but for contemporaries it hardly mattered whether external and internal wars broke out simultaneously or sequentially; either way resources and stamina were stretched and sometimes failed. In the reign of Domitian, for instance, war was waged in Germany against the Chatti probably at the same time as an offensive campaign was in operation in Britain. In both cases the Romans were the aggressors, supreme, unchallenged, confident of success, but the euphoria was short lived. There followed a series of disasters on the Danube, inflicted by the Dacians, who defeated two Roman armies and were not completely subdued even at the end of the war. Before he could follow up his victories properly, Domitian had to deal with a revolt led by Saturninus in Germany. The Emperor Domitian would probably have found a sympathetic audience in Gallienus or Aurelian, had they been able to compare notes. Fourth-century Emperors, too, would have found much common ground with their predecessors. Usurpations or attempts to usurp were nothing new in the third century, nor did they cease in the fourth century after Constantine defeated Licinius. Rome never did enjoy total supremacy over internal and external enemies. What was it, therefore, that made the third century different? It was not an isolated phase, totally out of line with what went before and what came after, but it cannot be defined merely by distilling the differences between the second century and the fourth, subtracting what we know of one epoch from what we know of another. The Empire rocked on its foundations in the third century, but it survived, admittedly in an altered form, for over a hundred years. The fourth century was one of recovery, the fifth was marked by final break up of the west. The establishment of the Gallic Empire, and of the kingdom of Palmyra, in the 260s, and the small British Empire of Carausius and Allectus, perhaps foreshadowed the fifth-century disintegration, but with important differences: in the third century the breakaway territories were Roman in all respects, governed by Roman officials, defended by Roman armies. Palmyra too was nominally Roman, and Odenathus was recognised as a Roman official by Gallienus, who was in no position to fight for supremacy. That was left for Aurelian, who fought it out with the successor of Odenathus, his wife Zenobia. In the fifth century, the emerging kingdoms were no longer truly Roman. Though Roman forms were preserved in law, civil government and language, allegiance to a wider Roman Empire was forgotten in the fifth century. In the third century the Empire was recovered and the separatist states were reintegrated.[6]

Throughout Roman history there was endemic disunity between the various component parts of the Republic and the Empire, latent for the most part, but on occasion requiring only a slight tilt of the scales to bring about a disaster, whether short or long term, superficial or intense. The Empire was never an entirely uniform, homogeneous entity. In the east, Romanisation did not penetrate right down to the grass-roots level of society, which had a much longer history behind it than Rome herself. The Syrian and Egyptian peasants, for instance, continued to use their own local dialects, though the language of the administration was Greek or Latin. Romanisation of the west was more intensive and widespread, but even in Spain and Gaul the local languages and customs were not totally absorbed to the point of obliteration. Provincial and regional differences across the Empire were often tolerated and even encouraged. Indigenous social and religious customs, artistic traditions and local languages were not deliberately effaced, unless some of those customs were in direct confrontation with Rome. The Empire was a conglomeration of territories, peoples, and military forces, corporately administered from regional centres under the aegis of the Emperor. By the third century, civil wars, military unrest and native rebellions, attempted coups, and internal squabbles in the Imperial household, had already highlighted the dissensions between the disparate elements that made up the Roman world. Some authors have traced this endemic disunity back to the early Empire, or the late Republic, or even to the foundations of Rome in the eighth century BC. If such is really the case, that the predisposition to disintegration was a congenital defect which Rome could not avoid, then it is nothing short of miraculous that the Empire staggered on as long as it did, and its protracted survival is a monument to the energy and pertinacity of the successive Emperors who repeatedly retrieved it from the brink of disaster, often at the expense of their own lives. It has been truthfully said that some Empires did not last as long as it took for Rome to fall.[7]

The crucial point is to define whether the Empire 'fell' at all. Those who argue that there was no such thing as the fall of the Roman Empire are constrained to point out the long-term continuities which underlie the gradual transformation, while those who argue for a collapse and regrowth highlight the differences. Both schools of thought still need to identify the point when the transformation or the collapse may have began, and scholars from both camps have alighted upon the events of the third century as the catalysts. Some of the ancient scholars detected a continuing decline after the reign of Marcus Aurelius. Gibbon thought that it all began to go wrong in the reign of Severus, largely because of the intransigent character of the Emperor himself rather than the milieu in which he found himself. This view presupposes that no one was able to halt the supposed downhill slide once Severus had set it in motion, which denies intelligence, determination or vigour to many of his successors. Our own view of the third-century crisis and its relationship, if any, to the eventual fall of Rome has undergone closer scrutiny and is subject to a greater diversity of opinion. From regional archaeological studies it seems that the various crises, political, military or economic, did not affect all places with the same intensity, nor was there a uniform perception of what was happening in the Roman world as a whole. In more modern times, the broad general picture has not been radically revised, but some of the details built into its fabric have been reconsidered, and there has been some reinterpretation of the political, social and economic factors in Imperial history, based on new pieces of evidence gleaned from various sources.[8]

SOURCES OF EVIDENCE

The lack of widespread, uniform evidence is the major problem that besets any study of the third century. Contemporary written evidence is not abundant, and ancient retrospective assessment is not renowned for its reliability. The narratives of Cassius Dio and Herodian, both of whom lived in the early third century, extend only as far as the 230s, but these two authors detected important changes for the worse when they compared recent times with the lives they had led in the past. Herodian looked back enviously to the period from Augustus to Marcus Aurelius, an era of universal peace, he claimed, without such a rapid succession of reigns or of military reverses, and free of turbulence among the civil population. Purists would take him to task under all those headings, because there very definitely were civil wars, military disasters, and civil upheavals during the supposed blissful period that Herodian describes, but the salient factor here is that he considered that the beginning of the third century was worse affected by all the problems that he listed than were previous eras. Dio shared the opinion that the changes he witnessed were deleterious, describing the age after Marcus Aurelius as all iron and rust, compared to the golden age of the adoptive Emperors.[9]

Other contemporary literary sources include legal texts, the panegyrics to the various Emperors, and the religious works of the Christians, much of which are concerned primarily with schisms and heresies and not with worldly events. There is a smaller corpus of purely literary works, such as the essays of Plotinus, probably written in the first half of the third century, and the poems of Nemesianus. These are not of foremost importance, but their existence testifies to the durability of traditional literary life in the Empire at a time when various ills and catastrophes had begun to make themselves felt. The very fact that writers had sufficient leisure to compose poems or send personal letters implies that not all parts of the Roman world teetered permanently on the edge of economic or military disaster.[10]

A selection of third-century legal texts have been preserved in the later law codes, such as the *Codex Theodosianus* (dated to 438) and the *Digest* of Justinian (534). These texts are obviously those which bore some relevance to the fourth- and fifth-century governments, with the inevitable result that much of the evidence for third-century legal activity will have been discarded and lost, so we are denied the main sources that might have elucidated the events of the third-century government. Nonetheless, the texts so far preserved, for example those of Julius Paulus, Ulpian and Papinian, provide certain glimpses of the problems of the third century. Occasionally the texts were edited to suit the needs of the later jurists, so once again authenticity is not firmly established beyond all doubt; but apart from epigraphic documents there are no better sources for legal matters of the third century.[11]

As for the extant body of panegyrics, the majority of the third-century Emperors either received no adulatory addresses, or if they did then the texts have not survived. With the exception of the laudatory address to Trajan, the panegyrics that do survive are all late third century, post-Diocletianic, and have a decided fourth-century flavour. Such speeches are by nature superlative and larger than life, so the facts as related in them must be reviewed with caution. Though they were designed to be heard by contemporaries, that is no guarantee of veracity; it is clear that at all periods of history, people are content to hear what they want to hear, and it requires fortitude or recklessness to oppose the dominant orthodoxy. Nonetheless, there are some common-sense facts to be garnered from the panegyrics, relevant to the turn of the third and fourth century. Wars and building programmes are not likely to have been invented from absolutely nothing, though they may have been tremendously exaggerated; but it would have been embarrassing to the most compliant of listeners to hear colossal lies of that nature.[12]

Religious authors of any persuasion usually had an axe to grind and were not above bending the facts a little to suit their own predilections. Whilst not necessarily concerned with documenting historical events, their attitudes speak louder than words. Lactantius, for instance, who lived from the mid-third century to about 320, witnessed all that went on from the reign of Gallienus to that of Constantine. He was a devout Christian and an ardent defender of the faith, so his particular enemies were those Emperors such as Decius and Diocletian, who persecuted Christians. Origen was another Christian author of the third century, but less of his work survives, and it is not so useful for documenting events. Eusebius' *History of the Church* and *Life of Constantine* provide more information, but Eusebius, who lived from *c.*260 to *c.*340, was concerned with wider themes and did not focus narrowly on the times through which he lived, except that as far as he and other Christians were concerned, the Emperor Constantine was by far the most important product of those times, the best thing, as it were, *before* sliced bread.[13]

Much use has been made of contemporary evidence contained in the valuable letters and discourses of Cyprian, Bishop of Carthage from about 248 until his martyrdom in 258. These writings are more immediate and spontaneous than the notorious fabrications of Herodian or the annalistic chronicles of Dio, and the intense detail that they contain is very welcome in a period normally devoid of minute particulars. Cyprian was an educated and highly experienced man, connected to a wide variety of correspondents in different parts of the Empire. He was well informed via his connections, and was level-headed enough to see causes and effects dispassionately, but not necessarily with detachment. He provides a glimpse of the whole Roman world instead of small parts of it, albeit for only a short time. Another valuable source is to be found in the fragmentary notes of P. Herennius Dexippus, whose main claim to fame is his organisation of the defence of Athens against the Heruli in 267–8. His lost works included a history of the Roman and Greek worlds down to about 270, and the *Scythica*, a history of the Gothic wars down to the reign of Aurelian. These texts survive only in fragments, culled from various sources. Some of them are quoted at second hand in the *Historia Augusta*, a source which is notoriously unreliable and fraught with difficulties.[14]

A considerable corpus of modern literature has grown up concerning the *Historia Augusta*. It has been dissected for its clues as to its authorship, its date, and its purpose. The work, as extant, purports to be an assemblage of Imperial biographies, continuing the tradition of Suetonius, by a collection of different writers, but from the nineteenth century onwards, beginning with Hermann Dessau, it has been argued that there was in fact only one author, whose scrupulousness and honesty are questionable. The consensus of opinion is that the work is fourth century, but which end of the fourth century has been hotly debated. Certain references to events of the reigns of Diocletian and Constantine, and dedications to these Emperors, have been used as evidence that the writer was a contemporary and that the work therefore belongs to the early fourth century, to a period just after Constantine, perhaps. Syme devoted much labour and ink to the *Historia Augusta*, and puts the date much later, at the end of the fourth century. Since there is never likely to be any proof of the date it must remain speculative, but it is an important point to try to establish because the date of the work puts it into context and reveals its likely bias and political sub-text. The sources of information used by the author are also important, but not yet proven beyond doubt. It has been shown that the lost work of Marius Maximus, the author of biographies from Nerva to Elagabalus, had a great influence on the biographer of the *Historia Augusta*, who quotes Maximus as one of his sources. This of course means very little, since the author quotes many sources, some of them imaginary, some of them real, and seemingly has no scruples about inventing information from any of his supposed sources. It was postulated that there was once some other common source, the so-called *Kaisergeschichte* or 'history of the Emperors', utilised by the author of the *Historia Augusta* and by other writers such as Zonaras and Zosimus, but this theory meets with less acceptance now than formerly. This ground has been dug over many times and it is not the purpose here to repeat or refute the conclusions reached by various scholars. The major problem must be underlined, of course. It is the authenticity of the information in the *Historia Augusta* that is in doubt. Which parts of it are to be accepted and which not? It is equally foolhardy to reject everything, ignoring the work altogether, as it is to give credence to everything without question. An evaluation is mandatory, but well nigh impossible in the absence of other corroboratory evidence. It is easy to fall into the habit of accepting all the facts that seem to support one's own ideas and to reject those which seem contradictory.[15]

In the later period, from the fourth to the sixth centuries, written sources are abundant but fragmentary and sometimes of dubious authenticity. Whilst contemporary written evidence is often the most telling, retrospective views can also add to our understanding. Later historians, not burdened with the dilemmas of living through the times about which they write, can offer dispassionate assessment of causes and effects, matters which are sometimes difficult to analyse at the time when events are actually occurring. On the other hand, authors of any period cannot help but be influenced by their own circumstances, so it is necessary to bear this in mind when evaluating retrospective analyses of the third century. In the second half of the fourth century, Aurelius Victor collected brief descriptions of the lives and reigns of the Emperors from Augustus to Constantius II. Another work, unfortunately anonymous, pretends to be an *Epitome* of these biographies, but in fact adds and subtracts so much that it is best to read it as a separate book. Another fourth-century compilation is the *Breviarum* of Eutropius, covering events up to 364, though its use for the third century is limited. Zosimus' *New History*, written in the late fifth century or perhaps the early sixth, covering the whole Empire from Augustus to 410, is more pertinent for events of the third century, but a considerable part of it is lost for the years after the reign of Probus, so for the reign of Diocletian other sources must be used.[16]

Apart from literary sources, Roman history is elucidated by a variety of other written methods. Epigraphy is a never-ending source, always susceptible to addition or revision when new inscriptions are discovered. Inscriptions cover a wide variety of topics, from proud Imperial proclamations to the humblest gravestone. It is not always possible to fit them into the known framework of Roman history, but on occasion an inscription can solve age-old problems, verify dates, or provide new perspectives. The personal inscriptions of all kinds provide an immediate link with the people and the age and place in which they lived, but for the Empire as a whole, an aggregate is needed to form any idea of trends and changes, an aggregate which is never free of gaps or problems. The epigraphic habit could be said to have declined in some parts of the Empire during the third century, but there is partial compensation in that several inscribed stones were used to construct city walls, a procedure which at least ensured the survival of most of them for future historians to read and debate.[17]

The bureaucratic leanings of the Roman government, both Empire-wide and local, ensured that day-to-day records of judicial proceedings, military affairs, and sometimes personal letters survived, most especially in the hot dry climates such as Syria and Egypt, where important collections of papyrological evidence have come to light. Even more than the inscriptions, these texts supply many insights into local administrative processes and personal lives, as well as the more cosmopolitan political events.[18]

Added to these sources of information there is the wealth of detail thrown up by archaeology, the only source that affords the same voice to native tribes and Romans alike, regardless of social status or wealth. Written sources and epigraphy speak for the educated upper classes or those with abundant wealth; archaeology speaks for almost everyone, but with a much more equivocal voice. It is not an exact science, and individual findings needs to be synthesised with many other individual results before meaningful conclusions can be drawn about trends or even about isolated events. Several new sites have come to light in the past few decades, and existing sites have been intensively studied, but the problems of establishing exact dates make it difficult to slot the documented histories of the sites into the larger historical framework. A ground plan by itself cannot necessarily define the uses to which a building was put, signs of burning may or may not be the result of nefarious action, and alterations to a building may depend upon whim as much as on historical circumstances. Finds of coin hoards or of valuable objects do not explain who owned these objects originally, whether they were part of a stolen haul or whether they were given as gifts, how the objects arrived at that particular place, why they were buried, nor why they remained buried. Archaeology is at one and the same time eloquent and mute, but cannot be ignored.[19]

THROUGH A GLASS DARKLY: LIMITATIONS OF THE EVIDENCE

All the types of evidence enumerated above form only a fragment of the overall pattern. Quite apart from the problems of veracity in the literary sources there is also the question of dubious semantics, lacunae, miscopyings in the various editions that have survived down the ages, and the unavoidable fact that some ancient writers had no firsthand knowledge of the things about which they wrote. For instance, everyday terminology, and especially military terminology, can be used misleadingly, either because the author did not recognise anachronisms, or could simply have been wrong – not because of a desire to confuse the issue, but because of a genuine misunderstanding. The way in which contemporaries used a particular word, precisely what an author meant by it, and what we now imagine that it means, are probably subtly or even appallingly different. As has been pointed out, the narrative histories, letters and speeches of the ancient authors for the most part represent a particular point of view: that of the upper classes; not everyone in the Empire is visible or audible in the historical record. The papyri and inscriptions allow conclusions to be drawn about life at a less elevated level, just as archaeology can explain how people lived, what they wore, what they ate, how they amused themselves, what they squabbled about, and how they died. With regard to all the types of evidence just described, the hackneyed phrase 'pieces of the jigsaw' is still a valid description for the disparate elements necessary for a reconstruction of the past; but for the third century the evidence is particularly fragmented, confusing and contradictory, so it is sometimes permissible to wonder if the pieces are really from the *same* jigsaw.

The third century witnessed momentous events and great changes. The problems faced by the early Empire and its later counterpart were not novel, hitherto unheard of developments. By the third century, Rome had seen it all before and in the fourth and fifth centuries she would see it all again. The significance of the third century lies in the fact that changes were taking shape not only within the Empire itself but also in the regions outside it – in the east where the Parthian Empire was replaced by the more vigorous Persian state, and in the vast northern territories beyond the Rhine and Danube where the tribesmen were more aware of Rome and where the great federations were steadily forming. These three major elements all reacted upon each other, generating conflict and co-operation, advances and declines, some successful modifications and some disastrous adjustments.

After the assassination of Severus Alexander in 235, the attacks on the frontiers, the movements of the tribes, the internal unrest, the revolts, usurpations, secessions and civil wars, financial and economic dilemmas, famines and plagues occurred in rapid succession, often contemporaneously, and sometimes across several provinces, leaving very few areas of the Empire completely unaffected by any one or all of these events. The problems of the third century were familiar, but intense and constant; the responses to them were mostly conventional, sometimes experimental, occasionally revolutionary, and the cumulative effect of these responses slowly turned the High Empire into the late Empire, the Principate into the Dominate, and the hegemony of Rome into that of Constantinople.

2

EMPERORS AND USURPERS
180–260

EMPIRE WITHOUT END

The Empire that Severus inherited was the product of several centuries of territorial expansion, accompanied by a continually evolving administration to deal with the steady accretion of provinces and peoples. The machinery of civilian government and military organisation had been tried and tested, sometimes with success and sometimes with a conspicuous lack of it; but lack of success was not always entirely detrimental. In adverse situations Rome was reasonably flexible and capable of improvisation, adaptation and change. By such a process the Republic had been transformed into the Principate, and in the course of the third century the Empire progressed from the Principate into the Dominate.

All new conquests brought Rome into contact with new peoples, altering the balance of power, sometimes creating the need for wider or deeper defence of the new boundaries, which in turn often ended in outright annexation. Rome's previous expansion had been undertaken for a variety of reasons. Sometimes the prime factors were undisguised imperialism, greed and opportunism, but on occasion Rome's remorseless Empire-building can be classified under the heading of the search for viable and safe boundaries. The Empire reached its greatest extent in the first decades of the second century AD in the reign of Trajan. After his death in 117 the period of aggressive expansion came to an end. There were some exceptions to this generalisation, but territorial acquisition after the reign of Trajan consisted for the most part of unrealised projects, or actual additions which were either abandoned or lost.

THE DEVELOPMENT OF FRONTIERS

It was Trajan's successor, the Emperor Hadrian, who called a halt to endless conquest. He immediately abandoned the recent acquisitions north of the Danube, and in the east, and he withdrew from a costly war with Parthia.

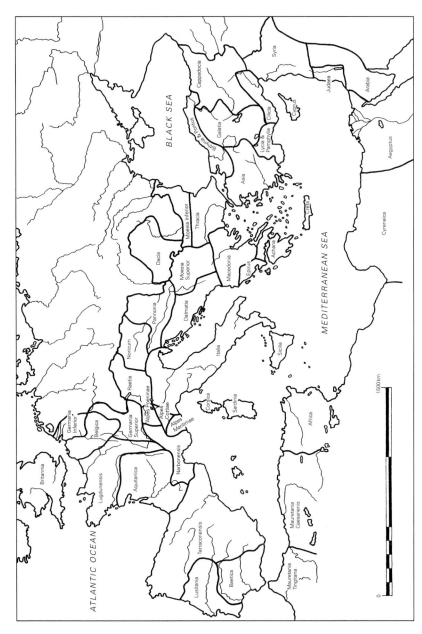

Figure 1 The provinces of the Roman Empire in the second century. (Drawn by Graeme Stobbs.)

He suffered considerable opprobrium as a result of his non-expansionist policy, but he was determined and consistent in his approach. He no doubt considered that the potential profits from newly conquered lands would be offset by the costs of administration and defence, perhaps even overstretching the resources of the Empire as a whole. On his accession, Hadrian had many reasons to call a halt to the war in the east. First and foremost he needed to secure his own position. His adoption by Trajan and his succession as Emperor were not welcomed by everyone. The details are murky but the few known facts suggest that Hadrian had only an insecure hold on his power in 117. One of his first acts was to execute four Senators, who may have been involved in a plot to remove him. It was not an auspicious start to his reign, so it would have been suicidal to embroil himself in a Parthian war at this juncture. At first, his withdrawal from the eastern conquests was probably not considered such a heinous crime by his imperial entourage, or by his opponents at Rome, because at first it would not be thought irreversible. What Rome had done before she could do again, at a more opportune time. However, Hadrian soon made it clear that he did not intend to take advantage of a more opportune time on any front. He set about enclosing the Empire, drawing firm lines around it, halting the continual absorption of new lands, opting instead for consolidation of what he thought Rome could successfully administer. It was the first time since Augustus' day that an Emperor had so resolutely turned his back on the concept of *imperium sine fine*, 'power without end', in both the temporal and territorial sense. After losing three legions in Germany in AD 9, Augustus advised his successor Tiberius not to expand the Empire any further. Tiberius complied, but the rest of the Julio-Claudians and then the Flavians reverted to the ideology of conquest. Hadrian was the first to make such a firm indication that the Roman world had reached an optimum size, more than enough for one man and his bureaucratic staff to administer. From the mid-second century onwards much of the Empire was enclosed within physical running barriers, or at least within plainly marked and protected boundaries which divided Roman territory from that of the various peoples who were now excluded from the benefits (or rapacity) of the *pax Romana*.[1]

There is still considerable argument among historians and archaeologists as to the prime purpose of the frontiers. Some scholars are of the opinion that the frontier lines, especially the physical barriers, were intended to be absolutely impermeable, and that all movement was halted. Others deny this, arguing that the Romans adopted a more flexible approach, in which movement and trade into and out of the Empire was directed, channelled, and watched. No ancient source states explicitly what the frontiers were intended to do, apart from Eutropius' somewhat platitudinous statement that in Britain, Hadrian was the first to build a wall to separate the Romans from the barbarians. The inevitable result is that argument about Roman frontiers rests ultimately on informed opinion and very little else. In addition to the lack of definite knowledge about any single frontier system, it is possible that the frontiers were custom-built, and that what was good for one province would not necessarily work in another. There is also the possibility that the Roman high command operated in slightly different ways at different times in the frontier zones. The one constant factor is that nobody thought of any truly radical alternative once the frontiers were established; Antoninus Pius, Marcus Aurelius, Septimius Severus, Diocletian, Constantine, and Valentinian all repaired frontier works, or established new ones in different locations on much the same pattern as before. In appearance the frontiers may have differed somewhat, and fort plans underwent some changes, but in essence the concept was the same.[2]

Hadrian's enclosure of the Empire was not a purely defensive measure, initiated under duress, nor did it obviate the need for trans-frontier campaigns or occasional adjustments of the boundaries. Antoninus Pius made some territorial advances in Britain and in Germany, but he did not depart from the established pattern. He built new frontiers exactly like those of his predecessor, the Antonine Wall in Scotland and the so-called outer *limes* in Germany. The latter survived until the third century, but the northern British conquests were quickly abandoned, and Hadrian's Wall became the frontier once more. Despite the construction of new frontiers to protect territory just taken over, and the occasional readjustment of boundaries, the Romans were not displaying signs of weakness, cowering behind their walls. Modern scholars have accused the post-Hadrianic Emperors of inertia and lack of initiative, because they did nothing to alter the system. But it is more likely that the Romans considered that there was no need to alter anything; as the saying goes, if it ain't broke, don't fix it. The Romans were definitely in the ascendancy when they erected the frontiers and remained so, even when wars were waged on more than one front. The system worked; in most provinces the hinterland could be demilitarised and peacefully settled, and the frontiers fulfilled their tasks for over a hundred years. They were not breached until they were overpowered by the onslaughts of the mid-third century, and even then, despite the demonstration that running barriers were not proof against determined assaults, the notion of frontier lines was not entirely abandoned.[3]

PRELUDE TO THE THIRD CENTURY

The third century crisis did not simply spring upon the world fully fledged and unexpected. Its roots obviously lay in the preceding century or centuries, each strand traceable to some point in the history of Rome, or in events in the non-Roman world. The quest for the origins of the crisis can be pushed as far back as any historian wishes, beginning with Romulus in the eighth century BC, but a useful starting point is the reign of Marcus

Aurelius, the breeding ground of the civil war that brought Septimius Severus to power. During Marcus' reign, all the afflictions of the third century began to surface, and many of the measures taken to deal with them provided a working basis for the Emperors who faced the worst of the crises, from Severus Alexander to Diocletian.[4]

After the death of Antoninus Pius several problems began to weigh very heavily on the state. By 162 the Parthian regime had gained enough strength to menace Rome by a potentially threatening interest in Armenia; after four years of war Roman arms prevailed, but almost immediately after the conclusion of peace in the east, there was a serious invasion of the Empire by tribesmen from across the Danube, resulting in prolonged warfare in that region. While the northern war was in progress, Avidius Cassius, a close personal friend of the Emperor and governor of the whole of Asia, led a tragic but brief revolt. He thought, mistakenly, that Marcus was dead, and therefore had himself declared Emperor. He had an ideal opportunity to take over the Empire, since he was already governor of the whole of Asia, and most of the eastern provinces declared for him; he took over Egypt, where he could strangle most of Rome's corn supply, but his rule ended with his death after three months and six days.[5]

Marcus' problems were not all military. Beginning probably in the 160s, there was a recurrent plague of unknown origin which carried off innumerable civilians and soldiers. As an undercurrent to all these problems, there was also the threat of bankruptcy, which Marcus partially alleviated by selling the Palace furniture and his personal valuables; the cash raised was rather less important than the cosmetic value of the noble gesture. Marcus' renunciation of worldly goods made his taxes slightly more palatable. Through all these simultaneous difficulties, the Empire displayed a great resilience. The Roman world survived in much the same state as it had begun, having acquired one or two innovative ideas in the process.[6]

Much of Marcus' governmental policy derived from the established practice of his predecessors. He brought to fruition developments which were already in evidence, but he initiated a new order and rationalisation in almost everything, nearly to the point of cold logic, sternly applied. There was an increasing regimentation of social distinctions, but without the snobbery that sustained the Roman world. Low birth was no longer an obstacle to promotion. For Marcus Aurelius social rank did not depend upon birth or noble ancestry, but was attached to the civilian or military posts held by each individual. He recognised talented people whenever he encountered them, and appointed them to posts best suited to their abilities, elevating them to the necessary social status to permit them to fulfil their tasks without offending too many people's sensibilities. He was perhaps the first Emperor to select and foster capable people, regardless of their origins, on such a large and consistent scale. Other Emperors had been known to promote a few individuals; indeed Augustus himself had laid the foundations for social mobility, but in a far more restricted sense. In the early days, promotion was rationed, and was not so rapid; it had to be earned and could be taken away as well as bestowed. Marcus Aurelius chose as wisely as he could, but broadened his base of likely candidates, and steadily built up a circle of government officials and army officers who blended meritocracy with aristocracy. He avoided offending the senators by deferring to their opinions, and keeping them informed of his ideas and policies. Eminently reasonable himself, he seems not to have provoked unreasonable reactions from the senators, while he promoted non-senators by adlecting them to the Senate, rewarding them for their services with legionary commands and in some cases with the consulship.[7]

The equestrian order was endowed with a new hierarchy, so hard-working or fortunate individuals could now progress from *egregius*, to *perfectissimus*, and then to *eminentissimus*. More administrative posts were created for equestrians, especially procuratorial offices. The Imperial civil service was expanded; the finance minister, *a rationibus*, was given a higher salary and an assistant. The *consilium principis*, previously an advisory body, was granted official status, and its members received the title *consiliaris*. The city prefect was given wider juridical powers, and the Praetorian Prefects were made responsible for keeping order in Italy. Perhaps the most far-reaching development was Marcus' employment of military officers, no matter what their origins may have been, whose valuable and visible expertise best suited them to ordinary or special commands. Equestrians, provincials, and even sons of freedmen, could rise to high office via the army, and then to even higher appointments through the equestrian and senatorial posts to which Marcus promoted them. Avidius Cassius was an equestrian, the descendant of an enfranchised provincial family, who eventually rose to the extraordinary post of governor of all of Asia. Publius Helvius Pertinax was the son of an ex-slave; after a varied early career, he joined the army, rose from the ranks, and became consul in 175. One of the most famous examples of an extraordinary career is that of Marcus Valerius Maximianus, an equestrian who was adlected into the Senate with the rank of praetor, and then given legionary commands in Pannonia, Dacia, and Moesia. In the reign of Commodus he was consul *in absentia* while he commanded a legion in Africa. During the Danubian wars, Maximianus was very active in a variety of special roles, including command of a fleet operating on the Danube to bring supplies to the Pannonian armies.[8]

When wars were in progress, special commands were necessary, sometimes giving the postholder great power and freedom of action. Inevitably, a corps of military men with wide experience developed in the process, men whose specialist knowledge and experience was very valuable. The careers of such men were almost exclusively military, involving only brief experience of civilian government posts. The separation of military and civil careers has been traced back to Hadrian or even further, not without dispute, but whatever the precise date when it began, from the Danubian wars of Marcus Aurelius the rift between the two career structures was much more pronounced. The growth of specialisation in the army made for a greater professionalism, but it also produced a few justly famous individuals with a preponderant influence over large armies; moreover, if those individuals were sent to several different provinces as military commanders they could build up a following of thousands of soldiers whose loyalties might be called upon in the future. Many of the soldiers would never see the Emperor except on coins or in sculptures, but they would see much of, and remember, their commanders, who would be far more real to them. Some of them they would hate, but others they would admire, and if it came to a choice between a distant man in Rome whose head was on the coins and an officer on the spot who could provide immediate benefits like ready cash and the promise of more in the future, it would probably not trouble the collective conscience too greatly to transfer allegiance to the man with the money. Defence of the Empire called for experienced men and large numbers of professional and well-trained soldiers, but the combination could be very dangerous if either or both of these parties conceived a desire for mastery of the Roman world.[9]

This was one of the problems of Empire which was never satisfactorily solved – the succession, and the overwhelming power of the army in deciding who should rule. Transfer of power had always been fraught with danger ever since the days of Augustus, and the decisive power of the army had made itself felt very early, but in the course of the third century military force in creating and destroying Emperors was much more brutal and overt. Numerous claimants to imperial power presented themselves, often simultaneously. Success did not guarantee survival; there were sixteen Emperors between 235 and 253, and the longest reign endured for five and a half years. The roots of this endemic disunity can be found in the very efforts of Marcus Aurelius to secure the succession, whereby he bequeathed to the world his son Commodus, and then civil war.[10]

THE REIGN OF COMMODUS

The succession of Commodus was the first true hereditary succession since Vespasian handed down the Empire to his sons Titus and Domitian. When the latter was assassinated in September 96, the Senate chose the aged and short-lived Emperor Nerva, who adopted his successor Trajan. From then on, the succession was by adoption rather than by strict dynastic means. Marcus Aurelius owed his Imperial status to Hadrian, who noticed him while he was still a teenager. Initially the childless Hadrian adopted as his son Lucius Ceionius Commodus, who took the new name Lucius Aelius Caesar. Unfortunately Lucius expired before Hadrian, leaving an eight-year-old son. In order to provide an immediate successor and also secure the transfer of power down to the next generation, Hadrian adopted Titus Aurelius Fulvius Boionius Antoninus, better known as Antoninus Pius, with the proviso that he in turn should adopt the son of Lucius Ceionius Commodus, who took the name Lucius Verus, and also the 17-year-old Marcus Annius Verus, better known as Marcus Aurelius. When Antoninus Pius died, these two boys both succeeded him, without faction or personal rivalry. They shared power equally, both adopting the title Augustus. Five years later, Marcus Aurelius' two young sons, Commodus and Annius Verus, were granted the title Caesar. Sharing power was not a new idea in principle. In the first century, Titus had been given the title Augustus along with his father Vespasian, but in this case it was quite unequivocal that the senior partner was Vespasian. Even if the driving force behind the Flavian dynasty in the later years was Titus himself, he operated through Vespasian as figurehead. Marcus Aurelius' measure was something rather different, taking the idea one step further. Just as Hadrian had indicated that the Empire was quite large enough, and the way forward was to consolidate and administer what it was feasible to hold, Marcus realised that in time of war or crisis the task was too large for one man. Consequently he persuaded the Senate to accept Lucius Verus as his equal. They were both invested with imperial power, and undertook independent military commands. The designated junior partners were Marcus' two sons, who were each of them given the title of Caesar. With two Augusti and two Caesars, the Empire seemed secure for the next two generations, and in this proto-Tetrarchy of two senior and two junior rulers there was an obvious precedent for Diocletian to follow. Diocletian may have arrived at the same system independently and applied it differently, but it was not a completely novel idea.[11]

Lucius Verus campaigned in the east against Parthia from 162 to 166, in theory as supreme commander but in practice heavily reliant upon his subordinate officers. At the close of the Parthian war there was a brief respite before the tribes from north of the Danube rushed into the Roman provinces, even reaching northern Italy. Lucius Verus and Marcus Aurelius set off to meet the threat together in the autumn of 167. They met with success, but Verus died, probably of the plague, in 169. Thereafter, Marcus ruled alone for several years, because there was no suitable candidate whom he could elevate or adopt to share power with him, and his son Commodus was still too young. As soon as Commodus reached the age of 16, he was made Augustus with his father. It was the only way to avoid jealous rivalries and even civil war. However unsuitable Commodus may have been, he was still young and it would perhaps be possible to influence and educate him, and he had the enormous advantage of being the undoubted heir. It was necessary to declare who would be the next Emperor in order to obviate speculation and to try to pre-empt potential usurpers. The example of Avidius Cassius, once a friend of the Emperor, showed that no one was immune to the prospect of becoming Emperor, and there would be many more like him, who were not necessarily friends, and who commanded soldiers and the resources to support a revolt.[12]

So it was for lack of anything better that Commodus became Emperor. When Marcus Aurelius died in 180, Commodus brought the Danubian wars to a close by diplomatic means. He arranged a treaty with the Marcomanni and Quadi, whereby the tribesmen contributed men for the Roman army. Although he has been accused of negligence because he did not carry on fighting, the peace that Commodus negotiated was a lasting one, not broken by the tribesmen for several years. There seems to have been more trouble with small-scale raids than serious attempts at warfare; a well-known series of inscriptions records the construction of watch towers to control the movements of robbers (*latrones*). There was no serious neglect of the frontiers or the army, and the provinces did not suffer under Commodus.[13]

His reign (180–93) began reasonably well but descended into farce and finally into terror, ending in the Emperor's assassination by the Praetorian Prefect and the palace chamberlain. Theoretically, Commodus ought to have been a model ruler. He was the son of a just and moderate Emperor who was as much a philosopher as a soldier and statesman, and almost from birth Commodus had been schooled to take over the Empire. Marcus Aurelius was the first Emperor since Flavian times to have a son of his own for whom the succession was clearly marked out. The precedent was not exactly a happy one, since the wily but wise Vespasian had designated his two sons to succeed him, and the unfortunate result of that master-plan was the very brief reign of Titus followed by the longer and infinitely more infamous reign of Domitian. Thus even a peaceful succession by a natural heir did not always guarantee peaceful success. The adoptive Emperors, Nerva, Trajan, Hadrian, Antoninus Pius, and Marcus Aurelius were for the most part sane and reasonable men, and whilst designation of an heir by adoption did not necessarily ensure a smooth succession, the choice of successor was perhaps marginally more objective than the automatic parental recommendation, since the selection was made from among mature young men who had no stiflingly close or emotional family ties. Marcus has been blamed for allowing Commodus to succeed him, but if he had designated someone else while Commodus was growing up, it is possible that the civil war of 193 would simply have occurred in 180 instead, as supporters of the natural heir and the successor nominated by the army fought it out among themselves. The era of the adoptive Emperors of the second century was in retrospect considered a golden age, and everything that came after was, as Dio described it, all iron and rust. There were alternatives to succession by natural or adoptive heirs, ranging from bribery and corruption, through the acclamation of a candidate by strong-willed soldiery, to full scale civil war. The third century was to become familiar with all of these methods of Imperial succession.[14]

THE RISE OF SEVERUS

Commodus had every opportunity to absorb and learn from his father and from events, and he inherited a circle of reliable advisers with considerable cumulative experience. Little by little he ignored or divested himself of these valuable tools of government, promoting his own personal and notorious favourites such as Perennis and then Cleander. Even allowing for the hostility of the sources it is apparent that by the end of his reign there were grave problems. Severus would be an interested observer of the entire reign and like everyone else he would have to curb any overt opposition unless he wished to ruin his career before it had begun. He entered the Senate at the age of 28 during Marcus' reign, and plodded dutifully through the normal appointments. He was quaestor in Rome in 170, and then served in Baetica, Sardinia and Africa. He was legionary legate of *IV Scythicae* in Syria, with Helvius Pertinax as governor. From 186–9 he governed Gallia Lugdunensis. His knowledge of the Empire was reasonably wide, but his career was not spectacular, and he had not seen much military action. He reached the consulship in 190 at the age of 45. It was not such a signal honour, since there were 25 consuls in that same year, which means that his experience of the office and all that it entailed would have been limited to about a month or even less. There were historical precedents for a large number of consuls in one year, on occasions when the Emperor wished to honour some of his supporters who had remained loyal in dangerous times, or when there was a dearth of eligible candidates for the proconsular offices that required some experience and the appropriate rank. Severus' appointment, however, fell under neither of these headings. According to Dio he was only one among many who were appointed by Cleander, and Dio was in a good position to know since he was in Rome at the time. He indicates that Cleander sold offices for personal profit. To varying degrees, this is no doubt true of nearly all influential members of the imperial household at any time, though in this particular instance it is not known for certain whether Severus bought his way into the consulship. It hardly matters. There were more portentous things to come, which made the purchase of a month's consulship seem quite unimportant.[15]

The influence of Cleander

In 190, Cleander was the most influential man in Rome. He had started out as a slave, but by a series of unrecorded events he had secured a position in the imperial household of Marcus Aurelius, ultimately achieving the status of imperial freedman. As Commodus' chamberlain he already possessed considerable power, but he acquired even more when the equally influential Praetorian Prefect, Perennis, was executed. There had always been many opportunities for the Praetorian Prefects to gain and maintain power, especially if the Emperor was weak or simply disinterested. Historically there had been the notorious example of Sejanus, but he had been removed and supplanted by the other Prefect (there were always two Praetorian Prefects, until the third century, when on occasion powerful individuals enjoyed sole power). For many years after the removal of Sejanus, succeeding Prefects failed to reach such an influential position, and so life went on as before. When Perennis was eliminated, Cleander stepped into the vacuum, but in a different guise. He was not a military man, he had no particular skills as a jurist or as a financial expert, and he had no noble lineage to give him a head start in the social hierarchy, but he managed to subordinate the two succeeding Praetorian Prefects to himself and rapidly became the fount of all power. Commodus was said to have given him a new title 'a pugione' or 'the dagger', indicating his position of supremacy; in modern parlance he would be called chief of security. It implied that he was on the most intimate terms with the Emperor. Selling offices and appointments would be the least part of his influence. If he had the power to elevate and promote, then he also had the power to terminate careers and even lives. Anyone who wanted to get on in life would have to know and be acceptable to Cleander.[16]

Dislike and distrust of him reached the inevitable conclusion. He had alienated too many people, with the result that even well-balanced, sane men who normally distanced themselves from politics and government were by now very disillusioned and willing to listen to ideas for removing him. He was finally brought down by means of an engineered food shortage for which he was held responsible. The Roman mob rioted on cue, and no one did very much to quell the riots. Commodus panicked, frightened by the prospect of an uncontrollable populace and the fact that the man upon whom he had come to rely was now powerless to help. He had Cleander executed. The lesson would not be lost on Severus. Commodus was justly criticised for ignoring the advice of his counsellors, and for allowing his subordinates to gain too much influence over him. Towards the end of his reign his disinterest in the Empire had tipped over into a detachment from reality, but long before then he had failed to curb the increasing power of his favourites and allowed them to get out of hand. It had been very clear to Augustus, and it would now be increasingly clear to Severus, that the Emperor must be the sole source of power and patronage, and that he must control his associates with a finely tuned sensitivity. On the one hand he must not allow them to become too powerful, but on the other he must not stifle all hope of advancement. He must somehow combine social mobility with a recognisable hierarchy whereby there were honourable and credible careers to be found.[17]

The end of Commodus

The years following the death of Cleander were very anxious ones for senators and equites alike. The Emperor was unpredictable and no one felt safe.

The Praetorian Prefects were removed, first Regillus and then Julius Julianus, after the latter had enjoyed a brief period as sole Prefect. Dio lists some of the other victims, saying that Commodus killed both men and women, but he gives no names, saying that it would be far too tedious to list them all. He probably did not exaggerate. Senators were surrounded by *clientelae*, drawn from all ranks from the city and from the rural population, from the provinces as well as from the city of Rome and from Italy, so their influence could therefore be very extensive, and to uproot this influence and avoid the possibility of a resurgence of power it was necessary to eradicate the entire circle of each senatorial victim. This may be what Dio implies when he says that many other people were killed as well as senators, including women.[18]

The activities of the Emperor became more and more bizarre. Identifying himself with Hercules, he devoted himself to gladiatorial pursuits, performing in public. Commodus had clearly tired of being Emperor. From birth, almost, he had been schooled for his task with all the noble tenets that his father could drum into him, without the luxury of free time and play. He had lived in a moral strait-jacket for a long time. Perhaps if Commodus had been allowed to enjoy a riotous youth without the ever-present knowledge that he would one day be responsible for the Empire, he would have got it all out of his system before he succeeded as Emperor. At the end of his reign the public gladiatorial performances were compulsory viewing. Senators were not given the option of boycotting the shows. They were even obliged to chant in unison, hailing Commodus as Lord, First Among Men, Victorious, and so on. At one performance, Commodus cut off the head of an ostrich, waving it at the senators as if to suggest that he could just as easily cut off the heads of everyone else. Dio describes how he took refuge in chewing laurel leaves so as to disguise the fact that he was laughing – a potentially fatal reaction if the Emperor happened to see it.[19]

This ridiculous state of affairs was lightened a little by the appointment of Quintus (some sources call him Marcus) Aemilius Laetus as one of the Praetorian Prefects. He hailed from north Africa, and seems to have been instrumental in appointing his fellow countrymen to posts on the northern frontiers – among them Septimius Severus, who was made governor of Upper Pannonia despite his lack of experience of the Rhine and Danube areas – or in the command of a fairly large province with an army. It was a fortuitous appointment. The garrison of Upper Pannonia comprised three legions, and the route into Italy was quite short. It was a time of great insecurity for everyone, and it was clear that sooner or later something momentous was going to happen. All the sources agree that Severus was extremely ambitious, and he almost certainly noted with interest all the potential opportunities when he took up his post in 191, even if he merely planned how to survive in a change of regime.[20]

It is not known how far in advance Laetus planned the assassination of

Commodus, nor is it known in whom he confided. The bald facts are that on New Year's Eve, 192, he and the palace chamberlain Eclectus murdered the Emperor, and shortly afterwards Publius Helvius Pertinax was proclaimed in his place. Dio and Herodian insist that the assassination was an *ad hoc* decision as Laetus seized his chance, and Pertinax was taken completely by surprise when he was declared Emperor. The *Historia Augusta*, normally suspect, is somewhat more credible in this instance, implying that Pertinax was party to the plot all along. Otherwise the audience is asked to believe in the unlikely scenario that Laetus killed Commodus in a fit of pique or panic, and then racked his brains looking around for someone who would be willing to take on the Empire.[21]

The reign of Pertinax

Pertinax was 67 years old, a man of wide experience. He started life as the son of a slave, and began his career in the army. In Marcus' reign he had been elevated first to equestrian rank and then adlected into the Senate. He had been governor of Lower Moesia, Upper Moesia, Dacia and Syria. He was a sterling example of the social mobility that had begun with the reign of Augustus. In the early years of the Empire it had been possible to rise from lowly origins to consul within three generations; Pertinax rose from the humblest rank to Emperor in one lifetime. The Senate accepted him without demur, probably frightened and perhaps unanimously deciding that any-thing was better than Commodus. All the usual titles were voted to Perti-nax, including *pater patriae*, 'father of his country', and his wife and son were offered the titles Augusta and Caesar. These last honours Pertinax rejected on their behalf. He succeeded in reconciling the Senate to the Praetorian Prefect Laetus, explaining that in obeying Commodus, Laetus did not necessarily condone his actions or behaviour. The Praetorian Guard itself was another matter. The men did not trust Pertinax. He was well known as a martinet, and the last thing the Guard wanted was an Emperor who made them toe the line. He had severely punished a rebellion in Britain when the soldiers there proclaimed him Emperor. Now, ironically, he was positively encouraging the Praetorians to do under coercion the very thing that he had previously punished the British soldiers for doing voluntarily. A payment of 12,000 sesterces per man assisted the Praetorians to make up their minds, but for an anxious moment it seemed that it would not work. At the cere-mony to take the oath of loyalty to Pertinax, some of the soldiers decided that a senator called Triarius Maternus suited them rather better, but their attempt to create a new Emperor failed, largely because their chosen candidate fled, minus his clothes.[22]

There was no bloody reprisal. Pertinax had other troubles, which he attacked in a series of common-sense measures. First he rid himself of the motley collection of slaves and hangers-on in the Imperial household, selling

Figure 2 Coin of Pertinax wearing a laurel wreath. Brass sestertius from the Rome mint dated to 193. (Drawn by Trish Boyle.)

all those slaves whom he considered to be superfluous, but according to Herodian a few concubines returned to the palace by the back door. In the Senate, Pertinax tried to undo some of the damage that Commodus and Cleander between them had done to various individuals. He took steps to reinstate exiles, and to assist the families of those who had been condemned or killed. His major problem was lack of funds, but he found the wherewithal to pay the donative to the Praetorians, and to the Roman mob, the two elements that it was wise to placate at the outset. He turned his attention to the coinage, which had been debased in 190–2; he brought the silver standard of the denarius back to the level it had enjoyed in the days of Vespasian. Commercial activity required a boost, so he reduced customs dues, and he tried to promote agriculture by granting titles of ownership to waste lands with ten years' tax exemption. There may be some confusion in the sources, since Hadrian's laws on waste lands were still in operation, but it is also possible that Pertinax hoped to speed things up. He did not rule for long enough for any judgement to be made about the likely success of his measures and his intentions, but Herodian thought that he would have changed the administration for the better, instituting 'sound and orderly government'.[23]

Unfortunately, he was not given the chance to prove himself. After 87 days as Emperor, he was murdered at the instigation of Laetus, who had now deleted two Emperors. He did not aim for power himself, even though after the death of Pertinax there was no immediately obvious successor trained up for total control of the Roman Empire. Pertinax had not been allowed sufficient time to cultivate anyone, and perhaps had even decided against doing so when the recent precedent of designating an heir and training him for rule had produced Commodus. In Rome the initiative remained with the

Praetorians, whose commanders and officers had from time to time gained a preponderant influence in political events. Since Laetus himself did not seem to want the job and was keeping a low profile (probably a wise choice since he knew better than anyone how Emperors could be removed), the Praetorians stood by while Flavius Sulpicianus, Pertinax's father-in-law and currently prefect of the city, tried to outbid Didius Julianus; but he was unsuccessful. Finally Julianus bought the Empire for the price of 25,000 sesterces per Praetorian Guardsman.[24]

SEVERUS IMPERATOR

In the provinces the casting vote lay as always with the army. As soon as the news of the death of Pertinax reached the frontiers, the armies and their generals were ready. Early in April, Severus was proclaimed Emperor by his troops at Carnuntum. There were two other rival candidates, Pescennius Niger in Syria and Clodius Albinus in Britain, each situated at opposite ends of the Empire and named for opposite ends of the spectrum: black (*niger*) and white (*albus*). The precise chronology of each proclamation is not established. Niger was proclaimed at some time before the end of May 193, while Clodius Albinus may have entered the scene somewhat later. The timing does not really matter. The crucial point is that there would be a brutal contest involving civil war. Severus decided to ignore the threats from east and west, and go straight to Rome to secure his position there. He had the advantage of being closer to Rome than the other two governors, and he probably also had the advantage of forethought and planning. His elevation cannot have been as spontaneous as it sounds, nor can it have depended entirely on good luck combined with speedy opportunism, though an element of both did enter into the whole picture. But loosely organised forward planning and not a little daydreaming along the lines of 'what if such and such a thing should happen?' will have played a more important part. Since he was not in a position to predict exactly what would happen, nor how events would fall out even if an opportunity should present itself, Severus could have prepared the ground very generally – for instance by establishing a large and loyal *clientelae*, by sounding out likely contacts outside his own group of clients, and creating networks of influential people ranging from army officers, wealthy senators and equites, down to the most lowly individual with specialised knowledge or particular talents. His marriage to Julia Domna, his second wife, had been carefully thought through, not simply because her horoscope contained the brilliant news that she was to be the wife of an Emperor, but also because her eastern connections were important, bringing more influential and wealthy people into Severus' circle. Networks had to be very wide, spread over as much of the Empire as possible as well as in Rome itself, providing eyes and ears for political and

Figure 3 Portrait of Severus in marble, *c.*195. The similarity to portraits of the Antonine Emperors was deliberate, promoting Severus' image as a descendant of Antoninus Pius and Marcus Aurelius. (Courtesy Ny Carlsberg Glyptotek.)

military developments. Information about who was friend or foe was absolutely vital in a regime like that of Commodus, simply as a survival tool, but it could all be turned to good use when the time came, as it assuredly would. No one could predict the precise moment and consequently no one would know who would be where and in what post when the crisis came, but it was obvious that there would be a crisis because there was no designated heir, and Commodus' behaviour was less and less conducive to longevity. It was highly likely that at some point the Empire was going to need an Emperor quite suddenly, and Severus had probably

29

thought about it long before Laetus chose Pertinax. One very important factor, perhaps the most important, would be to amass wealth, either by and for himself, or to arrange very rapid access to cash when he needed it. The next most important consideration would be to monitor at all times the mood of the soldiers, and to investigate the sympathies of the other provincial governors in the neighbouring and distant provinces. He would need to know whether there was support for him, or at least no overt opposition, so that he would not have to fight a premature civil war before he had even crossed the Alps. The technique would, of course, be much more subtle than this cursory description makes it appear. He would not invite a group of officers and senators to dinner and ask casually over the last course if they would be behind him in a bid for the Empire, but he would woo them thoroughly, make a favourable impression, drop hints, and after that make veiled promises of better things to come. Severus was in correspondence with other provincial governors early in April 193 after the death of Pertinax, but that will not have been the first time that he sounded them out. According to the *Historia Augusta*, the legions of the Rhine and Danube declared for him, encouraged by their generals, and when he established himself as Emperor in Rome Severus issued coins specifically honouring many of these legions by their individual names. The evidence is not conclusive, but it will bear the interpretation that Severus had thoroughly prepared the ground long before his acclamation. His investment paid off because sometime later, when civil war began in the west, the governor of Lower Germany, Virius Lupus, stood firm for Severus and opposed Clodius Albinus when the latter reached Gaul. Prepared and waiting, Severus was probably quite ready to take over as Emperor when Commodus was murdered at the beginning of 193, but the transition between old and new Emperor was rapid, leaving no room for Severus to act before the accession of Pertinax. He was fortunate that he did not act too soon and then find himself in opposition to the new Emperor. Thwarted for the moment, Severus would swear allegiance to Pertinax, then he would rethink, realign, follow a normal career, and wait upon events.[25]

Since Pertinax had promised a brighter future for the Empire and it had looked as though he might have been able to stabilise the government if he had survived long enough, Severus chose to enter Rome as his avenger, even adopting his name to demonstrate solidarity and continuity with the previous regime. His first coins bore the name Imperator Caesar Lucius Septimius Pertinax Augustus. By dint of this approach, Severus not only definitely disassociated himself from Commodus, but also cast himself in the role of selfless leader doing his duty to the state, rather than as an opportunistic general racing to the top. Later, when he was more secure, his attitude towards Commodus had to change because he wanted to establish a firmer basis for his power by connecting himself with the house of Marcus Aurelius and Antoninus Pius, but for the time being it was politic to act as he did, praising Pertinax as the worthy successor of the eminently unworthy Commodus.[26]

Severus faced three potential problems as he marched on Rome, in the form of the legitimate Emperor Didius Julianus, the Praetorians, and the Senate. Fortunately, there was little unity or cohesion among these three elements, so it would probably be easy to deal with them separately, or to set one against the other. Julianus took hasty steps to defend himself as soon as he knew that Severus was approaching Italy. He executed Laetus and Commodus' mistress Marcia, and persuaded the Senate to declare Severus a public enemy (*hostis*), but the Praetorians circumvented both Julianus and the Senate by opening up negotiations with this so-called enemy. The Senate, never fully committed to Julianus in the first place, bowed to the inevitable, condemned Julianus to death and declared Severus Emperor.[27]

There remained the Praetorians, and those senators who had supported Julianus. Severus dealt with the Praetorians before he entered Rome, summoning them to a meeting where he surrounded them with his legions and pounced on them, dismissing them all with dishonour. They seem to have been taken by surprise, with no inkling of what was to happen to them. They had been the first to negotiate with him, and probably expected to be handsomely rewarded, but Severus did not want to be in the dubious position of owing his power to them, since he had seen how extremely fickle they were. He mastered them from the start, and created a new and larger Guard when he was ready, recruited from the legions and not just from Italians – a factor bemoaned by Dio, who blames Severus for the abundance of unemployed Italians causing trouble later on. But the Praetorians had become an arrogant body of men, terrorising people and abusing their privileges. There will have been one or two cheers, possibly a little muted, when the Guard was disbanded, sobered perhaps by the realisation that whatever Severus had in mind might not be all that much of an improvement.[28]

The Senate was conciliated somewhat by Severus' studied actions of respect. Although he brought his troops to Rome in full armour, he entered the city in civilian dress. He promised to rule like Marcus Aurelius, and never to put any senator to death without first bringing him to trial by his peers in the Senate. He placated the soldiers and the Roman populace by a timely distribution of cash. Clodius Albinus was forestalled from taking any hostile action, if indeed he intended to make war at this stage, by the offer of the title Caesar, which according to previous usage now designated him as Severus' successor. He called himself Decimus Clodius Septimius Albinus Caesar, and seems to have been content with that title. It has been questioned whether he really believed that Severus was genuine and that he really would be the next Emperor. He must have known that Severus had two sons, but he may have reasoned that they were very young and did not represent a threat. History portrays him as a bit of an idiot, duped by the wily Severus, but this is probably inevitable because ultimately he was the loser. If he had won, he would probably have earned a reputation for crafty and calculated planning, waiting until the right moment had come before committing himself to a war. In reality he may have had much more common sense and been much more prescient than has been depicted. Knowing that he was not ready to give battle and needing to make proper arrangements in Britain so as not to leave total chaos behind him, he may have played the game as well as he could, accepting the name of Caesar gracefully, pretending to acquiesce in the arrangement while all along he was simply stalling for extra time to prepare, a sort of Roman precedent for a British 'Peace in our time'. He had the choice of abdicating altogether and perhaps being lynched by his own legions, or of waiting in Britain at the head of his own private Empire as Carausius did a century later, or he could meet Severus somewhere in Gaul or Germany and hope to defeat him there. If he made no move at all he could be sure that Severus would eventually come after him, so he could not sit still. On the other hand he was handicapped by having to leave at least some form of secure garrison behind him before he could begin, and then cross the channel to ferry troops onto the continent. He needed time for his preparations if he was to leave Britain. Far from being the dupe of Severus, it is just as likely that Clodius Albinus was grateful to have reached what he may have regarded as a temporary stay of execution, and breathed a sigh of relief knowing that Niger was to be the first to receive Severus' attentions.[29]

ELIMINATION OF RIVALS

Pescennius Niger

Severus was now ready to turn eastwards and face Niger, whose hold on the eastern provinces with their considerable resources gave him a tremendous advantage, greater than any advantage within the reach of Albinus, and therefore rendering him potentially the more dangerous of the two rivals for Imperial power. Had it been the other way round, with Clodius Albinus in the more advantageous position, no doubt Severus would have offered the title of Caesar to Niger to mollify him while he dealt with the other opponent. Speed was essential, because Niger must not be allowed too much time to gain strength. If he extended his control over north Africa and Egypt he would also gain control over the corn supply, much as Vespasian had done in 69–70. Niger already had powerful adherents in the east, and Egypt did indeed fall into his hands. Severus did what he could to protect the corn supply, and ordered troops to watch the western border of Egypt and prevent the legion there (*II Traiana*) from sending help to Niger. In the east, Niger's prospects looked reasonable. The proconsul of Asia, Asellius Aemilianus, had declared for him and had occupied Byzantium, but for the moment he could not advance further because the western provinces were firmly held by Severus. This equilibrium could alter at any time if Severus seemed less than energetic, so he set off overland as soon as possible, via Pannonia and Moesia, but to save time he sent orders for the troops in Moesia to set off ahead of him. He probably was not present himself when his general Candidus won a victory over Aemilianus at Cyzicus. Byzantium did not surrender even though Aemilianus was eliminated. Consequently the city was put under siege, which lasted until the end of 195.[30]

Niger withdrew into Syria, not yet in defeat but unfortunately his move was construed as the beginning of the end. Some cities previously loyal to him decided that it was time to change their allegiance since Niger seemed unable to stop Severus' advance, and if Niger was to be finally vanquished Severus would not deal kindly with the cities which had supported his rival. Laodicea was probably the first city to break away from Niger, spurred on by jealousy of its main rival, Antioch, Niger's headquarters. By the spring of 194, the war was over, brought to an end on the plain of Issus, where centuries earlier Alexander the Great fought Darius. Severus' Illyrian troops were invincible, and the cavalry proved decisive. Niger fled, allegedly to try to make contact with the Parthians, but before he could do so he was overtaken and killed. Severus sent his head to Byzantium to demonstrate that there was now no leader to rally behind, but the city still refused to surrender. The inhabitants probably feared retribution for having held out against Severus; rightly so, because when the city did fall at the end of 195 Severus destroyed everything, including the defensive walls. The action was deemed necessary as an example to others, but he and successive Emperors well knew the importance of Byzantium and eventually it was rebuilt.[31]

Retribution and rewards were put into operation on the eastern provinces. Laodicea and Tyre, and other cities which had declared for Severus, were well paid, but those which had sided with Niger were heavily fined, especially Antioch. Niger's adherents, embracing senators, equites, officers and soldiers alike, were severely punished, and as a result were driven into the arms of the Parthians where they found ready employment as engineers, builders, arms manufacturers, and so on. When Severus found that Roman expertise was being taken across the Euphrates, he stopped the punishments and concentrated instead on restoring Roman control and influence on the eastern frontier. The Parthian king, Vologaeses, had been sympathetic to Niger, and the city of Hatra had sent help to him. Elsewhere the civil war between two contesting Romans precipitated rebellion against Roman control in Osroene and Mesopotamia, where it was considered a propitious moment to strike while Rome was otherwise engaged. Roman garrisons were ejected, and the city of Nisibis in Adiabene, in Roman hands since the expedition of Lucius Verus, was besieged. Severus quickly restored order, making Osroene into a province in the charge of a procurator, and leaving king Abgar to rule over the capital city of Edessa and its surrounding territory. As a reward for its loyalty, he elevated Nisibis to the status of a *colonia*, thus bestowing upon it rank and privilege.[32]

For his successes in the war with Niger and for taking the army across the Euphrates, Severus took the titles *Parthicus Arabicus* and *Parthicus Adiabenicus*, and received from the troops six further Imperial acclamations, raising the total to seven. Fostering good relations with the army, in 195 he declared Julia Domna *mater castrorum*, literally 'mother of the camps', elevating her to the position of colleague in Imperial power. She had accompanied him on his campaigns and the soldiers respected her. Ideally, Severus would have continued the campaigns until he had brought them to a conclusion, consolidating his gains in the east by more demonstrations of strength or by further aggressive warfare, which is what he did three years later in the second Parthian campaign. In the first campaign he could achieve only so much, and for the time being he took what steps he could to secure the east temporarily so that he could then attend to the west. Albinus could not be stalled for ever, and he enjoyed considerable support in the Senate. From the very beginning, Severus knew that sooner rather than later he would have to deal with his officially appointed, but always redundant, Caesar.[33]

Clodius Albinus

Severus laid the foundations for a war against Albinus while he was still in the east, where he needed to ensure that there would be as little trouble as possible while he marched away. He had not strengthened the eastern frontier as he would have liked, but for the time being relations with Parthia were stable enough, and for his coming campaign in the west Severus needed to ensure that they would remain so. He dropped *Parthicus* from his victory titles, since at this moment spear-rattling and provocation of the Parthian king were not advisable. In any case, he probably felt that the titles were rather empty, not at all a true description of what had been achieved. Dropping them from his titulature meant that he could reopen the eastern campaign with justification, and earn them all over again. Perhaps now, rather than later, he divided the province of Syria into two smaller provinces. Niger had access to the legions and resources of the whole of Syria, which was clearly large enough and wealthy enough to permit another governor to emulate him. Henceforth the territories were to be smaller and there were to be no more than two legions at the disposal of one governor. Severus divided Syria into two unequal parts and renamed them, the larger northern part being Syria Coele with two legions, and the smaller southern province being Syria Phoenice, which retained one legion. The date of this division has been disputed but it seems more sensible for Severus to have put it into effect immediately after the defeat of Niger, rather than to wait until after the second Parthian campaign.[34]

The chronology of the breakdown of relations between Severus and Albinus is not crystal clear. At the end of 195, or perhaps at the beginning of 196, Albinus decided to take his promotion into his own hands and declared himself no longer Caesar but Augustus. The situation may have been engineered by Albinus himself, or his senatorial supporters may have encouraged him, or there may have been a spontaneous outcry by his army, but however it came about the end result was that he had now set himself up as an aggressive rival to Severus and war would definitely follow. Severus embarked upon alienation of Albinus perhaps even before he had heard that his rival was now styling himself Augustus. It may have been his intention to break with him as soon as he was free to do so, for he presumably knew perfectly well that Albinus would not be content with the title Caesar and the promise of greater things unless greater things came his way quite quickly and kept on coming. Severus was a parvenu compared to Albinus, who 'excelled in education and family' according to Dio. Even if Albinus himself could be ignored, the combination of his troops, his *clientelae*, and his senatorial supporters could not. Either as a provocative act prior to Albinus' self-promotion, or perhaps in response to it, Severus appointed his eldest son, Septimius Bassianus, as Caesar. The message for Albinus was clear, that he would never be Severus' colleague and heir, and he would not gain power unless he fought for it. Some sources say that Severus put this plan into operation at the end of 195, others say that he waited until the beginning of 196, so it is not definitely known which of the two Augusti provoked the other into war.[35]

In advertising a rift with Albinus, Severus sought for a firmer foundation for his supremacy, and also for a guarantee of survival for the dynasty he intended to establish. Continuity with the short-lived regime of Pertinax was important when he entered Rome for the first time as Emperor, but now he needed deeper roots. Marcus Aurelius was the last known respectable and respected Emperor, whose achievements and solid Roman attitudes were worth emulating, so Severus announced his connections with this Imperial house by declaring himself the son of Marcus and by giving his own son Septimius Bassianus the new names Marcus Aurelius Antoninus. Despite all his various other names, Severus' son is better known to posterity by his nickname Caracalla, given to him by the plebs after the Gallic hooded cloak that he habitually wore. His official name was Antoninus, reflected in inscriptions and documents. By determined and decided actions in connecting himself with the previous dynasty, Severus announced to the world his intention of founding a second Antonine dynasty without any assistance from Clodius Albinus. In spring 196 he had the army declare Albinus *hostis*, an enemy of the people.[36]

The rift between Albinus and Severus was now complete, though it still had to be made to seem that it was Albinus who had broken off relations first, in order to justify Severus' war against him. The unknown factor is Albinus' character, which some ancient sources insist was trusting and docile; but however docile he may have been in 193, by the end of 195 it would have been clear that Severus was not trustworthy. The ancient authors repeated the story that Severus sent messengers to kill Albinus, which may contain an element of truth, even if only in the sense that Albinus distrusted him to that extent, or that later audiences found it credible that Severus would stoop to such a subterfuge. Knowing that his days were numbered unless he acted, Albinus may have moved quite quickly as soon as he heard that Niger had been defeated. Indeed it would have been remiss of him to fail to take advantage of Severus' absence at the opposite end of the Empire. He moved troops into Gaul and established himself at Lugdunum (modern Lyons), where he began to issue coins in his own name as Augustus. His army was a mixed assortment of troops from Britain and soldiers recruited in Gaul. Individual units of his army are not known; the only certainty is that *Cohors XIII Urbana* from Lyons joined him. If he had hoped to win over the Rhine legions, he was disappointed, and it seems that the Spanish legion, *VII Gemina*, refused to help him, since it was rewarded with the title *pia* by Severus. How many soldiers Albinus took from Britain is debated. He presumably did not remove all of them, and would probably have arranged for the protection of the cities and the coasts in case he was driven back to the island. What he did on the northern British frontier is problematic; a few factors seem to point to a large-scale evacuation of Hadrian's Wall: firstly, it could be argued that there was trouble in Britain as a result of the withdrawal of troops, followed by the expedition that Severus undertook in Britain from 208 to 211 to restore order in the north of England and to subdue Scotland, but the fact that there was no Imperial activity on this scale for over a decade rather negates the urgency of the affair. Secondly, archaeological investigations reveal that Severus undertook large-scale repairs to Hadrian's Wall; and thirdly, the Wall garrisons of the late second century are not represented in the lists of units which are known for the third century, all of which makes it seem as though all the troops had been removed and then new ones reinstated. Detractors accuse Albinus of stripping the garrison of Britain to the bone to provide a large enough army with which to face Severus. The three British legions and the auxiliary troops would not provide anything like the numbers he needed, even if he took all of them across the channel. But Britain was not totally lost after Albinus' expedition, so it is assumed that he left some sort of garrison there, and then augmented his army by recruiting more men in Gaul.[37]

In preparing for the defence of Italy Severus closed and garrisoned the Alpine passes to prevent a sudden invasion by Albinus from Gaul. Contemporaries in Severus' entourage referred to the 'Gallic conspiracy' which cast Albinus in the role of usurper, an enemy of legitimate power. The situation could have escalated into something much more serious, almost a forerunner of that faced by Gallienus in 260 when Postumus was proclaimed by his troops and took over Gaul and the German provinces. But Albinus did not have the same degree of success or support. The governor of Gallia Lugdunensis would not back him and left the province, and Virius Lupus the governor of Lower Germany made a stand against him, unsuccessfully as it turned out, but ultimately the effectiveness or otherwise of his action was not as important as his demonstration of support for Severus. His reward was to be made governor of Britain. Not all of the cities in Gaul were enthusiastic supporters of Albinus, though they could not afford to demonstrate against him actively, putting armies into the field as Lupus was able to do. Nonetheless, they could refuse to send him help or supplies. Trier seems to have held out, and perhaps other cities followed suit.[38]

After a very brief visit to Rome, Severus marched via Pannonia, Noricum, and Upper Germany into Gaul. The issue was decided at the battle of Lyons in February 197. Albinus conveniently committed suicide, and infamously, Severus allowed his troops to sack Lyons, an event from which the city never really recovered. The episode demonstrated, not for the first or last time, just how easily a Roman army would turn against other Roman troops or against a Roman city, and it highlighted the overwhelming power of the army in co-operation with the Emperor. The mutual dependence of the soldiers upon the Emperor for their pay and perks, and of the Emperor on the soldiers for their corporate support, had always been a fact of Roman life, but it had perhaps never been so blatant as it was under Severus. The aftermath of this civil war involved the execution in Gaul of several of Albinus' supporters, just as in the east Niger's followers were hunted down. Herodian implies that it was at this juncture that Severus divided Britain into two separate provinces, just as he had dealt with Syria after the defeat of Niger; and for the same reasons: to prevent any other governor from gaining access to large numbers of troops under one command. The exact date is not known and is therefore open to debate. Most scholars prefer a later date, perhaps after Caracalla's settlement in 208, or even later at some time after 213. If Severus divided Britain immediately after Albinus' defeat it would make perfect sense, but evidence for two separate governors and for the status of the two provinces is lacking until post-Severan times.[39]

THE SEVERAN DYNASTY

As soon as Severus arrived back in Rome he embarked upon a programme of retribution against Albinus' supporters. He addressed the Senate, making a speech praising the severity of Sulla and Marius, and especially of Augustus. The first two were not especially commendatory role models, but the comparison with Augustus lent credence to what Severus was doing, since he reminded everyone that even leaders of impeccable reputation sometimes could not avoid bloodshed and turmoil, all for the ultimate benefit of the state. The sources disagree as to the number of senators killed during the Severan proscriptions, but perhaps the discrepancy arises from the use of different criteria and timescales for counting up victims. Some senators had presumably left Rome some time before to join Albinus, and so met death somewhat earlier than those who rather unwisely remained in Rome, where Severus and his henchmen could eventually find them.[40]

Just in case there may have been a shadow of doubt about his dynastic plans, Severus underlined them when he returned to Rome by giving Caracalla the title *Imperator destinatus*. He did not promote his younger son Geta as rapidly as Caracalla, nor did he bring to prominence his own brother Septimius Geta, who had been governor of Lower Moesia in 193, and may have been appointed to govern Dacia during the war with Niger. Perhaps Severus hoped to keep things simple by concentrating on Caracalla on centre stage and leaving other members of his family in the wings, patently available in case of emergency but not in major roles. The designation of Carcalla as the next Emperor took care of the future succession, but he still had to attend to the retrospective dynasty. In connecting himself with Marcus Aurelius there remained the problem of what to do about Commodus, whose memory had been damned by the Senate. It would have provided the opponents of Severus with ready ammunition to use against him if he tried to gloss over the fact that in his newly adopted ancestry there was an Emperor whose reputation was positively detrimental. To remedy this defect he requested the Senate to deify Commodus. This move had the dual advantage of pacifying the army, since the soldiers had been more than ready to turn Commodus into a god, and also of making Severus' Imperial lineage legitimate, seamless and unblemished.[41]

Consolidation of power

By a combination of good luck, good management, keenly alert opportunism and ruthless determination, Severus had arrived at unchallenged supremacy. His reputation for cruelty, well established by now, perhaps served as a deterrent to other candidates for Imperial rule for which Pescennius Niger and Clodius Albinus had already bid unsuccessfully. The aftermath of the civil wars necessitated a reshuffling of personnel in provincial and central government posts, and in the army. In tandem with punishments for opponents, rewards for supporters were just as useful in setting an example, and besides, Severus was only too aware that what he had done in Pannonia in 193 could be done by anyone else if the circumstances were favourable, so it was important to make the correct choice of provincial governors and army commanders, especially since he knew that his work on the eastern frontier was not finished and he would have to absent himself from Rome once again. It was vital to leave behind him responsible loyal men who would look after his interests and obey his commands in return for his patronage and steady promotions in the social, political and military spheres. The centre of government was wherever he was himself, but if he could trust his provincial governors and military officers in the rest of the

Roman world while he campaigned and carried on government elsewhere, so much the better. The Russian historian Rostovtzeff laid all the blame for the crisis of the Empire squarely on Severus' shoulders, for putting into practice his ruthless policies without scruples of any sort, setting the Empire on a path to the oriental despotism of Diocletian and Constantine. It must be noted that Rostovtzeff had a large axe to grind, so his theories were propounded on a specific basis of contemporary political doctrine, but Gibbon, definitely lacking the socialist background, also identified Severus as the major villain of the piece and the author of all the later problems that beset the Empire.[42]

Attention to the soldiers was a priority all through Severus' reign. It may have been in 197 when he put into effect his army reforms, in particular his pay rise. The date is disputed, and the exact amount of the pay rise is not known. It created great disapproval, but apart from his realistic attitude to the mainstay of his power, Severus knew that most Romans wanted defence at an impossibly cheap price. The last substantial pay rise had been granted over a century earlier by Domitian, so it was well overdue. So also was the recognition of the soldiers as people, with the right to marry and reasonable prospects of promotion, which is what Severus gave them. Marriages had been forbidden, but unsanctioned liaisons with local women near the camps had always occurred, so the new legislation merely acknowledged the existing situation.[43]

Just as he controlled the provinces, it was essential to keep a firm grasp on Rome and Italy while he was on campaign, for which task he relied upon his government officials and the army. He had reconstituted the Praetorian Guard, larger now than in previous reigns, and he also installed a new legion at Alba (modern Albano), not far from Rome. This was *II Parthica*, raised at an unknown date, but it was definitely in existence and in Italy when Severus went on campaign against the Parthians. The units of the new Praetorian Guard, combined with the new legion, provided Severus with an army of about 30,000 men all under his immediate control. It was a heavy handed but effective means of ensuring that no one could threaten him while in Italy or indeed in any other part of the Empire. In order to secure himself even further, Severus appointed loyal supporters to key posts. That of city prefect was held from *c.*196 by Cornelius Anullinus, one of Severus' associates. Perhaps the most notorious commander of the Praetorian Guard after the infamous Sejanus was Severus' close personal friend and fellow countryman Caius Fulvius Plautianus, whose previous post had been prefect of the *vigiles* from 193 to 196–7. At the beginning of 197, possibly before the campaign against Albinus, Plautianus was rewarded with the post of Praetorian Prefect. Normally there were two Praetorian Prefects, but Plautianus was something of an anomaly from the moment Severus appointed him to his first post. He rid himself of his colleague quite promptly, enjoying sole command of the Praetorian Guard for the rest of his career, until his

Figure 4 Gold aureus of 206 from the Rome mint. The legend runs IMPP INVICTI PII AUGG, and the portraits show Severus and Caracalla, wearing laurel wreaths, and cloaks over their cuirasses. The Emperors are not named on the coin, and for identification they rely solely on their reputation – this is unusual and was not copied by later Emperors. The reverse (not shown) has the legend VICTORIA PARTHICA MAXIMA celebrating the victory over the Parthians in 198. (Drawn by Trish Boyle.)

downfall and death in 205. But at the outset of Severus' reign there was not even a hint of these future troubles; at this stage Severus experienced very little trouble from the men whom he appointed. He democratised the army, enabling common soldiers to rise from the ranks to equestrian status and beyond, and in addition he opened up more military commands and governmental posts to the equites, continuing a trend already set in motion by previous Emperors. The three new legions that he raised, all named *Parthica*, were commanded by equestrians instead of senators, and he appointed more equestrians as the governors of the new eastern provinces created after the Parthian campaigns. The equestrian class in general experienced a whole new impetus under Severus, while the influence of the senators remained static; there were still many prestigious appointments for them to fill, but whilst it is not valid to speak of a decline, neither was there an escalation of senatorial power. Severus did not set out to damage the Senate, though he curbed it by making it clear that he would have what he wanted with or without its co-operation, but if senators felt neglected or threatened, it was rather that events overtook them, and the new social mobility that brought rough commoners to prominence eroded or even negated their position of privilege and prestige. Severus did not rely on the Senate, but tolerated it; he did not pander to the senators' collective sense of importance, nor did he care much for the feelings of the Roman mob. He consolidated his power by means of his sole control of the army, and to a lesser extent by means of the promotion of the equites. He had made himself the source of all patronage and advancement, he held the purse strings of the whole Empire, he was the fount of jurisdiction and the commander-in-chief of the armed forces. For the time being, the city of Rome was firmly under his control, and he had done all he could to ensure the succession to power after his death. When he set off for the second Parthian campaign in early summer 197 he was at the apex of his Imperial rule.[44]

Parthia and the east

From the Roman point of view there was a pressing need to attack Parthia. Vologaeses had occupied Mesopotamia and laid siege to Nisibis, but it did not fall, being ably defended by Laetus (not the same person who assassinated Commodus). The coming Parthian war was therefore a just one, as it was a matter of urgency to restate Roman claims on the east; had it not been so easy to find a cause for war, Severus would have had to work a little harder to prepare for it, but Parthia was the traditional enemy, so drumming up support would not have been too difficult, even though the *Historia Augusta* states that it was thought that Severus was influenced more by his desire for glory than by necessity. The war itself seemed all too easy, which perhaps gave rise to the rumour that Severus simply undertook the campaign to enhance his own reputation. Roman operations against Parthia did not always run so smoothly, as the Republican examples of Crassus and Marcus Antonius had shown. This time though, there was virtually no opposition. The Parthian Royal House was itself split into factions, and the brother of Vologaeses accompanied Severus and his army. Vologaeses retreated before the advancing Roman army, abandoning the siege of Nisibis. Like Trajan, and like Avidius Cassius commanding Lucius Verus' troops, Severus aimed for the Euphrates valley and followed its course. He encountered no resistance at Seleucia or Babylon, and only a slight problem at the Parthian capital Ctesiphon, which he took and sacked. There the campaign ended, because the point had been made. Severus had no intention of pursuing Vologaeses into the depths of his kingdom. He had no plans to remain in occupation of the capital city, nor to annex Parthian territory. It had been a demonstration of strength to deter the Parthians from interfering in Roman administrative arrangements on her eastern borders. In 198 Severus brought the army out of Parthia by a different route from that of the invasion in order to avoid traversing the area where he had used up all the food supplies during his advance. The army was in high spirits, acclaiming him Imperator for the tenth and eleventh time for these successful campaigns, and proclaiming Caracalla joint Augustus with his father, while Severus' younger son Geta became Caesar in his turn. The process was probably not spontaneous, or at least if it appeared so it would have been the result of careful preparation, thought out some time before. On his coinage

41

Severus added his new title *Parthicus Maximus*, a rather greater honour than the simple *Parthicus* that he had enjoyed for so short a time in 195.[45]

The only resistance that Severus experienced during this expedition came from the city of Hatra, which he besieged on his way back from Ctesiphon in 198 and again in 199, without success. Dio describes the two sieges, laconically indicating that they were disastrous, costly, and wasteful. Severus called off the sieges when it was clear that nothing would be gained from them. He then went on to Egypt, via Mesopotamia, Syria, Palestine and Arabia. He remained in the east perhaps until the end of 201, or the beginning of 202, for there were many administrative details to attend to in the old and new eastern provinces and on the frontiers. He had created the new province of Osroene in 195, but had been unable to do more because he had first to deal with Albinus in Gaul. Now he brought to fruition a scheme originally adopted by Trajan but abandoned by Hadrian, by annexing the new Roman province of Mesopotamia in 198. The connection with Trajan, who had also earned the title *Parthicus*, had been emphasised all through the campaigns. At the beginning of 198 Severus had chosen 28 January to make sacrifices for the success of his expedition, which date also happened to be the centenary of Trajan's accession, his *dies imperii*. It was a deliberate choice, to demonstrate solidarity and continuity with the past, and most of all with an Emperor of such tremendous renown. There could be no better spiritual guardian for the army than the perennially perfect and now divine all-conquering Emperor, and in the continual search for stability on the eastern frontier there could be no better precedent than the project of Trajan for the re-creation of the province of Mesopotamia. Severus entrusted the province to a procurator for a short time and then to an equestrian prefect, with the capital at Nisibis. The garrison comprised two of the newly raised legions, *I* and *III Parthicae*, both of which were commanded by equestrians, stationed respectively at Singara near the river Tigris, and at Rhesaena.[46]

Adjustments were made to the province of Syria Phoenice, where some territory at the southern extremity was ceded to Arabia. The eastern frontier was stabilised for the foreseeable future, the upper Euphrates was encased within Roman provinces, and the desert protected the approaches to Syria Phoenice and Arabia. The power of the Parthians was weakened from 198 onwards and remained so for the next two decades, which afforded Rome a breathing space and a short spell of relative peace and quiet. But when the Parthian Arsacid dynasty was overthrown and replaced by the more robust and energetic Persian Sassanids, Roman ascendancy was once more seriously challenged. The annexation of Mesopotamia as a Roman province was costly to the Romans and a constant thorn in the side of the Persian kings. It was certain that there would be a confrontation between them and the Roman Emperors who succeeded Severus.[47]

On his way to Egypt, Severus visited various cities in Syria and Palestine, bestowing upon them the rank of *colonia*; Sebaste in Palestine and Eleutheropolis and Diospolis in Judaea were among these, and it is probable that Palmyra was also made into a colony at this time. In Egypt, Severus reviewed and reformed the administration, and also became an Imperial tourist, visiting sites simply to see them, and apparently deriving tremendous pleasure from his excursions. He visited the tomb of Alexander the Great at Alexandria, and then closed it to other visitors. In each of the chief cities of the nomes, or the ancient administrative districts of Egypt, he instituted a council. The wealthier members of the community thus became liable to perform the local and Imperial liturgies, or public duties, the cost of which was borne by themselves, so perhaps not surprisingly there was a reluctance to serve on the councils. The city of Alexandria was always a distinct entity in Ptolemaic and Graeco-Roman Egypt, but it had not been given a council of its own. Augustus had placed it under the control of an equestrian *juridicus*; now Severus endowed it with a council, of the same type as those of the *municipia* of the Roman Empire.[48]

Return to Rome

In spring 201 the daughter of Plautianus, Plautilla, was betrothed to Caracalla and given the honorary title Augusta. That same year Severus left Egypt and went by sea to Antioch, where it is said he remained until January 202, when he entered the consulship with Caracalla as colleague; Christol has challenged the dating, because it is known that Severus was back in Rome by April 202, which would mean that he journeyed there in the winter between January and the end of March, across the high Anatolian plain. A departure in autumn 201 is perhaps more likely, especially since it is known that Severus passed through the frontier provinces of Moesia and Pannonia, where he took especial interest in the settlements around the legionary fortresses, known as *canabae*. At Viminacium, it is recorded that he and Caracalla reconstructed the *canabae*, and at Carnuntum and Aquincum the *canabae* were given colonial status. Birley speculates that he may have been at Carnuntum on 9 April, his *dies imperii*, reliving the events that made him Emperor.[49]

Entering Rome as conquering hero, Severus ordained that his Parthian campaigns should be recorded in a series of paintings, and publicised his conquests on his coinage with the legends *Victoria Parthica Maxima*, reflecting his new title *Parthicus Maximus*, and *Impp Invicti Pii Augg*, in the plural to include Caracalla as co-Emperor. *Invictus*, 'unconquered', was to feature widely on his coins and in his titulature from this time onwards. He celebrated a triumph in which his sons Caracalla and Geta played a prominent part, in order to remind onlookers that there were to be successors to his regime, which had endured until the tenth year, something of a remarkable feat after the calamitous events during the reign of Commodus and

43

especially after his demise. Justly proud of himself, Severus accordingly made a great celebration of his *Decennalia* with appropriate pomp and ceremony, public festivals and distributions of cash to the people of Rome. It had been customary since Augustus' day to celebrate the *Decennalia*, as the name suggests, every ten years, and Severus was concerned to emulate Augustus in many ways. The most durable celebration of his ten-year reign and his military achievements is the arch named after him in the Forum in Rome, erected near the Senate house on the spot where, in a dream before he became Emperor, Severus had seen Pertinax fall from his horse, which he then mounted himself. Superstition was combined with uncompromising realism in Severus' plans for the arch, which were made in connection with his triumph and the *Decennalia* in 202, though the project was not actually completed until 204. Every time the senators entered the Senate House and emerged from it, they would come face to face with a highly visible reminder of who was master of the Roman world. For the most part, the sculptures of the arch represent Severus' military victories in Parthia, and the inscription states that the monument was erected by the Senate and People of Rome in recognition of the restoration of the Republic and the extension of the Empire. The arch was placed opposite that of Augustus commemorating the return of the Roman standards from Parthia in 20 BC, a diplomatic success of the first order for Augustus, who claimed to have restored the Republic and to have rescued it from the brink of destruction by warring factions. The similar claims on the arch of Severus that he had restored the Republic were something of a contradiction in terms when juxtaposed with such an obtrusive reminder of his Imperial powers, but the parallels with Augustus and the civil wars that brought him to sole rule would not be lost on the Roman people and senators who were credited with setting up the arch.[50]

Africa

After the celebrations were over, and after a short stay in Rome, Severus and his whole family, including the Praetorian Prefect Plautianus, embarked on a voyage to Africa, the Emperor's homeland. A native of Lepcis Magna, Severus favoured fellow Africans in his government and in his army, just as he promoted men from the east, Julia Domna's homeland. While he was on campaign in Parthia, Severus' generals had been busy in the African provinces, extending the frontiers, taking in more territory, rationalising boundaries, protecting routes, and building new forts.[51]

Though there were some frontier works in the Roman provinces of north Africa, there was no continuous running barrier of the type already established in the Rhine and Danube frontiers. The territories under Roman control were vast, and yet the number of forts and military units in north Africa was almost negligible compared to the densely packed frontier installations in Britain, Germany and the Danube provinces. Hadrian had toured the African provinces and organised the frontiers according to the needs of the day, and now Severus continued his work with spectacular success, through his governors and generals, in particular Quintus Anicius Faustus, a native of Africa and legate of *III Augusta* from 197 to 201. Faustus was responsible for building new forts in Tripolitania and in the south of Numidia, generally concerned with providing greater protection for the Roman territories. On the edge of the Roman provinces there were highly mobile tribes, some of whom periodically carried out raids across their borders, and some of whom practised seasonal transhumance from winter to summer pastures. It was important to be able to deal effectively with troublesome raiders and to distinguish them from the more law-abiding but restless pastoralists, and to protect the settled farmlands from both groups. It seems that in Mauretania Caesariensis the frontier lines around the Hodna mountains catered for the movement of transhumant tribes into and out of Roman territory, so that the pastoralist groups were not prevented from following their customary routes, but could be super-vised while they did so, and other less well-intentioned groups could be fil-tered out and dealt with accordingly. Policing small-scale raids had been a constant problem from the early Empire. Hadrian had done much to ratio-nalise and stabilise the frontiers. In Numidia he had moved *III Augusta* from its base at Ammaedara to a new fortress at Lambaesis, and he had con-structed watch towers and small posts on the frontiers of Mauretania Cae-sariensis and Tingitana. Commodus continued the work by building outposts to give advance warning of raids.[52]

Severus took the process further by extending Roman control southwards over a much larger area, earning for himself the title of *propagator imperii*, known from several inscriptions in Africa. In Mauretania Caesariensis he made a tremendous advance south of the old Antonine frontier, taking in territory with a new frontier commemorated on inscriptions as the *nova prae-tentura*. This was begun by Octavius Pudens, an African like Anicius Faustus, in 198. To the west of the same province Severus filled the large gap between Caesariensis and Tingitana by moving garrisons into what had been a no man's land; the absence of existing settlements with recorded names is indicated by the fact that the places where the units were stationed were named after them, at Ala Milliaria and Numerus Syrorum.[53]

When Severus visited Africa, most of this work had been completed; Anicius Faustus had returned to Rome and served as suffect consul at the end of 198 or the beginning of 199. He would go on to govern Upper Moesia from about 205. Severus rewarded faithful and successful generals well, just as he rewarded his home town of Lepcis Magna and other African cities. Auzia in Mauretania Caesariensis was made a colony, but otherwise Severus concentrated on the eastern African provinces, returning to Rome in summer 203.[54]

Rome and Italy

Further Imperial and dynastic festivities marked the year 204, when Severus celebrated the Secular Games. The ceremony was rooted in the Roman past, combining religious ceremonial with games and festivals, occurring once every 110 years, so that no one ever witnessed more than one celebration in a lifetime, or *saeculum*. Augustus had laid great emphasis on the Secular Games of 17 BC, using the occasion to mark his achievements and to consolidate his influence and power. Severus followed the Augustan pattern quite closely, marking the occasion on his coinage, and bringing out his whole family on display, visible at all the ceremonies and taking an active part in them. The *domus divina*, attested as such on inscriptions, denoting the Imperial household as an entity, sacrosanct and unassailable, was now firmly established in Roman consciousness.[55]

While in Rome, before and after his visit to Africa, Severus devoted some time to the administration of the law. A number of his decisions and pronouncements concerned with a wide range of legal matters are preserved in the law codes, especially the *Digest*. Severus earned praise from Dio for his keen interest in the law, his patient attention to the speakers in court, and his willingness to allow his advisers to have their say. In the years between the Parthian and the British campaigns, there was a major problem, of which Severus himself seemed to be wilfully oblivious, concerning the Praetorian Prefect Plautianus, whose vast accretion of power and his unashamed exploitation of it had turned him into something worse than a combination of Sejanus and Cleander, and apparently far more to be feared. The ancient authors relished the scandal of Plautianus and his tremendous powers, his cruelty, and his influence over Severus. The two men had been friends from early youth, and it is on record that Severus wrote in a letter that he loved the man so much that he prayed to die before Plautianus. He loaded his friend with honours, making him a senator and appointing him consul in 203. Petitions began to arrive for Plautianus as a member of the Imperial household, and his name appears on several inscriptions alongside the Emperors themselves. In the east and in Africa there were tensions among the Imperial family and Plautianus, who treated Julia Domna with contempt, driving her to seek solace in philosophy, withdrawing from public life as far as she could. The situation is very odd, possibly highly distorted in retrospect, but it is indicative of the personal susceptibilities of Roman Emperors and the opportunities that presented themselves to their closest associates to acquire wealth and preponderant influence. All the clues that forewarned of trouble were in already in place towards the end of the second Parthian campaign, when Plautianus successively eliminated men of good reputation and distinguished service. The first to go was Laetus, who had been with Severus since 193, and had fought in the east against Niger and against Clodius Albinus in Gaul. It was probably easy to persuade Severus that Laetus was less than loyal, since it was said that he hung back at Lyons to see whether Albinus or Severus would win. Laetus was killed in 198. Tiberius Claudius Candidus, who had been the first to see action against Niger's troops, soon followed. Next, Plautianus eliminated Quintus Aemilius Saturninus, a former Prefect of Egypt and now his colleague as Praetorian Prefect. Severus acquiesced in all these actions, which made Plautianus unassailable, preventing anyone from trying to enlighten the Emperor about the dangerous trends. He was finally made aware of what was happening by his brother Septimius Geta, who denounced Plautianus on his death bed, and then Caracalla took proceedings into his own hands, persuading his father that there was a plot to remove the entire Imperial household, and that Plautianus was at the centre of it. On 22 January 205, Plautianus was killed.[56]

Two Praetorian Prefects were appointed in his place, Quintus Maecius Laetus, who had been Prefect of Egypt 200–3, and Aemilius Papinianus, an Imperial secretary with a good reputation as a jurist. He may also have been *praefectus annonae*, and in this dual capacity of administrator and jurist he foreshadowed the later role of the Praetorian Prefects whose main concerns, among many others, were the military food supply and administration. Severus emerged from the removal of Plautianus with his reputation intact, seemingly with no damage to his dynastic intentions. There was virtually no mention of Plautianus, who was wiped from the record. It was observed that Severus' preoccupation was now with the dissension between his two sons, and some said that he embarked on his British campaign in order to occupy them, and to gain even greater glory for himself. Whatever the reason, it cannot have been merely a whim that made the ailing Emperor, travelling in a litter because of his gout or possibly arthritis, leave Rome for the outermost province on the north-western edge of the Empire.[57]

Britain: *expeditio felicissima Britannica*

There is considerable controversy about the postulated disturbances in Britain in 197, after Albinus took troops to Gaul to face the armies of Severus. The governors Virius Lupus, Valerius Pudens and Alfenus Senecio had carried out rebuilding and repairs to several forts in the north, but it is not proven beyond doubt that these repairs were necessary because of destruction by British tribesmen. The post-197 situation in Britain is variously depicted, ranging from one of extreme gravity to perfectly normal routine. Dio informs us that Lupus the governor was forced to buy peace from the Maeatae, who lived 'near the wall that cuts the island in half', by which it is normally assumed that he meant the more northerly Antonine Wall. Beyond the Maeatae there were the Caledonians, and according to Dio both tribes were hardy and hostile. In consequence of this hint of unrest, some archaeologists have interpreted any signs of destruction at the forts in northern Britain as enemy action. It may be true that Albinus' departure in 197, taking large numbers of troops from the garrison, was viewed as an opportunity to reassert British strength, but the problem is that it is not clear from Dio's narrative whether the natives crossed the more northerly Antonine Wall or Hadrian's Wall, nor how far south they may have ranged. If there was trouble in Britain in 197, largely repaired by the governors Virius Lupus and his successors Valerius Pudens and Alfenus Senecio, it is difficult to explain why there was a long gap before any repair work was done on Hadrian's Wall. If the troubles were continuous from 197 onwards, fully occupying all three governors with constant fire-fighting and leaving them no time to carry out repairs to the Wall, it is odd that nine years elapsed before the Emperor himself appeared in the island, especially since for the last few of those nine years Severus was not engaged in a major war elsewhere. Frere suggests that Severus left his generals to proceed at their own pace and that by 207 the north of Britain was fully reoccupied and quiet, so all was ready for Severus' expedition to conquer Scotland. Dio affirms that Severus intended to conquer the whole island. No one since Julius Agricola had succeeded in this project, and so the conquest would be another glorious achievement for Severus, matching his conquest in the east.[58]

The Imperial armies arrived in Britain in 208 and Severus set up his headquarters at York. He brought his two sons with him in order to occupy them and give them experience, and he was accompanied by his *comites* and chosen specialists. He not only planned and executed the British expedition from York but also governed the whole Empire, so he needed the Imperial secretaries and freedmen and all the attendant bureaucrats, as well as British specialists who would be useful during the campaign. A few of the personnel are known, and some of them did not survive the expedition. As part of his campaign army Severus brought troops from the Rhine and Danube armies, possibly *II Parthica* from Italy and detachments from the Praetorian Guard.[59]

The literary sources for the expedition are not of great value. Birley dismisses Dio's and Herodian's accounts as not much more than travellers' tales, and the *Historia Augusta* as almost worthless. The archaeological traces of Severus' two campaigns are slightly more useful than the written evidence. Severan supply bases have been identified at Arbeia (modern South Shields), at Coria (modern Corbridge) and at Cramond on the Forth. At Carpow on the Tay Severus established a legionary base, where tiles of *VI Victrix* have been found. Two lines of marching camps have been traced in the north leading into Scotland, and though dating evidence is not unequivocally established they are usually identified as those used by Severus' army. There were two campaigns, the first in 208–9 led by Severus himself and the second in 210 led by Caracalla alone. Geta was left behind in York on both occasions, but there was some compensation when he was finally made Augustus and became an equal-ranking colleague of his father and brother.

The Imperial family did not enjoy harmonious relations. Caracalla had an obvious wish to rid himself of his brother long before he achieved the deed in 211 or 212, a wish that Severus recognised only too clearly. It may also be true that Caracalla tried to kill Severus while they rode out together to meet the Caledonians to arrange a truce. Dio says that Caracalla reigned in his horse, pulled back and drew his sword as if he was about to stab his father in the back. Shouts from spectators warned the Emperor, who ignored the incident, finished the diplomatic business and then called his son to him in the evening, placing a sword within easy reach and settling back to await upon events. Caracalla did not avail himself of the opportunity on this occasion.[60]

There was hardly any need for haste; Severus was already ill. He had been incapacitated in 210 when Caracalla led the northern campaign, and in February 211, on the brink of preparing a third campaign, he died at York. According to Dio he told his two sons not to disagree with each other, to pay the soldiers and to despise everyone else. His achievements in Britain have been variously measured according to preconceived ideas of his purpose. Historians have represented his campaigns as ultimate failures, but this is true only if the intention was to subdue the whole of Scotland and occupy it in force. Severus established no permanent forts in the Scottish lowlands, so it is more likely that he intended to mount a determined demonstration of Roman power in the north in order to secure the frontier of Hadrian's Wall, which he restored so extensively that in the nineteenth century it was thought that the Wall itself was in fact the Severan frontier, and that Hadrian's contribution was limited to the Vallum, or large ditch, on the south side of the Wall.[61]

Caracalla may have mounted a third campaign in 211, before he concluded peace and returned to Rome. He has been accused of indecent haste in leaving Britain, but the frontier remained stable for the next 85 years, so whatever arrangements he made presumably had some worth. By analogy with other occasions when the Romans conducted campaigns and then withdrew, there was most likely a treaty with the Caledonians and possibly with the Maeatae, whereby they would contribute troops for the Roman army, which served the dual purpose of removing restless young men from the north and filling gaps in the armies. This is the sort of arrangement that Commodus made with the Danube tribes when he made peace after the death of Marcus Aurelius. A further development in Britain, which is possibly due to Caracalla at some time after 213, is the division into two provinces, already mentioned above (p. 37). In 213 or 214 Caracalla readjusted the boundaries of the two Pannonias, placing Brigetio and its legionary garrison in Pannonia Inferior. This meant that instead of three legions in Superior and one in Inferior, there were two in each province, with less opportunity for the governor to raise rebellion by calling upon larger numbers of troops. It is possible that Caracalla was pursuing a consistent policy at this time with regard to the frontier provinces, dividing

Britain, and dividing the legionary forces of Pannonia to create a more equitable arrangement.[62]

THE SUCCESSORS OF SEVERUS

Very soon after the arrival of the Imperial party in Rome, Caracalla murdered Geta, perhaps at the end of 211 or at the beginning of 212. The brothers had been at variance for some time, each with a body of supporters who perhaps had much to gain if one or the other became sole ruler of the

Figure 5 Portrait of Caracalla, one of a famous series of similar portrayals. (Courtesy Ny Carlsberg Glyptotek.)

Empire. It was said that the brothers continually plotted against each other, so after Caracalla had lured Geta into Julia Domna's apartments and killed him there in cold blood, it was probably at least half credible when he dashed off to the Praetorian camp explaining that he had narrowly escaped an attempt on his life and had killed Geta in self-defence. It was no secret that armed force made the Emperors what they were: Augustus would have found it much more difficult to establish himself without the control of most of the troops; Vespasian would never have become Emperor without his armies to back him up; and Severus had made the army the mainstay of his power. A combination of uncompromising realism and insecurity motivated Caracalla when he appealed to the troops. For the first few hours after Geta's death Caracalla's future survival was not necessarily assured. The Praetorians did not rally to him spontaneously, and not all the soldiers were happy to forget that they had sworn allegiance to Geta; but cash payments, coupled with the promise that Caracalla as their sole benefactor would treat then well, made it so much easier for them to edit their memories to match the new orthodoxy.[63]

In order to complete the process and leave no source for future retaliation, Caracalla eradicated all his brother's supporters, killing a large number of people, including the Praetorian Prefect, Papinianus. All over the Empire, orders went out to obliterate the memory of Geta, whose name was chiselled out of inscriptions, and whose portraits and statues were destroyed. Depictions of the Imperial family are known in which there is an obvious gap where Geta's figure or head used to be. Contemporaries no doubt blocked out all memory of Geta too, since it was declared a crime to mention him. Even papyri were edited for any reference to Geta. Apart from the human psychological interest inherent in the episode, the assiduous, Empire-wide obliteration of Geta's name demonstrates the thorough, centralised, all-pervading power of Roman Imperial administration.[64]

Constitutio Antoniniana

Taking the name of Severus, Caracalla began to install his own supporters in influential posts. A few names are known of those of his adherents who filled administrative offices, such as Quintus Marcius Dioga who was the head of the finance office in charge of revenues and expenditure (*a rationibus*), and Sextus Varius Marcellus who managed the privy purse (*ratio privata*). Caracalla's government of the Empire is not known in detail. Dio's account is strongly influenced by his dislike of Caracalla and by Caracalla's hostility to the Senate; of all the passages of Dio's history, those concerning Caracalla have the most insistent hints of a firm grip on the stylus, a sweating brow and tightly clenched teeth. The most famous administrative measure of Caracalla's reign, giving rise to endless discussion, is the *Constitutio Antoniniana*, traditionally promulgated in 212. By this edict, Roman citizenship was granted to all freeborn inhabitants of the Empire, and since it was usual to take the name of the man who enfranchised new citizens, after 212 there were a great preponderance of men and women all over the Empire with the family name Aurelius. The motives behind this almost universal enfranchisement were several and varied, and the effects were profound. The tendencies of Severus' reign were towards a more egalitarian policy, embracing all the inhabitants of the Empire, so it could be said that Caracalla was merely bringing to fruition the policies of his father. He has also been accused of shoring up his regime by appealing to a wider public who would be grateful and would therefore support him, especially after his act of fratricide. Religious motives have been suggested, though with less conviction. The levelling effect of the *Constitutio* in theory subjected all free peoples in all the provinces to Roman law, though in practice local customs remained intact and difficult to eradicate, and financially it broadened the base of the inheritance tax, paid by all citizens. This is the motive most favoured by Dio, who says that Caracalla was driven to this desperate measure because of greed and mismanagement of funds, because he gave all his money to the soldiers. It is reported that Caracalla used to say that nobody except himself should have money, so that he could pay the armies. Dio is no doubt correct, but only in part, about Caracalla's purpose.[65]

There may have been some resentment about the equalising tendencies of the Severans, culminating in this cheapening of Roman citizenship, once a prize to be valued for its legal privileges and access to the higher offices in civilian and military careers. The citizenship had slowly lost its status and value over the years, and after 212 it was no longer confined to an elite group. Consequently a new elite evolved, while the old one declined. Instead of Romans and provincials, or citizens and non-citizens, class distinction became the yardstick. The new divisions were between upper and lower classes, *honestiores* and *humiliores*, without any clear legal definition, hereditary or financial, to distinguish one group from the other. What began as a social distinction was soon crystallised in law. *Honestiores* were possessed of greater legal privileges than *humiliores*, for whom punishments were much more severe.[66]

The Rhine and Danube frontiers

Severus had not totally neglected the frontiers of Upper and Lower Germany and Raetia while he had been occupied with various wars elsewhere, but he had not given these areas his close personal attention. On slender coin evidence it used to be thought that he had repaired or rebuilt Hadrian's original timber frontier enclosing the Taunus and Wetterau in Upper Germany, erecting instead a new turf wall like the Antonine Wall in Britain. More recently Schönberger has cast doubt on the dating, preferring to attribute the new turf wall to Commodus. For several years there had been no serious trouble in the north, but in 212–13 Upper Germany was threatened. In the epitome of Dio's text, the tribesmen responsible for the unrest are called 'Alamanni', meaning simply 'all men'. It denotes a federation of different tribes who chose to adopt a non-ethnic name for themselves, though it is disputed whether the federation was already current as early as 213. The tribal name may not have appeared in Dio's original third-century text; the relevant passages survive only in epitomised form, perhaps edited to suit a much-later audience who knew about the Alamanni (see pp. 208–14).[67]

Caracalla responded to the danger by conducting a campaign for which he appears to have prepared very thoroughly. In Raetia considerable numbers of new milestones indicate that the network of roads was repaired and increased; troops were collected from various sources. Not since Domitian's day had so many soldiers been collected together between the Rhine and Danube; detachments from *II Adiutrix* from Upper Pannonia and from *II Traiana* from Egypt are attested there. There is no evidence that the tribes had destroyed any installations along the German or Raetian frontier, and there is not much information, save for the prayers of the Arval Brethren for the success of the expedition and the safety of the Emperor, as to exactly what Caracalla did or where he campaigned. What he achieved was perhaps a pre-emptive strike before any trouble could develop, and it seems to have been effective since there was peace for two decades thereafter. Caracalla took the title *Germanicus Maximus*, and received his third acclamation as Imperator. At some of the forts in Raetia inscriptions reveal that the Emperor made a personal visit after the campaigns, notably to the temple of Apollo Grannus at Faimingen, where he hoped to elicit the aid of the god to eradicate his illnesses, which are not fully elucidated in any source. He repaired the frontier works in Raetia, and rebuilt the *Limestor* or gateway through the frontier at Dalkingen, which may have been a customs post as well as guard house, on a route from Roman territory into Free Germany. In 214 or thereabouts Caracalla adjusted the boundaries between the two Pannonian provinces, thereby equalising the distribution of legions, denying the governors of each province access to more than two legions, but also elevating Pannonia Inferior to consular status. His frontier policy seems to have been a combination of open warfare and demonstrations of strength, followed by organisation of the frontiers themselves. He may have paid subsidies to the tribes after his campaign, and in other cases he stirred up one tribe against another to keep them occupied and their attentions diverted from Roman territory.[68]

The east

As a dedicated admirer of Alexander the Great, Caracalla could not fail to be drawn to the east, whether or not there were opportunities or a need for Roman intervention. The Parthian Royal House was still disunited.

Vologaeses V and his brother Artabanus were at odds with each other, which provided Caracalla with sufficient excuse for mounting a campaign. After the German wars he returned to Rome for a short time, preparing for the eastern war by summoning King Abgar to Rome and then imprisoning him, taking over the kingdom of Edessa, which he made into a colony, intending to use it as a military base. He also summoned the king of Armenia, but was less successful in taking over the kingdom, and met resistance from the population. When he was ready he marched to the east by way of the Danube provinces, attending to affairs in Dacia, making some sort of alliance and probably raising troops, arriving in Macedonia towards the end of 214 and spending the winter there. Vologaeses diplomatically avoided all action which would put him in the wrong with regard to the Roman Emperor, so Caracalla was hard pressed to find anything to fight for. He was in any case distracted by trouble in Alexandria, where it seems that there were serious problems which demanded the Imperial presence. Leaving the Parthian campaign to his general Theocritus, who was sent to attack Armenia, Caracalla went to Alexandria where he is credited with killing many people in 215–16. At the end of 216 he returned to the east, where the situation had changed. Theocritus' expedition had been disastrous, and Vologaeses had been replaced by his brother Artabanus V. Roman ascendancy was no longer assured, even though Artabanus was not in a very much stronger position than his brother had been. Instead of mounting a quick campaign, Caracalla tried to negotiate a marriage between his daughter and the son of Artabanus. The offer was refused, politely. This ineffective inaction was resented by the troops, who no doubt compared Caracalla to his father, remembering the successful Parthian expedition some years earlier. Rumours began to circulate, foremost among them the prophecy that the Praetorian Prefect Macrinus would succeed Caracalla. The Emperor heard of it, and Macrinus began to fear for his life. At least, that was his story after he had murdered Caracalla early in April 217.[69]

The reign of Macrinus

The Praetorian Prefect Marcus Opellius Macrinus was the first non-senator to become Emperor. He was a native of Mauretania who had been closely associated with Plautianus, but he had survived the fall of his patron. He was declared Emperor by the army in the east – after a suitable delay, in an attempt to avoid the charge that he had killed Caracalla so that he could take over the Empire. He started out with three disadvantages: he was not of the correct social class, he owed his elevation to the army, and he was not in Rome when he became Emperor; nor could he abandon the east to travel there straight away. Other Emperors had faced one or two of these disadvantages in the past, but not all of them at once. Vespasian had been declared Emperor by the army in Egypt and then the east, and his

immediate ancestors were equestrians, but he was himself of senatorial rank
and was able to leave the war in Judaea to his son Titus while he went to
Rome. Pertinax had started his career as a freedman, but when he became
Emperor he was a respected senator with an illustrious career behind him,
and being conveniently in Rome at the time he could establish himself more
easily *vis-à-vis* the Senate and the Praetorians. Macrinus was an equestrian
and had not made the transition to higher rank via adlection to the Senate, and
he considered that he could not leave the eastern campaign hanging in the
air while he set off to establish himself in Rome. Perhaps because he ruled
for only 14 months, and perhaps because he had reached a respectably high
equestrian rank, his reign is not presented as a turning point in Roman
history to the same degree as that of Maximinus Thrax, who was Emperor
for longer (over three years) and had risen through the ranks of the army
from lowly peasant stock. There is in any case no single date which can be
identified as a turning point in the third-century Roman Empire. The year
217 would be as artificial as 235 or 260, but the former date is largely
ignored while the two latter dates have become accepted markers whereby to
divide history into manageable portions. The rise of Macrinus ought to have
created waves in the Senate and throughout the Roman world, but as Dio
explains, the senators were so relieved to be rid of Caracalla that they did not
notice at first that the new Emperor was not of the relevant social rank.[70]

Macrinus took the name of Severus to imbue his reign with some continuity with the previous regime, just as Severus had taken the name of Pertinax, and then the name of Marcus Aurelius for his son. In a letter to the
Senate, Macrinus announced his adoption of the Severan name and gave
himself the additional titles of Pius Felix Augustus. Dio's account is particularly valuable because he witnessed the events of which he writes, or at least
he was the equivalent of the Rome correspondent while Imperial history
played out in the east, though he does not always write of these events with
total impartiality. He points out that Macrinus knew perfectly well that it
would have been more fitting to wait for the Senate to bestow these titles
upon him, but he chose to act on his own authority. On the subject of Caracalla, everyone proceeded with circumspection. Macrinus did not declare
him an enemy of Rome, nor did he deify him at first, because he knew that
while the Senate and people hated Caracalla, the soldiers had liked and supported him. In Rome too, the senators did not dare to vote for damnation of
Caracalla's memory because of their fear of the soldiers in the city. The
divergent interests of the civil population and the military were highlighted
very clearly, and, just as clearly, the preponderant influence lay with the
soldiers. It was as though the different elements of the Roman world had
forgotten that they had originally been part of the same firm. Aims, motives
and needs had become very different.[71]

In keeping with Imperial practice, Macrinus was consul in 218, with
Oclatinius Adventus as his colleague. Adventus had also been his colleague

as Praetorian Prefect, and had been first choice as Emperor after the death of Caracalla but had refused the honour on account of his age. His appointment caused resentment, according to Dio, since Adventus' origins were extremely low. He was an uneducated ex-mercenary who had been a member of the *frumentarii* or secret police. To add insult to injury, Macrinus made him city prefect, replacing him soon afterwards by Marius Maximus, perhaps because of public disapproval but more likely because Adventus was an old man who had seen long service. Other appointments of Macrinus were criticised because he employed non-senators in positions of responsibility which more usually went to consulars, or in other words he chose men he knew and trusted and gave them tasks which he considered that they could fulfil, regardless of social standing or rank. He removed Caracalla's adherents Sabinus and Castinus from their posts as governors of Pannonia and Dacia, and installed in their stead his own men Marcius Agrippa and Deccius Triccianus. The former was a slave who had been convicted and banished, and the latter was once door-keeper to the governor of Pannonia, rising to commander of *II Parthica* and then to provincial governor. These appointments are mentioned in Dio's account because of their irregularity, but serve to reveal that Macrinus took his role seriously and did attend to Imperial government while also finishing off the Parthian war, which was by no means over. King Artabanus had seized his chance and launched an offensive against Mesopotamia. The Romans were off-guard and not very effective, and at one point the Emperor himself was in danger. He prepared for a counter-offensive, but the war was ended by negotiation and some readjustments of territorial boundaries. The Armenian question was solved for the time being by giving up some of the territory previously taken over by Rome, but also by installing Tiridates as king under Roman control. Macrinus also paid indemnities to Artabanus. It was considerably easier and more sensible to buy peace in this way than to engage in a war at this particular moment. Macrinus was not a military man, despite his appointment as Praetorian Prefect; he was an experienced jurist, an administrator with a wide knowledge of how the Empire functioned and most likely a realistic idea of his own capabilities in conducting a war in the east, of the state of preparedness of the army to fight such a war, and of the multiple problems he would face if he concentrated on an attempt to defeat Parthia instead of attending to his own needs and those of the Roman Empire. Sufficiently satisfied with the outcome of the eastern campaign, he awarded himself the title *Parthicus Maximus* in his report to the Senate.[72]

The rise of Elagabalus

In attempting to provide for the future succession, Macrinus bestowed on his young son Diadumenianus the title Caesar, which was confirmed by the Senate, and also the name Antoninus. This was in deference to the army, to

Figure 6 Billon denarius from the Rome mint, with the legend DIVO ANTONINO MAGNO denoting the deification of Caracalla. The Syrian princesses relied strongly upon the supposed descent of Severus Alexander and Elagabalus from Caracalla, so it was very much in their interests to deify him, but it is not certain which Emperor was responsible for the deification. (Drawn by Trish Boyle.)

illustrate the connection with Caracalla, who was eventually deified. The army was essential as the main prop for his regime, but he needed to strike a balance. Macrinus tried to curb the expenses of the army, without unduly offending the troops. He ignored the arrangements made by Caracalla, adhering to the Severan regulations as far as he could, enrolling new recruits on Severan terms. Whilst he did not attempt to withdraw any privileges, he reverted to the Severan rates of pay, ignoring the rise that Caracalla had awarded the army, a measure which may have pleased the Senate and people but certainly did not please the soldiers, who were accustomed to the lavish rewards given them by Caracalla; it was comparable to offering a nice juicy steak to a lion and then, just as the jaws closed around it, suddenly removing it with the explanation that there would not be any more. The Emperor then proclaimed a victory over Parthia, but did not celebrate it by gifts to the army; the discontented troops began to murmur. Dio says that Macrinus ought to have distributed the individual units over the eastern provinces in winter quarters instead of allowing them to remain together, where the potential for rebellion was enhanced. The presence of the large eastern army made it easier for rival claimants to power to ferment a rising. Communications with the troops were easier and quicker, sounding out loyalties was facilitated, so when relatives of the Severan family made their move the ground had been well prepared. Julia Domna did not long survive her son Caracalla, but she had a sister, Julia Maesa, whose ambitions were no less ardent than her own. Julia Maesa's two daughters, Julia Soaemias and Julia Mammaea, each had a young son, and Maesa was determined that the elder boy should be Emperor. She persuaded the soldiers that the true father of Soaemias' son Varius Avitus Bassianus was Caracalla, and on 16 May 218 the army declared the boy Emperor, with the name Marcus Aurelius Antoninus, thus bequeathing to the Roman world the detested ruler nicknamed Elagabalus after his devotion to the eastern god of the same name. Macrinus persuaded the Senate to declare the usurper an enemy of the state, and elevated Diadumenianus to the rank of Augustus. These measures availed him nothing. The troops deserted him, and he was forced to flee. He and his son were killed. Elagabalus entered Antioch early in June and wrote to the Senate as Emperor. Like Macrinus he did not wait for his names and titles to be voted by the Senate, styling himself Imperator Caesar Antoninus, grandson of Severus, Pius Felix Augustus. Establishing his connection with Severus and the Antonines did not give him sufficient security as Emperor; he declared himself a descendant of Nerva as well. He gave the soldiers 2,000 sesterces each to persuade them not to sack Antioch, another indication of the ease with which a Roman army could turn against a city, whether it was hostile or not. Fourteen months later Elagabalus entered Rome, at the end of September 219, bringing with him the strange and passionate cult of the god after which he was named. As priest of this cult Elagabalus would not be persuaded to wear suitable Roman clothing, and had ordered a painting of himself in his priestly robes to be sent on ahead to Rome and placed in the Senate house, so that everyone would become accustomed to seeing him and not be shocked. Even with these visual aids, it is possible that the Senate and people of Rome, in accepting the penultimate member of the Severan regime, had no inkling of the character of the new Emperor, nor of the overpowering influence of the Syrian princesses.[73]

Probably before he arrived in Rome Elagabalus embarked on the usual round of reshuffling military and government officials, disposing of Macrinus' followers and installing his own. P. Valerius Comazon was made Praetorian Prefect, though according to Dio he had absolutely no experience. He rose even higher, quite rapidly attaining the rank of consul, which had become the usual form for Praetorian Prefects, but then like Plautianus he was actually made consul, counting this as his second term of office because he had previously obtained the *ornamenta consularia*. It was all very irregular, but even worse developments followed. Comazon was appointed city prefect, an office which he held three times – quite unprecedented for anyone even if he originated from the correct social rank, so it was considered positively scandalous for an equestrian who had once been condemned to the galleys. The senator responsible for condemning him to the galleys, Claudius Attalus, did not long survive Comazon's appointment as Praetorian Prefect. Other victims were despatched as quickly; Dio lists some of them: Triccianus, Castinus, Valerianus Poetus, Seius Carus, Silius Messalla, and Pomponius Bassus.

The last two were condemned because they opposed what the Emperor was doing, suggesting that not everyone was totally compliant, or at least that there were one or two men willing and able to raise objections. The gesture was wasted, because the Senate as a whole condemned them after Elagabalus had killed them. As if the deaths were not enough, there was a more sinister development in that Elagabalus did not always bother to go through the proper formalities in every case; he simply had people murdered without making a statement to the Senate before or afterwards.[74]

For the reign of Elagabalus the focus of the ancient sources is on Rome itself, with the result that knowledge of what was happening in the provinces is not clearly elucidated. The enormities of the reign hold all the attention. Elagabalus was unable or unwilling to shake off the controlling authority of his mother Julia Soaemias, and he was a confirmed homosexual, despite his several marriages. It was not so much his outrageous sexual behaviour that caused offence as the fact that he was strongly influenced, to the exclusion of all else, by the men with whom he associated, such as Zoticus and Hierocles. Julia Maesa tried to control her grandson without success, and soon found a way of supplanting him by her other grandson, Gessius Bassianus Alexianus, the son of Julia Mammaea. She arranged his formal adoption by Elagabalus, who was only a few years older than his cousin. The Senate ratified the adoption, fully aware of the ridiculousness of it all. Alexianus was renamed Alexander, becoming consul in 221. Before long Elagabalus was intriguing against his cousin, but found that Alexander was too well protected by his grandmother and the Praetorians. The end was not far off. On 6 March 222 the soldiers killed Elagabalus, his mother, and many of his adherents, including Fulvius the city prefect. Once again Comazon filled this sudden vacancy for his third term as city prefect. He was perhaps the only one of Elagabalus' court to survive. Alexianus Bassianus, still a teenager, was declared Emperor, taking the name Marcus Aurelius Severus Alexander.[75]

Severus Alexander

Reforms and reparations were badly needed. One of the first appointments was Domitius Ulpianus, or Ulpian, as Praetorian Prefect. He replaced the two Praetorian Prefects Flavianus and Chrestus, and seemingly did not have a colleague throughout his short-lived appointment. He was not a military man, but was another jurist like Papinian, for at this time administrators and legal experts were required to a greater extent than soldiers, though that was soon to change when almost perpetual war began on the eastern and northern frontiers, and military expertise was then vital. Ulpian was part of Julia Maesa's circle, perhaps with long-established connections with the Severan dynasty. He had been *praefectus annonae* at the beginning of 222, becoming Praetorian Prefect in December of the same year. His

achievements were worthy. According to Dio he was not only appointed
Praetorian Prefect but was put in charge of 'the other business of the
Empire' and 'corrected many wrongs'. He was killed nonetheless. Traditionally it was believed that Ulpian was murdered in 228, but it now seems
certain that he lasted only from the accession of Severus Alexander in 222
until the spring of 223, and he may have been a casualty of the three days of
rioting in Rome, as fighting broke out between the populace and the Praetorians, when the soldiers of the Guard burned down some buildings in the
city. Dio does not elaborate on this theme, but adds in a later passage that
when he was consul with the Emperor as colleague, probably in 229, he was
advised not to come to Rome in case the Praetorians caused trouble. After
seven years of rule by Severus Alexander and the Syrian princesses, it is clear
that not all was well in Rome, but the sources are of very little use in trying
to discern exactly what was happening.[76]

The dearth of reliable information is the greatest drawback in any account
of the reign of Severus Alexander. Herodian witnessed the events he
described, but he was writing for the Greek east, where his audience was not
always familiar with the details of Roman administration, which he sometimes has to explain; his history is sometimes melodramatic but it is short
on analysis and rather superficial. Dio, another contemporary, is to be preferred when it comes to historical evidence, but unfortunately his account
peters out at precisely this period because he was appointed governor of
various provinces and spent some time away from Rome. The biography in
the *Historia Augusta* is mostly if not completely fictitious, perhaps an exercise in rhetoric aimed at the Emperor Julian, as a portrait of the perfect
prince. 'It will not be imagined ... that the author [of the *HA*] was much
concerned with the truth of his facts', says Crook in his analysis of the *consilium* of the Emperor, but it is possible that the sources used by the insouciant
author were better than is usually supposed. As always, the problem is to
identify which sections are authentic and which are spurious.[77]

Throughout the reign of Severus Alexander, the Syrian princesses Julia
Maesa and, after her death, the Emperor's mother Julia Mammaea, were the
guiding forces in the government. Mammaea was honoured with several
titles which gave her no actual political powers but extended her influence.
In particular she took on the role that Julia Domna had held with regard to
the army, with the title *mater castrorum*, or mother of the camp. Not content
with that alone, eventually she was known as *mater Augusti et castrorum et
senatus atque patriae*, indicating that her influence if not her authority
extended over most aspects of Roman life, including the Senate. This sort of
influence worked through connections and favours, not via political procedures, but it was just as effective. The Syrian princesses took care to sur-
round the young Emperor with the best-qualified advisers, choosing 16 of
the noblest senators to guide him. These may have acted as part of his
council, which included 70 members if the passage in the *Historia Augusta* is

correct. The names of some of the councillors are listed in the *HA*, but they are not otherwise identifiable since they are not corroborated by other evidence, and may be imaginary. Crook concluded that the council, whatever its size, did not prepare business for the whole Senate, nor did its membership rotate to refresh its composition. As to the issues that preoccupied the Emperor and his council, and the enactments that were carried out, there is virtually no information. Herodian's bland statement that all unworthy men were removed from office, and the correct men installed in posts for which they were trained, is somewhat platitudinous; more detail and some discussion would have been appreciated. It is fortunate for the young Emperor and his advisers that there was a peaceful interlude until 230, during which the policy of expansion and aggressive warfare was dormant, taking second place to reparation and restructuring of the government. The eight or nine years before war broke out in the east enabled a new aristocracy to establish itself, after the upheavals of Caracalla's reign, the eliminations of Macrinus, and the enormities of Elagabalus. Some of the old Severan notables re-emerged during the 220s, infiltrating government posts and the Imperial court.[78]

While the Romans had been concentrating on their internal problems the Parthian Royal house was under threat from a powerful new lord, nominally a vassal of Artabanus V. This was Ardashir, or Artaxerxes, of Iranian lineage. At the beginning of the third century the seeds of rebellion were already sown, culminating in a complete take-over in 224, when the Sassanid Persian dynasty with Ardashir at its head supplanted that of the Parthian Artabanus, after the latter was defeated and killed on the battlefield of Hormizdagan. Within a few years, Ardashir had begun to expand his empire to incorporate the states around the old Parthian kingdom. This naturally brought him into contact with Roman frontier territories. The first news of trouble on the eastern frontier reached Rome probably in 229 when the Persian king attacked Hatra. By 230 Severus Alexander was preparing for an eastern expedition, recruiting in Italy and the provinces according to Herodian. He left Rome in spring 231.[79]

There was trouble among the troops when Severus Alexander arrived in the east. The Mesopotamian legions had murdered the governor Flavius Heracleo, and the Egyptian troops among Alexander's army were restless. These problems were dealt with before the campaign began. Coins were issued proclaiming the loyalty of the army (*Fides Militum, Fides Exercitus*), more an indication of wishful thinking than reality. There seems to have been an overall strategic plan for the attack on Ardashir. Using Antioch as a base, Alexander attacked in three columns, leading the central one himself, while the others marched to the north and south, one to Armenia and then into Media, and the other towards the city of Ctesiphon. The results were mixed, with huge losses on both sides, but especially to the Roman troops which marched back through the hostile heights of Armenia. Alexander was blamed for his timidity in his slow advance and lack of support for the other

Figure 7 Severus Alexander portrayed on a brass sestertius from Rome, issued in 231 as the Emperor was about to depart for the Persian campaign. The reverse (not shown) bears the legend PROFECTIO AUGUSTI, and depicts the goddess Victory walking before the Emperor on horseback. (Drawn by Trish Boyle.)

two columns, and at some point there was an attempted usurpation by a certain Uranius, who was quickly suppressed. All was not well with the Roman army, but the details are not clear, obscured perhaps by sources hostile to Alexander and his mother. Yet his achievements were perhaps not as abysmal as they have been painted; the Persians remained quiet after the campaigns, not causing any serious trouble until the 240s under Ardashir's successor Shapur. Alexander took the title *Parthicus Maximus*, or *Persicus Maximus* (both are attested), probably with more justification than he has been allowed.[80]

While he was still in Antioch, Alexander received news of disturbances on the Rhine and Danube. He had troops in his eastern campaign army whose bases were on the northern frontier and in the Illyrian provinces, and these men became agitated about the safety of their homes and families. There had been attacks on the frontiers at several points: in Upper Germany in the region of the Wetterau, where there were productive farmlands, and in Raetia in the region of the Altmühl valley. Even the legionary fortress of Strasbourg had been threatened. Without concluding an official peace with Ardashir, Alexander wound up the war and returned to Rome at the end of 232 to celebrate a triumph, and then to begin preparations for the war on the northern frontiers. He took with him troops which had fought in Mesopotamia, such as the archers from Osroene and the units of Moors, as well as the legionaries and auxiliaries who had formed the detachments sent to the east. As part of the preparations he placed an experienced officer, C. Julius Verus Maximinus, in command of the recruits, with the responsibility

Figure 8 Portrait of Julia Mamaea on a gold aureus of about 225 from the Rome mint. Julia and her sister were the driving forces behind the throne. (Drawn by Trish Boyle.)

for training the troops for the coming campaign. The destruction of several forts along the Taunus–Wetterau frontier in Germany has been dated to 233 or thereabouts, suggesting that this area was where the German tribes concentrated their attacks, an assumption corroborated by the fact that Severus Alexander chose Mainz as his base, launching an offensive in 234 against the German tribes who were by now calling themselves the Alamanni. So far all had gone well, but instead of pursuing the enemy and eradicating them, Alexander began to negotiate, allegedly offering money and perhaps food tributes to buy the tribesmen off. He may have assessed the situation correctly, analysing what it was that the tribesmen needed, preferring to give it to them before they came to take it; but the troops saw it differently. There would be many reasons why the army was discontented. Having been granted a whiff of action and then stopped before their enthusiasm had run its course they would still be keyed up, eager for glory and booty. Those whose relatives had suffered would seek revenge, and would be very much opposed to withdrawal and then subsidy payments to the tribesmen, who now seemed to be rewarded for attacks on Roman territories and possessions. The Emperor's policy caused much resentment. Perhaps he would have done better to wage a brief and bloody campaign and when honour and revenge were satisfied he could have offered immediate peace and ongoing subsidies. Whether or not his policy was well- or ill-advised, in early spring 235 Severus Alexander and his mother were murdered.[81]

THE END OF THE SEVERANS: MAXIMINUS
THRAX BECOMES EMPEROR

The Pannonian soldiers declared Maximinus Emperor. He was better known to the troops than Severus Alexander, with a proven military record. He was a Thracian who had joined the army and risen from the ranks, the first soldier to become Emperor, only a few decades after Septimius Severus had opened up military careers, broadened the base of recruitment and facilitated promotions for outstanding soldiers and junior officers. Maximinus Thrax was perceived by the Senate as a barbarian, not even a true Roman, despite Caracalla's edict bestowing citizenship on all freeborn inhabitants of the Empire, and perhaps unworthy to become Emperor. These perceptions did not prevent the senators from passing the necessary decrees to invest Maximinus with Imperial powers. Without a senatorial army to back them up it would have been foolish for the senators to refuse to recognise the new Emperor, and would have angered the soldiers gathered on the Rhine who perceived Maximinus as an energetic commander who would teach the barbarians a lesson. He did not disappoint his supporters, going to war almost at once, but he was not allowed to concentrate solely on the campaign. Even in the Rhine and Danube armies not everyone was unanimous in support of his rule; there were squabbles among the military officers, who were thwarted one way or another. The Osroenian archers, led by a certain Macedo, elevated Quartinus, one of their own men, a friend of Severus Alexander, but Macedo had second thoughts and killed his Imperial candidate, hoping to be rewarded by Maximinus; his reward was execution. A group of officers decided to rid themselves of Maximinus and declared for a senator called Magnus, but failed to achieve their aims. The effect of these disturbances was to produce or rather to accentuate in Maximinus a healthy distrust of everyone, especially senators. His son C. Julius Verus Maximus was quickly declared Caesar, though he was still very young, in order to lend some stability to the regime and prepare for continuity. The immediate entourage of Severus Alexander was removed. This time it seemed that there was no wholesale murder or rapine, even though Herodian accuses Maximinus of cruelty after the revolts against him. Some men were relegated to lower grade posts and commands, such as the equestrian Timesitheus, one of the close associates of Alexander, who survived but was sent out of the way to a provincial command.[82]

By the end of 235, Maximinus was calling himself *Germanicus Maximus*, and in 236 he had transferred the army to Pannonia, basing himself at Sirmium to fight against the Sarmatians and Dacians, adding *Sarmaticus* and *Dacicus* to his titles. There is little information on the battles that preceded these declarations of victory. Archaeologically the evidence suffers from lack of firm dates, but several inscriptions from Pannonia referring to soldiers killed in a Dacian war, or to a Dacian expedition, can be dated to the reign

Figure 9 Caius Julius Verus Maximinus, better known as Maximinus Thrax, Emperor 235–8. Marble bust of unknown date. (Courtesy Ny Carlsberg Glyptotek.)

of Maximinus. Occupied with these northern wars, Maximinus did not enter Rome to reaffirm his rule and shore up his regime. If he could not appear in person because his presence was needed in the war zone, he could have sent messengers or representatives to explain his policies, to try to win at least some members of the Senate to his side. Instead he ignored the Senate and concentrated wholly on the frontiers, consuming vast amounts of money to pay the soldiers. The usual taxes did not prove sufficient for his needs, but to be fair to him income had not matched expenditure for some considerable time, so he had inherited a problem at a time when he required vast sums to pay the army. If he had been like the first Augustus, he would have packaged the necessary taxation and confiscations much more succinctly, either personally or by sending envoys to explain why he required money. Communications were as efficient as they could be in the ancient world, and propaganda was not unknown to the Romans. Maximinus could have stressed the importance of containing the northern tribes, outlining the consequences if he and the army failed. Perhaps if he had tried he could have limited the financial damage caused by his taxation policies, or altered perceptions of it, but in concentrating on the matter in hand he did not seem to care about other sectors of the community, laying himself open to charges of cruelty, greed and corruption. He complicated matters by giving the soldiers a pay rise, never a popular move because the inhabitants of Rome, secure now for many years, did not experience at first hand the threats to their frontiers and probably did not worry about it very much until there was a sudden scare, as in the reign of Marcus Aurelius when the Germans reached Aquileia in the north of Italy. To the Romans of Rome and the more peaceful provinces, the army was far away, full of foreign-sounding, semi-barbarous men who were troublesome and greedy. It was no longer a case of their own young men marching bravely away to fight in defence of the Empire, then coming home in various states ranging from heroic corpses, through walking wounded, to healthy heroes. When the Empire was smaller, the army was a part of the state, consisting of neighbours and friends, but now it was literally a foreign body, and despite the work that the soldiers did the army was not appreciated, particularly when money was wrested from unwilling hands to pay for its services. The financial dilemma had important consequences, provincial in origin but affecting the whole Empire. Some of the wealthy nobles in Africa rebelled against the extraordinary harsh tax collections, killing the procurator in Thysdrus (modern El Djem), and from there going on to realise that in order to prevent Imperial retribution they would need an Emperor of their own. The octogenarian proconsul M. Antonius Gordianus Sempronianus was persuaded to take on the task, immediately sharing it with his son of the same name; they are known to modern audiences as Gordian I and II.[83]

THE THREE GORDIANS

At the beginning of April 238 the Senate confirmed the Gordians in power, damned the memory of Maximinus and possibly deified Severus Alexander at the same time. The chronology of the rapidly shifting balance of power is difficult to establish precisely, especially since important events took place in various parts of the Roman world, perhaps simultaneously or as near to it as to make no appreciable difference. In Rome the Praetorian Prefect Vitalianus, loyal to Maximinus, was killed by agents of the Gordians, and the city prefect Sabinus was despatched by the Roman mob in a riot. In Africa, the two Gordians were routed and killed by the governor of Numidia, Capellianus, who was loyal to Maximinus, and who was fortunately not sufficiently interested in seizing power for himself. The Empire was now officially leaderless, though Maximinus and his troops would take issue with that judgement. The Senate was faced with two main courses of action. On the one hand there was the unpalatable choice of approaching Maximinus and admitting that there had been some mistake when he was accidentally declared an enemy of the state, or on the other hand there was the rather more acceptable possibility of finding a rival candidate to take on the Empire. The Senate acted with promptness and resolution, electing 20 of its most respected members to take charge of the government of the Empire (*vigintiviri rei publicae curandae*). The term *res publica* does not refer to the old Roman Republic, but translates as public business, or government as an abstract whole, so the senators were fully conscious that they had not restored the Republic. That was an impossibility now. An Emperor had to be found, but the Senate compromised by electing from the *vigintiviri* two Emperors, M. Clodius Pupienus Maximus and Decimus Caelius Calvinus Balbinus. The elevation of dual Emperors harked back to old times, as if the new Emperors were regarded as mega-consuls, each checking and balancing the other, and sharing the burden of Imperial government. When the people and the soldiers of the Praetorian Guard agitated in favour of the thirteen-year-old M. Antonius Gordianus, the nephew of Gordian II, the Senate recognised the boy as Caesar, conceding that he was marked out as the successor of the two senatorial Emperors.[84]

Very rapidly, the Senate and the two new Emperors were involved in civil war as the outlawed Maximinus approached Italy. Balbinus remained in Rome, while Pupienus Maximus marched north to meet Maximinus coming from the Danube. He won a victory of sorts. At Aquileia, where Maximinus was besieging the town, his army was disaffected. Food supplies were low and morale was even lower. Eventually the soldiers of *II Parthica*, thinking of the safety of their families at Alba, not far from Rome, took the law into their own hands. They killed Maximinus and his son. Everything fizzled out; Pupienus Maximus took over all the troops, keeping the German contingents as his bodyguard, and sent the others back to their bases, then returned to Rome. His employment of German guards made it seem as though he was aiming for sole power, so his colleague Balbinus felt a little put out, and the Praetorians began to worry that Pupienus might supplant them altogether and institute a German guard unit instead. In the event, the experiment with two equal Emperors failed because of mutual jealousies and their inability to win over the soldiers of the Praetorian Guard, who brutally tortured and then murdered both Pupienus Maximus and Balbinus, and declared Gordian III Emperor.[85]

Gordian III

The main sources for the history of Rome up to this point now expire altogether or lose themselves in fantasy. Herodian's account stops with the accession of the teenage Gordian, and the *Historia Augusta* is like the curate's egg: good in parts, fictional for much of the time, but reliable in those passages which are derived from Dexippus, who lived through the attacks on Greece and described how Athens withstood an attack by the Heruli in 267–8. Fragments of this account and of his other historical works survive in the form of quotations or precis in the *Historia Augusta* and other sources; the problem is to identify these fragments if the author who used the passages does not directly acknowledge his source material; this is a painstaking and detailed exercise, giving rise to a well-established secondary literature. Despite the quantity of extant works stemming from the pens of the ancient authors, the reign of Gordian III is not well illustrated. Even his ancestry is not properly documented, the parentage in the *Historia Augusta* being discredited. His mother's name is given as Maecia Faustina, but it is not at all certain that this is correct. Unfortunately the lady in question does not appear on the coinage or in other sources, so corroborative evidence is lacking. It seems that whoever she was, the mother of Gordian III was the sister of Gordian II, which means that the elderly Gordian I was the young Emperor's grandfather. The hereditary principle had therefore held good for the first time since the transition between the reign of Severus and that of Caracalla, but only because the Praetorians and a large part of the army endorsed it this time.[86]

Besides the soldiers, the nobles also rallied to Gordian, as did the populace, possibly because his accession brought a temporary peace after a long period of unrest, and measures were taken to put right the several wrongs that had plagued the state since the reign of Caracalla. Attempts were put in hand to ameliorate the financial situation of the inhabitants of the Empire without compromising the state treasury. The ranks of the sycophants and informers were considerably thinned, and control of the army was tightened up. For a brief period it seems that there were fewer equites in posts that were traditionally held by senators, though it is not possible to talk of a reversal of Severan policy or anything so definite, partly because the known samples do not represent the whole picture over the whole Empire, and partly because these social changes were fluid, not the sort of events that had clearly defined start dates and end dates.[87]

As part of the tightening up of control of the army, *Legio III Augusta* in Africa was disbanded for its part in the defeat and deaths of the first two Gordians. Capellianus, who had led the troops, submitted to the new Emperor. But without the legion to keep order and to take charge of defence, trouble broke out afresh in Africa. A certain Sabinianus made a bid for power; the governor of Mauretania Caesariensis restored order. It was only a brief interlude but it proved that not all the inhabitants of the Empire were loyal or satisfied, and that the path to power was by now a well-trodden one, continually embarked upon, despite the known risks, by soldiers and officers, Romans and Romanised provincials, sane well-intentioned individuals and not a few madmen, all over the Empire. Gordian III was hardly of an age to rule by himself, so the question must be asked, how and by whom was the Empire governed? After 241 the leading figure was Timesitheus, who was appointed Praetorian Prefect and to all practical intents and purposes directed policy and military matters. Before that date certain individuals are known, including some of those men who had been among the elected *vigintiviri* while the Senate assumed command and fought against Maximinus. Among the other influential men are some of the Severan aristocracy who resurfaced intact during Gordian's reign.[88]

The Imperial peace did not last long over the whole Empire. Internal as well as external troubles beset the provinces. In some areas there was dissension between the civilian population and the soldiers, as the famous inscription from the Thracian village of Skaptopara (in Bulgaria) demonstrates. The villagers petitioned the Emperor Gordian in 238 to protect them against the predations of the soldiers of the nearby garrisons, who descended upon them demanding *hospitium* (in Greek *xenia* or *xeinie*), literally 'hospitality' but implying much more than that. It was not exactly an illegal procedure, having its roots in Republican and early Imperial practice when soldiers were quartered not in barracks but in official lodging houses; in the case of Skaptopara it descended into blatant exploitation, because the soldiers seem to have interpreted it very loosely to embrace anything and everything that they wanted, all extracted free of charge. Gordian replied to the villagers but referred them to the governor of the province. It is not easy to quantify to what extent the complaints of the inhabitants of Skaptopara may have been symptomatic of similar problems elsewhere, but if armed soldiers decided to exert pressure to gain their own ends in any province, similar scenarios would result, unless their officers were particularly conscientious. Externally, there were ominous signs of disturbance in the Empire. In the west coin hoards deposited in the years 238–44 indicate some kind of trouble, usually interpreted as unrest originating from incursions of tribesmen from beyond the Rhine. It seems that there was some destruction in north-western Gaul, and in some parts of Germany, where coins and other objects were buried between 241 and 244 at Kösching and Gunzenhausen, and the fort at Künzing was destroyed. Further east, Pannonia was quiet and untroubled, but in Moesia and Dacia the Carpi and the Goths had erupted into Roman territory. The Emperors Pupienus and Balbinus sent Menophilus to restore order in 238, and he succeeded in doing so, repairing roads, fortifying Marcianopolis, and establishing a mint at Viminacium. He brought the tribes to terms and arranged a treaty, more favourable to the Goths, who received subsidies, than to the Carpi, who did not. It may have been a deliberate ploy to set one tribe against another and divert attention from Roman territories, but it sowed seeds of discontent for the future.[89]

While the Romans fought each other, the Persian king Ardashir took advantage of his enemy's preoccupation. As early as 239 he attacked Dura-Europos; he may have captured Hatra. He overran the greater part of Mesopotamia, ready to cross the Euphrates, threatening Syria. A gap in the coinage of Antioch from 240–1 implies that he may have attacked or even taken the city; if so, an embarrassing situation for the Romans. No official peace had been concluded with the Persians in the 230s, but in Rome preparations for war were made very formally in 241, the same year that Timesitheus became Praetorian Prefect and his daughter was married to Gordian III. When all was ready, the doors of the temple of Janus, closed only when the Empire was at peace, were ceremonially opened. Timesitheus prepared well for the eastern campaign, using his long military and administrative experience, especially in logistics and supplies. But there was a delay; before he could concentrate on the war with Ardashir he was forced to attend to the Goths and Germans in Illyricum. The tribesmen were restless after Timesitheus had disgraced and removed Menophilus in 241 for reasons that are not fully elucidated, but their restlessness may have resulted from the fact that tribesmen in general were much more comfortable in making treaties with an individual rather than with a state, and so when Menophilus, whom they trusted, was swept aside the tribesmen probably felt that betrayal of their treaty arrangements was imminent. Timesitheus conducted a short war in 242, probably recruiting tribesmen for the eastern front as he concluded peace. The date when he and Gordian III arrived in the east is disputed; it was probably in the last months of 242, thus delaying the start of the Persian campaign until the spring of 243. By now Ardashir had raised his son Shapur as his colleague in power, and the latter may have taken over Edessa. Timesitheus wrested Osroene from Persian control and restored Abgar X to power. After a battle at Rhesaena the Persians left Nisibis and Singara, but at this high point of the war Timesitheus died. The Romans did not recover from the blow, though Gordian III and the Praetorian Prefect Marcus Julius Verus Philippus, better known as Philip the Arab, followed the original plan and marched to Ctesiphon. Events are now clouded in obscurity. The upshot is that Gordian III died, somehow. Philip has been blamed for his death, but he may have been innocent; there are four different versions in the ancient sources for Gordian's demise, so it seems that even the historians were not sure of the facts. The more recently discovered source, the so-called *Res Gestae Divi Saporis*, insists that Gordian was killed in battle, approximating to the story of Zonaras that the Emperor broke his thigh and died afterwards.[90]

PHILIP THE ARAB

Philip was declared Emperor by the troops. Like many another newly elevated Emperor after the sudden death of the previous one, he was in an awkward position in more ways than one. He gave out that Gordian's death was from natural causes, and treated the dead Emperor with the greatest respect, transporting his ashes to Rome, insisting upon his deification, and negotiating carefully with the Senate, gaining recognition as Emperor in the process. Meanwhile he had to extricate the army from the clutches of the Persians while retaining some credibility and, more importantly, his head, in both the physical and emotional sense. The negotiated peace was not so ignominious, despite the accusation that he lost territory. It seems that he held onto Timesitheus' reconquest of Osroene and Mesopotamia, but he had to give up all pretence of controlling Armenia and pay an indemnity to the Persians of 500,000 denarii. It is possible that he also agreed to pay regular tribute in addition to the initial payment, but this is not proven and has not found corroboration except in Persian sources. Philip issued coins proclaiming that he had made peace with the Persians (*pax fundata cum Persis*), but the fact that he had bought his way out of a tricky situation was not well received at Rome, so despite his proud statement on his coinage, he is accused of hastening back to Rome without settling the east, since an inscription seems to indicate that he was there by July 244; this has been questioned, especially since Aurelius Victor says that he organised the east before he left, placing his brother Priscus in command. Priscus was Praetorian Prefect, and an equestrian, so it was perfectly acceptable to appoint him Prefect of Mesopotamia, but documents show that he was also governor of Syria, which was a consular command. An inscription reveals that he held the title *rector Orientis*, which while not signifying an actual office does indicate that he held wide-ranging powers over the east, powers which he used firmly if not brutally since Zosimus says that he caused offence among the provincials, especially on account of his financial measures.[91]

Once arrived in Rome, Philip made his son Caesar, though some authorities place the event in 246, followed by the boy's elevation to Augustus in 247. The Emperor's wife, Otacilia Severa, was named Augusta. As a further insurance policy for his regime Philip deified his father Marinus, even though he had never been Emperor. This was an unprecedented measure, but it was perhaps less artificial than trying to claim descent from any of the previous Emperors, none of whom had been particularly admirable or worthy as ancestors, and it would stretch the facts from suspension of disbelief to outright farce to try to manufacture a family tree that connected Philip, born in Arabia, to the household of Severus. Philip enjoyed good relations with the Senate, and from the outset of his reign he reaffirmed the old Roman virtues and traditions. Defence of the Empire was his first priority, and from 246–7 he fought the Carpi and Quadi on the Danube, taking

Figure 10 Gold aureus with the legend SAECULUM NOVUM dated to 248. The goddess Roma is shown in her temple, to mark 1,000 years of the city and Empire. The coinage of Philip the Arab was largely devoted to this theme and emphasised the splendour and magnificence of the festivities of the Secular Games. The obverse shows a portrait of Philip's wife Otacilia Severa Augusta. (Drawn by Trish Boyle.)

the titles *Germanicus* and *Carpicus Maximus*. In 248, back in Rome, he celebrated the Secular Games, always a significant festival for the Romans, marking their development and power over the centuries. This time the celebrations were even more meaningful, since it was the first millennium of Rome, an occasion worthy of celebration, highlighting the fact that Rome if not the Empire had existed for a thousand years. There were multiple celebrations, theatrical and musical events, spectacles in the Circus and the amphitheatre, literary and artistic displays. Strictly, the Secular Games were not due to take place for over sixty years, since there was supposed to be a gap of 110 years between each festival to ensure that only one celebration could be witnessed in one lifetime, and Severus had already celebrated the Games. But the ritual religious purifications associated with the Games were probably felt by some to be long overdue. The festival was not simply a backward-looking, self-congratulatory exercise; despite the long catalogue of wars, both victorious and disastrous, the usurpations, and the cataclysmic changes of fortune, it probably seemed that Rome would go on for ever. The coinage proclaimed at one and the same time her title and her destiny, *Roma Aeterna*. Philip could look forward to putting into operation reforms and innovations, forewarned at least of the problems and of what not to do by the mistakes of Maximinus. Philip's internal policy had little time to unfold, and the details are lost. The document that used to be accepted as a glowing account of his reign, the so-called *Eis Basileia* (*To the King*), has been re-examined and redated, and in one case attributed to Gallienus instead, though the text, full of commonplace rhetorical exercises concerning good government, is not precisely attributable to any specific reign.[92]

Firm in his policies towards the Goths, Philip stopped paying their subsidies in 248, with the result that by 249 the tribes had formed a coalition, united in adversity. They invaded Moesia and Thrace, and laid siege to Marcianopolis. Two revolts also broke out among the army commanders in the north and the east, and Philip lost his nerve. One of the usurpers, Pacatianus, had been given an extended command over Pannonia and Moesia, though it is not specified exactly where his authority lay. His command is symptomatic of the need to combine the armies in defence of large areas, since the enemies of Rome now ranged far and wide, moved rapidly and could not be dealt with by one provincial governor acting alone and within his own defined territory. The corollary to this requirement was that usurpation was rendered more feasible when such commands over large areas and large numbers of soldiers were instituted. Pacatianus issued coins during his brief reign, as did Jotapianus, the other usurper in the east, declared Emperor in Cappadocia, or possibly Syria, at the end of 248 or the beginning of 249. Neither the date nor the place are confirmed in any reliable source, and only a few pieces of evidence attest to his attempt to become

Figure 11 Philip proclaims CONCORDIA AUGUSTORUM on this medallion of 247 from the Rome mint. The succession had become a persistent problem, so Philip was anxious to advertise the fact that he had strongly unified family. His wife Otacilia Severa is depicted at his side, and his son faces them. The succession ought to have passed down without interruption, but civil war decided the matter. (Drawn by Trish Boyle.)

Emperor. Philip was oppressed by these events and offered to resign, but the Senate made a show of solidarity, shored up by a senator called C. Messius Quintus Decius, who declared that the revolts would be short lived. He must have sounded confident and convincing, since Philip entrusted the defence of Moesia and the Balkans, and the command against Pacatianus to him, with mixed results. Decius put down the revolt but was declared Emperor by his troops. Civil war followed, despite Decius' attempts to avert disaster and come to terms with Philip. Two Roman armies, one from Rome and the other from the Danube, converged on the north of Italy. They clashed at Verona. An alternative version, derived from the account by John of Antioch, is that Philip was on his way to Byzantium when he heard of the revolt and was killed at Beroea in Thrace; modern scholars have interpreted this to a place of the same name in Macedonia. Wherever the battle was fought Decius was the victor. Complications about the succession were avoided when Philip's eleven-year-old son was murdered by the Praetorians in Rome.[93]

DECIUS

Decius was confirmed as Emperor towards the end of 249. The exact date is uncertain, but by autumn 249 he was fully established. He was faced with several difficult tasks on more than one front, and started off by attempting to reunify the Roman Empire. As one of the means of doing so he reaffirmed the old Roman religion, not just reinvigorating the cult practices and rituals but also attending to the restoration of the temple buildings and their internal and external decorative elements. An inscription from Cosa bestows on him the title of *restitutor sacrorum*. As a consequence of his policies he marginalised or outlawed the cults that he saw as most threatening to unity, chiefly Christianity. Philip had been tolerant towards the Christians, earning himself a reputation in the process, completely unfounded, that he was the first Christian Emperor, a thesis that is generally discredited nowadays; but his reign was the calm before the storm, and the new persecution came as a surprise to the Christian community. It came in the form of an order to sacrifice to the gods of the Empire, an order that was rigorously enforced throughout the Empire. Compliant participants were issued with a certificate to prove that they had obeyed the order, and not a few Christians perhaps did so with no trouble, rendering unto Caesar what was his due but privately continuing undeterred in their Christian beliefs. St Cyprian complained that many of the flock crumbled in the face of the authorities and did as they were told. The edict had the advantage of singling out those who were not prepared to conform, and executions followed. Pope Fabian was among the first to be killed, on 20 January 250. Other trials and executions took place all over the Empire; some people ran away and found refuge in lonely places. The trials embraced not just the lowly adherents, but was aimed at the chief officials of the Church, so the name of Decius has been preserved as the arch-tyrant in the works of the contemporary Christian authors who survived and of those who wrote at a later time; the writings lost nothing in the way of umbrage with the passage of time.[94]

For the persecuted Christians it was seen as divine retribution when the Carpi attacked Dacia and the Goths invaded Moesia in 250. Decius was granted the name of Trajan by the Senate when he became Emperor, so the parallel with the erstwhile conqueror of Dacia will have been apparent to anyone with a sense of history when he cleared the Carpi from the Roman province, earning himself the title *restitutor Daciarum*. His campaign had begun well, but he faced a more resolute enemy in the Gothic leader Cniva in Moesia and Thrace. The Goths sat down in front of Nicopolis, and whilst they could not be said to be experts in siege tactics, they had learned a lot on their travels; they later succeeded in taking Philippopolis. Decius could not dislodge them, but could only wait for them to start to move. Meanwhile, he made his son Herennius Etruscus, already Caesar, his colleague in an attempt to provide stability for his regime; his younger son Hostilianus was in Rome with a respected senator, P. Licinius Valerianus (the future Emperor Valerian), in charge of the civil administration while Decius himself led the army. The presence of a respected senator delegated by the Emperor did not however prevent the Roman mob from raising a candidate of their own to replace Decius, whose name they removed from inscriptions in the city; this was another senator called D. Julius Valens Licinianus, whose name is known from St Cyprian's letters. His candidacy was short lived, mainly because the Roman mob had no army behind it to make their choice of Emperor more legitimate, or at least respected. Decius was probably too embroiled in the struggle in the Danube provinces to notice. In 251 the Goths began to move northwards, so Decius followed, fighting battles but unable to bring them to final confrontation until he reached the Dobrudja. He risked battle at Abrittus (modern Razgrad, Bulgaria) and was killed. Herennius Etruscus may have been killed in one of the earlier skirmishes, though some sources have him eliminated with his father at the last battle. There was now a power vacuum which the legions were not slow to fill, declaring for the governor of Moesia, C. Vibius Afinius Trebonianus Gallus.[95]

TREBONIANUS GALLUS

It was rumoured that Gallus had stood by while Decius fought, and from this assumption inflated stories began to circulate that he had actually betrayed Decius and had gone over to the Goths. When he made peace with the Goths it certainly seemed that he favoured them. He resumed their

subsidy payments and allowed them to go free, taking their booty and prisoners with them. It demonstrated that he did not feel strong enough to
bring them to their knees, and he was not about to repeat the mistakes that
Maximinus made in continuing the war and remaining in the war zone to do
so. Gallus went to Rome to establish himself in power. He eventually
adopted Decius' son Hostilianus and raised his own son Volusianus alongside him, making them Caesars and then Augusti. The chronology of this
episode is very confused, so it is not certain whether Gallus regarded Decius'
son as senior to Volusianus, or whether he hoped to avoid problems with the
succession by treating them in exactly the same fashion. It seems that he
raised them in echelon, with Hostilianus in the lead, so that when the boy
was made Augustus, Volusianus became Caesar. In these troubled times,
when the armies of various provinces declared for the man of the moment
and then disposed of him at the first suspicion of failure, this arrangement
could only have led to disaster; in more peaceful times, however, it might
have provided for a long and successful dynasty with the succession worked
out in advance for several years. In the event it hardly signified very much
because of the brevity of Gallus' reign. The most immediate crisis, nearer to
home than the war zones, was the plague of 252–3; Hostilianus succumbed
to it, leaving Volusianus and his father as Emperors. In spite of his wide
authority Gallus was powerless to stop the spread of disease, or to raise
morale. Making little progress against the Goths, it also seemed that Gallus
could not solve the problems of actual or potential invasions from across the
Danube and was not prepared to deal with the eastern question either. He
may have made preparations to conduct a campaign from Antioch, where
the mint began to issue a large quantity of antoniniani, the coins used to pay
the soldiers, as if in preparation for a gathering of troops. But Shapur moved
more quickly than the Romans. He took Nisibis and probably Antioch
itself, apparently causing much destruction, if Zosimus is correct. In these
circumstances the inhabitants of the affected provinces naturally look to
someone in the immediate vicinity who can help them without delay; in this
way the usurper Uranius Antoninus seized power and began to issue coins in
253.[96]

The revolt of Aemilius Aemilianus

The Danube frontier was hardly less pressured, so there the troops chose the
governor of Lower Moesia, Aemilius Aemilianus, as Emperor. He put an end
to the subsidies to the Goths and won a victory over them. According to the
ancient sources, this usurper recognised that one man alone was not sufficient to deal with the administration of the Empire while he was also fighting major wars, and not quite altruistically he recognised that his claims
would be received in a much better light if he adopted a more than respect-
ful attitude towards the Senate. Regardless of the fact that Trebonianus

Figure 12 Caius Publius Licinius Valerianus was in his sixties when he became Emperor in 253. There are very few portraits of Valerian, but his image on the coinage makes identification of this bust certain. The grim determined look had already entered Roman portraiture of the mid-second century. (Courtesy Ny Carlsberg Glyptotek.)

Gallus was the legitimate Emperor, Aemilianus sent a letter to Rome suggesting a division of responsibilities, explaining that while the Senate itself should exercise supreme power, he would be the general-in-chief in command of the Danube and the east. There will have been a multiplicity of reasons why he suggested this measure, among them the fact that he had more than enough to occupy him in trying to defend and control the areas he had chosen for himself.[97]

The army proclaims Valerian

Gallus sent Valerian with the Rhine legions against Aemilianus as the latter chose to march on Rome, but either the legions chose Valerian as Emperor, or he engineered his own acclamation. He had survived the transition between Decius and Gallus intact, because Gallus did not embark upon an elimination of the supporters of Decius and tried instead to reconcile them and the Imperial family. This time, though, the transition, if there was to be one, might not be so smooth, and before there could be any change at all there would have to be some fighting. Valerian perhaps reasoned that he might as well fight on his own behalf as on the part of an Emperor who seemed to be losing control of the Empire at an accelerated rate. The outcome of this year of four Emperors all converging once again on the north of Italy was that the troops of Gallus and Volusianus realised that they were too few in number to fight Aemilianus, so they killed the Emperor and his son. Quite soon after that Aemilianus was eliminated by his troops, leaving Valerian as Emperor. He set about confirming his power immediately; it seems that the Senate declared his adult son P. Licinius Gallienus *nobilissimus Caesar* and that when Valerian arrived in Rome he made Gallienus his colleague as Augustus. Now at last there were two Emperors who would be able to deal with the problems in two halves of the Empire at the same time, Gallienus taking the west and Valerian going to the east as soon as he could to combat the Persian menace.[98]

VALERIAN AND GALLIENUS

In 253 Shapur turned his full attention on Armenia. The unfortunate King Chosroes was killed and his son Tiridates fled, leaving Armenia wide open to Persian domination. Shapur may have captured Antioch in the same year, which would explain the interruption of the coinage there in 253. The Romans soon reinstalled themselves; on his arrival in the east Valerian set up headquarters at Antioch and started rebuilding. The mint reopened, and damage to the surrounding Syrian territories was repaired. From 253 to 255 the situation in the threatened provinces of both east and west slowly improved. Gallienus celebrated victories over the Germans in Illyricum. By 256 it seemed that Rome was in the ascendancy again, until the new threat from the Franks broke out in Gaul and Germany. Gallienus left the Danube provinces, installing his son Valerian the younger at Viminacium as Caesar, while he established his headquarters on the Rhine frontier at Cologne. He opened a mint there, which soon began to issue coins naming Gallienus as *restitutor Galliarum*.[99]

An inscription from Aphrodisias reveals that Valerian, Gallienus and Valerian the younger were at Cologne in August 257. The Frankish invasions were serious enough to warrant the Imperial presence in strength, and though the Franks were expelled, there would be much to do by way of mopping up to repair the damage and to restore confidence. A tour of the frontier provinces by the two Emperors and their young Caesar in 257 is not out of the question. For reasons which are obscure, Valerian embarked upon a widespread persecution of the Christians at this juncture. St Cyprian was exiled, but he returned to Carthage and was finally executed in September 258. One of the best sources for the events of the mid-third century was thus eliminated in this renewed assault. Without secure evidence of the sort that Cyprian's letters provide, the chronology of the years *c.*256 to 260 is disputed, and is not yet capable of resolution from any other unequivocal contemporary source; much depends upon the date of the capture of Valerian in the east, which some modern authors place as early as 258, at the very outset of the eastern campaign. This author opts for 260 as the date of the disaster, while the relevant footnotes outline the opinions of other authors. By the spring of 258 Valerian returned to the east by way of Illyricum, where he reinstalled Valerian the younger. He arrived in Antioch in May. In the meantime Gallienus was forced to leave Cologne that same year to oust a usurper called Ingenuus, whose troops had proclaimed him Emperor in Illyricum. It is probable that the younger Valerian was killed in this revolt. Personal disaster was followed by Imperial crisis, on three fronts if not four. Valerian was fully occupied in the east fighting against Shapur, and Gallienus was re-establishing his authority over Illyricum, but now there were more invasions by the Goths threatening the Black Sea coastal cities, and the Alamanni were restless on the frontiers of Germany and Raetia. The defence of all the western provinces at the same time was impossible. Gallienus had placed his younger son Saloninus at Cologne as the new Caesar. Leaving him there, he himself returned to northern Italy and set up his headquarters at Milan, where he established a mint. As events unrolled in the year 260, it probably seemed that there would never be any end to the disasters piling up one on top of another. In the summer of 260, Shapur captured the Emperor Valerian, perhaps by treachery. The Persians were now free to dominate the entire east, because there was no one to stop them. Usurpers appeared in several places, possibly as a result of the removal of one of the Emperors and because self-help on the frontiers had become the only alternative. At Carnuntum the soldiers chose Regalianus to lead them against the Iazyges and Roxolani; in the east Callistus (also called Ballista in some sources) and Macrianus took charge of the remnants of the army; neither Macrianus nor Callistus declared themselves Emperors, but Macrianus did not waste time in affirming his position, raising his two sons, Titus Fulvius Junius Macrianus and Titus Fulvius Junius Quietus, to Augusti. The west reacted just as rapidly. Though the facts are disputed it seems that it was only after the news of Valerian's defeat and capture was known in Gaul that the governor Postumus was declared Emperor. An inscription found at

Augsburg clarifies the date; it has been suggested that the victory over the Juthungi described in the text could have occurred as late as 261. The inscription also vindicates the statement made by more than one ancient source that under Gallienus, Raetia was lost. The domain of Postumus extended over this area as well as the Rhine frontier and the Gallic provinces; Britain was with him and Spain came over to him later. Thus the Emperor Gallienus was backed into a corner in Milan, with only a fraction of the armies of the Empire at his disposal. With these troops and reduced resources he faced his multiple problems. There were three usurpers in different parts of the Empire in command of sizeable armies. The Persians were at liberty to raid the whole of the east, and for the first time in Roman history an Emperor had not only failed to check them but had been ignominiously captured. The Goths were on the rampage in Moesia and Thrace, poised for attacks elsewhere, having learned by now how to use boats for successful hit-and-run raids on rich cities, and the Franks and Alamanni and other assorted tribes were poised to attack the Rhine and the upper Danube. The problems taken together probably seemed insuperable, and a lesser man might have collapsed under the strain. An Emperor immersed in traditional ways could not have begun to reverse the situation. Gallienus was forced to use the limited resources that he had at his disposal. Lateral thinking, continual adaptation to circumstances, and changes in operational and organisational methods were the first priority if Rome and the Empire were to survive.[100]

3

SCHISM AND REUNIFICATION
260–84

GALLIENUS SOLE EMPEROR

After the capture of Valerian, Gallienus was sole Emperor. Although he could have elevated other members of his family to share power, he chose not to take a colleague, and indeed kept his surviving relatives out of the limelight. He pursued a somewhat single-minded ruthless course from now onwards, largely dictated by necessity. He did not attempt to rescue his father or to ransom him. A military expedition to the east was out of the question unless he wanted to sacrifice the rest of the Empire to usurpers and the tribes from the north. Money was at a premium too, not to be squandered on paying huge sums to the Persians for the return of one man. Responsible Emperors could not afford to put personal considerations before those of the state, so Gallienus sacrificed his father and let his captors go unpunished. His detractors could accuse him of a lack of filial devotion, especially since he ignored or reversed much of what Valerian had attempted to do. Gallienus put an end to his father's persecution of the Christians, partly out of humanitarian reasons, perhaps, but also because he had nothing to gain from persecution of one particular sect, except to alienate yet another group of people. He had quite enough dissidents to deal with in the political and military arenas without creating more in the religious sphere as well. It has been said that Valerian's motives in persecuting the Christians were predominantly financial in that he sequestered fortunes of the condemned, but this is a standard sideline of the persecution or proscription of any group in the Roman Empire. Gallienus may have had to adjust his financial policy slightly to accommodate the shortfall from Christian sources, but it is unlikely that he noticed the lack in the chaos that reigned in that sphere.[1]

From the reign of Gallienus the Roman world entered upon a period of change, and though the changes may not have been intended to be permanent, by degrees they became entrenched and in some cases irrevocable. Forced to make the best use of what was immediately to hand, with no time for vacillation or trial runs, Gallienus adapted old and established methods and produced something new, sometimes sacrificing hallowed traditions if

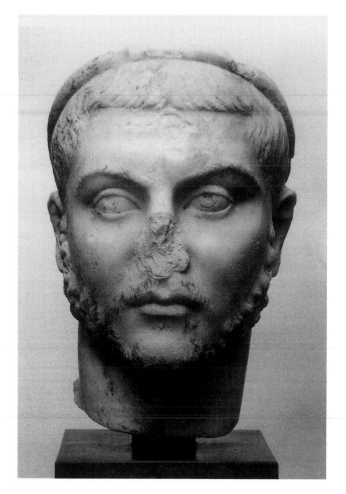

Figure 13 The young Gallienus sporting a moustache and light beard. There is a resemblance to the bust of his father Valerian, with whom he was co-Emperor until 260. (Courtesy Ny Carlsberg Glyptotek.)

they were not suited to his current circumstances. For want of a better description historians speak of Gallienus' reforms of the army and the administration, and indeed the changes he made warrant that description, but the full agenda of the term 'reforms' implies that deliberate and co-ordinated policies must lurk somewhere in the background, all planned out at leisure and implemented in good time by due process of law. Gallienus was not granted the luxury of forward planning, being for most of his reign engaged in fire-fighting rather than planning, lucky if he stayed one step ahead. His measures were taken with extremely short-term aims in mind, principally survival, with defence and reparation following close behind.[2]

Gallienus' achievements laid the foundations for the development of the late Roman Empire. Ancient authors recognised his importance; Aurelius Victor devoted more words to his reign than to most others, certainly as many as he employed to describe the events under Diocletian and Constantine. Subsequent Emperors selected and fostered those elements of Gallienus' policies which best suited their purpose. This is not to say that the transition between the regime of Gallienus and the new Empire of Constantine followed a smooth course, progressing ever onwards and ever upwards, building logically upon precedent after precedent, with never a retrograde movement or a low moment. Political and military necessity always dictated what must be done; circumstance, ingenuity and means always dictated what could be achieved. Modern authors justifiably identify the reign of Gallienus as central to the survival of the Empire in the third century, and the Emperor himself as the originator of several of the institutions of the Late Empire, but there was no straightforward linear development leading directly from Gallienus to Constantine. Whilst Claudius Gothicus, Tacitus and Aurelian did not fundamentally change any of Gallienus' measures, Probus departed from the assiduous care and attention to the army, and Diocletian remoulded his policies, or diverted from them. Constantine brought them back. Alföldi equated Diocletian with Decius, and Constantine with Gallienus, whose policies he brought to fruition. Van Berchem outlined the distinctions between Gallienus, Diocletian and Constantine, drawing upon the close parallels between Gallienus and Constantine, who were both fighting for control of the Empire against several enemies at once with limited resources to hand, while Diocletian was the anomaly who emerged supreme for a while, finally arriving at a point where he had time to spare, policies to adopt and systems to implement.[3]

The army

Gallienus' prime concern was, and always remained, the army. Whether he was to defend his diminished Empire against attacks from external or internal enemies, or whether he was to try to regain control of the territories that were lost to him, he needed an army. To varying degrees Roman Imperial power was always founded on armed force and depended upon the loyalty and support of the troops. Every Emperor from Augustus knew it, but Gallienus had more need than most of an efficient and loyal army, while at the same time he possessed few of the other advantages that previous Emperors had enjoyed to enable him to engender and sustain that loyalty. He was not in control of the resources of the whole Empire either politically, militarily, or financially. He could not assume the lofty dignity of Antoninus Pius, proclaiming the advantages of the *pax Romana*, when most of the provinces were threatened one way or another with existing or impending wars. He could not emulate Hadrian, touring the provinces to boost morale among provincials and troops, since parts of the Empire were closed to him and his presence was needed where revolts or invasions occurred – more often than not in two places at once. He was in an even less enviable position than Severus in 193. Like Gallienus, Severus was faced with enemies in both east and west, but he was able to eliminate them one at a time, beginning with Niger in the east, relying upon the fact that the western provinces were not solidly behind Clodius Albinus and probably never would be. Gallienus did not have this tenuous advantage, since all the Rhine legions and a large part of the population and, more importantly, the legions of Gaul seemed to support Postumus. There was no possibility of an attempt to forestall Postumus by persuading him that he would share the Empire with him. The historical precedent was too recent, so the ruse would have been too transparent, especially after the murder of Gallienus' son Saloninus at Cologne. Hemmed in on east and west, with only the military and financial resources of the Danube provinces and Italy to draw upon, Gallienus needed to apply fast and effective lateral thinking, adaptation and innovation. Fiscal and social policy, political and military traditions, everything in fact, were all subordinated to the needs of the army.[4]

He set about welding together the troops that were with him, vexillations mostly, drawn from the Rhine and Danube legions, gathered together alongside some auxiliary units. In general his army was a motley collection, consisting of soldiers whose loyalties may have been torn by their oath of loyalty to their Emperor on the one hand, and on the other hand to their attachment to their home bases where they may have had families, or to their parent units where they may have had close friends, or possibly even to other generals in other places. Various authors have attempted to identify the troops that made up the Imperial army, primarily using coin evidence. The Praetorians and 17 legions feature on the coinage, and the distribution of the legionary coins and their much-discussed reverse legends have been used in support of theories about the make-up and the whereabouts of Gallienus' army. The find spots range from Britain to Yugoslavia, but so far there are no finds in the eastern provinces, corroborating the evidence that the army was split between Gallienus and Valerian before the latter began the Persian campaign. In support of the theory that Gallienus did not command whole legions, it is pertinent that the coins are not found among the other coins at the home bases of the legions in question. The *Pia Fidelis* legends on the reverse of the legionary coins, numbered in sequence I–VII, have posed problems for archaeologists and historians, some of whom conclude that there were several issues struck at irregular intervals to commemorate individual victories and honour the troops that took part in them. This in turn requires that the victories be identified and connected to documented battles or actions, and it also requires that some explanation must be found as to why four of the legions seemingly lacked the honour of *VII Pia Fidelis*. It was suggested that these legions had joined the rebellion of

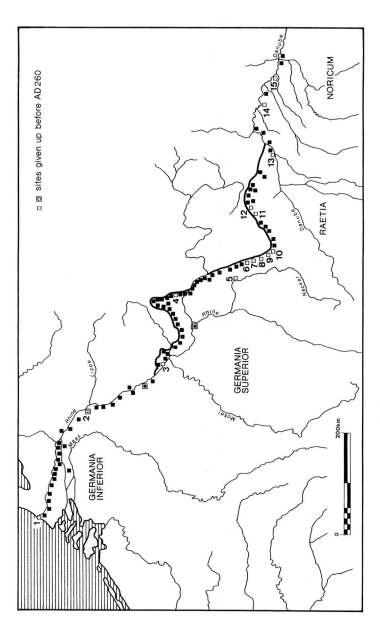

Figure 14 Map of the frontier of Germany and Raetia showing the few sites which had already been given up some time before 260. The frontier was still held in strength until the reign of Gallienus. (Drawn by Graeme Stobbs.)

Key: 1 Brittenburg, 2 Xanten (Vetera II), 3 Heddesdorf, 4 Marköbel, 5 Neckarburken, 6 Öhringen, 7 Mainhardt, 8 Murrhardt, 9 Welzheim, 10 Lorch, 11 Ruffenhofen, 12 Dambach, 13 Kösching, 14 Straubing, 15 Künzing.

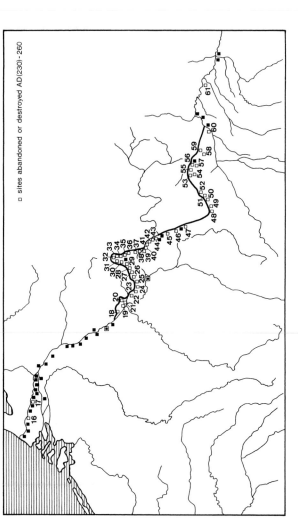

□ sites abandoned or destroyed AD(230) - 260

Figure 15 Map of the frontier of Germany and Raetia showing the main areas of destruction in the 230s and 260s. In many cases it is not possible to distinguish between damage caused at either or both of these dates. At some forts repairs were carried out after destruction in 230. The pattern of destruction, whichever are the true dates, reveals that the focus of the attacks centred around the Taunus and Wetterau frontier, which guarded fertile, easily drained lands that were probably rich in crops of all kinds. It may be that these areas attracted hungry tribesmen whose goals were limited to food and portable wealth, rather than that the frontier was weak and badly defended. (Drawn by Graeme Stobbs.)

Key: 16 Alphen-Zwammerdam, 17 Utrecht, 18 Niederbieber, 19 Niederberg, 20 Arzbach, 21 Bad Ems, 22 Hunzel, 23 Holzhausen, 24 Kemel, 25 Zugmantel, 26 Hefrich, 27 Kleine Feldberg, 28 Saalburg, 29 Kapersburg, 30 Langenhain, 31 Butzbach, 32 Arnsburg, 33 Inheiden, 34 Echzell, 35 Oberflorstadt, 36 Altenstadt, 37 Ruchingen, 38 Gross-Krotzenburg, 39 Seligenstadt, 40 Stockstadt, 41 Niedernberg, 42 Obernberg, 43 Wörth am Main, 44 Trennfurt, 45 Walldürn, 46 Osterburken, 47 Westenbach, 48 Schirenhof, 49 Böbingen, 50 Aalen, 51 Rainau-Buch, 52 Halheim, 53 Gunzenhausen, 54 Gnotzheim, 55 Theilenhofen, 56 Ellingen, 57 Weissenburg, 58 Pfünz, 59 Böhming, 60 Pförring, 61 Steinkirchen.

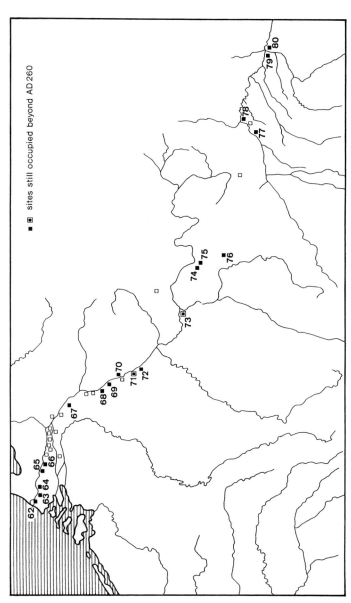

■ □ sites still occupied beyond AD 260

Figure 16 Map showing the parlous state of the German and Raetian frontier after 260, when virtually all the forts had been abandoned and the term 'frontier' was no longer applicable. (Drawn by Graeme Stobbs.)

Key: 62 Valkenburg, 63 Leiden-Roomburg, 64 Alphen, 65 Woerden, 66 Vleula De Meern, 67 Altkalkar, 68 Neuss, 69 Dormagen, 70 Köhn-Deutz, 71 Bonn, 72 Remagen, 73 Mainz, 74 Miltenberg-Altstadt, 75 Miltenberg Ost, 76 Jagsthausen, 77 Eining, 78 Regensburg, 79 Passau, 80 Passau-Innstadt.

Regalianus, but this theory must be revised in the light of new finds which suggest that the four legions did not lack the title, but instead the coins simply had not been found until recently. Okamura suggested that the *Pia Fidelis* legends commemorated not victories, but Gallienus himself as Imperator in the west, the first five acclamations as co-Emperor while Valerian still reigned and the sixth in 260 when Gallienus was hailed as sole Emperor. More significant for a reconstruction of Gallienus' army the coin evidence suggests that the core of the troops available to Gallienus in 260 were those which he had collected together for the Rhine campaign in the 250s, including the Praetorians and *II Parthica* from Italy, accompanied by vexillations from the legions of the British provinces, Upper and Lower Germany, Raetia, Noricum, Upper and Lower Pannonia, Upper and Lower Moesia, and the three Dacian provinces.[5]

Gallienus needed to foster goodwill among the soldiers to bind them to himself, and as part of this programme he issued the well-known *Fides Militum, Exercitum* and *Equitum* coins proclaiming the loyalty of the army. He endorsed and furthered Severus' policy of allowing the *principales* among the troops to wear white clothing, extending this distinction to all the soldiers. Public elevation and praise of the troops such as these messages proclaimed were backed up with more solid care and attention to the welfare of the soldiers, to their monetary rewards and to their social prospects. Though the democratising tendencies of successive Emperors such as Hadrian and Severus had gradually advanced the prestige of the army, it was Gallienus who broadened the career prospects of ordinary soldiers; each man could look forward to the possibility of promotion, to become junior officers, then perhaps to equestrian status, and from there to the highest social rank, all earned through distinguished service in the army, much as the *grognards* of Napoleon's army each carried, potentially, a marshal's baton in his knapsack.[6]

The mobile cavalry

This is the most famous and perhaps least documented change that Gallienus made to the army. The need for rapid response and therefore for increased mobility was ever more pressing, and campaign armies made up of vexillations did not immediately answer Gallienus' purpose. Based in northern Italy, he needed to be able to reach the Danube provinces, the Rhine provinces if he could win them back, and to guard the Alpine passes against invasion by tribesmen from the north, whilst also defending the western passes against troops of Postumus from Gaul. He could not be sure that Postumus would not attempt to invade. It has been said that this was the principle reason why he based himself and the cavalry at Milan, to prepare for invasion by Postumus and for his own counter-attack, but in 260 another perhaps more realistic consideration was the presence of the Alamanni actually in the Alpine passes, poised to descend into northern Italy. Milan and the plain of the Po constitute good horse country, with good grazing and cavalry-friendly terrain. There is reasonably good access from Milan through the Alps northwards and eastwards to the Danube, and westwards to Gaul. Gallienus would have several good reasons, besides protecting himself against Postumus, for basing his mobile cavalry army in Milan. This separate army of Gallienus was a new departure. The amalgamation of horsemen in this way, not brigaded in auxiliary units based in the frontier posts, or attached to any provincial army, able to fight wherever the Emperor wished, was somewhat different from the usual collection of vexillations drawn together for a particular campaign. The cavalry was given an individual commander, answerable directly to the Emperor, making it quite distinct from other elements of the army. The first commander, Aureolus, is attested in more than one source, but it is Zosimus who specifically links him with his headquarters at Milan when he finally rebelled against Gallienus.[7]

The troops that Gallienus was able to muster after the capture of his father and the loss of the Gallic and Rhine provinces will have included cavalry units, consisting of regular *alae* and *cohortes equitatae*, and perhaps some remnants of the Mauri and Osroeni brought to Germany by Severus Alexander for the Rhine campaign of 235. Their subsequent history after the death of Severus Alexander is not documented, so it is equally possible that their numbers had not been kept up by recruiting, either from their homelands where natural-born horsemen were available, javelin men in the case of the Moors, and archers from the Osroeni, or from the Rhine provinces where men could have been drafted in and trained to fight and ride in the same manner as the original horsemen. Gallienus could also draw upon the *equites Dalmatae*, troops from the province of Dalmatia. Opinion differs as to whether these were ethnic units of Dalmatian tribesmen, or whether they were from regular mounted units, but since there were few units in Dalmatia, it is impossible to pinpoint the troops from which they may have been detached. The likelihood is that the *equites Dalmatae* were tribesmen recruited for their skill in horsemanship, and not least because they may have arrived complete with their own horses, relieving the military suppliers at a time when finding remounts was no doubt very difficult. The Dalmatians, the Moors and the Osroene were most probably the units employed in Gallienus' mobile cavalry army. It is known that Aurelian employed Dalmatian horsemen to good effect, so it is not unreasonable to assume that he inherited them from the army of Gallienus. In addition to the native horsemen, Gallienus seems to have gathered the legionary cavalry together from each of his vexillations, and amalgamated them into the mobile army. These are the *promoti*, their name perhaps denoting their transfer from legionary cavalry to cavalry army, a step which was probably considered an upgrading.[8]

It is disputed whether this army is the true forerunner of the mobile armies of the later Empire. The Byzantine chronicler George Cedrenus says that Gallienus was the first to employ a mobile cavalry army, as though he were the founder of such an army. Such a feature would be familiar to ancient writers after the opening of the fourth century, so Cedrenus' statement ought to be examined with caution, since he may have applied anachronistic judgement. Modern opinion embraces the fact that the sources that he used dated from a much earlier time, and were in general quite reliable. Continuity cannot be traced with any certainty. The fate of the cavalry army after Gallienus' death is only imperfectly known; it survived him and is probably traceable on an inscription dating to the reign of Claudius Gothicus, mentioning *vexillationes adque equites* under the command of Julius Placidianus, the prefect of the *vigiles*, fighting in Narbonensis in an effort to gain control of the Gallic Empire. On this inscription, a distinction is made between the two elements, detachments and cavalry, suggesting that the horsemen were not considered part of the vexillations and did not fight under the same standard. The cavalry was perhaps used to good effect by Claudius Gothicus against the Goths, and by Aurelian, but it seems that after about 285 it was no longer at Milan and is not definitely attested as a separate entity. It is possible that Gallienus himself had no intention of keeping the cavalry together after the battles were over, if he foresaw a time when the fighting would end. It is equally possible that even if he did intend to form a mobile army, this intention was not upheld by his successors, and that the cavalry was disbanded after Gallienus' death, as if it were after all just another vexillation assembled for a series of campaigns, thus leaving Diocletian and Constantine the choice of discovering its usefulness all over again.[9]

The Protectores

The title of Protector first appeared in the joint reigns of Valerian and Gallienus, and was used much more frequently after the latter became sole Emperor. Though the terminology suggests that there may have been some intention on the part of the Emperor to form a new bodyguard, in addition to or possibly instead of the Praetorians, the officers who were distinguished by the title were from diverse units and followed diverse careers, so they were not amalgamated into a distinct body of men. Senators were excluded from the award of the title, so it is thought by some scholars that the increased use of it must coincide and develop from the exclusion of senators from army commands. Protector did not denote a rank, but it proclaimed an acknowledged loyalty to the Emperor and was in general a mark of distinction, which men were proud to mention on career inscriptions or to have inscribed on their tombstones. Having removed members of the aristocracy as commanders of the army, it is possible that Gallienus was keen to establish a new kind of aristocracy of military men with proven ability, rewarding

them for their loyalty to himself and marking them out as future commanders in one and the same operation. Some scholars have suggested that all
officers in the army received this title from Gallienus once they had reached
a certain rank, and indeed in the fourth century the term became synony-
mous with centurion. The suggestion that the Protectores were members of
a staff college is supported by the fact that at least one man is named as *princeps Protectorum*, and the distinguished Protectores whose later achievements
are known went on to higher offices, so that it is clear that the conferment of
the title was a indication that such men were marked out for splendid
careers. At first, under Valerian and his son, the distinction was reserved for
the Praetorians, and under Gallienus alone it seems to have been conferred
upon legionary prefects and tribunes of the Praetorians, then upon centurions. Men who had risen from the ranks were not excluded. Usage spread to
troops outside Italy, so it seems that there was no limit to the numbers of
men who could earn it, but Christol has argued that the title Protector indicates those officers who had been with the Emperor in his campaign armies,
serving close to him.[10]

The equestrians

Controversially Gallienus employed men of equestrian rank to a much
greater extent than Severus had done. He appointed them to high commands which had previously been the almost exclusive domain of men of the
senatorial class, and in particular he fostered military men who had risen
from the ranks to equestrian status. These were the men he knew and
trusted, in so far as it was possible to trust anyone in the circumstances.
They were also professional soldiers of long military experience; they had
concentrated almost exclusively on the army and had not served their time
simply in order to advance their political careers. It was military experience,
professionalism and permanence that counted at that moment, and those
commodities were to be found in the equestrians who had risen from the
ranks, or in the born equestrians whose careers had been focused on the
army. What Gallienus did not need was a transient corps of upper-class officers with little experience of war, fortuitously placed in positions of authority where their potential for making the wrong decisions was dangerous and
their reliability questionable. Soldiers who might be asked to risk life and
limb might tolerate such a situation in times of relative peace, but when
wars were to be waged, when tribesmen were poised to invade, or actually
did invade, or when troops were asked to fight against other Roman troops,
then the men needed to know that the officers they followed were trustworthy, that they had the best interests of the unit or units at heart, that
they would share their dangers and, most of all, that they knew precisely
what they were asking the soldiers to do.[11]

The senatorial military career had already begun to wane before Gallienus

91

became Emperor. At all periods there was always a considerable number of senators who were not interested in following such a career. Many of them were content with senatorial rank and prestige, without engaging too fiercely in the political scene or in military affairs. For the rest, there was a succession of administrative posts and military offices leading to the prized goal of the consulship and for a fortunate few the even more prized goals of the important provincial commands. In the early Empire ambitious senators usually combined their urban and civilian posts with a term of service with the army, as tribunes in a legion, then later as legionary legates, without necessarily gaining much military experience along the way. These military appointments were nowhere near the pinnacle of their existence, but merely a stepping stone to a more glorious political career as governor of one of the smaller provinces, then the consulship, perhaps leading to even more prestigious appointments as governor of one of the large, wealthy provinces, or to other lucrative commands in the gift of the Emperor. The third century witnessed changes to this established pattern. As early as the mid-250s, the *tribuni laticlavii* had already disappeared. Gallienus gave the *coup de grâce* to senatorial military careers, probably in the form of an edict to remove senators from command. The only ancient author who refers to this edict is Aurelius Victor, who says in one passage that Gallienus removed senators from the command of the army, and in a later passage comments that the situation could have been reversed in the reign of Tacitus, but the senators were simply not interested in service in the army, preferring to keep their fortunes and lands intact. Since this almost casual reference is the only evidence, there is room for doubt about the existence of anything quite so complete or as official as an Imperial pronouncement, but current opinion accepts the Edict as fact. It cannot be said that the intention behind this measure was to separate military and civil careers, either completely or permanently. As a trend, the feasibility of pursuing a career based on almost exclusively military or exclusively civil appointments had already begun to manifest itself as early as the reign of Hadrian, and the preference of a number of equites and senators alike for such focused careers, with little or no experience of soldiering on the one hand, or civil administration on the other, had contributed to the development of specialisation and professionalism. After the promulgation of the Edict removing senators from military command, this trend for separate careers and specialisation in one particular sphere would become the norm, but it was not one of Gallienus' priorities to put this into effect. Another spin-off from the Edict was the fact that equites who would perhaps have gone on to enter the Senate and take up administrative careers now no longer needed to do so to enjoy satisfactory careers with promotions and rewards; they could by-pass the Senate altogether, especially through close association with the Emperor, thus diminishing the supremacy that the Senate had always enjoyed in the past.[12]

Equestrian praefecti legionis

Whether or not he promulgated an edict, it is clear that Gallienus divorced senators from military commands, preferring to put experienced equites in charge of legions, not as *legati* but as *praefecti*, a title with an established history dating from Augustus' settlement of Egypt, where Octavian (as he then was) rigorously excluded senators from the new province. The governor of Egypt, *Praefectus Aegypti*, was an equestrian from the very beginning and the equestrian commander of the legion was not *legatus legionis* but *praefectus legionis*. Severus gave his equestrian legionary commanders of the three Parthian legions the same title of prefect. Gallienus built on these precedents, installing equestrian prefects at the head of all the legions in the provinces where his control was unchallenged. In the Gallic Empire, Postumus retained the senatorial legionary commanders. Gallienus had no intention of eventually reinstating the senatorial legates, but at the same time there was no sudden clean break with the past to produce something revolutionary and possibly inflammatory. The post of legionary legate was not swept aside; it was transferred intact from senatorial to equestrian postholders with a different title. It has been suggested that the new prefects may have been drawn from the *praefecti castrorum*, but it is unlikely that the camp prefect was simply promoted to the overall command in every legion; there will have been variations. The terminology that was regularly employed reflects the fact that the prefect was acting as substitute for the legate: *praefectus agens vices legati*. This meant that the prefect exercised the full powers of the legate, and according to the law codes it seems that without the full title the prefect would lack certain legal prerogatives.[13]

Equestrian provincial governors

There were respectable precedents for Gallienus' appointment of equestrians as governors of some of the provinces, excluding of course those areas which Postumus controlled. On occasions in the past, equestrians had filled temporary vacancies as provincial governors, for instance when the original governor died or was killed and there was a need for someone to take over until a new governor could be appointed. The usual title (*agens vice praesidis*) made it clear that the equestrian substitute possessed full authority to act on behalf of the provincial governor. From about 260 onwards, equestrian *praesides* were appointed to certain provinces not as temporary substitutes but as authentic governors, ousting the senators who until now had enjoyed exclusive rights to these posts. Examining senatorial careers, Christol concluded that by 262 the exchange had already been made in several provinces throughout the Empire. Exactly how it was effected is not elucidated. Gallienus probably did not wait until respective terms of office had expired, so it may not have been by natural wastage that equestrians replaced senators in the provinces, but by deliberate decision with immediate effect. There will have been perhaps successive batches of equestrians going out to replace senatorial governors. This in turn evokes the scenario of supplanted senators trekking back to Rome wondering whether they could look forward to a future career. Unfortunately there is little evidence to shore up this imaginative screenplay; after 250 fully documented senatorial careers decline in number. The evidence does show that the provinces to which equites were appointed were those which were under the greatest duress, threatened by the tribesmen from beyond the frontiers, or where potential internal unrest posed a problem. For the most part these were Imperial praetorian provinces with only one legion, where the legate was responsible for both military and civil affairs. In addition, Gallienus sometimes appointed equestrians as governors in Imperial consular provinces when there was a military crisis or perhaps whenever he considered a particular candidate was the best man for the task, but in contrast to his treatment of the Imperial praetorian provinces he did not adopt a consistent policy of substituting equestrians for senatorial governors. The statistics reveal that the number of senatorial governors far outweighed the equestrians in the Imperial consular provinces, so it cannot be said that Gallienus was motivated solely by his hatred of the Senate when he appointed equestrians as legionary legates or as *praesides*. His concerns were military, and the removal of senators from army commands and from provincial government sprang from no other agenda, hidden or otherwise. Where there was no impending danger or where there was no opportunity for senators to command troops, Gallienus did not blindly pursue his policy of placing equites in charge, since that was not his purpose. The senatorial governors of large provinces with two legions were not affected, principally because they did not directly command the army, which was in the hands of the equestrian prefects; similarly Gallienus made no changes in the provinces where no troops were stationed, nor in the senatorial provinces, where he allowed senators to continue as proconsuls.[14]

Gallienus and the Senate

Despite the portrayal of Gallienus as an arch-enemy of the Senate, relations between the two parties were never perpetually or consistently strained. The Emperor knew and associated with many senators individually, and received honours from the Senate corporately, so it cannot be said that there was a state of war between them. Though the Senate undoubtedly lost political power and influence in the third century, Gallienus did not annihilate it altogether. Senators still retained their prestigious status, and indeed, as described above, they still fulfilled many of the customary governmental posts. The removal of senators from military commands would not have arisen if there had been peace over most of the Empire. Everything could have continued as before, but the old methods were no longer appropriate.

Many of the senators who became legionary legates and those who governed the praetorian provinces simply did not possess sufficient or relevant military experience at a time when such experience was of paramount importance, so Gallienus looked for it elsewhere and found it in his serving officers of equestrian status. Once he had embarked on this course, the lack of military experience among senators was exacerbated, because they were now removed from the possibility of gaining any, so the choice of equites as military officers was perpetuated. It was not the fault of the senators as a class, nor was it ingrained rivalry between the senators and the equestrians that prompted Gallienus to act as he did. It was certainly not blind prejudice on the part of the Emperor, who needed all the allies he could find, and he did not set out to alienate an entire class. It was the system that was at fault, outmoded and out of touch with the requirements of the times. Senators were not deprived of wealth, prestige and honour, nor were they persecuted or molested unmercifully during the reign of Gallienus, but retribution was swift if there was a suspicion of revolt. As mentioned above, the military interests of the senators had been declining for some time. Even during the Marcommanic wars, Marcus Aurelius had found it difficult to find a sufficient quantity of suitable senators with ability and military experience. In peacetime generally, and in times of crisis especially, there was a lack of qualified men to fill all the posts that government and defence of the Empire demanded. For some time before the reign of Gallienus there had been an increasing trend for individual senators to concentrate on either purely civil or purely military careers, and it became possible to succeed without gaining the all-round experience, mixing army and civil governmental posts, such as senators of the early Empire had occupied. By the mid-third century senatorial careers had undergone considerable change; the junior magistracies disappeared, except the quaestorship, so that senatorial participation in the government of the Empire diminished. Equestrians carried out many functions in administration and finance, and the Emperor controlled the army, the purse strings, and significant appointments which were in his gift, so that there was little that was left to the Senate. The senators who suffered were those with aspirations, which were now were curbed, so that a core of disappointed ambitious men would perceive the Emperor as the villainous tyrant, as he was portrayed in the later sources. The main effect on senatorial careers after Gallienus' reforms was the severe disruption of the normal *cursus honorum*, whereby the appointment as governor of a praetorian province paved the way to the consulship and then to further appointments. This stage in the career structure was now withdrawn. Christol enumerates the losses: 25 posts as legate of a legion disappeared, along with 12 posts as provincial governor of praetorian rank. The inevitable result, after the closure of these posts, was that those who had reached the rank of praetor tended to concentrate on civil appointments in Rome itself or in Italy. Divorced from posts in Imperial praetorian provinces and from commands in the army, senators had to find alternative routes to the consulship. Even after this, consulars were restricted in the choice of further posts that were still available to them, and required the personal assistance of the Empire to further their careers. The goal now was the second consulship, and the lucrative provincial government posts that were still open to senators. But there was far less opportunity now, with appointments separated by a number of years, usually about 15 between the consulship and an important appointment like the proconsulship of Asia, and probably 20 to 25 years between the first and second consulship. To compound the situation, the Emperor and members of his family often monopolised the consulship, reducing the vacancies even further. From the mid-third century a spectacular senatorial career depended upon a good relationship with the Emperor, a situation to which Gallienus was probably not entirely antipathetic.[15]

Financial policy

Gallienus had the army exclusively in mind in his monetary and financial policies. For a long time, income had failed to match expenditure, and there was no budgetary system to speak of in the modern sense. In the mid-third century these two related aspects of Roman Imperial finance caused an escalating degeneration. While revenues declined in quantity, and were also restricted because of the Emperor's lack of control of the whole Empire, in inverse proportion expenditure climbed to new heights. One response was to debase the currency and issue more of it, and both Valerian and Gallienus consistently adopted this procedure. The silver coinage suffered the most. In the decade between 258 and 268, the silver content of the most common coin, the antoninianus, was reduced to a shadow of its former self. The result was a rise in prices, the full effects of which were not apparent until after Gallienus' death, beginning around 270. But purchasing power definitely declined, so the cash payments to the army and some taxes were partly transmuted into payments in kind. From the third century the *annona* became more of a regular institution, but at first its regulation was inconsistent and spasmodic. Cash payments to the army were taken from the central treasury, but requisitions in kind fell most heavily on those areas where the troops were operating. Some areas could be denuded in a prolonged continuous war, or if successive short campaigns were fought over the same terrain before the next harvests could be brought home. Coupled with destruction by the northern tribes, the requisition system had an unfortunate result in that the frontier zones suffered most.[16]

Direct taxation, the source of much of the state revenue, fell most heavily on the wealthy landowners in Italy and the provinces. In dealing with government of the praetorian provinces, Gallienus placed civil, military and financial matters in the hands of the *praesides*, so that collection of the taxes was the responsibility of the new equestrian officers. Senators with sufficient power and influence could evade taxation and so reduce the revenues even further, though the problem of powerful lords forming pre-feudal mini-states within the Empire did not manifest itself until later, in the fourth century. Income from the mines also decreased during the third century, and it was out of the question to embark on conquests of new metal-rich territories, as Trajan had been able to do by finally finishing off the Dacian wars and taking over the lucrative Carpathian mines. One source of revenue that Gallienus exploited was the traditional contribution from the provinces whenever the Emperor proclaimed a victory – the *aurum coronarium*. It has been said that he celebrated his repeated victories on the coinage and in his titles simply in order to increase the number of contributions of this nature. The accusation may be true, but at least his victories had some claim to reality, whereas Caracalla allegedly invented a few here and there for the purpose of raising money.[17]

With regard to the payment of the army, Gallienus founded several mints near the various military headquarters at Milan, Sirmium, Siscia, and Smyrna, which reduced the risks involved in transporting coin across the Empire, and ensured the regularity as far as possible of distributions of cash to the troops. Whenever Gallienus himself was present at the frontier areas, the mints produced good-quality gold coins and medallions, so some authors have assumed that he brought supplies of gold with him. The benefits to the soldiers were supreme, so the multiplication of mints was a well-judged policy, but for the Empire as a whole it meant that there was less consistency or uniformity in the production of coins. Values were not standard, so somewhere along the way the plot was lost. People generally would not accept the coins at face value, and had recourse to older, shrewder methods: as far as they were concerned the worth of an aureus depended upon what it actually weighed, not upon what Imperial power said it was worth. In the short term the consequences of Gallienus' financial policies were satisfactory, at least from his point of view. The army was well rewarded and functioned as the Emperor wished, and the rest of the Empire managed as best it could. In the long term the policies were disastrous, and Gallienus did not survive long enough to reverse them.[18]

The Gallic Empire

At an unknown date, probably in 260 when the capture of Valerian by the Persians was known in the west, Marcus Cassianus Latinius Postumus, governor of Lower Germany, was proclaimed Emperor by his troops. The Rhine army had no confidence in the ability of the legitimate Emperor to protect the provinces from invasion, and chose the man whom the soldiers thought most capable of doing so. Thus was the Gallic Empire created, based on Roman institutions, with annually elected consuls, an Emperor who assumed tribunician power each year, and protected himself by means of a

97

Praetorian Guard. Sources for this period in the history of the western provinces are poor. The literature that has survived hails from the ancient authors of the east, and it was naturally the east that interested these writers most. Postumus is described in the *Historia Augusta* as courageous and wise – but it is the bias against Gallienus that is predominant, not the wish to provide a true depiction of the first Gallic Emperor. Nevertheless Postumus did survive intact for a decade, and did what he could to set the provinces in his charge back on their feet. The two Germanies, the whole of Gaul with the possible exception of Narbonensis, then Britain and Spain joined him. He set up his headquarters at Cologne, after the murky episode when Gallienus' son Saloninus was murdered. Detractors of Postumus lay all the blame upon him for the death of Saloninus; supporters claim that he was totally innocent; they prefer to blame the Gauls for the murder, which they say was carried out because of the general detestation of Gallienus. In actuality, that had nothing to do with it. One Emperor was out of action, as a prisoner in the east; the other, preoccupied with usurpers and the Danube provinces, was unlikely to be able to assist in defending the Gallic provinces for some time. Once the rebellion began, there was no possibility of compromise, and once he had embarked on the road to Empire Postumus could not retract; Saloninus had to go, but who gave the order is not proven.[19]

Postumus' ultimate aims are not elucidated. His immediate concern, indeed his *raison d'être* and the basis of his power, was the reparation and defence of the Rhine frontier and the hinterland, a task into which he launched himself with vigour, earning the respect of the ancient authors, who proclaim that he restored the security that the provinces had enjoyed in the old days. He promoted himself just as Gallienus did, advertising his successes; he issued good-quality coinage that proclaimed him restorer of Gaul (*Restitutor Galliarum*) and the bringer of security to the provinces (*Salus Provinciarum*). The restored provinces were somewhat different, battered now and fearful of what the future might bring, and restructured according to current needs. Archaeologists have shown that many if not all the frontier forts were abandoned after 260, and there is evidence of widespread destruction. Though it was not apparent until later, city authorities began to think very seriously of strong walls and fortified gates. The magnitude of Postumus' task is perhaps easy to exaggerate, but it occupied him fully for many years, perhaps preventing him from turning his attention to Rome and the struggle for supreme power over the whole Empire. It is debatable whether he ever intended to usurp Gallienus or whether he was content to rule the western provinces, and no amount of discussion as to Postumus' ambitions, or of Gallienus' perception of Postumus' ambitions, has ever solved this problem definitively. The basis of Postumus' power, as stated above, was the defence of the Rhine provinces and Gaul, so it could be said that if he marched away in pursuit of greater glory, taking troops with him to fight for his stake in the government of the Empire, then he was in dereliction of

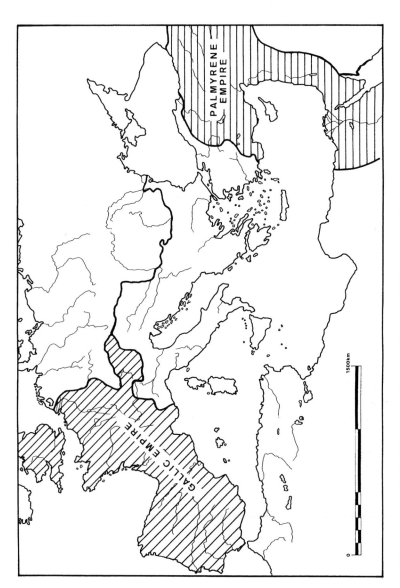

Figure 17 Map of the Roman Empire in 260, with the legitimate Emperor Gallienus confined in the central sector flanked by the Gallic Emperor Postumus in the west, and the Palmyrene Odenathus in the east. Postumus seems to have controlled all or most of Raetia, thus hemming in Gallienus in the north of Italy as well as in the west. (Drawn by Graeme Stobbs.)

duty. There are arguments for and against Postumus' intentions to proclaim himself Emperor of the whole Roman world, but in the end argument remains academic. The facts are that Gallienus never recognised Postumus, and tried to win back the Gallic provinces, probably in 265; but Christol postulates that there were two attempts, in 261 and 266. Gallienus controlled the exits from the Alpine passes and protected the route into Italy, and he may have succeeded in regaining control of Raetia, but ultimately he failed. He was wounded at Trier; it was said that Aureolus, the commander of the cavalry, may have made a secret alliance with Postumus, and therefore did not pursue him or press him too hard, but this is probably all slander, founded on nothing. Aureolus was loyal until 267, so the fact that neither Gallienus nor his lieutenant achieved anything against Postumus speaks eloquently for the latter's ability to avoid defeat. He did not carry the war against the legitimate Emperor from defence to aggression, however; neither Postumus nor his successors made a march on Rome to fight it out with the legitimate Emperor. What is certain is that the situation could not have continued indefinitely. As Christol points out, disunity was a threat that would have to be addressed sooner or later, leading inevitably to conflict.[20]

Palmyra and Odenathus

After the capture of Valerian by Shapur the Roman army was extricated by Macrianus, an equestrian who had been put in charge of logistics and supplies for the campaign as *praepositus annonae expeditionalis*. He later broke with Gallienus, proclaiming his two sons Augusti, eventually marching on Rome with the younger Macrianus, leaving the other son, Quietus, with Callistus or Ballista in command of the eastern provinces. Aureolus, Gallienus' general and cavalry commander, defeated the two Macriani in Pannonia, while Ballista and Quietus were eliminated by the Palmyrene Odenathus, who had pursued and attacked Shapur himself as the Persian army headed back across the Euphrates laden with booty.[21]

Palmyra owed its existence and its wealth to its fortunate geographical position astride the eastern trade routes, where taxes could be levied on the caravans passing through, and a lucrative secondary source of wealth could be gained from accommodating the traders themselves. Palmyra was, of course, very much more than a large customs post or the ancient equivalent of a motorway service station. It was a city of culture with an established nobility, of which Odenathus was one of the foremost members. His postulated ancestor of the same name has now been discredited, but it seems likely that Odenathus hailed from rich noble stock. His father Hairan had been granted Roman citizenship by Severus, and on inscriptions Odenathus calls himself Septimius. He was considered of senatorial rank, even if he was not actually a Roman senator, and by 258 he was of consular status (*vir consularis*). This probably means that he had been awarded *ornamenta consularia*, rather than the actual consulship, by the joint Emperors Valerian and Gallienus. Thus he had already come to prominence and the attention of Gallienus before Valerian's capture.[22]

Debate centres around the relationship between Gallienus and Odenathus. In 260 Gallienus was in no position to refuse the help of Odenathus against either the Persians or the usurpers, but Roman sensibilities were offended that a foreigner, whom the Romans labelled barbarian, should be the one to take charge of the east. It was not at all certain just how much Odenathus' loyalty to Rome outweighed his self-interest. Sandwiched between the Empire of Rome in the west and the rising power of Shapur and the Persian Empire in the east, it was possible that the Palmyrenes could turn either way, and it was thought by later chroniclers that Odenathus initially made overtures to Shapur before he began to act on behalf of Rome. Gallienus perhaps suspected such a situation, but he was not even capable at this juncture of despatching another general to supplant Odenathus or to bring him to heel, and he certainly could not afford to mount a campaign of his own to win back the east; a better option was to allow Odenathus to continue as he had begun. Consequently Gallienus readily recognised him, granting him a military command, *dux Romanorum*. This title is attested for his son Vaballathus and assumed for Odenathus, who was now legally in command of troops in the east, but it is not clear exactly how his command operated with regard to the existing military officers in the eastern provinces and to the provincial governors. He probably took over the remnants of the army of Valerian, but many of these troops would have departed with Macrianus and his son to meet defeat later at the hands of Aureolus in Pannonia. Was Odenathus in command of all the Roman government personnel in the east, and all the troops, or did he operate independently with a substantial military force, comprising his own and some Roman soldiers? There are unsubstantiated hints of a treaty between Gallienus and Odenathus, supported by an inscription of 262–3. It is very likely that both the Roman Emperor and the Palmyrene would attempt to establish a few ground rules before taking any action, though the arrangement may have been loosely organised to allow Odenathus a certain freedom of action within defined parameters.[23]

From 262–3, and again in 267, Odenathus launched campaigns against Persia, reaching Ctesiphon and liberating Nisibis from Persian domination. Only Zosimus writes of two Persian campaigns, but it is conceivable that he was correct. It was presumably after the first one that Odenathus began to style himself king of kings, in emulation of the Persian rulers. Gallienus took the title *Parthicus Maximus* for himself, granting to Odenathus the title *Imperator*, and *corrector totius Orientis*. Precisely what this implied is not known for certain; it probably did not mean that Odenathus was in total charge of the civil and financial administration, nor even command of all the troops in the east, but though he perhaps did not involve himself with the day-to-day routine, he would probably be the ultimate authority to whom

101

queries and problems would be addressed. Deference to the legitimate Emperor did not seem to be anathema to him, and the fact that Gallienus awarded him titles after successful actions suggests that communications were effective if not rapid. Odenathus also hurried to meet the Goths when they invaded Roman territory in Asia Minor. The evidence supports the theory that Odenathus was a loyal ally of Rome, but doubt has been cast on his true intentions. Initially he was suspected, as mentioned above, of sounding out Shapur, so there was always the possibility that he might one day find an alliance with Rome's enemy more compatible than an alliance with Rome herself. When he was murdered, probably in 267, though the date is not established beyond doubt, it has been suggested that he may have been ready to turn against Gallienus and to seize power in the east. It has also been suggested that Gallienus was the instigator of the plot to remove Odenathus, either because he had got wind of the grand designs of the Palmyrene, or because he always intended that Odenathus should be removed as soon as it was convenient when the east had been pacified and the Persian threat reduced. None of these theories can be proved, but it is a valid question to ask how Gallienus would have regained control of the east if Odenathus had refused to step down and be relegated to the background, loaded with honours, supremely important but powerless.[24]

After the death of Odenathus and his eldest son Hairan/Herodes, it is possible that Gallienus could have reunited the eastern provinces with the rest of his Empire, but at that same juncture invasions by the northern tribes across the Danube preoccupied him. Zenobia, the energetic and ambitious wife of Odenathus, stepped into the power vacuum with her two younger sons, Herodianus and Vaballathus. They managed to expel or embarrass Heraclianus, the Praetorian Prefect sent by Gallienus to take charge of the east, and from then onwards Gallienus was too hard pressed to retrieve the situation. It may be significant that Heraclianus is mentioned as one of Gallienus' assassins; perhaps he harboured a grudge arising from his unavenged treatment at the hands of the new Palmyrene rulers. To onlookers it would seem that Gallienus was weak and spineless, unable to assert Roman supremacy over non-Roman upstarts. That was a task bequeathed to Aurelian, and because he did it so well and knew how to use victories for self-promotion, Gallienus would recede further into the background as a failure.[25]

THE BATTLE FOR THE EMPIRE: GALLIENUS TO AURELIAN

The last years of Gallienus

The changes that Gallienus made in the army and the government of the provinces were not carried out all at once before an attempt was made to regain control of the fragmentary Empire. He could not afford to waste time in pre-planning. His policies were the product of an ongoing adaptation, meeting problems with hastily contrived solutions, progressing empirically, working in a somewhat hand-to-mouth existence. Circumstances dictated that he must place his trust in a few deputies to take care of urgent tasks or groups of provinces that he could not attend to himself. The names of some of his close associates are known, all military men, perhaps the most famous besides the cavalry commander Aureolus being Lucius Petronius Taurus Volusianus, a man of low birth who became consul in 261, then prefect of the *vigiles*, prefect of the Praetorian Guard, and city prefect in 267–8. The *Historia Augusta* names others, such as Theodotus, Heraclianus, who is variously titled *dux* and Praetorian prefect, and Marcianus, the general to whom he entrusted the campaign against the Goths. These were some of the men to whom he gave special tasks while he focused on the most important items on his agenda, little of which he had been able to set for himself. He was not even in a position to make a list of urgent priorities in a clear descending order. There were several priorities, to which it would have been tempting to give equal weight, but he could attend to only one thing at a time. The inevitable result was that while he was absent fighting battles in one part of the Empire, the people in the other areas where there was also an urgent need for action felt that their interests and their lives were being sacrificed for the benefit of people elsewhere. The blatant favouritism shown to the army was not seen for what it was, the way to salvation, but as an unnecessary expense which drained money from all quarters while everybody else except the soldiers had to suffer from a chronic lack of cash coupled with rising prices due to inflation, and the hardships that all this entailed. The rift between the army and the civilian population of Rome, Italy and the provinces was nothing new, but during the reign of Gallienus it widened, despite his coinage announcing *Concordia* between the soldiers and the people.[26]

The dangers which offered direct threat to himself or to Rome were the ones that occupied Gallienus first. For the time being, he ignored the Gallic Empire under Postumus, and the east under the Palmyrene Odenathus, while he concentrated on other matters. If he can be accused of selfishness or lack of initiative, then so can his successor Claudius, who likewise ignored both east and west while he tried to repulse the Goths. It was only under Aurelian that the Empire was pulled back together, but without the efforts of Gallienus there may have been no Empire to reassemble. The Alamanni were soundly defeated near Milan in 260, and notably caused no trouble until after the death of Gallienus in 268. The chronology of events in the reign of Gallienus is far from clear. The revolt of Regalianus in Pannonia was ended when he was killed in an invasion by the Iazyges and Roxolani, while that of Macrianus was dealt with by Aureolus in the west and Odenathus in the east. Gallienus' general Theodotus put down another attempt at usurpation by Aemilianus in Egypt from 261–2. Gallienus had to quell

Figure 18 Gold aureus dated to *c.*267 from Rome, showing Gallienus wearing a lion skin, identifying him with the god Hercules. The reverse (not shown) proclaims the loyalty of the army (FIDES MILITUM). (Drawn by Trish Boyle.)

an attempted mutiny in Byzantium at about the same time. Once these upheavals calmed down, it seems that by the middle of 262 Gallienus had re-established control over most of the Empire save for the extensive territories still loyal to Postumus. Though the east was still in the hands of Odenathus, the Palmyrene ruler was nominally Gallienus' chosen deputy, *dux* and *corrector*, just as between 257 and 258 Marcus Cornelius Octavianus was appointed *dux per Africam Numidiam Mauretaniamque* and *correctores* were established in Egypt; these appointments were made even before the capture of Valerian, so the titles granted to Odenathus and the powers that they conferred on him were not without precedent. The loyalty of the east was not in question at this moment; the Antioch mint coined for Gallienus, not for Odenathus, from 262 onwards.[27]

In that year Gallienus returned to Rome where he celebrated his Decennalia. It was a notable achievement to have survived for ten years in such an era, the chief hallmark of which was the rapid turnover of Roman Emperors. It was even more noteworthy that Gallienus was able to celebrate his ten-year rule in a time of relative peace, in a position of ascendancy, though it was clear that the Empire had a long way to go before unification was complete. Like the first Augustus, Gallienus knew how to present himself in the best light, and turn adversity into advantage. He associated himself with the powerful gods such as Jupiter and, most especially, Hercules; he declared himself to be under the special protection of Apollo and Diana, and of Sol, the sun god. Throughout his reign he honoured all these gods on his coinage, whose legends proclaimed the successes of the army, and the onset of peace. As time went on, portraits of the Emperor became more idealised, as he elevated himself above the realm of ordinary men. Several authors have commented on the spiritual quality of the portraits of his sole rule, which seems all the more ethereal when combined with the unrealistic, almost rigid style that prefigures the later Byzantine portraiture. Gallienus gazes heavenwards rather than at the viewer; his mind is clearly on a higher plane than the mere mortal. Titles such as *Invictus* appeared on inscriptions, and the legends of his later coins presented him as superhuman hero and saviour of the state.[28]

During the few years of relative peace between 262 and 265, Gallienus found time to devote to philosophy, promoting Platonism via his favourite Plotinus. He toyed with the idea of granting land in Campania to Plotinus and his followers to found a sort of study centre, but members of his court advised him against this plan. Nonetheless, the school of Plotinus still flourished and received many followers. Culturally, Gallienus' interests were not confined to this particular branch of philosophy. He encouraged literature and the arts, and indulged himself as a confirmed Graecophile by visiting Athens where he was made exarch of the city and was initiated into the Eleusinian mysteries. His visit was not regarded benignly in all quarters. The Empire was still not united and the Gothic threat to the Danube provinces was not eradicated, and though he had done what he could to establish peace in the diminished Empire, he was not visibly devoting himself day and night to winning back the lost territories; instead he enjoyed a holiday in Athens. This is one reason why his detractors accuse him of negligence; the Emperor proclaimed victories and successes, but did not finally deliver all that was proclaimed or promised. Disgruntled perception distorts the overall picture, and the sources concentrate on the Emperor's inactivity and failures, disregarding what Gallienus had achieved. The inactivity was not to last for very long. In 265 the Emperor embarked on his ill-fated attempt to reconquer the Gallic Empire, and in 266 he was called to the Danube to combat the Goths, basing himself at Siscia. The first campaign produced no tangible result, and in 267 it seemed that the whole of the Roman world from Moesia to the Mediterranean was at the mercy of several tribes, all labelled indiscriminately 'Scythians' by the ancient authors. The main groups were the Goths, pouring across Moesia into Thrace, and the Heruli threatening Athens, Sparta and Corinth; another group laid siege to Thessalonika. The Emperor and the army could not be everywhere at once, and the provincial troops were not sufficient in number to meet the invading bands and drive them out. Self-help was the only answer, so various communities built walls around their cities. Aquileia in northern Italy had more than once been the first rendezvous of the tribesmen emerging from the Alpine passes, and had been threatened during the reign of Marcus; as early as 238 the city authorities built a fortified wall. During the reign of Gallienus the city of Verona was enclosed in 265, and the cities of Moesia followed suit. Sometimes it was necessary to arm the civilian

Figure 19 Gold aureus from Rome, dated to 267 towards the end of the reign of Gallienus. The reverse emphasises once again the loyalty of the army. (Drawn by Trish Boyle.)

inhabitants; the Augsburg inscription refers to civilians fighting alongside the troops. The mid-third century was the age of enforced self-sufficiency; it is the context of the defence of Athens by Dexippus, who resisted valiantly but still failed to save his city from capture, a fact which is subsumed in the rhetoric. Gallienus could not clear the whole of this vast area of the invading tribesmen, and concentrated on Illyricum where he defeated one group of Heruli under their leader Naulobatus. The remainder surrendered and were incorporated into the Roman army. Gallienus moved on towards Philip-popolis, now besieged by the tribesmen. He defeated them again, at Nestus, but the exact location of the victory is not clear and has become confused in some sources with that of Claudius Gothicus a short time later at Naissus. The ancient sources deny that Gallienus had any success at all, but archaeo-logical and epigraphic evidence illustrates the wide-ranging army manoeu-vres, and the groupings and regroupings of troops. The finer details are lost, but Gallienus cannot be accused of inactivity. He was unable to follow up the recent victory because news arrived that Aureolus had raised a revolt in Milan.[29]

One of Gallienus' generals, Marcianus, 'a thoroughly experienced soldier' according to Zosimus, was left in command of the campaign against the Heruli and the Goths, while the Emperor himself hastened back to Milan where he besieged Aureolus. A plot was hatched, led by Heraclianus, to remove Gallienus while he conducted this siege. There are conflicting ver-sions of the assassination. The most dramatic is that of Zosimus, who says that an accomplice of Heraclianus called Cecropius, the commander of the Dalmatian cavalry, lured the Emperor outside his tent by announcing that Aureolus was approaching with his army; not waiting for his bodyguard, Gallienus dashed out unprotected and Cecropius killed him. It was July or

Figure 20 Stylised portrait of Gallienus from Rome, dating from late in the Emperor's reign. (Courtesy Ny Carlsberg Glyptotek.)

August 268. The reason for the assassination is not clear. Zosimus does not elaborate. It is possible that Heraclianus bore some sort of grudge against Gallienus, but that is only speculation, and the theory that one general was disgruntled does not account for the apparent readiness of Claudius II to condone the assassination and then consent to becoming Emperor himself, nor for the complicity of Aurelian in the plot. The generals who had risen to prominence under Gallienus had become disenchanted with him or his policies or both, and thought that they could govern the Empire rather better. Judging by the energy that Claudius Gothicus and then Aurelian devoted to pulling the Roman world back together, their aims may have been as

107

altruistic as they were personal. It was said that Claudius had always been marked out as the designated successor of Gallienus, being one of his closest advisers and most experienced generals. When he was declared Emperor there was little dissent. There was apparently no stigma attached to his association with the previous Emperor, so it does not seem that there was a conspiracy to remove the whole court circle and the top generals, and then start again with a new faction. It was Gallienus himself and his immediate family who were the targets of the plot. His brother and son were killed shortly afterwards. When and where the plot originated is not recorded. The generals had at some point divorced themselves from the Emperor, and pre- sumably begun to talk to each other, on the alert for opportunities. The sources are rather coy about the precise role and the extent of involvement of Claudius in the conspiracy, because of the favourable bias applied retrospec- tively when Constantine the Great laid claim to Claudius Gothicus as one of his ancestors. But it is hard to believe in the complete innocence of Claudius; even if the actual assassination was the result of a hastily con- structed plan, the transition from Gallienus to Claudius was smooth enough to be almost seamless. The only glitch was that the army reacted badly to the murder of their benefactor, and had to be calmed with cash rewards. After the elimination of Gallienus it was the turn of Aureolus, who tried to surrender to Claudius but was put to death.[30]

Claudius II Gothicus

The new Emperor Marcus Aurelius Claudius was an Illyrian army officer whose career had blossomed under Gallienus. His early career as documented in the ancient sources is probably fictitious; both the *Historia Augusta* and Aurelius Victor declare that he was in command of all the troops in the Balkans under Gallienus, but precisely what rank he held is uncertain and the path by which he arrived there remains obscure. Claudius survived for so short a time that he had no chance to undertake sweeping reforms or to estab- lish coherent policies in the military, financial or social spheres. Consequently he neither changed nor reversed any of Gallienus' policies. Whilst he may not have endorsed everything that Gallienus had done, it seems that there were no glaringly obvious mistakes to rectify, which suggests that the reign of his predecessor had not been as dire as it was later portrayed.[31]

Whether or not Claudius was really Gallienus' chosen successor, the army officers who elevated him were determined to have him as Emperor. When the rank and file soldiers expressed dismay at the death of their Imperial benefactor, they were bought off with donatives. The Senate ratified the army's choice and conferred the name of Augustus on him, though it was more a case of being swept along by events than an act of volition. Claudius' relations with the Senate were at least cordial, but once again the retrospec- tive favour shown him by Constantine may have improved and embellished the picture somewhat. Avoiding the mistake that Maximinus Thrax had made by staying on the frontiers with the army, and careful to observe the formalities, Claudius went to Rome, where he persuaded the Senate to deify Gallienus, though the first inclination of most senators was to damn his memory for ever. By this act, Claudius implied that the murder of Gallienus was unjust; but there was no witch hunt, and only Aureolus had been put to death when he tried to surrender to the new Emperor.[32]

Military necessity dictated that Claudius should spend nearly the whole of his reign fighting Rome's external enemies, and like Gallienus he had no opportunity to devote his energies to winning back the western provinces or to solving the Palmyrene problem in the east. He sent the prefect of the *vigiles*, Julius Placidianus, to begin the task of bringing the Gallic Empire back into the Imperial domain, and it seems that this officer won over the eastern part of Narbonensis and regained control of the Rhône valley, but successful though this was it was not the focal point of Claudius' reign. There could be no full scale war here because the bulk of the army was committed to the defence of the Empire against the Goths and the Alamanni. The Goths had already discovered the advantages of seaborne transport to ferry the tribesmen from one zone to another, and had by now adapted to the idea of using ships to carry out raids and make a rapid exit with booty and prisoners. The situation had worsened in the east when the Goths began to threaten the Mediterranean coastal cities and to disrupt shipping. The numbers of ships and men that the Goths could muster is probably grossly exaggerated in the sources, but whatever the true figures the impact was immense. Claudius entrusted the Prefect of Egypt, Tenagino Probus, with command of a fleet based in Greece to sweep the seas clear of the Goths and to protect the coasts. Probably at this moment Zenobia, the wife of Odenathus, more and more confident of her power, decided to take advantage of the preoccupations of the Emperor and Tenagino Probus to extend her control of the eastern provinces. Towards the end of Claudius' reign her armies swept into Egypt. The Prefect was defeated and killed himself. The Palmyrene Royal House was therefore in command of most of the east and, more important, in charge of the bulk of Rome's corn supply.[33]

The chronology of Claudius' campaigns is debatable. According to some sources he fought the Alamanni in the north of Italy and then campaigned against the Goths, and according to others his battle with the Alamanni was sandwiched between two separate campaigns in the Danube provinces. It is likely that as soon as he was able to do so Claudius marched to the Danube, to conclude what Gallienus had partially finished. Marcianus had been left in command after the victory at Nestus, and had achieved some success, but Thessalonika and Marcianopolis were still under siege. Claudius claimed a victory at Naissus, which may have been confused with Gallienus' battle at Nestus. Once again there was no conclusion to the campaign; the Goths dispersed after the battle, ready to fight another day.[34]

After the death of Gallienus, the Alamanni erupted once again into north-ern Italy. They had been quiet since their defeat in 260, and it is probable that they had entered into a treaty with Gallienus. There was a story prob-ably current in the third century that the Emperor had made a treaty with the Marcomanni, taking the chieftain's daughter Pipa as his wife. This was an arrangement that the tribesmen would recognise on their own terms. It was usual for the Romans to draft some of the young men into the army as part of the peace treaty. The important factor to note is that the tribesmen regarded the treaty as a personal affair rather than an agreement made between states; from their point of view it was a pact between their chief or chiefs and the Roman Emperor, the chief of the Romans. Now that Gal-lienus was dead, it was likely that the Alamanni would regard the arrange-ments made with him as invalid, and besides they had had time to recoup their losses and to recruit new warriors. There may have been a dispute over subsidy arrangements, too. Aurelian dealt firmly with the Alamanni some time later, refusing to reinstate subsidies when the tribesmen asked for them. Claudius brought the tribesmen to battle near Lake Garda, taking the title *Germanicus Maximus* after he defeated them. In summer 270 Claudius was engaged on a campaign against the Juthungi and Vandals in the Danube provinces, based at Sirmium, but before he had achieved anything he died of the plague that broke out in that year. For a short time his brother Quintillus stepped into the vacancy as Emperor, surviving long enough to issue coins, though the sources vary on how long Quintillus remained Emperor. He probably reigned for a few months rather than the few days allotted to him in one source. But he did not have the support of the whole army, and he had no opportunity to go to Rome and win over the Senate and people; within a very short time the rival contender, Aurelian, was proclaimed by his soldiers, and carried all before him.[35]

THE EMPIRE RESTORED: AURELIAN

It is testimony to his obscure origins that no one knows where Lucius Domitius Aurelianus was born. According to the *Historia Augusta* he was a native of Sirmium, but other sources are less certain, hedging their bets by opting for an indefinite point somewhere between Moesia and Macedonia. Aurelian's elevation from obscurity to supreme power is also eloquent testi-mony to the effectiveness of the new social mobility based on military prowess. Soldiers could rise to supreme heights if their abilities brought them to the notice of the generals or the Emperor himself; personal ambi-tion, determination, and being in the right place at the right time, ensured that no opportunity should be missed. When Claudius died Aurelian was in the field on campaign, probably against the Juthungi and Vandals. The exact date of his proclamation is not recorded; it was probably in November

270, but certitude about the timing is not as important as the inevitability of his elevation. It cannot have been entirely fortuitous, nor can it have taken him by surprise. He was one of the most important officers in Claudius' entourage, and he would have built up connections of his own, political, social, and not least, military. One of his first acts after the army proclaimed him was a purely practical measure; he seized the mint at Siscia, where he struck gold coins to enable him to pay adequately grateful or adequately persuasive donatives to the soldiers.[36]

Aurelian had already achieved a reputation for determined and energetic activity, earning the nickname, even before his reign began, of *manu ad ferrum*, hand on hilt, or sword in hand; perhaps a more pertinent idiomatic, if loose, translation to illustrate his uncompromising nature would be an iron hand in an iron glove; there was no equivalent of the velvet touch in Aurelian. Before the end of his reign his reputation for cruelty was so well established as to be indelible; Eutropius describes him as *saevus et sanguinarius*. Perhaps in less stressful times he would have avoided such a charge, but the second half of the third century was not a time when kindness and mercy could prevail against all problems, or weaklings could hope to flourish. Activity and determination were the keystones of his reign, which was brief but eventful. Aurelian's priorities were to conclude the wars with the Juthungi and Vandals, and bring about the swift elimination of Quintillus and any other rival claimant. The initial vigour of the Juthungi was probably already exhausted; they swept out of northern Italy towards their homes, weighed down with their stolen goods; Aurelian caught up with them in Raetia. He refused to grant them the peace treaty they asked for but

Figure 21 Gold aureus bearing a fine portrait of Aurelian, issued in 270 from the Rome mint. (Drawn by Trish Boyle.)

111

allowed them to continue homewards unmolested. According to Dexippus they contributed 40,000 horsemen and 80,000 soldiers for the Roman army. In the campaign against the Vandals Aurelian devastated the territories all around them to deny them food. giving orders that anything consumable was to be taken into the towns; this harsh strategy brought results. The tribesmen were starved into submission; Aurelian extracted 2,000 cavalry for the army, and made peace, giving food to the remaining Vandals so that they could return home.[37]

When a temporary peace was restored Aurelian journeyed to Rome. The chronology of his reign is unclear, so the recorded events can be described individually but it is not always possible to be certain how one event might have influenced another or what preceded or was consequent upon different episodes. Though the date is disputed, the ancient sources indicate that one of the first problems that Aurelian dealt with was the revolt at the mint in Rome, where the workers had achieved a high degree of independence that tipped over into insubordination. There was a great deal of corruption among the mint workers, who were interested in lining their own pockets as much as anything else. Aurelian made an initial attempt to reform the finances in the early part of his reign, and it may have been the prospect of firm discipline and too much penetrating curiosity on the part of the Emperor that triggered the revolt. On the other hand the revolt may have had much deeper roots; there may have been senatorial interests represented at second hand by the actions of the mint workers, and it is possible that the ringleader at the treasury, Felicissimus, who occupied the post of *rationalis*, was merely a tool of more influential men who saw the revolt as a way out of their problems. It is quite possible that this disturbance is to be dated somewhat later, when Aurelian had suffered a defeat at the hands of the Alamanni and there was widespread panic in Rome, or later still in 274 when he began his reform of the currency and the financial system; traditionally, though, the revolt of the moneyers is placed at the very outset of the reign. Whenever it occurred, the revolt flourished only very briefly and was put down with a firm hand. Aurelian, never a man to vacillate or compromise, closed the Rome mint. Felicissimus was killed, somehow, in the rioting, or by someone sent to remove him; no one seemed to know or care.[38]

The attempted usurpations of Septimius or more properly Septiminus, Domitianus, and Urbanus, were quickly detected and eradicated. Suspicion was all that was necessary to condemn them, and whether they were guilty or not, the point was made that Aurelian would not tolerate opposition and was moreover powerful enough to stamp it out. It seems that all of these potential troublemakers appeared and disappeared early in Aurelian's reign, perhaps all of them in 271, possibly even before he arrived in Rome. As mentioned above, chronology is not one of the strong points in the documentation of the period from Gallienus to Diocletian, and for Aurelian's reign it is singularly confused, and consequently much debated. Exactly what the Emperor did on the way to Rome is not known and there is some disagreement about how long he stayed once he had arrived; all this confusion is connected to the Juthungian wars, described below (see next paragraph). Consolidation of his supremacy with the Senate and people of Rome were Aurelian's main concerns when he reached Rome. Though the Roman mob no longer possessed the coercive power that it once had, it was always a wise move for new Emperors to cultivate the goodwill of the populace; Aurelian distributed donatives of 500 denarii each and issued coins with the legend *Genius Populi Romani*. The Senate was nervous and unsure of what the hardened soldier-Emperor would do. Not only was he a military man, he was obviously turning out to be a populist as well. He cancelled debts to the Treasury, making a bonfire of all the records and gaining much popularity as a result, and according to Ammianus he descended on the rich 'like a torrent' when he raised taxes. Not knowing that all this was coming, but instinctively wary of him and his intentions, the senators bestowed the usual powers on him; all of those present at the meeting of the Senate were no doubt fully aware that this was a formality that Aurelian could circumvent if necessary. Already a weakened force, under Aurelian the Senate lost its privilege of issuing the bronze coinage, and its legislative powers were absorbed and disappeared as the Emperor evolved into totalitarian ruler and lawgiver.[39]

Before very long, Aurelian was called upon to fight the northern tribesmen once again. In 271 he was faced by the most serious incursions of the Juthungi and the Alamanni, joined this time by the Marcomanni. The sources vary with regard to the tribes whom he fought and exactly when he did so. Tribal names in the Latin and Greek sources are not reliable, and may overlap. The *Historia Augusta* speaks of battles with the Suebi and Sarmatians, and with the Marcomanni; Zosimus labels most tribes with the all-embracing terms Scythians and Alamanni; Dexippus calls the tribes Juthungi and Vandals. It is unlikely that these names represent seven completely different groups, all fighting against Aurelian successively or at the same time, but it is not possible to be pedantic about which tribes in Zosimus' account are the equivalents of other tribes in the *Historia Augusta*, and which of the tribes in both accounts correspond to those described by Dexippus. It has been debated how many times Aurelian waged war against the Juthungi; scholars thought that there were two wars, then the theory was challenged in favour of only one war, with the supposition that accounts were so mangled in the sources that they split into separate fragments, so that it only *seemed* that there were two wars. Recently the case has been restated for two Juthungian wars. Whatever the number of campaigns, it is apparent that throughout the early part of Aurelian's reign there was a hectic pace of rapidly changing military actions and wide-ranging movements of troops. In 271 the Juthungi reached Milan. Perhaps not ready or not willing to commit himself to fighting running battles on Italian soil,

Aurelian proposed a peaceful settlement. The tribesmen met with him but went away discontented, then attacked by night near Placentia, taking the Romans by surprise and inflicting a severe defeat. Panic ensued in Rome; the Senate ordered sacrifices and purification to appease the gods. In northern Italy Aurelian chased the tribesmen from battle to battle. It is indicative of the extremely mobile nature of the war against them that the Emperor caught them up and defeated bands of warriors in at least three different places: at Fanum Fortunae, Metaurus, and on the Ticinus near modern Pavia. The tribesmen did not necessarily choose a battleground and then stand still to fight, and though they might lose a battle they were not defeated; they regrouped and kept on coming back. They were not fighting on behalf of a state, as was the Roman army; they were unpredictable, with no readily discernible objective because they were not conducting a military offensive as the Romans understood the operation. Tribal numbers and organisation fluctuated, and the tribesmen could split up into several different groups and go their separate ways. Finding them, keeping track of them, discerning which was the most dangerous, and then catching up with them stretched the intelligence networks and the marching capacity of the Roman troops. In aggressive wars across the frontiers and in defensive campaigns in the Rhine and Danube provinces the Roman army had gained considerable corporate empirical experience of this sort of warfare. Misjudgement and mistakes in these circumstances, far away from the capital, were costly, but had only limited effects on Rome itself; but now Aurelian was chasing the tribesmen in northern Italy, where mistakes as to the whereabouts of the enemy were more damaging to Rome and the Italians, and therefore magnified. More importantly, from Aurelian's point of view, failure was potentially lethal to the Emperor's career prospects and survival. The initiative had passed to the tribesmen, and Aurelian had to try to second-guess their next moves. When some semblance of order was restored, not by pitched battles but by running the tribesmen to ground, Aurelian returned to Rome and proclaimed a German victory. He knew well, as did everyone else, that his victories did not mark an end to war. He had gained a temporary respite, nothing more, and Rome was still vulnerable.[40]

The walls of Rome

The Romans had bitter experience of another invasion of Italy, long ago, but it was recorded in the history books and still vivid in folk memory. The depredations of the Gauls in the early Republic had been belatedly but finally avenged by Caesar's conquest of Gaul, but the fear and loathing had never been obliterated from Roman consciousness. For centuries since those days Rome had stood supreme, unwalled, having long ago outgrown the old Servian walls that enclosed the early city. Now in the late third century circumstances were much different. It had been demonstrated that the frontiers were permeable, not proof against determined onslaughts by large numbers of tribesmen; indeed, they were never meant to withstand attacks. The prime purpose was to avoid attacks in the first place, and this was achieved largely by psychological intimidation, to control the movement of peoples on the other side of the frontier by means of alliances, gifts and subsidies, by patrolling, intelligence gathering, occasional aggressive wars. Police work such as the frontiers now demanded was costly, time consuming and labour intensive, and Rome could not afford the time and manpower to control movement into and out of the Empire. Time and time again the army was successful in battle against the tribesmen, but once inside Roman territory the tribesmen did not necessarily gather to fight pitched battles; they moved very rapidly and it required only small numbers of men to create lasting havoc. Once the tribesmen were across the Alps the road to Rome was open and within easy reach. Aurelian called a meeting of the Senate to discuss the project of building a wall round the city.[41]

Civilian workers were mobilised, because there were not enough soldiers to spare for the purpose of building the wall. The *Historia Augusta* greatly exaggerates the work (as though it were not a monumental enough task to begin with), declaring that the wall was 50 miles long, which is quite ridiculous; it is a dozen miles at the most. It is true, however, that the circuit was too long to defend adequately, given that the entire garrison of Rome including the Praetorians, the Urban cohorts and the *vigiles* amounted to about 25,000 men, but the intention was not necessarily to enable the city to withstand a prolonged siege by troops equipped on the same scale as the Roman army. The tribesmen did not generally attempt to besiege cities, because they did not have the ability to supply themselves for a long time in one place; their forte was speed, enabling them to make hit-and-run raids, and they sought rapid results. If rapid results were not forthcoming they moved on. Thus the dubious defensibility of the walls of Rome was far outweighed by the feeling of security that the existence of a protective enclosure afforded to the inhabitants of the city. The building of the walls was carried out remarkably quickly. The work was speeded up by the incorporation of standing buildings within the circuit, and by the fact that the new walls did not attempt to take in the full extent of the city sprawl; even so, the walls were not finally completed until the reign of Probus.[42]

The reunification of the Empire

Palmyra

The extension of Palmyrene control over Egypt was very serious for Rome, not least because the bulk of Rome's grain shipments came from Egypt itself and from the provinces of north Africa, so that anyone in command of the country with access to a fleet could completely disrupt the food supply.

While Aurelian was fully occupied on the Danube and also with the problems in Rome, he acquiesced in what amounted to a shared rule with Vaballathus, as demonstrated by the coins issued by the Alexandrian mint, bearing on one side the head of the Roman Emperor in the first year of his reign, and on the other that of Vaballathus in his fourth year. The titles that Vaballathus awarded himself derived from those of Odenathus, *corrector totius orientis* and *dux Romanorum*. The more elaborate and wider concept embraced by the sweeping title *Rex regum*, king of kings, was an old-established eastern concept, used to notorious effect by Cleopatra on behalf of her son Caesarion; Vaballathus' mother Zenobia liked to model herself on Cleopatra. All of this was just tolerable, based on old or relatively recent precedents, but in 272 when she knew that confrontation with Aurelian was inevitable, Zenobia broke with precedent and with pretence. Vaballathus became Imperator Caesar Augustus, a direct challenge to Aurelian which he could not ignore.[43]

Already on his way to the east in 271, Aurelian was waylaid by the Goths under their leader Cannabas or Cannabaudes, who may well be the legendary Cniva of Gothic renown. The fighting resulted in Roman victory, leaving Aurelian free to continue to the east. In the meantime, according to the *Historia Augusta*, the future Emperor Probus reconquered Egypt; this may be an error, since Probus was probably active in the west, where he was later put in charge of reconstruction of the frontier provinces. Paschoud suggests that it was more likely Marcellinus, whose command lay in the east, who reconquered Egypt. At any rate, whoever was responsible for the reconquest, by August 271 the Alexandrian mint was coining for Aurelian alone, indicating that Egypt was once more incorporated into the Empire. The principal source for the Egyptian episode and the second Palmyrene campaign is Zosimus, who devotes considerable energy and verbiage to describing the final surrender of Palmyra in 272. Having been delayed by the Goths, Aurelian probably wintered at Byzantium in 271, moving into Asia Minor at the start of the next campaigning season. The city of Tyana closed its gates to him and risked a siege; Aurelian lost patience and gave orders that when the city finally fell nothing and no one, not even a dog, was to be left alive. In the end the city fell to him by treachery and he contented himself with having the traitor put to death, sparing the other human and canine inhabitants. Not surprisingly, perhaps, other cities in his path opened their gates and avoided bloodshed. Aurelian came face to face with Zenobia and her army, commanded by her general Septimius Zabdas, at Immae, just over 40 kilometres east of Antioch. Aurelian resorted to a ruse to draw the Palmyrene heavy armoured cavalry (nicknamed *clibanarii*, literally 'ovens') into an ambush. He ordered his Moorish and Dalmatian horsemen to turn tail and run when they saw the *clibanarii*. The stratagem worked. The heavy horsemen were defeated, leaving Zenobia the choice of staying to be captured or to flee for her life. She left a garrison at Daphne near Antioch, but it did not hold up Aurelian for long.[44]

116

The final battle was at Emesa. After his victory Aurelian marched to Palmyra and besieged the city. During the action he was wounded by an arrow, but not seriously. His main problems concerned supplies, which were not abundant in the middle of a desert miles from anywhere; there was a chance that Zenobia might outlast his ability to feed his troops, and then their roles would be reversed as he tried to retreat and the Palmyrenes picked off his troops as they marched back towards safety. He came to a successful arrangement with the desert tribes and secured his communications, and the siege did not last long. Before the city fell Zenobia fled once again, heading for the Euphrates and Persia, but she was caught by the Romans before she could reach the sanctuary of the Persian court. The city of Palmyra was split by factions, the anti-Roman diehards ranged against those who were willing to compromise. It was only a matter of time. Aurelian waited. He took the city in the summer of 272.[45]

The army wanted the death of Zenobia, but Aurelian wanted her alive to march through Rome in his future triumph. Zosimus says that she died by suicide or because of an illness, but it seems that this is either a mistake or a deliberate falsification. Zenobia survived, and after the triumph she lived in Italy, respectably married, so it is said, to a Roman senator. The house where she lived was remembered in ancient times, a place of note for Roman tourists.[46]

Aurelian placed Marcellinus in command of what was left of the province of Mesopotamia, and on the way back to Rome he met and fought the Carpi on the Danube. He earned his title *Carpicus Maximus*, but he was not granted the opportunity of finishing this war satisfactorily because the successes of the Palmyrene war quickly evaporated. There would have to be another eastern campaign. This may be the context of the evacuation of Dacia and the creation of the new province of the same name south of the Danube. Soon after the Romans left Palmyra, the anti-Roman faction led by Septimius Apsaeus agitated for a revival of the family of Odenathus, producing a very distant relative of the Royal family called Antiochus, whom Apsaeus proclaimed king. At about the same time in Egypt, a certain Firmus, a wealthy merchant at Alexandria, also rebelled against Rome. This cannot have been a coincidence. Firmus did not declare himself Emperor or try to create a limited kingdom for himself based on Egypt; it is almost certain that the Palmyrenes were behind his revolt, trying to reconstitute the extension of power that Vaballathus and Zenobia had attempted to bring about. The Empire-building tendencies of the Palmyrenes were demonstrated by their interest in Mesopotamia. Antiochus and Apsaeus tried to persuade the Roman governor Marcellinus to join them in rebellion against Aurelian. To his credit, Marcellinus remained faithful to the Emperor and warned him of events in Palmyra, while stalling for time and avoiding a fight by taking no definite stance for or against the Palmyrenes. He must have experienced a few tense moments, trying to balance loyalty and prudence, before Aurelian marched back with the army.[47]

According to Zosimus the reappearance of Aurelian in the east was so sudden that the Palmyrenes were stupefied; minus the rhetoric, the heroics and the *topoi*, the statement probably retains a great deal of truth. The Palmyrenes do not seem to have done anything to rebuild the city defences that the Romans had slighted in the first campaign, which indicates either that they had not had sufficient time, or that they had been very remiss and tremendously over-confident in their planning, or both. Aurelian was not noted for patience or clemency, except perhaps when he could gain something in return. When he captured the city this time, he razed it. There would be no resurgence of Palmyrene power.[48]

Next it was the turn of Egypt. Alexandria was treated very severely. Firmus took his own life, and his partisans were eradicated. Aurelian took revenge on the Egyptians by raising the taxes on their principal products, a measure that had the added advantage of bringing revenue into his depleted coffers. The whole eastern campaign was over in a few months, and brought longer-lasting results than the first one. At the end of it Aurelian promoted his image as restorer of the east, *Restitutor Orientis*, as his coins proclaimed him.[49]

The Gallic Empire

The Empire that Postumus founded had lasted for over a decade, and was now beginning to experience discord and fragmentation. Postumus held the provinces together by his promise, backed up by his ability, to defend the Rhine frontier and keep the inhabitants safe from pillage and destruction, by the northern tribes and by his own soldiers. His government was sound, his coinage was of a better and more reliable quality than the legitimate Emperor's, and he had held out against the attempts at reconquest by Gallienus and his deputies. Dissension began in 269 with the revolt of Laelianus. Postumus defeated him, only to face another usurper, Marius. While engaged in the struggle against the latter, Postumus refused to allow his soldiers to sack Mainz. If the story is true, it reveals the extent of the army's detachment from provincial concerns, and the preoccupation of the soldiers with themselves and the immediate gratification of short-term aims. For his refusal to fall in with their demands the troops killed Postumus.[50]

Victorinus, who had been Postumus' colleague in the consulship in 268, was proclaimed Emperor in October or November 271. Shortly after his accession, the legitimate Emperor Claudius II sent Placidianus to south-east Gaul; part of the Gallic Empire reverted to Rome. Perhaps now, the city of Autun revolted against Victorinus, possibly imagining that the arrival of Placidianus signified the end of the Gallic Emperors. If so, their rebellion was badly timed; Victorinus besieged and took the city and punished it severely.[51]

Not long afterwards Victorinus' reign was brought to an end by his murder, probably an act of thoughtless revenge rather than a political plot. Victorinus was a womaniser and had tried to seduce the wife of one of his officers, Attitianus. This lady did not succumb to him and informed her husband, who found a somewhat drastic way out of his dilemma. Beyond the removal of Victorinus, no one seemed to have thought of the next move, so for a while the mother of the murdered Emperor, Victoria, filled the power vacuum and brought to the attention of the troops, along with substantial amounts of cash, the senatorial governor of Aquitania, Esuvius Tetricus, who earned the dubious distinction of being the last Gallic Emperor. Victorinus administered from Cologne; eventually Tetricus set up headquarters at Trier. He was recognised in Britain and the whole of Gaul, save for Narbonensis where Placidianus had won back some territory under Claudius Gothicus. Spain wavered and decided on reintegration, as did the city of Strasbourg. There is some evidence of fighting against the German tribes, after which Tetricus celebrated a *Victoria Germanica*, but little else is known of his activities. The problems he faced were exacerbated by the growing discontent with the regime. Strasbourg declared for Aurelian. Invasions across the Rhine and along the coasts continued unabated, and the only response that Tetricus could make was to abandon forts and withdraw the troops. A serious incursion of Germans reached the Loire. There was no sign of any end to these raids, no matter how many German victories Tetricus proclaimed. At least some of the coin hoards in northern Gaul must relate to this period of endemic insecurity. Even if a proportion of the coins were buried because of economic upheavals, there are too many to be accounted for from this single cause. Aurelian mobilised against Tetricus perhaps late in the year 273, though some authors prefer to date the beginning of the campaign to the early part of the year and the final outcome to the autumn. The story goes that the opposing armies seemed to be ready to fight each other when they met at Châlons-sur-Marne, but neither of the two Emperors were committed to risking a battle. It was said that they had already been in contact, and that despite the wishes of his soldiers Tetricus sent his famous message to Aurelian, quoting Virgil: *'eripe me his invicte malis'*, 'rescue me undefeated from these troubles'. More recent authors have doubted the veracity of this tale, insisting that there was indeed a battle at Châlons-sur-Marne and that Tetricus did not necessarily give up immediately after it. Whatever is the true version, it does not alter the fact that the history of the Gallic Empire came to an end probably in March 274, when the mint at Lyons changed from coining for Tetricus and began to issue coins for Aurelian, declaring him the restorer of the east, and indeed the restorer of the world. The hyperbole was customary, but very apt for the circumstances; the time for Imperial modesty had long gone.[52]

The Empire was unified once more, not without certain false starts. A usurper called Faustinus was proclaimed Emperor at Trier, probably while

Tetricus was facing Aurelian, but the rebellion was soon quelled. Britain returned to the fold voluntarily. In Gaul the army was split up and put into different garrisons, and the reliable Probus was put in charge of the frontier zones, which required reconstruction. Aurelian held a splendid triumph in Rome, in which Tetricus and Zenobia featured as part of the display. Both of them survived, Zenobia as a guest of the Roman Empire, and Tetricus in an official post as *corrector Lucaniae*, preserving his fortune and his status intact.[53]

The evacuation of Dacia

The date when Aurelian took the troops out of the Dacian provinces is not known, and is therefore much discussed. The sources do not elaborate very much on Aurelian's activity, some of them tending to throw all the blame for the abandonment on Gallienus. Five out of the six authors who touch on the subject say that there was an evacuation of Dacia, partial or complete, under this maligned Emperor. Since nothing was too preposterous or outrageous to lay at Gallienus' door, it is even possible that at least one or two authors wished to describe the evacuation of Dacia as a reprehensible act, but did not wish to blame the worthy Aurelian for it; such convoluted thinking was not beyond the Latin and Greek authors. Rather than embroil themselves in this conundrum, Aurelius Victor and Orosius opt for silence, with not even a hint of Aurelian's part in the translation of Dacia to the right bank of the Danube. The sources which do credit Aurelian with the event favour a date towards the end of the reign; modern scholars have argued for the opposite, round about 270–1 at the beginning of the reign, and yet others prefer 272–3. There is a tenuous case, therefore, for any and every year in Aurelian's reign when Dacia was abandoned. The case for 272–3 is perhaps the most convincing, just before the second Palmyrene campaign. There is no solid evidence as such, but there are strong indications. There may be a link with Aurelian's war against the Carpi, when he earned the title *Carpicus Maximus*, gained when he stopped the advance of the tribesmen at the end of 272. A coin hoard from Romania containing 260 coins from the mints at Milan, Cyzicus and Siscia has a cut off date of 272. While he was still in the field against the Carpi, news reached Aurelian that all the successes of the first Palmyrene war had been overturned; everything would have to be done over again, and this campaign would possibly be more protracted than the first. Egypt was once again in the hands of Palmyrene sympathisers, and the city of Palmyra was in full revolt under a relative of Odenathus. Engaged against the northern tribes and unable to spare the time to follow up his victory and arrange a full settlement, it is probable that Aurelian evacuated the Dacian provinces and brought the troops out at this juncture. He placed them on the right bank of the Danube and created a new province called Dacia, carved out of territory that had belonged to the two Moesian provinces. It was something of a desperate measure for an Emperor who was bent on restoring the Empire, and was perhaps undertaken in a moment of duress, not intended as a permanent arrangement but unfortunately never reversed. Some time later, before 285, the single province was split into two smaller ones, called Dacia Ripensis and Dacia Mediterranea.[54]

Archaeology reveals that life in the old Roman province of Dacia continued to 272 without any discernible decline or expectation of termination. Even if there had been a partial evacuation under Gallienus, which is itself disputed, it did not seem that the population was clamouring for removal to another part of the Roman world. The decision to take the troops out was most likely a military measure for the better defence of the Danube and Aurelian's rear while he marched to the east. The capital of the new province was at Serdica (modern Sofia), on the road connecting Viminacium with Byzantium. The old fortresses of Ratiaria and Oescus were strengthened, and the forts guarding the Danube crossings were retained, at Drobeta, Sucidava and Barbosi. The territory that had been abandoned was now open to the Goths and Carpi, who would be kept busy while they occupied it, settled in it and squabbled over it. This process would hopefully delay their forays into Roman territory. There may have been a treaty with the tribesmen whereby they acted as defenders of the evacuated territory and kept it free from other incursions, but there is no evidence for such an arrangement, only the shallow hints that some authors have discerned in the story that when the Goths moved into Asia Minor in the reign of Tacitus they said that Aurelian had called upon them to fight in the east, which is quite different from asking them to protect the evacuated province.[55]

The question of how many of the civilian population came out of Dacia in the wake of the army is probably unanswerable. There would be many who would remain in their homes, even though the political intentions and accompanying propaganda may have represented the removal as total. Epigraphic evidence speaks for a continued Romanised population after the evacuation. How these people assimilated the Goths and Carpi, or if they were assimilated by them, remains unrecorded; likewise it is not known how the influx of the inhabitants of the new Dacia affected the population of Moesia, if at all.[56]

Aurelian's reforms

Superlatives began to enter the titulature of the Emperor from 274 onwards, after he had reunified the Empire and he had become in truth the restorer of the world, albeit a world that was somewhat different from the Empire of Hadrian and Severus. The frontiers that were once so clearly marked were now a little ragged, untenable in parts, and territory had been lost. Nonetheless, the situation was such a vast improvement on the previous two decades that it probably did seem as though Aurelian was not just victorious but *victoriosissimus*, not only glorious but *gloriosissimus*, conqueror of the Carpi, the Germans, the Arabians, the Persians and the Palmyrenes. Aurelian progressed from the sterling qualities of a mere mortal to outright divinity in a few easy steps; in inscriptions he is eternal, invincible, the personification of Hercules, divine, and finally a god in his own right, *Imperator deus et dominus*. This godly status was assumed, or perhaps thrust upon him, in return for his services to the state, deriving from his achievements as an adult, but the final step was soon taken when his divinity was backdated to his birth, *deus et dominus natus*. He took to wearing a diadem, and demanded obeisance of his subjects; obviously he had learned a lot in the east. Aurelian had a developed sense of his own importance, or to be fair, of his position as leader of the state. He took his role very seriously, projecting an image of power and protection, magnificence and majesty, invincibility and immortality. It was important that Romans should believe in him, and that enemies should fear him. The time of rough soldier-Emperors sharing their soldiers' meals, marching with the lads, caring little for politics and statesmanship, was over. As it had always been, the Emperor needed to be all things: general, politician, statesman, psychologist, performer, and god. For this it was necessary to create echoing distance between ruler and ruled, to be remote, lofty, an ideal rather than real. Aurelian knew how to do it, and would have been more than a match for Constantine.[57]

Although the Empire was reunified territorially, there were many things to put right within the state. Inflation had reached ridiculous proportions; the monetary system had foundered, not helped by Gallienus' financial policies. It required a strong hand to set it on course again. Aurelian had attempted a partial reform in 271, but he had not time to devote to a long-term plan, and his ideas had not been totally effective. In 274 he began again. Unification brought in its wake increased revenues, and new taxes were raised, some of them on Egyptian goods after the second revolt under Firmus was put down. Aurelian taxed the wealthy men of the Empire, justifiably in his view since everyone ought to contribute to the well-being and defence of the Empire. It was resented of course; Ammianus Marcellinus lapses into hyperbole to describe the rapaciousness of the Emperor, but in truth Aurelian had no choice. The Treasury was empty, drained by wars and mismanagement, and by the temporary loss of control over the western and eastern extremities of the Empire. The re-establishment of control of these areas meant that a greater quantity of precious metals flowed in once again, nowhere near in the same scale as in the early Empire but sufficient to enable Aurelian to reform the coinage. He adhered to the three-metal currency of tradition. Possibly in connection with the revolt staged by the workers at the mint, the right to issue bronze coinage was wrested from the control of the Senate. The silver and gold coinage was improved in precious metal content, and Aurelian tried to withdraw all the old silver antoniniani of

Figure 22 Radiate bust of Aurelian on a billon antoninianus of 274 from the Ticinum mint. This coin is important both for its portrayal on the reverse of the Sun god Sol, with whom Aurelian identified very strongly, and for the mint mark XX, which also appears on other coins as XX.I, XXI, or KA. The mark has been variously explained by modern scholars, but most probably refers to the 5 per cent or one-twentieth silver content of the coins. (Drawn by Trish Boyle.)

negligible weight; he succeeded in eradicating the bad coinage in Rome and Italy, but was less successful in the provinces and not at all successful in Britain or Gaul. The next step was to establish a standard weight and value for the silver coinage over the Empire. The antoninianus was replaced by billon coins marked XX, XX.I, XXI, or KA in Greek. The significance of these marks is disputed, but seems to be related to the 5 per cent silver content of the coins, indicating the fraction one-twentieth. It is sympto-matic of the chaos of the monetary system that a 5 per cent silver content could be regarded as an improvement.[58]

The food supply of the Roman plebs also claimed Aurelian's attention. He may have put an end to the *alimenta* inaugurated by Trajan to provide suste-nance for the children of Italy; the last known official in charge of the *ali-menta* is Postumius Varus who was prefect of the city in 271. If he did suppress this food distribution system, he most likely intended to put into effect a more radical reform. Probably after his triumph he reorganised the corn dole for the city, distributing bread instead of grain, and adding salt and pork to the rations, as well as oil, and wine free or at a reduced cost; these arrangements continued under successive Emperors. The substitution of a bread ration for the corn dole was an innovative step. It involved a series of operations all under the supervision of the *praefectus annonae*, covering col-lection of the goods and transport by sea and by land, storage, processing and distribution. Grain was levied from Egypt as part of the taxation system, and delivered to the bakers free of charge; the weight of the loaves was increased but the price was held for the benefit of those who could afford to buy. The distribution of wine revitalised the struggling viticulture of Italy, and the transport of all the various goods encouraged the shippers, the *navicularii*. The rudiments of the guilds and corporations of the later Empire derive from this reform of Aurelian's, but he probably did not intend to impose the inflexible rigidity that developed as part and parcel of the state control of the various component parts of the *annona*.[59]

Religion was another sphere where Aurelian's reforming zeal introduced changes. The old gods had not been neglected by previous Emperors, but there was a certain lack of coherence and cohesion, not to mention the disruption caused by Elagabalus' attempt to supersede Jupiter and the whole structure of Roman religion with an eastern god whose cult practices were weird. Without making the same mistake of trying to overturn the religious structure, Aurelian introduced the sun god as the supreme being. In the east he had seen the unifying force of the sun as a divinity. The sun was a real entity, a universal symbol and a single powerful force that all people, civilians and soldiers, Romans, Italians and provincials, could believe in without betraying their other gods. The cult of the sun god offended the least possible groups of people and excluded hardly anyone. There were precedents in the reign of Claudius Gothicus, whose coinage had featured the sun god Sol. Aurelian's coinage accentuated the attributes of the sun god, with legends such as *Sol invictus, Sol conservator, Sol Dominus Imperii Romani*, celebrating the unconquered sun, the saviour of the state, and the lord and master of the Roman Empire. Since no cult could function without the focal point of a temple, Aurelian built one on the Campus Agrippae in the seventh region of Rome. Work may have started as early as 271; the temple was finally consecrated in 274. It was extremely ornate, and housed the trophies from Palmyra brought back to Rome after the two campaigns. The priests of the cult were drawn from the aristocracy, so that the bruised prestige of the upper classes was revived by the knowledge that the control of the state religion, if not of the state itself, was in their hands. Aurelian's religious policy was to restore old values in a new guise, to unify the Empire, to exclude no one except the most intransigent, and to support his own regime with himself as earthly but divine intermediary between the supreme god and the people of the Empire. He was granted little time in which to develop the theme of one state, one god, a theme that Constantine was heir to and chief architect after Aurelian. Had Aurelian lived longer he would have found himself and his ideas in conflict with other societies who worshipped one god, and who were not willing to assimilate the god Sol with their own cults. There was no suppression of other gods, and Aurelian did not persecute the Christians or the Jews, but Lactantius, trusting none of the Emperors except Constantine, was certain that had Aurelian lived he would have persecuted Christians with the same thoroughness as he employed in all his other tasks.[60]

The end of Aurelian's reign

From Republican times, eternal glory for Rome was always attached to attempts to defeat Parthia, now remodelled as Persia. There was a score to settle after the defeat of Valerian, which was still unavenged, and Aurelian was a great admirer of Trajan, whose eastern campaign was still the definitive version. Towards the end of 272 the Persian king Shapur died, and was succeeded by Hormizd who did not long survive him, dying at the end of 273 or at the beginning of 274. The new king Vahram had much to do to keep his Empire together and was not likely to launch an aggressive campaign against Rome. It was a favourable time for Aurelian to attack instead. Rome was reunified and stronger than she had been for some time, and Persia was relatively weak. Fair play did not enter into the matter; Aurelian was aware that if he did not kick other states when they were down he may not get another chance.[61]

In the summer of 275 he set out for the east. Details are lacking for his campaign army, but the redeployment of the Dacian legions would have released troops for other theatres. According to the *Historia Augusta* he assembled his army in Illyricum, and declared war on Persia. He never reached his objective. On the march through Thrace, at a place called Caenophrurium, a plot was hatched, or came to fruition, to kill Aurelian. Zosimus relays the most detailed version, not necessarily accurate despite the elaboration, naming a court official called Eros as the instigator of the plot. Afraid that Aurelian would punish him severely for a mistake, he used his talents for forgery and drew up a fictitious 'hit list' of army officers, and showed it to the supposed victims, who swallowed it whole and decided to remove Aurelian before he removed them. Other sources do not name Eros, but describe the perpetrator of the conspiracy as a minor official, or *notarius*, and one source gives the name of the murderer as Mucapor. These garbled versions probably conceal a much more complicated situation than the facile story of Zosimus suggests, perhaps a smouldering resentment or a long-standing disaffection, though of what nature it is impossible to elucidate. The theory that the officers who were named on Eros' list readily accepted, without question, that they were to be eliminated suggests that they all had guilty secrets and were afraid of being found out, and that Aurelian's reputation for uncompromising cruelty was so deeply embedded that no one was prepared to give him the benefit of the doubt. It is possible that for many men, even among his immediate circle, relations with him had either broken down or were on shaky ground to begin with. On the other hand, the fact that there was no candidate ready and waiting in the wings to take over the moment that Aurelian was dead supports the suggestion that the conspirators acted suddenly, in blind panic. There may also have been a few officers who were glad to rid themselves of both the Emperor and the need to go and fight the Persians.[62]

Aurelian's promising career was terminated before he had been granted the opportunity to follow up his successes in pulling the Empire back together; or perhaps before he threw away all his credit by losing the war against Persia. The outcome of that campaign may have settled the eastern frontier for some time to come, or it may have considerably damaged Roman interests and compromised her in the west as well as the east. As it was, Aurelian's death left a legacy of unfinished business. But that was not his fault; he had achieved what he set out to achieve and deserved his title *Restitutor Orbis*; building on the unacknowledged work of Gallienus and Claudius Gothicus, Aurelian paved the way for Diocletian, who absorbed most of the credit that was really due to his predecessor. Aurelian was the first Emperor not to be interred in Rome; his funeral was arranged in Thrace. He was eventually deified, at the request of Tacitus, though it is permissible to enquire how such an honour could have bettered the situation of one who was already a living god on earth.[63]

THE SUCCESSORS OF AURELIAN: PROBUS TO DIOCLETIAN

Tacitus and Florian

The soldiers were very displeased at the murder of their Emperor and made it clear that they did not intend to proclaim any of the generals in Aurelian's place. There was no heir, nor was there an obvious successor marked out by Imperial favour during Aurelian's reign. Despite the assertion to the contrary of the *Historia Augusta*, even the future Emperor Probus enjoyed no privileges or special attention from Aurelian. The important generals were dispersed in various parts of the Empire, so for a short time the Roman world seemed poised for complicated civil wars as the leaders of various armies fought among themselves until one of them emerged victorious. But this time there was no war. The sources all agree that the soldiers sent to Rome to ask the Senate to choose an Emperor, and the result, after some delay while the soldiers and the Senate threw the responsibility back at each other, was that the aged senator Tacitus was persuaded to shoulder the task. Zonaras says that the army and the Senate chose the Emperor, by which he probably means the Praetorians. Between the murder of Aurelian and the accession of Tacitus there will have been a delay of perhaps two months or more, an interregnum which has been confused in some sources and expanded to six months. Syme thought that this 'interregnum' referred not to a period without any Emperor at all, but to the months that elapsed between the death of Aurelian and the accession of Probus, dismissing the contribution of Tacitus and his half-brother Florian as though they never existed.[64]

Marcus Claudius Tacitus was in Campania when his name was put forward as Emperor. It was said that he had requested that Aurelian should be deified as soon as it was known that the Emperor was dead, and then he had left Rome while it was being decided who should take over the Empire. He was not a young man, but on the other hand he was probably not as aged as some sources would suggest – Zonaras says he was 75 years old, but this may be an exaggeration. His previous career is unknown. He was a senator, perhaps a middle-class eques who had been adlected to the Senate, but probably not a military man. Syme speculated that he may have been an Illyrian soldier, perhaps one of Aurelian's generals, but there is not enough evidence to support or disprove the theory. Nor is there enough evidence to confirm that there was a momentary revival of senatorial influence under Tacitus. The reign was too short for any resurgence to be effective. There was no sudden rash of senatorial appointments or any indication that if Tacitus had lived longer there would have been a reversal of Gallienus' policy of employing military men and equestrians as legionary commanders and governors of provinces, and this was where the real power lay. Some legal privileges may have been restored in the short term, but in the long term there was no appreciable difference in senatorial power and privilege. The Emperor Tacitus executed the assassins of Aurelian, though exactly who these men were is not specified, and presumably some of them escaped punishment since it was left to Probus to round up the rest and kill them. Tacitus spent most of his short reign fighting the Goths, earning the title *Gothicus Maximus* for a victory or victories that have escaped documentation. He died after a mere six-month reign, at either Tyana or Tarsus, probably in suspicious circumstances. His death may have been caused by disease or by an accident, but according to Zosimus he was killed because he had appointed one of his relatives called Maximinus to command in Syria; for everyone concerned, Maximinus was too severe. The situation mirrored that of Philip the Arab, who had appointed his brother Priscus to the eastern command only to face potential rebellion because of Priscus' cruelty. The implication in 276 is that the army had not totally accepted Tacitus. He had made his half brother Florian Praetorian Prefect, and left him in command against the Goths. On the death of Tacitus the troops proclaimed him Emperor, but probably at the same time Probus, who now commanded in Syria, Phoenicia and Egypt was also declared Emperor by his troops.[65]

Florian did not wait for the approval of the Senate, but assumed power as if it were his hereditary right, an action which illustrates just how effective the supposed revival of senatorial power had been under Tacitus. Florian no doubt felt hard pressed to make a decision quickly, rather than to waste time waiting for a reply from Rome, since the east was almost wholly behind Probus; indeed Egypt, one of the most important provinces, seems to have declared for him immediately. Following ancient Egyptian tradition, regnal years began on 29 August, and documents show that the Egyptians reckoned Probus' first year from the death of Tacitus (not known in Egypt until July) until 29 August 276, when his *second* year began. There was no mention of Florian as Emperor in the interim. The conflict between the two Imperial candidates ended at Tarsus, where Florian decided to face Probus. He may have done better to ignore Probus and go to Rome, consolidate his position and then attend to his rival in the east, as Severus had done, but Florian was not comparable to Severus. His soldiers were not accustomed to the eastern climate and began to suffer ill health; in direct proportion to their suffering, their commitment to the cause declined. Probus had only to wait, without giving battle. Florian's troops killed him, or perhaps suggested very strongly that he should commit suicide.[66]

Probus

The reign of Probus was longer than that of Aurelian, and almost as important for the reconstitution of the Empire, but describing the events of his rule and his policies has been compared to making bricks without straw. The written evidence is largely anecdotal, not really evidence at all; the best source is Zosimus, but his work is lost half way through a description of the reign, just at the point where he is about to launch into an evaluation of Probus, 'a good and just Emperor'. Other sources such as the *Historia Augusta*, Aurelius Victor and Eutropius, corroborate some of the stories in Zosimus' work, but not all of them, and though they agree with each other on some points, they each relay different stories or details for which they are the sole authority. Crees compared and contrasted each of the major sources in useful tabular form, highlighting their similarities and divergences. Chronology was not a priority for the ancient writers, whose prime purpose was to tell a good story and to strive for literary excellence, with varying degrees of success. Thematic structure with a moral point to press home was often considered more important than annalistic documentation. Probus' coins display his titles, making the usual claims that the Emperor is invincible, unconquered, and emphasising the Emperor's *Virtus*, but the coinage does not help to establish dates for recorded events. The result is that the salient factors of Probus' reign can be described in broad outline based on the dubious foundation of a few overlapping statements in the works of the main authors, but chronology, cause and event, and consequence can be reconstructed only on the even more dubious foundation of modern speculation.[67]

Probus benefited greatly from the achievements of Aurelian, but he still had many loose ends to tie up. It was not a restful reign. The frontiers of the Roman Empire required immediate attention. The Rhine and Danube were still under threat despite Aurelian's victories, and the Persian campaign that had been aborted on the Emperor's death was not regarded as redundant. Much of Probus' energies went into clearing Gaul and the Rhine frontier of the tribesmen who had invaded, to refurbishing the cities which had been damaged and re-establishing some of the forts. He fought and defeated the Longiones, who may have comprised the Lugii familiar to the writers of the early Empire; he captured their chief called Semno, but on the return of all prisoners and booty he let him go again. Zosimus reports that another chief of the Longiones, called Igillus, did not return booty and prisoners, and Igillus was captured and punished. The captives from this expedition were sent to Britain, where they were useful later on in suppressing a revolt. Zosimus is the only source for this story, which sounds suspiciously similar to the story of the chieftain Semno, but it may be that like Aurelian in northern Italy Probus had to chase different groups of tribesmen over the same territory until he had eradicated them. There were certainly wars on more than one front; Probus was victorious with the help of his generals against the Franks on the Rhine; he fought the Vandals and Burgundians, and carried the war into territory beyond the frontiers and established forts *in solo barbarico*. It was said that no less than nine barbarian kings submitted to him. Beyond these brief notices very little detail is known. The identity of the nine kings, the tribes they represented, and the location of the forts that he established presumably to watch over the subdued tribes, cannot be listed. It can only be said that the Romans had returned, however briefly, to the ascendancy, and that reparation was now feasible. Destruction in Gaul had been extensive, but not so deep rooted that the infrastructure had not disappeared. Rebuilding could now begin. Probus reputedly restored 60 towns and cities in Gaul, a number which increased to 70 in the probably spurious letter, supposedly written by Probus himself, quoted in the *Historia Augusta*. Little of this energetic activity can be securely dated; it is probable that the campaigns in Gaul and Germany occupied Probus from his accession until the end of 278, and that in the new season beginning in the winter of 278–9 he turned to the Danube.[68]

Probus had other ways of dealing with the tribes, apart from fighting them. According to Zosimus, he settled 100,000 Bastarnae in Thrace, 'where they lived in the Roman manner'. The *Historia Augusta* credits Probus with the settlement of Vandals, Gepids and Greuthungi inside the Empire. Whilst these settlements potentially secured peace for at least one generation, providing a good source of recruits for the army and a partly Romanised zone between the Empire and the tribes outside it, the schemes did not always produce the desired results; the Franks were given lands, probably in the Danube area, but were too restless to stay put. They first swept through Greece and then commandeered ships, sailing to Sicily and Africa, pillaging their way round the coast, through the Straits of Gibraltar and back to the Rhine and their original homelands. This expedition typifies the sort of problems that Probus had to deal with – not full-scale wars limited to a relatively small area, but small-scale actions in localised zones, all of them nonetheless very disruptive, dispiriting and demoralising. Since it went against propaganda to broadcast the fact that there was trouble of different sorts over much of the Empire, the cumulative picture would be known only to the Emperor himself and his generals, but the people in the several different provinces where there were raids and rebellions would perceive only that Rome was failing in her duty to protect and nurture, despite the brave propaganda proclaiming eternal peace and prosperity. The other side of that particular coin was that Rome was not watching as closely as she once did, so in the absence of strict law and order the unscrupulous law breakers flourished. Brigandage was by no means a new problem; from the Republic and throughout the Empire infamous rebels and gangsters entered history, earning a grudging respect once they were defeated. In Probus' reign it was Lydius and/or Palfuerius (sometimes rendered as Palfurius), who may or may not be one and the same person. Argument still continues about these two names, and whether there were two or only one bandit who has been recorded under two distinct identities. The *Historia Augusta* reports that in the east the Isaurian robber (*latro*) Palfurius was captured and killed, while Zosimus describes at some length how the Isaurian Lydius rampaged over Pamphylia and eventually took control of Cremna in Lycia, withstanding a long siege, betrayed eventually by one of his own men.[69]

Zosimus devotes a high proportion of his work to describing these events, but dismisses in a couple of lines the rebellion of the people of Ptolemais in Egypt and their alliance, forced or otherwise, with the Blemmyes, tribesmen who had always been ready to harass the province from time to time. The rebellion was squashed by Probus' generals. Attempts at usurpation in the east and in Gaul do not seem to have greatly inconvenienced Probus in that they were extinguished very quickly. A general called Saturninus was declared Emperor, either in Egypt or more probably in Syria; the sources are confused as to exactly where his command lay and where he chose to stage his rebellion. According to the *Historia Augusta*, Aurelian had placed him in command of the eastern frontier, and he was proclaimed Emperor at Alexandria, then returned to Palestine. Aurelius Victor, Eutropius and Orosius all place his attempted coup in Egypt. Alternatively Zosimus says that he was governor of Syria, and that the eastern troops killed him before Probus reached the scene. The story is not further elucidated, but is eloquent of confusion in the eastern provinces and dissension in the army. Saturninus had failed to win over all the troops, possibly because he had also failed to prepare the ground properly and secure enough cash. At Cologne there were two potential Emperors, Bonosus and Proculus, who were both eliminated seemingly without much trouble. What does emerge from these scantily described events is that over most of the Empire Probus' government was working well enough. Governors of provinces and military officers did their loyal duty to the Emperor, communications were secure, the focal point was still Rome, and the army was ultimately successful when engaged in pitched battles, in suppressing other Roman generals, or in guerrilla warfare against plundering tribes.[70]

Figure 23 Gold aureus of Probus minted at Lyons *c.*281. It celebrates a victory, probably in Gaul; the reverse (not shown) proclaims VICTORIA AUG. (Drawn by Trish Boyle.)

Probably in 281, Probus celebrated a triumph. For the time being he had achieved peace over the Empire, dealt with usurpers, pirates and brigands, and could turn his attention to more peaceful pursuits. One of his reforms is mentioned in more than one source: the encouragement of vine growing in Gaul, Pannonia and Moesia. In the latter province, according to Eutropius, he set his soldiers to the task of planting the vines on hillsides. He used them also on drainage projects in the Danube provinces; the fact that he had soldiers to spare for such tasks, when Aurelian could not spare any to build the walls of Rome, testifies to the success of the long campaigns from the 270s to the early 280s. Indeed, Probus is said to have remarked that very soon the Empire would have no need of its armies. The report may be based on truth. In propaganda terms, a promise that there would be no more need for fighting had great value. It was a proud boast that would satisfy the war-weary inhabitants of Rome and the provinces, but it was not news that the army wished to hear. If he had also remembered to say that it would be possible to reward the soldiers for long service, pension them all off with lands, money, slaves, and everything they could wish for, perhaps he would have survived longer. Scepticism on the part of the Roman army was not without justification; in all periods before and since, and in all places, soldiers have often been treated in the same fashion, lauded when there is something to be saved from, reviled when they fail, and discarded without a thought when the danger is past.[71]

Perhaps the army need not have been concerned for its future, since Probus had decided upon a Persian campaign. While he was otherwise engaged on the northern frontiers he had come to a peaceful if temporary arrangement with Persia, compatible with both sides because Vahram was not in any position to ward off a Roman attack until he had consolidated his position at home. After the successful campaigns against the northern tribes, Probus was in a position to attack, as Aurelian had been. And as Aurelian had been, he was killed before he started; this time the assassination took place at Sirmium, where the Emperor was killed by his own soldiers.[72]

Carus and his sons, Carinus and Numerianus

Dissatisfaction in the army probably had a long incubation period before it came to a head with the murder of Probus. The Praetorian Prefect Marcus Aurelius Carus, commanding troops in Raetia and Noricum, rebelled before Probus' death, and the troops sent against him joined him without a fight. He was declared Emperor at the end of 282, urged on, it was said, by the soldiers; Probus was killed at some time between September and December of that year. It was also said that Carus took power with no reference to the Senate, or so Aurelius Victor complained when he pinpointed this moment as the one where the army finally wrested from the Senate all right and privilege of bestowing power on the Emperor. Modern scholars take issue with this statement. Although Carus did not go to Rome for ratification of the army's choice, he did not ignore the formality altogether. Zonaras affirms that the intention to travel to Rome was always present, but events did not unfold in that way; besides, Carinus, Carus' elder son, came to northern Italy early in 283 for his marriage, and he visited Rome in his father's place. Emperors had been made by the army before, and more than once the Senate had acquiesced in the army's choice and ratified it, formally bestowing all the usual powers, but Aurelius Victor felt that there was something different about this occasion, perhaps because there had been a brief spark of senatorial influence when Tacitus was made Emperor, and from the rebellion of Carus onwards the role of the Senate was again curtailed, and there was never any reversal of the trend thereafter.[73]

Carus' early career is unknown but the sources assure us that he was an experienced military man. This is probably true, but by the late third century it had become a prior necessity for the Emperor to have a military background. As Praetorian Prefect Carus had not risen to the consulship as had Volusianus under Gallienus and Placidianus under Aurelian. Lack of consular experience and power need not hinder him, however, and he possessed what should have been a distinct advantage in that he had two sons and ought to have been able to secure the succession and found a dynasty that might have ensured peace and prosperity, building on and bringing to completion the work of Aurelian and Probus. Carus elevated Carinus and Numerianus to Augusti – Carinus early in 283 to take charge of the western provinces when the Persian campaign began, and Numerianus towards the end of the Persian campaign, perhaps in conjunction with the first victories.

When Carus died the existence of two Augusti, one in the east and one in the west, ought to have ensured a smooth transition of power, but it did not; nor did it cause a premature and irretrievable split into two separate Empires. It might seem that Carinus in the west had clearly demarcated territories to govern with distinct boundaries while Carus and Numerianus conducted the Persian campaign, but the arrangement was not a prefiguration of the division of the later Empire; it was more like a reiteration of the situation when Gallienus was left in charge of the west and Valerian embarked on his disastrous eastern war. Carus fortunately met with considerably more success. The Persian regime was not as strong as it had been under Shapur; Vahram II was still in the throes of establishing his authority over his Empire, so he did not put up much of a fight, allowing the Romans to march into Seleucia and Ctesiphon almost unopposed. The title *Parthicus Maximus* was awarded to Carus.[74]

At this juncture, Carus died unexpectedly. He was in his sixties, and could perhaps have succumbed to a sudden stroke or heart attack. It was said that he had been struck by lightning; more likely he was struck by an instrument, blunt or sharp, wielded by his Praetorian Prefect Lucius Aper. This individual was the father-in-law of Numerianus, and ambitious as well. During the withdrawal from Persia the young Augustus died, but Aper concealed the fact and gave out that the Emperor was suffering from an eye complaint and consequently had to travel in a closed litter as protection against light and dust. When the corpse began to emit an unsavoury aroma, as is the way with corpses especially in hot climates, Aper's subterfuge was discovered. The tale is fantastic bordering on the ridiculous, and all sorts of explanations are possible. Perhaps if Carus had indeed died accidentally or from disease without any assistance from Aper, then it would have been doubly difficult for the Praetorian Prefect to try to make the soldiers believe that his son-in-law had suddenly died of disease too. Perhaps Aper panicked and was unable to decide what to do, but he must have known that he could not travel very far with a dead Emperor in a closed litter before some sort of decision was made for him. The man who helped him to make a decision was the commander of Numerianus' guard, the *protectores domestici*, a stalwart soldier called Diocles.[75]

4

A WORLD GEARED FOR WAR
284–324

DIOCLETIAN: THE EMPIRE STRIKES BACK

Soon after becoming Emperor, Diocles changed his name to Gaius Aurelius Valerius Diocletianus, rounded down by modern scholars to Diocletian, the name by which he is known to history. Whether or not he was implicated in a plot to remove Numerianus remains a matter of conjecture; perhaps he merely stood by while Aper did the work and then muscled in as righteous avenger, condemning Aper to death. He executed him personally, in full view of the troops, thus fulfilling the prophecy of a wise woman in Gaul who had told him that he would be Emperor after killing his boar (*aper*). More likely this is a story fabricated after the event to demonstrate that he was following his destiny, marked out for him by the gods long ago. The process whereby Diocletian was raised to the purple cannot have been as straightforward, simplistic or as spontaneous as the extant ancient narrative makes it sound. He survived long enough to ensure that certain parts of his history were rewritten in accordance with the official version, which would be silent on the issues of his ambitions, whatever they were, and on the intrigues that brought him to power. Consequently, the retrospective restructuring of the historical narrative has masked for ever the details of what happened in 284 and no doubt in the ensuing years as well.[1]

The soldiers proclaimed him Augustus on 20 November 284. For the remaining part of the year he made himself consul with a senator called Caesonius Bassus as his colleague. The path to sole power was not yet assured, since there was still a legitimate Emperor in the west. Carinus would contest the issue rather than offer an alliance, and in any case an alliance would not furnish a solution that would be compatible to both sides. At some point Carinus had to put down a revolt staged by Marcus Aurelius Julianus (probably the same man who is called Sabinus Julianus in some sources), who had been appointed *corrector Venetiae* in northern Italy. The date is disputed, as are so many other dates of events at the end of the third century. Aurelius Victor's account makes it seem that Julianus' revolt occurred just before the death of Carus; but modern scholars date it to the

period immediately after the death of Numerianus and the accession of Diocletian. From northern Italy Julianus extended his authority into Pannonia
and began to issue coins from the Siscia mint, setting himself up as
Emperor, promising liberty. This was grist to Diocletian's mill, because it
cast a bad light on Carinus, whose rule was allegedly oppressive and whose
cruelty was extreme. The inhabitants of northern Italy, if of nowhere else,
would rally to the cry of freedom, so for Diocletian it was only a matter of
waiting in the wings while Carinus or Julianus emerged the victor, then
stepping in to eliminate the survivor, not only with impunity but with
laurels and applause. It would be a case either of fighting the cruel Emperor
Carinus who did not deserve to reign, or reluctantly putting down Julianus,
the leader of a revolt against the legitimate ruler. Either way Diocletian was
the winner in the moral sense, if not in the battle. In the end Diocletian and
Carinus fought each other in the valley of the Margus. The ancient sources
cannot agree on the location, which is given variously as Marcus in Moesia,
which is improbable, or Margus near Belgrade, which is more likely. The
battle went badly for Diocletian at first, but then the balance was tilted in
his favour by the defection of Carinus' Praetorian Prefect and colleague in
the consulship, Aristobulus, who is suspected by modern scholars of killing
Carinus. The contemporary story was that the Emperor was killed by one of
his officers whose wife had been forced into an affair with him. It seems a
glib excuse, moreover one which had been used before. It is more probable
that Aristobulus had seen which way the wind was blowing and made his
mind up to join the candidate with the support of the eastern provinces
behind him; even if Carinus won this particular battle he would probably
not win the war. Aristobulus did not lose by his decision. Far from treating
him as a traitor and executing him, Diocletian confirmed him in his office as
Praetorian Prefect, and as consul for the rest of 285.[2]

Consolidation of Diocletian's power began with the oath of allegiance
sworn to him by the remnants of Carinus' army. Next he may have been
embroiled in battles against the Quadi and Marcomanni, which prevented
him from going to Rome to meet the Senate and to have power conferred on
him with the appropriate ceremonial. It has been said that he deliberately
avoided going to Rome as part of his policy of divorcing the Senate from
government and marginalising the city of Rome itself, which was patently
not the strategic centre of the Empire any longer. The absence of Diocletian
from the city has been disputed by Christol who points out that the coinage
issued around this time looks very much like a series celebrating the *adventus*
of the Emperor. The point is academic, since even if he did arrive very
briefly in Rome just after his accession, he could hardly have remained there
for very long, and he spent the next two decades attending to urgent
business elsewhere in the Empire.[3]

Among his other aims, one of Diocletian's first priorities was to re-
establish internal law and order in the beleaguered provinces and to restore

the frontiers of the Empire. With regard to fulfilling these aims Diocletian was aware of several prerequisites which he could not furnish entirely by himself. He was a soldier but not an experienced general. The Empire in its current situation was too large for one man to govern effectively, so trusted helpers would be needed to deal with all the problems of administration and defence. Delegation in one form or another was inevitable, and at the end of his reign he would require successors to continue the work he had begun, because no one could realistically imagine that he would finish the task of reconstituting the Empire in one lifetime. And he had no sons. All these factors pointed towards power sharing on a more or less permanent basis. Joint rule had an established history, usually kept in the family. Marcus Aurelius had shared the burden with Lucius Verus and then with his son Commodus; the Severans had followed the same example, and the Emperor Carus had tried to establish a dynasty by elevating his sons to Augusti. The Emperors who were childless had frequently adopted an heir or heirs to mark out their intended successor while they still lived, using the same techniques that the dynastic Imperial families had used to promote their sons, first as Caesar, then as Augustus. Frequently the Emperors had employed their sons or adoptive heirs in different theatres of war in the east or the west while they themselves attended to other problems, allocating tasks as they arose, rather than fixed areas with definite boundaries. The division was one of labour rather than territory, dictated arbitrarily by necessity, with temporary headquarters set up at strategic locations over the Empire. All the measures to try to ensure the succession and to share the tasks of government and defence were in place long before Diocletian adapted them to his needs. He proceeded very cautiously, just possibly working to a far-sighted preconceived plan, but more likely feeling his way forward little by little as circumstances dictated, steadily building upon precedent. His first move, very soon after the battle of Margus, was to appoint his fellow soldier Marcus Aurelius Maximianus as his Caesar. Maximian added the name Valerius to his nomenclature, and it has been claimed that he was linked to Diocletian as *filius Augusti*. More recently doubt has been cast on this theory, which arises from a misreading of a papyrus. Even if it is correct that Maximian was regarded as the son of Diocletian while he was Caesar, the concept changed when he was made Augustus, when he and Diocletian were described as brothers. Their relationship was couched in religious terms, in a deliberate revival of the old Roman tradition, probably as soon as Maximian was designated Diocletian's partner, though whether this was when he was created Caesar or Augustus is debatable, and the debate can be complicated further by the suggestion that Maximian was made Augustus immediately, and his apprenticeship as Caesar is nothing but a myth. Whatever the date, it is clear that the earthly association of the two men was equated with a partnership of the gods, Diocletian taking the name Jovius, and Maximian that of Herculius, names which were also applied to military units, and eventually, during the Tetrarchy, to the Caesars attached to each Emperor. Jove or Jupiter was the chief of the Roman gods, and Hercules was his assistant, which mirrored the relative positions of Diocletian and Maximian. The partners in government each had designated tasks to perform as a matter of urgency. From 285 onwards Diocletian was occupied on the Danube, and then in the east, until 288. Maximian took charge of the west.[4]

Gaul and Britain

The Bagaudae

Gaul was beset by internal and external problems, the internal ones probably inspired or exacerbated by the external ones. The Bagaudae were infamous for their lawlessness, destruction and pillaging. It is generally believed that these gangs were composed of displaced peasants, probably deserters from the army, and a motley assembly of desperate people whose fortunes had been ruined by the invasions of the tribesmen from across the Rhine. Bandits had always existed in the Empire, sometimes coming to prominence and enjoying a niche in history, usually after they had been eliminated by the proper authorities. The Gallic bandits of the third century were perhaps typical of the sort of society in which law and order have broken down to the point where everyone has to fend for himself, and where an honest living is impossible to achieve. All those who are at liberty to do so invariably escape to a better place and a better life, leaving the more unfortunate people who cannot leave the area to make a living as best they can, usually by plundering. The leaders of the Bagaudae, or at least one group of them, were Amandus and Aelianus, about whom very little is known apart from their names. They probably did not aspire to ruling the Empire, or even a part of Gaul, although they are listed under the heading of usurpers because some scholars consider that they intended to make a bid for the Empire. In reality they perhaps do not strictly belong in the category of usurpers. Maximian's successes against them are not fully documented; this was not a glorious war of conquest after all. It would be interesting to know how he located the Bagaudae and hunted them down, what measures he took to alleviate the economic position of the displaced and landless classes to prevent the lawlessness escalating again, or even if he was fully successful in eradicating the menace. The few references extol his virtues and successes, without going into detail; the panegyric of 289 generalises about Maximian's own particular blend of harshness and leniency in dealing with the poor people who had been forced into brigandage by dire circumstances, but this simple summing up is telling enough about the situation. The word 'Bagaudae' does not appear in this contemporary description. A large element in Maximian's success will have been the promise of a constant military presence on

137

the Rhine frontier and defence against further invasions; confidence in the government can restore more than just morale, provided it is backed up quite quickly by good results.[5]

Carausius

By 286 Maximian was able to begin to concentrate on eliminating the Frankish and Saxon pirates who threatened the coasts of Britain and Gaul, and the Rhine mouth. No one had yet been able to attend to this endemic problem in force, though it is possible that Carus and Carinus had already appointed the Menapian Carausius to his command of the fleet, and of the coastal forts on both sides of the English Channel. If he was not already in post, then Maximian appointed him soon after he took up his own command. Carausius' status is not known; it has been argued that he could have been the last prefect of the *Classis Britannica*, or the very first *dux tractus Armoricani et Nervicani*. It seems that whatever his title and job description, whatever the extent of his command, and however long he had held the post, Carausius' work was satisfactory. It has been suggested that Diocletian's victory title *Britannicus Maximus* was taken on account of Carausius' achievements, probably in 285, but the title is not securely dated. It is

Figure 24 Carausius in Britain attempted to gain recognition as an equal by Diocletian and Maximian, hence this coin with the hopeful legend CARAUSIUS ET FRATRES SUI – 'Carausius and his brothers'. Diocletian as senior Emperor is in centre place, flanked by Maximian and Carausius. This coin was minted in Britain, but at which town is uncertain. Candidates include Clausentum (modern Bitterne), Colchester or Cirencester. (Drawn by Trish Boyle.)

possible to argue that the epithet *Britannicus Maximus* is much more likely to belong to the successful campaign of Constantius in bringing Britain back under Imperial control in 296, but the fact that Diocletian later dropped the title strengthens the argument that he took it for Carausius' successful actions against the pirates, or for bringing Britain under firm control. When Maximian decided to arrest Carausius, precipitating the formation of the independent British regime, Diocletian probably drew a veil over the so-called British victory to avoid the irony of proclaiming success in an area where he clearly had no control at all, and also to disassociate himself from the man who was labelled in contemporary literature as a rebel or even pirate. While he achieved his successes against the real pirates Carausius was perhaps securing his own future, by means of personal alliances in the army in Britain and Gaul, and among the government personnel. His knowledge of the Channel waters and defences was intimate, and his reputation with the troops on both sides of the Channel was well entrenched. It began to be said that he also knew a little too much about the timing of the Frankish raids, standing by while they plundered, and then descending on them on their way home, relieving them of their booty which seemingly never found its way back to the original owners. He had hired Frankish soldiers to swell his army, so it was assumed that he was using his illicit gains to pay them. The rumour may have derived from nothing more than malicious gossip, but whether it was true or not it presented Maximian with a problem that

Figure 25 By 293 Carausius had begun to issue coins in his own name, making a break with the legitimate Emperors after realising that he would never gain recognition from them. The legend proclaims him as Augustus: CARAUSIUS P F AUG. Gold aureus from the London mint. (Drawn by Trish Boyle.)

139

he had to be seen to resolve, so he proposed to arrest Carausius. He missed his chance. Carausius slipped away to Britain, secure behind his coastal defences and protected by his fleet. He had the upper hand because Maximian's ships had been mauled by the pirates, while Carausius possessed ships with experienced crews and had conveniently arranged an alliance with the Franks. For the time being Maximian had to leave the situation as it was with Carausius in unchallenged possession of Britain, the port of Boulogne on the coast of Gaul, and command over some of the Continental troops.[6]

Most of the evidence for Carausius' *Imperium Britanniarum* derives from his coinage, which was generally of good quality. A sound coinage was a prerequisite if the army and the influential people in Britain were to have any faith in him. By means of the legends on his coins Carausius established and promoted himself, on one occasion quoting from Virgil (*expectate veni*) to indicate that he was the one whose destiny was to lead them. To Diocletian and Maximian he made it clear that he considered himself their equal, issuing coins which can be dated to 290, proclaiming that he ruled with 'his brothers' (*Carausius et Fratres Sui*). The sentiment was not shared by Diocletian and Maximian, who never formally recognised Carausius or his claim to Britain and the coast of Gaul. If the extent of his original official command is not known, after he declared his independence it is even more debatable how far Carausius' influence stretched over the troops and bases on the Rhine and the coasts of Gaul. He certainly held Boulogne, and seems to have commanded some of the legions, or parts of the legions, on the Continent.[7]

The forts of the Saxon Shore

The strength of Carausius' position in Britain derived, among other considerations, from the fact that anyone who wished to make war on him had to gather a fleet and run the gauntlet of a Channel crossing in the face of his experienced sailors and the soldiers of the coastal forts. The Saxon Shore forts are known to modern archaeologists by their collective name, which gives rise to a spurious sense of an ordered defensive system along the south and east coast of Britain of long-established antiquity. This is not the case. The Saxon Shore was probably not labelled as such when Carausius created his British Empire. Most of the forts will have existed by his day, but they were not part of a unified plan for coastal defence. Archaeology shows that the forts are not all of one design, and moreover that they were built at different times, probably for different purposes; they are dated to the half century between 250 and 300. Reculver and Brancaster are generally considered to be the earliest in the series, conventionally planned like the majority of forts built in the first and second centuries in Britain. Burgh Castle and Dover may have been next, then Lympne, Richborough and Portchester; the strangely un-Roman ovoid fort at Pevensey was probably a late addition. In the *Notitia Dignitatum* (*Oc.* XXVIII) the forts are listed as a part of the command of the Count of the Saxon Shore, so by the time this document was drawn up (and the date of the British entries in this document is a subject with a respectable bibliography of its own) there was a corporate system utilising all nine forts of different periods on the British coast. The command extended to the coasts of Gaul as well, a situation that was partly foreshadowed by Carausius' continued control of Boulogne. The question that no one has yet been able to answer is at what point this unified Saxon Shore command came into existence, and there are those who suggest that it may have been Carausius who welded the so-called Saxon Shore forts of Britain into a functional whole. He had, after all, two groups of enemies to watch for, in the shape of the pirate ships and the Imperial Roman fleets, so perhaps more than any of his predecessors who governed Britain he required a strong defensive line of forts to guard and keep watch over the potential points of access to the island.[8]

Maximian Augustus

In an entrenched and virtually invulnerable position, Carausius could not be prised out of his stronghold until Maximian could amass a considerable force against him, and a fleet. That was not possible until the Franks and the Alamanni were defeated and the Rhine and Gaul were safe. There was probably more immediate danger to the Gallic provinces from these tribesmen than there was from Carausius, who indeed never attempted to launch an attack from his base at Boulogne and seemed content to remain supreme in his own British Empire. It is a matter of opinion, then as now, as to what Carausius' ultimate intentions were. Diocletian was not prepared to condone the secession of Britain from the Empire, so ultimately there could be only one outcome, which would be decided by war. Knowing this, Carausius might strike first. The potential threat posed by Carausius in Britain has been viewed as one of the most important factors in the elevation of Maximian to the rank of Augustus. Seston thought that Diocletian would never have taken this step if it had not been for the rebellion of Carausius. One consideration may have been that Diocletian needed to find a way of binding Maximian more closely to himself, with the promise of adequate rewards, to pre-empt the possibility that he might join forces with Carausius, combining the armies of the west against the armies of the Danube and the eastern provinces. If that happened, the situation in the east and on the Danube would have to be neglected or delegated to someone else to deal with, while the usurpers were brought down. Progress on all fronts would be delayed, probably even fatally, so the loyalty of Maximian had to be secured, and he would have to be granted authenticated empowerment to enable him to operate independently and with credibility while Diocletian attended to his own problems in the eastern half of the Empire. In 286, probably as early as

1 April, Diocletian declared Maximianas Augustus, and his full colleague in Imperial rule. As noted above, though this date meets with the acceptance of many scholars it has also been suggested that Maximian became Augustus at the very beginning of Diocletian's reign. The chronology is not established beyond doubt, but it is possible that when Maximian was made Diocletian's colleague, Carausius had not yet declared himself Augustus, so he may have done so as a response to Diocletian's elevation of Maximian, interpreted by Carausius as justification that he may as well aim as high as possible in the hope that he would be accepted into the Imperial college, as he anticipated on his coinage. The army officers and government officials in Britain may have felt that they were now so far compromised that they had reached the point of no return, and so they threw in their lot with him.[9]

During the rest of the year 286 Maximian fought the Franks and Heruli on the coast of Gaul and around the Rhine mouth. He was at Trier in January 287, and probably began his campaign to clear the tribesmen from Gaul and the Rhine frontier in the spring of that year. There are virtually no details and certainly no firm dates for his work, but in broad general outline it can be said that Maximian secured the Rhine and Gaul between 285 and 288. A few inferences from the panegyrics can be made to fit the circumstances. In the panegyric of 289 addressed to Maximian himself there is emphasis of the insecurity of the frontiers and praise for the Emperor's prompt reactions, and in the panegyric to Constantius a few years later there is mention of the lands of the Alamanni devastated from Mainz to the Danube. The context is most likely the campaigns of 287 and 288, the first perhaps limited to driving the tribesmen out of the Roman territories and the second, more ambitious, to carry the war across the Rhine and Danube into the lands claimed by the tribes. It is known that at some point Maximian received the submission of King Gennobaudes and all his people on the lower Rhine, and that he settled Friesians, Franks and Chamavi between the Waal and the Rhine, with obligations to protect their newly awarded lands from attack by other tribes and to provide men for the Roman army. The exact date of the operations leading up to these settlements is not known; it may have been part of Maximian's work of 286, brought to completion in 287. While Maximian fought in Gaul and on the Rhine, Diocletian had defeated the Sarmatians on the Danube in 285 and then marched to the eastern frontier, where he successfully completed a diplomatic mission which, temporarily at least, brought peace in 287 (see p. 242). He was thus relieved of the necessity of gathering a campaign army for a war against Persia, and perhaps was able to spare manpower for a war in the west. Bringing troops with him he joined Maximian, probably at Mainz, and the two of them embarked on a joint campaign against the Alamanni. Maximian operated from Mainz and Diocletian from Raetia, probably burning and destroying crops and food supplies as they went to deny the tribesmen sustenance or rest, much as Marcus Aurelius had dealt with the Marcomanni and the

142

Quadi in the second century. By these brutal but effective methods Diocletian and Maximian cleared the *Agri Decumates* of the tribesmen who had
overrun the area when the frontiers fell under Gallienus.[10]

In 289 Maximian was ready to tackle Carausius. Nothing came of his
plan; whether it was aborted or failed is not known. The author of the panegyric addressed to Maximian in 289 is confident that the campaign will
succeed, but the next speech, dated to 291, contains no mention of Britain
or Carausius, an omission which is generally taken as proof that the campaign had failed. The panegyric addressed to Constantius Chlorus makes
brief mention of the failure, which is tactfully ascribed to the bad weather,
perhaps to play down the contrast between Maximian, who failed, and Constantius, who some years later succeeded in putting an end to the independent
British *Imperium*.[11]

The Danube and the east

Immediately after his accession Diocletian was embroiled in war against the
tribes of the Danube, chiefly the Sarmatians, who demanded assistance in
regaining their former territories or the right to pasturage inside the
Empire. Diocletian refused all their demands and made war on them, but
like most of his predecessors he won battles but was unable to eradicate the
problem entirely. Whatever the arrangements he made at the end of the
campaign, the pressures on the tribes for land or survival had not been eased,
and four years later Diocletian had to fight the Sarmatians all over again.[12]

At the end of 286 and the beginning of 287 Diocletian journeyed into
Thrace and then into Syria. A confrontation with the Persians was avoided
by diplomatic arrangements, whereby Rome was the beneficiary. Carus'
victory was momentous for the Romans, justly famed in later literature, and
because it came at a time when the Persian regime was beset by internal
troubles, a temporary peace of unpredictable duration was guaranteed for
both great powers. There was no actual treaty as such, but hints in the panegyric of 289 to Maximian suggest that the Persians negotiated and sent gifts
(*dona Persica*). Diocletian seized the opportunity to strengthen Rome's position. He did not follow up Carus' success with aggressive warfare in an
attempt to eradicate the Persian problem altogether. That would have been a
dangerous and time-consuming process. But he did all that he could
without provoking aggrieved retribution. Mesopotamia was re-absorbed into
the Empire, the Syrian frontier was reorganised, Circesium on the Euphrates
was fortified, and the Roman candidate for the throne of Armenia, Tiridates,
was installed without opposition. This non-violent settlement of the east
conserved manpower and resources, which Diocletian was not yet ready to
commit to the east, because he considered it a greater priority to employ
troops in the west in a combined offensive with Maximian against the
Alamanni during the year 288. Diocletian was probably based in Raetia,

Figure 26 Portrait of Diocletian on a gold coin worth two and a half aurei from the Rome
    mint. It dates to *c.*293. The reverse (not shown) depicts Victory offering a crown to
    Jupiter, with whom Diocletian identified himself, while Maximian was associated
    with Hercules. (Drawn by Trish Boyle.)

striking into the Alamannic territories while Maximian attacked from
Mainz. By the following year, the Sarmatians had regrouped, and another
war loomed. No details survive, but victory for the Romans was probably
rapid. Inscriptions show that Diocletian took the title *Sarmaticus Maximus*
four times altogether, the second time after the campaign of 289.[13]

At some time in 290, Diocletian fought a campaign in the east against
the Saracens, or Arabian tribes, but next to nothing is known about this
campaign. By the end of 290 the Empire was more or less stabilised and
secure, firmly under the control of the two Emperors, with the glaring
exception of the regime of Carausius in Britain and his embarrassing hold on
the port of Boulogne. Diocletian and Maximian had survived longer than
most of the Emperors since the end of the Severan regime, and though there
was still much to do, it was time to advertise themselves, their solidarity,
and their achievements in the service of the Empire. The year 291 was
dedicated to celebrations, with the important difference that, unlike other
events of this nature, the festivities were held not in Rome itself but nearer
to the potential troublesome zones, in Milan. Maximian journeyed through
Gaul and Diocletian met him for a leisurely progress through northern Italy.
Senators travelled to meet them in Milan. More than ever it underlined the
fact that the city of Rome was not conveniently situated for the effective
government of the Empire when it was under threat from any of the frontiers, for whatever reason. Gallienus had based himself in Milan when he
faced invasions from tribesmen from the north and Roman armies from
Gaul. Journeys to and from Rome took far too much time, news from the

frontiers was subject to delays, and response time was sluggish; though Rome remained supreme as an ideological concept for many years, the nerve centre of government revolved around the Emperor and his court, wherever that happened to be. This was not the final break, but it paved the way to Constantine's decision to move his headquarters and seat of government to the east.[14]

The formation of the Tetrarchy

The Tetrarchy is not a term that Diocletian would have used to describe his regime; though it was used in the Greek world to describe a territory divided into four areas, the derivative word 'tetrarch' used to describe the person who controlled such an area eventually commuted its meaning to denote a subordinate ruler, so Diocletian and his colleagues would hardly have been flattered to hear themselves addressed as tetrarchs. In recent times Tetrarchy has been applied by modern scholars to describe the rule of four that Diocletian imposed on the Roman world in 293. Debate still has not solved the problem of how and when the Emperor conceived this new regime, whether it was a master plan formed in its entirety at the very beginning and put into operation in stages, or whether, as is much more likely, it was a response to circumstances, adapted when they changed. Some authors have suggested that it was a measure that was forced upon Diocletian by the successes of Maximian in the west that made it politic to promote him, and others envisage that Maximian's power-hungry ambitions for himself and for his son-in-law Constantius forced Diocletian to acknowledge him and then elevate a candidate of his own to redress the balance. Seston writes of Diocletian's bad grace in elevating his colleagues, suggesting that the whole idea was an attempt to alleviate the bitter rivalry between the various rulers, but there is no evidence that this was the case, nor that Maximian was disloyal at this stage. If Diocletian was at the mercy of squabbling subordinates at least he came up with a solution that at one and the same time provided generals to attend to the different parts of the Empire, and also provided successors.[15]

Though there was a temporary peace over most of the Empire, Diocletian was aware that none of the successes of the recent past had solved the problems of the northern and eastern frontiers. He was also aware that he would never be allowed the luxury of finishing one war before he had to embark upon another, and these simultaneous outbreaks required more generals who could be trusted to concentrate on the conduct of the war instead of their own advancement. If the generals he appointed were assured of their relative positions and of their promotion prospects, then perhaps they could be relied upon to perform their tasks with full concentration and also to suppress anyone else who aspired to rule the Empire rather better than they were ruling it themselves. One individual could not simultaneously direct

Figure 27 The famous portrait of the Tetrarchs from Piazza San Marco in Venice. It is paralleled by another more primitive sculpture depicting the two Augusti, from Rome. (Photo David Brearley.)

wars, fight all the battles, govern the Empire, and watch out for usurpers as well. Even with two Augusti operating in different parts of the Empire, there would have to be some delegation to cope with the other large territories under their control, or not under their control as the case sometimes was. In other words and in modern idiom Diocletian had a staffing problem, so in 293 he increased his establishment by 100 per cent, by elevating to the rank of Caesar two younger colleagues, Constantius and Galerius. The appropriate ceremonies took place simultaneously on 1 March 293, in different parts of the Empire, probably at Sirmium, where Diocletian invested Galerius, and at Milan where Maximian did the same for Constantius. The

146

two Caesars adopted the names Flavius Valerius Constantius and Gaius Galerius Valerius Maximianus. The changes of name illustrated their family connections with the two Augusti, connections which had already been reinforced by marriage alliances, before the Tetrarchy was established in 293. Constantius had been married, officially or unofficially, to Helena, a tavern keeper's daughter from Naissus. It was an alliance he had formed as a soldier, and it was to have momentous consequences for the future of the Empire, since Constantius and Helena were the parents of Constantine. When his career began to revolve around the Emperor's court, Constantius divorced Helena and married Theodora, the step-daughter of Maximian, perhaps in 289. It is not known when Galerius married Valeria, Diocletian's daughter, divorcing his former wife in the process. Marriage alliances had always been regarded as an important part of Roman political life, a way of cementing agreements and an attempt to secure loyalty. From early Republican times and all through the Empire, marriage alliances had never averted civil wars once political issues and individual egos had outgrown the original agreements, but the custom was never abolished.[16]

The four men who ruled the Empire were all Illyrians, and all of them had started their careers in the army. It was perhaps inevitable that Diocletian would choose men he knew either personally or by reputation from his own circle. His own position in the rule of four was as the undoubted senior partner, distinguished by the fact that he held one more German victory title than Maximian; the two Augusti were titled Imperator Caesar, and they both held the priestly office of Pontifex Maximus. The Caesars were not given the title Imperator and did not share the high priesthood, but all four men shared the same victory titles, whether or not they had participated in the relevant wars. Rivalry over titles was therefore pre-empted as far as possible. Constantius was equated with Maximian and adopted the name Herculius while Galerius was associated with Diocletian and became Jovius, but Constantius was still the more senior of the two Caesars; on official documents he took precedence, being always mentioned first. The appearance of four Emperors did not necessarily involve a fourfold division of the Roman world, though it seems from their attachment to certain groups of provinces as if each Caesar and each Augustus controlled an allocated portion of the Empire; indeed Aurelius Victor specifically states that this was the case, but in fact there were no strict boundaries between the four quarters of the Roman world where each man operated, even though there were four cities which became their headquarters, or capitals. Lactantius complained that everything had been multiplied by four as each of the Tetrarchs tried to outdo each other, increasing their armies, bodyguards, Imperial staffs and so on, but he exaggerated in order to condemn the regime that persecuted Christians, as opposed to his hero Constantine who founded the Christian Empire. A division of the Empire into four distinct units would seem perfectly reasonable to those authors who compiled their histories during the fifth century and later, when officially established territorial boundaries were the norm. It would seem logical to them that this had also been the case during the Tetrarchy, but at the turn of the third and fourth centuries the four Emperors were assigned to regions as and when they were needed, and not to specific areas as part of a fixed geographical plan. It is not known how far each of the Tetrarchs could act, take decisions or legislate in the areas where the others were operating, but it is fairly certain that Diocletian could override protocols and take decisions in any part of the Empire, commensurate with his seniority.[17]

The system as described implies a certain amount of rigidity of planning, with mathematical checks and balances that took no account of human idiosyncrasies. Sooner or later, in most works dealing with Diocletian, the word 'pragmatism' makes an appearance, and indeed it is a very apposite description of his methods. He adapted to circumstances and made arrangements accordingly, but this implies that he was perpetually limited to short-term planning. Having survived for a decade he perhaps now looked further ahead. With regard to the succession, once again it is not known whether Diocletian prepared for his abdication well in advance. The Caesars were clearly marked out as the successors of the Augusti, but in 293 it may be that Diocletian had not yet made any firm plans as to how or when this was to take place. In normal circumstances the succession would be by natural selection when an Emperor died or was killed, so it could be said that Diocletian had prepared as well as he could for this eventuality, but whether or not he had always intended to abdicate along with Maximian is unknown; that too may have been a pragmatic decision taken when he felt himself unable to continue through ill health. As has been pointed out, he presumably looked forward to living in his palace at Split, which was built for the specific purpose of housing him, and could not really be described as a vital strategic centre of the Empire. Since it could not have been planned and built in the single year when he decided to retire, there is some support for the argument that he always intended that at some point he would withdraw from public life and let others take over. The Tetrarchy was an anomaly in the government of the Empire, a short-lived experiment that succeeded in rebuilding the Roman world in an altered form, but ultimately, as a self-perpetuating system, it was a failure. It worked while Diocletian was in control and while the Empire was under threat from various sources, but eventually broke down and degenerated into civil war when personalities clashed.[18]

A world at war: 293–305

A strict chronology for the events of the decade or so after the establishment of the Tetrarchy has not yet been agreed upon by modern scholars, who must work with an incomplete body of evidence. Epigraphic sources are not as abundant as they are for the earlier Empire, and contemporary written sources are largely confined to the panegyrics, a form of address that did not entail the recording of exact dates for posterity because that was not the purpose of the works. Nevertheless, what emerges from the debatable sources is that the Empire was fully stretched at certain times, with wars of reconquest or aggressive punitive campaigns going on in the east and west while the northern frontiers were harassed. For the first few years Diocletian and Maximian recede into the background while the younger men went on campaign, but they reappear on the war front in 296–7.[19]

Immediately after his elevation to the rank of Caesar in 293, Constantius launched himself into the eradication of Carausius' hold on Boulogne and the Gallic shores, a task in which he succeeded quite rapidly, also cutting off Carausius' access to any more Frankish troops. Despite the fact that the loss of his Gallic port reduced Carausius' credibility and led to his assassination by his finance official Allectus, Constantius did not follow up this success with an immediate invasion of Britain. That came three years later, after operations in Gaul, a battle or battles against the Alamanni and at least one journey to Italy. The situation in Britain probably deteriorated. Carausius had defended his little Empire well, including the northern frontier, but Allectus may not have been so competent. The reasons for Constantius' campaign in northern Britain may have derived from endemic upheavals after the death of Carausius and the defeat of Allectus. While Constantius fought against the Alamanni, Galerius was in Egypt, where a revolt had broken out, probably as early as 293. There was also some action on the Danube against the Sarmatians in 294. Tantalising literary references indicate that forts were built in barbarian territory opposite Aquincum and Bononia (*in Sarmatia contra Acinco et Bononia*). These forts have been interpreted as bridgeheads guarding the approaches to the main forts on the Roman side of the Danube, but others see them as forts built well inside Sarmatian territory – outposts rather than bridgeheads. Mócsy points out that there is some corroboration from references to forts *in barbarico* in the *Notitia Dignitatum* (*Oc.* XXXII, 41; XXXIII 48). This description is unusual, in that it is not one that is normally applied in that document to bridgehead forts. Consequently it can be postulated that Diocletian fought a successful campaign and occupied the territory of the Sarmatians, building forts to keep them under surveillance. Unfortunately there is as yet no archaeological proof of the whereabouts of these forts.[20]

During the course of 294 there was disturbing news from Persia, where the warlike Narses had seized power. He sent an embassy to the Romans, and for a while there was no action, but in 295 the Persians invaded Armenia and ousted Tiridates. This was a classic move, and it was not a situation that the Romans could tolerate for long, so after his operations in Upper Egypt, Galerius embarked on a war against Persia in 296, as Constantius was preparing to invade Britain. Diocletian was occupied in a struggle with the Carpi on the Danube and Maximian came to the Rhine to relieve Constantius of the task of guarding the area. The successes of the campaign in Britain offset the losses of the other against Narses. Galerius was soundly thrashed, in a humiliating defeat not far from Carrhae where Licinius Crassus had notoriously met disaster and death towards the end of the Republic. Constantius on the other hand, aided by his Praetorian Prefect Asclepiodotus, defeated Allectus and massacred the Frankish mercenaries who had fought for Carausius. According to Constantius they were about to sack London, and he saved the city from its fate. He issued the famous medallion from the Trier mint, proclaiming that he had brought back the eternal light to Britain (*Redditor lucis aeternae*). Given that Carausius had remained in power for several years seemingly unopposed, that he had as far as possible looked after the interests of the merchant and land-owning classes, had issued a high-quality coinage and protected the northern frontier of Hadrian's Wall as well as the coasts, there may have been some inhabitants of Britain who questioned whether they had really been in such terrible darkness.[21]

During the next two or three years the theatre of action shifted from the west to the African and eastern provinces. Maximian campaigned in Mauretania, Diocletian suppressed a revolt in Egypt and Galerius collected another army, mostly from the Danube, and attacked Persia. It is testimony to the ability and goodwill of the army and the efficacy of Diocletian's system that the Empire was able to sustain warfare and police work for so many years on such a scale. The long-range movements of the army are illustrated by the Danubian troops that Galerius took to the east, and the German units that accompanied Maximian to Mauretania. The supply of food, armour and clothing, and above all of recruits to keep the army up to strength, will have taxed the resources of the Empire tremendously, but the loyalty of the troops and their adherence to the ideology of Rome and the Emperor did not seriously break down. The revolt in Egypt was probably a residual offshoot from the troubles that Galerius had dealt with from 293 to 295. The leaders were Domitianus, who declared himself Augustus, and Aurelius Achilleus, self-styled *corrector* of Egypt. Their sedition led to a prolonged siege of Alexandria that prevented Diocletian from joining Galerius in the east.[22]

The next four years saw an upsurge in Rome's fortunes and the achievement of peace on most frontiers. The siege of Alexandria was over by the summer of 298, and when the dust settled Diocletian went on a tour up the Nile, visiting Oxyrhynchus and Elephantine. The administration of Alexandria and Egypt was tightened up; the census that may have sparked off the riots did take place, and Alexandria lost its special status and the right to issue independent coinage. According to the ancient sources Maximian conducted two campaigns in Mauretania, one around the city of Sirta and another in the mountains, which were probably part of a constant search and find exercise, and a series of skirmishes rather than a pitched battle. In

Figure 28 A stylised portrait of Diocletian on a gold 10-aureus piece, minted at Nicomedia, his favourite residence before he retired to Split. Realism and characterisation have disappeared in favour of anodyne standardisation. (Drawn by Trish Boyle.)

298–9 the Persian campaign was crowned with success. Diocletian and Galerius led the army together; it has been said that Diocletian remained behind in Syria, but he protected the southern flank of Galerius' army while the latter attacked through Armenia and into Media and Adiabene, very much along the lines of the plan that Marcus Antonius had tried over three centuries earlier. Where Antonius failed, Galerius succeeded. He defeated the Persians near modern Erzerum. The sources do not specifically state that he took Ctesiphon, but it is assumed that he did, not least because he is said to have captured Narses' wife and children, but where exactly this occurred is not recorded. Triumphantly he marched back along the Euphrates and into Mesopotamia, where Diocletian was encamped with his army. Negotiations followed. Diocletian travelled to Nisibis where he and Galerius formulated a treaty with the Persians in 299, one which was highly favourable to Rome. Tiridates was installed once again on the Armenian throne; Mesopotamia was recovered. Apart from the political significance of the treaty, it also carried great economic importance; all trade was to pass through Nisibis, which was under Roman control.[23]

Diocletian probably spent the next year at Antioch. Galerius was given a heroic welcome there but he was soon occupied on the Danube fighting the Marcomanni and the Carpi. His exploits in Persia were recorded on his triumphal arch at Thessalonika, significantly enough not in Rome itself but in the city from which Galerius carried out most of his administration. While Galerius campaigned on the Danube, Constantius was likewise engaged on the Rhine against the Franks. The northern frontier wars are not well documented, but were deserving of victory titles using the generic names Germans and Sarmatians. Save for some problems on the Rhine that occupied Constantius, peace seems to have been established by 303. In that year Diocletian and Maximian celebrated their 20-year rule, their *vicennalia*, in the city of Rome. If the two Caesars went with them, it is not recorded. The celebrations were recorded on the coinage; on one issue the Romans were exhorted to rejoice (*Gaudete Romani*), an instruction which practically begs for the addition 'or else'. There are some hints that while in Rome Diocletian persuaded Maximian that it would be politic for the two of them to renounce their powers together and let their junior partners progress from Caesars to Augusti, taking new Caesars of their own. It is said that Maximian swore to uphold Diocletian's plan in a ceremony in the temple of Jupiter.[24]

Lactantius records that Diocletian did not like the Romans because he found them too brash and too free of speech. It may be true, since the Emperor left as soon as he could to go back to Nicomedia. He was already quite ill; at the beginning of 304 he collapsed. At some unknown date, probably after this crisis, Maximian went to meet Galerius. The reasons behind their meeting can only be guessed, and what they agreed upon, if anything, cannot be discerned. Constantius may not have been invited; or if he was, then he could not attend because the Franks were causing trouble on the Rhine. Lactantius insists that it was Galerius who forced Diocletian to abdicate; the most likely explanation is the Emperor's illness, but it is still debated whether it was always part of Diocletian's master plan to abdicate eventually. Galerius persecuted Christians with extraordinary zeal, so on that count alone Lactantius' statement is not to be trusted. If Maximian hoped to forge some sort of alliance with Galerius to maintain his position as Augustus, he renounced it in 395 when Diocletian abdicated and stepped down. Constantius and Galerius became Augusti. Diocletian retired to the famous palace at Split, while Maximian went to Lucania in southern Italy. Though technically outside political life, ensconced in quiet backwaters, it may be significant that they established themselves in different halves of the Empire: one in the west and the other in the east, but close enough together to be able to communicate.[25]

The new Caesars were Severus in the west under Constantius, and Maximinus in the east under Galerius. Both men were colleagues of Galerius, which gave him the edge if it came to squabbling with Constantius. Severus was an experienced military officer from Pannonia; Maximinus had served in the Imperial guard. It has been suggested that Diocletian intended that each Augustus would reign for 20 years, if he survived for so long, and then hand over to the Caesars, repeating the pattern of 305. The system, if such there was, relied upon co-ordination and harmony between the four men who ruled the Empire. Diocletian and Maximian had achieved a close working relationship which went well for nearly two decades. They put all their ener-gies into protecting the Empire and restructuring the way it worked. They succeeded in redressing the balance so well that a purely defensive stance could be turned into an offensive policy in taking the war into the territory of their enemies; they campaigned beyond the Rhine and Danube, and into Persia; Constantius as Augustus could think of mounting a campaign in northern Britain. Not too many years before, it would have been impossible even to think of turning attention to Britain. If Constantius and Galerius could achieve the same harmonious relationship as Diocletian and Max-imian, with their Caesars able to take on the wars or administrative tasks that they could not attend to themselves, there was no reason why the system could not go on for several decades. But there were two other protag-onists who had so far been overlooked when Severus and Maximinus were promoted: Maximian's son Maxentius and Constantius' son Constantine; between them they would soon tilt the balance.[26]

Diocletian's reforms

One of the advantages of Diocletian's long reign was that military, adminis-trative and financial reforms could be set in motion, tested over time, and brought to conclusions. The greatest disadvantage for historians and archae-ologists is the lack of contemporary evidence for any of these reforms; most of the literary, epigraphic and papyrological information derives from the immediate post-Diocletianic period, or more often from the reign of Con-stantine, with the result that it is difficult to disentangle the authorship of the original reforms. Nor is it possible to document the successive stages leading to the fully evolved versions of the late-third-century to early-fourth-century procedural changes, so no one can confidently assert that it was Diocletian who established this or that system, and Constantine who embellished it, or that Diocletian had nothing to do with it and it was Con-stantine who thought of it all. The only statement that can be made is that as a result of the work of these two Emperors the Roman world was irrevoca-bly changed. Previous Emperors whose reigns had been cut short had no time to attend to anything but the most pressing problems. Those who, like Aurelian and Probus, had begun to reorganise had to start at such a disad-vantage, and even though both these latter Emperors had felt strong enough to attack Persia, neither of them was able to carry out their project, and neither was able to get to grips with the finances, the army, or provincial organisation. Diocletian had several threads to pick up that his predecessors had left dangling. Aurelian had tackled the coinage and paved the way to the ideology of the remote and sanctified Emperor. Diocletian took over where he had left off, but at the same time reverted to traditional Roman values and religion to provide the infrastructure for his regime. Jupiter and Hercules replaced Aurelian's Sun god, but the magnificence, the cloth of gold, the diadems, the *adoratio* or obeisance all remained and were refined into a deliberately elaborated system. The Emperor-god was a concept that found ready acceptance in the east; in the west the sacrosanctity of the Emperor had been established by Severus. The distance of the Emperor from his subjects did not extend to refusing to listen to them; Diocletian and his colleagues took a personal interest in legal proceedings and numerous rescripts survive, many of them concerning minor cases. But the increasing rigidity of ceremonial and pomp served to regulate an ever-growing court circle, where simple soldierly affability would have been out of place and counter-productive, no match for the complex machinations of practised court officials. The projection of superhuman status may also have served as a tool to subdue the tribesmen outside the Empire, who understood heroic leadership with all its trappings better than they understood negotiation with an ordinary mortal who did not look much different from his assistants.[27]

The army and the frontiers

Source material for Diocletian's reconstruction of the frontiers is so slender and so general that all that can be said is that he rebuilt forts on the Rhine and Danube and on the frontier from Egypt to Persia. Archaeology can help to identify only a few of the forts mentioned in the sources, and cannot provide all the details of the broader picture to verify or negate the sweeping generalisations of the ancient writers. Archaeologically it is often difficult to distinguish the work of Diocletian from that of his predecessors or his successors. For instance, the Emperor Probus is credited with work on the forts of the Saxon Shore, probably continued by Carausius, and with the establishment of the new frontier connecting the Rhine and the Danube, currently termed the Rhine–Iller–Danube *limes*. Diocletian probably consolidated the work begun here. He campaigned beyond the Danube and may have established forts in the lands of the Sarmatians, and Maximian advanced beyond the Rhine, but there seems to have been no permanent advance beyond the Rhine–Iller–Danube frontier line. In the east, the *Strata Diocletiana* is the classic Diocletianic or Tetrarchic frontier system, consisting of a road marking the boundary, protected by closely spaced forts, backed up by fortifications in the hinterland. In advance of the Danube the earthworks known as the Devil's Dyke, which cannot be even approximately dated to a specific century, have been attributed to Diocletian. The lines run eastwards from the Danube bend opposite Aquincum, and then turn southwards to rejoin the river at Constantia and Viminacium, enclosing a vast tract of territory. It is possible that the forts *in barbarico*, mentioned above, were built inside the lands enclosed by these earthworks and that patrols were sent out to police the area, but for this there is no evidence, only speculation.[28]

Forts themselves began to change their appearance in the later third century, diverting from the classic playing-card shape of the earlier Empire, as the Romans adapted to changed circumstances. Gateways were blocked up, sometimes by projecting towers for better surveillance of the walls. U-shaped towers were built at intervals along the walls, and on the Danube distinctive fan-shaped corner towers were built, allowing for greater protection of the defences. It is possible that this work is part of the Diocletianic refurbishment of the frontiers. The Emperor probably also attended to the various road posts, watch towers, *burgi*, and fortified harbours, repairing existing structures and building new ones. Such features had always been part of the Imperial defence system where interior policing and exterior protection were necessary.[29]

There was no corporate policy for the fortification of the cities of the Empire, where initiative was left to the inhabitants. From the reign of Gallienus there had been an increasing number of cities which had acquired walls; protection was required against threats from three major sources: from invading tribesmen, from lawless bands such as the Bagaudae in Gaul, and on occasion from Roman troops who had chosen a different leader from that of the city authorities. Insecurity is difficult to quantify or rationalise, and once it has taken hold it is difficult to eradicate, so whilst it may have been an overreaction to build walls round cities that had previously managed without them, the phenomenon is indicative of the lack of faith in the central government to protect the provincial population.[30]

Diocletian's army at the beginning of his reign was essentially the same army that had defended the Empire from the first century onwards, with the exception that the cavalry had increased in importance since the reign of Gallienus. There had been considerable movement of troops during the third century as various campaigns were fought and civil wars were waged. Campaign armies were drawn from the frontier units as they had always been in the early Empire. There had been an army in the field somewhere in the Empire almost without interruption from the reign of Marcus Aurelius, and the fact that Rome had been able to sustain almost continuous, sometimes very intense, military activity for several generations attests to the efficiency of the armies and their generals, and also the support systems such as recruiting, training, logistics, and not least the overall loyalty of the individual soldiers. On the negative side, the power of the armed forces, which was necessary to keep order in the provinces and peace on the frontiers, also contributed to their ability to make or break Emperors. This was one of the problems that Diocletian was faced with, ensuring that generals did not use the troops at their disposal to raise rebellion. He needed to disperse the vexillations and mixed troops that comprised the expeditionary armies and send them back to the frontiers, and reorganise the command structure of the frontier armies. Unit size and the size of the composite army are the subjects of great debate among scholars. Lactantius' complaint that Diocletian quadrupled the army can be ignored, but that does not help to establish what the Diocletianic and Tetrarchic armies were like, nor their overall size. The auxiliary units of the early Empire were either 500 or 1,000 strong on paper, but in fact numbers may have varied considerably according to availability of manpower, casualties, disease, and desertions. The losses that the army sustained in the third century, of whole units as well as individual soldiers, cannot be documented since there is no contemporary information with which to reconstruct the history of Diocletian's army. Only the *Notitia Dignitatum* can help, but this document was compiled almost a century after the demise of the Tetrarchy, so the locations of the troops listed in it cannot be taken as evidence of Diocletian's dispositions for the defence of the Empire, nor for the size of his auxiliary units. It is possible that he split existing units into smaller groups, dividing them up between different forts, and that newly created units were smaller.[31]

The same assumption is made about the size of the legions. Originally 5,000 to 6,000 strong in the early Empire, the Diocletianic legions may have been only 1,000 strong. This makes it easier to understand how the Emperor could afford to add over 30 new legions to the existing 34 that he inherited. The fourth-century evidence from the Danube shows that men from *III Italica*, which was raised by Marcus Aurelius, were distributed over five different forts and also contributed a unit to the campaign army. This may mean that the 6,000 men were divided into six groups of 1,000, so that there was no reduction in size of the old legion. The new legionary fortress at El Lejjun on the *limes Arabicus* could not hold 6,000 men, but the smaller forts nearby could have held detachments. The evidence from these and other sites is not conclusive, but it is a strong possibility that the newly created Diocletianic legions were only 1,000 strong, with the old legions remaining at their original strengths.[32]

By the fourth century the mobile campaign army was an established institution, but there is controversy over its origins. Though Roman armies had been permanently occupied on some campaign or other for many years, the composition of the expeditionary armies had not changed. Detachments known as vexillations were taken from the frontier armies to supplement the numbers of men already available in the region where the war was to be fought. These detachments usually went back to their original provinces once the campaign was ended, but on occasion they could be split up and distributed among other depleted units, and at least in one case the vexillation became a permanent auxiliary unit. There was no permanent campaign army, in addition to the frontier troops, ready to fly to threatened zones. Severus had created three new legions, one of which, *II Parthica*, he stationed in Italy some distance from Rome, but it could not be described as a mobile reserve army, nor as an expeditionary force. Its purpose was to support Severus, and perhaps to help to police Italy, where brigands were rife. In 260 when Gallienus was left with a depleted Empire and reduced resources, he amalgamated the troops at his disposal and welded together the cavalry units drawn from several different sources, placing the resultant force under a single commander. How this cavalry fought, how it was administered, and what happened to it later are not elucidated, but to the Byzantine chronicler George Cedrenus it was the forerunner of the later mobile army. Cavalry had become more and more important, sometimes decisive, in the latter half of the third century, eventually finding its evolved form in the *comitatenses* of the later Empire – the mobile cavalry field army as distinct from the frontier army. Diocletian's role in the formation of the *comitatenses* is debated. The argument revolves around the *comitatus*, or groups of friends and picked soldiers that accompanied any Emperor on campaign. There is no doubt that such a body went on campaign with Diocletian, and probably also with each of the other Tetrarchs, but it is less certain exactly what the *comitatus* was, how it was composed and what its function was. Whether it was an embryonic mobile cavalry army or simply a bodyguard at this stage is not fully established, but the balance of probability is that it was what it had always been: a group of the Emperor's advisers and friends, and picked soldiers acting as guards.[33]

Diocletian's achievements are difficult to evaluate because most of the evidence for military and other reforms derives from the reign of Constantine or later Emperors. In broad general terms it can be said that Diocletian concentrated on reconstituting the frontiers and replacing units in forts to strengthen and protect the frontiers. He probably did not establish the mobile army, which was Constantine's contribution to the defence of the Empire; nor did Diocletian create a separate frontier force, tied to the land, that evolved into the later *limitanei*. The term is used anachronistically by fourth- and fifth-century authors, projected retrospectively into previous reigns, so that it seems that the *limitanei* had a long history – for instance they are mentioned in the *Historia Augusta* in the life of Severus Alexander, as though he commanded frontier troops similar to those of the later Roman army. Some authors who have assessed Diocletian's army reforms have described his system as defence in depth, with troops stationed on the frontiers supported by fortified road posts and depots in the hinterland. It is postulated that invasions were to be dealt with by allowing the trans-frontier peoples access to the provinces and then converging on them and fighting them inside Roman territory. The theory ignores the fact that the Romans had conducted campaigns in advance of the frontiers, and had shown that they did not intend to take the passive role all the time, waiting to be attacked and then reacting once the invasion had occurred. In the end the argument turns on perception and semantics, whether Diocletian intended to adopt a system as such, or whether he was simply reconstituting what had gone before in a different guise.[34]

Administratively, Diocletian did set the trend for later years in that he finally separated military and civil posts. There had been a growing tendency for many years for men to specialise in only one branch of the service without gaining any experience of the other, so soldiers and officers remained in the army and civilian administrators remained in civil posts. Thus civilian and military careers had been steadily diverging at least from the reign of Hadrian, and though successive Emperors had not forestalled the trend by forcing through any compulsion to serve under both headings, at the same time no one had set up a framework to crystallise the process whereby military and civilian posts were separated for ever. Diocletian's measures finally achieved this separation. Henceforth, except for a few small provinces where the governor was also the military commander, all armed forces were under the control of the *dux*, who was an equestrian officer whose authority often extended over more than one province, so that there was a unified command over frontier zones regardless of who the civilian governors were. The military commander and the governor had to co-operate with each other with regard to supplies, but the duties of the *dux* were purely military and the duties of the *praeses* were purely civilian, judicial and fiscal. It meant that the wide-ranging workload for governors and military officers was lessened, demanding less broad-based diversity and more specialist knowledge. Later Emperors did not see fit to make radical alterations to the division of military and civilian commands. It is often stated in this context of the separation of commands that senators were completely ousted from their customary posts, but it has been shown that senators were not totally eradicated from provincial government. The power and influence of the Senate had declined, and since the reign of Gallienus senators had been divorced from military command. This, and the fact that Rome was no longer the centre of the universe, had adversely affected senatorial careers, but there is no evidence that Diocletian severed all relations with senators or forbade them to hold governmental posts. One other military reform can be attributed to Diocletian. Though they are first attested only under Constantine, it was probably Diocletian who established the *scholae* or Imperial guards. The Praetorian Guard still existed, but its power was much reduced and did not long survive the accession of Constantine.[35]

Finance and taxation

Though complex financial transactions were regularly undertaken in the Roman Empire, the government had not hitherto conceived of an annual budget to raise the resources to meet expenditure. Income was derived from taxes, spoils of war, the produce of mines and so on, but the economy was predominantly agriculture based, so if production declined the income from taxation also declined. As for expenditure, by far the largest expense was the upkeep of the army and the buildings associated with it. In addition, Diocletian was accused of building mania, ruining the state by squandering huge sums on public and private projects, including the huge baths in Rome and the palace at Split. But it was and always had been the army that absorbed much of the state revenues. Defence did not come cheaply, a point which Severus recognised when he increased army pay. The inability of the state to pay the troops increased during the third century, with the result that arrears of pay became the accepted norm, and in some cases payment in kind was substituted for cash payments. Weapons, clothing and food were originally paid for out of the soldiers' wages, deductions being made for these items, and for compulsory savings, at each pay parade. In the third century these essential items became part of, and sometimes the whole of, a soldier's pay. The *annona militaris* originally involved compulsory requisitions by order of the Emperor when the army was on campaign; items were (theoretically) paid for as the army passed through each designated area, but more frequently as the third century progressed the system was abused. There was less and less regulation when the cash payment system broke down and hungry troops in need of food and clothing requisitioned whatever they lacked. Provincials were unable to protest effectively against armed men, and, to make matters worse, when the army operated in areas where there had already been considerable devastation the extra burden only added to the general disruption.[36]

This sort of abuse threatened to split the Empire, setting provincials against the army that was supposed to protect them, and landowners and city councillors against the state that threatened to bankrupt them. One of the problems of the taxation system was to find some method of assessment that spread the burden fairly and ensured that all provinces contributed to the defence of the Empire. Italy had for long enjoyed exemption from the tax burden, but this came to an end with Diocletian's reforms. Now liable to make tax contributions, Italy was in effect downgraded to the status of a province. Rome itself was exempt, including territory around the city up to a radius of 100 miles. In a predominantly agricultural world taxation could be based only on production, which naturally varied from region to region, depending on the quality of the soil and the type of crops produced on it. Diocletian introduced a system of assessment based on an agricultural unit called the *iugum*, which was not a standard measurement rigidly applied over the whole Empire. It varied according to the type of land and crop, and the amount of labour required to produce enough for one man to make a living. The labour (*caput* – literally head) was also assessed; it was not strictly a poll tax, relative to the numbers of people on a farm or estate; for instance a woman's labour was usually, but not always, assessed as half a *caput*. The *iugatio* and *capitatio* were inextricably related, and both were needed to make the fair assessment of taxes due from an area. Livestock was also included in the assessments, as the *capitatio animalium*.[37]

For the purpose of assessment and recording a census had to be conducted. It was to be renewed every five years to keep track of changes. The dates when the various provincial censuses were taken are not known. There is some information for Syria and Egypt, but none for the western provinces.

It is possible that all the censuses were undertaken quite early in Diocletian's reign, in Egypt perhaps as early as 287. It used to be thought that it was the taking of the census, or the mere threat of it, that had caused the riots there in 296, and that once they were quelled by Galerius, the Prefect of Egypt then issued his edict to inaugurate the tax system, documented on an extant papyrus, in 297. Some scholars now suggest that the edict of 297 was a secondary stage in the process and that the whole system was well established by then. It is perhaps inadvisable to date the commencement of the census over the whole Empire to 287 on the basis of the evidence from one province.[38]

When the annual requirements for the state were set, the Praetorian Prefects were responsible for apportioning the amounts to be collected from each province. The municipal councils were then charged with the collection of the taxes. Any shortfall had to be made up by the members of the councils; this could be a potential disaster for the city and town councillors, who could be rapidly impoverished if production slumped. Since all agricultural land was attributed to the towns and cities, it became a matter of urgency to find people to cultivate vacant lands. Various Emperors had tried to solve the problems of deserted land, sometimes offering incentives to farmers in the form of tax exemptions to help them to get started. Tribesmen had been settled in their thousands on vacant lands within the frontiers; it seems that there was never any lack of vacant lands in the Empire, so it is highly unlikely that the maximum potential production was ever reached.[39]

Under the heading of finance Diocletian attempted to reform the currency and to tackle the problem of inflation by curbing prices. The coinage had suffered during the third century, and Aurelian's measures had not solved the problem entirely. He had tried to fix the value of the coins and therefore their purchasing power, but traditionally coins were worth only as much as their metal content. While coins were issued with less and less precious metal, good coins were hoarded and disappeared, and prices inevitably rose. Diocletian restored the three-metal coinage and issued better-quality pieces. The denarius was dead, and it was not revived in its old form, but Diocletian issued a 25 denarius piece. The predominant coins were bronze, admittedly with little enough metal content; he tried to fix the value of the *nummi*, the common coins currently in circulation, at half their original value. He issued an edict concerning the revaluation, but it did not have the desired effect. The revaluation or currency edict anticipated the price edict by only two or three months. Prices were still rising, so Diocletian took action designed to stop them from rising further. The famous edict *de pretiis* is known from several versions, providing archaeologists and historians with invaluable information about products and their relative values at the end of the third century and the beginning of the fourth; it has a fascination far beyond its original purpose, and now has a bibliography of modern works devoted to all its aspects. In the preamble, Diocletian reminds inhabitants of the

Empire that wars have been fought with unremitting energy on their behalf, the problems of barbarian invasions and internal unrest have been successfully tackled, and tranquillity has at last been achieved. There is an exasperated tone to the synopsis of the present evils that trouble the state, namely the greed of unprincipled men who will not renounce their profits; the implication is that if it were not for these the world would be perfect. The edict goes on to list in minute detail products and their recommended retail prices that must not be exceeded. Various penalties were laid down for transgressions. But it is easy to make laws and quite another matter to enforce them, especially over a collection of diverse provinces such as those that made up the Empire. Application of the principle would be very uneven, and the measures that the edict was intended to enforce were widely resisted. The price edict was allowed to sink into oblivion; it died quite soon after it was issued, to the amusement of Diocletian's enemies. Lactantius lapsed into hyperbole about the terrible effects of the edict, which caused goods to disappear from the market and fisticuffs to break out over the smallest items; he wrote of deaths, which may be true but sounds like exaggeration. It would certainly have been an emotive subject, and where emotions rule, the law is powerless. Diocletian backed down.[40]

Control of products and services

Supplies for the army and the administrative staff were not fully provided for via the taxation system. Money payments did not die out altogether, but a large proportion of payments were made in kind; the requisitioning of produce of all descriptions became a prime concern of the government. Mines and quarries had been under partial state control since the early Empire, but manufacturing businesses were for the most part in the hands of private individuals. Those manufacturers which had the slightest bearing on military functioning were now closely scrutinised by the state. The agricultural produce destined for the army and raw materials once garnered still had to be processed, so factories, especially those producing arms and armour, textiles and clothing, were managed and operated by military personnel. Skilled craftsmen, whose expertise was vital, were conscripted to work at their trades. In order to retain specific skills in any sphere, it became compulsory for craftsmen to join a guild or corporation and to train their sons in their specific skills. No one was allowed to move to another profession, nor were their descendants allowed to take up a different trade or to move to another area. The consequent loss of personal freedom gradually extended to all walks of life. Though the compulsory membership of craft guilds did not come into full force until later in the fourth century, it was Diocletian who set the scheme in motion. Freedom of choice and social mobility were subsumed by state-imposed obligations. Much the same arrangements were made in many countries during the world wars of the twentieth century, but these arrangements were temporary and lasted only slightly longer than the duration of the wars; Romans of the fourth century remained in that condition for the whole of their lives.[41]

The rural population was no less constrained. The *colonus*, originally much more of a free agent, became too important to lose, because when compelled to stay on his land he produced, and the produce could be taxed. Bad harvests and insecurity had forced many small farmers off the land, because as rent-paying individuals without any corporate infrastructure behind them the small men could not weather the storm. The *coloni* needed influential people to provide the support systems, and the social security that would enable everyone to survive bad harvests or fight off importunate tax gatherers. Landowners needed workers to ensure that their farms were staffed and fully stocked, so it was inevitable that the two would get together; in fact they had been doing so for some time – for instance in Egypt where the peasant farmers were already closely associated with the landlords through whom they paid their taxes. Diocletian did not invent the system nor did he impose it on an unwilling population, but he confirmed a situation that was already established, and Constantine tightened the bonds. As the fourth century progressed more landowners abandoned the cities where their obligations were becoming too onerous; the *coloni* gradually came under their control. Security was dearly bought, and what became almost captivity was far from gilded. There was little alternative, except perhaps to join the army, and on occasions landowners and the military competed for manpower.[42]

Central administration of the Empire was the largest service industry, and that too became militarised and regimented. In fact the term *militia* was applied to the administration by contemporaries, and to distinguish the civil service from the military, the term *militia armata*, armed service, was used. The administrators were organised in ranks, just like the military, and Diocletian overhauled the organisation. Separate departments to deal with specific sections of the administration had existed since the early Empire, and had grown and expanded as the Empire grew. Diocletian divided the administration into departments, called *scrinia* after the boxes used to carry the relevant documents for each section. *Magistri* were placed in charge of each section; these were perhaps not completely new personnel, but the existing ones were perhaps issued with new names. The *magistri* were members of the Imperial council, the *consilium*, which may have also been called the *consistorium*, but there is no unequivocal evidence for this term from Diocletian's reign, except for a reference to one of his constitutions in the *Codex Justinianus* which may well be an interpolation made at a time when *consistorium* was in established usage. There is debate about when the *consistorium* was instituted, since *consilium* was still in use in the reign of Constantine. Whatever it was officially called, Diocletian's council was closer in spirit to the later consistory than it was to the original early Imperial *consilium*. Augustus employed the council much as any head of household employed his own *consilium*, as a circle of advisers. The first Emperor could have governed without the benefit of a council, but he drew senators and military men together as a cosmetic exercise to make it seem that his government was corporate, not autocratic. By means of a constantly changing membership of the *consilium*, many men could be made to feel that they were playing a part. The equestrians and freedmen who ran the offices behind the scenes were not members of this council. Diocletian's *consilium/consistorium* was in effect the government, directed ultimately by the Emperor himself, but its make-up included the administrators and heads of departments.[43]

The elaboration of court ceremonial went hand in hand with the evolution of the administration and the growth of the court circles around the Emperors. The complex organisation of the civil service, staffed by numerous personnel, would have been at odds with an Emperor who lived in a modest house on the Palatine in Rome, or who sat round the camp fire and ate the same rations as the soldiers when on campaign. Hauteur, magnificence and echoing distance from ordinary mortals was called for in the man who directed this vast machinery. Autocratic government was not invented by Diocletian but it was developed by him to its full potential, and with it he also developed a screening system that filtered all physical approach to him. Public appearances were stage managed to the ultimate degree; sumptuous costume and jewellery enhanced the Emperor's image; Imperial residences were designed to overawe and intimidate; stylised rituals governed all public activities. *Adoratio* or obeisance illustrated the relative position of Emperor and subject. Court ceremonial, ethics and custom crystallised ranks and social position; advancement depended upon remaining on good terms with a number of officials and above all with the Emperor, the source of all benefits because the gift of appointment was in his hands. Many a monarch, including Henry VIII of England and Louis XIV of France, could have taken lessons from Diocletian, the last Emperor of the Principate and the first Emperor of the Dominate.[44]

Provincial reorganisation

As with his military reforms, the initial dates of Diocletian's provincial reorganisation cannot be discerned, because all the evidence so far revealed is Constantinian or later. There were two major alterations to the provincial administration. As a preliminary measure Diocletian grouped together several existing provinces into new administrative units which he called dioceses, and installed equestrian officials called *vicarii* in control of the dioceses. In its literal sense the word *vicarius* simply means 'substitute' and it was used in this sense during the early Empire when an official acted on a temporary basis on behalf of the appointed provincial governor, in his absence, or on occasion when the governor had died. The precedent for the use of the

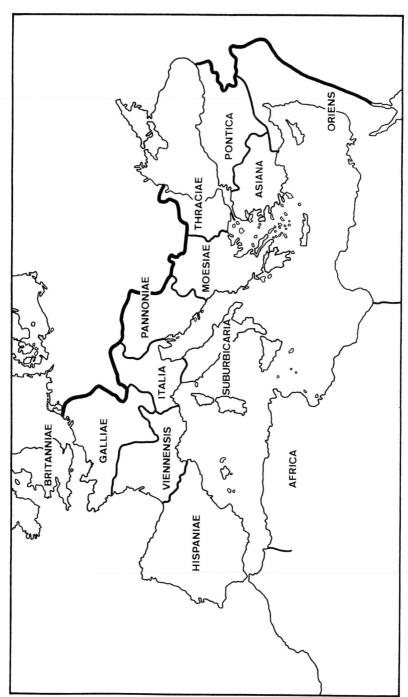

Figure 29 Map of the dioceses of the Roman Empire created by Diocletian. (Drawn by Graeme Stobbs.)

title was already set, but Diocletian made the post permanent. These new officials represented an extra step in the administrative hierarchy. They were directly responsible to the Praetorian Prefects, and their function was to supervise the provincial governors. The hierarchy was not strictly observed all the time, since the Emperor and the Praetorian Prefects could communicate directly with the provincial governors or with the *vicarii*, and vice versa. One can only hope that whenever this direct communication was undertaken, copies of all proceedings were sent to both the governors and the *vicarii*, otherwise everyone would find themselves acting at cross purposes, unaware of requests and instructions winging their way across the Empire that might be contrary to their intentions. The potential for chaos when there is a multiplicity of officials and a lack of communication is immense, even in a tiny office, let alone a large Empire.[45]

The next step was to reduce the size of individual provinces. Severus had split Britain into two provinces, Aurelian had created the new Dacia by carving a new province out of parts of Moesia, but in general the provinces remained the same as they were during the High Empire. The number of provinces almost doubled in the reign of Diocletian, which meant that the number of officials also increased, giving rise to criticism that there were more officials than taxpayers. As mentioned on p. 157, military and civilian commands were now separated, with the equestrian *duces* responsible for all the troops in the province, even if the governor was a senator; in some cases the *dux* commanded troops of a large area comprising more than one province. Only in a few cases in the smaller provinces was the governor also in command of troops. The date of the changes in provincial administration cannot be ascertained; the document known as the *Laterculus Veronensis*, a list of dioceses, the *vicarii* in charge of them, and of the provinces and their governors, is the nearest evidence available for the Diocletianic system, but some of the entries have been shown to be Constantinian in date, thus masking for ever what may have been different arrangements under Diocletian. It is likely that the provincial reorganisation was carried out over a prolonged period. How it was done is not known; the existing governors may have been allowed to serve their full terms before they were replaced, the boundaries redrawn, and then two or even three new governors installed in the area occupied by the old province. If it is correct that the dioceses were created before the provinces were divided, the *vicarii* may have undertaken the duties of the governors as they were replaced, until new officials were appointed. Continuity would be important while the provincial reorganisation was being carried out. The benefits of the subdivision of provinces were that each governor could devote more time to supervising the cities, transport and communications, and the food supply, and to hearing judicial cases from a smaller number of people. They could exercise a tighter control over a smaller number of taxpaying provincials than would have been the case if they had still governed larger areas. Control was the order of the day, as was

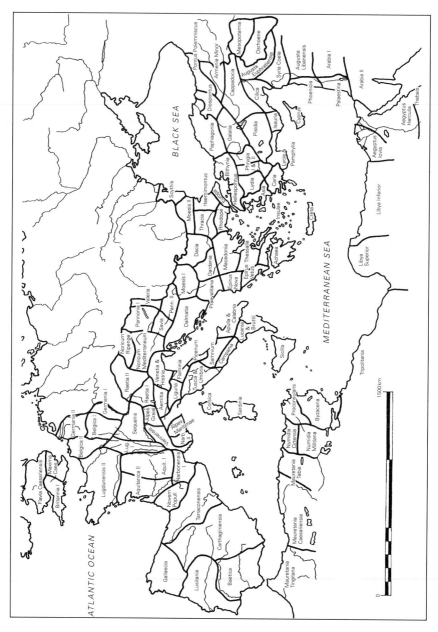

Figure 30 Diocletian's reorganisation of the provinces at the end of the third century. (Drawn by Graeme Stobbs.)

the prevention of rebellion; some authors state that the creation of smaller provinces was designed to make usurpation that much more difficult; but even the unarmed provinces were subdivided, and if the division was ever intended to prevent rebellion then the attempt to stamp out such activities by reducing the power of the governors was not necessarily successful. The provinces did not increase in size after Diocletian, so governors did not gain more power, but usurpation as a regular Roman recreational activity ceased in the fourth and fifth centuries.[46]

The persecution of the Christians

The edict of 303 aimed at the Christians represented not just a hardening of anti-Christian policy but a complete change. During the early part of his reign Diocletian was preoccupied with wars and had no time to devote to witch-hunting to root out subversive elements. He revived and strengthened the old Roman religion but did not go so far as to enforce universal observance. Even Eusebius acknowledged that the beginning of Diocletian's reign was peaceful as far as the Christians were concerned. The first onslaught against religious sects came with the attacks on the Manichaeans, who were firmly entrenched in the eastern provinces, and were numerous in Egypt and north Africa. They followed the teachings of Mani, who was considered a heretic by the Mazdean priests of Persia. Shapur had forbidden the persecution of religious groups, among them the Manichaeans. For this reason the Romans suspected that they were sympathetic towards the Persians, possibly forming a fifth column in the Roman provinces of the east. In particular it was suspected that they were the agitators behind the Egyptian revolts. Nothing specific was done to eradicate them until 302 when Diocletian visited Egypt. He issued an edict against the Manichaeans that same year. The text is known; how it was put into effect is not elucidated.[47]

From the Manichaeans Imperial attention turned to the Christians. For some years there had been isolated examples of Christian intransigence, particularly with regard to the army. In 295 a certain Maximilian appeared before the proconsul of Africa because he refused to enlist in the army; a purge of the army was attempted to remove any Christians who might refuse duty. It was said that Galerius reduced Christian officers to the ranks. If there was such a purge it was not total, nor could it prevent enlisted soldiers from converting to the new religion, for in 298 a Christian serving in the army, a centurion named Marcellus, refused to take part in the celebrations in honour of Maximian, which presumably involved sacrifice to the Emperors as gods, or to Jupiter and Hercules. This matter of sacrifice became the litmus test of a Christian's attitude to Imperial rule. Unwillingness to serve in the army was subversive enough, and it seemed that there was no way round this problem. If it spread, recruitment for the armies all over the Empire would be compromised, and if the Christians were to be officially excused from military service there was nothing to stop those whose resolve was already weakening about military life to undergo sudden conversion, and then refuse to serve. The universal principle of sacrifice to the chief gods of Rome was also dangerously compromised. Most religious groups who were accustomed to the worship of several gods, or aspects of gods under different names, would not find any difficulty in sacrificing to the Emperor or to the gods of Rome; the Christians, unfortunately, could not tolerate gods other than their own, and their missionary spirit meant that they were not content to live quietly in the background without drawing attention to themselves. A conflict was inevitable.[48]

At the beginning of the fourth century the Emperors applied themselves to eradicating Christianity. The blame for the anti-Christian policy is laid at Galerius' door. He was in a strong position after his victories in the east and on the Danube, and was said to have been violently anti-Christian throughout his career. Those who wish to exonerate Diocletian fall back on the assumption that he merely yielded to pressure from Galerius, and as the successive edicts grew in severity Diocletian was too ill to control his Caesar's enthusiasm. The first edict was timed for 23 February 303, the festival of the Terminalia at Nicomedia. The church was destroyed and panic ensued in the city. Mysterious fires broke out twice in the Imperial palace, and Galerius ostentatiously left the city rather than be murdered by the Christians. Others said that he had started the fires himself to put the blame on the Christians and provide the excuse for persecuting them. So far the persecution was unfocused, but in the summer of 303 another edict was issued aimed at the clergy, who were to be imprisoned. When the prisons were overflowing and it was clear that it was impossible to carry out the terms of the edict, a third one was issued ordering compulsory sacrifice to the gods. The diehards would be weeded out, or they would have been if the terms of the edict had been strenuously applied over the whole Empire. The west escaped lightly because Maximian limited his efforts to closing churches and confiscating books, and Constantius did even less to eradicate Christians. No one was executed. Constantius and Maximian did not share Galerius' zeal for burning people alive, a penchant for persuasion that Diocletian apparently managed to avert in his Caesar. The uneven treatment of the Christians ensured that the edict could never achieve its goal; it was enforced rigorously in some parts of the Empire where enthusiasts in positions of power tried to force Christians to sacrifice by all manner of unspeakable tortures, lovingly described by Eusebius and Lactantius. Elsewhere officials told the Emperors what they wanted to hear, reporting that everyone had sacrificed without bothering to check, and heroic acts were recorded where pagans sheltered Christians from the worst of the persecution. At the time of Diocletian's retirement, the Christian problem had not been solved.[49]

CONSTANTINE: THE EMPIRE RESHAPED

From 305, when Diocletian abdicated, until Constantine became sole Emperor, and indeed throughout Constantine's reign, recorded history depends almost totally upon the version that this ambitious ruler endorsed, little tempered by alternative sources. Strict chronology is not easy to ascertain, so cause and effect likewise cannot always be established. Some cardinal facts are obscure, for instance no one knows exactly when Diocletian died, and although he ceased to play a major part in the political arena after his abdication, his presence influenced Galerius sufficiently to invite him to the conference at Carnuntum in 308, where he tried to persuade him to take power again, or at least to arbitrate among the rival factions that had grown up in the few years that had elapsed since the two Augusti had retired.[50]

When the two new Caesars were proclaimed in 305, Constantine was at the court of Galerius at Nicomedia. His father Constantius was about to start his British campaign, and allegedly sent for his son because he was ill; this may be true, since Constantius was dead by the next year. Galerius seemed reluctant at first to release Constantine, no doubt reasoning that without his hold on Constantius' son he would have no bargaining power with his colleague. Constantine for his part treated his release with deep suspicion, and proceeded as fast as he could to the west. It is alleged that he melodramatically killed or maimed all the horses whenever he changed to fresh mounts at posting stations so that he could not be pursued. It is indicative of the man. Perhaps he had already developed an inflated sense of his own importance, or was prepared to go to elaborate lengths to throw

Figure 31 Constantius Caesar receives the submission of London after his campaign in Britain. The legend on the reverse states immodestly that Constantius is the Restorer of the Eternal Light (REDDITOR LUCIS AETERNAE). Gold 10-aureus piece from the Trier mint, issued in 296. (Drawn by Trish Boyle.)

blame onto Galerius for putting his life at risk. It is uncertain to what degree he thought that he was in danger.[51]

The rise to power of Constantine

Constantine arrived at his father's camp on the northern coast of Gaul, just as the British campaign was about to begin. Father and son proceeded to the far north of the island, but archaeology has little to show for this campaign. Only very slight traces of Constantius' progress are visible, and none of the many temporary camps in Scotland have been authoritatively assigned to this campaign. The similarities with Severus' British wars have been highlighted by several authors, especially since both Emperors took their sons with them, and both died at York. The reasons for the war and what Constantius may have achieved in Britain is overshadowed by the fact that the army declared Constantine Emperor in July 306, perhaps with a little encouragement from Constantius, and not a little from Constantine himself. The hereditary principle had not died out as far as the army was concerned and Constantine was not about to pass up the opportunity and nobly revert to the Tetrarchic principle of non-dynastic promotion, which might eventually fall to him, all in good time, if circumstances and ability warranted it. He did not have the time to risk all that, and probably always intended to become Emperor by whatever means were made available to him. He tried to reconcile his new status with Galerius, and wrote to him to say that he had no choice but to concur with the wishes of the troops. Galerius compromised and made him Caesar; Constantine acquiesced. His fortunes were to rise and fall in the same fashion once more before he became Emperor, but he had made it to the first rung of the Imperial ladder, and bided his time.[52]

Complications arose in October 306 when Maxentius, the son of Maximian, was declared Emperor in Rome itself, gaining much support from senators and the Praetorians. There followed a general mêlée and scramble for survival over the next few years. Alliances were made, broken, and made again. Galerius sent Severus to retrieve the situation, while he and Maximinus looked on from their respective parts of the Empire. Maximian reappeared, either on his own initiative, or perhaps he was invited to become Emperor again by his son; both versions are relayed in the sources, but the truth may have involved an amalgamation of the two. Severus failed to dislodge Maxentius, and was besieged in Ravenna, soon to be forced to kill himself. Constantine cannot have failed to note that there was one down and four to go. Even Galerius, the conqueror of the Persians, could not prevail against Maxentius in Rome, which perhaps attests to the effectiveness of Aurelian's walls. Galerius returned to his provinces, leaving Italy in the hands of Maxentius. Allegiances shifted in the west. When Maximian offered Constantine an alliance cemented by the hand of his daughter Fausta, the two concluded an amicable agreement. It is said that Maximian

170

promised to make Constantine Augustus. This may have been the clinching factor, though Constantine will have known perfectly well that the path would not be smooth, leading to conflict with Galerius and Maximinus, or Maxentius, or all of them, at some point in the future. Some authors dispute the fact that Constantine became Augustus under Maximian, but in the end his title does not affect the power he had attained and was steadily accruing.[53]

On the occasion of Constantine's marriage to Fausta in 307, probably in September, the panegyric to him and Maximian was pronounced at Trier. At this stage Maximian was the senior partner, and the author of the panegyric glossed over the fact that according to the Diocletianic plan he was not supposed to be Augustus at all; in fact he was nothing more than a usurper, so Constantine's dependence upon him, for such it was, cast a dubious light on his career. He disassociated himself from these less than perfect beginnings as soon as opportunity arose. Maximian was his own worst enemy, and some of his actions are not easy to explain, except in so far as he had clearly not renounced the desire for power when he abdicated. After Galerius left Italy Maximian and his son quarrelled. Maximian tried to depose his son, but had reckoned without the support that Maxentius could call upon in Rome and ended by fleeing himself, heading for Constantine's court at Trier. For some time, Constantine remained in northern Gaul, attending to the Rhine frontier. A campaign or campaigns against the Bructeri are recorded, and there was activity at Cologne where Constantine built a bridge; he had also perhaps begun to build the fort opposite the city at Deutz, though the archaeological evidence suggests that it belongs to the period after the battle of the Milvian Bridge in 312.[54]

The Carnuntum conference in 308

While Constantine and Maximian were in Gaul, Galerius arranged the famous meeting at Carnuntum which took place on 11 November 308. An inscription set up in the Mithraeum at Carnuntum records the fact that the Emperors were reunited. The Tetrarchic system was repaired, and adjustments were made that were unfortunately to have no long-term effects. Diocletian would not be persuaded to rule the Empire again; this is the occasion of the famous quotation, when he said he gained more enjoyment from growing cabbages in his retirement. Rome certainly did not take second place to cabbages in Maximian's ideology, but he was forced to retire once again. Constantine was relegated to the position of Caesar, along with Maximinus. The vacant slot for another Augustus was taken by Licinius, a colleague of Galerius'. Maximinus was not happy with this decision, and presumably nor was Constantine, who never ceased to style himself Augustus. Maxentius was not consulted because he was considered a rank outsider.[55]

The demise of Maximian and Maxentius

By 310, Constantine had rid himself of Maximian, who had allegedly begun to intrigue against him. Constantine marched to southern Gaul and put his erstwhile ally under siege at Marseilles. Maximian died in suspicious circumstances that were passed off as suicide. That was two down, but with the elevation of Licinius there were still four to go. Diocletian was excluded because he was a sick man, probably without influence since he had declared himself uninterested in becoming Emperor again. Constantine now purged himself of all connection with Maximian and sought for more respectable ancestry, insisting on the divinity of his father Constantius, and, by some inexplicable convoluted reckoning, he attached himself to the house of Claudius Gothicus. The Tetrarchic principles were flouted in favour of hereditary power, which had a longer history. Licinius countered by attaching himself to the house of Philip the Arab. At about the same time as he created his new lineage, Constantine also departed from the Jovian–Herculean religious support structure, and turned instead to Apollo, and increasingly to Sol Invictus as Aurelian had done. Constantine was emerging as an independent entity.[56]

Fate now took a hand in the inexorable rise of Constantine. It is possible that Diocletian died in 311; Lactantius' statement can interpreted to support this date. There is no absolute certainty, and some scholars prefer the date of 313, or even 316, but the later date is less likely; when Licinius ordered the deaths of Diocletian's daughter Valeria and his wife Prisca at the end of 313 or in 314, it is more than probable that Diocletian was already dead. It is well attested that Galerius fell ill and died in 311, probably in April or May. Before he expired he reversed the persecution of the Christians, issuing the edict of toleration that restored Christian places of worship and reinstated the clergy. Only Maximinus refused to obey the edict, and continued to persecute Christians as before. By 311, therefore, Constantine could count three down, and three to go; Severus, Maximian, and now Galerius were all dead. The surviving contestants, Licinius, Maximinus and Maxentius, were powerful enough and all commanded armies, but fortunately for Constantine they were far from united against him. None of the four rulers of the Roman world trusted each other, so there was a period of watchful suspicion while they decided who would ally with whom. Licinius was betrothed to Constantine's half-sister Constantia, so in theory he was allied to Constantine, but if he suddenly threw in his lot with either of the other two the balance would tilt, so Constantine took action as soon as he could. He turned his attention first to Italy in 312. Maxentius had extended his power and now, in addition to Italy, he effectively ruled the African provinces and had their agricultural resources at his disposal. After securing the Rhine, Constantine mobilised against him before he could gain any further powers. The causes of the civil war are in reality the intolerance of

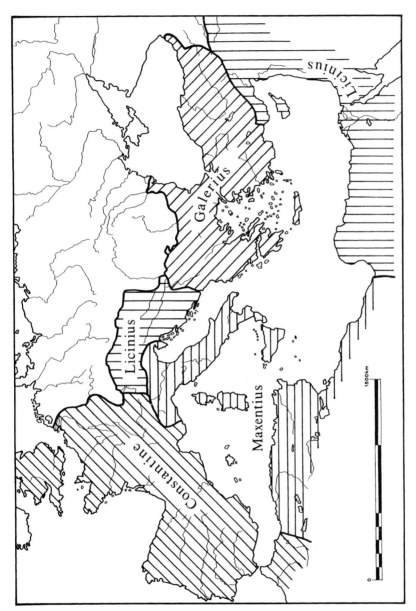

Figure 32 Map showing the Empire divided between Constantine, Maxentius, Galerius and Licinius. (Drawn by Graeme Stobbs.)

one Emperor for the other, and the grudges they held. Even though he had quarrelled with his father, Maxentius wanted to avenge his death, since Maximian had more than likely been murdered by Constantine. On the other hand it was clear to contemporaries that Constantine wanted to rule the Empire, so he now represented himself as the saviour of Rome from the tyrant who was after all a usurper. He marched from Gaul to the Alps with a conglomerate army that has never been fully documented, smashing through the troops sent to guard the Alpine passes by Pompeianus, Maxentius' Praetorian Prefect. He stormed the town of Susa (ancient Segusio) where Maxentius had placed a garrison, but his own troops were held back and there was no bloody massacre or looting. It was an important point, and attests to Constantine's iron authority and command of his soldiers. This was going to be portrayed as a war to save Rome and the Empire from the unsuitable elements who had taken control, so it would have been extremely detrimental to the cause to behave in a worse fashion that the supposed tyrant Maxentius. At Turin where Constantine's troops defeated the guard that Maxentius had placed there, the town was once again spared. Assured of lenient treatment, other towns welcomed Constantine. Milan opened its gates to him. His eventual arrival at Rome was assured.[57]

Figure 33 Constantine wearing a laurel wreath depicted with a radiate crowned Sol, on a gold piece worth 10 solidi from Ticinum minted in 313. He assumes Sol's title INVICTUS and also styles himself MAXIMUS AUGUSTUS, a title voted to him by the Senate, leaving no doubt about his seniority; on the reverse, he acknowledges Licinius by the legend FELIX ADVENTUS AUGG NN, indicating that two Emperors share the Imperial power. The coin celebrates his victorious entry into Rome after the defeat of Maxentius. Though it was claimed that Constantine was persuaded towards Christianity by his vision of the cross, or of Christian symbols, before the battle of the Milvian Bridge, there is no reference on this coin. (Drawn by Trish Boyle.)

174

Maxentius decided to meet him outside the city, even though he had strengthened the Aurelian fortifications. It was a mistake to let Constantine get so far without stopping him, and then when he had arrived it was a mistake to offer battle so soon; but Maxentius had already lost some of his popularity, despite his studied promotion of Roman values and traditions, partly because his building programme was proving expensive. If he had risked a siege of Rome he would merely have lost even more support in proportion to the length of time the siege went on, and when the food was running out and Constantine offered a better choice, his fate would have been sealed. So Maxentius met Constantine at the battle of the Milvian Bridge and lost. His troops were backed into the Tiber and he was drowned along with many of the soldiers. His death was convenient because now that he was removed Constantine could portray him as a tyrant, and more importantly everyone could choose to believe the propaganda without the embarrassing living reminder that he or she was betraying the erstwhile Emperor. Besides there was an inevitability about it all; Constantine's victory was god-given, though which god had given it was not as apparent at first as it later became. The authenticity or otherwise of Constantine's Christian vision before the battle will never be proven. The tales are too deeply embedded in Christian iconography to be uprooted now by modern speculation, and such a pastime is doomed to failure because the various versions of what he saw and when he saw it are so inconsistent; they range from a simple cross in the sky some days before the battle, to a complicated chi-rho symbol, combining the first two Greek letters X and P of Christ's name, seen or dreamed on the night before the battle. Allegedly he was informed that in this sign he would conquer, and allegedly he ordered the soldiers to put this Christian device on their shields, which conjures up the scenario of lots of soldiers milling about looking for some paint when they could have been getting a good night's sleep. Veracity is not the important point; it is the legend and the use that Constantine made of it that count, because he reshaped the Roman Empire and, by extension, the western world.[58]

The elimination of Maximinus and Licinius

Shortly after the battle, when he was established in Rome, having conciliated as many groups as possible with promises that he was just as Roman as other Emperors, Constantine wrote to Maximinus to try to persuade him to end the persecution of the Christians in his territories. His letters were probably ineffective. Maximinus was steadily marginalised as Constantine and Licinius drew closer together. Early in 313 the two met at Milan, where Constantine's half-sister was married to Licinius, and an edict was issued declaring toleration of all religions. Licinius' part in this undertaking is overshadowed by the glory of Constantine's later reign, and because towards the end of his life Licinius resorted to persecution of the Christians again, but in 313 he deserved as much credit as his brother-in-law.[59]

Equality was never in Constantine's personal vocabulary for long; in his own territories inscriptions made it clear that he was the senior Emperor, and he began to describe himself as Maximus Augustus, or at least he made no move to prevent others from addressing him as such. Licinius acquiesced, perhaps because he thought that he could eliminate Maximinus and build up a power base in the east that would secure him against anything that Constantine could put into effect against him. He picked a fight with Maximinus because the latter had invaded Thrace; Licinius won the victory and took over Maximinus' provinces. He also made sure that few of Maximinus' family or adherents survived; no risk of any resurgence in his name was to be countenanced, and whilst he was about this grisly business Licinius seems to have decided to remove any possibility that Diocletian's or Galerius' families might make a bid for power. Whatever his reasons, in 313 or perhaps in 314, Diocletian's daughter Valeria, the widow of Galerius, and Prisca, Diocletian's widow, were killed. Maximinus fled to Tarsus and committed suicide. Constantine hardly needed to count now; there was only one main rival.[60]

Relations remained stable enough through the following years. In 315 Constantine celebrated his ten-year rule. The festivities of the *decennalia* were crowned by the dedication of the arch of Constantine, still visible in Rome near to the Colosseum. It was magnificent but somewhat second hand, in that some of the sculptures were borrowed from other monuments. The text outlines Constantine's achievements, in phrases not unlike the beginning of the *Res Gestae* of the first Augustus, who advertised the fact that at the age of nineteen he had raised his own army to save the Republic from faction; Constantine attributes his success to inspiration of the divinity and his own noble-mindedness, by which he was enabled to save the Republic from the tyrant and his faction. This refers to Maxentius, but could just as well be taken as indicative of any other dissenting elements. Consolidation of his power was achieved in the west. There remained the east, and Licinius. Constantine waited upon events until 316, when he appointed his brother-in-law Bassianus as his Caesar. This man's brother Senecio was a friend of Licinius, and Constantine probably used this relationship to weave a little intrigue. It was said that there was a plot against him, engineered perhaps by Senecio, perhaps by Bassianus, possibly with the support or encouragement of Licinius. It was all rather mysterious, no doubt by design to increase the aura of subterfuge. Bassianus was executed, and Constantine asked Licinius to surrender Senecio. This was the test of his loyalty, perhaps; he refused to hand him over. Manoeuvring began. Licinius moved up with his army to the borders with Constantine's territories. He appointed an Augustus of his own called Valens. The inevitable war resulted in defeat for Licinius, and a compromise. He ceded territories to Constantine, the frontier province of Pannonia, part of Moesia, and part of the Balkans. The unfortunate Valens was eliminated, and in his place three Caesars were appointed, two of them the sons of Constantine, the fourteen-year-old Crispus, the son of his first wife, and the infant Constantine; Licinius' son, not yet two years old, became Licinius Caesar. The hereditary principle was restated, since these Caesars could not yet play any part in government as the Tetrarchic Caesars had done.[61]

Sole rule for Constantine was now not far away. From 317 to 323 there was a sort of entente cordiale while each Emperor attended to his own domains, but consulships were shared. In 318 Licinius and Crispus were consuls, and in 319 the young Constantine and the young Licinius shared the honour. During the same year, Constantine was in the Danube provinces while his son Crispus campaigned against the Franks on the Rhine. It seemed as though the Tetrarchic system might prevail after all. Licinius departed from Constantine's plan when he began to persecute the Christians, which gave Constantine the opportunity to champion their cause. Relations deteriorated, and when Constantine crossed the boundaries of his own territories into Thrace while he was campaigning against the Goths in 323, Licinius reacted badly, perhaps because he thought that Constantine was about to launch an invasion. His predilection for taking over territory had already been revealed in 317. By way of response, Constantine was reasonable; he said that he had defeated the Goths and thrown them back across the Danube, so the methods by which he had accomplished this were less important than the result. On the face of it, he was right; he and Licinius were after all supposed to be working for the same firm called the Roman Empire.[62]

Preparations for war escalated; Licinius appointed yet another Augustus, Martianus, as he had done in 317. His reasons may have been to provide himself with administrative assistance, freeing him to concentrate on the war, but it is notable that Constantine kept any promotions within the family, giving the command of his fleet to his son Crispus. Licinius and Constantine faced each other at last in July 324 at Adrianople. Licinius was defeated and fled to Byzantium, but Constantine's fleet under Crispus forced its way through the Hellespont, threatening him with blockade or capture, so he moved on. The final battle was another victory for Constantine at Chrysopolis, opposite Byzantium. Licinius' wife Constantia persuaded him that her half-brother would be merciful, and he surrendered. The terms were that he ceded all his territories to Constantine in return for a life of leisure under house arrest. The promise lasted for some months, then Licinius and his son, and Martianus, were killed. It had taken nearly two decades for Constantine to extend his rule over the whole Empire. His path had not been easy or direct, and there had been many casualties, but he had achieved sole rule. From 324 the name of Constantine is almost a synonym for autocracy.[63]

From *Roma aeterna* to *Roma altera*

In the next decade Constantine brought together all the threads of the mid-third-century developments, of the adaptations of Gallienus and of the Diocletianic and Tetrarchic innovations, and created a new world. Once he had all the Empire under his control, Constantine could rewrite his origins, his achievements, and his policies. His press agents were Christian writers, notably Lactantius, who wrote *de Mortibus Persecutorum* probably before 314 and certainly before the defeat of Licinius; and Eusebius, who wrote his *History of the Church* at around the time of the defeat of Licinius, and then the *Life of Constantine*, which was completed after Constantine's death. Several authors have noted the change of tone concerning Licinius in Eusebius' *History of the Church*, where Constantine's rival is portrayed in a more favourable light before 324 and in an inimical fashion thereafter. Constantine's promotion of the Christian Church is his most enduring achievement, and the one that has received the most attention from the ancient authors and many modern scholars. His first allegiance to a single god, Sol Invictus, never faded entirely, so it is a matter of opinion whether he believed in the Christian message or whether he used it for his own ends. To some authors he was a true convert to the Christian faith, and to others he wished only for some kind of unifying force and used Christianity to achieve it, but since the early Church was rent by schisms from its infancy it was not perhaps the most effective unifying force that he could have chosen. Constantine took an active part in the councils and synods of the Church, the most famous being the Council of Nicaea in 325, which at first seemed to produce all the answers to thorny questions of doctrine and to quell the factions within the Church, bringing about the hoped for unity. It did not prove wholly successful on this score, though the Nicene creed still forms the basis of Christian belief. The Church was favoured by Constantine and used by him, but it never emerged from a position of dependence on him. Though he allowed the clergy considerable freedom he remained the master while calling himself the servant; if he had changed his mind, he still had the power to outlaw Christianity, and would probably have succeeded. The fact that he did not do so indicates that the Church gave him what he wanted. In return he encouraged the foundation of Christian churches; most new foundations were on Imperial lands.[64]

His social policies were bound up with his attitude towards the Christians. He exempted the clergy from their municipal obligations, while at the same time tightening his hold on those decurions who were eligible to serve. Such a policy was divisive and bound to cause resentment, especially since more and more people sought a way out of their municipal burdens by entering the Church, reducing still further the number of people who could serve their communities in the practical sense rather than the spiritual sense. Whilst paganism was not stamped out and did not die of its own accord, the officially sanctioned state religion was Christianity, which meant that personal alliances and networks could be built up within Christian circles in the Imperial administration. Belonging to the group would be seen as a distinct advantage. It has been suggested that as a means of conciliating the pagan aristocracy of the Empire, Constantine created new senators, bestowing senatorial rank without the obligation to live in Rome or to attend meetings of the Senate. Rank and privilege rather than a share in the government of the Empire had contented many senators for generations. Constantine employed these senators as prefects of Rome; he appointed them as governors of the consular provinces, and as *correctores* in Italy. Gradually, long after Constantine's death, the equestrian class which had risen to prominence under Hadrian and Severus, was eclipsed by the new aristocracy, but it took a long time, and Constantine did not alter the arrangements that Diocletian had made with regard to the provinces. He did not attempt a full-scale removal of the equestrians as governors and did not radically alter provincial boundaries. The large numbers of experienced personnel demanded for the government of the provinces and command of the armies made it unlikely that he could turn his back on equestrians as a source of supply. Perhaps for similar reasons he did nothing to halt or reform the crystallisation of professions; his policies did not include liberating the inhabitants of the Empire from their hereditary obligations. The *coloni* continued their descent from free men to virtual slaves.[65]

The army was a different matter. There he did make some changes, though controversy still reigns over who created the mobile field armies. The balance of probability is that Constantine remoulded Diocletian's armies and developed something new. The pagan author Zosimus accused Constantine of destroying Diocletian's system, because the latter had secured the frontiers by putting the troops back into their forts, while Constantine took the troops away again and put them into the cities, where they were not needed in the first place. That was perhaps how it seemed to contemporary observers as the mobile cavalry armies (*comitatenses*) and the more static frontier armies (*limitanei*) were developed. The new deployment of the armed forces was reflected in the new military commands, the *magister equitum* in command of the cavalry and the *magister peditum* in command of the infantry. Constantine's contribution to the protection of the Empire was not radically altered by his successors.[66]

The evolved central administration was Constantine's contribution to the government of the Empire. The Praetorian Prefects had already been given tremendous responsibilities in the administration of the Empire, and under Constantine they lost all their military functions. The Praetorian Guard was abolished after the battle of the Milvian Bridge, and replaced with a new bodyguard called the *scholae*, first established by Diocletian. This bodyguard was not commanded by the Praetorian Prefects, but by the chief of the civil administration, the *magister officiorum*, who was in charge of all the departments of the administration.[67]

Figure 34 Colossal head of Constantine, originally from a seated statue of which only fragments remain. It is now in the courtyard of the Palazzo dei Conservatori in Rome.
Constantine wears a detached other-worldly expression, elevated above normal
humanity, preparing for divinity. (Photo David Brearley.)

Apart from introducing Christianity as the official religion Constantine's
next most famous or notorious innovation was to reinvent Rome in the east,
at Byzantium. It was not a complete surprise since the Emperors had not
lived in Rome for many decades, and some of the short-lived Emperors never
even saw the capital city. New capitals had been established at different
cities nearer to the frontiers at Trier, Milan, Sirmium and Nicomedia; Constantine had chosen Serdica (Sofia) as his residence, and now his choice was
Byzantium. Strategically this city offered tremendous advantages. It was
eminently defensible; Septimius Severus had reduced it only after a long
siege. Supplies could be brought in directly by sea, unlike Rome which had
to be supplied from the port of Ostia. And it was close to the eastern

180

provinces and the Danube; these were prime requirements for defence of the Empire. Byzantium officially became the city of Constantine, Constantinople, in 330, but there is evidence that it was already labelled *altera Roma* at least four years before the official foundation date. So far the establishment of yet another Imperial headquarters only imitated what had happened in other provinces; in itself it was not a revolutionary move. What was revolutionary was that Constantine transported to his new city the whole of the government administrative machinery. He gave his new capital a Senate, a Forum, everything that mirrored Rome itself. In Italy there was a shadow of what had gone before. Senators still lived out their lives in Rome, debates were still held in the Senate House, and some senators took up provincial posts. But the government of the Empire was no longer centred on Rome. It was the concept, not the actuality, that was shocking. For many years the administrative machinery had not been located in Rome, but lumbered after the Emperor wherever he was; as Herodian recognised at the beginning of the third century, Rome was where the Emperor was. The citizens of Rome perhaps did not feel the absence of the central government until it was permanently relocated in another city at the eastern end of the Empire, and then it probably seemed catastrophic. Rome declined in the physical realm, and became a backwater remote from the action, the repository of nearly eleven centuries of memories. But in the end, Rome did not lie down quietly and die. The new Christian Empire revolved around Constantinople, but today it is the Roman Church. After a long and distinguished history at the centre of the Byzantine Empire, Constantinople survived as a city, while Rome still survives as an idea. Rome is everywhere in the ideology and the infrastructure underpinning the fabric of western society.[68]

5

BEYOND THE NORTHERN FRONTIERS

INTRODUCTION: THE IMAGE OF THE 'BARBARIANS'

First, the obligatory note on terminology. The choice of descriptive names for the peoples beyond the frontiers is subject to all kinds of debates under several headings. Some scholars prefer the Latin *gens* to identify a specific people, usually with the cautionary footnote about the problems of trying to impose a close definition on an entity so diverse as to defy such a process. In this work, the similarly imprecise words 'tribe', 'tribesmen' and 'peoples' are used where others would employ *gens*. On a more emotive issue, the use of the term 'barbarians' has to be explained. It has acquired an unsavoury aspect nowadays. Its derogatory tone implies inferiority, or at least an inherent value judgement condoning inequality, separating acceptable groups of people (us) from unacceptable groups (them). Throughout history, such ideology has usually meant that the latter groups (them) have no share in the same rights and benefits as the former (us), which in turn implies that the unacceptable groups can be exploited or disposed of in any manner currently fashionable among the acceptable ones. Superiority is a comfortable human goal, but it is rarely achieved by striving ever onwards and ever upwards, allowing room for all people to achieve the same goal; instead it is usually achieved spuriously by self-delusion, by finding another group to look down upon, sometimes within the community, but more often outside it. In the Roman world there were many sub-groups of 'us' and 'them' whose interests were in conflict with each other, besides the wider-ranging 'us' and 'them' of the Romans and the so-called barbarians, and superimposed on the contemporary Roman view there is the modern view, which by force of circumstance must milk the available evidence and fill in the gaps in order to reconstruct the mindset of the Romans and their neighbours. The relationship between the Romans and the barbarians has been variously depicted according to fashions of time or place, from the days of Julius Caesar to our own era. When writing about any historical period it is impossible to shake off every vestige of the all-enveloping mantle of contemporary attitudes to

182

produce an absolutely impartial account. Judgements creep in, evaluations are formed, all based on upbringing and subjective experiences. Thus there are many subtly different barbarian and Roman worlds in the literature of the last two centuries.[1]

Not so very long ago, authors could use the word 'barbarians' with impunity, without regard for the connotations outlined above; the residual trappings of imperialism and colonialism were deeply embedded, to the point where the subtler shades of meaning were not even noticed or could be ignored. The word itself is a Greek invention sneeringly applied to outsiders who could not speak Greek, but made unintelligible bar-bar-bar sounds instead. The concept has not entirely died out in modern life, of course. It is still an accepted ploy for speakers of one language to raise a laugh by reproducing the sounds made by speakers of a different language, but hopefully the process ceases with the vaudeville act and stops short of racism. The Romans readily adopted the description 'barbarian' and applied it in the same spirit as the Greeks to anyone who was not Roman, no matter where the so-called outsiders originated, or the level of civilisation they represented. As has been pointed out, to the Romans, the King of Parthia was a barbarian. Aided by popular culture in the form of novels, films and free imagination, modern understanding of 'barbarians' immediately conjures up a picture of wild tribesmen, inevitably from the northern regions, mostly long-haired, possibly fur-clad, trousered, axe-wielding, sword-wielding, intent on destruction, sweeping all before them in murderous raids. Cartoons and jokes about a spot of pillage and rape do nothing to dispel this image; despite their detachment from reality, they somehow confirm that rape and pillage was what barbarians did best, all the time. Historians and archaeologists must keep on repeating that although destruction, pillage and rape are definitely attested, that was not *all* that the barbarians did, all the time. Furthermore, though there is a tremendous emphasis on the northern tribes, there were other groups of people all round the Empire who were equally mobile and just as potentially dangerous. All these tribes surrounding the Roman Empire, whoever they were, consisted of people like anyone else, with individual identities, names and families, personal and corporate histories, hopes and ambitions, fears and disappointments. At the same time, whatever modern state-of-the-art phraseology is employed to put this wider message across, there is no escaping the fact that the Romans called the tribes *barbari*, and from the third century onwards they labelled the lands beyond the frontiers *barbaricum*. Exercises in modern semantics will not alter these facts. All that has changed is the current estimation of the attitude of the Romans to the barbarians, and whether they were justified or not in their sometimes brutal treatment of the tribes. The pendulum of opinion has still not come to rest impartially in the middle; as Dauge points out, the current elevation of the so-called barbarians, timely though it is, has been achieved at the expense of the Romans, who are cast as the villains.

Until all the peoples inside and outside the Roman Empire are regarded as equal but different from each other, it will be impossible to avoid taking sides.[2]

ROMANS AND NATIVES

A more profitable line of enquiry would be to try to establish precisely what the Romans themselves meant by these terms *barbari* and *barbaricum*. This is yet another subject for debate. The use of any word changes over time, acquiring different attributes and subtle nuances as time goes on, so it is likely that the words conveyed different ideas to different peoples at different times in the Roman Empire. One reason why the Romans used the generic term *barbari* to describe the peoples beyond the Empire was the lack of a long-term national identity among the tribes, in the way in which modern nations understand it. Tribes were not static in either the territorial or genealogical sense. Whole peoples known to Caesar or Tacitus either disappeared or were subsumed by other tribes by the third century. Affiliations could change rapidly, and so could territorial location, either by migration or by slow encroachment on new lands, successively cultivated and then abandoned. Caesar thought this was an annual process. He may have witnessed such annual movements, but what he saw perhaps does not apply to all peoples at all times. If the soils were not exhausted and there were no other pressures, there was probably no movement of settlers. Surplus population may have moved on from time to time, thereby extending the tribe's territorial location.[3]

There were no new tribes as such, only new combinations and new names for groups of people, which belies the supposed continuity and the expected links between the older and more recent groupings. This fluidity made it difficult for the inhabitants of an established state such as Rome, accustomed as they were to fixed boundaries and fixed names, to apply anything other than broad general descriptive terms to collections of peoples, whose complicated relationships probably did not interest them in the slightest. They knew of 'Germania' covering very roughly the lands beyond the Rhine, and 'Sarmatia' beyond the Danube, but where one shaded off into the other was probably only a matter of opinion. Similarly the names of peoples sometimes merged, without regard to tribal origin. In the eastern parts of the Empire the Sarmatians were often called Scythians, a name which passed into widespread use in the later Empire, applied to all and sundry, no matter what the tribal affiliations of the peoples so described. Uncertainty over tribal names is not confined to the literary record; it enters the epigraphic sphere as well. An altar to Victory found in 1992 in Augsburg refers to barbarians of the tribe of Semnones or Iouthungi (*ob barbaros gentis Semnonum sive Iouthungorum*).[4]

On the most simplistic level in Roman terminology, *barbari* meant, as it always did, those who were not Romans, and *barbaricum* meant 'out there', obviating the need to be specific about an area which probably did not have a firmly established regional name. Territory beyond the frontiers was labelled *barbaricum* much more frequently from the third century onwards, and perhaps reflects the fact that native unrest had disrupted the patterns of settlement and tribal groupings that the Romans knew without yet replacing those patterns with anything concrete or stable. There need not necessarily be any qualitative judgement inherent in the term *barbari* apart from the intention to highlight the non-Roman character of the peoples so described. If a qualitative or judgemental aspect were required, then the Romans had many other words with which to convey ferocity, savagery, brutality, or any of the other connotations with which modern people imbue the description 'barbarian'. There was a whole arsenal of *topoi* with which to describe the barbarians, derived from Rome's long past. The memory of the Gauls and their invasion of Italy in the fourth century BC never faded, nor did the terrible insecurity imposed by the migrations of the Cimbri and Teutones. It is to Rome's credit that she did not allow those memories to colour all her dealings with the tribes beyond the frontiers.[5]

By the mid-third century the Romans had acquired long experience of dealing with the various native peoples surrounding their Empire. Throughout the centuries from the foundation of Rome there had been an awareness, sometimes vague and shadowy, sometimes rather more vivid, of the tribes from the north, whose sudden movements and tremendous fighting force were terrifying, all the more so because they were unpredictable. Romans and tribesmen met on several occasions, so by the third century there had been a long time for the perception of the barbarians to sink in. Some of the early chroniclers labelled the tribes 'plunderers', because that was all they saw or heard of them. But not all the barbarians were tarred with the same brush and treated as enemies. Tacitus delineated the sterling qualities of the Germanic peoples, whose customs and morals he considered highly commendable, though of course he used the morality of the Germans as a telling contrast with the highly immoral Romans of his own day; praising one community, Tacitus roundly condemned another by mere inference, without actually having to say it all. His work was designed to be read out loud, performed almost, and he was making a statement to a Roman audience, not a Germanic one.[6]

Roman perception of the tribes beyond her frontiers was not blindly monolithic or prejudiced. Rome was capable of judging each case on its merits. Dio considered that the barbarians were adaptable and would readily adopt Roman ways, so that assimilation into the Empire was possible. He had witnessed the influx of rough-looking barbarian soldiers into Rome, and though he did not approve of their appearance he was not totally prejudiced against them. The superiority of Roman culture was self-evident to him;

there was no question of meeting the natives half way. Romans had always assumed this superior attitude, whilst extracting what they wanted. From the earliest times in the expanding Roman world, the tribesmen were employed by the Romans as part of their armies. Native leaders were acknowledged and promoted, and given Latinised names, and the particular military specialisms of their followers were welcomed. The Gauls provided excellent horsemen, and so did the Numidians who rode without the use of elaborate harness. In the east, the expertise of the Syrian and Palmyrene archers was immediately recognised and readily employed. The Gallic Emperor Postumus employed Franks to fight invading Franks; in Britain, Carausius and Allectus employed them against raiders from the sea. Sometimes Alamanni and Franks combined to raid the Empire, but at other times they co-operated with Rome against each other. Where there was opportunity or need, Rome employed tribesmen, sometimes integrating them into their army units, at others for shorter periods, without imposing rigid uniformity upon them. In the later Empire, as in the very early Empire, tribesmen fought under their own leaders with their own weapons. For the most part, the native peoples in Rome's employ were loyal and served her well, but the exceptions when rebellions broke out have received much more attention and therefore tend to obscure the more successful encounters between Romans and tribesmen. The reputation of the Roman government was not always stainless, but nor was it entirely despicable. Ruthless and exploitative at times, Rome could also be magnanimous and tolerant, provided of course that she was always in supreme command. This predominant factor should be borne in mind when examining the theory that Roman rule in the west collapsed as a direct result of the progressive barbarisation of the army. It is true that from the third century onwards the Roman army underwent changes culminating in the reforms of Diocletian and Constantine, and it is also true that tribesmen were increasingly employed in these successive armies, but there is no need to charge Rome with criminal negligence in allowing her armies to be swamped out of existence by barbarians, almost by accident, because no one could think of anything better. The Romans had always employed natives in their armies, so in the third and fourth centuries they were merely following and developing long-established practice in the continued use of natives. The resultant armies were different from the classic first-century armies, but were not necessarily any less effective or any less loyal.[7]

Study of the native peoples on the periphery of the Empire has gained much ground in recent years, but it is uneven in its coverage. The northern peoples from beyond the Rhine and Danube have received more attention from European scholars than the African or smaller eastern tribes, partly because any history of the formation of modern Europe must take into account the development, movement and settlement of the northern tribes and partly because there was a great deal of sporadic but frenetic Roman and native activity on the northern frontiers. Comparison between the long but sparsely garrisoned and thinly populated African frontier and the more densely militarised northern frontier highlights the intensity of the interactions of Romans and natives in the north. With the exception of wars against the Parthians and then the Persians, it was against the northern tribes that the Roman government of the third and fourth centuries expended most of its resources and energies.[8]

Any investigation of the non-Roman tribal population is hampered as always by lack of reliable all-round source material. Whilst there is a relatively large amount of evidence, tantalising and infuriating though it is, with which to reassemble the lives of the Romans, by comparison the natives in and around the Empire have left fewer traces of their existence. The classical documentary sources in particular are of only limited use; the information they offer about tribes outside the Empire is scanty. Besides, literary and epigraphic sources illuminate only the Roman world, or more precisely the Roman view of the world, and are restricted for the most part to the upper classes or the wealthy. Then, as now, large numbers of people would live their entire lives leaving scarcely any record of their existence, but at least for the reconstruction of the daily lives of the Romans and the Romanised provincials there is the advantage of background knowledge of political and social history, and certain accepted norms of provincial lifestyle, which provides a tentative framework against which to set the lesser-known details. For the tribesmen outside the Empire, the larger framework is more shifting and more dimly lit. There is no contemporary voice to speak for the tribes from their own milieu, so the knowledge that we have of them derives either from purely Roman sources of different periods, with all the inherent problems ranging from bias to anachronism and error, or from later histories, such as those of Jordanes for the Goths and Gregory of Tours for the Franks. The later tribal histories were composed long after the eventual settlement of the tribes, and, in striving to give some cohesion and provide a continuous narrative thread to events which were not necessarily so easily described, such works are often unreliable or even fictitious. Only archaeology gives the natives a contemporary voice of their own, revealing their lifestyles and documenting their movements and regroupings, by comparing house types, clothing, weapons and accoutrements, and by analysing burial customs. The tangible remains and artefacts bring the tribes closer as real people but cannot illuminate tribal structure, actual personalities or patterns of thought. Thus, there are no sources of direct or unequivocal evidence for the history of the tribes which can be adopted without hesitation.[9]

The Romans did not produce a team of anthropologists whose task it was to study the tribes at first hand and then to draw up impartial accounts, or if they did then no record has survived. While the Empire was growing, there was a certain diffidence if not hostility about the tribes around the Roman world, and an assumption that they were all uncivilised and untameable. Caesar was the first to describe objectively what he saw or heard of the Germanic tribes, accepting their customs without the missionary zeal to convert them to Romanitas, and recognising their intelligence. Tacitus documented the same peoples at second hand, though he may have used accounts written by Pliny, who went on campaign against the Germans. Apart from these two sources, there is only the evidence contained in Ptolemy's *Geography*, composed in the second century, and then silence. The third-century historians Dio and Herodian did not attempt to repeat Tacitus' survey by studying or merely listing the various tribes of their own day, which leaves a great deal to be desired because by the beginning of the third century so much had changed since Tacitus wrote his account, in both the Roman and barbarian worlds. The interaction between the two worlds contributed to the change, even if it did not precipitate or accelerate the process. Attitudes were different by the mid-third century. When Tacitus described the Germans, he wrote of something distant, far away and for the most part contained, threatening only the periphery of the Empire. The early history of Rome comprised several encounters with the barbarians and some disastrous defeats at their hands, but in the late first century and the early second, there was still a strong belief in Rome's capacity to control the tribes, or to recover from defeats and regain supremacy. The Marcomannic wars of Marcus Aurelius' reign prove the point. There had been panic in Rome when the tribes had penetrated as far as northern Italy, but the invasion had been short lived. There had been no permanent tribal foothold in Italy and Roman armies rapidly pushed the invaders back beyond the frontier. Thereafter the wars were lengthy and protracted, but that was because of the nature of the two opposing parties. The Romans converted the war from a defensive one to an offensive one, but it was more of a guerrilla war than one of decisive battles, involving a series of skirmishes until the tribes were worn down. They wanted to migrate, but Marcus would neither let them move nor settle. Exhaustion and hunger completed the process. When Commodus made peace he was derided for it, but there were two decades of peace on the frontier as a result of the long years of warfare. Roman supremacy had been restated; there was no need to ask for more.[10]

Roman contact with the tribes

Client kings and promotion of the elite classes

There were certain well-defined methods of dealing with the tribesmen, which had evolved throughout Rome's history. Contact with the tribes occurred on several different levels via embassies to and from Rome, via the system of client kingship, via trading activities, and occasionally in open warfare. In newly assimilated territories Rome cultivated and promoted the local elite classes who were prepared to be friendly. On the other hand they made every effort to suppress those elements which were hostile. Outside the Empire the same procedure was followed, since it was much preferred to establish cordial relations with the nearest neighbours than to achieve control by going to war. How far Roman influence extended outside the Empire is debatable. The fact that the third-century invasions seemed to take the Romans by surprise perhaps indicates that the Emperors were content to keep a watching brief only on the peripheral tribes, and knew very little of what was happening some distance away from the immediate frontier areas. Even if the Emperors, via their governors and troops, did have a finger-on-the-pulse approach to wide areas of non-Roman territory, there would not be much warning of the hit-and-run raids across the frontiers, which by their very nature would begin clandestinely and erupt very suddenly. It was probably impossible to pre-empt those kinds of attacks, but on a wider scale it would be important to know who wielded the most influence in any particular tribe, and whether there were internal native rebellions in the offing. This sort of intelligence would enable Rome to take action promptly before adverse situations got out of hand. It has been argued that Roman intelligence networks developed in tandem with the defence of the frontiers, and that as the boundaries were fixed and frontier installations became static the administrative machinery was set up in relevant locations to facilitate the collection and processing of information. It is suggested that the *beneficiarii consularis*, stationed at various places on the frontiers, were responsible for gathering intelligence from a variety of civilian and military sources, and passing it on to provincial governors, the military commanders and the Emperor.[11]

This makes perfect sense. Delicate shifts in the balance of power and changes in native society could be monitored as closely as possible. Occasionally the reigning Emperor could install a ruler favourable to Rome, who could be supported and promoted perhaps by gifts and subsidies, or even by armed expeditions to secure the authority of the chosen ruler. In this way Rome had tried to influence the loyalties of the various eastern kingdoms from the late Republic onwards. The technique was applied to the native kings of Africa and in the northern parts of the Empire. Antoninus Pius, for instance, celebrated on coins his achievements in installing kings to rule over the Quadi and over the Armenians. The system worked better in areas like the east, where there was a tradition of established boundaries and administration conducted from permanent central places. The Rhine and Danube tribes were not accustomed to administering from a town or city, nor did they necessarily exercise total or permanent control over their people.[12]

Tacitus noted that the Germanic kings were chosen from among the nobles, and their warrior leaders from among those of proven valour, all of which seems deceptively simple until the terminology and the circumstances are examined more closely. Nobility and kingship can be interpreted very differently by modern audiences, by the Romans, and by the tribesmen whom Tacitus was discussing. Having only Roman sources by which to judge, it is not possible to penetrate fully the inner meanings and finer nuances of the social structures of the tribes. The Romans recognised the difference between kings, whom they called *reges* or *reguli*, and warrior leaders, whom they commonly called *duces*, but there was no strictly rigid classification into two mutually exclusive groups. Tacitus' account makes it seem as though the two types of leaders, king and warrior, commonly existed side by side, fulfilling different functions. Wolfram has re-examined this view, arguing that the two forms of leadership succeeded each other. Indeed the interaction between the Romans and the tribes beyond the frontiers probably instigated and accelerated the transition, because the Romans preferred to exercise control indirectly through a leader who was favourable to them, and it would not really matter too much whether the leader's origin was from among the nobility or from the men or proven valour, provided he satisfied the first criterion of partiality towards Rome. It has been suggested that Roman diplomats would need to know the difference between a *rex* and a *dux* in order to deal properly with the various problems that arose, and that they would always adhere to the definitions whereby a king ruled the people (or *gens*) and a *dux* was purely a war leader at the head of his following of warriors. This is an ideal situation, but humanity has the happy knack of crossing the boundaries of strict definitions in favour of diversity. A king could be a war leader, and sometimes the Romans referred to a leader who had started out as a *dux* as a king, either because he seemed more regal than a war leader or because he aspired to and achieved royal status. The most famous example of such a personage who began as a political and military leader and graduated to kingship is Maroboduus, or Marbod, who welded together the Marcomanni in the reign of Augustus. His domination was not universally accepted by all the tribes, and he was eventually toppled by another leader called Catvalda. Tiberius allowed Maroboduus himself to settle in Ravenna, where he survived for 18 years, perhaps not too miserable at his lost status. Catvalda did not long survive him as ruler of the tribesmen. The Hermunduri soon evicted him. The followers of Maroboduus and Catvalda were resettled on the north bank of the Danube, where the Romans installed Vannius, a tribesman of the Quadi, as their king. This is the first recorded instance of the Quadi, who came to greater prominence as the adversaries of Marcus Aurelius. For three decades, with Roman assistance, Vannius enlarged his kingdom, built strongholds, and successfully fought off opposition from within and without; then he, too, was defeated and came to settle in Pannonia. The same process was observed in Dacia, in the first century AD when first Burebista and then Decebalus gained control of their tribes, posing a considerable threat to Rome. The Emperor Domitian fought them, but was unable to follow up his victory; Trajan required two major campaigns to bring the Dacians under Roman control. The emergence and disappearance of strong native leaders, the fluctuations of tribal gatherings and affiliations, and the consequent disturbance of the balance of power were well-established phenomena by the third century, but the struggle was for the most part an internal one, with tribesmen fighting against each other. This situation was greatly to Rome's advantage, and cost her very little. If the struggles began to threaten Rome, the resources of the Empire were mobilised and concentrated on the area concerned for as long as it took to establish peace.[13]

In designating their allies as king or *dux*, Roman pride may have played a part in the choice of label, especially if the choice was made to promote and support the war leader as if he were a king, through whom the Romans hoped to control his followers and keep other tribes at bay. Since protection and defence of the tribe was a prime consideration, then permanent readiness for war was of paramount importance. The establishment of a band of warriors following a military leader, in tandem with, or perhaps instead of, the king chosen from the nobility, was a deeply rooted tribal custom which Tacitus recognised when he described how the leader could not maintain his entourage except by constant violence and war. There may be a thinly veiled reference to developments in Rome in this statement. Imperial power rested in control of the armed forces, and in many ways the Romans themselves had trodden the same evolutionary path as the northern tribes. Far back in their history the Romans had rid themselves of kings and replaced them with a Republican government, but although they could never again countenance kings, they were gradually taken over by strong military men operating extraneously from the normal governmental system, culminating in the dominance of Julius Caesar and Augustus. In the days before the frontiers were fixed, with the troops stationed in permanent forts and fortresses, the Roman military leader needed access to a standing army both to support his own power and to defend himself and Rome from external threats. In times of peace, when older custom dictated that armies should be abandoned, Caesar and then his great-nephew Octavian–Augustus had kept control of their troops by seeking out wars. After the battle of Philippi, when Caesar's assassins were finally vanquished, the power struggle narrowed down to two men, Octavian and Mark Antony. While Antony controlled the east and kept his army together with the intention of subduing Parthia, Octavian manufactured a war in Illyricum to gain military renown and to retain legitimate command of his own army. The war leaders of the Germanic tribes may seem poles apart from the Roman Emperors, but the overall comparison is valid, since they built up power bases founded on military successes and the accretion of armed forces. The warrior *duces* wielded genuine power, and the Romans, inveterate realists, recognised power when they saw it. The only criterion thereafter was whether they could use it to their own advantage.[14]

Gifts and subsidies (annua munera)

Having chosen the native leader most likely to succeed, the Romans supported him and rendered whatever assistance was deemed necessary, including prestige gifts, cash payments, food supplies, and even the loan of engineers and architects to build Roman-style palaces, bath houses and fortifications. Gift exchanges were a recognised feature of tribal society, in which the Romans participated as both recipients and givers. It was not unknown for tribal chiefs to send diplomatic gifts to the Emperors. As for Roman gifts to tribal leaders, without the advantage of specific literary evidence it is difficult to identify with any certainty where, when and to whom the prestige gifts may have been sent. The archaeological evidence can be milked for only a few facts. Whilst the provenance of such prestige goods can be ascertained without much difficulty, the presence in non-Roman territory of coins, gold and silver jewellery and vessels or any other objects does not automatically equate Roman gift-giving with specific Germanic recipients. Legitimate purchase, or booty carried off from Roman territory or from one tribe to another, has also to be taken into account.[15]

Gift exchanges differ slightly from regular subsidies, but the two procedures were still rooted in Germanic culture. Rome used the native traditions to her own advantage, adapting to circumstances, and was always ready to review the situation and make changes. With regard to annual money payments, Bursche suggests that the English term 'subsidies' ought to be rendered as *annua munera*, the phrase used by Jordanes. The payment of regular subsidies, and the occasional payments to buy peace by tribute could be viewed in different ways by contemporaries. Modern terminology also conveys different viewpoints, because the words contain subtle shades of meaning. The term 'subsidies' evokes images of noble-minded aid programmes from a wealthy dominant state to a less fortunate one; 'tribute' conjures up a sub-text of cash payments after defeat, or of ignominious bribes to pre-empt attacks from a stronger power. Some of Rome's payments did fall into this second category, but they were usually regarded as stopgaps until the tables could be turned. The labels changed, depending upon circumstances. While in the ascendancy, Rome could be magnanimous and naturally construed her payments as gifts from a greater to an equal or, more often, to a lesser power. When Rome was temporarily in retreat but refused to acknowledge the fact, her payments to the tribes were still called gifts, with some bluster and propaganda. When strong enough to reverse the situation, war-mongering Emperors changed the labels, acknowledging that the payments constituted shameful tributes and should be stopped. Payments to the Goths seem to have evoked this sort of behaviour. Julian dismissed Constantine's subsidies as tributes, and even Themistius, who advocated assimilation of the tribesmen, classified the payments to them as a shameful bribe to ward off attacks. Thus in the Roman world, mood and circumstance dictated whether the payments to the tribes were construed as dishonourable and cowardly, or as potent symbols of Roman domination. There was naturally a certain amount of bias towards the particular Emperor who authorised the payments. Those Emperors who enjoyed a sound reputation were usually considered to have been unassailably correct in their payments of subsidies, while Emperors with a bad reputation were considered to have been disastrously mistaken. Caracalla was censured by Dio for paying unadulterated gold to the 'barbarians', while the currency he issued to the Romans was debased, and the assassin of Caracalla, the Emperor Macrinus, accused him of paying more to the barbarians than he did to the soldiers. For many reasons the subsidies were neither continuously maintained nor consistently applied. Moods changed in Rome or in the frontier provinces, Emperors were created by the armies which wanted to see action, or the tribes did not keep their side of the bargain, so the subsidies either petered out or were abruptly stopped, occasionally with good results from the Roman point of view, and occasionally with disastrous consequences. Pertinax managed to put a temporary end to subsidies to the northern tribes, and he even succeeded in reclaiming payments in gold that were already on their way northwards, escorted by the tribesmen themselves. There were no grave consequences as a result of this determined show of force, so Dio could rightly use it as a demonstration of Pertinax's upright character. On the other hand the subsidies paid to the Goths after the treaty of 238 were stopped as soon as the Romans considered themselves in the dominant position in the 240s. The result was the development of the coalition under the Gothic leader Cniva, followed by the serious invasions of the 250s when Cniva took advantage of the rebellion of Decius to attack while the Romans fought each other. Gradually Rome brought the situation under control. Trebonianus Gallus defeated Cniva and made a treaty reinstating the payments of subsidies, but then shortly afterwards Marcus Aelius Aemilianus stopped the payments and went to war. Cniva disappeared from the record, but then so did Aemilianus, hailed as Emperor by his troops and then assassinated by the same troops when the Emperor Valerian's army approached.[16]

The subsidy system was a useful device which served several purposes. On a purely practical level, disadvantaged tribes could be sustained by gifts of Roman cash, food or clothing. It would be rare for Rome to expend her energies in such an exclusively altruistic way. In return for her subsidies to certain tribes or warrior leaders Rome achieved a position of dominance, whereby the recipient and his followers were dependent on her for support and, theoretically at least, were likely to be co-operative. The arrangement was often reciprocal, in that the tribes provided recruits for the Roman army for as long as the agreement lasted. Symbiotic relations between tribesmen and the Romans were built up in this way, until the distinguishing factors were blurred and a meld of cultures began. The levying of recruits could be annual, or sometimes irregular. Commodus made a peace treaty with the Marcomanni and Quadi in 180, waiving the annual levy in favour of a large influx of recruits all at once. The removal of a large number of young men would reduce the tribes' capacity to make trouble, and would fill the gaps in the Roman armies after prolonged periods of warfare. Thus the Romans adapted to circumstances. After the treaty with the Goths in 238 it is likely that subsidies were given in return for troops, and that recruitment for the Roman armies began immediately, for there were Goths in the army in the 240s.[17]

The subsidy payments could be regarded as a form of defence of the Empire, since the friendly king or leader who was sure of maintaining his following and his dominant position via the wealth provided by Rome would also be better able to avert or control rebellion within his own tribe and to beat off attacks from neighbouring tribes. The subsidised tribes could therefore act as buffers between Rome and the tribes further afield. In some cases the subsidy could be regarded almost as a fee for guarding the tribe's own territory in the interests of Rome. Direct references to such a system are not found in the early Empire, but historians of the late Empire found no difficulty with this ideology and it is highly likely that it was an established procedure rooted in the past. Zosimus describes annual subsidies paid to the Bosporans in return for holding back the Scythians, and Procopius refers to payments in gold to the Huns and Saracens for guarding their lands at all times. In other cases there may have been a deliberate and devious intention to play one tribe off against another, subsidising one but ignoring the other, causing dissension that would divert attention from raids across the Roman frontier. The Carpi, for instance, complained to the governor of Moesia Inferior, Tullius Menophilus, that they were worth much more than the Goths, who received subsidies while they were left empty handed. Whether this was deliberate third-century policy or whether it was a simply a fortuitous outcome is not established, but divide and rule was after all a well-established Roman doctrine. Another way of controlling the tribes and averting attacks on the frontiers was to pay food subsidies to tribes who were hungry. It was an easier and cheaper method of pre-emptive defence than any show of arms.[18]

All these types of subsidy were employed at one time or another by the Romans, embracing the eastern and African peoples as well the northern tribes. The actual mechanism of payment is not well-documented. Annual subsidies are mentioned in the sources, but not all of them were necessarily paid on this basis. The system presupposes fixed calendar dates, pick-up points, convoys, small tribal gatherings and Roman military guards, but the sources do not elucidate events in great detail. There is some evidence to suggest that although the subsidies were authorised by the Emperor, neither he nor the provincial governor were closely involved in the process. It was probably the provincial procurators who held responsibility for collection and delivery of the subsidies, and it is likely that the money, food, or whatever the subsidies included, were collected mostly in the provinces nearest the frontier and not delivered directly from Rome or Italy.[19]

Trade

A long-standing connection had always existed between Rome and the tribesmen surrounding the Empire, dating from the earliest times, well before the establishment of frontiers. Tacitus distinguished two groups of people with regard to trading activity: firstly the peoples nearest to the Empire who were accustomed to Roman goods and monetary systems, and secondly tribes further afield where the economy was more natural, based on exchange and barter rather than money. The Roman coins found in *barbaricum* bear out his assertion that the Germans preferred silver to gold; there are very few aurei, compared to an overwhelming preponderance of denarii found in *barbaricum*. Whether the coins represent booty, ransom payments, gifts or subsidies is arguable; the coins found in the Ukraine have been interpreted as payments to slave dealers. The bronze coinage found in tribal territories is less likely to have arrived there as gifts from other tribal leaders or from Rome; the low-denomination coins suggest that the tribesmen did in fact use them for commercial purposes, but not necessarily with Roman traders. It is possible that the Germans of Tacitus' day who relied upon barter had begun to use money for limited purposes by the second century, not in the modern sense of purchasing ordinary commodities but perhaps to pay retainers for their services or to use as part of gift exchanges. The events of the late second century and early third, brought about some changes to the distribution of Roman coins. In western Russia the supply slowed down after the reign of Commodus, and in the third century the Scandinavian lands were cut off from supply altogether. Although coins continued to arrive in free Germany in the third century, they seem to have been mostly older issues, which were more valued. Indeed, Roman coins of the first and second centuries remained in circulation for the next 200 years, being found in hoards of the fourth and fifth centuries.[20]

The peoples who practised the 'natural' economic systems did not eschew the use of Roman goods. There was a considerable mobility of Roman arte-facts, distributed by one means or another – just how far Roman goods pene-trated the interior of the non-Roman lands is revealed in a growing corpus of studies from Poland and Russia. The perennial problem that besets the study of Roman goods in *barbaricum* is exactly the same as the difficulty of distinguishing Roman gifts and subsidies from booty or native exchanges. No one can say with any certainty whether the Roman items found in native contexts arrived there as a result of trading activities or by one of many other different methods. Much has been made of the prehistoric amber routes from the Baltic to the Rhine and Danube. Amber has been described on the one hand as the principal precious commodity carried into the Roman Empire

195

from *barbaricum*, but on the other it has even been doubted whether the amber trade was a major one. The importance or otherwise of amber is not the salient point in this context; rather, it is the routes that are important: via Vetera and Mainz from the Rhine to the Baltic, then via Carnuntum from the Danube to the Vistula. From the end of the second century new routes had opened up through Olbia and Tyras via the river Bug to the Vistula. Whatever the trade items carried in each direction along them, these routes were well known, and were to be used later as invasion routes by the Goths, Franks and Alamanni.[21]

Difficult as it is to establish the existence of trading networks, the problems do not end even if those links can be clearly demonstrated. The major dispute is about the importance or otherwise of trade in the tribal set-up. The lack of evidence on this score allows scholars to take completely opposed stances on the importance of trade to the natives. Some authors have argued that trade with the Roman Empire was vital to the existence of the tribes, or at least to their leaders, because control of trade and production gave the leading families a preponderant influence within their tribes.[22]

Other scholars deny that trade between Rome and *barbaricum* had any importance at all, highlighting the very low volume of artefacts that crossed the frontiers. Trade is a two-way process, as attested by the fact that most of the loan-words which crossed the Germanic/Gothic and Latin/Greek boundaries were concerned with commerce, or denoted items which were traded. Trade could be important to the tribesmen and tribal leaders under two headings: firstly to make profit by selling surplus produce to the Romans, most especially to the Roman army; secondly to obtain Roman luxury goods and everyday items such as pottery, glass and textiles. Neither of these theoretical scenarios is capable of absolute proof. Examples which seem to support the first theory, where natives beyond the frontiers may have established trading links by selling their surplus produce to the Romans, include the villages of Feddersen Wierde (near Bremerhaven in Germany), and Wijster and Bennekom in Holland. These villages enjoyed a lengthy occupation of some 500 years, beginning in the first century BC, and they prospered during the Roman period, especially in the third and fourth centuries. They collapsed in the fifth century, when Roman power in the west declined, a factor which strongly suggests that they were closely bound up with the fortunes of the Empire. The great uncertainty about this postulated trade with the Empire is that there is no surviving evidence of the food supplies, or textiles, skins or furs which may have formed part of the trading arrangements. Concerning Roman goods in *barbaricum*, attempts to classify them into readily discernible groups are doomed to failure from the start, despite the temptation to interpret high-luxury goods as prestige gifts to client kings, the lesser articles as gifts from Rome for the client king to distribute to his followers, and the lowly items such as pottery as the product of trading activities. This is ludicrously simplistic, allowing for none of the multifarious variations of which humans are capable. The mundane middle-of-the-road view is probably nearer the truth, namely that trade was vital to certain leaders at certain times, that there would be growths and declines; there would be fluctuations in the amount of traded goods coming into native lands, and at different times and at different places there would be increases or decreases, depending on fashion, availability of goods, and the personnel whose business it was to carry the goods. Unfortunately there is insufficient information to elucidate the details. The available evidence suggests that after the Marcomannic wars trade with Rome fell off in Bohemia but increased north of the Carpathians. Whether these two facts are related awaits demonstration.[23]

Those who argue that trade was not a fundamental feature of tribal life must account for the restrictions that Rome placed on it. Marcus Aurelius restricted the number of places where the Marcomanni and Quadi could conduct their trade with Rome; Diocletian made a treaty with the Persians in 299, stipulating that the sole place of trade was to be Nisibis. The Goths too were restricted to designated locations along the Danube for engaging in trade, and the terms granted to them in the treaty of 332 are considered very unusual in that trade was authorised at any place on the frontier.[24]

These restrictions on trade were derived from considerations of safety, and no doubt encompassed fiscal reasons as well. If the days for trading were designated in advance and the places where it could be carried out limited to only a few, then the supervision of the gatherings of people could be much better organised. Policing would have been a foremost consideration on the frontiers, even in peacetime, so any arrangements that facilitated policing would be welcomed. The other security measure concerned spying; if trade was carried out only at a few locations, the tribes from beyond the frontier could not carry away too much information about the province and its military organisation. Probably the most important consideration from the point of view of the Roman government was that, hand in hand with policing, the machinery of the taxation system would be far better equipped for its operations if trade was conducted in only one or two designated places, at stipulated times. Laws of the later Empire reveal that goods were taxed at their exit points from Roman territory, supervised by the *comites commerciorum*; it is reasonable to suppose that the Romans were not slow to realise the importance of taxation on trade with the natives, and that they exercised close control over it before, during and after the third century.[25]

Trading rights with Rome (*ius commercii*) were regarded as a privilege bestowed upon her neighbours, one which could be withdrawn if necessary. Similarly export and import of certain items could be banned, and trading activities between Rome and the tribes outside the Empire would be restricted by the laws regarding these bans. The existence of the laws banning export of certain goods has been taken to imply that there was an illegal trade across the frontiers, especially in Roman arms. In the third century, Roman-style swords became fashionable in *barbaricum*, perhaps as possessions of the elite groups of warriors. Sometimes genuine Roman swords were altered and adapted to native use, as for instance the large numbers of swords with a ring at the end of the hilt, commonly described by modern archaeologists as *Ringknaufschwerter*. Many other examples of Roman-style swords found in tribal territory are copies, produced locally. The old problem surfaces once more, in that no one can discern how the swords arrived in native territory. The significance of these finds from the point of view of trade lies in the illegality or otherwise of their presence in *barbaricum*. The laws regarding the ban on exports, of bronze, iron, gold, and weapons, have been taken as a blanket ban on all exports to all the tribes outside the Empire, applicable at all times. Recently, Boris Rankov examined these laws to conclude that they have been misinterpreted, and that too much has been read into them. For the most part the laws refer to enemies of the Roman people. Only one law specifically bans the sale of weapons, or the means to make them, to natives from outside the Empire. It dates to the 450s, and refers mainly to the Eastern Empire. Rankov suggests that in fact there was no blanket ban of exports of metals and weapons, but instead laws were made to deal with specific circumstances at specific times, and then only to ban sales to enemies. It goes without saying that not all tribesmen fall automatically into this category of enemies. The reinterpretation of the ban on exports narrows the existence of the supposed illegal trade and restricts it – if indeed it ever existed – to the aforementioned specific circumstances and times; sword-running to the Germans and Scythians may have been as fabulous and fantastic as gun-running to the Commanches and the Sioux in Westerns.[26]

Settlement on the land

For various reasons during the history of Rome, tribesmen had been settled on lands inside or on the frontiers of the Empire. Pressures on the natives who asked for admittance to the Empire included exhaustion of their lands and resultant food shortages, or aggressive domination by another tribe or tribes. This was not a phenomenon confined to the third century. Julius Caesar allowed the Usipetes and Tencteri from across the Rhine to settle in Gaul, because they were harassed by their neighbours. A short time later Marcus Vipsanius Agrippa brought the Ubii to the west bank of the Rhine to protect them from attacks by more rapacious tribes beyond the river. According to some sources, pressure from more distant tribes was a direct cause of the Marcomannic wars. When such displacements began, Rome had only limited responses in her repertoire, specifically war or resettlement, or sometimes war followed by resettlement. The process was constantly repeated throughout the history of Rome. MacMullen collected the main references to settlement within the Empire: Augustus brought 50,000 Getae from across the Danube into Moesia; Tiberius settled 40,000 Germans in Gaul and on the Rhine; Nero received more tribes from across the Danube into Moesia; Marcus Aurelius allowed 3,000 Naristae into Roman territory; Probus settled 100,000 Bastarnae. The numbers are probably wildly exaggerated but the settlements are not fabricated; the unexplained factor is that there was so much land available within the Empire, from the earliest times onwards.[27]

These official settlements of large groupings of families, complete with women and children, and probably animals as well, served the multiple purposes of reducing pressure on the tribesmen, draining off manpower and thereby hopefully avoiding war, providing potential recruits for the Roman army from among the settled communities, and finding people to cultivate the land inside the Empire. It was a recurring theme in Imperial administration to attract people to unused lands. Hadrian passed a law concerning the problem of uncultivated waste, which was still in force when, according to Herodian, Pertinax devised a scheme to sign over neglected land to private owners. This by itself was apparently not sufficient to attract hordes of claimants, since Pertinax had to dangle bait before his potential new landowners in the form of security of tenure and immunity from taxes for ten years. The problem had not been solved by the reign of Aurelian, who tried to shift the onus for finding landlords for empty lands onto the city councils: either they installed people on the wastelands to cultivate them, or they paid the tribute that would have been due if they were under the plough. There seems to have been plenty of room for tribesmen to settle as farmers within the Empire, without causing an outcry from established farmers in the provinces concerned. The numbers of settlers quoted in the ancient sources may be suspect, and even the ancient authors themselves sometimes abandoned any attempt to provide an accurate head-count, falling back on the noncommittal vagueness of 'many' or 'a lot' (*plurimi*, *multi*). Nevertheless, though the numbers may be unreliable the principle is sound. Settlement of tribesmen and their families within the Empire was a regular practice, and it was not necessarily considered a dangerous one because Rome was capable of dealing with troublesome elements. For instance, Marcus Aurelius encountered rebellious tribesmen settled in Ravenna. They seized the city for a short time, but the event seems to have been something of a damp squib and did not escalate into anything more serious. Marcus evicted them, along with all the other tribesmen who had been brought into Italy.[28]

The later history of these immigrants into the Empire is not known in detail. Assuming that the tribes would settle in reasonably large groups, and that they would retain some if not all of their ethnic identities, MacMullen attempted to trace them from archaeological sources; generally, the finds do not bear out the supposedly large numbers of immigrants who came into the Empire. There are many possible reasons why the tribes left only a little evidence of their settlements. In some cases it is possible that the numbers were inflated in the sources, and in reality only a few families settled; in other instances the settlements may have been small and scattered, so that archaeological traces of them depend upon long-term cumulative results. Most of the settlers would perhaps have been absorbed seamlessly into the Roman way of life, thus becoming indistinguishable from the rest of the provincials. MacMullen's hypothesis is that this sort of assimilation was feasible in the first and second centuries, but ceased to be viable in the third century when new types of settlers appeared, probably from the Tetrarchy onwards, in the form of the *laeti*. These groups of people were confined to Gaul and Italy, with no regard for ethnic distinctions. The *laeti* were culturally and ethnically diverse, and according to some authorities they had the status of *dediticii*, denoting people who had surrendered to Rome. These notions have been challenged, together with the assertion that some of the *laeti* were Roman prisoners of war. Despite these studies, the origins of the *laeti* remain obscure, and even the name is shrouded in mystery. There are several opinions as to its derivation and meaning. *Laetus* may be related to a Germanic word, roughly translatable as 'serf', meaning a category of person who was neither slave nor free, which at least fits the known facts – namely, that the *laeti* were not free to do as they liked, but were under an obligation to provide men for the army. Another theory is that the military obligations of the *laeti* included defence and policing of the regions where they settled. In Gaul for instance, where there were settlements of *laeti* near Amiens, Beauvais, Troyes and Langres, one of their duties may have been to protect the countryside from the depredations of the Bagaudae, outlaws and landless men who plagued the inhabitants of Gaul in the third century. By the mid-fourth century if not earlier, the *laeti* were supervised by officers with the title of *praepositus*. At the beginning of the fifth century their lands were called *terrae laeticae* in the law codes, and Zosimus seemed to think that the name *laeti* denoted a specific tribe in Gaul. This attests to the long-term success of the arrangements pioneered by Diocletian.[29]

These new schemes did not completely supersede settlement en masse within the Empire. Constantine brought more than 300,000 Sarmatians across the frontiers, and dispersed them in different areas in Thrace, Italy, Macedonia and Scythia. The orator Themistius (*c.* 317–88) declared that settlement of tribesmen was better than war, and that Thrace would be better filled with farmers rather than corpses. The Empire had always been faced with tribesmen on the periphery, requiring assistance or demanding lands, and for the most part accommodated them in a civilised manner. In turn the tribesmen served Rome in several ways, entering the armies or by cultivating the soil and paying tribute. There were many variations on this theme but in the main it was a mutually beneficial relationship, interspersed with wars, sometimes short and sometimes protracted, which Rome usually won in the end. In the third century the relationship was tipped off balance; the northern tribes began to pose different and more serious threats, and Rome was forced to adapt herself to meet them.[30]

Service in the Roman army

From the earliest times the Romans had employed native troops in addition to her own armies. Warriors fighting under their own tribal leaders were often engaged on a temporary basis while campaigns were fought, and then released from service once the wars were over. This reflected the regular practice of the late Roman Republic and the early Empire, before permanent standing armies were established; the Roman troops were themselves dismissed when there was no further need for them. After the reign of Augustus the army developed into a permanent feature of the frontier provinces, with stipulated terms and conditions of service. Use of tribesmen continued when the standing armies were formed; the Romans were frequently able to employ one tribe to fight against another, taking advantage of the lack of national unity among the Gauls, Germans and Scythians. The barbarian traditions of heroism and glory in battle created excellent fighters, and the custom of fighting for a tribal leader allowed them to adapt easily to fighting for their tribal leaders on behalf of the Romans, or directly under the command of a Roman leader. It was more or less the same arrangement: personal loyalty to a warrior in return for booty and glory could be painlessly transmuted into loyalty to a soldier in return for pay and similar glory. Caesar recounts how Ariovistus fought on the Roman side during his conquest of Gaul. He was a German, not a Celt, and spoke a different language from the Gauls, but he would fight other Germans when occasion arose. Caesar recognised him as 'king and friend of the Roman people' (*rex et amicus populi Romani*), and 'king of the Germans' (*rex germanorum*), though the terminology reflects Caesar's viewpoint rather than an exact description of Ariovistus' status among his own people.[31]

Other tribal leaders who feature in the early Imperial army include Arminius, who brought his warriors to fight for the Romans in Tiberius' German campaigns; Civilis a 'prince' of the Batavians; and Maroboduus. Arminius was rewarded with Roman citizenship and equestrian status, but eventually turned against Rome and tried to assert his independence; Civilis commanded his men as a Roman officer and used his influence during the civil war of 69 to incite the aggrieved Batavians to revolt; Maroboduus entertained more wide-ranging ambitions and went on to carve out a kingdom for himself. All three men had the advantage of knowledge of the Roman army when they became enemies of Rome.[32]

Recruitment of tribesmen took several forms. Voluntary enlistment of individuals is not well documented but it can be assumed that it occurred. Service in the army has been construed as highly attractive to tribesmen, since they would be paid and allowed other opportunities for amassing wealth. The presence of Roman coins in *barbaricum* has been interpreted as evidence of trade, gift exchange, or booty, but some authors prefer to see the coins as evidence of military pay brought back by men who had enlisted in the army. Active recruitment drives may have taken place in *barbaricum* from time to time; the various interpreters who have left traces of their activities beyond the frontiers may have been multifunctional, combining the tasks of merchant, soldier, intelligence gatherer and/or recruitment officer for the army. Given that there would be considerable wastage from disease, accident, desertion and many other causes besides battle, the army as a whole would consume inordinate numbers of men, so the possibility of active recruitment beyond provincial boundaries should not be discounted.[33]

The levying en masse of large numbers of tribesmen could be on a voluntary basis, or, more likely, as Rome expanded, it was by treaty arrangement, often after the conclusion of a war. The payment of subsidies often involved military service, via the contribution of a number of men on an annual basis or all at once on conclusion of the treaty. After the Batavian revolt, the practice of installing newly recruited tribesmen in places near their homelands was changed in order to avoid local unrest and the possibility of rebellion. In Flavian times, or perhaps under Trajan (rather than as previously thought under Antoninus Pius), Britons were recruited in unknown numbers and sent to the frontier of Upper Germany. Marcus Aurelius sent 5,500 Sarmatians to Britain. They may have been kept together, as the Britons on the German frontier seem to have been, since there is some evidence from a later period of Sarmatian units in Britain. The 13,000 Quadi and the smaller number of Marcomanni recruited by Commodus in 180 may have been split up and distributed among existing units to fill gaps in the ranks. The status of these tribesmen may have differed, according to the terms of the treaties made at the conclusion of hostilities. The Britons and Sarmatians could have been considered *dediticii*, and as such not entitled to the privileges of the time-served auxiliary soldiers, while the Quadi and Marcomanni may have been enlisted as auxiliaries, eligible for the grant of citizenship on discharge, though there is no evidence to prove these theories. Whether correct or not, it is certain that many tribesmen entered the army in one way or another after wars with the Romans, and it is entirely possible that there was no standardisation in the way in which Rome dealt with them; the arrangements to accommodate them were probably tailored to suit the needs of the moment and each individual circumstance. At the end of the third century, as has been mentioned, the *laeti* entered the scene, perhaps representative of a new method of dealing with defeated tribesmen by settling them on the land with obligations to provide soldiers for the army.[34]

During the third century when invasions across the frontiers increased in number and intensity, the recruitment of natives was not abandoned. The so-called barbarians were much too useful to the Romans as a ready source of manpower. The pressures caused by wars on more than one front sometimes occasioned the need to recruit wherever men could be found, so many tribesmen became soldiers of Rome and fought far from their homes. There were Goths serving in the army of Gordian III during the Persian campaign, possibly recruited as part of the treaty of 238. The tribesmen from beyond the Rhine and Danube served Rome loyally. Towards the end of the third century Germans were commonly employed in all branches of the army, particularly in the new style *scholae*. During civil wars between Roman commanders, rival claimants to the throne often used barbarian troops to swell the ranks of their armies, so there was abundant employment for tribesmen throughout the third and fourth centuries. The Gallic Emperors and the British usurper Carausius both used Frankish mercenaries in their armies. Constantine gathered large numbers of natives when he was assembling an army for the final campaign that ended in the battle of the Milvian Bridge, and by so doing he consolidated an already established procedure. By the fourth century it was common to find Alamannic and Frankish soldiers in the army, many of them serving as officers.[35]

THE THIRD CENTURY AND AFTER

By the end of the second century, the Roman government and Roman armies had learned a lot about the peoples around the Empire. The process was reciprocal. Tribesmen had learned much about Rome, often by serving in her armies. Each knew the other's strengths and weaknesses. The forte of the warbands lay in rapid movements and sudden strikes, but there was a lack of long-term cohesion. Roman offensive attacks or defensive responses were slower and more ponderous, but very thorough and quite relentless. Staying power often proved its worth in the end, making up for any amount of heroic dash.[36]

As the second century progressed into the third, important changes had taken hold in Roman and tribal society. Firstly, the gradual expansion of Rome and then the stabilisation of the frontiers imposed an unaccustomed permanence upon the more naturally fluid structure of the tribes nearest to the Empire. The presence of Rome both attracted and repelled, but could never be ignored, and even with only minimal interaction between Romans and natives the ripple effect would be felt far beyond the frontiers. The Empire represented different ideals to the tribesmen. To some it was a source of food and life support, to others a place of refuge, and to others a source of portable wealth with the opportunity for rich pickings, glory and adventure.[37]

Secondly, in the northern half of the Empire the Germanic tribes beyond the frontiers were reaching towards state formation, though the process was in only very rudimentary stages in the third century. The warrior bands had developed a greater cohesion, under stronger and more influential leaders;

the great federations were forming, detached from the usual tribal affiliations. The presence of Rome influenced the course of events in tribal society, and developments among the tribes in turn had great bearing on Rome; her responses had to be adapted accordingly. It is not possible to apply the concept of 'change' wrought upon tribal society by Rome, and vice versa upon Rome by the tribes, because it is merely academic to speculate what may have been the outcome in tribal development if Rome had not existed, or what might have become of Rome if the lands all around her had been totally empty. The parallel existence of Rome and the northern tribes ensured that they developed in concert with each other and influenced each other directly or indirectly.[38]

The multiple attractions of the Roman Empire and the unpredictable conditions facing the tribes brought about encounters of diverse kinds, ranging from peaceful migration into the Empire to hit-and-run raids across the frontiers with no concerted plans for conquest or settlement. Wholesale migration of large numbers of people bringing with them their families and possessions was not an everyday occurrence and was brought about only in the direst circumstances. Either by slow encroachment upon new lands as old ones were exhausted, or more commonly by rapid displacement by warring neighbours, successive groups of desperate people arrived at the frontiers asking for admittance. Settlement of tribes within the Empire on this basis has already been discussed. Even when the impetus and initiative for settlement derived from a decision of the tribesmen, it was always carried out on Roman terms. Invasion and conquest, cunningly planned in advance with the object of seizing lands, was not part of tribal mentality. It required organisation and tenacity of purpose to carry it out, and demanded greater tribal cohesion for a longer term than was usually the norm. For instance the Alamanni overran the *agri decumates* but did not settle there immediately. The Goths did not settle immediately in the eastern provinces. These bands were geared to raiding and making war, but not to settlement at this period. That came later.[39]

Movement of tribes or groups of tribesmen could be precipitated by a number of causes, such as food shortages, oppression by aggressive neighbours, or warfare. At the beginning of the third century there is some evidence of both climatic change and endemic warfare affecting what is now north-western Europe. In Holland wetter weather on a prolonged scale reduced the areas available for agriculture. The archaeological evidence reveals that by AD 300 the settlements in the west of Holland had virtually disappeared, and even those in the eastern parts had been significantly reduced. Excavations at the military vicus around the fort of Katwijk, north of the Rhine, showed that layers of clay sediment built up during the third century. The sea levels rose as a result of the so-called Dunkirk transgression, caused the flooding of many low-lying areas of the western coasts, and the pollution of adjacent lands by salting. There was a consequent detrimental effect on agriculture in the areas north of the lower Rhine, creating food shortages and the need to find more productive lands. The search for lands could be a peaceful process but more often involved encroaching upon other settlements.[40]

More telling is the discovery in Denmark and Jutland of extensive weapon deposits, probably votive, which have been interpreted as signs of large-scale, continuous warfare, beginning around AD 200. The best known finds are from Nydam and Illerup, where staggering quantities of armour and weapons were buried, probably representing hundreds of warriors either killed or captured. The locations of the votive offerings outline the probable area of warfare as being in Funen and southern Jutland. The effects of the wars can be seen in the desertion of lands. The major settlements of the western Baltic, previously flourishing, wealthy and agriculturally prosperous, were all at once abandoned in the early third century. Economic and climatic factors may have had a part to play, but endemic warfare is thought to be the main cause of this decline. Coastal settlements disappeared, and large tracts of territory in north-western Europe returned to uninhabited waste, dotted with nucleated settlements gathered together, perhaps in defensive groups.[41]

The emergence of the tribal federations

Tribal society embraced the concept of warfare as naturally as breathing in and out. The most obvious reason for the growth of a martial mentality was the need for defence of home and hearth, and for carving out new territories as population expanded or lands and soils became exhausted. Any tribe without its warrior bands would quickly be overwhelmed or become extinct. Defence was a prime necessity, but the ideology went far beyond that. Success in war was the one true test of valour, honour and heroism. The warrior bands surrounding a king or military leader could be drawn from different tribes, but they were normally bound by close ties to the kinship groups and operated within those parameters. By the end of the second century there were traces of newer, different organisations, fostered and encouraged by the developments of the third century. War was waged as a natural process in the tribal world, but one of the main ends in view was for extension of control. Enterprising families exploited the power vacuum to pursue the accumulation of wealth and influence. Wealth bestowed power, which in turn bestowed a controlling influence over the tribe or divisions of tribes, control over the agricultural lands of the group and over all of the agricultural production, over trade and most importantly over the warrior bands. The possession of a private army dedicated to supporting the aims and aspirations of its leader, and the ability to reward the warriors to ensure their loyalty, in turn ensured the maintenance of control and permanent access to resources. This is the context for the appearance of the richly endowed princely graves in northern Europe, the Fürstengräber. Their occupants represented dominant families who were able to exploit personal connections and monopolise wealth and imported goods. The distribution of these graves in the period corresponding to the early Roman Empire shows a widespread dispersion, but in the later period there was a concentration in more centralised locations indicative of a regrouping, perhaps of a redistribution of lands, and certainly of the emergence of elite groups, separated from the rest of society and enjoying economic and military predominance.[42]

The process could continue independently within tribal society but was also nurtured in part by Roman influences. Rome preferred to deal with a designated leader, whom she supported via gifts, subsidies, and the weight of her moral superiority, blazoned for all to see in her attitudes, her armies and her obvious wealth. The attractions of what Rome could offer were considerable, because Roman wealth greatly facilitated the path to power. With Roman aid, all kinds of wealth could be accumulated with which to attract warrior bands to serve the prospective leader. The old-style kingship or military leadership thus became more and more attuned to Roman ideals, accelerating its divergence from the kinship organisation of the tribe. The disruptions of constant warfare in the north and the simultaneous restrictions on food production opened up ideal opportunities for enterprising families to build up power blocs.[43]

The climatic influences on food production may have been overestimated, but agricultural production was never reliable at the best of times and tribal society was constantly on the brink of famine. When bad harvests and loss of fertile lands combined with endemic warfare, the result was hardship and shortage of the necessities of life, and the consequent creation of a number of landless displaced persons, who looked to an influential personage for support, for food, for lands and for protection. In the third century conditions were ripe for the creation of new groupings of tribesmen, ethnically mixed, owing allegiance to the leading families who had seized the opportunity to take control of production and trade, and thereby cement new alliances. A new division of society into aristocrats and peasants was created.[44]

There is no evidence which irrefutably links these climatic, social and military developments outlined above with the later invasions of the Roman Empire, but the theory is worth investigation. Tribal society was undergoing a reformation in the face of hardships beyond human control. Adaptation and initiative were the order of the day. As new groupings emerged and a new type of kingship evolved in the more settled societies, in parallel the warrior bands also evolved into more independent units, detached from the tribal bonds, serving whichever leader happened to be the strongest, ranging far and wide in pursuit of their aims, which were various and usually focused on the gratification of short-term needs. Leagues could be formed to find food, to search for booty, to form raiding parties which descended on tribal neighbours or the Roman Empire according to whim. These leagues were transitory, constantly changing in their groupings as tribesmen joined and departed, ethnically mixed, capable of instant division into newer, smaller groups under new leaders, or of equally instant amalgamation under one successful strong leader.[45]

Roman intelligence would scarcely be able to keep up with such amorphous, rapidly changing groups. Names of leaders might be noted but before the ink was dry there would be another leader. The Roman equivalent of a card index would be out of date before it was completed. It was impossible to keep track of who were the tribal leaders, or where the groups were. There was no time to negotiate a successful alliance with any leader before the group had split up into smaller units, or the tribesmen had elected a new leader who better suited their purpose. Such groups of warriors lived off the land, owing no allegiance to any central place, so the tactic of destroying the homelands and burning out the tribesmen was not an option for the Romans. They were forced instead to try to pre-empt attacks, a task at which they failed miserably, or to try to locate, pursue, and smash the groups once they had entered Roman territory. Though the leagues formed at the end of the second century among the Marcomanni and Quadi foreshadowed the third-century problems, they were subtly different from the warrior groups who plagued the Empire from the first decades of the third century. In the prolonged Marcomannic wars, Marcus Aurelius had been able to contain the tribesmen, ejecting them from the Empire and then keeping them at a safe distance beyond the frontiers. In the face of the new ethnically mixed tribal groupings, which were highly mobile, unencumbered with baggage and families, not seeking lands upon which to settle, and probably not excessively large, the frontiers did not perform very well. The nature of Roman warfare and defence had to change.[46]

These new federations of tribesmen served under military leaders to whom they owed everything. They faced pressures on food supply and the constant spectre of starvation, and subscribed heavily to the native tradition of warfare and glory. Coupled with the immediate accessibility of wealth just over the Roman frontier, all these factors combined to produce the threat to the Imperial provinces within reach of the highly mobile tribal warbands. Contemporaneously, at a time when radical rethinking and adaptation to the requirements of the day were absolutely paramount, Rome's usual thoroughness and resilience was diluted by several simultaneous internal and external problems. The stage was set for conflict, as the power of one of the contending sides increased in strength and organisation, and the power of the other was momentarily compromised.[47]

The names of the new tribal federations

The names by which we know tribal groupings, such as the most famous examples of Alamanni, Franks and Goths, give the immediate impression of distinct, ethnically homogeneous tribes whose existence was rooted in the deep past but whose origins were obscured by lack of definite knowledge. The names also convey the idea of centrally organised tribes, operating as a unit under one leader. Such is not the case. Firstly, tribal names which have come down to us are not necessarily those by which the tribes knew themselves. Sometimes the names which found their way into the ancient Greek and Latin sources were applied by outsiders to the tribes in question, and the tribe's original name for itself is sometimes lost. The Romans tended to use all-embracing terms to describe tribes or groups of tribes, without bothering too much about minor ethnic distinctions. Most Germans were labelled 'Suebi', which is a generic name meaning 'the people of one law'. Most of the tribesmen north of the Danube were called 'Scythians', until the term 'Goths' was substituted for the earlier name. Secondly, the new names applied to the federations were not necessarily always derived from ethnic names. The name 'Goths' has been interpreted as 'human beings'; the Franks derived their name either from a word meaning 'the free', or possibly 'the fierce', depending upon which particular etymological root word is considered to have been chosen to describe them. The Alamanni are usually said to encompass 'all men'. Many of the groups of people designated by generally accepted single names never comprised ethnically undiluted tribes; they were always mixed. When the sources describe attacks by these named peoples they are not to be taken at face value. For one thing the historians of a later age were not sure of the identity of the tribes they were attempting to describe, and at no time were the Roman authorities dealing with the entire 'tribe' under one leader.[48]

Another problem with names of people concerns not just the meaning of the words but also the origin of the labels. For some groups it is not known whether their names were chosen by the groups themselves or whether they accepted labels chosen for them by outsiders. Descriptive terms such as 'the free' or 'all men', with their connotations of proud separatism, may attest a conscious decision taken on behalf of the new groupings by the leaders or the participants in the groups to find a new denomination pertinent to all group members. If large numbers of men were drawn together for reasons of hardship or for common cause, their particular ethnic identities would probably never be forgotten, but would be submerged in the new identity, freely imposed as soon as the group began to feel a long-term cohesion. The adoption of names for the new federations was much more significant as a political act than as a naming process.[49]

The Alammani

The date when this group first appeared is disputed. The ancient sources attest that Caracalla fought the Alamanni as early as 213, but the authenticity of the name Alamanni at this early stage has been disputed. One of the sources is Dio, who wrote about 220 and had witnessed the events that he described under Severus and Caracalla, so it might seem that this author is the most reliable. The problem here is that all the passages where he mentions the Alamanni may not represent his actual words. Much of the text of Dio's history is put together from that of his later epitomisers, so the descriptions of the Alamanni could be retrospective interpolations made by writers who were familiar with the name by the time they came to read and use Dio's works. Similarly the *Historia Augusta*, the other source for Caracalla's battles against the Alamanni, is suspect on many counts, and was written (whatever the date of its composition) long after the events. The Emperor did not celebrate his victories by calling himself Alamannicus; in all sources his victory was over Germans. The Arval Brethren in Rome gave thanks to the gods for the victory on 6 October 213, naming Caracalla *Germanicus Maximus*. The title appeared on coins and inscriptions in the following year. The contemporary evidence recording the campaigns of the early third century reveals absolutely nothing about the federation of the Alamanni.[50]

The first properly attested use of the name Alamanni dates from a panegyric of 289, referring to a victory over the '*Burgundiones et Alamanni*' by Maximian in 286. Even so, there is room for disagreement on the date of the formation of the league of the Alamanni. Some authors project backwards as far as the reign of Severus, while others prefer a much later date. Christol favours 256, and yet others opt for a date after the invasions of 259–60 for the first appearance of the Alamanni as a named group. This does not deny the existence of a federation before any of these dates, of course. The groupings could have occurred much earlier, under other names now lost to us, before the title 'all men' was adopted. The ethnic composition of the Alamanni is generally taken to be mixed, and, among others, the Hermunduri and Naristae may have been absorbed into the group rather than being completely eradicated when the Alamanni swept over their lands. The Romans knew that the parent group was the Suebi or Suevi, to which the Juthungi also belonged. The Juthungi operated independently at first, as inscriptions attest; they first appear on the recently discovered inscription from Augsburg, where they are equated with the Semnones. The inscription is securely dated, since the text informs us that the stone was dedicated in September 260, recording battles fought in the previous April. The Juthungi merged with the Alamanni towards the end of the third century. By the sixth century, the author Agathias knew that the Alamanni were a mixed group, composed of different tribes. His source was a third-century author, Asinius Quadratus, who may have provided the information about the polyethnic nature of the Alamanni, or at least did not actually contradict the idea. Unfortunately this work is now known only in fragments.[51]

The Alamanni had no single leader or central organisation. They did not operate as one group. They had no fixed homeland until much later when

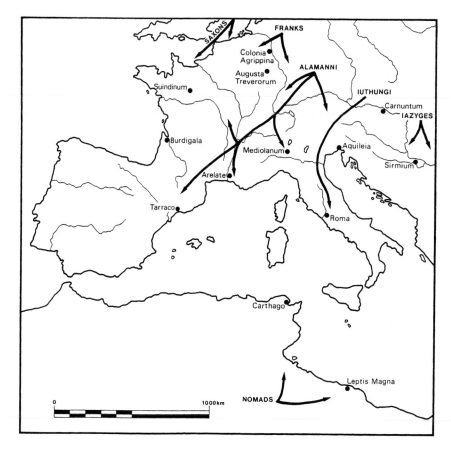

Figure 35 The Franks and the Alamanni first appeared in the 260s and 270s when they pene-
trated the Rhine and Danube frontiers. They were mobile and rapid movers, but
they had no strong central organisation and could split into several different groups
once they had crossed into Roman territory. Full documentation of where they
went and the damage they caused cannot be achieved, but a combination of literary
evidence and archaeological finds indicates that the effects of the invasions were felt
in southern Gaul and Spain. (Drawn by Graeme Stobbs.)

they eventually settled the areas they had overrun and devastated. When
they did settle the terrain prevented easy communication and was not conducive to unity. Independent kings and princes ruled over sections of
the Alamanni, but none of them could boast ancient lineage. The organisation is redolent of new assemblages of tribesmen, brought together by circumstance, clustered round opportunistic leaders who set themselves up as
kings or princes on an equal footing with other like-minded leaders. This is
to go beyond the evidence, but the evidence, such as it is, will bear that
interpretation.[52]

210

When the attacks were made on the Roman provinces, the numbers of men who broke through the frontier at various points may not have been enormous. Considerable damage can be done by relatively small groups of men, especially if they are daring enough and highly mobile. The attacks on Roman territories did not involve the whole people, nor even the entire subdivisions ruled over by the kings and princes. Nor were the descents on Roman territory carried out with the purpose of migrating into and settling in the Empire. The purpose was for individual gain, to plunder what could be carried off and to destroy what could not be moved. Modest numbers of men moving rapidly, with the advantage of surprise, wreaked havoc on the undefended countryside. The archaeological evidence reveals destruction of farms and houses and buried hoards of coins and precious metals in Raetia and Gaul, interpreted as proof of the passage of the Alamanni by some authors, and just as readily rejected by those who point out that even if destruction deposits and coin hoards can be dated, the sum total of the evidence does not necessarily prove that the direct causes behind it all were the invasions of the Alamanni or any other group.[53]

There is little archaeological evidence to support an invasion or any fighting in 213 under Caracalla. The first serious invasion which did leave traces of the passage of the Alamanni occurred in 233, coincidental with the expedition to the east under Severus Alexander. It is likely that significant numbers of troops had been removed for the campaign against Persia, and that the northern frontiers were consequently weakened. The Alamanni crossed the Rhine and Danube frontiers at several points, threatening Gaul and Raetia. Signs of burning at Regensburg, and traces of destruction accompanied by coin hoards at sites in the Bavarian Alps, have been associated with the invasion. More grisly evidence comes from the fort at Pfünz, where the soldiers guarding the south tower were killed *in situ*, having been given no chance to defend themselves. In the vicus, the temple of Jupiter-Dolichenus yielded a hoard of silverware and coins, the latest of which dates to 232. It has been questioned whether the destruction here was done by the Alamanni, and the dating has been challenged; the fact that the soldiers in the fort seemed not to have had time to defend themselves may have come about because the attackers were other Romans, during the revolt of Maximinus, who perhaps took the fort by treachery. But the evidence for destruction elsewhere is too strong for the presence of the Alamanni to be discounted altogether. Several sites in modern Bavaria have produced coin finds which end with those of Severus Alexander or with those of his mother Julia Mamaea. Whilst the coin evidence is not by any means conclusive, other evidence suggests that the invasions took the Romans by surprise. The case of Pfünz has already been mentioned. In Upper Germany, the Romans were not prepared for immediate attack, and were confidently rebuilding a shrine in the vicus at Öhringen and the fort baths at Walldürn. If there had been imminent danger the soldiers would surely have been refortifying and attending to the fort defences. The sum total of the archaeological evidence does suggest that the Alamanni swept through Raetia, causing fear of destruction if not actual destruction. They penetrated as far as Trier in the west and from the Danube they reached the northern Alps, perilously close to Rome itself. Maximinus Thrax repelled them, and pushed them back beyond the frontiers, celebrating his victory on coins with the legend *Victoria Germanica*. The invasions may have erupted again in the 240s while Gordian III was in the east. At the fort at Künzing, a large hoard of iron work was buried, including a magnificent collection of daggers. A bronze coin in mint condition was found with the deposit, dating to the reign of Gordian. Yet again in the 250s, more hoards of coins and treasure were buried in Raetia. In the autumn of 260, the Alamanni repeated the process. The Raetian frontier was overrun, and signs of destruction at Augsburg, Kempten, Bregenz, Grenoble and Lausanne have been associated with this invasion. The Emperor Valerian was in the east, where he was defeated and captured by the Persians – probably in the late summer of 260. When the news of his father's defeat reached him, perhaps followed or maybe preceded by the news of the attacks by the Alamanni, Gallienus was unable to go to the rescue of Raetia and Gaul. He was soon preoccupied with events in Pannonia, where the usurper Ingenuus had claimed the throne. When he was free of other problems, Gallienus brought the Alamanni to a halt near Milan in 260.[54]

It has been pointed out that the timing of the raids by the Alamanni and other tribes was perhaps not merely fortuitous, since they were often carried out at times when the Emperor was compromised in some way with other battles in other places, or with financial crises or with unrest in the provinces. It is not beyond the bounds of possibility that the tribesmen beyond the frontiers kept watch on events in the Empire and knew when there was trouble. They may not have known all the details, but they would be able to observe that troops were being removed, and could identify weak points fairly easily, exploiting them to the full. Some scholars are sceptical about the ability of the tribesmen to assemble information on the movements of the Roman troops, postulating instead constant raids or attempts at invasions which succeeded only when there was a lapse of Roman vigilance. Each case demands investigation on its own terms, since some occasions would be more likely than others to influence events on the other side of the frontiers. The defeat and capture of Valerian, previously mentioned, may have little bearing on the invasions of the Alamanni. Knowledge of the chronology of events in 260 is not precise enough to be certain that the invasions occurred subsequent to the receipt of information about the Roman disaster in the east. The news reached Egypt at some time in September 260, so it may have been known in Raetia and Germany by the late autumn. Probably, though, it had no bearing on the invasion of the Alamanni, whose needs would probably be more immediate and may have concerned a shortage of food: the invasion occurred when the crops would have been harvested and therefore the food would have been more easily portable.[55]

One of the most hotly debated questions concerning the Roman frontier is the date when the territory north of the Danube and west of the Iller was given up. In the ancient sources all the blame is thrown upon Gallienus for the loss of Raetia (*sub principe Gallieno Raetia amissa*), but he is not credited with doing anything constructive about the loss. The fully evolved Roman frontier based on the Rhine, Iller and Danube rivers is the composite creation of several Emperors who built and rebuilt fortifications and adjusted various details. Its initial conception is normally attributed to the Emperor Probus, but it is just as likely that the original idea and the foundation of this frontier belongs to Gallienus. The sources were hostile to this Emperor, and loath to grant him any credit, so it was perhaps natural that Probus, who came upon the scene less than a decade later and who perhaps finished off what Gallienus had started, should take all the praise for the establishment of the frontier. Gallienus refortified the old legionary fortress of Vindonissa (modern Windisch) guarding one of the main routes through the Alps; the commencement of rebuilding at this site is dated to 260 by an inscription later removed from the site and built into a wall at Altenburg. There is room for argument that the reoccupation of the first-century fortress of Vindonissa may have been carried out as a response to the invasions, but there are some scholars who think that Gallienus may have taken steps to fortify the area by a pre-emptive measure, and that the reconstruction may even predate the invasion of the Alamanni in 260. Probably at the same time, Gallienus put troops into Augusta Raurica (modern Augst), Castrum Rauracense (modern Kaiseraugst) and Basilia (modern Basel). All these sites have yielded a great number of coins from the reign of Gallienus.[56]

After the troops were withdrawn from the old frontier and the new frontier was created, the territory north and west of it, the *agri decumates*, was never reclaimed by the Romans. It is unlikely that the area was entirely deserted, but some inhabitants presumably relocated within the new confines of the Empire, and the Alamanni were slow to settle in the area they had overrun. The archaeological record shows that it was a poor area with regard to Roman imports after 260, so the area was perhaps impoverished for many years after the raids.[57]

The Alamanni remained peaceful during the rest of Gallienus' reign, but they were a constant perceived threat. The Emperors and the army were overstretched and could not protect all parts of the Empire. Insecurity was now a fact of life, and measures were taken, presumably on the part of individuals, to avoid attack by the Alamanni. In the Jura mountains hilltop refuges were occupied. Some of these hilltop sites yield only a few finds and so were perhaps inhabited for only a short time; other sites, such as Wittnauer Horn, have produced a greater quantity of finds, including pottery, which suggests that they were occupied on a more permanent basis. In 268 groups of Alamanni crossed the frontier again and entered Italy via the Brenner Pass. Another group repeated the raids in 271, joined this time by the Juthungi. Aurelian stopped them, but only after an initial defeat near Placentia. An important demonstration of the moral effect of the raids is the fact that Rome itself was hemmed in by walls for the first time since she became a power to reckon with in Italy, many centuries before. Numerous sections of Aurelian's walls of Rome remain on view, and are still impressive for their height and robustness.[58]

In 275, after the death of Aurelian, the Alamanni and Franks burst into Gaul, where for three years they enjoyed almost free rein to pillage, living off the land. They were brought to terms by the Emperor Probus, who arranged the return of prisoners and booty. He allegedly settled 400,000 tribesmen and extracted 16,000 men for the Roman army. This may be the origin of the *ala I Alamannorum*, the *cohors V Pacata Alamannorum,* and the *cohors IX Alamannorum* mentioned in the *Notitia*, along with the *ala I Juthungorum*, and the *cohors IV Juthungorum*. Nine kings submitted to Probus; no one can be certain if they were all from the Alamanni, since there would be many sub-groups who joined the main one when raids took place. An inscription from Augsburg (Augusta Vindelicum) praises the Emperor Probus for restoring the province of Raetia (*restitutor provinciae*).[59]

About a decade later in 286 Maximian won a victory over the Alamanni and Burgundiones, which was celebrated in a panegyric composed and delivered in 289. An inscription from Augsburg records Diocletian as *'fundator pacis aeternae'* or founder of eternal peace, a bold claim which may not have derived solely from encounters with the Alamanni, but the presence of the inscription in Augsburg suggests that the Roman armies were there during the campaign against them. A panegyric of 291 records victories over the Alamanni and Burgundiones once again, and in 302 the Romans won another battle near Vindonissa. Thereafter it seems that there was peace with the Alamanni, and it is not without significance that as the name of the group, Alamanni, declines in the sources, the place-name Alamannia is attested for the first time. It appears in the written sources, on a victory monument, and on coins. At the end of the third century the tribal name is last used by the author Arnobius; then the sources begin to celebrate victories over a territory, not over a people. The *agri decumates* is named on later maps and in later sources as Alamannia, so it may be that at the turn of the third and fourth centuries this area was settled and recognised as such, and the Romans fought the Alamanni on their own ground instead of inside the Empire. The presence of the Alamanni has never been forgotten in neighbouring Gaul, whose modern inhabitants, descendants of the Franks, label all Germans 'Allemands', and their country 'Allemagne'.[60]

The Franks

The early Imperial Roman authors such as Tacitus and Pliny did not know of the Franks, whose history began in the third century when they first appeared as raiders from across the Rhine. The Frangiones mentioned by Cicero in a letter to his friend Atticus have sometimes been suggested as possible forerunners of the Franks, but it is now considered that they were a different group of people who had nothing to do with the Frankish league of the third century. There is no reliable chronicle of the origins of the Franks. Their name may derive from adjectival descriptions meaning 'fierce', or 'the free', or, as has been argued, perhaps both names applied at different times, and meanings changed as different people came into contact with the Franks. The late Roman historians and later authors, all writing about events long before their own day, tried valiantly to give the Franks a respectable and retrospective ethnic identity. Gregory of Tours maintained that the Franks hailed originally from Pannonia, and came to settle on the right bank of the Rhine. Later chroniclers became even more fabulous in their search for origins, claiming that the Franks came from Troy, sharing their mythic foundation stories with the Romans themselves. In fairness, it could be that there was some confusion arising from mangled versions of the place-names with which the Franks were associated on the lower Rhine, where the most important city was Colonia Ulpia Traiana (modern Xanten) which may have been corrupted into Troiana. Even so, the lack of consistency in the authors who could not decide upon a single foundation myth argues very strongly for the fact that no one really knew when, where or how the Franks became a people.[61]

The Franks, like the Alamanni, were not an ethnically distinct tribe but a federation of smaller groups of people such as the Chamavi, Chattuarii, Bructeri, and Salii, all of whom are listed in the late third-century sources as Frankish. Other groups included the Batavi, Tubantes, Usipi and Tencteri. These were small tribes, most of them already known to the Latin and Greek authors. Individually these tribes were ineffective but in combination they would be much more powerful and could defend themselves against their aggressive Germanic neighbours. The Frankish league, whether it was formed on a progressive basis or on a sudden rapid impulse, was the outcome of a conscious social and political act. This is not to say that the above-mentioned tribes suddenly decided to amalgamate and place themselves under one leader. There was never any such unity or consensus. The Franks who broke through the Roman frontier in the 250s were not whole tribes working together. They were more likely bands of warriors serving their individual overlords, and the groups could split off and go their separate ways once inside the Roman Empire. The composition of these warrior bands was not limited to members of specific tribes. Any warrior, no matter what his ethnic origins, could join the group provided he found acceptance and would obey the leader.[62]

Traditional dating for the Frankish raids across the frontiers places the first of them in 253–4 when the Emperor Valerian was fighting in the east, and the second series of invasions in 256–7. More recently opinion has veered from this traditional viewpoint, inclining towards an abnegation of the invasions of 253–4; if there were such attacks they left little evidence of destruction behind them, whereas the archaeological traces of the invasions of 265–7 show that they were much more serious and caused widespread damage far from the frontier. The Franks pushed their way into Gaul, moving steadily southwards. Some of them reached Tarragona in Spain, where it was said that they remained for about a dozen years. It is thought that some groups may have taken ship and sailed to north Africa. The only literary source is Aurelius Victor, but a third-century inscription from Tamuda (modern Tetuan, Morocco) recording raids by unnamed barbarians has been interpreted as evidence of Frankish attacks.[63]

The traditional scenario depicts Gallienus as dilatory in his response to the danger and then quite ineffective against the Franks in 253–4, having to do all his work again three years after the first battles. Much depends upon the dating of Gallienus' three German victories, which have been interpreted as evidence of battles against the Franks, then against the Goths, all in keeping with the traditional dates for the Frankish invasions across the Rhine. Recently the dates of the victories and the actions of Gallienus have been reinterpreted, revealing the possibility that, far from being dilatory, the Emperor responded very rapidly to the Frankish threat, which in fact broke out for the first time in 256. Taking the evidence even further, Christol has suggested that the formation of the leagues of both the Franks and the Alamanni is to be dated to 256 and no earlier. According to this new interpretation, the first German victory celebrated by Gallienus has nothing to do with a battle against the Franks, but probably refers to a campaign against the Marcomanni in Pannonia in 254. Gallienus was at Viminacium (modern Kostolac, Yugoslavia) in 255, so the dating and location of the war is perfectly feasible. The second German victory is to be assigned to battles against the Franks in 256, and the third to the war against the Goths. In 256, responding quickly to the danger, Gallienus left Illyricum to hurry to the Rhine frontier, which had suffered considerable damage. He brought more troops to Germany, basing some of them at Mainz, and set up his headquarters at Cologne, to where he transferred the mint from Viminacium to facilitate paying his campaign army on the Rhine. There was some hard fighting and a Roman victory, possibly near Cologne, but Gallienus could not follow it up before he had to rush back to the Danube to attend to problems there. He left his young son Saloninus at Cologne, with M. Cassianus Latinius Postumus, perhaps as governor of Lower Germany, in command, though his exact appointment is not certain.[64]

The Franks were still on the loose, ravaging Gaul, and the frontier was in dire straits. The fort at Niederbieber on the lower Rhine was destroyed and given up about 258–9; the latest coins in the destruction deposits were dated to 258. Gallienus could do nothing to help, since he was by now facing the Alamanni in northern Italy. He won a victory at Milan in the spring of 260, but meanwhile the army in Gaul was growing impatient. The danger from the Franks and the absence of Gallienus were two contributory factors in the elevation of Postumus as rival Emperor in the summer of 260. He confined his ambitions to the west, where he was fully stretched, defending what rapidly became the Gallic Empire. The Franks took Xanten, and menaced Cologne, but for some reason spared Trier. Taking to the sea, they raided the coast of north-western Gaul and the estuaries of the Somme and the Loire. It took three or four years for Postumus to gain the upper hand, but by 264 he was celebrating his new status as *restitutor Galliarum*, restorer of Gaul. According to Aurelius Victor, Postumus recruited Franks to fight Franks, which is perfectly feasible and based on solid Roman practice. There is no question of betrayal of their Frankish compatriots when Franks entered the service of Rome. They had no sense of nationhood or ethnic unity, and they served Roman leaders as faithfully as they served their own. It is not known whether these newly recruited Frankish soldiers were used to fill gaps in the ranks of existing units or whether they fought as individual units under their own leaders. It was more likely that they were dispersed among Roman units; when the Goths were recruited to fight under their own leaders by treaty arrangement it was thought worthy of comment.[65]

Small-scale Frankish raids continued while the Empire was split into factions. The legitimate Emperor Claudius II fought off the Alamanni and the Goths, while the Gallic Emperors struggled with problems of their own. Postumus and then his replacement Victorinus were assassinated, and Tetricus took over. He seems to have had some successes against the Franks, if his coinage proclaiming *Victoria Germanica* is to be believed. Shortly after Aurelian won back Gaul for the Empire, he left for the east, perhaps taking some of the Rhine troops with him. The Franks and the Alamanni seized the opportunity, pouring into the Empire in 274–5. It was said that 70 towns were destroyed in Gaul, which may be an exaggeration, but it is clear that the damage was extensive. Only those towns and cities which were fortified, such as Trier, Cologne and Toulouse, survived intact. Coin hoards on the Cologne–Tongres–Bavai route have been interpreted as evidence of the passage of the Franks. The Moselle valley was also affected.[66]

The Emperor Probus finally restored order by 278. He strengthened the Rhine frontier and built bridgehead forts to watch the territory north of the river. In order to remove the aggressive members of the Frankish league he recruited widely, filling gaps in his armies, and sent some groups of prisoners to settle on the shores of the Black Sea at the mouth of the Danube. These Franks were not subdued, however, and decided to go home. They stole ships, crossed the Black Sea, the Aegean and the Mediterranean, rounded Spain and reached the mouth of the Rhine. Their exploits excited

Roman imagination and admiration. The homing instincts may have arisen from an increasing identification with an area and a people. It has been suggested that after 276, when the lower Rhine frontier was virtually unprotected, the Franks exchanged their customary hit-and-run raids for a policy of permanent settlement within the Empire, or at least on the left bank of the Rhine.[67]

Not much is known of any action against the Franks immediately after the assassination of Probus. His successors Carus and Carinus proclaimed German victories on coins and inscriptions, but at least some part of the fighting was against the Quadi, so it is not certain what the title *Germanicus Maximus* is intended to celebrate. The energetic Maximian had considerable success against the Franks, and was suitably lauded for it. The panegyric addressed to him records the capture of a Frankish king, Gennobaudes, and a treaty made in 288 or 289 by the terms of which the Franks were to return all their prisoners. Some Franks were settled around Trier and perhaps near Bavai, and the first settlements of the *laeti* were organised near Amiens, Beauvais, Troyes and Langres.[68]

In the meantime, Carausius had been entrusted with the defence of the Channel coasts, but he broke away and declared himself Emperor in Britain. He perhaps did not aim at dominance of the whole Roman world, but his separatism was tolerated only while the legitimate Emperors were too preoccupied to fight him. Frankish warriors were recruited to fight on behalf of Carausius; they were still in evidence when Allectus succeeded Carausius, but it is not known what happened to them after Constantius Chlorus won back Britain for the Empire. Chlorus turned to the Rhine frontier where there was bitter fighting, continued sporadically under his son Constantine who was better able to marshal resources and power once he had eliminated some of the problems facing him. If the sources are accurate they show that the Romans had lost patience and had become extremely brutal in their struggle against the Franks. Two captured Frankish princes were made to fight against wild animals in the amphitheatre at Trier. To them their deaths may have been honourable, totally in keeping with the warrior tradition, but to the Romans it was an ignominious demise, designed to dehumanise the victims.[69]

Constantine recruited a great number of tribesmen, forming them into units which appear later in the *Notitia Dignitatum*. Most of the Frankish units, and those of the individual tribes who formed part of the Frankish league, were probably recruited originally by Constantine. Frankish soldiers could rise to officer status or even enter the armies as officers. The short-lived Emperor Silvanus was the son of a Frankish officer called Bonitus.[70]

The Frankish menace was not taken lightly even when there was no fighting and no invasions across the Rhine. There was a member of the Imperial household based at Trier and watching the Rhine frontier almost permanently during the first decades of the fourth century, despite the equally dangerous presence of the Goths on the Danube frontier. When Constantine died in 337, the Franks were still quiet for a while, but invaded in some strength in 341. These were allegedly the Salian Franks settled by Constantius Chlorus in the Netherlands, forced out by the Saxons. They were resettled in the Brabant, in an area called Toxandria, and the frontier, properly garrisoned and well guarded, was at peace for the next few years.[71]

The Goths

The Romans of the second century knew of a people called the Gutones situated north of the Danube, settled near the Vistula. The last-known mention of these people dates from about 150, when Ptolemy listed them in his *Geography*. Between then and the early third century there is no hint of any tribe under the name Gutones or Goths. The Romans were preoccupied with their various wars and other problems, and the peoples far beyond the frontiers were not included in the mainstream developments of the Empire. Only in 238 did the Romans become fully aware of the presence of the Goths, and even then they did not necessarily know them by that name.[72]

The history of the Goths was not written down until the early sixth century, when Cassiodorus, secretary to Theodoric the Great, was asked to produce an account of the Gothic people. This he did, probably during the years 526–33. Cassiodorus had a strongly vested interest in creating a seamless junction between Gothic and Roman society, and in order to imbue the Goths with a past that would be recognisable to the Romans he equated them with the Getae and Scythians, placing them north of the Black Sea and along the east bank of the Vistula. Cassiodorus may have had access to another source, the much-disputed history of the Goths by Ablabius; this must remain in the realms of conjecture, since there are some scholars who deny even the existence of Ablabius. Jordanes, writing in the mid-sixth century, may have used the work of Cassiodorus. He shared the same aims of fusing Roman and Gothic culture, but goes further in proclaiming a more distant origin for the Goths in Scandinavia, which he calls Scandza. He bolstered up his claims with references to Ptolemy's work and to that of Pomponius Mela. The suggested Scandinavian origin of the Goths has caused dissension among scholars. The German archaeologist Kossina found no difficulty in accepting the story, but much more evidence has come to light since his day, and later scholars are more cautious. The idea of a sudden migration from Scandinavia is generally rejected, usually in favour of a series of gradual encroachments on neighbouring lands over a long period of time, but the archaeological evidence cannot demonstrate the unadulterated purity of Gothic culture during these slow movements. As Heather points out, it is a false premise to try to find early 'Gothic' burials and monuments in Scandinavia, and traces of a later 'Gothic' presence extending towards the Vistula neatly illustrating a progressive migration. As the tribesmen moved they would meet many outside influences over a long period of time, and changes would occur perhaps with each new generation, subtle and not far reaching but enough to generate differences in culture and daily life after several years. On this basis it is not to be expected that replicas of the Scandinavian Gothic settlements, burial customs and artefacts will be represented in the archaeological record of the Gothic settlements in Poland.[73]

Kazansky summarises the arguments and proposes a solution that does not violate any of the main ideas. The Scandinavian origins of the Goths may be based on truth, and the migration probably took the form of a prolonged series of gradual movements as lands became exhausted or population increased. Archaeologists in Poland have discerned traces of Scandinavian culture imposed on the natives living near the Vistula. In Pomerania there are several burials of Scandinavian type, but dated to a later period than the original Scandinavian examples. It is postulated that the Goths arrived at the Vistula perhaps in the second half of the first century, which is not at odds with the statements of Jordanes or Ptolemy.[74]

The type site for early Gothic settlements is the village in east Prussia known as Willenberg-Wielbark, which has given its name to the so-called Wielbark culture. It was never exclusively Gothic. The people of the Wielbark culture did not share a common language, nor was there any political unity. The most distinctive Gothic trait was that warriors were buried without weapons; but the graves of the Wielbark culture display a variety of customs. The Goths were formed from a composite society, made up of different tribes. Nor was it a fixed society; men could come and go. It is not without significance that the name probably means simply 'men' – as in mankind, not necessarily gender.[75]

At the end of the second century and the beginning of the third, the Goths began to move. They spread slowly round the basin of the Vistula to the river Bug, to the Carpathians and the Ukraine. From Pomerania they spread out, moving into and blending with the Sarmatian settlements of the region around Cherniakhov, near Kiev, where another type of site giving its name to the whole culture was discovered and investigated in 1900. This culture was also a mixed racial one, but more technically advanced than the Wielbark culture. The people of the Cherniakhov culture were materially better off, and imported Roman goods as well as producing high-quality pottery and metalwork. There was also an intermix of tools and weapons like those found in the Gothic settlements of the Vistula, so it is supposed that the Goths were moving into this area in the second century. By physical movement or by absorbing knowledge of the Roman way of life, the Goths gradually came closer to the Roman Empire. They were not directly involved in the Marcomannic wars, but the Romans probably knew they were there, poised in the north. The source is the *Historia Augusta*, where it is indicated in the life of Marcus Aurelius that there were more tribes pushing southwards, precipitating the movements of the Marcomanni and

Quadi. Some modern scholars take this for an anachronistic analogy with the Huns of the fourth century, but others have postulated that the Goths were already known to the Romans of Severus' day and may have been recruited into the army.[76]

Early contacts with Rome, whenever they were established, would reveal to the Goths what was available across the frontiers. They traded with Rome, and developed a taste if not a need for oil and wine, and all kinds of prestigious luxury goods. The desire for more of the same may have motivated their descent on the Empire. On their travels they met with other tribes, such as Thracians, the ubiquitous 'Scythians' and other Germans, who joined them, seemingly operating with Gothic kings at their head. The strength of Gothic kingship seems to have been more pronounced than in other tribes, with much more authority and longer-lasting powers of

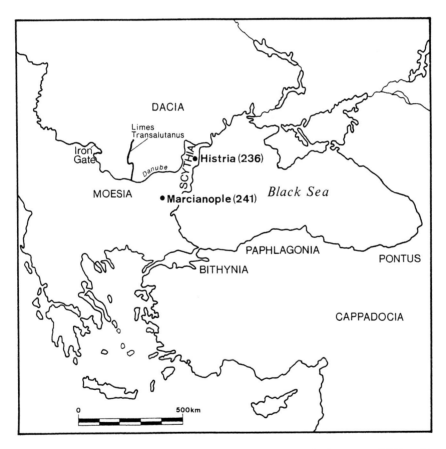

Figure 36 Map showing the main thrust of the Gothic invasions in the 230s and 240s, with battles at Histria and Marcianople. They quickly adapted to using sea transport, threatening the Black Sea coastal towns. (Drawn by Graeme Stobbs.)

221

unification. They used their powers skilfully, a factor which made their raids slightly more like military attacks than the hit-and-run skirmishes of a disorganised rabble. The Goths were also assisted by the fact that they had fairly easy access into the Empire, to Thrace, Macedonia and Greece.[77]

In 238, alongside the Carpi, they emerged from beyond the Danube to attack Olbia and Tyras, where they caused considerable damage. The coinage of Olbia disappeared altogether, and that of Tyras was interrupted for a long time, indicating cessation of all commercial activity. The Empire was in no position to mobilise all its resources to stop the invasions, being entangled in a complicated series of civil wars and usurpations. The chronology of the various Roman military actions and the invasions of the Goths cannot be easily equated, but it is sufficient to enumerate what was happening in the year 238. The Emperor Maximinus, chosen by the soldiers in 235, marched to Italy intending to eliminate his rivals Pupienus and Balbinus, chosen by the Senate. In Africa the revolt of the Gordians broke out and subsequently collapsed in a matter of months. All contenders for the throne were killed, leaving the young Gordian III as sole Emperor. Before the gruesome end of their 99–day rule, Pupienus and Balbinus despatched their general Menophilus against the Goths. He restored order and seems to have made a treaty, paying subsidies to the Goths but not to the Carpi, who were greatly offended. In return for the subsidies it is likely that the Goths contributed men for the Roman army.[78]

For the next decade there was more trouble from the Carpi than the Goths. The Emperor Philip celebrated victories over Germans and Carpi by his titles *Germanicus Maximus* and *Carpicus Maximus*. The Goths remained quiet, but in 248–9, ostensibly because Philip stopped paying their subsidies, they invaded again. After some probable but unknown successes against them, Decius declared himself Emperor and marched to Rome, no doubt taking troops from the Danube frontier with him. The opportunity was seized by a new federation of different tribesmen under the Gothic king, Cniva, who led an attack on Dacia and Moesia in 250. He besieged Philippopolis (modern Plovdiv), which fell to him in summer when the usurper Priscus handed the city over on the mistaken assumption that the Goths would do no harm. They sacked it. Meanwhile, Decius, now Emperor, fought the Carpi in Dacia and pushed them back, then turning to the relief of Philippopolis. Cniva outwitted him, attacking while he was on the march. Battered and unable to sustain another battle, Decius reformed his army at Oescus, then early in 251 he marched to intercept Cniva and the Goths who were heading for home. At Abrittus (modern Razgrad, Bulgaria) Decius and his army met the main Gothic force. The result was a disaster for the Romans. Decius and his son were both killed. The general left in command, Trebonianus Gallus, extricated his troops and allowed the Goths to continue on their journey. He could do nothing to rescue the prisoners marching with the Goths or to retrieve the booty stolen from the Roman settlements. It is possible that he agreed to pay subsidies as well. It was a black day for Rome, and though Gallus was declared Emperor, he never lived down the reputation for cowardice and even treason.[79]

Detailed information is lacking for subsequent Gothic invasions. The governor of Moesia, Aemilianus, stopped the payments of subsidies and started a war that he did not finish. The Goths attacked Thrace and Moesia, and in retaliation Aemilianus attacked across the Danube. Then he was declared Emperor by the troops and headed for Rome. Perhaps because they themselves were exhausted, and the lands through which they attacked certainly were exhausted, the Goths do not seem to have caused too much damage in the next few years, but by 255 they had learned how to use ships to descend on the coasts from the sea. For three years bands of Goths ravaged the towns and cities round the Black Sea. Trebizond fell to them in 256 because the soldiers guarding it panicked and fled. It has been suggested

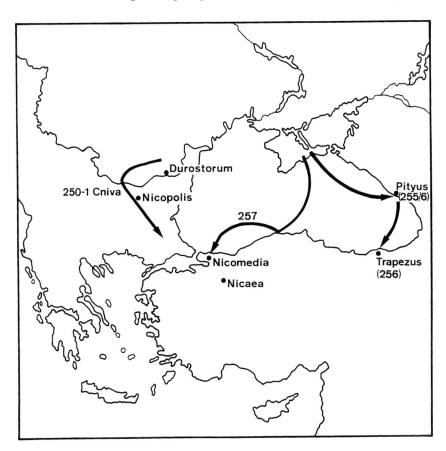

Figure 37 In the 250s and 260s the Goths resumed their attacks over land and sea routes. (Drawn by Graeme Stobbs.)

that the Goths turned to the sea because the land routes had been effectively guarded, so their progress was blocked. The use of ships also shows that the Goths were adaptable and easily learned new skills. After the first year, when they simply used ships to reach distant territories, then disembarked, left the ships behind and went on their plundering expeditions, they soon learned about the advantages of combined operations from land and sea so that they had some chance of getting home again. Eventually they tried their hand at sieges too, but were not as successful as besiegers as they were as sea raiders.[80]

The raids carried in their wake concomitant troubles caused by the vagaries of human behaviour. It is clear from the letter written by Gregory Thaumaturgus, Bishop of Neocaesarea, at some unknown date in the mid-third century, that the repercussions of a Gothic descent on Roman territory involved a great deal of underhand activity on the part of the inhabitants of

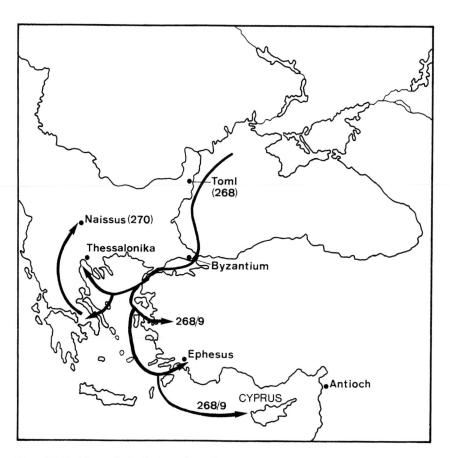

Figure 38 Gothic attacks in the late 260s and 270s. (Drawn by Graeme Stobbs.)

the provinces concerned. Goods seized and carried off by the Goths sometimes came into the hands of other provincials, who could claim that they
had 'found' things, including captives who were sold into slavery with no
questions asked. On occasion it seems that some provincials attacked their
neighbours and blamed it on the Goths, and, worse still, some provincials
joined the Goths. No one was safe, either from the tribesmen or their own
neighbours. Lawlessness engendered insecurity, which in turn engendered
desperation. Gradually, the situation was retrieved, and the Romans gained
the upper hand. When the Goths invaded using different routes in 268, they
tried and failed to take Tomi and Marcianopolis. Similarly they were beaten
off from Cyzicus and Byzantium. As the Goths learned about the Romans,
the inhabitants of the threatened provinces had also learned about the
Goths. Cities did not automatically fall when they approached. The year 268
was a turning point for the Romans and the Goths. Three groups of tribesmen split off from each other and went different ways, and were individually
defeated in successive years. Gallienus met one group at the river Nestus in
Thrace and won a decisive victory. Another group was driven back from the
Aegean. Finally Claudius II, who was the first to take the title *Gothicus
Maximus*, crushed the Goths at Naissus. On account of the similarity of the
names, detractors of Gallienus have conflated his battle of the Nestus with
Claudius' battle at Naissus, and have denied that Gallienus had any success
against the Goths. There is no reason to doubt his part in the Gothic wars,
which required remorseless fighting over a number of years. The follow-up
to these battles came in 271 when Aurelian, on his way to the east, carried
the war across the Danube and defeated and killed the Gothic king,
Cannobaudes (which may be an alternative form of the name Cniva).
The Roman victory was complete.[81]

Some scholars have argued that it was at this point that Aurelian gave up
the province of Dacia, settling the inhabitants in a new Dacia, carved out of
the old province of Moesia on the southern bank of the Danube. Others
prefer to date this event to 273, in the context of the war against the Carpi,
broken off suddenly because news arrived that the Palmyrenes, who had
recently submitted to Aurelian after the fall of their city and the capture of
their queen, had revolted again and had set up another ruler in the east.
Worse still, Egypt was in the hands of a Palmyrene sympathiser, so Rome's
food supply was threatened. The situation demanded the presence of the
Emperor in the east and an able deputy in Egypt, and large numbers of
troops would have to be gathered for the second Palmyrene and Egyptian
campaigns. One rather drastic way of leaving the northern frontier quiet and
protected in his rear while Aurelian fought elsewhere was to take the legions
out of Dacia and install them on the Danube. On balance, this date for a
hasty evacuation of Dacia is preferable (see Chapter 3). It may not have been
intended as a permanent arrangement; had he survived beyond 275 Aurelian
may have returned to Dacia. Perhaps he regarded it as a short term measure,

operable until he had finally conquered the east and made the Parthian frontier safe. Whatever his long-term intentions were, he surrendered what was left of the old province of Dacia for the Carpi and the Goths to settle in and fight over, no doubt reasoning that while the tribesmen battled against each other for vacant lands their attention could be diverted from Rome. The Goths emerged as the victors, but it took them a few years to eject their main rivals – first the Bastarnae, who were settled in the Empire by Probus, and then the Carpi, who appealed to Galerius for help. The Goths settled on either side of the Carpathians, and the division into two branches was crystallised thereafter. The western group formed the Tervingi or Vesi (Visigoths), and the eastern group were the Ostrogothic Greuthungi. The history of these Goths belongs to a later period. From the point of view of the Romans, the Gothic occupation of Dacia after Aurelian's crushing victory provided a long breathing space in which the Goths did not disturb the peace for 'centuries', according to Ammianus Marcellinus, whose hyperbole can perhaps be brought down to 'many years'.[82]

6

BEYOND THE EASTERN
FRONTIERS

Rome's relations with her strongest eastern rival had never been stable. The Parthian Empire of the Arsacids, founded by Arsaces *c.*250 BC, was subject to the same disruptions as the Roman Empire: internal unrest, external threats and the ever-present possibility of usurpation. Arsaces himself had won his throne by force, driving out the previous dynasty of the Achaemenids and taking over their territories by right of conquest. Just as in the Roman world, there was always the threat of dynastic squabbles and military risings; the Parthian Empire was a conglomerate of different peoples and tribal groups, not all of whom submitted easily to Parthian rule. Vassal kings sometimes rebelled, aiming for independence or alliance with other powers, and nomadic tribes on the borders occasionally invaded the more settled territory. From the late Republic onwards a mutual tension between the two powers had occasionally erupted into war, and Rome always kept one eye on events in the east. Great expeditions had been mounted against the Parthians, sometimes in response to a perceived threat and sometimes in response to direct provocation, as for instance when Mark Antony's generals were attacked in Syria, Judaea and Asia Minor. These Parthian expeditions had always cost a great deal in money and personnel, and were not always successful. Some were disastrous, most infamously that of Marcus Licinius Crassus, who was defeated and killed by the Parthians in 53 BC. Antony fared no better when he tried to dash through Armenia and come upon the Parthians from the north. Augustus avoided war altogether, and by a much celebrated diplomatic tour de force he managed to retrieve the Roman military standards that Crassus had lost. Diplomacy did not suit all Emperors. Whenever Rome was free of other serious pressures, organising an attack on Parthia was a customary demonstration of strength, and likewise the eastern power made demonstrations whenever there was opportunity. Each side monitored the problems of the other, sometimes choosing a moment to attack when there were external threats or internal rebellions to distract the attention of the current ruling house. Tremendous resources and effort went into Rome's eastern campaigns, sometimes without tangible rewards.[1]

Control of the kingdoms sandwiched between Rome and Parthia was of paramount importance for both antagonists. As fortunes varied for one or the other, kingdoms and territories like Armenia, Media, Mesopotamia and Osroene were cultivated or sometimes taken over by whichever power was the stronger. Rulers, princes and kings were installed and uninstalled according to their loyalties to one or the other superpower, while various portions of smaller kingdoms were occasionally hacked off and appended to a different smaller kingdom. The inhabitants of the borderlands and small kingdoms probably witnessed several types of government and overlords in one lifetime, perhaps not knowing who would be coming to collect the taxes from one year to the next. Some of these rulers, installed by one side or the other, managed their affairs so well that they were able to retain a degree of independence while satisfying both opposing sides, convincing them that they were loyal and true. The Armenian kings were especially adept at this. Rome made some inroads into the client kingdoms and allied states, annexing large or small areas as and when convenient. Vespasian took over Lesser Armenia and attached it to the province of Cappadocia. Trajan annexed Armenia itself, and also Mesopotamia, but Hadrian abandoned much of his predecessor's eastern conquests. In the reign of Marcus Aurelius and Lucius Verus there were more campaigns beyond the Euphrates, and garrisons were left in cities that had once been wholly Parthian possessions, the most famous example being Dura-Europos, established as a Roman frontier garrison in 165. But it was left to Severus to expand the Roman Empire further eastwards. He created new provinces which he called Osroene and Mesopotamia, though the latter did not encompass the whole territory normally designated by this name, only the part of it nearest to the Roman provinces. Thereafter Roman Mesopotamia was a thorn in the side of the Parthians, since it had always been their preserve to colonise and exploit the area. Now Rome had forcibly extended her influence further east than ever before, and it probably seemed to the Parthians as though the Romans were intent not only on remaining but perhaps even advancing. The ancient sources recognised that the legacy of Severus' annexation of Mesopotamia was constant and costly war.[2]

THE RISE OF THE SASSANIDS: ARDASHIR DEFEATS THE PARTHIANS

The successors of the Parthians construed the presence of Rome in the east in the same fashion as their predecessors. Just as Rome was undergoing changes in the third century, so was the eastern power. The Parthian regime was weakening at the end of the second century. Lack of strong central control, combined with aggressive attacks by the Romans, led to anarchy – a state of affairs that was exploited by minor but ambitious kings at the eastern end of the Parthian Empire. The Iranian Ardashir had begun to establish his power while the Parthian Royal House was fully occupied in fighting the Romans at the western extremities of their Empire. Severus and then Caracalla both conducted campaigns against Parthia, so for some years the Parthian king could not abandon the western frontier with Rome. While the wars with Rome progressed, Pabag, an Iranian noble traditionally descended from the house of Sasan, together with his two sons Ardashir and Shapur, had successfully staged a revolt against the king of Istakhr, near Persepolis, elevating themselves to the kingship seemingly without much opposition. This was probably in 208, though the date is not established beyond doubt. Exactly how Ardashir, as the second son of Pabag, managed to become king himself is not fully elucidated; after the death of Pabag there may have been a quiet fratricide in the palace at Istakhr, though tradition has it that Shapur died after an accident: a wall fell on him, or in another slightly different version a stone from a wall fell on him. It may have been aimed, not simply dislodged. For the next few years Ardashir assembled an army of his own, augmenting it each time he took over another state. He concentrated on extending his power over the neighbouring territories, some of which were provinces of his newly won kingdom based at Stakhr, and some of which were independent states. What they all had in common was their relationship to the Parthian king himself, to whom they were all subject as his vassals or allies. The blatant empire-building in the east of the Parthian state was a direct affront that Artabanus V could not ignore, but unfortunately he was fully occupied with the Roman offensive of Caracalla. The revolution grew in strength as Ardashir consolidated his conquests and allied with other discontented kings. At first he may have been one among many, but he soon assumed the leadership and afterwards he rewrote his own history in glowing heroic terms. He did not reach power unopposed; he failed to take over Media, could not reduce Hatra, and made no headway in Armenia, but in c.220 he and his allies marched into Mesopotamia, threatening the city of Seleucia-Ctesiphon on the Tigris. Having captured the city he made it his capital, and was eventually crowned king there when he had eliminated the Parthian Royal House. The brother of Artabanus, Vologaeses V, was killed at the end of 222 or the beginning of 223. Ardashir now had only one obstacle in his way to supreme power. When Artabanus V finally marched against him in 224, Ardashir had an experienced army and several allies at his back, though little enough is known about his army and how it operated. Normally the army would be assembled for a specific campaign and would be disbanded once the campaign was over, but it is likely that Ardashir kept his troops together. He had welded all the allied forces into one and used them to good effect in the final battle against Artabanus. At a place that cannot be identified today, called Hormizdagan, Artabanus lost the battle, his throne, and his life. The revolution was completed. Some of the Parthian troops under Artavasdes, the son of Artabanus, fled to the mountains to continue resistance, but they were all captured and brought to Ctesiphon to be executed.[3]

Ardashir's government and state religion

By 226 Ardashir had made himself *Shahanshah*, king of kings, establishing a new dynasty in full control of the old Parthian Empire. From the early third century onwards it is convenient to label the new dynasty that of the Persians, signifying a return to the old regime of Darius and Xerxes, the arch enemies of the Greeks, but a more accurate appellation is the dynasty of the Sassanids, derived from the name of the grandfather (some versions say the father) of Ardashir: Sasan or Sassan. Persian tradition imbues Ardashir with recognisable heroic traits even before he was born; the story was told that Sasan was a guest of Pabag, who predicted that any offspring of this illustrious guest would achieve great successes, so he lent him his wife for the night and the result of the union was Ardashir. This is retrospective embroidery of the kind that most usurping regimes require in order to establish firm roots for their power. When the Romans finally became aware of Ardashir's rise to power they interpreted his ambition as a desire to reconstitute the old Empire of the ancient Persians; Herodian specifically says that he set out to regain all the territories that had once formed part of the Persian Empire. It is more likely that Ardashir was a realist and an opportunist, rather than a man with a mission to be realised at all costs. The new regime was vigorous and well organised, replacing the loose Parthian administration with a much more centrally controlled government – not quite so regimented as the Roman Imperial system, with its provinces and manned frontiers, but still comprising tighter control of the vassal states and allies than ever before. Government of the states and kingdoms around the core of the Empire was controlled by the king of kings himself, and army commands were kept within the Royal family. A strong unifying force in this central control was the spread of worship of Mazda, or Ahuramazda, the supreme and singular Iranian god. The people of ancient Iran had a long-established tradition of Mazdeism, or Zoroastrianism, so the elevation of this tradition into a state religion did not need to be a violent, coercive procedure. It was a particularly benevolent and tolerant religion; Christian and Jewish communities flourished, for the most part unmolested, until the persecutions during the reigns of Vahram II and Shapur II, the first orchestrated by the high priest Kartir. This individual gained a high position at court and is shown on many of the Sassanid rock carvings, accompanying the Royal family. He was active from the time of Shapur I but came to prominence during the reign of Vahram II (276–93), when he launched a campaign to eradicate cults that were not devoted to the worship of Ahuramazda. The Parthian kings had also zealously endorsed the worship of Ahuramazda, but it seems that it was the Sassanid Ardashir who co-ordinated the official state Church and put it onto a firm footing. The priests and magi who had been suppressed by the Parthians were called out again to serve the state religion. Ardashir is credited with gathering together all the sacred texts of the *Avesta*, the repository of the Zoroastrian doctrine and wisdom, whose origins were oral rather than textual, perhaps reaching as far back as the beginning of the first millennium BC. About 500 BC the first written sources appeared. At some time in the Sassanian period the first authorised edition was produced, and although there is no positive proof as to which of the Sassanid kings was responsible for the new edition it may well have been Ardashir who concentrated on tracing and collecting all the fragments and texts. He derived his power directly from Ahuramazda, depicting his investiture by the god in three great rock carvings at Firuzabad, Naqs-i Rustem, and Naqs-i Rajab near Persepolis. His son and grandson, Shapur I and Vahram I, imitated these portraits of their investiture by Ahuramazda, underlining their political and religious authority. Technically Ardashir was a usurper, whose claim to rule rested solely upon right of conquest and not upon long-established royal lineage. It would have been of great advantage to him to found and promote a state religion at the outset of his career, with himself as the head of the Church, worshipping an all-powerful, kindly god, one of whose main attributes was the protection of kings.[4]

The Parthian and Sassanid army

The most striking disadvantage that hampered the Parthians, from the Roman point of view, was that their army was never put onto a permanent footing, nor did the Sassanids alter the military system to create the sort of standing paid army that the Romans could put into the field. In the accounts of the wars with Rome, it is easy to assume that the Persians had a readily available standing army such as the Romans had always possessed since the late Republic. This was not the case, and though there may have been an army in the field for very long periods, and there may have been a few places that were under guard on their western frontier, the Persian kings were in a position much more akin to the feudal Normans, who had to assemble an army for each campaign, relying upon the nobles to marshal their retainers and take command of sections of the army under the overall command of a prince of the Royal House. In the Sassanid army, though there were plenty of warrior-nobles, there was no permanent cadre of officers with military experience, and no system of perpetual recruitment to keep individual units up to strength, because there were no standing units. The soldiers who were brought into the various wars were of doubtful quality, untrained for the most part and reluctant to leave their homes and farms. In consequence, both the Parthians and the Persians had to hire mercenaries. All things considered, the Persians held their own very well against the Romans, whose armies were permanent and supposedly more professional.

Another disadvantage for the Persians arose from the vast distances over which their army and mercenaries were drawn together from different parts of their Empire. Distance equals time, which in turn limited the effectiveness of their response to threats from the Romans on their western border. But knowledge of their own territory and the vastness of the Persian domains could also assist in defence, the equivalent of the vastness of Russia in modern European warfare. In these situations it is difficult enough to invade, even more difficult to make the enemy fight the decisive battle, then impossible to remain, and impossible to retreat without heavy losses. The Romans more than once reached the capital city of Ctesiphon and could have taken it, but they did not annex it or do anything meaningful to consolidate their brief conquests. Sooner rather than later they had to retrace their steps, over ground where they had eaten all the food and used up all the resources, or over different routes but with just as many problems of supply. Reciprocally, the Romans too had to assemble large campaign armies from their other frontiers and were unable to respond rapidly to any threat emanating from the Persian attacks on their territories if these attacks overwhelmed the forces at the disposal of the provincial governors. A mutual distrust between the two powers ensured that there could never be peace where their territories adjoined, only extended periods of armed truce.[5]

THE ROMAN EASTERN FRONTIER

Rome's response to the perceived threat from the Parthian and then the Persian kings was to strengthen her frontiers and fortify strategic points, committing troops to the permanent defence of the eastern provinces. Not too many troops, because governors of large provinces with masses of troops at their disposal tended either to entertain delusions of grandeur or have delusions entertained on their behalf by a coterie who came to the conclusion that the governor would make a better Emperor than the one who was currently ruling. Partly for this reason, Severus had divided some provinces into smaller units, notably in Syria and on the Danube frontier in Pannonia. The eastern frontier was not guarded by running barriers like the northern frontiers of Britain, Germany, and Raetia, and though frontier lines have been traced in the eastern provinces they function more as protected communication routes rather than defended barriers. The degree of military action on Rome's eastern frontier in the third century has been disputed, with some scholars taking it for granted that there would be perpetual skirmishing, while others dismiss this theory as untenable and unproven. There may have been a constant need for policing on the long eastern frontier, in response to raids, thefts, sporadic homicides, frequent cases of grievous bodily harm, drunken brawls between soldiers and civilians, between civilians and other civilians, and the like; but none of this need represent military action on the part of the Persians. Nor is it necessarily representative of attacks or concerted aggression by any particular tribes or sections of the communities on the non-Roman side of the frontier. From the third century onwards there is much talk in literary and epigraphic sources of 'Saracens', but this does not denote a united ethnic tribe or identifiable homogeneous group. Anyone who caused trouble or committed lawless acts of varying degrees, on either side of the frontier, was labelled a Saracen, perhaps in much the same vein as some inhabitants of the English-speaking world refer to destruction by vandals (written in lower case and not to be confused with the tribesmen who eventually carved out a kingdom in north Africa). Police work was a normal task for the multifunctional Roman army. The soldiers fulfilled all the duties that in modern times are performed by different uniformed units, such as customs guards, security corps, traffic wardens, police, as well as purely military personnel whose main purpose was to defend the provinces and go to war beyond them. Warfare between the Romans and the Persians was endemic in the third century, but it was not continuous, due in part to the disadvantages that the Persians suffered. More often than not it was Rome who was the aggressor, sometimes with disastrous consequences.[6]

THE REIGN OF ARDASHIR (224–41)

The opening rounds of the third century left Rome in the ascendancy, with the campaigns of Severus ending on a reasonably successful note, his lack of success at Hatra eventually offset by the annexation of Mesopotamia and Osroene. The Romans did eventually take Hatra, perhaps in 230. But despite Severus' achievements there had been no lasting treaty, guaranteed to ensure peace for some time thereafter. Caracalla achieved little, not even finding an enemy to fight on his last expedition. Even if it had been possible to force a battle and to win it, the disaffection with the Emperor would probably not have been avoided, and the assassination of Caracalla would have altered the state of affairs; it made the Romans attend to their own problems for a while. In 217 the new Emperor Macrinus extricated the troops and bought peace from Artabanus after an indecisive battle, strictly speaking a Roman defeat, near Nisibis in Mesopotamia. He ought to have dispersed his army immediately, secured the frontiers and gone to Rome, but before he could do so the women of the Severan house emerged supreme, establishing Elagabalus as the true successor to Caracalla. For a short time the unfinished business of the eastern frontier had to be shelved, until the young Severus Alexander could return to it in 231. In the meantime everything had changed. By this time Ardashir was in full control of an increasingly centralised state; he had been king of kings for four or five years, relatively secure on his throne since he had a son who was old enough to succeed him. This was Shapur, destined to be even more of a deadly enemy of Rome than his father. In 230 Ardashir was ready to face Rome with a much more aggressive policy than his predecessors. He invaded Mesopotamia and put Nisibis under siege, an important city for control of communications and most of all for trade, not to be relinquished lightly to the Romans if the Persian Empire was to be put onto a solid footing. These considerations clashed with Roman interests, upsetting the fragile balance of power and threatening client states and allies of Rome. Diplomatic missions and negotiations produced no agreement, so the Romans had to go to war if the aggressive activities of the new Persian regime were to be stopped. Severus Alexander assembled a campaign army, which he led in person like Trajan, Severus and Caracalla before him; from the end of the second century the Roman Emperors had to command the army and be present in the war zone, especially in the east. There was no lack of competent, experienced generals to conduct the wars on the frontiers, but the pattern was rapidly becoming established whereby the victorious commander was declared Emperor and had the choice of marching on Rome. Instead of waiting for that to happen the Emperor went on campaign, running the alternative risk of being deposed and assassinated in the war zone rather than in the Imperial palace in Rome. Another reason why the Emperor had to be present at the wars was that the terms of peace treaties, if it came to the point where they could be arranged, were best debated in person than via delegates at a vast distance.[7]

The result of Severus Alexander's campaigns of 232 was a stalemate. The initial plan to attack in three main columns, with the Emperor in the centre and two other armies to north and south was sound, but it failed to bring decisive success. The Romans were prevented from mounting another campaign in the following year by the outbreak of war on the northern frontier. Had they been able to start again on the offensive in 233–4 there is a remote chance that they would have gained the upper hand, because although Ardashir had defeated one of the three Roman columns – the one led by the Emperor himself – the Romans fared better in Media, and for about six or seven years the Persians were not ready to attack again once the Romans had withdrawn to fight their wars on the Rhine and Danube. For whatever reason, Ardashir did not feel strong enough to challenge Rome by continuing his invasion of the Empire, or there was nothing that he wanted or hoped to gain by doing so. Although Herodian speaks of a truce, once again there was no peace treaty or any negotiation, and the absence of a firm conclusion to the war ensured that this was not the end of Roman and Persian conflict.[8]

THE REIGN OF SHAPUR I (241–72)

By the end of 238 or the beginning of 239, the Persians were ready for another assault on the Roman east. They attacked and took several cities in

Syria and Roman Mesopotamia. Hatra fell to them, probably in 240. It was another two years before the Roman government took action against the Persians. The young Gordian III and his Praetorian Prefect Timesitheus mobilised in 242, preparing for a campaign in 243. It was a fortuitous time to start the campaign, since Ardashir died in 241, and on his accession his son Shapur was preoccupied with rebellion among the conquered peoples on the periphery of his Empire. He subdued the rebellions and was crowned king of kings in 242, so when the Romans arrived he was ready to face them. For this period the evidence is not limited to the works of the Roman or Greek historians, presenting the Roman point of view, since Shapur recorded his exploits in the so-called *Res Gestae Divi Saporis*, the famous inscription from Naqs-i Rustem, carved on the rock face in three languages. Parthian, Persian and Greek. Shapur first establishes exactly who he is, the Mazda-worshipping king of kings, son of Ardashir. Then he carefully documents all the territories that he commands. The next entry is a laconic account of the war with Gordian III, who marched against him with an army drawn from the whole Roman Empire and from the Goths and Germans. There was a great battle at Meshike, in which Gordian was killed, and the Romans made Philip their Emperor. Then the new Roman Emperor made peace, paying 500,000 denarii to buy it. It is assumed that there was a treaty between the two powers. Meshike was renamed Peros-Sabour in honour of Shapur's victory; the Romans called the place Pirisabora (modern al-Anbar). Shapur depicted his defeat of the two Emperors on several rock carvings, notably at Bishapur, where Gordian III is shown lying beneath Shapur's horse, and Philip kneels before the king of kings.[9]

The Romans left, proclaiming that peace had been made with the Persians (*pax fundata cum Persis*). Philip made novel arrangements for the government of the east, installing his brother Priscus, who was already Praetorian Prefect, as *rector orientis*. Shapur was the most vigorous and the most hostile king of kings, representing much more of a threat to Rome than the Parthian kings for many generations, so Philip tried to counter the threat by leaving behind him a reliable deputy who could watch for further developments in the east. Shapur did not remain quiescent for very long after the treaty of 244. In the early 250s, perhaps even earlier, he was involved in a struggle over the control of Armenia, whose king, Chosroes, may have raised a revolt against him. It is possible that the Romans backed the revolt or encouraged it because it was in their interests to foster internal warfare on the borders of Shapur's territory. Shapur resorted to subterfuge, disposing of the king by having him murdered and then establishing control over the kingdom. He departed from the usual tradition; instead of installing a pro-Persian king of his own choice he subjected the country to direct military rule, creating a territorial province as the Romans had tried to do from time to time. In the meantime, the son of Chosroes, Tiridates, had fled the country, his most likely destination being the Roman Empire. The sources do not fully corroborate this supposition, merely attesting that he went to Greece, but it is more than likely that he had Roman support when he returned to Armenia, allegedly ousting Shapur's troops with great slaughter.[10]

According to Shapur's account 'the Roman Caesar [who is not named] lied and did wrong over Armenia', which perhaps refers to Roman support for the revolt of Chosroes or for his son Tiridates. There may have been an agreement in the peace terms with Philip that the Romans would not intervene in Armenian affairs. The context is uncertain, and the Emperor to whom Shapur refers may be Philip, or possibly Trebonianus Gallus. Next, Shapur says that he made war on the Romans, inflicting a severe defeat on a large Roman army of 60,000 men at Barbalissos. This may mean that in the course of invading Syria, the Persians wiped out a provincial garrison, perhaps exaggerating the numbers; the Roman sources are either unaware of this disaster, or more likely contemporary annalists decided to gloss over it. There is no Roman tradition of a full-scale war in the east until the campaigns mounted by Valerian, and even then the dates of these events are only approximate. The main focus of Roman activity in the second half of the third century was on the Danube and in the provinces threatened by the Gothic raids across the river. The Emperor Decius was killed in 251 whilst fighting against the Goths; his successor Trebonianus Gallus, formerly governor of Moesia, fought desultorily but then made peace and returned to Rome with Decius' son. The apparent lack of effort against the Goths incensed the Roman army, so they readily proclaimed Marcus Aemilius Aemilianus Emperor when he took over as governor of Moesia and began to fight the Goths with some success. Aemilianus left the frontier and marched towards Italy to fight it out with Trebonianus Gallus, and though the potential civil war was averted by the intervention of Valerian and the death of Aemilianus, the rapid turnover of Roman Emperors did not cease. Shortly afterwards, Gallus died; the army raised Valerian and his son Gallienus as joint Emperors. There was a recurring tradition of striking the enemy when there was trouble elsewhere; while the Romans fought amongst themselves Shapur seized his chance. It may have been in 252, as Gallus made peace with the Goths and returned to Rome, when Shapur attacked Armenia, though some authorities date this to the following year. As the rebellion of Aemilianus was played out, Shapur turned his attention to Antioch and may have captured the city in 253 when the Roman coinage temporarily ceased. The mint reopened in 254, which is taken as an indication that the Emperor Valerian had re-established Roman control of the city.[11]

The capture of Valerian and the supremacy of Odenathus

There is little enough detail to elucidate Roman or Persian activity from 254 to c.260. Whatever gains that Shapur had made within Roman territory, most of them may have been quickly given up after 254, though not before all the portable wealth and several captives had been removed; just as the Romans sometimes reached but never remained in Ctesiphon, the Persians did not usually colonise on a permanent basis when they invaded Roman territory. They did take Dura-Europos, which fell in 256 or 257, and they may have briefly taken Antioch again, but since Roman coin production did not cease at Carrhae and Nisibis it seems that the Persians did not take these cities. Even if they had done so, it is unlikely that the Romans would have been able to mount an immediate expedition to restore the situation. During the years between 254 and 260, Valerian was fully occupied in repelling Gothic attacks, and his son Gallienus was similarly occupied on the Rhine. It may be that Odenathus of Palmyra was one of the principal forces upholding Roman rule in the east at this early date, while the Emperors were fighting elsewhere. Odenathus hailed from a pro-Roman family that had connections with Severus, as witnessed by their adoption of the name Septimius. He was acknowledged as *vir consularis* by 258. It is unlikely that he had been made consul, but it may mean that he had been awarded *ornamenta consularia* for some contribution to the Romans at some time before 258. The nature of this contribution and its date must remain hypothetical, but it is at least possible that Odenathus helped to stabilise the

Figure 39 Drawing of a cameo now in the Bibliothèque Nationale, Paris, showing Shapur's victory over Valerian. The king grasps the hand of the Emperor, an indication that Valerian has submitted to him. (Drawn by Trish Boyle.)

situation in 253 before Valerian arrived, and continued to monitor events thereafter.[12]

Though there were no Imperial campaigns during the late 250s, the war between the Romans and Persians had never formally ceased, and hostilities broke out again towards the end of the decade. Without giving a precise date, Shapur records that he embarked on a third campaign against the Romans in which he besieged Edessa and Carrhae, took the Roman Emperor Valerian prisoner, and acquired several cities of the Romans together with their surrounding territories. It was an unparalleled success for Shapur, who made much of his achievement via the sculptured reliefs at Naqs-i Rustem, Bishapur, and elsewhere. It was also an unparalleled disaster for the Romans, worse even than the defeat of Crassus in 53 BC. After the death of Crassus and the loss of his army, there was no immediate offensive, but the eastern provinces were not occupied and annexed by the Parthians. In 260 Shapur had actually captured Roman cities, but there was no possibility of a Roman campaign against him to recover them. Valerian's son and successor Gallienus did not attempt to mount one, not even to rescue his father. Though Shapur claimed that he took several Roman cities, he may have exaggerated the number of places that fell to him; in the end his territorial gains do not seem to have been tremendous. He boasted of having burned and destroyed vast stretches of Roman territory and had probably caused great damage to property and crops. Retrieval of the east devolved upon Odenathus of Palmyra. Already *vir consularis* by 258, Odenathus acquired more power and independence after the capture of Valerian. It was rumoured that he had tried to forge an alliance with Shapur, but if this is true it came to nothing. Palmyra did not turn away from Rome, though it is not clear whether Odenathus received any official appointment as governor of an eastern province or region with a command over Roman troops, or whether he stepped into the breach voluntarily, acting independently with an army of native levies. He did Rome good service in whatever capacity he operated. He fought the Persians as they retreated across the Euphrates, dealt with the usurper Quietus by besieging him in Emesa and finally killing him, and he also repulsed a Gothic attack. He is credited with a campaign into Persian territory, where he reached Ctesiphon, in 262 or 263. He was the most energetic figure in the Roman east, and the most successful. Gallienus rewarded him, probably with specific powers, but unfortunately it is not known precisely what these powers might have been. He was *dux totius orientis* or *corrector totius orientis*, commander of the whole east, but the interpretation of exactly what the words mean is a tortuous question. The titles applied to Odenathus are derived from those assumed by his successor Vaballathus and perhaps are projected backwards in an effort to provide tangible roots for Palmyrene power. But the lack of contemporary sources for Odenathus' titles does not alter his situation. It is fairly certain that he was the man of the moment in the east after the capture of Valerian, and that Gallienus recognised this fact;

Figure 40 Rock carving from Naqs-i Rustem detailing the triumphs of Shapur, from the second half of the third century. It is significantly sited just below the tomb of Darius. The two Roman Emperors defeated by Shapur are shown in the same relief, distorting chronology somewhat. Philip the Arab, cloak flying, stretches out his arms to the king, almost kneeling in supplication, while Valerian is depicted standing by the king's horse, with both his hands held by Shapur and one hand covered by his sleeve; this denoted submission to Shapur. Identification of the three figures as Romans is assisted by the efforts of the artist or artists who carved the reliefs to illustrate the differences in their clothing compared to the Persians, but there is disagreement about which Emperor is which. Vanden Berghe (1984, 69–74) is of the opinion that the kneeling figure in this relief and those at Bishapur is Valerian and the one held by the arm is Philip the Arab, but this is less likely when it is considered that Valerian was indeed held captive, while Philip merely had to agree to terms and pay an indemnity. (Drawn by Trish Boyle.)

but, hard pressed as Gallienus was, instead of trying to re-establish his own authority over the eastern provinces he was content to allow the Palmyrenes under Odenathus control of the area, at least for the time being. By 262 the eastern provinces seem to have reverted to business as usual; inscriptions reveal that building work was going on and religious dedications were being made at some Roman sites, and Antioch minted coins for Gallienus. Odenathus never seems to have overstepped his brief, whatever it was, by attempting to take over more territory, setting himself up as a completely independent king in opposition to Rome. That was a feature of the next few years after he was murdered in 267. His wife Zenobia and his son Vaballathus extended their control over the eastern provinces, including Egypt, creating in effect a Palmyrene Empire within the Roman Empire, attempting to reconcile their actions with the Emperor at first but finally emerging

Figure 41 Detail from the rock carving from Bishapur celebrating the triumphs of Shapur. On either side of the gorge at Bishapur, two almost identical rock carvings tell the story of Shapur's triumph over three Roman Emperors. The scene on the right side of the gorge is very worn, but there is enough detail to ascertain that the same characters are depicted in this scene, which is the better preserved of the two from the left side of the gorge. The Emperor Gordian III lies dead beneath the hooves of the king's horse, and his successor Philip the Arab kneels before the king. The Emperor Valerian is held captive, his arms firmly grasped by Shapur, similar to the way in which Valerian is held in the rock carving from Naqs-i Rustem (fig. 40), and on the cameo (fig. 39). (Drawn by Trish Boyle.)

as rulers in their own right, a situation that Aurelian could not tolerate for long. He crushed them in 272 and almost obliterated Palmyra.[13]

THE SUCCESSORS OF SHAPUR:
HORMIZD I (272–3), VAHRAM I (273–6)
AND VAHRAM II (276–93)

There was little or no harassment from the Persians while Aurelian made war on Zenobia. If there had been a concerted effort on the part of the Palmyrenes and the Persians, either as allies or separate forces, Aurelian would have found it a much harder task to reconstitute the Roman Empire. But in 272 Shapur died. After such a strong and determined rule, lasting for three decades, the sudden lack of central direction rendered the Persians momentarily weak. Shapur was a hard act to follow, and his two sons, Hormizd I and Vahram I were not of the same calibre as their illustrious father, nor did either of them enjoy such a long period of rule. In a reign of one year and ten days, Hormizd I scarcely had time to achieve anything, nor did Vahram I find the time or resources to attack the Romans. The extent of Roman control in the eastern territories in the 270s is debatable. Despite his successes in attacking the Persians, it is not clear whether Odenathus had regained control of Osroene and Mesopotamia. When Aurelian planned his campaign against Parthia, assembling a large army in Illyricum, it may have been that the recovery of these provinces was his main agenda, but he was assassinated before he had a chance to mount the campaign. Probus suffered the same fate in 282. It has been pointed out that there is no numismatic evidence for this projected Persian war, but it could be that he intended to stabilise the kingdom of Armenia by installing Tiridates on the throne as a Roman dependant. The war against the Persians that Probus may have planned fell to Carus. He may have embarked upon it either as a con- tinuation of Roman Imperial policy, or possibly in response to a Persian assault mounted by Vahram II, who perhaps saw an opportunity to attack just after the murder of Probus. The most probable reason for the Roman attack was the rebellion of Vahram's brother Hormizd, who attempted to set up an almost independent kingdom in the eastern half of the Persian Empire. Vahram eventually put the rebellion down, and recorded the battles on rock carvings at Naqs-i Rustem, but in the meantime the Romans cap- tured his capital city. Most sources agree that Carus' expedition was emi- nently successful, and if he had been able to follow up the victory he would perhaps have achieved a lasting peace had he not inconveniently died just as he reached Ctesiphon. It was said that he had overreached himself, and that the gods were angry with him, because he promised that he would reach the Persian capital, but his ambitions were for even greater things and he had exceeded his brief from the gods.[14]

Vahram II was in the seventh year of his reign when Carus invaded. He seems not to have retaliated aggressively when the Romans retreated, perhaps because a negotiated settlement and the departure of the Roman army gave him all that he wanted while he dealt with rebellious subjects in his Empire. There was probably no formal peace treaty between Romans and Persians at this time, but a safe passage may have been granted to allow Numerianus, or more likely the Praetorian Prefect Aper, to withdraw. The reign of Vahram II is notable for the rise to political prominence of the high priest Kartir, and the reversal of the hitherto tolerant religious policy in an effort to expel or eradicate Jews, Christians, Manichaeans, and other sects whose adherents did not subscribe to the official state cult of Zoroastrianism.

Perhaps the lack of recorded activity of Vahram against the Romans was due to internal problems, involving a sort of witch hunt within the state to ensure that Persia was for the Persians, and loyal ones at that. If that were the case, there would be little time for aggressive external wars. Similarly, Vahram II would be fully aware that after the death of Carus the Romans were fighting their own battles, until one strong Emperor emerged in 284. Even then, Diocletian was not in a position to organise an eastern campaign, and it was to be another three years before he came to a diplomatic under-standing with the Persians. In 287, the settlement went in Rome's favour and was widely regarded as a victory over the Persians, the main achieve-ment being that the Roman candidate Tiridates III was placed on the throne of Armenia. The Persian king sent valuable gifts to Diocletian, and the Roman sources insist that he submitted voluntarily to the Romans.[15]

VAHRAM III (293) AND NARSES (293–302)

Vahram II died in 293 and was succeeded very briefly by Vahram III, who was removed after only four months by his great-uncle Narses, a younger son of Shapur. Like the Roman Emperors, few of the Persian monarchs enjoyed the advantage of a long reign and peaceful succession. Narses had been governor of territories in eastern Iran, and just as several Roman provincial governors emerged at the head of armies to challenge the Emperor, Narses made a successful bid for the throne. After he had estab-lished himself he challenged the Roman hold on Armenia by invading the kingdom and ousting Tiridates III. He was evidently well prepared for Roman retaliation, at least at first, but the Roman government had increased its senior personnel and acquired new generals with Imperial rank, with two Augusti, Diocletian and Maximian, and two junior Emperors as Caesars, Galerius and Constantius. It has been suggested that Diocletian perhaps made these new appointments as a direct result of the Persian threat, but the chronology as well as the probability is questionable. The accession of Narses will have been known to the Romans, and his probable intentions with regard to Armenia may also have been crystal clear, but it is more likely that Diocletian had already framed his plan to appoint two Caesars as understudies to himself and Maximian, and the news about changes in the Persian Royal House merely confirmed him in his conviction.[16]

It was not until 296 that Galerius was able to mount a campaign to redress the balance that had been upset by the Persian invasion of Armenia. He had been in Egypt, where a revolt had broken out, and he had been fully occupied in suppressing it until 295. His first Persian expedition was not successful; in fact Narses decisively defeated him not far from Carrhae. The Romans had to withdraw once again, with their territorial losses still not recouped. Armenia was in Persian hands, control had not been regained over Mesopotamia and Osroene, and now the whole of the eastern frontier was vulnerable. But Narses had not the military resources of the Romans, who laid low while they recruited another army. In 298 Galerius captured the Persian treasury and the royal harem, and Narses was forced to negotiate. The Roman victory was the most decisive for many decades, and the subsequent treaty, perhaps negotiated in 298 and ratified in 299, defined the frontier between the two powers for some years to come. All the territories that had been lost, all the debatable lands, and control of Armenia through the reinstatement of Tiridates III, were now in Roman hands. The terms of

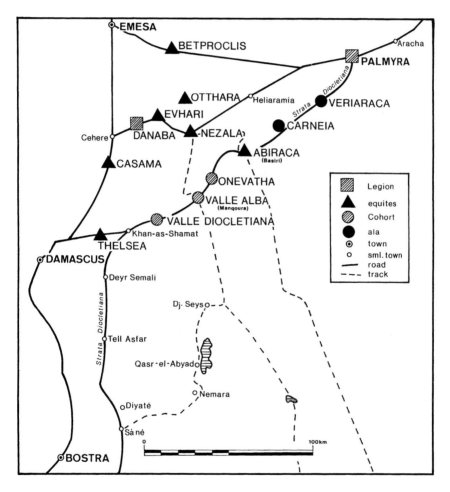

Figure 42 Diocletian's eastern frontier route, the *Strata Diocletiana*, as reconstructed by van Berchem (1952) from documentary and archaeological sources. (Redrawn by Graeme Stobbs.)

the treaty have been preserved by Petrus Patricius. The new frontier arrangements were detrimental to Persia. The boundary between the two states was to be the Tigris, thus bringing back into Roman control Mesopotamia and Osreone, with the added provision that territories beyond the Tigris should be governed as Roman dependencies, stretching Roman influence as far as, or further than, ever before. The boundary of the kingdom of Armenia was to be Zintha, on the Median border. Rome did not administer Armenia directly by annexing it, but presumably felt secure enough with the pro-Roman ruler Tiridates on the throne. A further clause of the treaty stipulated that Nisibis was to be the sole place of trade, filling the vacuum left by the destruction of Palmyra, the city that had hitherto controlled most of the eastern and western trade between the two empires. Though the territorial boundaries were fixed and Roman influence secured beyond them, there seems to have been no immediate policy of fortification under the Tetrarchy in the forward zones of Mesopotamia and Osroene, despite the fact that Ammianus Marcellinus, 60 years later, describes forts and road posts for the protection of Mesopotamia. The fortified road known as the *Strata Diocletiana* is the major work that can be attributed to Diocletian, though he did not construct it from nothing. He joined up, extended, and strengthened elements that were already constructed by previous Emperors, with the result that some sites have complicated archaeological histories, and it is not always possible to identify all the Diocletianic work. Van Berchem studied epigraphic, literary and archaeological evidence to reconstruct the frontier, and archaeological investigations have refined the details. How the frontier was intended to operate is a matter of debate, largely because the nature and level of the real and perceived threat is only imperfectly understood. Policing and protection of travellers and convoys will have been part of the functions of the troops guarding the road, but since the road was not thrust far forward in juxtaposition with the limits of the Persian Empire, it presumably had as much to do with internal security as defence of the Roman Empire against the eastern power.[17]

HORMIZD II (302–9) AND SHAPUR II (309–79)

The arrangements made in 299 proved long lasting, despite the fact that they represented a humiliating defeat and loss of face for Narses. His revenues were reduced, a situation which unsettled his subjects and gave cause for his subordinate nobles to become restless. Until his death in 302, he was probably fully stretched in simply keeping order in the Persian Empire. Galerius' military victory was endorsed by Diocletian's economic achievement. The seven-year reign of Hormizd II is not well documented. It seems that there may have been some military action with Rome, but it cannot have been anything approaching a full-scale war involving an Imperial expedition. He may not have renewed the treaty of 299, since it was made person to person between Diocletian and Narses, but even if he repudiated it Hormizd II did nothing to disturb the peace. When he died in 309 he was succeeded by his son Shapur, who was only a child. The government was in the hands of the boy's mother and her council, who perhaps tried to regain some of their losses in two campaigns; for reasons imperfectly understood Maximinus and Licinius were active on the eastern frontier in 311–12 and 313–14. When Shapur II was about sixteen years old he resumed hostilities against the Romans. For some time his elder brother Hormizd had been in captivity, but now contrived to escape and to flee to the Romans. Licinius received him in 324 but did not lead any expedition to place him on the Persian throne. In the same year Constantine emerged the victor in the civil wars and Licinius was removed from power. Shapur sent an embassy to him and war was avoided, even when in the following year Shapur led an army against the Arab tribesmen of the Persian Gulf. He approached the Roman frontier, but there was no fighting. Ten years later when control of Armenia was once more an issue after the death of Tiridates, Constantine sent his son Constantius to defend Mesopotamia from incursions and to secure the throne of Armenia by placing upon it his nephew Hannibalianus. There was an heir of Tiridates who had sought refuge with the Romans, but Constantine preferred to establish more direct Roman control of Armenia, a point which could only have antagonised the Persians, who responded by sending an embassy to reclaim certain territories. Unwilling to cede anything, Constantine prepared to go to war but his death in 337 prevented him from undertaking a campaign. Shapur seized the opportunity at Constantine's death to besiege Nisibis, but had to withdraw because of lack of supplies when it did not fall after two months. In Armenia, the Romans were forced to compromise after Constantine's attempt to rule the kingdom directly; by mutual agreement the heir of Tiridates was made king. Throughout the first half of the fourth century there was no major campaign on the part of either the Romans or the Persians, and there was no real redress for Shapur until the disastrous expedition of Julian in 363, when the Roman Emperor was killed and the Persians regained some of the losses that they had sustained in 299.[18]

7

THE EMPIRE TRANSFORMED

The Christian Roman Empire of the successors of Constantine was the heir of the pagan Roman Empire. There was a certain family likeness, but this next generation Empire differed from the original series in that it was the product of cumulative evolutionary changes, some of them naturally progressive taken at their own pace, and some of them accelerated by the circumstances of the fraught middle years of the third century. In adapting to these circumstances Gallienus and Diocletian set in motion some of the administrative changes discernible in the substructure of the later Roman Empire, but it was Constantine who produced the final version. His work was not simply a direct continuation of that of his predecessors. Though he completed most of Diocletian's reforms, he abandoned the attempts to fix prices throughout the Empire and to stabilise the silver coinage. In religious terms Constantine was diametrically opposed to what Diocletian started, and as soon as he could do so he turned his back on the Tetrarchy. Constantine was a product of his time, a man for whom the trite stock epithets come readily to mind: ruthless, determined, and decisive. He knew what he wanted, never wavered in his purpose and set about achieving it as soon as there was opportunity; once he had achieved sole rule he had the advantage of a lengthier reign than most of the Emperors of the last hundred years, and could sift and sort the governmental procedures that he inherited. Constantine rejected or reversed some of the trends that had shaped the century, and accentuated others that consolidated his power and supported his regime. This was not personal selfishness in ensuring his own survival. He was the embodiment of the state, and it was his duty to ensure that it would continue after his death. He would not have recognised any pejorative intention behind the label 'autocrat', and would not have understood the distaste of the modern world for the concept of autocracy.[1]

EMPERORS

With the exception of Macrinus, the Emperors of Rome up to the time of Severus Alexander were senatorial aristocrats, not necessarily from Rome

246

itself but from the higher-ranking provincial families who had gained recognition via their careers in a succession of administrative and military posts. The aberrant Elagabalus was everything an Emperor should not be, at least in public, but he was still an aristocrat. When Maximinus Thrax was made Emperor by his troops it was regarded as a turning point by ancient historians. The man was a soldier, which in itself was scandalous enough from the aristocratic point of view; worse still, he made it clear that he did not even pay lip service to the authority of the Senate. Emperors who came to power via the army, or after rebellions, still had their power conferred on them by the Senate; there was a time-honoured ritual to be observed, despite the fact that the Senate had no executive powers to speak of and the Emperor could force his way to the top with the armies at his back without all the ceremonial senatorial fuss. Maximinus was too busy keeping the frontiers together and did not even go to Rome. Subsequent Emperors faced the same problems; first of all, some of them had never even seen the city that they served; secondly, they did not have the senatorial upbringing and connections that would have helped them to form a sympathetic power bloc within the Senate during their absence; thirdly, constant wars kept them away from the city for most or the whole of their reigns, so there was no time for the diplomacy and local self-advertising campaigns in Rome that would have smoothed the relations between Emperor and Senate. On occasion, senatorial Emperors surfaced, with divergent degrees of success, as illustrated in the careers of Pupienus and Balbinus, the Gordians, Decius, Valerian and Gallienus, and Tacitus. The Senate perhaps deserved more respect from the military men who ruled Rome in the mid-third century, and likewise the soldier-Emperors deserved credit for fulfilling their tasks in defending the Empire, often at the expense of their lives. The various usurpers who flashed into prominence were for the most part concerned with the proper defence of their own territories which the legitimate Emperor could not defend, rather than with toppling the Empire. This is not to say that there would have been no attempts to usurp the throne if the Roman world had been at peace for generations and no external wars had threatened nor internal strife had arisen; but there may have been a less rapid turnover of successful and unsuccessful bids for Empire.[2]

The relative accessibility of the Princeps from Augustus onwards had been one of the remarkable features of the early Empire. Some Emperors like Augustus, Claudius and Vespasian thrived on it, while others like Tiberius and Domitian positively abhorred the idea. Official and unofficial screening of suppliants, requests and visitors will have been a normal part of the Emperor's existence, much like a greatly enlarged version of the Republican magnate's household. The Emperor had as his clients the whole population of the Roman Empire; he was the man upon whom the burden and benefits of rule had been bestowed, responsible for the welfare of the inhabitants of the Empire, the man to whom appeals could be made as a last resort when injustices could not be remedied locally or immediately. Even while the Emperors were becoming more and more grandiose, elevated above ordinary mortals, this sort of contact was still possible. Diocletian was assiduous in answering appeals and delivering judgements, but even during his reign all trace vanishes of the relatively informal procedure of answering requests by rescripts, or handwritten replies at the foot of letters of appeal. Contact with the Emperor from the end of the third century onwards would be very much at second hand, via a host of officials of graded ranks. Constantine did nothing to diminish the distance between himself and his subjects, but paradoxically he applied himself to the promotion of an outward display of accessibility to all.[3]

The increasing remoteness of the Emperor was signified by the elevation from the mortal realm to the divine. The Imperial cult had begun with Augustus, and deification of Emperors after their deaths was routine, except for those whose memory was damned. In the east the worship of the living ruler as a god was perfectly acceptable, deeply ingrained in the eastern consciousness, but in Rome itself and in the western provinces it was not the norm to worship the living Emperor directly; the Imperial cult circumvented the worship of the man and concentrated on the spirit or *genius* of the Emperor. Those Emperors who departed life with ignominious reputations had gained little from attempting to be gods. Caligula emphasised his divinity; Domitian aspired to godhead in his title *Dominus et Deus*; Commodus too thought he was a god on earth. Their ideology did not find ready acceptance among their contemporaries. All were assassinated and their memories were damned forever by the Senate; Severus reversed the decision in the case of Commodus because he required divine ancestry, attaching himself to the house of Marcus Aurelius and through him Antoninus Pius; the embarrassing hiatus of Commodus' reign had to be rectified. From the reign of Severus onwards the Imperial house became the *domus divina*. Emperors were already sacrosanct by dint of their tribunician power, but they had acquired something more; Severus Alexander was described as *sanctissimus*, as was Gallienus. Aurelian became a god with divinity backdated to his birth, and Diocletian and Maximianus were *dii geniti et deorum creatores*. Such Emperors were far removed from the ordinary. Earthly divinity demanded ceremonial, elaborate ritual, superb dress, imposing architecture, an ostentatious court with numerous gradations of staff. Grandeur requires a massive infrastructure.[4]

As the Emperors distanced themselves their evolutionary path towards autocracy was perhaps inevitable. The wise Emperor had always been the sole source of benefits and advancements; the unwise Emperor allowed others to assume an all-powerful intermediate position, acting in his name, like Commodus with Cleander, and the usually shrewd Severus with

Plautianus. Wise Emperors also maintained the fiction that they were not autocrats, that others had a part to play and a voice in political developments; their *comites* could advise or perhaps persuade, with potential rewards in the form of influential and prestigious posts and lucrative financial gain. While Emperors could spend much of their time in Rome, not pressured by external events, proper debate could take place, personal appointments could go through the proper channels, long-term policies could be framed. The military needs of the mid-third century precluded these arrangements. Decisions had to be made quickly without prolonged debate, and far away from Rome; the responsibility fell on the Emperor alone. Autocracy was a natural development, the only solution to the rapidly changing and challenging needs of the third century. It was also inevitable that as the century progressed the Emperors became the fount of law. Until the first quarter of the century the jurisconsults formed the laws of the Empire under the eye of the Emperor, relying upon their experience and accumulated authority; thereafter they ceded their lawmaking capacity to the Emperor himself, losing the capacity to formulate the law and taking on instead the role of compilers and interpreters. Certain Emperors, notably Severus and Diocletian, took a very conscientious view of their legal responsibilities, and their cumulative pronouncements formed the basis of law in the later Empire, collected together in great codices drawn up by Diocletian himself, and by Theodosius and Justinian.[5]

Outgoing Emperors expired or were removed in a variety of ways, bequeathing a corresponding variety of problems to incoming Emperors. The succession was a perennial concern. True hereditary succession was rare and was not necessarily successful or uncontested when it happened, as the examples of Commodus and Caracalla reveal. Emperors with less than perfect claims to power usually tried to shore up their regimes by elevating their sons to the rank of Caesar, and then to Augustus, or occasionally directly to Augustus, even though some of these associates in power were children. These schemes did nothing to ensure the continuity of the Imperial house. Diadumenianus, aged ten, was killed after his father Macrinus was defeated and eliminated by the army of Elagabalus. Marcus Julius Severus Philippus was proclaimed co-Emperor with Philip the Arab and died at the age of about twelve at the hands of the Praetorians. Decius' sons fared little better: Herennius Etruscus being probably killed in battle, and Hostilianus being taken under the wing of Trebonianus Gallus and allegedly dying of plague. Power-sharing had been a feature of the Roman Imperial government from the time of Marcus Aurelius and Lucius Verus, and then Marcus and Commodus. In theory it seemed a logical step to take a colleague in order to govern the vast territories that comprised the Empire, especially when wars were fought on two fronts. Sometimes these colleagues were not given any territorial responsibilities, as in the case of Caracalla; conversely, close relations could be put in charge of territory without being given

Imperial collegiate powers, such as Philip's brother Priscus who was made *rector Orientis*. Brothers of Emperors such as Quintillus and Florian did not long survive after the deaths of their Imperial kin, no matter whether they had or had not been designated Caesar or Augustus. Even when there was an undoubted heir to the throne, rival contestants were not discouraged from rebellion. When Valerian was captured in the east, his adult son Gallienus was in command as Augustus in the western half of the Empire, with sons of his own to succeed him, but that did not prevent one of Valerian's officers, Macrianus, from attempting to take over in the name of his two sons, backed by the troops in the east. Possibly at about the same time Regalianus raised revolt in Upper Pannonia, and Postumus took over the Gallic provinces. The circumstances were complex and extreme, and secure dates and a chronology are not fully established for the capture of Valerian and for the rebellions, but even if an exact chronology were available it does not alter the fact that the succession ought to have been straightforward and uncontested. Diocletian's experimental collegiate government, intended to facilitate administration and defence of the whole Empire, and to provide two Emperors and two understudies, failed to solve the succession problem. Constantine's absolutism, combined with his long reign, provided a temporary respite, and it seemed that in Crispus he had a worthy successor, but in 326, for reasons that are not perfectly understood, he executed his eldest son and also his own wife. In the fourth century the battle for the succession still continued.[6]

New Emperors evidently considered that continuity was important; they rarely founded a completely new dynasty unrelated to previous regimes. Severus manipulated genealogical truth to connect himself with the house of Marcus Aurelius, even though it meant that he had to deify Commodus in the process to legitimise his claim. Deification of the previous Emperor and respect for his name and his house smoothed the transition for some of the incoming Emperors. Philip insisted on the deification of Gordian III; Trebonianus Gallus deified Decius. Sometimes connection with the previous Imperial household was decidedly not an asset, so deification would be out of the question. Continuity was then achieved at second hand by historical reference to other Emperors; for instance Decius was awarded the honorary name of Trajan.[7]

USURPATION OR REGIONAL SELF-HELP?

Rebellions and attempts at usurpation were occupational hazards of Emperors at any time; the third century witnessed an increase of this activity in different regions. When an Emperor died or was removed, usurpation became increasingly normal as a method of succession. Usurpation is an emotive term with many shades of meaning. Definition should take note of the extenuating circumstances. Succession via usurpation was on occasion merely an uncontested take-over, without the bloodshed and mayhem involved in slaughtering the family and friends of the deceased Emperor. When the succession was contested, usurpation takes on a more significant aspect. Only a small proportion of the men who were declared Augustus by their troops achieved the ultimate goal; those who were already in the entourage of the Emperor and still upright after his death, like Maximinus Thrax after Severus Alexander and Philip the Arab after Gordian III, stood a better chance of surviving than those who were elevated by other armies removed from the Imperial household, or those who were proclaimed while the reigning Emperor was preoccupied elsewhere. The rivalry of the different armies or even the Senate sometimes produced multiple choices all at the same time. In 238 there were Emperors on the Rhine, in Africa and in Rome, set up in opposition to Maximinus. Ten years later, Philip was unscathed by the rebellions of Jotapian and Pacatian, who were proclaimed by the troops in Cappadocia and on the Danube, but then he succumbed to Decius without much prolonged fighting. Usurpers who failed to become Emperors were often represented as brigands, especially if they were short lived and ultimately unsuccessful. Their motives and long-term aims must remain conjectural, especially since the only notice of their existence is from a hostile disapproving source, framed in few words almost as a footnote in history. On some occasions the object of the rebellion was simply the protection of the immediate area from external threat. It is questionable whether some of the newly declared Augusti were determined to take on the whole of the Empire. Even though they amalgamated large territories under their control, neither Postumus nor Odenathus made any sudden march on Rome to take over the whole Empire. Odenathus governed the east as a Roman official, though his exact status and his titles are only inferred from those of Vaballathus, and it is not known whether he commanded Roman troops. Postumus declared himself Emperor and appointed consuls and magistrates, but his administrative officials and army officers were confined to what later writers called the *Imperium Galliarum*. Neither of them departed from Roman ideals and forms of government. Over two decades later Carausius adopted the same pattern, looking to his own small empire in Britain. In his case there was to be no emulation of Clodius Albinus, who challenged Severus in a battle for the Empire and lost.[8]

This kind of usurpation classifies more readily as self-help, which featured more prominently from the second half of the third century and into the fourth. When external raids and internal unrest reached dangerous and intolerable proportions and no help was forthcoming from Rome or the troops in nearby provinces, the only course when the legitimate Emperor could not defend the area was for the inhabitants to take on the task themselves. Dexippus' defence of Athens is well documented, chiefly by himself, but the novelty of civilians fighting either alone or with the army is not confined to Greece. Postumus had civilians in his army when he fought the Alamanni, and so did Ingenuus, governor of Lower Pannonia, when he defeated the Sarmatians with an army of peasants and urban inhabitants. It has been suggested that the *praepositus vexillationum* Castus, in Lycia in 256, may have been a civilian leading a militia that he had raised for the purpose of defending the area; there were no auxiliary troops in garrison in Lycia at the time. MacMullen comments on the increasing readiness of the provincials to do what Rome could not do for them.[9]

Active fighting was not always an option, but passive defence was a priority in some areas. City walls were erected in the late third century around many of the hitherto unwalled cities in the western provinces. The psychological value of city walls was probably just as important if not more important than their effectiveness in defence. Some of them were built over a long period in a seemingly leisurely fashion, perhaps as an exercise in local politics where the governing class had to be seen to be responding to the potential attacks from tribesmen, internal rebels like the Bagaudae, or even plundering Roman armies. When there was Imperial assistance building probably progressed more rapidly, and where there was a prolonged Imperial presence, cities like Arles, Cologne, Trier, Milan, Sirmium, Nicomedia, Thessalonika and Serdica benefited greatly. The fortification programme in Gaul was seemingly fairly uniform, and since it was too vast an undertaking for the local decurions to sustain it is suggested that it may have stemmed from an Imperial project, perhaps even funded by the central government. Probus is credited with restoring the towns of Gaul, and coin evidence suggests that he may also have assisted in the construction of the defences of Athens, where the damage caused by the Heruli was not repaired but efforts were concentrated on defending the Acropolis. Diocletian may have inherited and continued the defence programme. The larger and more important cities and towns, especially those on main routes and those where the large granaries were eventually established, were included in an Imperial defence plan; elsewhere, in lesser towns, fortification seems to have been left to local initiative. As the third century progressed, hilltop refuges were established in those areas under most threat from raids or invasions; they were just as much a feature of fourth-century life as of the later third century. Fortified villas also appeared, not on a vast scale, but these too featured in the fourth century, as documented by Ausonius in the Moselle region. Large estates also appeared in Pannonia, where the constant presence of the army brought wealth into the region and ensured some protection. In some parts of the Danube provinces it is probable that the civilian population was allowed into the forts, as at Eining and Regensburg. Such measures were local and specialised, and cannot be taken as evidence of dire circumstances and decline over the whole Empire. Historians and archaeologists are generally at a loss to explain why defence was a priority in some areas and considered unimportant in others. Some cities never received walls – even those in the direct path of potential invaders, like Lauriacum and Virunum on the Danube. Other cities started to build walls and took an extremely long time to complete them, or never finished them at all. The evidence is not standard from east to west in the Roman world.[10]

The differences between the various regions of the Empire were never more plain than in the third century, when some areas suffered badly from unrest and invasions and others remained relatively unscathed. The Empire was never a homogeneous whole, unified by a common culture. There was certainly a main Roman theme running through all parts of the Empire and all aspects of life, but there were many variations upon that theme at a regional level. Romanisation was probably not proactive, many arrangements being left to local initiative. Native customs were not supplanted or eradicated. Variations of climate, agricultural practices and techniques, differences in religious observances and the degree of urbanisation, all ensured that complete uniformity could never be achieved. Regionalism had never been discouraged, but in the third century it surfaced on a larger scale. Attachment to a province or group of provinces in some instances merely indicates that the sense of homeland was stronger than the ideal of Rome; thus the Pannonians in the eastern campaign army of Severus Alexander wanted to go home when they heard of the raids across the Danube by the Goths. Defence of a province merely attests to the devotion to duty of the inhabitants and Roman military personnel, not to any megalomaniac ambition to rule the Empire; thus an inscription from the mid-third century records a *defensor provinciae suae*; the addition of the possessive, 'his' province, puts it firmly in the local realm. It is debatable how much the stresses of the time and the necessity for self-help contributed to a lessening of the ties with Rome, and whether narrowly focused local interests represented a transitory phenomenon or a deep-seated desire to throw off Roman rule. It is suggested by some scholars that in most cases where self-help was the only option there was generally no intention of breaking away from Rome on a permanent basis. Though opinions differ about the aims and intentions of the Empire builders such as Postumus, Odenathus and Carausius, it is probable that they looked first to their own territories and not to becoming Emperor themselves. Military men in command of troops on the frontiers were placed in very awkward positions when invasions threatened and no Imperial help was available; in some instances there was probably no thought of rebellion as such. It was simply that people would appeal to the generals on the spot, calling them Emperors because all they wanted was a saviour with the power and authority to protect them. The number of Imperial titles appearing in the third century, such as *restitutor, renovator, conservator*, does suggest rather strongly that even after the hyperbole there was a great and widespread need for restitution, renovation and conservation, and that Emperors were determined to take the credit for it.[11]

THE SENATE AND SENATORIAL CAREERS

The Senate's influence waned considerably during the third century. There are two aspects to consider, the Senate as a body and the individual senators who made up that body. From the foundation of the Empire under Augustus the Senate never recovered its Republican strength and status. The apathy that set in because of the lack of influence resulted in reduced attendance at meetings. Augustus had to lower the quorum in order to pass resolutions before the Senate; Claudius tried to encourage debates to indicate that freedom of speech was allowed, but there was not much improvement. In the third century the influence of the Senate descended to an all-time low. Severus made it clear that the army was where he looked for support. This had always been a factor in any Emperor's reign, but now the brutal truth was more overt and the Senate ran second to the army; it was still the Senate, though, that conferred power on the Emperor according to time-honoured tradition. The Emperors were themselves senators, with the exception of Macrinus, until the middle of the third century. There was supposedly a revival of the fortunes of the Senate and senators under Severus Alexander, but the degree to which the revival took hold is disputed, and in any case the Emperor who succeeded Severus Alexander broke the monopoly of the senators on the Imperial scene. The potential for senatorial revival under Tacitus can be dismissed as wishful thinking; predominantly the story was included as an opportunity for Aurelius Victor to point out that many senators were more interested in their landed estates than in politics. From Gallienus to Constantine no Emperor made significant efforts to restore political power to the Senate; Aurelian deprived it of the right to produce bronze coinage; Diocletian continued Gallienus' policy of employing equestrians as provincial governors, and did not see fit to install senators as *vicarii* in charge of the new dioceses.[12]

Maximinus Thrax and the soldier-Emperors who followed him spurned the Senate as a body. Soldiers knew very well where the source of their power lay and it did not matter so much to them whether or not the Senate conferred power on them. What mattered was whether the realities of power enabled them to command the troops, defend the Empire, and remain alive. The military needs of the Empire forcibly distanced the Emperor from Rome, and therefore from the Senate if not from individual senators. Maximinus and later the Emperor Carus did not make the journey to Rome to have power conferred on them, though Carus may have sent his son Carinus. It was said that Florian, the brother of the recently deceased Tacitus did not wait for the official confirmation of his status by the Senate, so it was not just the soldier-Emperors who bypassed the Senate. Contact between Imperial ruler and Senate was ruptured from the first decades of the third century onwards and was never repaired.[13]

The senatorial career was modified and then curtailed from the reign of

Severus onwards, following a slow evolutionary path that can be linked with, but not wholly ascribed to, the gradual rise of the equites under successive Emperors, beginning in the early Empire. The watershed occurred in the 260s when Gallienus removed senators from military commands, and it seems that some of the junior magistracies disappeared at the same time. The *triumvir monetalis* died out in the reign of Severus Alexander; the vigintivirate is not heard of after the 260s, and the post of tribune of the plebs came to an end. The higher echelons of the senatorial career survived, especially the prestigious post of *praefectus urbi*. If political influence had been stripped from the Senate, wealth, prestige and privilege still remained to senators. Individuals were sent on special missions, and towards the end of the third century it was senators who were chosen as *correctores* in Italy.[14]

When Constantine came to power there were tangible changes. He increased the number of senators, probably to 2,000, but did not impose any obligation to attend meetings in the Senate House. In other words he bestowed rank and privilege without any executive powers, and once having removed the centre of government and the court circle to Byzantium he could afford the gesture of allowing the senators of Rome more privileges without much fear of opposition. Any usurper in Rome was surrounded by provinces with armies under Constantine's command, and he had a good track record when it came to attacking and taking Rome. He recruited widely to fill the newly enlarged Senate, promoting Italians and provincials as the earlier Emperors had done. As sole Emperor Constantine opened up careers to senators, basing the magistracies on earlier precedents but with altered functions. The quaestorship had always been a kind of apprenticeship for the aspiring senator, but now it was downgraded somewhat and given to senators' sons, the legal qualifying age being sixteen. The praetorship was reduced in influence; having already lost its legal functions, it became an office primarily concerned with organising the games. The consulship was still a goal worth aiming for, but the suffect consulship was not regarded as highly as it once was. The ordinary consuls were appointed by the Emperor himself, so it was necessary to come to his notice, and presumably it was more than ever necessary to say and do all the right things in order to rise. Significantly, the provincial government returned to senatorial hands, the larger or more important provinces being governed by consulars.[15]

THE EQUESTRIAN CAREER

Social mobility for the equites had developed steadily from the first century. Augustus opened up administrative posts and military commands, and established the four great prefectures that marked the uppermost echelons of the equestrian career. He began by appointing an equestrian as the Prefect of Egypt after the battle of Actium and the fall of Alexandria. The Praetorian

Prefects were established probably by AD 2, the *praefectus vigilum* followed in AD 6, and the *praefectus annonae* in AD 8. Within 50 years equestrians with sufficient capital were regularly advanced to membership of the Senate, a process that was marked by the relatively swift rise to senatorial status of Vespasian's family in only three generations. The equestrian order was less restricted in its activities than were the senators, who were forbidden to engage in trade and therefore employed equestrians to operate and oversee their business interests. Besides being able to engage in all kinds of business enterprises without incurring the social stigma that attached to senators who did so, equestrians were more versatile in their choice of occupation, ranging from civic functionaries in the cities and towns all over the Empire, to administrative officials in central government, and army officers, all of whom would be under the scrutiny of the Emperor and could rise (or fall) according to their perceived merits. At some time in the mid-second century equestrians acquired titles denoting their rank: *egregius* for the lower officer, *perfectissimus* for those who had reached distinguished posts such as Imperial procurators or the prefects of the corn supply, the *vigiles*, or the prefecture of Egypt. The Praetorian Prefects were *viri eminentissimi*. These descriptions regularly appear on dedicatory inscriptions and tombstones, so they were clearly of importance to the men who were awarded the titles. By the mid-third century it had become common practice for Emperors to adlect equestrians into the Senate, but except in a few cases equestrians did not hold military or administrative posts reserved for senators. Eminent army officers could hold special commands, sometimes acting independently for a time, but these were exceptional cases. It was Gallienus who advanced the careers of the equestrians by employing them in the roles normally occupied by senators, as provincial governors and as commanders of the legions. Senators were divorced from military posts, and there was also a separation of civil and military commands, a tendency towards specialisation that has been traced back to Hadrianic times or earlier. Diocletian did not radically alter these arrangements, except to divide the provinces into smaller units, grouping them together in his new dioceses and installing the *vicarii*, also equestrians, over the provincial governors, predominantly equestrian officers (*praesides*), while other equestrians (*duces*) also commanded the frontier troops of one or more provinces. From the reign of Gallienus to the reign of Constantine, the equestrians enjoyed considerable influence, some of them rising to the rank of Praetorian Prefect and then going on to be awarded consulships and to enter the Senate, some of them even becoming Emperors in times of crisis. Constantine accepted most of the administrative arrangements that had evolved from Gallienus to Diocletian, not finding it necessary to redesign provincial government, except that he reinstated senators in place of equestrians. He did not reverse the separation of civilian and military careers. His immediate circle of friends, the *comites*, contained mostly senators, whose careers he promoted. This was not necessarily designed to eliminate the equites, but he started a process of levelling down that resulted at the end of the fourth century in the disappearance of the equites as a class.[16]

THE PRAETORIAN PREFECTS

The developing role of the Praetorian Prefects was connected to both the equestrian and senatorial career paths. In the third century the prefecture was still the ultimate goal of the equestrians, and the Prefects themselves accrued power and influence as the century progressed. They were in the position of second in command to the Emperor, sometimes making and breaking Emperors and occasionally taking on the Empire themselves. Plautianus was quite exceptional in his day, becoming consul while still in office; the curriculum vitae of Comazon was likewise extraordinary. Some of the Prefects were awarded *ornamenta consularia* without actually holding office, but it was perhaps counted as an office in certain cases; Q. Maecius Laetus was awarded *ornamenta* in 205, and when he became consul he counted it as his second term of office. The award of *ornamenta consularia* elevated the Prefects who received it to *clarissimi*. The culmination of the process can be seen in the career of L. Petronius Taurus Volusianus, who became consul in January 261 while still Praetorian Prefect and went on to become *praefectus urbi*. Under Diocletian the Prefects were still equestrians in origin but the trend to power was not reversed. Aristobulus and Asclepiodotus became consuls and then pursued a senatorial career, both of them becoming *praefectus urbi*. The functions of the Prefects changed under Constantine. In 312 after the battle of the Milvian Bridge he abolished the Praetorian Guard. Unlike Severus who disbanded it and then reconstituted it by recruiting the Danubian legionaries, Constantine replaced the Guard with something different; the *scholae* became the bodyguards, and the Praetorian Prefects lost their military functions, except in so far as they were responsible for the supply and welfare of the armies. Henceforth they were the chief administrators of the Empire, in charge of highly complex organisations. Perhaps inevitably, from the significant date of 324 when Constantine achieved sole rule, the Praetorian Prefects were all senators.[17]

THE PROVINCES

The effects of the multiple problems of the third century were naturally varied across the Empire. There was no standard set of responses because there was no standard set of problems in each of the provinces or in each Emperor's reign. Two Imperial regimes sought to control the provinces more closely by subdividing them; Severus divided Britain into two new provinces, and Pannonia was probably divided by his son Caracalla. When Diocletian embarked on subdivision of the provinces it was a much more thorough exercise, not only creating smaller provinces but also grouping the new provinces into dioceses, and installing a *vicarius* in command of each diocese and the provincial governors within his territory. The old-style administration where the governor was at once the civil and military commander also changed. Specialisation evolved, and eventually civil and military matters were divorced; the frontier armies came under the command of the *duces*, and the civil administration was the realm of the *praesides*. Tighter control of smaller areas and the fostering of military specialism were responses to the mounting third-century problems. The classic scenario involves internal insecurity and external invasions resulting in loss of life, property, agricultural produce and livestock; unreliability of some of the troops who instead of guarding the inhabitants of the provinces oppressed them; rampant inflation of ludicrous proportions and economic ruin; government control of vital industries that reduced everyone to a form of servitude. Undoubtedly painful, casting a shadow over most aspects of the second half of the century, the gloom and doom cannot have been universal or permanent, but the very lack of literary, epigraphic, artistic and architectural sources for the second half of the third century does suggest that life in the provinces, as the inhabitants of the Roman world knew it in previous centuries, was definitely on hold.[18]

The western provinces probably suffered most from the upheavals of the third century. Fluctuation in regional prosperity was unavoidable even in peaceful times, and it has been shown that Italian manufacturing industries were already in decline in the second century, as entrepreneurs expanded industries further afield in Gaul; then in turn the central Gallic industries declined as manufacturing and trading enterprises moved further out to the Rhine and northern Gallic towns. Cisalpine Gaul suffered when the wine trade moved to new centres. When the third-century invasions began, Gaul was attacked several times; the north-western parts suffered most; farms were abandoned and not resettled. In central Gaul, though there was resettlement, it was not on the same sites as before; small farms were abandoned and villages grew up in their place; only a few of the cities recovered the prosperity of Antonine times. By contrast the British provinces were not nearly so badly affected and suffered no invasions, though some of the towns acquired walls nonetheless. In general the British provinces became self-sufficient and more insular. The archaeological record from the Pannonian and Moesian provinces displays an upsurge of prosperity at the end of the third century and the beginning of the fourth. On the Danube, the presence of the army helped to increase security, and army pay ensured the influx and the circulation of wealth, at least among the upper echelons of society, marked in Pannonia by the growth of large defended villas. Similarly in Spain, which was not directly threatened to the same extent as Gaul and the

Danube, the rich landowners were better placed to withstand adverse economic conditions. Towns declined and large villas grew up in their place. Spanish traders were hit hard, as long-distance trade fell away and the ports declined; the internal markets turned to local products. Conversely the north African provinces were beset by raids from the tribesmen along the borders, but suffered no serious or long-lasting consequences. Stagnation set in but did not tip the balance towards decline. After the reign of Diocletian the stagnation ceased and growth resumed; and the fourth century was one of tangible prosperity for Africa, noted in the literary sources and attested archaeologically in the enormous villas. Much of the land in Africa was always in the hands of a few wealthy men, so what seems to be happening in Gaul and Spain, where wealth inexorably regrouped into fewer hands, already had a head start in Africa. The fate of the western provinces in the third century varied: some were devastated and did not recover; some adapted well to changed circumstances and after a period of hardship they revived; others carried on almost unaffected.[19]

The eastern provinces suffered several invasions by the Persians, cities fell or were captured, some were destroyed during the wars. But the economic base of cities in the east was more robust and not so easily destroyed. Antioch, for instance, fell into Persian hands twice or possibly three times, and was damaged by fire, but in the early fourth century it was once again flourishing. The main bones of contention between the Persians and the Romans were the control of Armenia and Mesopotamia and the struggle to find a mutually acceptable boundary to divide the two Empires. Stability eluded both parties, since when one power was weak or compromised the other extended control across the shifting boundary. The Persians made a limited number of expeditions into Syria, Cappadocia, and Mesopotamia, but never did reconstitute their former Empire and did not remain in occupation of the cities they gained for very long. In contrast, the tribesmen who invaded the western provinces and swept across the Danube were not united in their purpose, and though they occasionally submitted to the rule of a powerful and charismatic leader like Cniva, they were not subject as the Persians were to the overlordship of a king of kings. They were not driven by the desire to create kingdoms and Empires; their needs were pressing and immediate, their aims limited to the short term and the achievable. It has been argued that the Persians were not interested in territorial gain and the complications of administration, but that they intended only to plunder and take captives, settling the latter in new cities in the Persian Empire. Though the results may have felt the same to the victims of raids into Roman provinces, there was a difference between east and west. The Persians desired static, organised wealth; the tribesmen were interested in food and portable wealth. The first results in little more in the long term than a change of dynasty, however temporary; the second results in destruction, some of it not redeemable.[20]

CITIES AND TOWNS

The cities of the Empire did not enjoy the same level of prosperity at any one time. The fate of cities, particularly in the west where the city was a relatively recent introduction, probably hinged on the enterprise and initiative of certain individuals. The same few families are documented in eastern cities time and time again as the magistrates and benefactors, and there is some evidence that there was a spontaneous and voluntary movement towards the establishment of a hereditary ruling class in many cities. There is no concrete evidence to explain why some towns and cities failed and others succeeded. As mentioned above, some had already entered upon a period of decline before the end of the second century, such as the Italian cities whose main industries subsided as those industries and the entrepreneurs with the expertise migrated to Gaul and beyond. For many reasons, sustainable growth, the buzzwords of twentieth- and twenty-first century lottery applications, was not achievable over the whole Empire at all times. Urban economies both waxed and waned, and the third century saw much of the latter process. The expenses incurred in governing cities and towns, normally met by the decurions who aspired to local office, became increasingly burdensome, and the complete stagnation of growth and the lack of fresh adornment in third-century cities has been noted and proclaimed one of the most compelling pieces of evidence for decline. The upsurge in the building of defensive walls has already been mentioned, and in those cities where defences were erected there may be a ready explanation why adornment ceased, but even towns which did not receive walls also stagnated or declined, with little trace of growth, improvement or decoration of any sort. The costs of building walls around cities cannot have been wholly met by the decurions, and the expense as well as the considerations of defensibility may have exercised a considerable influence on the extent of the circuits. The walls of western cities usually enclosed a much smaller area than the city limits of the second century; there is some argument about what this actually means. Where new defensive walls were built in Gaul, parts of Spain, Raetia and the Upper Danube provinces, enclosing a reduced area, it has been argued that the circuits were built on the most easily defensible ground, containing the area that the citizens could hope to hold, according to their resources and manpower. It is postulated that the majority of the population lived outside the walls, taking refuge inside the city when danger threatened. Evidence from some of the cities in Gaul argues against this theory; in some cases large gardens and open spaces disappeared; buildings encroached upon the streets and public spaces, and in some cases rooms were subdivided, all of which suggests overcrowding and the inclusion within the new walls of most of the population that previously lived on the outskirts. At Tours and Tournai the lie of the land precludes any settlement outside the walls, so it seems that in these instances at least the cities had in

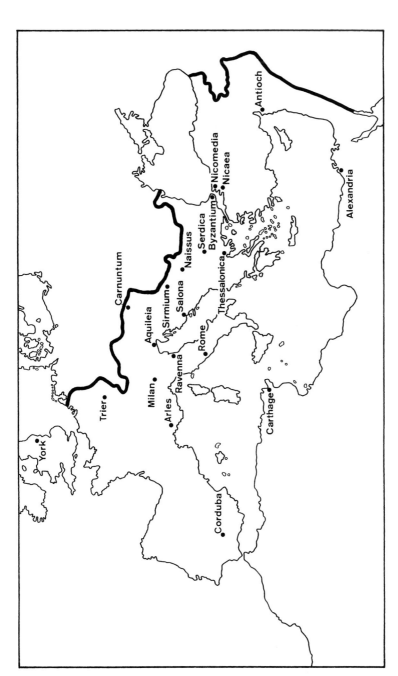

Figure 43 Imperial residences where Emperors set up their headquarters and courts at various times in the third century. The presence of the Imperial household and entourage brought prosperity to these cities, and the Emperors themselves were responsible for some improvements and adornments. (Drawn by Graeme Stobbs.)

fact shrunk and the population had shrunk with them. Despite the argument that the reconstructed cities were perhaps central citadels or refuges with many of the inhabitants still living outside the perimeter, some authors argue for a considerable drop in population in the second half of the third century, with the most serious results being apparent in the countryside. St Cyprian writes of the shortage of agricultural workers in the mid-third century, as well as the shortage of sailors and soldiers.[21]

Communities already in decline were in no position to recover rapidly from destruction of their surrounding areas, unless there was an injection of ready cash. As mentioned above, those cities where there was a direct Imperial interest, or better still a prolonged Imperial presence, survived the third-century crisis and prospered in the following century. Cities that were on major routes were fortified and the routes themselves were protected by means of watch towers. Elsewhere it was a matter of chance. If some of the towns themselves escaped relatively unscathed, too often the rural areas did not, and the dependence of cities and towns upon their agricultural territories has been emphasised by scholars. The severity or otherwise of the effects of the destruction of crops depends upon the region, the type of crop, and the social and economic conditions in which recovery is attempted. Variables such as climate, type of soil, agricultural technique, and collapse or survival of the market also have a bearing on the rate of revival. Recovery of cereal crops can be made within a year; vineyards take longer, and olive groves, with a crop only every second year, require about a decade to re-establish. The relationship between cities and agricultural producers was symbiotic. Cities depended on the countryside to supply them as much as the farmers depended on the existence of markets to sell their surplus, thus raising money to pay taxes and to buy other goods. When the local surplus production ceased to be exchanged via urban markets the economy of the cities began to unravel.[22]

The desperate plight of the decurions whose task it was to govern the cities in the third century has attracted both ancient and modern discussion. Examples of reluctance to serve on city councils can be found as early as the second century, but the phenomenon became much more widespread during the third century. The burdens fell upon the same families and their descendants in some cities, and especially in the east there was a tendency towards hereditary membership of the city councils some time before Diocletian's reforms crystallised the arrangement. Snobbishness precluded anyone from the lower classes or anyone engaged in trade from entering upon office, even when it proved difficult to recruit new councillors. The third-century lawyer Callistratus explains that such individuals are not forbidden by law from becoming councillors, but he thinks that the councils would be degraded if such low-class people were admitted to membership. In modern terms, wealthy businessmen might seem to provide the answer for struggling councils whose collective wealth was declining, but in the Roman Empire trade could never provide the sort of wealth that ownership of land could provide. The emphasis on landownership resulted in a reduction of the size of holdings as the qualifying figure, so that men with as little as 25 *iugera* were made councillors; these men could scarcely sustain the costs of office in towns and cities. The rule that council members should have served in a magistracy before entering the decurial class was waived, which broadened the recruitment base; but the measure still did not solve the problem. Eventually, under age boys were appointed councillors when the shortage of candidates was extremely severe. Inevitably, people began to avoid taking office if they could do so. Some gave up all pretence to property ownership so that they did not qualify, others extricated themselves by retiring to their estates, becoming as far as possible self-sufficient magnates, developing unassailable power bases which enabled them to avoid making contributions to the cities. The alternative to withdrawal was to extract wealth from the lower classes, oppressing them in the process. Evidence from the fourth century suggests that this is how some decurions found an answer to their problems.[23]

THE THEORY OF DEPOPULATION, DESERTED LANDS AND THE DECLINE OF AGRICULTURAL PRODUCTION

Depopulation has been postulated as the result of the third-century decline, and the cause of it; nowadays questions are asked whether there really was an actual decline in agricultural production, and whether depopulation had any part to play. The chicken-and-egg conundrum perhaps does not apply, since both ideas probably contain an element of truth. Statistics on population figures are simply not available, and no amount of scholarly speculation on the matter can ever graduate to proven fact, but the assumption is probably correct that in some areas the internal insecurity and the invasions caused deaths, with a resultant flight of survivors towards less threatened areas. Loss of life was not limited to invasions and attacks by brigands. There were serious plagues during the reign of Marcus Aurelius, and in the 250s and 260s, which were said to be serious and Empire-wide. The effects on the countryside and the cities are not quantifiable in terms of numbers. The apparent shrinkage of the cities is not a reliable guide.[24]

Just how widespread and frequent was the flight from the land in the third century is a subject that has occupied scholars for decades. Desertion of the land was an old, old story. The Roman Republic was constantly beset by land issues, and efforts to attract farmers to settle or resettle and put land back into cultivation were recurrent themes in Roman history. During the later Empire Pertinax offered tax immunity to encourage farmers to settle on empty lands; Aurelian ordered town councils to find cultivators or be responsible for the taxes that the lands would have yielded. Clarification of precisely what is implied by the phrase 'deserted lands' is probably impossible to achieve, but it seems to embrace on the one hand marginal lands that had never been fully cultivated and on the other once prosperous farms that had been wasted, with every variant in between the two extremes. The rhetoric of the panegyrics envisages tribesmen being officially settled on the very lands that they or their compatriots had destroyed. Some of these large-scale settlements had two purposes: to put land back into cultivation and to provide men for the army. In Gaul and northern Italy communities known by the collective term *laeti* were settled on the land with the obligation to furnish recruits. The process may have begun under Probus, and was certainly established by the Tetrarchic period. Originally the *laeti* may have been prisoners of the tribesmen brought back into the Empire; the word itself may derive from a Germanic root, denoting half-servile status. By the mid-fourth century the *laeti* were under the command of *praepositi*, and a law of the late fourth century refers to *terrae laeticae*. The literary references for the settlement of various tribes within the Empire, however much the numbers of people may be exaggerated, give the impression that there was always a supply of empty lands available with vacant possession for the tribesmen to farm. When archaeological excavation shows that there was a gap in occupation and then a reoccupation of some farm sites, this may on occasion reflect the settlement of tribes on vacant lands where the original inhabitants had moved away or been killed, but it is impossible to be certain about who was responsible for the reoccupation. It has been argued recently that the desertion of land was not as widespread as it has been portrayed; in at least one region in Gaul the villas were abandoned but the cultivation of the land continued, so there was presumably a restructuring of living accommodation but no loss of production. The phenomenon is visible in some parts of Britain today, where farms are either empty or occupied by non-farmers who sublet their lands, or where farmers have diversified, making their main businesses the farm shops and bed and breakfast concerns. The land, however, is still under crops of one kind or another, planted and harvested by commercial firms or other farmers, or the pasture is still grazed by sheep and cows. In parts of Roman Gaul, the demise of small farms and the growth of medium-sized ones and of small villages may mean that there was a regrouping of families or neighbours for reasons of security and for the pooling of resources. Some parts of the northern provinces were unable to adopt this method of survival. It is clear that lands were indeed deserted and never resettled in northern and north-western Gaul, and in some parts of north Italy, largely because the invasions from across the Rhine, and in the case of north-western Gaul from the sea as well, endangered and impoverished the territories so that it became untenable to live there any longer. This abandonment on a large scale has not yet been found elsewhere in the Empire, but small-scale desertion of lands may have occurred for reasons other than tribal invasions. Climatic change, increased rainfall, and a rise in sea levels affected the coasts of the north-western provinces; in other areas soil exhaustion may have brought production to a standstill. What brought the agricultural problems to a head in some areas was the taxation scheme of Diocletian. Firm evidence of this comes from Autun, where the siege and reduction of the city under the Gallic Emperor Victorinus had irreparably damaged the resources of the area. The panegyric to Constantine delivered in 311 makes more than a passing reference to abandonment of lands because men could not meet the tax demands; as a result Constantine reduced the burden.[25]

The postulated decline in agricultural production is more difficult to prove or disprove than the depopulation theory. The example from Gaul cited above, where cultivation of the land did not cease even though some of the farms were deserted, can perhaps be extended to other areas, but even if there was a clustering of population and a continuation of cultivation the levels of production may have dropped, remained the same, or increased, and there are few reliable ways of estimating yields. The old-fashioned theory that lack of freedom among the agricultural workers reduced production has been challenged; it was formed at a time when oppressed workers of the nineteenth and twentieth centuries were beginning to find a voice, and to project their problems backwards into various historical circumstances. The largest corporate consumer of agricultural produce will have been the army, but little is known about the supply system of the third-century army. Whether the presence of troops stimulated production has been debated, but most of the discussion concerns the more static army ranged along the frontiers, and then the field armies and frontier armies of the fourth century. The transitional period, when the various frontier armies were involved in both external and civil wars – some of them uprooted from their forts, and some of them split off from their parent units – was a time of constant movement, where supply will have been as much a matter of fortuitous local requisition as of convoys from distant regions.[26]

ECONOMY AND FINANCE

To write of the Roman economy gives the erroneous impression that there was a uniform economic system over the whole Empire, which in fact consisted of a collection of regional economies, each of them slightly different, but all affected by inflation and taxation. The rate and severity of inflation and its effects on the provinces is difficult to establish, since there is a lack of coherent evidence with which to reconstruct the fluctuations in any one area. The most commonly cited indicators of inflation are the prices of wheat and the rates of army pay, because these are the best-documented sources. The price of wheat rose only very slowly from the first century BC to the beginning of the third century AD, and thereafter accelerated sharply, most severely after 260. Despite the outflow of cash to the army, pay of the soldiers did not keep up with inflation. It was finally commuted into payments in kind in the form of goods and services; in the interim the short-term palliative chosen by hard-pressed Emperors was to debase the coinage. The purer coins paid in taxes could be called in, recycled and reissued with a reduced precious metal content, providing more pay for the troops without the matching expenditure. The symptoms revealed themselves early. Marcus Aurelius and Commodus adjusted the weight of the silver coinage; Pertinax attempted to improve it, but Severus and Caracalla once again reduced the weight to enable them to pay the troops. Caracalla issued the new antoninianus, which masqueraded as a double denarius but in reality contained only 50 per cent more silver than a single denarius. The result was that the good denarii began to disappear as people began to hoard them, and prices rose because the new coins were not accepted at their imposed values. Prices current in the early second century had more than doubled by the first half of the third. Confidence in the coinage waned rapidly after 235, as debasement to pay the costs of war increased and the profits normally associated with wars of conquest ceased because wars were now defensive and desperate. Reinstatement of the coinage after debasement could no longer be funded by foreign booty. Only after Gallienus and then Claudius Gothicus had halted the Goths, and Claudius had regained control of Spain, could the smallest of improvements be attempted. Even after the Empire was reunited by Aurelian and some concerted effort could be put into reforming the coinage, the supply of precious metals was still adversely affected by its removal by various means from the open market; for instance, hoarding of the good silver coins tied up silver reserves, especially as many hoards were never recovered during the Empire.[27] Subsidies paid to the Germanic kings and to the Persians drained gold reserves, which never returned to the Roman world; the cash payments made by Philip the Arab were melted down into Persian dinars.

The debasement of the silver coinage had an adverse effect on the gold coinage; weight standards were lowered steadily until in the mid-third century an aureus was only half the weight of its first-century counterpart. Aurei of different values were in circulation simultaneously, so exchange rates were calculated at different levels for these successively reduced gold coins. Though the weight was reduced the gold content was kept up to standard as far as possible because Emperors did not wish to jeopardise the effectiveness of their donatives to the troops. Similarly the bronze coinage was adversely affected by the debasement of the denarius, which itself was eventually degraded to a bronze coin washed with silver. Aurelian introduced a new bronze sestertius, and Diocletian introduced new denominations that are only imperfectly understood; successive Emperors found it too difficult and expensive to issue a token bronze currency. The demise of the bronze coinage was not reversed until the mid-fourth century, when the currency reverted to the three-metal standard, with pure gold and silver coins and four different sizes of bronze coins.[28]

While the transition between the degraded currency of the late third century and the improved coinage of the fourth was in progress the market suffered from a dearth of small change. Certain provinces suffered from a dearth of coinage in general; it is well known that coinage did not reach the former Gallic Empire or Britain; despite Aurelian's reforms of the currency, the circulation of coinage was not regular or even. In southern Gaul there was a shortage of coins, but no widespread issues of imitation coins; in the northern parts of Gaul imitations abound, presumably to supply the local markets and perhaps to pay the troops. If central government was paying the soldiers, then the coinage ought to have circulated more widely. The personnel such as government officials and the soldiers, who were paid in cash, found that their money bought less and less. Pay could not be raised, so people resorted to underhand survival methods. Corruption spread rapidly among government officials and the army used its position of power to intimidate people to requisition goods and services, legally or illegally. The Praetorians in Italy reputedly terrorised the civilians at the beginning of the third century, and the famous plea of the inhabitants of Skaptopara illustrates what happened when the soldiers bullied the provincials. The more acceptable reverse of this coin is the fact that in many areas the army was the authority to which people appealed for justice, and were not necessarily exploited in the process.[29]

The decline of trade in the third century adversely affected the urban centres. Long-distance trade diminished sharply, one reason being the endemic insecurity of the land and sea routes. This does not imply the total collapse of civilisation; trade did not come to a complete standstill, but was restructured on a local basis. Even cities as far apart and diverse as London and Ostia lost international trade and catered for local markets. Urban markets declined because the relationship between the farmers and the market traders had vanished. The old system of converting surplus produce into money via the urban markets had been radically altered when tax payments were converted from monetary mode to payment in kind; the urban markets depended on an interchange of cash payments for various goods. As self-sufficiency became the order of the day the urban markets were perhaps replaced by rural markets, some of them centred on villages, others on large estates. The polarisation of wealth that concentrated most of it in the hands of the owners of these large estates ensured that economic and political power accrued to the landowners. The poor got poorer and the rich got richer, and the small shopkeepers and traders, who never had much of a co-ordinated or coherent voice in the historical record, disappeared. Throughout the Empire there was never any commercial enterprise that could compete with the ownership of land as a source of wealth. This is not to say that the small peasant farmers were better off than the shopkeepers and traders; such small-scale ownership hardly counts. Landownership properly embraces only the upper classes. Landowners, who were not exclusively men, generally counted their estates in multiples, often spread over several provinces. These individuals were in a better position to survive the third-century disruptions, and the workers on their estates were firmly enmeshed in the self-sufficient environments that traded labour for security. Whether these estate systems developed into pre-feudal establishments is a matter for debate; archaeology cannot answer the questions of where the surplus food was sold or exchanged, nor how restricted were the workers.[30]

THE ARMY AND THE FRONTIERS

Socially the army had undergone radical changes, not necessarily related to the structural reorganisation at the end of the third century. The Emperors had always depended upon the army for the support of their regimes from Augustus onwards; to be Emperor without control of the armed forces would have been unthinkable. As the Empire expanded and the armies were moved out towards the periphery and began to recruit from the local population in the provinces where they were stationed, the links between the citizens of Rome and Italy were severed. Wars of conquest or of defence were no longer conducted by the young men of Rome, who brought home cart-loads of spoils and tales of foreign parts. When some of the soldiers did come to Rome in the early third century, their rough appearance, strange apparel, and guttural speech, all so horribly alien, repelled the sensitive inhabitants of the city. However much the rough frontier soldiers may have seemed outlandish and foreign, these men were increasingly necessary not only to the Emperors but for the defence of the Empire, and they served Rome well. Severus raised their pay and improved their conditions of service, recognising the importance of attracting men to join the ranks. Even so, Romans, Italians and provincials still did not flock to join the ranks, so recruitment of tribesmen continued and increased, as the frontier wars depleted military manpower. The famous and fierce Illyrians were recruited because of the lack of military interest among the inhabitants of other provinces; the Illyrians were among the most vigorous soldiers who ever served in the Roman armies, and it is not surprising that some of them went on to become Emperors. The so-called barbarisation of the army has been advanced as one of the causes of the decline of Rome, whereas in fact it was one of the strengths of the Empire that it was able to tap into a source of recruits, ready, willing, and able, and for the most part, loyal and effective as a fighting force. Tribesmen were employed to fight other tribesmen, and on occasion the same peoples were at one and the same time enemies of the Romans and also employed as their soldiers; for instance, the Juthungi were recruited into the army to battle against the Alamanni. Carausius employed Franks to protect Britain, and Constantius employed them to protect Gaul. During the third century, the tribesmen were trained and regimented as Roman units, commanded by Roman officers, fighting with Roman weapons. During the later Empire this changed; tribesmen fought under their own chiefs, using their own weapons, not always integrated into the structure of the army, so that in effect they were not Roman armies any longer. This did not detract from their fighting abilities, and the armies performed successfully when they were led by strong and charismatic men.[31]

It cannot be denied that the army sometimes became alienated from the population that it was supposed to protect. The expense of keeping the various armies in readiness for war was burdensome to the population; taxes were naturally resented, but that was nothing new. People wanted their defence cheaply. When economic hardship increased, the burdens became intolerable in some areas, because the army was as hard pressed as everyone else but the soldiers could use their power to browbeat people, overzealously requisitioning goods and services that they were not entitled to. During the civil wars a Roman army could sack a Roman city with apparent nonchalance; to the inhabitants, one army would begin to seem like any other, all of them representing potential threat. Armies could make or break Emperors, of their own volition or by coercion or persuasion. Soldiers who had never seen Rome fought for the Emperor or the aspiring general with the most credibility, or the most cash, or both. Despite the soldiers' corporate reputation for love of gain rather than duty, the army served Rome well on the whole. There is no comprehensive list of deceased Roman servicemen, such as there is for the last two world wars, to impress historians with statistics of those who died defending the Empire, either in battles or from disease or by accident; if there were, such a list might balance the stories that have survived of truculent soldiers and rebellious armies who made Emperors and broke them. When they could see the point in what they were asked to do the soldiers generally did it, but when Probus asked them to plant vines and dig drainage ditches they did it under sufferance; then, when he proclaimed that there would be universal peace and no need for armies, the soldiers nearest to him rebelled. This reveals that there was something to be gained by soldiering, or at least that the alternatives to soldiering were not as appealing or as profitable. Social mobility via the army was gradually increased under successive regimes but reached its zenith in the third century, especially after Gallienus put equestrians into military commands and provincial government posts. The army was a social entity in its own right, and was for many men the starting point of a long career. The rank and file could become officers, and rise to important commands, reach equestrian status, and from there follow a splendid career without needing to enter the Senate. The army was largely self-sufficient, providing many of the military commanders and administrators of the third century.[32]

In the early Empire the officers had wide experience from the usual inter-mix of civilian and military posts, but they were often strongly focused on their political careers and did not become specialists in one field or the other. From the second century onwards, the civilian and military career paths began to diverge, so that anyone who wanted to remain in one stream could do so. As the third century progressed, specialism and professionalism in military affairs were needed to ensure continuity and to pool experience; the army diverged even more from civilian interests. Gallienus removed senators from command of the armed forces; Diocletian and Constantine crys-tallised the process by finally separating civil and military careers. Diocletian retained the equestrian *praesides* as governors of the provinces, but for the most part divested them of any military functions, installing army officers with the title *dux* (plural *duces*) in command of the troops. *Duces* were known from the beginning of the third century, but the title was not strictly a rank; like the *praepositi*, the *duces* were usually employed on special mis-sions; for instance they commanded mixed troops in transit, or filled tempo-rary active posts. Diocletian formalised the system; from his reign onwards the title *dux* denoted a high rank, bestowed on experienced professional army officers. The *duces* were sometimes put in charge of the armies in several provinces, to protect an extended stretch of the frontiers; this is reflected in the title *dux limitis*, but it does not seem that there were fixed ducal commands which were immutable; appointments were made with the specific situation in mind, so in times of danger, the command of the *duces* could be enlarged to include the troops of neighbouring provinces, and in times of peace they could perhaps be reduced. Most of the information about the *duces* derives from the later Empire when the system was fully evolved. The law codes reveal that the primary concern of the *duces* was defence of the frontiers. They were in charge of all the troops, including the mobile forces and the legions and auxiliary units of the province or provinces in their com-mands. They were responsible for military administration, including juris-diction over soldiers who had committed crimes, and all other matters such as keeping the units up to strength, inspection and acceptance or rejection of recruits, supervision of the collection and distribution of supplies. They had no control over supplies other than distributing them, since the Praetorian Prefects were in charge of the *annona militaris* and army pay. The *duces* were answerable to the *magister militum*, and also had to make quarterly returns to the Praetorian Prefects. It could be argued that in dividing the provinces into smaller units, Diocletian had reduced the opportunity for governors to raise revolt, and had then promptly negated this measure by placing mili-tary men in command of large numbers of troops, but the administrative system ensured that the *duces* were supervised by the *magistri*, the Praetorian Prefects, and were probably watched by the *vicarii* in charge of the dioceses. On occasion, in the smaller provinces, the *duces* undertook civilian duties as well as supervising military matters, and the *praeses* sometimes commanded

270

troops, but in general, from Diocletian's reign onwards, the frontier commanders were always *duces*.[33]

At the beginning of the third century the Roman army was recognisably that of the preceding 200 years, a system that first-century Romans would have understood, apart from the innovation of solid running barriers marking the point where Roman administration ended. By the fourth century the army had evolved from the legions and auxiliary forces of the early Empire into the *comitatenses* and *limitanei*, the mobile field forces and the frontier troops. Which Emperor was responsible for the change is debated. Gallienus was credited by a Byzantine author with the establishment of the first mobile cavalry army, which in itself is probably correct in that he did gather together the cavalry forces of different units, welding them into a composite force under a single commander. To the Byzantines this would look familiar, and so it would be accepted that the mobile forces came into being when the Empire was under extreme stress and Gallienus was faced with the impossible task of reuniting it. Modern scholars are not so confident that Gallienus' cavalry army was the forerunner of the mounted *comitatenses*. The continued existence of the cavalry cannot be traced with certainty; it was still a distinct force under Claudius Gothicus, when Aurelian commanded it, and it is said that it was this cavalry force that was used to good effect against the Palmyrene heavy armoured horsemen. After 285 it was no longer based at Milan, and its whereabouts, if it was still an operative force, are unknown.[34]

The *comitatenses*

The mobile field armies of the later Empire grew out of the turmoil of the end of the third century. The main problem is to decide whether it was Diocletian or Constantine who was responsible for the development of the field armies, and whether either of them adapted the mobile cavalry, or created the *comitatenses* independently of any legacy from Gallienus. Diocletian had with him on campaign a *comitatus*, perhaps merely a group of advisers and friends, or perhaps a mobile army that was the precursor of the *comitatenses*. No one can be pedantic about the answer to this dilemma because the evidence is circumstantial and open to dispute. It is not established whether the other three Tetrarchs also had a *comitatus*, though even if that was known beyond doubt it would not help very much because it can be argued that the word changed its meaning between Diocletian's reign and the middle of the fourth century. On balance it is likely that Diocletian was not the direct founder of the mobile armies of the fourth century, but that Constantine adapted his predecessor's ideas and whatever else was at his disposal, and came up with something new. It has been pointed out that after the battle of the Milvian Bridge Constantine was in a very similar position to Gallienus. He had consolidated his command of the central parts of the Empire, but had to face opposition from other quarters, with a mixed bag of troops drawn from the Rhine provinces, Britain and elsewhere. He had the motivation and the opportunity to look with fresh eyes on what he needed his army to do and how it was performing, and, more important, at the beginning of his reign he needed troops clustered around him and under his command. The *comitatenses* probably began life as a single and perhaps fairly small army following the new Emperor, and went on to become the main attack and defence force of the Empire. New posts were established to command the new army, the *magistri equitum* for the mounted contingents, and the *magistri peditum* for the infantry, but there is no evidence for any Constantinian *magistri*, so it still cannot be proved that it was Constantine who invented the entire system.[35]

The *scholae*

The Imperial bodyguard also changed under Constantine, who abolished the Praetorian Guard after the battle of the Milvian Bridge and put in its place the *scholae palatinae*, which were under the direct command of the Emperor. No ancient source confirms that it was Constantine who created these units, but he would require a bodyguard of some kind after ridding himself of the Praetorians, and it is characteristic of him to avoid the risk of installing an intermediate commander of the bodyguard, who could achieve enormous power in such an influential position, just as some of the Praetorian Prefects had done in the past and as Aureolus and Aurelian had done in command of the cavalry army. The later *scholae palatinae* were 500 strong, but the strength of the Constantinian units is not known. The Praetorian Prefects survived the abolition of the Guard, but their role was henceforward an administrative one.[36]

The *limitanei*

The frontier armies in the early Empire were similar in constitution whether or not they were stationed behind physical barriers, or guarded a river or a boundary marked by a road lined with small posts and watch towers. Broadly speaking the legions occupied strategic positions some distance behind the frontiers, while the auxiliary forces of cavalry and infantry units were stationed in forts nearer to or, in the case of Hadrian's Wall in Britain, actually on the frontiers. At what point the frontier armies separated from the field armies is not known, but once the repair of the frontiers had begun and the expeditions into tribal territory had subdued the tribes for a while, the reorganisation of the army could proceed. Zosimus praises Diocletian for repairing the frontiers and putting the armies back into the forts, and by contrast he accuses Constantine of taking them away again and putting them into the cities which did not need defending. In the east the presence of soldiers in cities was not an innovation, but for Zosimus, despite the rhetoric, it was Constantine who made some far-reaching changes in military organisation that were not reversed. Documentary evidence has been brought to bear on the date of the establishment of the frontier armies, the allegedly static counterparts of the more mobile *comitatenses*. The first evidence that there had been a change from the normal arrangements of legions, *alae* and cohorts stationed in frontier forts is indeed Constantinian in date; it is to be found in a law of 325 which distinguishes between three classes of troops, the *comitatenses*, the *ripenses*, and the *alares* and *cohortales*, with the unwritten implication that the *ripenses* rank lower than the *comitatenses*. It is likely that the evolution of the mobile field armies and the frontier troops was gradual, conceived perhaps in one session but put into effect in stages. The *ripenses* include the legions and the auxiliary troops along the frontier, showing that the old distinction between *legiones* and *auxilia* had disappeared by 325. At that date the term *limitanei* had perhaps not yet come into fashion; it embraces all the troops of the *limes*, but has shades of meaning that changed over time. It appears anachronistically in the biography of Severus Alexander, making it seem to the unwary that such troops existed in the early third century, but it is used by an author who wrote much later, and applied the words that were current when he wrote. In the sixth century the *limitanei* were tied to their forts as a kind of militia, who combined defence of the frontier with cultivation of the lands allotted to them. The fourth-century troops, whether they were called *limitanei* at that stage or not, were not restricted in this way; some of the frontier units fought with the field armies on expeditions.[37]

The frontiers

The way in which the frontiers worked has been much debated. One of the connotations firmly embedded in the term 'frontier' is that it will naturally have a military function, but a variety of other functions have been suggested for all the frontiers of the Empire: as customs barriers, intelligence bases, aids to police work inside and outside the provinces, fortified communication routes and, not least, the delimitation of Roman territory. There is argument as to whether the running barriers that formed the frontier lines were intended to be impermeable to all assaults, or whether they were intended to function as aids to a policing system that relied heavily on moral supremacy for its effects. There was no single blueprint for all the frontiers of the Empire, since regional variations such as climate, terrain, and – most of all – perceived threat were the determining factors in frontier design and function. Though there is archaeological evidence to support the theory that Roman frontier societies were perhaps distinct from both the provincial hinterland and the lands beyond the frontier, the idea has been disputed and it is assumed by some authors that Roman influence did not cease entirely at the frontiers. In the early Empire it is probable that there was a no-man's land immediately beyond the frontier line, where no one was allowed to settle. Watching and patrolling beyond the frontiers, to pre-empt large gatherings that might lead to attacks, would make very great sense to modern minds, but except in those cases where outpost forts existed, as in the lands north of Hadrian's Wall in Britain, it is very difficult to prove that there was an unrelenting Roman influence in non-Roman territories. Patrolling and intelligence gathering leaves little trace. Besides, these activities are effective only if there is a great psychological ascendancy, and must be backed up by a strong military presence with no weak points. After 260 it could not be said that Rome had those advantages on all frontiers.[38]

The northern frontiers

The mid-third century witnessed a collapse of the Imperial system that had operated successfully from the reign of Hadrian. Patently, the barriers were not capable of forestalling the determined onslaughts of the tribesmen from the north. The causes of the raids and invasions were probably varied, sometimes involving the search for food or the longer-term need for settlement, sometimes involving purely warrior ethics. Political correctness has banished the use of the word 'barbarians' because of its connotations of lack

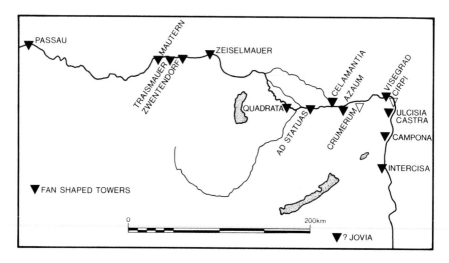

Figure 44 Map showing forts on the Danube where fan-shaped towers were added in the late second and early third centuries. These additions were probably undertaken in the Tetrarchic period, or possibly under Constantine. The Danube became the main focus of Roman attention as threats mounted in the later third century, demanding a refortification programme and perhaps altered internal arrangements in the frontier forts, reflecting changes in army organisation. (Redrawn by Graeme Stobbs from Johnson 1983.)

of civilisation, but that does not alter the fact that in many societies, even so-called civilised ones, there are groups who simply like fighting, destroying and plundering, who make a lifestyle out of it according to their own code of honour, and who cause problems to the official forces sent to control them because of their extreme mobility and unpredictable behaviour. The Rhine and the Taunus–Wetterau defences and the frontiers of Raetia were attacked in the 230s and 240s, and though there are signs of rebuilding and recovery after the first assaults, by 260 the frontiers had collapsed. Forts were destroyed either by the tribesmen, or possibly by rival Roman armies, and some were abandoned. Some territory was given up between the Rhine and the Danube. Aurelian abandoned Dacia and brought people out of the old province into parts of Moesia. Probus is credited with repair of parts of the frontiers, particularly with the establishment of the Saxon Shore in Britain and the line of the Danube–Iller–Rhine *limes*. Diocletian is better served in the literature, and credited with a full-scale reparation of all the frontiers, though archaeologically his work is hard to trace beyond doubt. In his reconstruction of the frontiers Diocletian created more legions; he may also have reduced the size of the legions from *c.*6,000 to 1,000, though

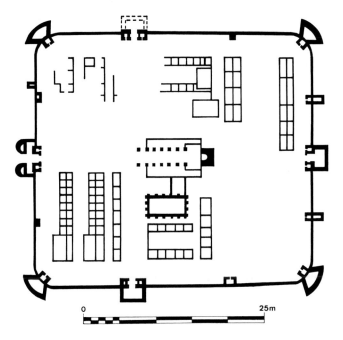

Figure 45 The fort at Drobeta on the Danube was strengthened by the addition of fan-shaped towers and blocked gateways. The barracks on this plan may not belong to the same late phase; it is not certain if there were altered internal arrangements necessitated by reorganisation of the garrison. (Redrawn by Graeme Stobbs from Lander 1984.)

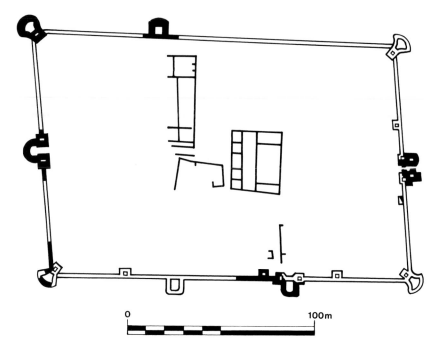

Figure 46 Plan of the fort at Ulcisia Castra, which was renamed Castra Constantia, on the Danube. Fan-shaped towers were added at the corners and all the gateways except one were blocked by additional defences projecting outwards from the flanking towers. (Redrawn by Graeme Stobbs from Fitz 1976.)

whether this means that he left all the old legions at their normal strengths and established new ones of a much smaller size is not clear. His reorganisation of the defence of the Danube provinces may have involved the redesign of the forts on this frontier, which from the end of the third century display a new style of fan-shaped corner towers, and U-shaped interval towers, sometimes taking in the old gateways which had been blocked. Constantine's work on the frontiers is imperfectly known and indistinguishable from that of the Tetrarchy by purely archaeological means. It is probable that he built the bridgehead forts across the Rhine and Danube, such as Deutz (opposite Cologne) and Celamantia (opposite Brigetio). His battles against the Franks and the Alamanni in Gaul and against the Sarmatians on the Danube will have necessitated the organisation of defence in these areas, but it is possible that Diocletian had already done most of the groundwork. One of the features of frontier defence under Diocletian and Constantine is that the pattern changed from one of reactionary defence inside Roman territory to occasional aggressive pre-emptive defence across the frontiers; it has been suggested that the central mobile army of Constantine and his successors was an instrument of attack rather than one of interior defence.[39]

276

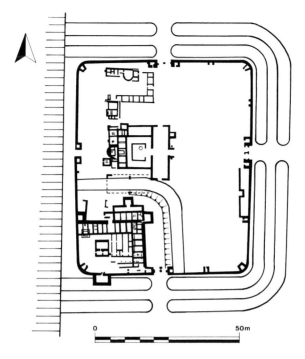

Figure 47 The addition of new defences and the blocking of gateways was not the only feature of later third-century forts. This fort at Eining on the Danube was much reduced in size, squeezed into the south-west corner of the earlier fort. This must reflect reductions in manpower or the splitting of units and redeployment in other forts. (Redrawn by Graeme Stobbs from Fischer and Spindler 1984.)

The eastern frontier with Persia

Relations between Rome and Parthia, which from the 220s was more accurately Persia, fluctuated according to the relative strengths of each contestant Empire. There was never any long-term stability, only armed and watchful truce arranged by mutual agreement or arrived at through mutual exhaustion. The Romans were the aggressors more often than the Persians, acting in response to real or imagined threats, often taking advantage of domestic difficulties when the current Parthian or Persian Royal Houses were preoccupied with internal rebellions or with trouble on their own eastern frontiers. Likewise the Persians took advantage of internal or external problems in the Roman state. The struggle between the two Empires was never resolved because one power never managed to defeat the other decisively, once and for all, and yet neither reached the point where it was too weak to keep on trying. Nor could the two parties arrive at a boundary line that was acceptable to both, consequently there was an ebb and flow of

277

territorial gain and loss. The eastern question absorbed much of the time and energy of successive Roman Emperors from Augustus onwards, in wars or in diplomatic wrangling.[40]

By the third century it was an established custom that important campaigns, especially eastern campaigns, must be led by the Emperor in person, and that Emperors had an overriding responsibility to go on expeditions to the east whenever the least trouble threatened and as soon as there was respite on the other frontiers. Keeping the Parthians or the Persians in check was not an optional accessory that came with the appointment; it was an obligation. Septimius Severus was able to subdue the Parthians in 197, carving two new provinces of Osroene and Mesopotamia from parts of the Parthian territory. Caracalla mounted an eastern campaign in 214; Macrinus spent the entirety of his short reign in the east. Severus Alexander's campaign in the 230s was mounted in response to the rise of Ardashir and the Sassanids in the 220s, and resulted in a victory in one battle and a defeat in another. From about 235 Ardashir and his son Shapur began to recoup their losses. Somewhere between 239 and 241 they took Hatra, seemingly intent now on regaining control of the territories they had lost when Severus redrew their western frontier with Rome. Gordian responded by invading in 242, but died or was killed in 244, leaving his successor Philip the Arab to arrange the best terms that he could, which involved paying large sums in gold to the Persians. In 252 Shapur invaded Syria and Cappadocia, and in 259–60 he attacked the Roman province of Mesopotamia. Valerian's expedition ended in what was arguably the worst eastern disaster for the Romans since Crassus' defeat at Carrhae. The Palmyrene Odenathus kept the Persians in check, but then after his death his wife Zenobia began to create an Empire for herself, prompting Aurelian's wars to reduce Palmyra. Aurelian took a Persian victory title, but did not by any means defeat the Persians. At the end of his reign, when he had dealt with all the other problems, he turned his attention to the eastern question. He embarked on his projected campaign to regain Mesopotamia in 275, but he got only as far as Thrace where he was assassinated. Probus also planned to reconquer the territory that Shapur had won, but he was assassinated before he had begun to march. The Romans mounted no major eastern campaign until that of Carus in 283. It was victorious but indecisive, and it was left to Diocletian and Galerius to defeat the Persians; but they did so only after an initial humiliating defeat. During all these third-century campaigns, the Romans were frequently successful, sometimes reaching and capturing Ctesiphon and/or other Persian cities, but beyond the Tigris they did not annex the territories they had overrun, and soon withdrew after a show of strength. Similarly the Persians did not hold onto their gains in Syria or Cappadocia. For a brief period in the 250s, Shapur reoccupied the mid-Euphrates, but the treaty between the Roman and Persian rulers at the end of the third century put the Romans back into the ascendant position. Galerius's and Diocletian's gains were lost in 363 in the disastrous campaign of Julian, but the bound-ary between the two powers that was established after this Roman defeat endured until the beginning of the sixth century.[41]

The kingdom of Armenia kept the Romans and the Parthians apart and also united them; as a buffer state (the term has been debated and disputed) and as the scene of mutual antagonism between the two Empires, Armenia was ruled by a succession of Roman and Parthian favourites, installed and deposed according to whichever Empire was the stronger. At the beginning of the fourth century the Christian tendencies of the people of Armenia alarmed the Persians, who saw in the religious developments an inclination towards stronger bonds with the Christian Roman Empire. A much greater source of antagonism in the third century was Severus' creation of the two provinces of Osroene and Mesopotamia, which involved a loss of territory for the Persians – one which they would never condone or accept. From the 220s Ardashir and Shapur adopted an aggressive policy. Dio commented that the acquisition of Mesopotamia was detrimental to Rome in the long run, because it upset the balance in the east, bringing Rome nearer to the potential enemy, lengthening supply lines and communications, while shortening the communications for the Persians. Severus' frontier, not a running barrier but a road with fortified posts strung out along it, ran from Palmyra to Damascus, on more or less the same lines that Diocletian's fron-tier would be laid out later, the *Strata Diocletiana*. Abandoning the legionary bases of his predecessors, Diocletian moved the troops up to the road, which was watched by small fortified posts, many of them dated epigraphically to his joint reign with Maximian or to the Tetrarchy.[42]

RELIGION

In the Empire that Severus inherited at the beginning of the third century the old Roman gods were worshipped in the old Roman way, and the Chris-tians were a relatively minor sect that had been recently persecuted by Marcus Aurelius. At the beginning of the fourth century, Constantine embraced Christianity, albeit somewhat ambiguously, and though he did not adopt any measures to suppress paganism, he paved the way for its eradi-cation. His successors began to turn their backs on the Roman and pagan gods towards the end of the century; pagan worship was finally outlawed in 391. It is not known whether this was Constantine's ultimate aim when he adopted Christianity. Even his own personal beliefs are questioned, and the veracity and validity of his conversion have been debated. Political expedi-ency probably weighed as much with him as religious sincerity. Like many converts, Constantine was not baptised until he was about to expire, so that the possibility of committing any sins between baptism and death was reduced. This was normal practice among early Christians, so it is not proof of his own uncertainty about his new faith. Whatever he believed, he did not patronise Christianity to the total exclusion of all else; he promoted the Sun god in tandem with the Christian faith; he issued coins honouring Sol until 322. He inclined towards monotheism, despite his ambiguous stance as to precisely which god he favoured.[43]

Monotheism as a philosophical rather than a religious concept had been gaining ground in the third century. Aurelian promoted the Sun god as the supreme deity; Mithraists worshipped a single supreme deity, and so did the Christians. The latter were accorded the same freedom as other minor sects in the Empire, and when they were persecuted it was not primarily because of their religious beliefs. It was their close-knit organisation and their networks spread over the Empire that caused concern to Roman Emperors, who saw that although the Christian communities were rent by heresies and internal squabbles, their membership included wealthy and influential people, and their hierarchical structure rivalled that of the Empire itself; the Christians owed obedience to their bishops to the same degree as to the Emperor, or possibly to an even greater degree. The connections of the Christian communities transcended regional, provincial or city loyalties. If the sect had been limited to one class of people, or to one or two small areas of the Empire, the Christians would probably not have come to the notice of the Emperors to such an extent, but it was clear that the community included all classes and extended over most of the Empire. Beliefs, religious practices, dogma, heresies, and endless debates about theological problems did not concern the Emperors, but loyalty and obedience did; the Christians could not guarantee either of these, so there was a conflict of interests from the start, which weighed more heavily when the Empire was under some threat. Significantly, it was the Emperors who battled on the frontiers who persecuted the Christians; Marcus Aurelius, Maximinus Thrax, Decius, Valerian, Diocletian and Galerius all tried to coerce the Christians to make at least a show of loyalty, or to outlaw them and eradicate them. But Christians thrived on martyrdom. Diocletian's persecution was probably the most violent and determined, for political reasons that were cloaked in subterfuge; it was said that the Christians had spoiled the sacrifices while Diocletian and Galerius attended a ceremony, then when fires broke out at Nicomedia, the blame was thrown on the Christians. Disunity of any sort was what Diocletian hoped to prevent, and for the same reasons he had already turned on the Manichaeans in the east because he considered that they were in league with the Persians.[44]

The persecution of the Christians was not carried out systematically over the whole Empire. Constantius was more lenient than his colleagues, so about a quarter of the Empire escaped rigorous punishment, and, more importantly, the populace in both eastern and western provinces were not sufficiently incensed about the Christians to support the schemes to suppress them. By 311 the persecution was rescinded and Galerius issued the edict of toleration; the wording of the edict as reported by Eusebius encapsulates the main problem that the Christians caused to the Emperors: it was said that they did not follow the ancient institutions, but made laws for themselves according to their own purpose. Two years later at Milan, the edict of toleration was confirmed and extended; Christians were granted privileges and legal rights, and anyone in the Empire was allowed to follow the religion best suited to his or her predilection. For some considerable time this freedom of belief and worship prevailed.[45]

Under Constantine there was no sudden and total conversion to Christianity. The Empire cannot be described as wholly Christian from 312 onwards, though undoubtedly the scene was set for Christianisation as the fourth century progressed. For some time the Roman and Hellenic gods were worshipped side by side with the Christian God, and although the pagan gods disappeared from the coinage by the second decade of the fourth century, the Emperors still assumed the role of Pontifex Maximus, chief priest of the pagan cults, until 381. The Imperial cult did not die out immediately, and Christians could partake in these cults without being compromised. In general the inhabitants of the Empire were unaffected by Constantine's conversion to and promotion of Christianity. It was the longer-term effects that counted, and the attitude of Constantine's successors that ensured the eventual supremacy of the Church. Imperial patronage, legal rights to hold property, and financial assistance all assured the prosperity and power of the Church. At the Imperial court, Christians began imperceptibly to rise in favour at the expense of pagans, though the rivalry did not begin to impede progress of pagan courtiers immediately after 312; the full effects were not apparent until paganism was banned at the end of the fourth century.[46]

Constantine adopted a new religious symbolism that appealed to both Christians and pagans, in the form of the chi-rho and the *labarum*. The chi-rho, the first two letters of Christos, had not been used in this way before Constantine adopted them; they had appeared in papyri, where they stood as an abbreviation for *chreston*, meaning good. The connection was perhaps not just fortuitous. The *labarum* was, according to Eusebius, like a cross consisting of a gold spear with a crossbar near the top, which supported a square of cloth. The chi-rho was usually situated inside a gold wreath at the top. The *labarum* was similar to the military standard, or *vexillum*, which would be familiar to everyone and particularly acceptable to soldiers. There is no agreement about the origins of the new standard, and no one knows whether the word derives from Greek, Latin or Celtic roots. Constantine probably fabricated it himself, seeking for a unifying symbol that was new but owed something to the past, so that it would not antagonise large groups of people. Unification of the Empire was Constantine's main purpose, but he wanted to achieve it with everything firmly under his control. He favoured the Christians, bestowing Imperial lands on them on which to build new churches; he fostered the religion by his own personal adherence to its tenets, without any real interest in the figure of Jesus or the dogma that divided the Christians. He favoured the clergy and allowed them privileges, exempting them from military service, but he controlled the bishops as he controlled his administrators and military officers, appointing them himself. He did not withdraw support from the pagan cults, and made no attempt to convert pagans or to force them to renounce their beliefs. Deity as a concept was left deliberately vague, and anodyne terminology was chosen to describe divinity, suitable for whatever anyone believed. Constantine made no formal statement about what he himself believed while he ruled the Empire, allowing others to form their own opinion. He was first and foremost a politician and a soldier, and Christianity was on his agenda because it served his purpose.[47]

To view the third century as a whole and in retrospect, especially when contemporary sources are lacking for precisely that period when the serious problems were at their height, is somewhat artificial. For the people who lived through the events of that crucial period this view would be limited both temporally and territorially; most people's awareness of history would stretch to three generations at the most, and there was no reason why a provincial living in Syria at the time of the Persian invasions should spare a thought for the provincials in Gaul who had just been attacked by the Alamanni or the Franks. The only individuals who would see the whole picture all over the Empire would be the Emperors themselves and the higher echelons of their court and their armed forces. The Emperor and his associates were the people who responded to each problem and formed policies for dealing with them, and the success or failure of their response depended upon their assessment of the situation. By far the most preponderant influence on the history of the third century was the movement of the tribesmen beyond the Rhine and Danube, and many of the other problems stemmed directly from that. A great proportion of Imperial time, energy and effort went into pacifying the northern frontiers. The tribal movements in the north coincided with the rise of the Persians under Ardashir and Shapur; individually, the threats on either the eastern or the northern frontiers might have been dealt with more quickly and efficiently, but serious fighting on two fronts used up manpower and resources, requiring two or more military commanders with authority and credibility – in short, more than one Emperor. It has been suggested that the inability of the central government to deal with the invasions gave rise to many of the so-called attempts at usurpation, with the consequent fragmentation of the loyalties of the troops and the provincial governors who tried to defend their own areas. The cost of supplying and paying the armies to defend the Empire escalated and was resented, and had a knock-on effect on every aspect of life within the Empire. The regimentation of production and distribution was the response of a beleaguered government towards the end of the third century; it has been claimed that its effects have been exaggerated, because it presents only worst-scenario information, unrelieved by other evidence that attests to the contrary. It is true that some parts of the Empire suffered hardly at all from the raids of the tribesmen, and not all provinces experienced drastic economic decline, but in general the instability of the northern frontiers undermined the whole Empire, if only for two or three decades. In historical terms this is a relatively short time, but to the generations of people who lived through them those decades represented most of their entire lives. To communities that had grown up with the ethic that Rome was the centre of the universe, the powerful protector as well as the framer of laws and the collector of taxes, the alternative reality that fragmentation was a possibility and the frontiers were not permanently exclusive will have seemed more serious than just a transformation. This is where life as the provincials knew it and life as historians understand it diverge. Historians know that the Roman Empire survived the third century by adapting to circumstances, and that some of the adaptations became permanent fixtures in civil and military organisation. There were some losses but also some gains, and when couched in these simplified and prosaic terms it might seem that the third century was after all simply a time of change.

NOTES

1 THE THIRD CENTURY: THE NATURE OF THE PROBLEM

1 On Severus in general see Birley (1988). Gallienus' policy was examined by de Blois (1976), and his cause is championed by Christol (1997, 131–65, esp. 143–52). On the reforms of Diocletian see Seston (1946); Williams (1985, 89–150); Barnes (1982). The third century crisis has received considerable attention; for a review of research 1939 to 1959 see Walser and Pekáry (1962); for overviews of the period see A. Alföldi 'The Crisis of the Empire' in *Cambridge Ancient History* vol. XII 1936, Ch. 6 pp. 165–231; Alföldi (1938; 1967); Petit (1974); Millar (1981, 239–48); Christol (1981; 1982); a synthesis of these last two references and the most up-to-date views are to be found in Christol (1997) who points out (1997, 69; 111 n.1) that the date of 235 and the elevation of Maximinus Thrax was chosen by the fourth-century historians (principally Aurelius Victor *de Caes*. 24.7–9) as a decisive and significant event because of its shock value, but there was a considerable gap between Maximinus and the later soldier-Emperors, and therefore no continuity of anarchic disruption, so it cannot be said that the acclamation of Maximinus was anything more than a historical accident. See also the introductory chapters in Vogt (1967) and Cameron (1993, 1–12).

2 Alföldi (1938, 7) argued that innovations and changes in the third century resulted neither from good nor bad Emperors, but were the results of a long process, and that there was an inevitability about everything that happened. Oliva (1962, 67–8; 130) places the beginning of the third-century crisis in the 160s when the Marcomannic wars began, and also blames the slave economy for weakening Roman society, quoting Liebenam (1900) and Hirschfeld (1913) who detected a definite decline in the second century in town and city life, and in agriculture. Millar (1981) is of the opinion that the fundamental changes in the Empire that came to prominence in the fourth and fifth centuries had already occurred by the end of the third century, and that it was the wars of that century that accelerated the changes. Vogt (1967, 61) comments that long-term defence planning was not an option granted to the Romans in the third century.

3 Millett (1981, 525–30) discusses what exactly the word 'crisis' means, and how modern interpretations have diverged; see also Alföldi (1938) and Cameron (1993, ch. 1). Mac-Mullen (1976, 1–23) examines contemporary views of the so-called decline, pointing out that there was considerable divergence of opinion even among those authors who lived through the events that they described.

4 Cimbri and Teutones are described by Strabo (7.292) and Caesar compares them to the tribes that he met in Gaul (*BG* 1.33; 1.40; 2.4; 2.29; 7.77). He also records at length the way in which he dealt with the Helvetii (*BG* 1.1–30).

5 Service in the Roman army familiarised both the tribesmen and their leaders with Roman fighting tactics. Arminius served as tribune, leading his own people, in the campaign army of Tiberius (Tac. *Ann*. 2.10.3). As reward for his services he was given Roman citi-

zenship (Vell. 2.118.2). Civilis served in the Roman army of the lower Rhine as cohort prefect (Tac. *Hist.* 4.32.3).

6 On the Gallic Empire see ch. 3 notes 19–20; Drinkwater (1987); on Palmyra and Odenathus see ch. 3 notes 21–5; Christol (1997, 146–7; 154–6; 160–1); Schwartz (1966); Will (1992).

7 Vogt (1967, 12; 16) emphasises the differences between the levels of Romanisation in the east and the west. Local dialects survived among the peasants of Syria and Egypt, whereas in the western provinces Latin took a deeper hold, albeit amalgamated with the Gallic and Spanish provincial languages. Elsewhere, Vogt (1967, 62) describes the divergence of cultures, artistic fashions, and social customs. Millar (1981, intro.) argues for unity and overall uniformity among the provinces of the Empire, while MacMullen (1966) highlights the discord and dissent within the state, all manifested in accordance with Roman customs, but nonetheless expressing 'energies both harmonious and hostile' (1966, 242). In the later Empire he envisages the growth of divergent forms in an Empire made up of 'homogeneous elements formerly suppressed but latterly vital' (1966, viii).

8 On the different views on the fall of the Empire see the essays gathered in Chambers (1970). On the collapse of the western Empire see Walbank (1969). MacMullen (1976, 10) suggests that it was the Christian authors who perceived decline and impending disaster, while the writings of the pagan authors do not present such an unwaveringly gloomy opinion; where these works survive it can be seen that the pagan authors react to individual events and perceive some changes for the worse, but do not feel obliged to predict the end of the world.

9 Cassius Dio was consul for the first time under Severus and achieved his second consulship under Severus Alexander in 229; he described the events of the early third century as an eye witness. For a general survey see Millar (1964). Dio perceived the age after Marcus Aurelius as 'all iron and rust' (71.36.4). On the value of Herodian as a source see Birley (1988, 204–5); like Dio, Herodian thought that the history of Rome up to the reign of Marcus Aurelius was more peaceful (1.1.4). See Alföldy (1971a and 1971b) for studies of Herodian, and Alföldy (1974a) for the crisis as seen by contemporaries.

10 Plotinus was born *c.*205 in Egypt and died *c.*270 in Italy. He wrote in Greek, his extant work being the *Enneads*, a collection of essays. Nemesianus lived in north Africa, and wrote Latin poetry in the late third century. He planned to write an epic on the achievements of Carinus and Numerianus, but never produced it. Vogt (1967, 30) dismisses the literature of the third century as almost non-existent, and highlights the jurists as the foremost writers of the time. All branches of learning suffered complete stagnation, from the point of view of original research. Compilations of existing knowledge were what survived.

11 For a study of the sources of Roman law and the extant texts see Robinson (1997). See Vogt (1967, 30) on the writings of the jurists as the only branch of literature that flourished in the third century.

12 Panegyrics as a form of adulatory address were part of a long-standing tradition, originating in Greek rhetoric and associated with the games celebrating the great festival of the Panathenaea, or the Olympic games. The *Panegyrici Latini* which have been preserved date from Pliny's address to Trajan through to the address to Theodosius in 389. They are commonly referred to as the 12 Panegyrics, but Gallétier chose to leave out Pliny's work in his edition of the *Panégyriques Latins*, so his three-volume work includes the 11 Panegyrics dating from 289 to 389. Concerning these late Roman Panegyrics, credence is sometimes stretched, but the wars and campaigns, resounding victories, building programmes and general achievements, all lauded to the skies in the various texts, could have been grossly exaggerated in importance, but it is unlikely that all these stories were complete fabrications. See Gallétier (vol. I, intro. xxv–xxix) on the historical value of the Panegyrics.

13 Born in north Africa, Lactantius spanned the second half of the third century and the first

half of the fourth, *c.*240–320. Noted as a Latin author who staunchly defended Christianity, much of his work is now lost; the most important of his surviving works are the *Divinae Institutiones*, and *de Mortibus Persecutorum*. Origen was probably born in Alexandria, and lived from *c.*185–*c.*253; he died in Caesarea in Palestine. He wrote in Greek, his most famous extant work being *Against Celsus*, championing the cause of Christianity and deriding paganism. Eusebius (*c.*260–*c.*340) was born in Judaea, and became bishop of Caesarea Maritima, where he had been educated; he wrote in Greek, and was a prodigious author, but he was more of a collector and compiler of knowledge and useful facts than an original thinker (Williamson 1989, xiii). The *History of the Church* is in ten books, beginning with the origins of Christianity and ending with the sole rule of Constantine after the defeat of Lactantius in 324. He was still working on his *Life of Constantine* when he died.

14 For an evaluation of St Cyprian see Alföldy (1973; 1974a). For text and translation of the extant correspondence see Bayard (1925). The correspondence covers the years 249 to 258, but despite the relatively short period of history, the letters are extremely useful for an overview of the state of affairs in the Empire, since Cyprian was well connected to a wide range of people in different parts of the Roman world. In particular, the persecution of Decius is well documented. Fragments of the literary works of St Cyprian are preserved in the quotations taken from them by other writers, such as Lactantius, St Augustine and St Jerome. Fragments of the work of Dexippus are gleaned from the quotations used in other ancient sources, and many of them were gathered together in the tenth century by Constantine VII Porphyrogenitus in a book called *Excerpta Historica* (Saunders 1992, 320); see also Millar (1969).

15 The *Historia Augusta* is such a fertile ground for debate that it now has a series of *Colloquia* devoted to it, and a full bibliography in no less than three volumes was published by Merten (1985–6). Millar (1964, 124) epitomises the difficulties of assessing this work: 'the problem of the *Historia Augusta* is one into which sane men refrain from entering'. Syme (1968, 220) labelled it a 'Serbonian bog'; elsewhere (1971a; 1971b; 1983) he devoted considerable effort to unravelling the mysteries of the *HA*; see also White (1967) and Barnes (1978). Birley (1988, 205–6) has a very useful synopsis of the *HA*, its various surviving editions and translations, and its many and varied exasperating problems. The so-called *Kaisergeschichte*, a supposedly lost work utilised by the writer of the *HA*, and by Zonaras and Zosimus, was first postulated by Enmann (1884), but it is not quite so widely accepted now (Schwartz 1983, 3–4). Johnson (1983, 58) discusses the rejection or acceptance of the facts related by the *HA*, concluding that the accounts of campaigns and building works are probably largely authentic, since there would be other extant sources available to contemporary audiences that would corroborate or refute the facts as related in the *HA*.

16 Historians of the fourth to the sixth centuries include Aurelius Victor, born in Africa in the first half of the fourth century. He had administrative experience of the Empire, rising to governor of Pannonia Secunda in 361 (Ammianus 21.10.6) and under Theodosius he was city prefect of Rome in 389. He wrote at least four works: *Origo gentis Romanae*, on the origins of the Romans; another work on the famous men of Rome (*de viris illustribus urbis Romae*); *Historiae abbreviatae*, better known as the Caesars, or *de Caesaribus*. An epitome of the latter, but not exactly a parallel text, was written later (*Libellus de vita et moribus imperatorum breviatus ex libris S. Aurelii Victoris*). This is better known as the *Epitome de Caesaribus*. Eutropius' history of Rome in ten short books, the *Breviarum*, covered the Republic and Empire from the foundation of the city to the death of Jovian in 364. Eutropius accompanied Julian on his Persian expedition, and was later a court official under the Emperor Valens. His work was translated from Latin into Greek several times. Zosimus, whose work may be early sixth century, wrote the *New History* in Greek, covering the Empire from the time of Augustus to 410. His sources included Dexippus, Eunapios, Olympiodorus, and Ammianus Marcellinus.

17 For an introduction to the use of inscriptions see Keppie (1991); the main collections of Latin and Greek inscriptions are *CIL*; *ILS*; *IGR*. A useful modern survey of source material pertinent to the third-century crisis is Loriot and Nony (1997).

18 There are many collections of papyri, amongst the most important of which are those from Oxyrhynchus in Egypt (*P. Oxy.* ed. Grenfell *et al.* 1898–date); for the army of the early third century see Fink (1971), and the papyri from Dura-Europos (*P. Dur.* ed. Welles *et al.* 1959). Other collections include those at the University of Michigan (*P. Mich.* ed. Edgar *et al.* 1931–date), and the Greek papyri in the John Rylands library in Manchester (*P. Ryl.* ed Hunt *et al.* 1911–52). Papyrological and epigraphical studies are covered by the periodical *Zeitschrift für Papyrologie und Epigrafik.*

19 Archaeology's contribution to the understanding of the third century is invaluable where there is no contemporary documentation. Archaeology assists in building up the composite history of the provinces of the Empire; for those in English with a synopsis of the third century events see Alföldy (1974b); Mócsy (1974); Rivet (1988); Salway (1991); Wightman (1985). For the frontiers of the Rhine and Danube, the various excavations of many fort sites produces an overview that would not otherwise be possible; see Johnson (1983); Maxfield (1987); Petrikovits (1971); Schönberger (1985, 401–25). The east and Africa: see Bowersock (1983); Daniels (1987). Civilian sites and agricultural environments across the Empire have also received much more attention in the last two decades; see among others Wightman (1985); Lewit (1991). This list is nowhere near complete.

2 EMPERORS AND USURPERS: 180–260

1 Hadrian withdrew from Dacia and Parthia (Birley 1997, 77; esp. 84f; 88; 96), and according to Dio (68.13.6) he destroyed the superstructure of Trajan's bridge across the Danube, allegedly fearing an invasion across the river. Execution of the four senators is described by Dio (69.2.5) who names them as Palma, Celsus, Nigrinus and Lusius [Quietus].

2 Eutropius' statement (8.6.2) that Hadrian was the first to build a wall in Britain is the only literary source for the erection of this frontier. On frontiers generally see Birley (1974a); Luttwak (1976); Whittaker (1994).

3 Many Emperors repaired frontier works after Hadrian established them, and even when territorial advances were made, the new frontiers were copies of the old ones. Thus when Antoninus Pius advanced from Hadrian's Wall in northern Britain into southern Scotland he built a frontier of turf instead of stone, but to all intents and purposes it was a new Hadrian's Wall some miles further north, and in Germany the new Antonine frontier was a copy of the Hadrianic one *c.*25 miles to the west. Both Severus and Diocletian devoted much time and energy and state resources to repairing existing frontiers or establishing new ones, and after them, Valentinian did the same in the fourth century. According to Mann (1974) inertia set in once the frontiers were established, so no one did anything to remove or improve them. But if the frontiers were not working properly, it is remarkable that the Emperors and army commanders did not notice, or even more remarkable if they noticed that there were tremendous problems but failed to invent a new system.

4 On Marcus Aurelius in general see Birley (1987). Dio says that when Marcus died and Commodus succeeded him history descended from a kingdom of gold to one of iron and rust (72.3.6.4).

5 Lucius entrusted the armies to Avidius Cassius, who was given command of all the east (Dio 72.2.2; 71.3.1 = book 72 in Loeb edn) He revolted when he thought Marcus was dead; Dio says that the revolt was engineered by Marcus' wife Faustina because she thought that her husband was going to die and Commodus was too young and simple-minded to be able to take on the Empire (Dio 72.22–3). As a result of this trouble in the east, Marcus summoned Commodus as his colleague, and was forced to come to

terms with the Iazyges (72.17), but he did not pursue or punish the senators who were associated with Cassius (72.28).

6 For the plague in the reign of Marcus Aurelius see Gilliam (1961). Marcus sold the Palace furniture to raise money (Dio fragments, between 72 and 73 Loeb edn) The financial crisis began in the reign of Marcus, foreshadowing the later problems, but did not yet reach serious proportions; although Marcus tried to avoid taxation by selling off his own possessions, new taxes had to be raised to finance wars against the Bastarnae, and the *annona militaris* is first heard of in Egypt (Petit 1974, 33).

7 Marcus was noted for utilising and elevating people who displayed particular talents, regardless of their social origins; 'so long as a person did anything good he would praise him and use him for the service in which he excelled, but to his other conduct he paid no attention' (Dio 72.34.4).

8 On the equites in general see Keyes (1915); Osier (1974); Brunt (1983); Pflaum (1960; 1982). For the *consiliares* see Crook (1955), and for the administrative reforms of Marcus Aurelius see Birley (1987) and Petit (1974). Knowledge of Maximianus' career and special commands derives from various inscriptions from the Danube frontier and from Africa (*CIL* III 1122; 13439; *CIL* VIII 2621; 2698 = 18247; 2749; 4234; 4600; *AE* 1933, 70; 1934, 40; 1956, 124); see Pflaum (1955, 135–54; 1960, 476–94; 982–3 no. 181*bis*). An inscription records the presence of Roman troops 125km north of the Danube (*CIL* III 13439 = *ILS* 9122). It is carved on a rock face in Trencin on the river Waag or Vag, now only visible from the window of the hotel backing onto the cliff.

9 Professionalism grew up among the ordinary soldiers from about the second century; they could follow a career with potentially greater rewards than in the early Empire, and a military society grew up with a hereditary tradition of service (Rémondon 1964, 80). Professionalism among the officer classes can be said to date from the wars of Marcus Aurelius, when 'a more concentrated effort was made to assemble and retain men of proven ability in senior commands' and equestrians who showed any talents could be raised to senatorial rank and appointed to commands normally reserved for senators (Campbell 1994, 61–2).

10 The role of the army in creating Emperors was already well known from the early Empire. Tacitus (*Hist.* 1.4) wrote of the 'secret of Empire' in the context of the death of Nero and the proclamation of Galba, Otho, Vitellius and Vespasian in the civil wars of 69–70. See Campbell (1994, 181–92) for the political role of the army throughout Roman Imperial history.

11 On sharing power as two equal Augusti see *HA* Marcus 7.5; Dio 71.1.1; Eutropius 8.9. Marcus was *consul ordinarius* with Verus in 161 (*CIL* VI 1984.22).

12 Dio (71.1.2) and *HA* Marcus 8.9 describe Verus' campaigns in the east. His departure (*profectio Aug.*) was celebrated on the coinage (*RIC* III 252). Commodus was made Augustus with Marcus Aurelius (*HA* Commodus 2.4), despite Marcus' reservations. Petit (1974, 17) says that it would have provoked civil war if anyone other than Commodus had been promoted.

13 Dio (72.33) describes the death of Marcus as not exactly from natural causes; though Marcus was ill, Dio says that it was not the disease that finished him but the doctors who wished to do Commodus a favour. According to *Epit. de Caes.* 16.2, the death occurred at Vindobona. After his death Marcus was awarded a gold statue by the Senate (Dio 72.34.1) and was deified (*HA* Marcus 18.3.5). Commodus concluded a peace treaty with the tribes across the Danube; see Demougeot (1969, 226–7); Lengyel and Radan (1980, 99); Fitz (1961). For the *latrones/latrunculi* inscriptions see Visy (1977, 6; 46); Mócsy (1974, 196; fig. 35); *RIU* 1136; *CIL* III 3330; 3332; 10312; 10313; *ILS* 395; 8913.

14 Dio lived through the reign of Commodus and was disenchanted from the start, describing it later as all iron and rust compared to the previous golden age (72.36.4). He also says that Commodus was given the best guardians and advisers that Marcus could provide, but he ignored them all (73.1.2).

15 On Severus' early career see Birley (1988, 37–80). Cleander (*PIR2* A 1481) appointed 25 consuls in one year, one of whom was Severus (Dio 73.12.4; see Birley 1988, 78).

16 Perennis was compelled by Commodus' lack of interest to become a surrogate head of state, according to Dio (73.9.1). Cleander hated Perennis (Dio 73.9.3–4). On Cleander's origins see Dio (72.12) and on selling privileges see Dio (73.10.2; 11.3). Ammianus (26.6.9) says that Cleander ruined many men's fortunes.

17 On the fall and death of Cleander: Dio (73.13); Alföldy (1989a); Birley (1988, 240 n.29; 263).

18 Removal of the Praetorian prefects: Dio (73.14.1); Birley (1988, 80–1). Sole prefect: *CIL* XIV 4378. Dio (73.4.1; 5.2–3; 7.3) lists some of Commodus' victims, and says that he killed both men and women.

19 Commodus insisted upon being addressed as Dominus, and by various heroic names (Dio 73.20.2). At the games where Commodus waggled the ostrich head as if to remind the senators that he could do the same to them, Dio and others chewed laurel leaves to disguise the fact that they were laughing (73.21). Herodian (1.15.5) also recounts the slaughter of ostriches.

20 On the appointment of Laetus see Birley (1988, 82–3). *AE* 1949, 38 reveals Laetus' *origo* (A.R. Birley 1969, 252). See also Jarrett (1972).

21 Murder of Commodus: (Dio 73.22; Herodian 1.17). According to *HA* (Pertinax 4.4) Pertinax (*PIR2* H 77) knew about the plot but Dio (74.1.1–2) implies that Laetus only went to Pertinax after he had killed Commodus, without any prior warning or discussions with Pertinax, who carefully went to view the body to make sure it was really true that Commodus was dead. Avidius Cassius had been caught out on that score, by taking action before he had checked that Marcus was dead, though in his case it would have taken a long time to receive accurate reports. Birley (1988, 84) says that Pertinax was Laetus' choice for Emperor before he killed Commodus; see also A.R. Birley (1969, 250).

22 Pertinax took the title *pater patriae*, or father of his country, on the same day that he was declared Augustus, and was the first to do so (*HA* Pertinax 5.6). The senatorial candidate Triarius Maternus fled rather than be made Emperor (*HA* Pertinax 5.5). Herodian (2.4.4) describes how the Praetorians had grown very arrogant and knew that their privileges were likely to be curtailed. Dio echoes the same sentiments (74.1.3).

23 On the government and achievements of Pertinax see *HA* (Pertinax 6.6–9.9) and Herodian (2.4.6). The army played an important part in sustaining Pertinax and he rewarded it well, paying the donatives that Commodus promised and then some payments of his own; the *HA* mentions payments three times in a short space, emphasising the importance of such measures (Pertinax 6.6; 7.6; 9.1). Pertinax tried to be fair and just; he was lenient to Falco who was accused of plotting against him (Dio 74.8.5; *HA* Pertinax 10.1–7), and he tried to promote ideas of equality (*BMC* V Pertinax 14–17; Christol 1997, 12).

24 Plots formed against Pertinax (Dio 74.8–9) and finally Laetus murdered him (*HA* Pertinax 10.8). Flavius Sulpicianus was Pertinax's father-in-law, and had been appointed city prefect (*HA* Pertinax 13.7). He and Didius Julianus bargained for the throne (Dio 74.11).

25 The armies of the various provinces proclaimed Severus, Clodius Albinus (*PIR2* C 1186) and Niger (Dio 74.14.3–4). The exact date when Severus was proclaimed is disputed; Dio gives no precise dates; *HA* Severus 5.2 says that it took place *Idibus Augustis*, the Ides of August, but this is better interpreted as a mistake for *Idibus Aprilis* or the Ides of April, which would mean 13 April. Paschoud (1971, 135 n.25) says it was 1 April. Severus was in touch with neighbouring governors from his *dies imperii*, 9 April (Christol 1997, 13), but he will have been preparing the ground before then. He made arrangements to secure the provinces he was leaving in his rear when he marched on Rome (*HA* Severus 5.3) and the Danube and Rhine armies declared for him under compulsion from

their generals (*HA Severus* 5.5). Whilst this is not solid evidence it supports the theory that he had sown the seeds for his bid for the throne. He honoured the legions on his coinage (*BMC* V Septimius Severus 7–25; Christol 1997, 13). Virius Lupus was governor of Lower Germany and suffered a defeat by Albinus (Dio 76.5.4), but he proved his loyalty to Severus and was rewarded by being appointed governor of Britain; see Birley (1981a, 149–51).

26 Severus was universally regarded as the avenger of Pertinax (*ultor Pertinacis*) (*HA* Severus 5.5), and he adopted the name of Pertinax, displaying it on his coins (Christol 1997, 13).

27 Julianus tried to defend himself in a manner in which Dio found ludicrous (74.16). According to *HA* (Didius Julianus 7.9–11) he resorted to magic and all sorts of strange rites. The Senate condemned him to death (Dio 74.16.4), and it was said that he had taken poison, but a soldier killed him in the Palace (*HA* Didius Julianus 8.8).

28 The Praetorians had learned to live well and had become accustomed to comfort and privileges (Dio 74.16.2). When Severus approached Rome he summoned the Guard, surrounded them with his legionary soldiers and dismissed them ignominiously (Dio 75.1–2; Herodian 2.13.1–9). See also Durry (1938, 383–5). Severus stopped the practice of recruiting men for the Praetorian Guard from Italy, Spain and Noricum, and according to Dio (75.2.5) he ruined Italian youth because they had no employment. He reconstituted the Guard, making it much larger at 15,000 men (Dio 75.2.6), and these new Praetorians recruited from the legions were boorish, uncouth and terrifying (Herodian 2.1.4.5), whereas the men from Italy, Spain, Noricum and Macedonia had been much more respectable in appearance (Dio 75.2.4). The new Guard was not given a new and different name, but still went under the name of Praetorians; inscriptions confirm that many of the new men were Illyrians (Durry 1938, 384; see also *CIL* VI 210 = *ILS* 2013).

29 Severus sent a letter by one of his trusted friends to offer Albinus the title Caesar, and Albinus believed he would share the throne with Severus (Dio 74.15.2). Severus also made him consul (*HA* Clodius Albinus 6.8). According to *HA* (Clodius Albinus 7.1–6) Severus sent him another letter after the defeat of Niger, calling him brother in spirit and on the throne. Severus is accused of duplicity by having this read out in public and planning to assassinate Albinus in private.

30 Herodian (2.14.6–3.2.5) describes the course of the war with Niger. *HA* (Niger 5.4) is the source for Severus sending troops to Africa; *CAH* XII, 6 suggests that Severus sent detachments of *III Augusta* to watch over the border between Egypt and the African provinces, and to prevent *II Traiana* from sending help to Niger. *HA* (Niger 5.7) says that Niger gave battle under Aemilianus, who is accused by Dio (75.6.2) of sitting on the fence, waiting for a favourable outcome; he met defeat at the hands of Severus' generals near Cyzicus (Dio 75.6.4). Candidus is not mentioned in these sources in connection with this battle, but he was instrumental in another that took place 'amid the narrow passes of Nicaea and Cius' where he rallied the Severan soldiers who had begun to give ground (Dio 75.6.5). For his career see *CIL* II 4114 = *ILS* 1140.

31 The cavalry played an important part at the battle of Issus (Christol 1997, 14). Niger intended to make his escape to the 'barbarians', i.e. the Parthians (Dio 75.8.3). Dio (75.12.2) says that the siege of Byzantium lasted three years, which would take it from 193 to 196; *CAH* XI 11 suggests that it must have been at the end of 195 when Byzantium fell; see also Birley (1988, 119). Severus destroyed Byzantium, including the defences, thus eliminating 'a Roman base against the barbarians from Pontus and Asia' (Dio 75.14.4).

32 Punishment of the cities that had aided Niger and rewards for those which had resisted him were cleverly combined, when the latter were elevated at the expense of the former, receiving lands and revenues that formerly belonged to the cities undergoing punishment. Nicaea was severely punished (Herodian 3.2.7–9). On Antioch see Christol (1997,

14; 61); Robert (1977, 22–35); Downey (1961, 241–2). Byzantium was placed under the authority of Perinthus (Dio 75.14.3; Herodian 3.6.7). Retribution towards Niger's personal adherents began as soon as the war was over, but despite the hysterical accusation in *HA* (Niger 6.4) that Severus killed countless senators (*innumeros senatores*) Dio is much more trustworthy when he insists that Severus did not kill any senators, but exiled them and sequestered their property instead (Dio 75.6.3–4). *HA* (Niger 6.1–4) says that Severus at first only exiled Niger's family but then executed them all when he heard that Albinus had raised a revolt in Gaul. An inscription honouring and recounting the career of Candidus (*CIL* II 4114 = *ILS* 1140) records the *expeditio Parthica* that Severus embarked upon after the war with Niger was concluded. According to Dio the reason for this campaign was that the Osroeni and Adiabeni had rebelled and laid siege to Nisibis, so Severus made war against them (Dio 75.1.2 = end of book 75 in Loeb edn pp. 194–6). Severus elevated Nisibis to colonial status and entrusted the city to an eques (Dio 75.3.2 = Loeb edn p. 198). An equestrian procurator was put in charge of Osroene; see *ILS* 1353 referring to C. Iulius Pacatianus, *proc. provinc. O[sr]hoenae*. For the date of the creation of the province see Christol (1997, 61 n.8) quoting recently discovered inscriptions *AE* 1984, 919 and 920; as Christol points out this epigraphic evidence leaves no doubt of the date of foundation of the province in 195.

33 Severus took the titles *Parthicus Adiabenicus* and *Parthicus Arabicus* after the campaigns (*HA* Severus 9.20; Eutropius 18.4; and see *ILS* 417 dated to 195), and received his fifth, sixth and seventh Imperial acclamations from the troops (Christol 1997, 14). He made his wife Julia Domna *mater castrorum*, which was the equivalent of taking an Imperial colleague (Birley 1988, 130).

34 According to *HA* (Severus 9.11) Severus refused a triumph for the campaigns in the east because it would seem as though he was celebrating a victory over Romans, and he dropped the title *Parthicus* so as not to injure the Parthians (*ne Parthos lacesseret*); as mentioned above (note 33) *ILS* 417 dated to 195 displays the titles *Parthicus Arabicus* and *Parthicus Adiabenicus*; *ILS* 418 dated to the following year displays only *Arabicus* and *Adiabenicus* without the '*Parthicus*'. The division of Syria into two provinces is most likely to be dated to the period just after the defeat of Niger (Birley 1988, 114; Millar 1993, 121; Christol 1997, 24. See also G. Downey *Berytus* 1939–41, 1ff).

35 The chronology of the break between Severus and Albinus is open to debate. Dio says that Albinus aspired to be Emperor but gives no details about dating (75.4.1 = 76.4.1 Loeb edn p. 203). Some authors prefer to date the assumption of the title Augustus to the end of 195, while Petit (1974, 46) dates it to January 196. Severus hailed from equestrian roots while the senatorial Albinus 'excelled in family and education' (Dio 76.6.2). He was descended from a rich family (Herodian 2.15.1), and he had already earned fame in the northern wars (Dio 73.8.1). For Albinus' career and governorship of Britain see Birley (1981a, 146ff), and for his bid for the throne see also *CIL* VIII 1549; 17726; 26498. Severus' son Bassianus was probably declared Caesar in spring 195 (Birley 1988, 122) and put on display to the army at Viminacium at the end of that year. Other sources place the event at the beginning of 196 when coins were issued to celebrate the event (Kent 1978, 304). *HA* (Severus) reports the event twice, at Viminacium (10.3) and after the defeat of Albinus (14.3), which was perhaps the date when the title was confirmed by the Senate. See also *CJ* 4.19.1; Herodian (3.10.5).

36 Continuity with the regime of Pertinax was important to Severus and he adopted the name (Christol 1997, 13). Connection with the house of Marcus Aurelius lent stability to his regime, and in 195–6 at the same time as he made Bassianus Caesar, he renamed him Marcus Aurelius Antoninus. See *BMC* 612 for the new name in 196; this is the name under which Caracalla appears on the coinage ever afterwards (Christol 1997, 15; 62 n.9). *HA* (Severus 10.6) says that Severus gave the name Antoninus to Caracalla because he wished to enter himself into the family of the previous Emperors Marcus Aurelius and Antoninus Pius.

37 Herodian (3.5.3–5.) says that Severus did not want to risk open war with Albinus, and decided it would be easier to kill him, so he accordingly sent messengers to Britain with instructions to speak to Albinus in private and kill him, or to poison him; the story is also found in *HA* (Clodius Albinus 8.1–9.1); see Birley (1988, 117–18). It is not known what arrangements Albinus made to secure Britain while he went to Gaul, but it is generally assumed that he left a skeleton garrison; Birley (1988, 124) estimated that the legionary force of the whole province would amount to 50,000 men and that Albinus would have taken *c.*40,000. Frere (1987, 155) says that it is conceivable that Albinus stripped Britain of every available soldier, presumably having made arrangements to protect the northern frontier, but it is not certain what happened to the original garrisons on Hadrian's Wall, most of which were changed at some time in the third century. For discussion of the problem see Frere (1987, 155–8); Salway (1991, 221–31; 1993, 165–7). Albinus' army was equal in size to Severus' according to Dio (76.6.1). *CAH* XII 14 suggests that Albinus recruited troops in Gaul to make up numbers, as does Birley (1988, 124), who adds that Albinus can hardly have had enough time to train the troops he raised in this way to make them effective against Severus' battle-hardened legions and auxiliaries. See also Herodian (3.7.2).

38 Severus 'sent a general with a force of soldiers to take control of the Alpine passes and guard the routes into Italy' (Herodian 3.6.10); the general is thought to have been C. Iulius Pacatianus (Whittaker 1969, 195 n.4; Birley 1988, 122). The phrase 'Gallic conspiracy' probably derives from Marius Maximus, who took part in Severus' campaigns and was made governor of Gallia Belgica after the defeat of Albinus (Birley 1988, 122). Virius Lupus, governor of Lower Germany, is most probably who is meant when Dio describes how Albinus defeated Lupus, one of Severus' generals (76.6.2); see Birley (1981a, 149–51) and Christol (1997, 16). Deserters from Albinus came over to Severus according to *HA* (Severus 10.8), but human nature being what it is this is a platitude as well as savouring of Severan propaganda. Trier may have held out against Albinus, which may be the reason why the city was honoured by Severus; see *ILS* 419, where the *civitas Treverorum* is mentioned while Severus is still named as Pertinax, a name which he never dropped altogether but which eventually went out of use in his official titles (Birley 1988, 199), but Caracalla is not yet Augustus, which dates the inscription prior to 198, probably just after the battles with Albinus.

39 Severus stayed a short while in Rome before going on to Gaul (Birley 1988, 123–4). The battle of Lugdunum is described by Dio (76.6) but he does not describe the sack of the city, whereas Herodian (3.7.6) says that the soldiers burned it to the ground. Executions of Albinus' followers began in Gaul (*HA* Severus 12.1–6). In Herodian's narrative (3.8.2) it is inferred that Severus divided Britain into two provinces immediately after Albinus was defeated, but the earliest attested inscriptions referring to the two provinces Britannia Inferior and Superior are post-Severan (*CIL* VIII 2080; 2766 = *ILS* 2762; 5180). See below (note 62) for discussion.

40 In his speech to the Senate Severus praised the severity of Marius, Sulla and Augustus (Dio 76.8.1). He condemned to death 29 senators (76.8.4), but allowed 35 prisoners of the noblest lineage who had supported Albinus to go free. *HA* (Severus 13.5) says he killed 41 senators, and gives their names, most of which seem to be invented (Birley 1988, 199). Alföldy (1976) examines the names for those which can be rejected and those which may be authentic. This passage in *HA* follows immediately upon a description of the war with Albinus, and the statement that Severus spoke about the mercy he had shown to Albinus' adherents. The discrepancy between Dio and *HA* may be caused by several other factors, including the possibility that in this sweep Severus also included supporters of Niger whom he had previously ignored; see Christol (1997, 17) and Jacques (1992).

41 In order to make it clear that Severus was to be succeeded by his son, Caracalla received the extra title *Imperator destinatus* (Christol 1997, 17; Sasel 1983; *ILS* 442; 446; 447).

Severus' son Geta and his brother Septimius Geta were not promoted so rapidly as Caracalla. When Severus marched to the east against Niger his brother Geta came to meet him, and was either sent back to Lower Moesia or appointed governor of Dacia, where he is attested as governor by 195 (*CIL* III 905). He may have hoped to share in the Imperial power, or for a field command (Birley 1988, 109). *HA* (Severus 8.10) claims that Geta had 'other hopes' (*aliud sperantem*). Severus' younger son Geta was only one year younger than Caracalla, but had to wait for several years before he was made Caesar, and several more before he was made Augustus; 12 years elapsed before he attained equal rank (Birley 1988, 186–7; 218). Dio recounts with distaste the fact that Severus compelled the Senate to deify Commodus, and that he called him 'brother' (76.7.4); he preserves (76.8) much of the speech that Severus made eulogising Commodus. *HA* (Severus 11.4) places the deification of Commodus just after the defeat of Albinus, when there was rumour of more rebellious feeling against him, so he did it 'to spite the Senate', which rather misses the point of the proceedings. See also *HA* (Commodus 17.11) where the deification is attributed to hatred of the Senate; in another passage (Severus 12.8–9) it is stated that Severus made a speech to the Senate and before the assembly of the people declaring Commodus a god, and insisting that Commodus had been unpopular only with the degenerate (*infamibus*). On the relationship between Commodus and the army see Speidel (1993)

42 See Graham (1973), Birley (1988) and Christol (1997, 26–8) for careers of Severus' adherents. The real seat of government of the Empire was wherever the Emperor was (Millar 1993, 121). Envoys came to Severus in Germany after the defeat of Albinus (*ILS* 1143); an ambassador from Ephesus came to Rome and then to Britain (*AE* 1971, 455); inscriptions make it clear that Imperial decisions were made where the Emperor was working at the time: *AE* 1986, 628 mentions a decision made at Eboracum, by Caracalla and Geta. Rostovtzeff (1957, 710 n.10) says that Severus entered consciously upon the new path, inaugurating a new phase in the history of the Empire; Emperors like Trajan, Hadrian and Antoninus Pius would have been able to prolong the peace but Severus pursued selfish aims. This prejudiced view is offset by the legislation that showed Severus' concern for the helpless and destitute people of the Empire, whose plight he tried to remedy; see Lewis (1996); Coriat (1997).

43 The army reforms are attested only by Herodian (3.8.4–5), who places the arrangements just after the defeat of Albinus. *HA* (Severus 17.1) says that he gave the army a pay rise, but it is implied that this happened just before the second Parthian campaign. It was the first for over a century and it was resented by the populace of Rome (Watson 1969, 188 nn.231–3; Campbell 1984, 185–6; Birley 1988, 128; 196). Herodian (3.8.8) says that Severus taught the soldiers to be greedy. The rise may have been granted to cope with inflation, but there is little evidence with which to reconstruct the likely percentage of inflation at this time, and there is some uncertainty as to whether the whole pay rise was in cash or whether some of it was in kind. Whittaker (1969, 308 n.2) points out that the Greek word used by Herodian for army pay literally means corn allowance, though he uses it in other contexts where the Latin equivalent *stipendium* is indicated. Dio (78.34.3) implies some system of payment in kind, and says that it was under Severus that the *annona militaris* was started, but it was nothing like the later fourth-century version. See Develin (1971) for further discussion. Smith (1972a, 493) suggests that Severus may have raised army pay by as much as half, from 300 to 450 denarii. Permission to marry recognised a situation already established, though it was legally permitted to the auxilia anyway (Whittaker 1969, 309 n.5). The measure was a successful one, and as forts became more permanent the vici outside them grew in size (Smith 1972a, 493). The gold ring did not confer equestrian status, and the privilege was granted only to centurions and *primipilares*; it indicated the possibility of social mobility, which was necessary to fill the administrative posts in the Empire, usually undertaken by equestrians (Whittaker 1969, 309 n.4). The reasons for the pay rise and the army

reforms were in part to keep the army loyal to Severus and his household, and to encourage recruitment into a service where conditions were not good. Severus had witnessed the problems caused by desertion and desired to make the army a more attractive proposition to recruits. Furthermore he had increased the size of the army, so there would be a greater need for more and more men to replace losses and retired veterans; see E. Birley (1969); Smith (1972a); Graham (1973).

44 Severus raised three new legions and left one of them, *II Parthica*, in Italy at Albano while he went on his second Parthian campaign (Birley 1988, 129; Benario, 1972). Herodian's claim (3.13.4) that the garrison of Rome was quadrupled under Severus is an exaggeration; with the Praetorian Guard and the legionaries of *II Parthica* it has been estimated that there were 30,000 troops in Italy (*CAH* XII, 26; Durry 1938, 82–9; Whittaker 1969, 352–3 n.2; Smith 1972a). The date when *I, II*, and *III Parthicae* were raised is not known for certain; Mommsen suggested that *I Parthica* was in existence by 195 (notes to *CIL* XII 1856). Smith (1972a, 486 n.28) points out that Severus would not have had time to raise and train three legions for the war with Niger, but it seems that C. Iulius Pacatianus was prefect of *I Parthica* before he took up command of the Cottian Alps to block the route into Italy from Gaul, so if this is correct it means that at least one of the new legions was in existence by 196. Smith suggests that Severus raised two of the legions from Niger's troops; *II Parthica* was made up predominantly of Illyrian soldiers, whereas *I* and *III Parthicae* were recruited from oriental troops. The city prefect while Severus campaigned was Cornelius Anullinus, one of the Emperor's friends (Birley 1988, 122; 129; 248 n.2). Plautianus was an African, and closely associated with Severus from his youth, some said as a boy-lover; see Dio (76.14–16) and Herodian (3.10.6–7). On Plautianus' career see Birley (1988, 128–9) and Christol (1997, 28–9).

45 Severus made war on the Parthians because they had overrun Mesopotamia (Dio 76.9.1), whereas Herodian (3.9.1) says that the excuse for the campaign was revenge on Hatra, which had aided Niger. Dio is the more reliable of the two sources. There was dissension on the Parthian Royal House, and Severus was accompanied by the Parthian king's brother (Dio 76.9.3; Birley 1988, 129–30). King Abgar provided troops and archers for the campaign (Herodian 3.9.2). Vologaeses retreated as the Roman army advanced, and Severus followed the course of the Euphrates, sending troops down it in boats (Dio 76.9.3). Although Severus captured Ctesiphon he had no plans to keep it, so it seemed that the expedition was undertaken solely for the purpose of plundering the capital city (Dio 76.9.4). The army acclaimed Severus Imperator for the tenth and eleventh times for the Parthian campaign (Christol 1997, 17). Caracalla was made Augustus and shared the throne with his father, and Geta was made Caesar (Birley 1988, 130); Herodian erroneously puts this event in Rome and says that both sons were made Augusti (3.9.1). The legend *Parthicus Maximus* appeared on coins to commemorate the campaign (Christol 1997, 17; *BMC* V Severus 265–6).

46 Only Dio gives an account of two sieges of Hatra (76.10.1; 76.11.1–12). Herodian's version (3.9.3–12) is different, and it has been suggested that he was following the order of events as depicted in the paintings that Severus commissioned in commemoration of the campaigns, or perhaps Herodian also used as his guide the sculptures on the arch in the Forum, which were executed later than the paintings (Whittaker 1969, 317 n.4, citing Picard *CRAI* 1962 7ff). Dio depicts Severus' campaigns as wasteful and not very effective, especially the sieges of Hatra. Herodian is also sceptical about the purpose of the war and says that Severus won prestige with this war more by good luck than good management (3.9.12). These two authors wrote in the old tradition of Roman expansionism, which was not Severus' aim in this war; Birley (1988, 132–3) suggests that it was not such a failure as has been assumed, in that it achieved all that Severus wanted. The connection with Trajan's *dies imperii* (28 January 98) would be especially significant for Severus a century later (Christol 1997, 17). Trajan's reputation was one of total perfection and he had dealt successfully with Parthia, so as a role model he was ideal, espe-

cially beneficial for the soldiers. The province of Mesopotamia was created in 198 (Birley 1988, 132; Christol 1997, 23). Equestrians were appointed as legates of the two legions (*I* and *III Parthicae*) stationed in the province; see note 44 above for the controversy over the dates when the legions were raised. The post of governor of Mesopotamia also went to an equestrian. The first governor was Tiberius Claudius Subatianus Aquila (Kennedy 1979; Christol 1997, 62 n.2). After the campaigns Severus went to Egypt (Dio 76.13.1).

47 Some territory from Syria Phoenice was ceded to Arabia (Bowersock 1983, 110f; Kennedy 1980; 1982, 69ff; Birley 1988, 134). The conquest of Mesopotamia was a constant drain on resources and because it brought the Romans into contact with neighbours of the Medes and Parthians it was the cause of further warfare, according to Dio (75.3.3). See Tyler (1975) for the effect of the later-third-century Persian wars on Roman finance and monetary policy.

48 Severus bestowed numerous rights and privileges on the people of Palestine (*HA Severus* 17.1). On creation of colonies see Birley (1988, 135). In Egypt Severus visited and then closed the tomb of Alexander (Dio 76.13.2), and he gave Alexandria a council of its own (Birley 1988, 137; *HA* Severus 17.2). Augustus had not allowed Alexandria such autonomy, placing the city under an equestrian *juridicus* (Dio 51.17.2).

49 Plautianus' daughter was given to Caracalla in marriage (Herodian 3.10.5), but Caracalla hated her (Herodian 3.10.8). The marriage took place in Rome with great festivities (Dio 77.1.2). On the way back to Rome Severus went via Moesia and Pannonia (Herodian 3.10.1). The timing of the journey is not known. Christol (1997, 29) speculates that the Imperial party left in autumn 201, despite the fact that traditionally Severus and Caracalla inaugurated the year 202 as consuls at Antioch. Birley (1988, 143) suggests that Severus may have been at Carnuntum to celebrate his *dies imperii* on 9 April 202.

50 Coins bearing the legends *Impp Invicti Pii Augg* and *Victoria Parthica Maxima* were issued to commemorate the Parthian campaign (Christol 1997, 30; *BMC* V Severus 44–245; 265–6). Severus celebrated a triumph and gave donatives to the people of Rome (Dio 76.1.1–5; Herodian 3.10). The *Decennalia* festivities cost 200 million sesterces, according to Dio (77.1.1–2), who says that Augustus had inaugurated the custom, as if renewing his power (53.16.2–3). For an in-depth discussion see Chastagnol (1984b). Severus had a dream in which he saw Pertinax fall from his horse, which he then mounted and rode (Herodian 2.9.5–6), so he placed his triumphal arch on that spot in the Forum, an advantageous position with regard to the Senate House and the arch of Augustus (Birley 1988, 155). On the arch itself see Brilliant (1967); Rubin (1975; 1980); Hannestad (1986); Birley (1988, 155); Christol (1997, 31).

51 Severus and his whole family, including Plautianus, travelled to Africa in 203 (Dio 76.14.2–5; Birley 1988, 137–8). Plautianus appears on inscriptions as part of the *domus divina* (*CIL* IX 4958; XI 1336), and received the title of *socer et consocer Augusti* (Christol 1997, 28–9). Severus favoured fellow Africans in his government, and also easterners because of their connection with the family of Julia Domna; there was an obvious increase in the number of African and Oriental senators in his reign (Whittaker 1969, 348 n.2); it is estimated that over 60 per cent of the new procurators that Severus created were of African or eastern descent (Birley 1988, 196).

52 Expansion in Africa pushed the frontiers further south (Christol 1997, 25–6; Birley 1988, 146–53); for an overview see Daniels (1987), and on Severus' frontier policy see Birley (1988, 151; 197). For Roman Africa in general see Raven (1993), and on Numidia see Fentress (1979). The majority of published works on Roman Africa and the frontiers are by French scholars, and there is an enormous literature; among others, see Benabou (1975); Le Bohec (1989, 391–8); Trousset (1974). Hadrian moved *III Augusta* from Ammaedara to Lambaesis (Birley 1997, 209). Quintus Anicius Faustus was suffect consul at the end of 198 or the beginning of 199 (*CIL* VIII 2550). He was appointed governor of Upper Moesia, and later became proconsul of Africa (Dio 78.22.4). See Pflaum *Libyca* 5, 1957, 65ff, and Eric Birley *JRS* 40, 1950, 62ff.

53 Several inscriptions in north Africa attest Severus' title as *propagator imperii*; these have been studied by Pflaum (1969) and Birley (1974b). The new frontier zone was called *nova praetentura*, and was put into effect by Octavius Pudens from Auzia (Birley 1988, 148; Christol 1997, 25–6). The province of Numidia, encompassing a much smaller territory than the land of the Numidians, was created sometime before 208 (Christol 1997, 63 n.7). The Severan frontiers of Mauretania Caesariensis and Tingitana have been studied by Salama (1953; 1955; 1977).

54 For Lepcis Magna see Birley (1988, 148–54; 212–21). Auzia, the home of Octavius Pudens, was made a colony by Severus (Birley 1988, 148; Christol 1997, 25–6).

55 On the Secular Games see *ILS* 5050a; *AE* 1968, 518–24; Birley (1988, 158–9); Christol (1971); Gagé (1934a; 1934b). The *domus divina* is attested on inscriptions (*CIL* IX 4958; XI 1336); Christol (1997, 18) discusses milestones where the title appears. Tertullian (*Apol.* 34) speaks of divine authority.

56 See Herodian (3.10.2); Birley (1988, 164–5) on Severus' legal work and his appearances in court. Coriat (1997) examined the legislative activity of the Severans and the Emperor as lawgiver at the end of the Principate. Lewis (1996) assembled the constitutions of Severus as represented in the law codes and the papyri that have come to light, concluding that Severus had a genuine concern for individuals; many of the constitutions derive from replies to complaints and appeals for help. On Plautianus: *PIR2* F 554. On his growing power see Dio (76.14.1–15.2a) who says that nothing was left unplundered by the Praetorian Prefect, and that petitions were addressed to him as though he were Emperor. Plautianus had a reputation for cruelty (*HA Severus* 15.4) and treated Julia Domna with contempt (Dio 76.15.6). Severus said that he loved Plautianus so much that he hoped to die before him (Dio 76.15.2). On the removal of Julius Laetus see *PIR2* L 69; Birley (1988, 131); Christol (1997, 29; 64 n.13). Claudius Candidus: *PIR2* I 754; Pflaum (1960, 548–9); Christol (1997, 29; 64 n.13). Aemilius Saturninus: *PIR2* A 403; Dio 76.1.4.1; Christol (1997, 29; 64 n.13); Birley (1988, 137). Septimius Geta denounced Plautianus just before he died (Dio 76.2.4), and Caracalla then manoeuvred to implicate Plautianus in a plot; Herodian's account (3.11.1–12.12) is unreliable; Dio's (77.3.1–4.5) does not survive in its entirety and has been preserved by his epitomators.

57 Two Praetorian Prefects, Q. Maecius Laetus and Aemilius Papinianus, were appointed after the death of Plautianus (Herodian 3.13.1). They are first attested in May 205 (*CIL* VI 228; Christol 1997, 35). Some of the officers of the Praetorian Guard were implicated in the alleged plot hatched by Plautianus, but the soldiers were left unscathed (Durry 1938, 386). The powers and functions of the Praetorian Prefects changed in the third century. After a short interlude when legal experts held the office, military men came into prominence once again as the need arose with the continual wars during the second half of the third century. By the end of the century the Praetorian Prefects had gained in influence and importance, combining three spheres of influence, as commander of the guard, as a member of the Emperor's tribunal with judicial powers, and as an authoritative figure in the *consilium*. The most important change that began with Plautianus was the entry into the Senate, but this did not become customary until some time later; in the interim, Praetorian Prefects after Plautianus commonly received *ornamenta consularia* without actually becoming consuls themselves (Durry 1938, 161; 187; Howe 1942, 3–4; Crook 1955, 79). Papinianus may have been *praefectus annonae* (Christol 1997, 35); see also Pflaum (1960, 583–4); Syme (1970; 1980). On Maecius Laetus see Pflaum (1960, 581–3). After the death of Plautianus, Severus merely made a short speech in the Senate, making no denunciation of his former friend, but some men were executed on account of their association with Plautianus (Dio 77.5.1–3). Dissension between Caracalla and Geta and their atrocious behaviour are recorded by Dio (77.7.1–2; 11.1; 14.1) and Herodian (3.13.3–6).

58 From 197 onwards the governors of Britain were Virius Lupus (Birley 1972; 1981a, 149f; 155f; 1988, 126; 171f; *RIB* 637; 730; 757; 1163), Valerius Pudens (Birley 1988,

171f) and Alfenus Senecio (Alföldy 1969; Birley 1981a, 188f; 1988, 170–7; *RIB* 722; 1234; 1462; 1909). Herodian (3.14.1) says that the governor of Britain sent a despatch to ask for more troops or the Emperor's intervention because the Britons were causing such destruction, but another reason for the expedition was to give Caracalla and Geta an opportunity to see military life and to keep them occupied. Birley (1988, 171) accepts that there was a serious invasion of the northern tribes in 197; Frere (1987, 157–8) discusses the dating problems and the long delay in repairing Hadrian's Wall, and the reoccupation of the north under the Severan governors, which he thinks was complete by 207. Salway (1991, 221–7) discusses the likelihood of an invasion of 197 after the withdrawal of troops by Albinus, preferring to interpret the need for wide-spread repairs to the military installations in northern Britain to the fact that there had been no major reorganisation in the province for many years. Dio says that Lupus had to buy off the Maeatae (75.5.4 = book 76, p. 217 Loeb edn) and in another passage (77.12.1) he says that the Maeatae 'live next to the wall that cuts the island in half', usually interpreted as the Antonine Wall. Shotter (1996, 100–1) points out that it is highly unlikely that Hadrian's Wall was overrun and destroyed, but the intricate diplomatic systems will have been neglected and broken down, allowing the tribesmen to break their promises and cause trouble. Lupus could not mount a full-scale expedition when he took over in Britain and therefore had to resort to paying the northern tribes to keep the peace, but Shotter sees no reason to interpret the reconstruction work in the north by Lupus and his successors as reparation of war damage.

59 See Birley (1988, 174–5) for the specialists accompanying Severus to Britain, and for the troops from the Rhine and Danube legions. Herodian (3.14.9) says that Geta was left behind in York while his father and brother went on campaign, to exercise jurisdiction over the provincial population and the civil administration of the Empire, with a council of the Emperor's friends to guide him. For the rescripts issued by the Emperors whilst in Britain from 208 to 210, see Birley (1988, 185; 256 n.26), citing the references in the *Codex Justinianus* (dated 208: 3.32.1; 8.25.2; 2.11.9; 3.28.4; 6.35.2; 8.13.4; 2.11.10; 6.53.4; 8.40.3; dated 209: 7.62.1; 8.18.1; 7.8.3; dated 210: 3.32.18; 6.4.1; 8.44.3; 8.37.2; 3.1.2). An ambassador from Ephesus came to Britain (Birley 1988, 256 n.26, citing *Die Inschriften von Ephesus* Bonn 1979–84, no. 881).

60 Birley (1988, 178; 182) considers that Dio and Herodian relayed little more than travellers tales, and that the *Historia Augusta* contains very little of historical worth. Stores bases were set up at Arbeia (South Shields), Coria (Corbridge) and Cramond (Frere 1987, 159–61; Birley 1988, 173). On South Shields see Dore and Gillam (1979). An inscription from Corbridge (*RIB* 1143) records that an officer was in charge of the granaries there 'at the time of the British expedition – *tempore expeditione felicissimae Britannicae*. On the fortress at Carpow see Birley (1988, 255 n.21); R.E. Birley (1962; 1963). Dio (77.14.1–7) describes Caracalla's attempt to kill Severus by stabbing him when they rode to meet the Caledonians. Herodian (3.15.2) says that Caracalla continually tried to persuade his father's doctors to hasten his death.

61 Dio claims to quote Severus' exact words to his sons as he lay dying: 'be harmonious, enrich the soldiers and scorn all other men' (77.15.2). Dio's final assessment of Severus is not at all derogatory (77.16–17).

62 On Caracalla and Geta see Calderini (1949, 69ff; 87–98). Frere (1987, 162) suggests that Dio's hostility to Caracalla made him suppress news of a third Caledonian campaign in 211. An inscription from Carpow (see *JRS* 55, 1965, 223) dates from 212 or later, demonstrating that when Caracalla concluded peace there was no immediate evacuation of Scotland. According to Herodian (3.8.2) the division of Britain into two provinces occurred just after the defeat of Albinus in 197, but there are reasons to believe that it was Caracalla who carried out the scheme, since the earliest known inscriptions attesting Britannia Superior and Inferior are dated after the death of Severus; see above (note 39). The problems of the dating and the administration of the

two provinces are discussed by Frere (1987, 162–4). Dio (55.23.3; 23.66) says that *VI Victrix* was in Britannia Inferior and the other two legions were in Superior. The status of Britannia Inferior, with only one legion, is disputed, since by analogy with other provinces it should have been a praetorian province, but as Frere points out (1987, 163), in Severus' reign there is evidence for the activities of consular governors in northern Britain. Either the whole of Britain was under a single command, or Inferior was originally consular and only became a praetorian province later (Salway 1991, 223), or it was under a procurator (Birley 1953). It is easier to put the division of the province in Caracalla's reign as part of his settlement when he made peace and returned to Rome (Salway 1991, 231; 1993, 171), or perhaps somewhat later in his reign, *c.*213 (Frere 1987, 164), though both of these solutions raise a different set of problems. See Birley (1981a, 166ff) for discussion; Birley suggests that Julius Marcus *c.*212–13 was the last governor of undivided Britain. Herodian (4.8.1) only hints at the adjustment of the boundaries between Upper and Lower Pannonia. The latest attestation that *I Adiutrix* at Brigetio was in Upper Pannonia is on an inscription dated to the end of 212, mentioning the 'three legions of the province' (*CIL* III 4452 = *ILS* 2382; Christol 1997, 66 n.15). At some date soon after that the readjustment of the boundaries placed Brigetio in Pannonia Inferior, so that there were only two legions in each province. Herodian (4.8.1) laconically describes the arrangement: as 'business with the garrison on the Danube'.

63 The murder of Geta is graphically described by Dio (78.1.4–2.6). Herodian compares and contrasts the characteristics of each of the brothers and describes their hostility towards each other (4.3.1–4.4.2) before describing the murder (4.4.3). The date is disputed, except that it must have occurred before 11 July 212; Dio's date depends upon certain knowledge when Geta was born; he lived 22 years and nine months, so if it is accepted that he was born 27 May 188, his death occurred 26 February 212 (Whittaker 1969, 392–3 n.1). Caracalla spent the night in the Praetorian camp for protection, winning over the men with promises of future gifts; according to Dio (78.3.1) he told them that he was in a position to do them all favours. Herodian (4.5.1) says that he gave money to the soldiers.

64 Dio (78.4.1) says that 20,000 people who were in any way connected with Geta were killed; Herodian devotes a whole chapter (4.6) to the people who perished.

65 For Dioga and Marcellus see Christol (1997, 37). On the *Constitutio Antoniniana* generally see Ulpian (*Digest* 1.5.17); Sherwin-White (1973a, 279–87; 380–93; 1973b) and Wolff (1978). *P. Giessen* 40 preserves tantalising details but raises more questions than it solves; from information in the papyrus it has been suggested that there may have been religious motives behind the enfranchisement. The date of the *Constitutio* is disputed. Sasse (1958) and Honoré (1962) prefer the traditional date of 212, Seston (1946) argued that it should be 213, and Millar (1962) suggested 214; see Christol (1997, 65 n.7). Dio (78.9.5) describes the enfranchisement in the middle of a passage devoted to financial matters, first outlining the taxes that Caracalla invented or increased, for instance the 5 per cent tax on emancipation of slaves, bequests and inheritances was increased to 10 per cent. Almost as an aside in the same passage Dio adds that Caracalla pretended to honour the inhabitants of the Empire but in reality he made them liable to pay the taxes that all citizens paid.

66 *Honestiores* and *humiliores*: the distinctions between upper and lower classes of the Roman Empire were as vague and loosely defined as they are in modern western societies, but from about the reign of Antoninus Pius the *honestiores* acquired more privileges than the *humiliores*. Individuals were not necessarily rigidly assigned to either class by pre-ordained legal definition. It was generally assumed that senators, equites, veterans and decurions belonged to the *honestiores*, and these were not subject to the harsher punishments meted out to the *humiliores* in the law courts. See Gagé (1964b); Garnsey (1970); Rilinger (1988).

67 Schönberger (1985, 410) casts doubt on the third-century date for the renewal of the frontier in Germany, attributing it instead to the end of the second century and identifying it as the work of Commodus. Dio (78.13.4; 15.2) mentions the Alamanni, but the term may be anachronistic because his text may have been edited by later epitomators to whom the name was familiar; on the Alamanni see ch. 5 notes 50–60. As Christol points out (1997, 65 n.9), the title that Caracalla took after the war was *Germanicus Maximus*, indicating that the tribes in question were still known to the Romans as Germans; see also Alföldy (1978); Chastagnol (1984a).

68 Caracalla attended to the road system in Raetia, as inscriptions attest (*CIL* XIII 9061; 9068; 9072; *AE* 1924, 19); see Schönberger (1985, 413 n.441); Dietz (1985; 1986). Dio (78.20.3) accuses Caracalla of deliberately stirring up the Vandili against the Marcommani, and of giving pure gold to other tribesmen while using debased currency at home (78.14.3). Herodian (4.7.3) describes how Caracalla won the loyalty of the Germans north of the frontier and recruited troops from them. See note 62 (above) for the new boundaries between Pannonia Superior and Inferior.

69 Emulation of Alexander was Caracalla's obsession (Dio 78.7–8). The Parthian Royal family were at odds with each other (Dio 78.12.2–3) so Caracalla planned a campaign against them, merely in order to have the title *Parthicus*, according to Herodian (4.10.1), but, as Whittaker (1969, 429, n.4) points out, Herodian glosses over the thorough preparations for the war, first ensuring that he had control over Edessa, the kingdom of Abgar, and attempting to gain control over Armenia (Dio 78.12.1). His route to the east took him through the Danube provinces and into Dacia, where he took hostages as part of the terms of an alliance; Macrinus returned them to Dacia (Dio 79.27.5). Caracalla progressed from there into Thrace, identifying more and more with Alexander (Herodian 4.8.1–3). He set up winter quarters in Nicomedia (Dio 78.18.1). He sent Theocritus to fight against the Armenians in 215 (Dio 78.21.1–4) while he himself went to Egypt in 215–16 allegedly to venerate the god Alexander, but after an initial friendly reception he turned against the Alexandrians because they had made jokes about him and seemed to favour his brother Geta (Herodian 4.8.6–9.3). Then he massacred a large part of the population (Herodian 4.9.8; Dio 78.22.2). He was back in Syria by May 216 (Christol 1997, 42), but others argue that the Alexandrian episode was all over by the end of 215 (*CAH* XII 1939, 49). Artabanus, who had succeeded his brother Vologaeses, refused Caracalla's offer of a marriage alliance (Dio 79.1.1; Herodian 4.10.1–5). Macrinus was Praetorian Prefect, having a good grounding in law but with little military experience, for which Caracalla often mocked him, making him very resentful (Herodian 4.12.1–3). Dio (79.4.1–2) reports that an African soothsayer had prophesied that Macrinus would become Emperor; Herodian (4.12.5) says that Caracalla asked Materianus in Rome to investigate the matter; Materianus replied by letter denouncing Macrinus, but Caracalla gave all the letters to Macrinus, so he opened it himself and read it, thus realising that he was in grave danger.

70 Marcus Opellius Macrinus (*PIR2* O 108; Pflaum 1960, 667–72 no. 248) was born in Mauretania in 164, and had been steward to Plautianus (Dio 79.11.2). He survived the downfall of his patron and became *procurator aerarii maioris* in 208 and Praetorian Prefect in 212 (*HA* Macrinus 4.7). He was with Caracalla in Parthia in 216 (*AE* 1947, 182) and was awarded *ornamenta consularia* in 217 (Dio 79.13.1). The army declared him Emperor (Dio 79.11.6; Herodian 4.14.1–3) but he allowed a few days to elapse before taking up the title because he did not want to be accused of having killed Caracalla simply to usurp the throne (Dio 79.11.4). He did not go to Rome but remained in the east to finish off the Parthian campaign (Dio 79.26.2). The people were so glad to be rid of Caracalla that they took no notice at first of the low rank of the new Emperor, imagining that anyone would better that the previous Emperor (Dio 79.18.4). The accession of Macrinus in 217 is not considered to be a turning point in the same way as the accession on Maximinus Thrax in 235; it was Aurelius Victor (*de Caes.* 24.7–9) who pinpointed

this date of 235 as a disaster, before which all was well and after which he considered that everything went downhill (Christol 1997, 69).

71 Dio (79.16.2) records that Macrinus wrote to the Senate announcing that he had taken the name of Severus and the titles Pius Felix Augustus, even though he knew that it would have been more seemly to wait for the Senate to award these titles. Millar (1964, 160–6) evaluates the usefulness of Dio as a contemporary source for this period. The problem of how to deal with Caracalla divided the Senate and people from the army, since the former groups reviled him and the latter adored him, so Macrinus made no move to deify him or to declare him an enemy, preferring to put the onus onto the Senate (Dio 79.17.2), but in Rome no one dared to make any suggestion of damnation of Caracalla's memory for fear of the soldiers (Dio 79.17.4).

72 Oclatinius Adventus was consul in 218 as colleague of Macrinus (*AE* 1953, 11; 1964, 229). He was of advanced age by the time he reached the consulship, and could not read very well both because his eyesight was failing and because he lacked education (Dio 79.14.1–4); on his career see Pflaum (1960, 662–7 no. 247). Dio (79.13.2) says that Macrinus dismissed Sabinus and Castinus from their provinces on account of their friendship with Caracalla. Deccius or Decius Triccianus rose from the ranks of the Pannonian army to become prefect of *II Parthica* under Caracalla, then under Macrinus he became governor of Pannonia (Dio 79.13.4; *CIL* III 3720) only to be murdered by Elagabalus in 219 (Dio 80.4.3). While the Romans were preoccupied with their internal problems, King Artabanus of Parthia invaded Mesopotamia (Dio 79.26.2). After some fighting there was a negotiated peace, and Macrinus awarded himself the title *Parthicus Maximus* (Dio 79.27.3; *AE* 1964, 229).

73 Macrinus' son Diadumenianus was appointed Caesar, nominally by the troops, but in reality it was Macrinus himself who did so. The letter from Macrinus outlining the events after Caracalla's death was read out in the Senate, after which the senators voted Diadumenianus the status of patrician, and the titles *princeps iuventutis* and Caesar (Dio 79.17.1; 19.1; *AE* 1953, 54; 1954, 8; 1960, 36). In an effort to curb expenditure Macrinus fixed the pay of the Praetorian Guard at the levels that Severus set for them (Dio 79.12.7), but did not reduce other privileges granted to the army. He wrote to the Senate to explain that it was impossible to pay the wages of the army and also the donatives that had been promised, the whole amounting to 280 million sesterces per annum, but on the other hand it was impossible not to pay it; he presumably added compelling reasons as to why the soldiers must continue to be paid but Dio's text (79.36.2–3) is too fragmentary at this point to discern what he said. On the Imperial finances during the reigns of Caracalla and Macrinus see Bellinger (1940); Callu (1969, 171–4); see also Develin (1971). Dio (79.23–4) describes the death of Julia Domna, cynically ascribing her mourning not to the death of her son but to the loss of her position of power and way of life. On the family of Julia Domna see Birley (1988, 221–4); Chastagnol (1992, 180–3). Macrinus kept the army together at a time when he should have split the units up and put them into winter quarters where they would be less dangerous (Dio 29.2), which would have made it that much more difficult for Julia Maesa to communicate with them; she began to plot against Macrinus while living at Emesa, though Dio (79.31.1–4) places the blame for the elevation of Avitus = Elagabalus on a certain Eutychianus, who presented the boy to the soldiers as a natural son of Caracalla without the knowledge of his family. Judging by the alacrity with which the Syrian princesses took to wielding Imperial power, it is extremely unlikely that they knew nothing of what was happening; in fact it is highly likely that they engineered or at least endorsed the whole series of events. The Senate complied with Macrinus' wishes and obediently declared Elagabalus, or the False Antoninus as Macrinus labelled him, an enemy of the state (Dio 79.38.1). On the defeat and death of Macrinus see Dio (79.39.1–40.5) and Herodian (5.4.7). On Elagabalus in general see Calderini (1949, 108–13). The first to apply this name of the god to the Emperor himself was Aurelius Victor (*de Caes.* 23.1).

The new Emperor bribed the army, giving them 2,000 sesterces per man to persuade them not to sack Antioch (Dio 80.1.1). The first historian to use the name Elagabalus, identifying the Emperor with his god, was Aurelius Victor (*de Caes.* 23.1). The new Emperor followed the example of Macrinus and did not wait for the Senate to vote him his titles (Dio 80.2.2). He declared himself a descendant of Nerva (*CIL* VIII 10347) and utilised his relationship to Severus, calling himself his grandson (*AE* 1961, 79; 1964, 269; 1978, 842). He arrived in Rome in 219 (Christol 1997, 50; *CIL* VI 31162), having sent ahead a portrait of himself in his priestly robes (Herodian 5.5.6). He brought the Holy Stone of Emesa to Rome (*CIL* VI 31162) and started to build a temple to the god Elagabalus on the Palatine (Dio 80.11.1–3; *HA Elagabalus* 3.4). The Romans would not have objected to the arrival of the eastern god in Rome if Elagabalus had observed his cult for himself and his followers, but he put him before Jupiter, thus giving great offence to the Roman people (Dio 80.11.1–2).

74 On Publius Valerius Comazon see Pflaum (1960, 752–6 no. 290), who points out that Dio's accusation that Comazon had no experience cannot have been true, and that Comazon had been prefect of a legion, probably *III Gallica*. Christol (1997, 51) suggests that Dio's account is biased. Comazon was Praetorian Prefect (*AE* 1955, 260) and then consul (*AE* 1950, 238); see also Chastagnol (1970, 64; 1992, 223). The despatch of Macrinus' followers is described by Dio (80.4.3–5.1). Elagabalus issued no statements about these murders (Dio 80.4.6). Herodian (5.7.6) lapses into hyperbole to explain how actors and circus performers were given official posts.

75 Elagabalus' sexual behaviour is the subject of several passages in Dio (80.13.2–15.4), who also mentions the preponderant influence of the Emperor's 'husband' Hierocles (80.15.4). Whittaker (1970, 61 n.2) points out that all sources agree that the dominant influence was always Julia Maesa, who persuaded Elagabalus to adopt Bassianus Alexianus (Dio 80.17.2), otherwise known as Severus Alexander. He was consul with Elagabalus (Herodian 5.7.4) and appears as co-Emperor on an inscription dated 1 June 222 (*CIL* VI 3069); Whittaker (1970, 58 n.1) questions the date. Elagabalus tried to stir up the Praetorians against Alexander, but to no avail (*HA Elagabalus* 13–15) and then plotted to kill him (*HA Elagabalus* 16.1; Dio 80.19.1a; Herodian 5.8.3–7). Eventually the soldiers took matters into their own hands and killed Elagabalus and his mother Julia Soaemias (Dio 80.20.2; Herodian 5.8.8). As the supporters of Elgabalus were eliminated, Comazon was made city prefect for the third time, taking the place of Fulvius who was killed; as Pflaum (1960, 755) points out, he was presumably held in high esteem by Julia Maesa and Julia Mammaea.

76 Dio says (80.1) that Ulpian was made Praetorian Prefect and put in charge of all the other business of the Empire. It was thought that Ulpian survived until 228, but it is now considered that he was killed in the summer of 223; Paschoud (1971, 138 n.34 citing *P. Oxy* 2565) says that Ulpian was dead before 224; Howe (1942, 100–5) opts for Ulpian's death in 223. Ulpian may have perished during the three days of battles between the Praetorians and the people (Christol 1997, 54; 68 n.13). Dio (80.2.5) describes these riots during which the soldiers set fire to some buildings in the city. In subsequent passages Dio says that Ulpian corrected many wrongs, but was killed nonetheless, as though the two events, the riots and the death of the Prefect, were related. A very similar story is told by Herodian (7.11–12), but his tale is set at a later date in 238, when the soldiers (again?) set fire to some buildings. Dio was consul as colleague of Severus Alexander in 229, but was warned against coming to Rome for fear of the Praetorians. After the supremacy of the jurists Papinian, Paulus and Ulpian, circumstances dictated that Praetorian Prefects with military experience were necessary (Crook, 1955, 79; Howe 1942, 3–4; Durry 1938, 161).

77 The sources for the reign of Severus Alexander are notoriously unreliable (Christol 1997, 55). The life of Alexander in the *HA* is probably wholly fictitious, aimed at Julian as a portrait of the ideal prince (Baynes 1926, 57–67; 118–44). The author would not be

very much concerned with truth, relying more upon literary effect (Crook 1955, 86). The task of identifying the *amici* of Severus Alexander is not helped at all by the list of names in *HA* (Severus Alexander 68.1), scarcely any of which are corroborated by any other source. Crook (1955, 90–1) points to Marius Maximus the historian as a member of Alexander's circle, and, of course, Dio. In a passage describing the accession of Maximinus Thrax, Herodian (7.1.3) says that the new Emperor disposed of all Severus Alexander's friends, members of the council appointed by the Senate. As Whittaker (1970, 150 n.2) comments, it is not clear in this passage whether it is the *amici* or the council members who were chosen by the Senate.

78 Herodian (6.1.1) says that the Syrian princesses Maesa and Mammaea tried to bring about a return to moderate and dignified government. Maesa is identified in all sources as the guiding spirit in all political developments (Whittaker 1970, 61 n.2). Mammaea tutored Severus Alexander even before he became Emperor (Herodian 5.7.5), and afterwards she and Maesa chose 16 senators to guide him (Herodian 6.1.2). According to *HA* (Severus Alexander 15.6–16.3) the young Emperor's *consilium* had 70 members; Crook (1955, 88) questioned the numbers, but concluded that the 16 senators formed only a section of the council and did not constitute the entire body, which seemed not to have prepared business for the Senate nor did it rotate its membership (Crook 1955, 87). Most of Herodian's chapter (6.1) is devoted to the reforms of Severus Alexander, but without specific detail; he says (6.1.3–4) that unworthy men were removed and the correct men for the relevant tasks were installed. Fine; but who? Dio (52.15.1–4; 52.33.3–4) invents a speech for Maecenas to deliver to Octavian–Augustus just as the latter was embarking on sole rule, often quoted as a homily on good government, which may have been aimed at Severus Alexander; Millar (1964, 102ff) argues that it was aimed at Caracalla, but Whittaker (1970, 79 n.3) finds this argument unconvincing. Syme (1971a, 146–62) identifies individuals whose careers had begun under Septimius Severus now coming to the fore again under Severus Alexander; see also Christol (1997, 55; 68 n.14).

79 On the rise of Ardashir = Artaxerxes see Herodian (6.2.1); Dio (80.3–4); Dodgeon and Lieu (1991, 9–16); Christol (1997, 73–4). Dio (80.3.2) says that Ardashir defeated Artabanus in three battles. Severus Alexander prepared for war but tried diplomacy first (Herodian 6.2.3). He recruited in Italy and the provinces, and specifically in the Illyrian provinces (Herodian 6.3.1; 6.4.3). Whittaker (1970, 102–3 n.2) says that Alexander left Rome in spring 231 and was in Antioch by summer.

80 The war in the east did not begin smoothly. The Mesopotamian legions were restless and killed the governor Flavius Heracleo, and there was a potential usurper called Uranius (Zosimus 1.12; *CAH* XII 69–70) who had to be suppressed first before Severus Alexander could begin his campaign, which is described by Herodian (6.5.1–6.6.6), and related in hagiographic terms in *HA* (Severus Alexander 55.1–3; 57.3). See Dodgeon and Lieu (1991, 23–9) for a compilation of the literary and epigraphic sources, and Christol (1997, 75–6; 111 n.4) for an overview. On the titles *Parthicus* and *Persicus Maximus* see Jardé (1925, 81–2); Whittaker (1970, 125 n.3) refers to a milestone with the title *Parthicus Maximus*.

81 News of the invasions of the German tribes reached Severus Alexander while he was in Antioch, according to Herodian (6.7.2.), who insists that the 'Illyrians on the borders of Italy' were in danger. This suggests that he meant Raetia rather than Upper Germany where most of the trouble seems to have been concentrated; see Schönberger (1985, 414–18) for the forts where destruction can be dated to *c.*233. The soldiers in the eastern army thought that they had been afflicted with a double tragedy, because in the war against the Persians many of the men had been killed or wounded and now their families were threatened at home (Herodian 6.7.3). Severus Alexander's triumph is described in *HA* (56–8), but Christol (1997, 76) questions the dating of September 233. Maximinus (*PIR2* J 407) was put in charge of the recruits on the Rhine in preparation

for the campaign (Herodian 6.8.1), but he was probably in command of more troops than just the new recruits. On Maximinus in general see Bersanetti (1940); Bellezza (1964); Walser and Pekáry (1962, 17–18); on his origins and early career, about which very little is known, see Loriot (1975, 668–70); Christol (1997, 112 nn.1–2). Syme (1971a, 185–6) suggested that Maximinus did not hail from Thrace itself, but came from the Thracian part of Moesia, the descendant of a soldier serving in the army of Dacia Ripensis (see below note 82). Severus Alexander took with him to the Rhine the eastern troops such as the Mauretanians, or Moors, and the archers from Osroene (Herodian 6.7.8; *CIL* XI 3104; XIII 6677a). The army was based at Moguntiacum (modern Mainz), from where the campaign was launched (Herodian 6.7.6–8), but after the initial onslaught Alexander tried to negotiate, offering payments to the Germans who were 'always ready to trade peace for gold' (Herodian 6.7.9–10). *HA* (Maximinus 7) makes Maximinus a party to the plot to kill Severus Alexander and his mother, as does Herodian (6.8.3–9.8), who puts the elevation of Maximinus before the murder of Severus Alexander. Zosimus (1.13.1) says that the Pannonian and Moesian troops were already hostile to Severus Alexander long before they revolted and declared for Maximinus; Jardé (1925, 90 and footnote) considered that this information derives from the work of Dexippus, and is therefore trustworthy because it is contemporary. For the proclamation of Maximinus as Emperor see *CIL* VI 2001.

82 Herodian (6.8.3) says that it was the younger men, the great majority of whom were Pannonians, who chose Maximinus as Emperor. Syme (1971a, 179–93) discusses the reign of Maximinus and the portrayal in *HA*, which he considers a 'rich fantasy'. Maximinus was afraid that the Senate would despise him because of his low birth (Herodian 7.1.2). Whittaker (1970, 131–2 nn.2–3) considers that Maximinus may not have been a citizen, but Syme (1971a, 188) suggests that he may have been the descendant of a soldier of the garrison of Dacia Ripensis. On the rebellions of Magnus and Quartinus see Herodian (7.1.5–8; 7.1.9–10); Loriot (1975, 672); Christol (1997, 112 n.4) identifies these as Caius Petronius Magnus, and with less certainty, Titus or Titius Quartinus, a friend of Severus Alexander; see *HA* (Maximinus 11.1). Herodian (7.1.12) says that the rebellions embittered Maximinus and made him more harsh than normal. *HA* (Maximinus 8.6) says that the total number of executions was 4,000, which is a tremendous exaggeration. Maximinus did execute most of Severus Alexander's immediate entourage as soon as he became Emperor (Herodian 6.9.7), and later he removed the members of Alexander's *consilium*, sending some back to Rome and removing others from their administrative posts (Herodian 7.1.3); see also Crook (1955, 92); Loriot (1975, 670–2). Timesitheus managed to survive the transition between Emperors with his life and career intact; see Pflaum (1960, 811–21 no. 317) and Whittaker (1970, 152 n.1) for a reconstruction of his career, recorded on inscriptions (*ILS* 1330 for the whole career; *AE* 1936, 151 procurator of Asia; *CIL* XIII 1807 procurator of Lugdunensis and Aquitania).

83 Herodian (7.2.1–9) describes the German campaigns in which Maximinus took part in person, fighting side by side with the soldiers. The war on the Danube is ignored by Herodian, except for the brief superlative statement (7.2.9) that Maximinus would have conquered all the barbarians and driven them back as far as the Ocean. See Christol (1997, 113 n.5; *CIL* V 7989 = *ILS* 487) on repairs to the roads into northern Italy, for evidence of recruiting, and for Maximinus as *Aquileiensium restitutor et conditor*. Loriot (1975, 674–5) discusses the Danube campaign. Maximinus used Sirmium as a base for the wars; *CIL* III 3336 mentions a Dacian expedition; in Pannonia several inscriptions refer to soldiers who died *bello Dacico* and *in expeditione Dacica* (*CIL* III 4857; 5218 = *ILS* 2309; *AE* 1909, 144; 1965, 223); see Loriot (1975, 675 n.149). Syme (1971a, 190–1) says that *Dacicus Maximus* in Maximinus' titles indicates war against the Carpi, and in 238 Maximinus was once again at Sirmium ready for battle with the Goths. The fiscal policy of Maximinus was very harsh, affecting not only the wealthy elite but producing an adverse effect on the whole population (Loriot 1975, 681–2).

Syme (1971a, 190) points out that the Emperor did not enlist civilian or ceremonial support for his regime. It seemed that he wished to extract money purely for the soldiers, and Herodian (7.1.3) says that Maximinus wished to be surrounded only by his troops with no nobles around him. He had little time and perhaps no opportunity to win over the people, single-mindedly applying himself to the frontier wars. Syme (1971a, 178) comments on Maximinus' failure to explain his policies before the Senate in Rome. The accusations that Maximinus confiscated properties is probably based on truth; Herodian (7.3.5) says that he reduced good families to penury then began to commandeer money being gathered for the food supply and for cash distributions for the people, and to strip temples of their treasures and ornaments; all this is standard stuff for unprincipled tyrants, but it also indicates that Maximinus put military priorities before civilian ones. Whittaker (1970, 169 n.3) finds it no coincidence that those Emperors who 'most successfully maintained the frontiers ... relied upon confiscations to pay the bills'. Herodian (7.4.2–3) pinpoints the moment when the rich young nobles in Libya rebelled against the severities of the procurator in Carthage, whose confiscations and exactions were too harsh. They gathered their retainers and supporters (Herodian 7.5.4; *HA* Gordians 7.3–4), marched on Carthage and killed the procurator, then looked for a way out of their problems by declaring the proconsul Marcus Antonius Gordianus Sempronianus Romanus Emperor (Herodian 7.5.1–8). See Kotula (1960) on the rise of the Gordians.

84 On the crisis of 238 see Loriot (1975, 688–723). The Senate confirmed the two Gordians as Emperors, conferring upon each of them the title Augustus (Herodian 7.7.2). The Praetorian Prefect Vitalianus was murdered by the partisans of Gordian (Herodian 7.6.6–9), then the people rioted and Sabinus the city prefect was killed (Herodian 7.7.4). Meanwhile Capellianus in Numidia defeated the two Gordians (Herodian 7.9.1–11). Loriot (1975, 703–7) discusses the 'senatorial revolution' when the Senate took charge of the state; Syme (1971a, 175–8) dismisses the idea that there had been a resurgence of senatorial power under Severus Alexander, favouring instead the opposite theory that the weak rule of Alexander had encouraged the pretensions of the leading senators, and there was no Emperor in Rome to keep them down. The senators met in the temple of Jupiter and chose 20 men to take charge of public business (Herodian 7.10.2–5). See *CIL* XIV 3902 = *ILS* 1186 for the full title *vigintiviri ex Senatus Consulto rei publicae curandae*; see also *ILS* 8979; Zosimus (1.14.2). Theodoridès (1947) examines the situation in 238 and the election of the *vigintiviri*, and the chronology of the events of 238 is discussed by Loriot (1975, 720–2). Aurelius Victor (*de Caes.* 26.7) specifically states that the election of the *vigintiviri* took place after the deaths of the two Gordians; for a contrary view see Syme (1971a, 165) who says that the 20 men were already elected and functioning when the Gordians were killed, and then after their deaths the Senate elected two Emperors. According to *HA* (Maximinus 32) the 20 men were to defend Italy against the Emperor Maximinus who was declared an enemy, and *HA* (Gordians 10.2) says that each of the 20 were assigned a particular area of Italy to defend, which is highly unlikely; see Whittaker (1970, 238–9 n.1). Syme (1971a, 162–5) recovers the names of six of these 20 men. Herodian (7.10.3–5) says that two Emperors, M. Clodius Pupienus Maximus (*PIR2* C 1179) and D. Caelius Calvinus Balbinus (*PIR2* C 126), were chosen by the Senate. He presumably meant that the two men were chosen from the *vigintiviri*; as Whittaker (1970, 226 n.1) points out, Herodian does not actually say that the new Emperors were chosen from the 20 senators, but his wording almost certainly refers to the *vigintiviri*. Loriot (1975, 703–7) reconstructs the careers of the two Emperors. The young nephew of Gordian II was living in Rome, and there were demonstrations in his favour, so the Senate acquiesced and made him Caesar (Herodian 7.10.6–9).

85 Maximinus' exploits in the north of Italy are described at some length by Herodian (8.1.6–5.7). Food shortages took effect at the siege of Aquileia quite quickly (Herodian 8.1.5) and before long the men of the Alban legion, *II Parthica*, decided to kill Maximi-

nus (Herodian 8.5.8–9; *HA* Maximinus 32; Loriot 1975, 711–13). Herodian (8.8.1–3) considers that Pupienus Maximus and Balbinus ruled well, but the Praetorians were angry, imagining that the German troops raised by Maximinus and taken over by Pupienus (Herodian 8.7.7) might supplant them; later Herodian (8.8.4) contradicts himself by saying that the two Emperors were not in complete agreement and each harboured a desire for sole rule; see Syme (1971a, 165–6). Herodian's narrative ends with the deaths of the two Emperors and the elevation of the young Gordian III.

86 The only sections of the lives of the three Gordians in the *HA* that can be relied upon are those that derive from the works of Dexippus (Syme 1971a, 170; Burian 1963; Loriot 1975, 724; Christol 1997, 93). Maecia Faustina as Gordian III's mother is otherwise unknown, and does not appear on official inscriptions or on the coinage (Syme 1971a, 169–70; Loriot 1975, 725–6; 727 n.539).

87 Loriot (1975, 727–9) enumerates the nobles who rallied to Gordian III and analyses the circle of intimates in the immediate entourage; see also Christol (1997, 90). After years of uncertainty and upheaval most people would be ready to settle for a period of calm (Loriot 1975, 726), especially since efforts were made to put reforms into action. The finances required and received attention (Callu 1969, 174–6; Loriot 1975, 732–2) and procurators were encouraged to be more lenient in collecting revenues (*CJ* 10.3.2). The number of equites taking up posts normally reserved for senators seems to decrease under Gordian III (Loriot 1975, 730 n.561) and there is a detectable rise in the numbers of officials from the Greek east (Loriot 1975, 740–2; Christol 1997, 90).

88 The date when *III Augusta* was cashiered is not known; Christol (1997, 90) places the event during the reign of Pupienus and Balbinus, but Gordian III would have more personal reasons for punishing the soldiers and their leader who had been responsible for the deaths of his relatives. Capellianus' name was removed from inscriptions (Loriot 1975, 734). Timesitheus' career is documented on an inscription put up in his honour at Lyons (*CIL* XIII 1807 = *ILS* 1330; see also *CIL* VI 1611 = 31831 from Rome; *AE* 1936, 151 from Bostra). These inscriptions and Timesitheus' career are discussed by Howe (1942, 78–9); Pflaum (1948; 1960, no. 317); Loriot (1975, 735–8). The ancient authors could not agree on Timesitheus' real name; in *HA* (Gordians) he becomes Misitheus; Zosimus (1.17.18) calls him Timesicles, while Zonaras (12.18) opts for Timesocles.

89 On the well-known inscription from Skaptopara (*CIL* III 12336 = *IGR* I 674) see Loriot and Nony (1997, 49 no. 20); Herrmann (1990, 18–27). *Hospitium/xenia* originally referred to ritualised friendship of a formal nature between members of different social groups; see the article in *The Oxford Classical Dictionary* under 'friendship, ritualised'; Livy (33.29.2) and Suetonius (*Tib.* 37.1) use the term *hospitium* in the context of military quarters. Coin hoards deposited in the Rhine frontier area between the years 238–44 indicate unrest from some unknown cause (Loriot 1975, 753–4), attributable perhaps to incursions by tribesmen from beyond the frontiers, or perhaps from unruly Roman soldiers and brigands within the province (Demougeot 1969, 487–90). At Kösching and Gunzenhausen in Raetia during the same years coin hoards were hidden (Kellner 1953) and the fort at Künzing was destroyed (Schönberger 1964; 1969, 176–7; 1985, 474–5 D123; 490 E95); see also Loriot 1975, 755). Tullius Menophilus was sent to fight Maximinus when the latter approached Rome from the north (*HA* Maximinus 21.6; 22.1; Herodian 8.2.5). According to Peter the Patrician (*FHG* 4.186.8) and *HA* (Pupienus Maximus and Balbinus 16.3) Menophilus was sent to round up the Carpi and Goths who had invaded from across the Danube; see also Loriot (1975, 755 n.730).

90 The paucity and unreliability of the historical accounts of the Persian war are emphasised by Loriot (1975, 757), but the papyri from Dura-Europos (Welles *et al.* 1959) and the discovery at Naqs-i Rustem in 1936 of the so-called *Res Gestae Divi Saporis* (*RGDS*), inscribed in Persian, Parthian and Greek languages (the Greek portions are the best preserved) throw more light on the events (Loriot 1975, 758; for translated passages

concerning the campaign of Gordian III see Dodgeon and Lieu 1991, 34–5; 45). *RGDS* has been studied by several authors; see Carratelli (1947); Guey (1955); Maricq and Hunigman (1953); Maricq (1958); Mazzarino (1971); Rostovtzeff (1943); see also the relevant passages in Chaumont (1969, 39–46); Ensslin (1949); Olmstead (1942, 251–6); Sprengling (1953, 79–84); Vanden Berghe (1984). Ardashir (see Loriot 1975, 759 n.766 on variant forms of the name) adopted an aggressive policy while Rome was preoccupied; he invaded Mesopotamia and occupied Carrhae and Nisibis (Zonaras 12.18; Loriot 1975, 717 n.471; 760 n.767). Dura was attacked *c.*239 (Loriot 1975, 760 n.768; Gilliam 1950, 220; 249–50; Fink 1971, 192–7 no. 50) and the tribune Julius Terentius may have been killed in the fighting (Welles 1941). The outbreak of war was caused by the capture of Hatra, which was allied to Rome (Loriot 1975, 760–1). See Winter (1988, 45–79) on the peace arranged in 230–1 and the importance to both major powers of Hatra and alliance with the Arabs. Maricq (1957) questioned whether Ardashir or his son Shapur took Hatra or whether it reverted to the Persians as a result of the peace concluded by Philip the Arab in 244. Gordian married the daughter of Timesitheus in 241 (Zosimus 1.17). Timesitheus had valuable logistical experience, having been in charge of supplies in Syria and Palestine during the expedition of Severus Alexander (Loriot 1975, 736), and he planned the eastern campaign 'minutely' (Loriot 1975, 765–6 n.800). After campaigning briefly in Illyricum Timesitheus recruited Goths for the eastern campaign (Loriot 1975, 766–7 n.810). *Res Gestae Divi Saporis* (1.6–7) refers to Gordian raising an army which contained Goths and Germans; see also Todd (1992, 150); Wolfram (1988, 44; 384 n.13; 397 n.59). There are four main versions of the death of Gordian III which differ quite widely; they are enumerated and evaluated by Loriot (1975, 770–2) as follows: *HA* (Gordians) 29–30 and Zosimus (1.18–19) have him dead before he reached Persia; the epitomators and abbreviators such as Eutropius (12.2.2), Festus, St Jerome, and Orosius recount his victories and have him murdered on his return; others, such as *Epit. de Caes.* (27.2), say that he was assassinated when he reached Ctesiphon; Zonaras (12.17) says that he broke his thigh and died, which version agrees most closely with *RGDS* where it is stated that Gordian III was killed in battle. See also Dodgeon and Lieu (1991, 35–45); Winter (1988, 83–97) on the various versions of Gordian's death; Hartmann (1982, 76–8) makes a case for the Emperor's death in battle.

91 Philip (*PIR2* I 461) was born in Arabia (Zosimus 1.18.3); he became Praetorian Prefect (*HA* Gordians 29.1) and *Epit. de Caes.* (27.2). His Imperial titles appear on *CIL* III 3203 as Imperator Caesar Marcus Julius Philippus Augustus; see also *CIL* VI 1097 = *ILS* 506. He was hailed as Emperor in March 244 (Zosimus 1.19.1; Zonaras 12.18; Eutropius 9.2.3). Timesitheus reconquered all of Mesopotamia (*HA* Gordians 26.3; 27.2–8), and in the peace with the Persians Philip probably kept most of it except for some fringe areas (Guey and Pékary 1961; Dodgeon and Lieu 1991, 45–6; Winter 1988, 97; 119). Coins from Edessa, Rhesaena and Nisibis continue unbroken from the reign of Philip through to Decius, indicating that the Romans retained control of these cities, but Armenia was lost and an indemnity was paid to Persia (Christol 1997, 98); according to *RGDS* (lines 9–10 Greek version) the Romans paid 500,000 denarii, and became a tributary of Persia (Dodgeon and Lieu 1991, 45; 358 n.25). This was arranged by treaty; a later treaty with the Persians arranged in 363 refers to the one made in 244 (Winter 1988, 97–8; 116); see also Zosimus (1.19.1; 3.32.4). Coins proclaimed *pax fundata cum Persis* (*RIC* IV.3 p. 76 no. 69). Philip took the titles *Parthicus Maximus* (*CIL* III 4634; 10619 = *ILS* 507) and *Persicus Maximus* (*CIL* VI 1097 = *ILS* 506; *AE* 1935, 27). An inscription (*CIL* VI 793 = *ILS* 505) indicates that Philip had arrived in Rome by 23 July 244, but Christol (1997, 99; 116 n.1) disagrees, citing Aurelius Victor (*de Caes.* 28), who says that Philip did not leave the east until he had organised it properly; see Trout (1989). Philip made his brother Priscus prefect of Mesopotamia (Zosimus 1.19.2), but his powers were much wider than that office would indicate, since in one

inscription from Philippopolis he is called *rector Orientis* (*CIL* III 141595.5 = *ILS* 9005; Christol 1997, 99–100; Dodgeon and Lieu 1991, 47–8). Zosimus (1.20.2) describes Priscus' administration as too harsh.

92 Philip made his young son Caesar, probably as soon as he arrived in Rome, perhaps before 15 August 244; the date is not precisely documented, but as Christol (1997, 99; 116 n.1) points out it would be more likely that Philip would take care of the succession as he arrived in Rome, rather than leaving it till later. The young Marcus Julius Philippus is attested as Caesar on inscriptions (*CIL* III 14191 = *OGIS* II 519 = *IGR* 598; *AE* 1960, 356); see Loriot and Nony (1997, 51–3) and Herrmann (1990, 28–33 no. 6). Philip's wife Marcia Otacilia Severa is named on another inscription (*AE* 1965, 346). Philip deified his father Marinus (Christol 1997, 99). Zosimus (1.20) briefly describes the war against the Carpi and Danube tribes. Philip's titles *Germanicus* and *Carpicus* are attested in two separate sources: *IGR* IV 635 (*Germanicus*) and *P. Lond.* 3221 no. 951 (*Carpicus*). Zosimus (1.20) describes how the Carpi were forced back and retired to a fortress where they were besieged, which Loriot and Nony (1997, 40 no. 12) link with an inscription (*AE* 1965, 223) recording the death of a Praetorian soldier at a fortress of the Carpi in a Dacian war. An honorary inscription (*CIL* III 8031) from Romula in Dacia Malvensis declares both Philip and his son *restitutores orbis totius*, restorers of the whole world: a slight exaggeration but excusable in the circumstances, brought on by relief that present dangers were averted; the text of the inscription then describes more prosaically the building of a defensive wall round the city. On the Secular Games see Christol (1997, 104–6); Loriot and Nony (1997, 183–5 no. 124); *CIL* VI 488 = *ILS* 4095; *HA* (the Three Gordians, 33.1–3). Coins with the legends *Roma Aeterna* (*RIC* IV 3 Philip 44–5; 65) and *Saeculum Novum* were issued to commemorate the festival (*RIC* IV 3 Philip 25; 86; 244). The date was 248, if Aurelius Victor (*de Caes.* 28.2) is to be taken literally when he points out that in 348 there ought to have been another festival; but this does not account for the usual interval of 110 years (see Gagé 1934a; 1934b). The work known as *Eis Basileia* has been attributed to Aelius Aristides and included in the corpus of his works. Its date and purpose are disputed; Keil (1898) included the text in his edition of Aristides' works, and dated it to Philip's reign; in his English translation Swift (1966) opts for the same Emperor, as do several other authors, including Alföldy (1974a); Oliver (1978); de Blois (1979). Faro (1980, 427–8) redates it to the reign of Gallienus.

93 When Philip stopped the subsidies to the Goths in 248 the result was a coalition of the tribesmen and an invasion in 249 (Demougeot 1969, 402–9; Wolfram 1988, 57–8; 408–9). Jordanes (*Getica* 89–100) describes the exploits of the Goths under their king Ostrogotha; the episode probably refers to Cniva and his unification of Gothic tribesmen in the 250s. The siege of Marcianopolis is described from the point of view of the Goths by Jordanes (*Getica* 89), and an account of its defence by Maximus the philosopher is preserved in a fragment of Dexippus' works (Petit 1974, 171 n.16; *FGrH* no. 100 Jacoby, vol. 2, 453). Pacatianus (*PIR2* C 929 and 930) had previously served as governor of Syria (*AE* 1933, 227), and in Philip's reign he was given command of more than one Danube province; Zosimus (1.20.2) says that the legions of Moesia and Pannonia supported him; see *CIL* III 2771; 2772; Christol (1997, 117 n.7); Peachin (1990, 34); Loriot and Nony (1997, 26–7 no. 4). On the revolt of Jotapianus, Zosimus (1.20.2) puts all the blame on the severity of Philip's brother Priscus; no one seems sure of where the revolt began. It was either in Cappadocia, or according to Aurelius Victor (*de Caes.* 29.2) in Syria; see also *CIL* IX 2004. Philip offered to resign (Zosimus 1.21.1) but Decius reassured him that revolts like this were usually put down quickly, with the result that Decius was appointed to the Danube command and rounded up the supporters of Pacatianus, whereupon the soldiers recognised him as a better general than Philip and proclaimed him Emperor (Zosimus 1.21.2–3). On the battle at Verona and the victory of Decius see Zosimus (1.22); Aurelius Victor (*de Caes.* 28.10); Eutropius (9.3); Zonaras

(12.19). Birley (1990, 67–8) has restated the case for Beroea in Macedonia as the place of the battle, rather than Verona as described by John of Antioch (*FHG* IV frg. 148, p. 597ff). Dusanic (1976) examines the end of Philip's reign. According to Jordanes (*Getica* 89) Philip was the first Christian Emperor predating Constantine, but this is now discredited and seen as a favourable retrospective view from the time of Decius' persecution of the Christians, looking back to the reign of Philip as one of peaceful tolerance.

94 The first known constitution of Decius is dated to 16 October 249 (*CJ* 10.16.3), and in Egypt a document of 28 November 249 is dated to the first year of Decius' reign (Christol 1997, 122). According to Aurelius Victor (*de Caes.* 29.1) Decius (*PIR2* M 520) was born in a village near Sirmium; *Epit. de Caes.* (29.1) says that he was a soldier risen from the ranks, from Budalia in Pannonia; see Barbieri (1952); Birley (1990, 59–60); Christol (1997, 166 n.4); Peachin (1990, 32–4); Syme (1971a, 194–6). On the Cosa inscription see Marelli (1984); Christol (1997, 166 n.5). On the general order to sacrifice to the gods and the certificates issued as proof see Loriot and Nony (1997, 54–5 no. 23). Eusebius (*History of the Church* 6.41.9) and Lactantius (*de Mort. Pers.* 4.2) describe the persecution of the Christians from the Christian point of view, rejoicing in Decius' demise. Saumagne (1962) describes the events in Africa using the correspondence of St Cyprian.

95 Decius was hailed as *restitutor Daciarum* (*CIL* III 1176 = *ILS* 514). For Cniva and the Goths see Wolfram (1988, 57–7; 408–9); Demougeot (1969, 402–9); Loriot and Nony (1997, 41 no. 12). Decius' sons Herennius Etruscus and Hostilianus are attested as Caesars on an inscription (*CIL* XIII 9123), but the precise month in 250 when Herennius was made Caesar is not known; some opt for May or June 250 after *CJ* (5.12.9) while Rea (1984) arguing from the evidence of *P. Oxy.* 3608 opts for September 250; see Christol (1997, 167 n.7). Herennius was made Augustus in 251 just before the final confrontation with the Goths. His younger brother Hostilianus remained in Rome with Licinius Valerianus in charge of civil government (Zonaras 12.20). The Roman mob, tired of the prolonged wars (Aurelius Victor *de Caes.* 29.2–3), chose an Emperor of their own, Julius Valens Licinianus (St Cyprian *Ep.* 55.9). The siege of Philippopolis was described in retrospect by Ammianus (31.5.17). Cniva defeated Decius at Abrittus (Jordanes *Getica* 101–3; Zosimus 1.23.3; Zonaras 12.10; Aurelius Victor *de Caes.* 29.4). The Christian author Lactantius (*de Mort. Pers.* 4.1–3) considered Decius 'execrable' and rejoiced that it was God who punished him at Abrittus for his sins against the Church. Loriot and Nony (1997, 41–2 no. 13) point out the conflicting accounts of the battle. Trebonianus Gallus hailed from Perusia; his full name and titles are given on *CIL* XI 1927 as Imperator Caesar Caius Vibius Trebonianus Gallus Augustus.

96 Zosimus (1.23.2) and Zonaras (12.20) represent Gallus in the worst light, saying that he betrayed Decius and joined the Goths; Paschoud (1971, 146–7 n.50) points out that Zosimus as an ardent pagan was favourable to Decius, and he and Zonaras are the only authors to portray Gallus as a traitor. The treaty with the Goths did nothing for Gallus' reputation, though he may have restored the subsidy payments on condition that the Goths should guard the Danube (Christol 1997, 127; 167 n.8; Wolfram 1988, 46). Paschoud (1971, 147–8 n.51) calls the peace 'disastrous' and Zosimus complains that the Goths devastated every province, leaving not one undamaged, because Gallus was lax and those in power thought only of Rome. When Gallus returned to Rome without trying to rescue the prisoners that the Goths took with them, the provincials can be excused for thinking in these terms. Hostilianus and Volusianus were made Caesars, but the chronology is confused; see Paschoud (1971, 147 n.51). Zosimus (1.25) says that Gallus adopted Hostilianus. The plague in Rome and the Empire is recorded by Aurelius Victor (*de Caes.* 30.2). Christol (1997, 128) thinks that the increased output of antoniniani from the Antioch mint implies that Gallus was planning a campaign in the east. The usurper Uranius Antoninus, attested on coins as Lucius Julius Sulpicius Antoninus (Christol 1997, 129; 168 n.15), may have become confused with the earlier

Uranius attested under Severus Alexander (see above, note 80), or he may have been a descendant of the same family. The coins are dated to the Seleucid year 565, or October 253 to October 254.

97 Aemilius Aemilianus was governor of Moesia (Eutropius 9.5) though Zosimus (1.28.1) says that he was in command of the Pannonian legions when he was declared Emperor, and that he had taken the victorious campaign against the Goths across the Danube and had released some Roman prisoners. This may refer to victories in Moesia and on the Danube, since the Goths had gone into Asia Minor (Ridley 1982, 140 n.53; Salamon 1971, 115). Zonaras (12.20) relates how Aemilianus wrote to the Senate proposing a division of labour and power, leaving the senators in charge of administration while he concentrated on the wars against the Goths and the Persians.

98 Licinius Valerianus was sent to gather the Rhine legions to fight against the usurper Aemilianus; he was declared Emperor in Raetia (Zosimus 1.29; Aurelius Victor *de Caes.* 32.1; Eutropius 9.7; Zonaras 12.22; Orosius 7.22.1). Christol (1997, 131), discounts the distinguished career outlined in the ancient sources for Valerian. According to all the surviving ancient authors, who presumably used a common source (Christol 1997, 131) Gallienus was immediately declared Augustus and co-Emperor by the Senate on hearing the news that the Rhine legions had declared for Valerian. Paschoud (1971, 151 n.58) outlines earlier doubts that Gallienus had ever been Caesar, now dispelled by the evidence from milestones from Numidia where Gallienus is named as such (Pflaum 1966, 175–9; Christol 1997, 131; 169 n.2). It is likely that the Senate on its own initiative declared Gallienus Caesar, and Valerian made him Augustus when he arrived in Rome; Eutropius (9.8.1) says that Gallienus was made Augustus with Valerian; *Epit. de Caes* (32.2) is more specific, stating that Valerian made his son Augustus; Zonaras (12.23) laconically says Gallienus was made Emperor (*Imperator factus est*). On a diploma (*CIL* XVI 155 = *ILS* 2010) Gallienus is named with all his titles, but he is still subordinate to Valerian. According to Zosimus (1.30.2) Gallienus attended to the western half of the Empire while Valerian went to the Persian front; Ridley (1982, 141 n.57) says that the dating is correct, and that Valerian set off for the east immediately in 253.

99 Shapur attacked Armenia in 253, and probably captured Antioch, which would explain the cessation of coin production in that year. When Valerian was on his way there, or as he arrived, the mint reopened in 254. The number of times and the dates when Antioch was captured by the Persians is disputed; it is probable that it fell three times in 253, 258–9 and again in 260, but whether the final occasion was before or after the capture of Valerian remains in doubt (Paschoud 1971, 149–50 n.54; 153 n.60; Ridley 1982, 141 n.57; Dodgeon and Lieu 1991, 53–4). Kettenhofen (1982) says that Armenia was a Sassanian province from 252, and dates the first capture of Antioch to 253. The usurper Uranius Antoninus disappeared when Valerian arrived, and the Emperor soon took the title *restitutor Orientis* (*RIC* V.1 Valerian 286). Zosimus (1.30) says that Gallienus attended to the tribes on the Rhine front who were threatening the Gallic provinces, as if this occurred in the same year that Valerian went east. Demougeot (1969, 491f) and de Blois (1976, 6) accept this early dating of 253–4 to 256 for the campaigns of Gallienus on the Rhine, and therefore date the earlier German victories to these events. Others such as Drinkwater (1987, 21–2). Fitz (1966a, 18–19) and Christol (1997, 132–5) prefer the interpretation that the first German victories were in the Danube area, and Gallienus did not arrive in Cologne until 256–7, when the mint was established there. The traditional date for the first appearance of the Franks in 253 may not be correct. Schönberger (1985, 422–3) dates the first invasion of the Franks to 257, though he admits that there is no strong and securely dated archaeological evidence to pinpoint where they broke through the frontier. Gallienus earned the title *restitutor Galliarum* (*RIC* V.1 Gallienus 27–35).

100 An inscription from Aphrodisias reveals that Valerian, Gallienus and Valerian the younger were at Cologne in 257 (Roueché 1989, 4–8 no. 8; Christol 1997, 136; 170

n.8). Valerian was back in Antioch by May 258 (Christol 1997, 135; *CJ* 5.3.5; 9.8.18). Valerian the younger was left in Illyricum while Valerian went to the east. He was probably killed during the revolt of Ingenuus; Christol (1997, 137) points out that on a papyrus dated February 258 (*P. Oxy.* 1717) Valerian the younger is mentioned, but he has disappeared by July 258 (*P. Oxy.* 2560). In his description of the revolt of Ingenuus, Aurelius Victor (*de Caes.* 33) refers to a *clades Valeriana*, which is normally interpreted as the capture of the elder Valerian, but since this would mean that Aurelius Victor was diverting attention from his main theme and then coming back to it again, it could mean that there was a disaster in Illyricum involving Gallienus' son (Christol 1997, 137; 170 n.1). Zosimus (1.31–35) describes the invasion of the Goths, usually dated to the mid-250s (de Blois 1976, 3), but dates are lacking in Zosimus' narrative; he mentions only one summer and the following winter (1.33.1; 34.2) as if everything occurred within two years. Ridley (1982, 141 n.61) dates the invasions to the years 255 to 258–9. Zonaras (12.24) describes how the Alamanni threatened the *agri decumates*; Gallienus set up headquarters at Milan, where at a later time Zosimus (1.40.1) mentions that Aureolus was stationed in command of the cavalry. The series of coins proclaiming the loyalty of the army and the loyalty of the cavalry (*Fides equitum* and *Fides militum*) were struck at Milan (de Blois 1976, 27; Alföldi 1927; 1929). The capture of Valerian by Shapur is recorded by most sources (Zosimus 1.36.2; Zonaras 12.23; *HA* Valerian 4.2; Aurelius Victor *de Caes.* 32.5; Eutropius 9.7; Orosius 7.22.4; Lactantius *de Mort. Pers.* 5). For the Persian account from *RGDS* (lines 19–37) see Dodgeon and Lieu (1991, 57). On the portraits of the Roman Emperors in the Sassanian reliefs see Macdermott (1954); see also Winter (1988, 340–1 plates 8–9) where Probus and Valerian are identified on the rock carvings. The exact date of Valerian's capture is not proven beyond doubt, but is narrowed to a choice of somewhere between 258 and 260 with the emphasis on the latter date. Périn and Feffer (1987, vol. 1, 31) argue that it was as early as 258 just after the campaign began, and the removal of one of the Emperors sparked off the invasions of 259 in the west; de Blois (1975, 10–11; 1976, 2–3) opts for 259 for the capture of the Emperor. Christol (1997, 139; 179 nn.4 and 7) points to papyrus evidence for the year 260: Valerian, Gallienus and Saloninus are mentioned together up to August 260 (*P. Oxy.* 2186), but by October 260 officials in Egypt were dating events by the regnal years of the two sons of Macrianus (*P. Oxy.* 1476). Dodgeon and Lieu (1991, 2; 57–65) also pinpoint 260 as the date when Valerian was captured. For discussion see Lopuszanski (1951). On Regalianus see Fitz (1966a); Göbl (1970); Christol (1997, 141). De Blois (1976, 33) says that fear of the barbarians prompted most of the usurpations. On Callistus = Ballista and Macrianus, and the two Augusti (Macrianus and Quietus), see Dodgeon and Lieu (1991, 65–6); Zonaras (12.24); *HA* (Trig. Tyr. 12.10; 18; Gallienus 1.3–5); *PLRE* (I 528); Eusebius (*History of the Church* 7.1.0.3). According to Zonaras (12.24) Postumus revolted over a difference with Silvanus, the tutor of Saloninus, on how to deal with the barbarian incursions into Gaul. He besieged Saloninus at Cologne, but according to Drinkwater (1987, 26–7) he was acting as a soldier, not a usurper, interested only in protecting the Gallic territories and not in marching to Rome to supplant Gallienus. See also de Blois (1976, 259–73). The extent of Postumus' Empire increased when Spain joined him, and the Augsburg inscription (*AE* 1993, 1231) indicates that his influence extended to Raetia (Bakker 1993; Lavagne 1994; Loriot and Nony 1997, 76–7 no. 36; Christol 1997, 171 n.6). König (1997, 348) says that the victory proclaimed over the Juthungi could be as late as 261.

3 SCHISM AND REUNIFICATION: 260–84

1 On the changes in the third-century administration in general see Malcus (1969). On Gallienus and his reign see *PLRE* (1, 383); Christol (1975). Gallienus did not rescue his father, and swept him aside by almost obliterating his memory (Paschoud 1971, 155–6

n.64). Zosimus (1.32.1) says that the Empire was abandoned and leaderless at the outset of the reign of Gallienus. Though the Emperor had a brother, Valerianus, who was consul in 265, and a third son called Marinianus, he did not share power with them or bring them into prominence. The only member of his family to be publicly acknowledged was his wife Salonina, whose portrait appeared on the coinage. Furthermore he departed from or even reversed some of Valerian's policies, because he had a completely different attitude to government, religion and culture (de Blois 1976, 25). He put an end to the persecution of the Christians begun by Valerian; he restored the use of churches, religious buildings and cemeteries to the Christians, probably as soon as he could in 260, thought the date is disputed (de Blois 1976, 175–84, esp. 177; 178–9). Eusebius (*History of the Church* 7.13) quotes the text of a rescript from Gallienus to the bishops of Egypt, and mentions another rescript concerning cemeteries without quoting from it; see Loriot and Nony (1997, 86–7 no. 42). It is not known for certain if Gallienus issued an edict of toleration. His motives may have been to remove a potential source of trouble at a time when he needed to pacify dissident groups, and he may have wished to influence the Christians of the eastern provinces to prevent them from turning to the Persians (de Blois 1976, 182–3; 185). The diminishing resources and reduced revenues available to Gallienus made his task especially difficult, and the situation was compounded by a decline in agriculture and trade, and continual tax evasion by the wealthy classes (de Blois 1976, 13–15; Petit 1974, 193–4; 198).

2 The changes introduced by Gallienus were the result of emergency measures, not coordinated and not really intended to be permanent. Gallienus' first task was to survive, and he progressed by trial and error, willing to sacrifice hallowed traditions if he could achieve what he wanted (de Blois 1976, 117–18; Petit 1974, 193–4).

3 Gallienus was not allowed time to plan constructively throughout his reign, since he was struggling to stay one step ahead, or fire-fighting as the modern terminology describes it. Aurelius Victor recognised the importance of the reign of Gallienus, devoting as much space to him as he did to Diocletian or Constantine (de Blois 1976, 86–7). The immediate successors of Gallienus did not change his policies (Petit 1974, 177), largely because his policies were adapted to the current circumstances and were successful even if only in the short term. Diocletian could introduce reforms which had been thought out in advance and applied more systematically (de Blois 1976, 118). Alföldi 1939 (*CAH* XII 231) described Decius and Gallienus as a pair of opposites, equating Diocletian with Decius and Constantine with Gallienus; van Berchem (1977a) points out that Gallienus and Constantine had more in common with each other than either of them had with Diocletian, since they were both isolated and reduced to fighting battles with the resources they had, and introduced changes on the basis of necessary adaptation, whereas Diocletian had time to think of the Empire as a whole, and to plan accordingly.

4 The constant wars of the period 250–75 engendered extraordinary measures in military and civil administration, resulting in an increase of the powers and importance of the men of military background, and their intrusion into provincial government (Christol 1986, 35–6; 45–6). The army was crucial in this period; it grew in size and importance as Gallienus attempted to deal with the wars, and without the army he could not have survived, since he faced more usurpers than any other Emperor (de Blois 1976, 13; 47; Christol 1997, 143–4). His whole government was devoted to the army, and fiscal, social, and political policies were subordinated to its needs (de Blois 1976, 117). See also Eadie (1980) on frontier policy.

5 Gallienus did not have whole legions in his army, but only vexillations from them, of unknown sizes; see Drinkwater (1971); Okamura (1991); Christol (1997, 143). Saxer (1967, 55–6, nos. 101–2) lists two inscriptions (*CIL* III 3228; *AE* 1934, 193) which reveal that vexillations from the legions of Germany and Britain were with the Emperor, possibly from the time of the Rhine campaign, and that detachments from *II Parthica* and *III Augusta* from Italy and Numidia, respectively, were with him in north-west Pannonia

at some time between 260 and 268. Other inscriptions (Saxer 1967, 56–7, nos. 103–6; *AE* 1936, 54–7) name detachments of *V Macedonica* and *XIII Gemina*; *AE* (1936, 57) names the equestrian *praepositus* in command of the vexillations as Flavius Aper. The *Pia Fidelis* coin series naming all 17 of the legions in Gallienus' army have been related to the number of Gallienus' German victories on the one hand (Alföldi 1959), and on the other hand to his acclamations as Emperor, the fifth being the last as joint Emperor and the sixth being the first as sole Emperor (Okamura 1991). Christol (1997, 143; 171 n.1) describes the pronounced military slant of Gallienus' coinage, extolling the victories and the *virtus* of the Emperor; see also Alföldi (1929 = 1967, 73–119); Göbl (1953); Fitz (1966b); King (1984).

6 Since there were many dissensions in the Empire Gallienus needed to ensure that the troops available to him remained loyal. The series of coins proclaiming the loyalty of the army have been discussed by several authors. Alföldi (1927; 1929) thought that the Praetorian series embraced the cavalry series (*Fides Equitum*) and that therefore the mounted units were subordinate to the Praetorian guard, but de Blois (1976, 29) considers that the coins dedicated to the cavalry were simply a part of the whole *Fides Militum* series. If the soldiers were to be bound more closely to him, Gallienus needed to reward them, and to give them privileges, or at least to promise such things. Grosse (1920, 12–13) recognised that the increasing privileges of the army had begun with the democratisation that Severus had brought about, upon which Gallienus built. Severus had allowed the *principales* to wear the white clothing of the equestrian class, and Gallienus took the final step by allowing all the soldiers the same privilege (*HA* Gallienus 8.1). In general, Gallienus favoured the ordinary soldiers, the NCOs and the lower civil grades in the administration (de Blois 1976, 55). He promoted men of proven ability (Osier 1977, 686). Since he was restricted to the Danube provinces for recruiting, the Illyrian soldiery were the ones who came to prominence during his reign (de Blois 1976, 56).

7 The cavalry army that Gallienus put together was a new departure. He probably assembled this mounted army for the Rhine campaign when speed and mobility were essential to stop the Germans from crossing the river (Zosimus 1.30). Alternatively the origins of the cavalry army may be found in the preparations for the battles against the Alamanni (de Blois 1976, 26–30). Some authors are of the opinion that the mobile army also contained some infantry (de Blois 1976, 30 n.33). The feature which makes the cavalry army unique is that it had one commander, Aureolus (*PLRE* 1, 138), an appointment hitherto unknown (Grosse 1920, 18). On Aureolus see Zosimus (1.40.1) and Zonaras (12.25). On the mobile cavalry in general see de Blois (1976, 26–30); Southern and Dixon (1996, 11–14); see also MacMullen (1976, 187) on the cavalry coins.

8 The troops that made up the cavalry army are known only by conjecture. It is possible that the units of Mauri and Osroeni brought to the Rhine by Severus Alexander (*HA* Severus Alexander 61.8; the two Maximini 11.1; 11.7; Herodian 7.21) were still extant, but they predated Gallienus by more than twenty-five years, and it is not known if the units had been kept up to strength. The *equites Dalmatae* are also generally considered to have formed part of Gallienus' cavalry; Osier (1977, 683) implies that the cavalry was composed solely of these mounted troops. See Grosse (1920, 16 nn.1–9) on the troops in the cavalry army; see also Zosimus (1.40.2) and *HA* (Gallienus 14.1) where it is said that during the war against Aureolus and the siege of Milan in 268 it was a commander of the Dalmatian horse (*dux Dalmatarum*), called Cecropius or Ceronius, who first deceived Gallienus into thinking that Aureolus was approaching and then killed him, which implies that these horsemen were close to the Emperor and trusted (see Ridley 1982, 143 n.74; Paschoud 1971, 158–9 n.68). Zonaras (12.25) gives two versions of the murder of Gallienus.

9 The sole authority who insists that Gallienus was the first to employ a mobile cavalry is the Byzantine chronicler George Cedrenus (*Compendium Historiarum* in Migné ed., vol. 121, p. 454). Grosse (1920, 15–16) says that Cedrenus is trustworthy because he used older, reliable sources. The question of permanence is debated; Ferrill (1986, 32) suggests

that Gallienus had no permanent policy in mind in his use of the mobile cavalry; de Blois (1976, 28–30) considers that the cavalry was used like any other temporary vexillation, brought together for a specific purpose, to be disbanded once the purpose was fulfilled. In this connection, the strategic function of Milan is also debated, some preferring the theory that it was held only so long as the Gallic Empire was still dislocated from Rome. The cavalry was seemingly kept together after the assassination of Gallienus; an inscription (ILS 569) dated to the year after his death mentions *vexillationes adque equites* as though the two were separate entities, so presumably the horsemen had not been absorbed into other units or merged with the vexillations. The cavalry was still employed under Claudius Gothicus (Zosimus 1.43.2; *HA* Claudius 11.9), and it was an important part of the army at Emesa under Aurelian (Zosimus 1.52.3). See also MacMullen (1976, 187). But after 284 it was not in evidence as a mobile reserve at Milan (de Blois 1976, 29; Seston 1946, 298–300; 305), though the concept that it was no longer strategically necessary because the Gallic Empire had been brought back into the Empire begs the question as to what was the true purpose of the cavalry army; whether it was gathered together for the narrow aims of defence against Postumus, or whether Gallienus had wider aims in view. Seston (1946, 298–300) considered that Carinus disbanded the cavalry army because its commander was potentially too powerful.

10 On the Protectores in general see Keyes (1915, 40); Southern and Dixon (1996, 14–15). The title Protectores appeared from about 253 onwards (Christol 1997, 394–5). It seems to have been confined to Italy during the joint reigns of Valerian and Gallienus, but extended outside Italy thereafter; see *CIL* III 3424 where a *praefectus a.v.l. II Adiutrix* holds the title. This was probably not a direct grant made to the officer while he served in this post; Christol (1977, 402) believes that the title was given to officers of the rank of centurion and above who were in the immediate entourage of the Emperor, and therefore in the mobile army. The award of the title marked a particular stage in officers' careers, before they went on to higher things. Two of the most famous Protectores were L. Petronius Taurus Volusianus who rose from the rank of *primuspilus* to Praetorian Prefect and consul (*CIL* XI 1836 = *ILS* 1332), and Traianus Mucianus, whose career inscription reveals his many talents and many military appointments (*I.G. Bulg.* III/2, 1570; Loriot and Nony 1997, 141 no. 85; Christol 1977). De Blois (1976, 85;106) says that the Protectores were assured of a good career, and points out (*ibid.* 53) that the title could be and often was awarded to men who had risen from the ranks; see also Grosse (1920, 13–15). For other career inscriptions of Protectores see *CIL* III 3424 = *ILS* 545; *RIU* III 871 = *AE* 1965, 9; *CIL* III 3529; *AE* 1965, 114; *CIL* III 1805 = *ILS* 5695. For the theory that the Protectores formed a staff college see Parker (1935, 180; 220). For the *princeps protectorum* see Christol (1977, 401 n.33).

11 On the rise of the equites in general see Keyes (1915); Osier (1974). Severus was responsible for the preliminary steps in the promotion of the equites (Chastagnol 1992, 207); for an overview from Severus to Gallienus see Devijver (1989 = 1992). Gallienus promoted military men and facilitated social mobility via military service for soldiers to enter the equestrian class (de Blois 1976, 37–44); he favoured equestrians who had risen from the ranks (Loriot and Nony 1997, 125), selecting men of proven ability (Osier 1977, 686). Since the number of equestrian military and administrative posts increased, so there was a greater need for trained and experienced men (Osier 1977, 674; 679; de Blois 1976, 38). The evidence for the so-called Edict of Gallienus derives solely from Aurelius Victor, who says (*de Caes.* 33.31–4) that Gallienus divorced senators from access to the army, and in another passage (37.5–7) that under the Emperor Tacitus the senators could have regained military power but they thought only of their personal fortunes and privileges. Chastagnol (1992, 208–9) says that the existence of the Edict is confirmed by epigraphy documenting the careers of senators; see also his note (1992, 208 n.16) on Aurelius Victor. On the Edict see also de Blois (1976, 57–8; 117); Thylander (1973) discusses Victor's statement, the Edict and the effect on senatorial careers.

12 Many senators preferred not to embark upon a military career, opting for non-political lives or for purely civil appointments (de Blois 1976, 60–1; 72–7). Christol (1986, 39–40) documents the waning senatorial career, while de Blois (1976, 68) quotes Thomasson (1960, 95) on the lack of experienced senatorial military officers and commanders as early as the Marcommanic wars. See also Keyes (1915, 49–54); Malcus (1969); Thylander (1973); Chastagnol (1992, 209). Some of those senators who did follow a career were not from strong senatorial backgrounds; Birley (1953, 206) points out that many of the administrators were drawn from equites who had entered the Senate.

13 On equestrian legionary prefects see Osier (1977). The last-known senatorial legionary legate was the commander at Caerleon (Christol 1986, 43–4 n.33). Grosse (1920, 4 nn.5 and 6) thought that the *praefectus castrorum* was elevated to command of the legions. The regular formula in the title *praefectus agens vice legati* was probably a legal necessity, and without the full title it is possible that the prefect did not have full legal powers (de Blois 1976, 47 n.108).

14 Gallienus appointed equestrian *praesides* to the most threatened provinces (de Blois 1976, 51), and after 260 more and more smaller provinces were governed by equestrians (*ibid.* 80–1). Christol's conclusion (1986, 45–6) after a study of senatorial careers was that the exchange of equestrian *praesides* for senatorial governors was completed by 262 in the praetorian provinces; inscriptions show that the last attested *legati Augusti propraetore* predate 262 in Noricum (*CIL* VIII 2615 = *ILS* 1194), Thrace (*AE* 1972, 724), and Arabia (Pflaum 1952). In the Imperial consular provinces there was no consistent policy of substituting equestrians for senators; there were examples where equestrian governors followed senators, but whenever it happened it was not an indication that it was to be a permanent change (Christol 1986, 49–50; de Blois 1976, 48). It was command of the troops that counted, so in Imperial consular provinces there was no senatorial influence in the army, which was commanded by equestrians (de Blois 1976, 80–1; Loriot and Nony 1997, 121).

15 Christol (1986, 17–18; 66) estimates that 25 posts as legionary legate were lost, and 12 as provincial governor of praetorian rank. Chastagnol (1992, 214) documents the general disappearance of senatorial administrative posts and junior magistracies, with the notable exception of the quaestorship; see also Loriot and Nony (1997, 122). The senatorial career was not so badly affected by the Edict divorcing them from military command, except in its extraordinary aspects (Christol 1986, 39), so the only senators to suffer were the really ambitious ones (de Blois 1976, 78). Senators still enjoyed considerable prestige and social influence even after the Edict (Rémondon 1964, 100). Arnheim (1972, 30) stresses the economic importance of the senatorial class, though as Ensslin points out (1939 *CAH* XII, 372) the Senate had no control over the finances of the Empire, since the treasury was in the hands of the Emperor, but senators could finance rebellions, and Gallienus thought that there had been senatorial backing behind the attempted usurpations of Ingenuus and Regalianus (de Blois 1976, 82). Gallienus' relations with the Senate were not totally bad; he remained on good terms with individual senators, and accepted honours from the Senate (de Blois 1976, 57–8). Senators of praetorian rank did not have sufficient military experience comparable to long-serving equites (de Blois 1976, 80–1); for the effects of Gallienus' Edict on the praetorian career and the subsequent concentration on posts in urban government in Rome and Italy, see Christol (1986, 47–8) and Loriot and Nony (1997, 122). Consulars had less opportunity for promotion in that there were fewer posts open to them (de Blois 1976, 59), but sometimes the Emperor could help careers by personal intervention (Loriot and Nony 197, 122). Chastagnol (1992, 214) estimates that 14–15 years would elapse between the first consulship and a post such as the proconsulship of Asia, and between the first and second consulship there would be an interval of about 20 to 25 years. Christol (1986, 89–90) says that the senatorial career began with the consulship, that is *consul ordinarius*, with the result that the suffect consulship declined in importance. All sources agree that Gallienus responded swiftly to threats if he suspected a plot (de Blois 1976, 144–5).

16 There was no budget as the modern world understands the term in the Roman Empire, so it is not possible to speak of monetary policy in modern terms (Loriot and Nony 1997, 159). For the financial policy of Gallienus the most important study is by Callu (1969), whose tables show that there was a complete lack of uniformity in weights or values of coins during the joint reigns of Valerian and Gallienus, and of Gallienus as sole Emperor; see also Petit (1974, 200). In his overview of coinage and money from the Severans to Constantine Crawford (1975) does not discuss the reigns of either Valerian or Gallienus in depth; their answer to the problem was to debase the currency and keep on issuing more of it; Callu (1969, 287) estimates that silver coin production rose by 700 per cent. The old antoninianus dwindled in value (de Blois 1976, 88), reaching an absolute nadir in the reign of Claudius Gothicus (Cope 1969; Harl 1996, 131); at the beginning of Aurelian's reign the antoninianus contained only about 1 per cent silver (Crawford 1975, 569). Similarly, the full effects of the rise in prices that began under Gallienus were not felt until about 270 (de Blois 1976, 89). The purchasing power of money fell sharply, with the natural result that payment in kind for the army was substituted for payment in cash; it soon became a normal institution in the second half of the third century. Callu (1969, 289ff, 482) describes the system as a natural economy, almost pre-feudal; see also de Blois (1976, 91), and on the growth of the *annona militaris* see van Berchem (1937). Egyptian papyri show that the system was already in operation before Gallienus became sole Emperor, and constantly mention payment of taxes in kind not cash; see Loriot and Nony (1997, 164–5); *P. Oxy.* 2282; 2346; 3109; 3111.

17 Evidence for the continued production from the mines of Spain dries up after the reign of Severus. Even if the mines were in full production, Gallienus was denied access to them, so he was reliant upon the Dalmatian mines instead; see Wilkes (1969, 267–8; 277–80); Loriot and Nony (1997, 160 no. 99). Gallienus stands accused of announcing victories in order to claim *aurum coronarium* (de Blois 1976, 90–1). There was also great promotional value for his regime in proclaiming himself victorious over his enemies.

18 On the new mints see de Blois (1976, 90) and Petit (1974, 198–200). Aurei almost ceased to function as coins since people resorted to weighing them (de Blois 1976, 90 n.253).

19 On the Gallic Empire generally see König (1981); Drinkwater (1987); Loriot and Nony (1997, 65–80). The term 'Gallic Empire' derives from Eutropius who called it the Empire of the Gauls (9.9.1). Aurelius Victor (*de Caes.* 33.6.4) lists all the Gallic Emperors. Postumus was *praeses* of Lower Germany in 259 (de Blois 1976, 7 n.21). His elevation by the army was recorded by *HA* (Thirty Tyrants 3.9.11); Zosimus (1.38.2); Aurelius Victor (*de Caes.* 33.7); Zonaras (12.24); Eutropius (9.9.1). Not mincing words, at least one writer declared that the usurpation of Postumus was tolerable because he stepped in when Gallienus was unable to defend the Rhine and Gallic provinces (*Pan. Lat.* 8 (5) 10.1–4). *CIL* II 4943 records Postumus' full name and titles; see also *CIL* II 4919; *ILS* 561–2. Postumus' Empire closely emulated the institutions of Rome, with annually appointed consuls and the Emperor counting tribunician years (Christol 1997, 147; Loriot and Nony 1997, 65). Drinkwater (1987) assumes that civil and military government went on as before and that no provincial boundaries were redrawn. Senatorial governors and army officers were retained by Postumus (Loriot and Nony 1997, 78 n.23), and the coinage was of a better quality than that of Gallienus (Loriot and Nony 1997, 69–74). The estimation of Postumus in *HA* (Thirty Tyrants 3.1–7) was that he was courageous and wise, and brought back the security of old, but some at least of this estimate stemmed from the strong bias against Gallienus. Epigraphic evidence shows that Britain joined Postumus (*ILS* 560) and later inscriptions mentioning Victorinus and Tetricus confirm that Britain and Spain were part of the Gallic Empire (*ILS* 564ff). For discussion of the extent of the Gallic Empire and the provinces where Postumus was recognised see Lafaurie (1975a), König (1981, 55–6 for list of inscriptions) and Drinkwater (1987, 27–8; 116–18).

20 Opinion about Postumus' ultimate aims is subject to variation, and there is no certain evidence as to his ambitions. According to de Blois (1976, 7) he never renounced his intention of conquering the whole Roman Empire. Drinkwater (1987, 34) assumes that Postumus made the initial decision to remain in the west and then clung to it, making it clear to Gallienus that he intended to focus entirely on the western provinces (*ibid.* 85). König (1981, 55) is convinced that Postumus was dedicated to the defence of the west, as the basis of his power, which would have been eroded if he turned towards Rome and removed troops to fight for the Empire. Schönberger (1985, 423) thinks that in general the whole frontier was given up about 259 or 260, given that some forts may already have been abandoned earlier, and some may have remained in occupation for a few more years, but not for very long. Gallienus tried to win back the territory under Postumus' command (*HA* Thirty Tyrants 3.5; Zonaras 12.24) but he was wounded at Trier (*HA* Gallienus 4.4–6) and put out of action. There may have been two attempts to defeat Postumus, in 261 and 266 (Christol 1997, 146); de Blois (1976, 7) dates the action to 265, as does Drinkwater who says (1987, 30) that preparations began at the end of 264. See also Elmer (1941); Göbl (1951; 1953). A fabulous story grew up that Gallienus challenged Postumus to a duel so the fate of the Empire should be decided by the outcome of a fight between the two of them, sparing the lives of the soldiers (Anonymus post Dionem, *FHG* IV, 194–5 ed. Müller). It was said that Aureolus was secretly in negotiation with Postumus and did not pursue the war vigorously enough (de Blois 1976, 7), but this is most likely a false accusation; Aureolus was loyal till 267 (Christol 1997, 145). Postumus followed the usual pattern of proclaiming his successes with titles on his coinage such as *Restitutor Galliarum* and *Salus Provinciae* (Christol 1997, 146); see also Loriot and Nony (1997, 72–4 no. 33). Whatever were the aims and intentions of Postumus and his successors in the Gallic Empire, the disunity of the Empire would lead inevitably to conflict in the end (Christol 1997, 147; Drinkwater 1987, 239–51; Sherwin-White 1973a, 437–44).

21 On Fulvius Junius Macrianus and his sons Macrianus and Quietus see *PLRE* I 528. The elder Macrianus was originally in charge of logistics and supplies during the Persian campaign, *praepositus annonae expeditionalis* (Petit 1974, 182). On the rise of the Persian Empire and the role of Palmyra see Gagé (1964a); Dodgeon and Lieu (1991, 68–83). Zosimus (1.39.1) describes how Odenathus attacked Shapur, combining his own troops with the legions that remained in the east.

22 On Palmyra and its rulers in general see Gawlikowski (1985); Will (1992); Millar (1993, 319–33); on the treatment of Palmyra in the *Historia Augusta* see Schwartz (1966). Odenathus (*PLRE* 1, 638; Dodgeon and Lieu 1991, 68–83) came from a distinguished family; Zosimus (1.39) says that he was judged worthy on account of his ancestry. It was once postulated that Odenathus had an ancestor of the same name, but this is now discounted (Will 1992, 172–4; Gawlikowski 1985). Paschoud (1971, 157 n.67) assumes that Odenathus' family rendered some assistance to Severus against Pescennius Niger, and received appropriate awards. The name Septimius was adopted by the family, and continued in use by Odenathus' successors (*AE* 1948, 120; Gawlikowski 1985, 254 no. 5 for Septimius Hairan, son of Odenathus; *ibid.* 256 no. 11 for Palmyrene text and statue of Odenathus erected after his death, dedicated by his generals Septimius Zabda and Septimius Zabbae). *IGR* III 1030 shows that Zenobia (*PLRE* 1, 990) took the name Septimia. Odenathus was *vir consularis*, but this probably meant that he had been granted *ornamenta consularis* and was not actually consul (Christol 1997, 148; Potter 1996, 283).

23 The relationship between Gallienus and Odenathus is portrayed by the ancient authors as one of master and assistant; Zosimus (1.39.1) says that the Emperor ordered Odenathus to take charge in the east, a theory repeated by Peter the Patrician (frg. 10) and John Malalas (297). The title *dux Romanorum* for Odenathus is attested by Zonaras (12.23) and from a coin of Vaballathus with the legend V(*ir*) C(*larissimus*) R(*ex*) Imp(*erator*) D(*ux*) R(*omanorum*) (*RIC* V.1 Aurelian no. 381). The title *dux* implied that Odenathus was in charge of mili-

tary affairs in the east; according to Hieronymus (*Chron.* 2282) Odenathus already commanded ymustroops of his own, and he presumably commanded the Roman forces as well. The extent of Odenathus' power is not clearly established, but probably embraced Syria, Palestine, Mesopotamia, Arabia, and the eastern areas of Asia Minor (de Blois 1976, 33–4). Besnier (1937, 217) considers that Gallienus delegated both civil and military power to Odenathus. There are hints of a treaty between Gallienus and Odenathus, dating from c. 262 (*CIL* VIII 22765; Zonaras 12.23; *HA* Gallienus 3.3). On Odenathus and the Palmyrene episode see also Millar (1993, 159–73).

24 For the background to Odenathus' campaign versus the Persians see de Blois (1976, 1–8). Of the ancient authors who describe the campaign (Zonaras 12.24; Eutropius 9.10; Orosius 7.22; *HA* Gallienus 10.12) only Zosimus (1.39–40) says that Odenathus marched to Ctesiphon twice. Gallienus took the title *Parthicus Maximus*, or *Persicus Maximus* according to some sources, in 264 (*PIR2* L 197 p.44). Odenathus was rewarded with the title Imperator and *corrector totius orientis* (Loriot and Nony 1997, 91–3 no. 46; Gawlikowski 1985, 256 no. 11; *OGIS* II 649; *IGR* III 1028). For a discussion of these titles see Potter (1996). Odenathus also fought the Goths in Pontus (de Blois 1976, 33–4), But despite these displays of loyalty to Rome it was also said that he had made an attempt to ally with Persia (Petr. Patr. frg. 10 ed. Müller; Paschoud 1971, 157 n.67). Cizek (1994, 78) thinks that by the time of his assassination Odenathus may have turned against Gallienus; the date of the murder of Odenathus is not certain, except that papyrus evidence shows that it occurred between 28 August 266 and 28 August 267 (Paschoud 1971, 158 n.67). He was probably killed at Emesa; see *HA* (Gallienus 10); Eutropius (9.13.2); Orosius (7.22). Petit (1974, 183) suggests that Gallienus connived at the assassination; see also Loriot and Nony (1997, 91).

25 Julia Aurelia Zenobia (*PLRE* 1, 990) later became Septimia Zenobia. She became regent for her son Vaballathus; see *HA* (Gallienus 13.1; Aurelian 38.1). Zosimus (1.39.2) says that she had the boldness of a man and with the help of her husband's friends she equalled him in careful administration. Vaballathus' full name was Lucius Julius Aurelius Septimius Vaballathus Athenodorus (*ILS* 8927). Heraclianus' titles and rank vary in the sources; in *HA* (Gallienus 14.1) he is *dux*; an inscription (*AE* 1948, 55) reveals that he was *praefectus praetorio*. See also Zosimus (1.40.2); *HA* (Gallienus 13.4–5); Bersanetti (1942); Manni (1949, 40); Bird (1971).

26 On Volusianus see *PLRE* (Volusianus 6); Pflaum (1960, 901–5 no. 347). *CIL* XI 1836 lists Volusianus' equestrian appointments, and *CIL* XI 5749 shows that he was *cos. ord.* in 261. From 267 until the death of Gallienus he was *praefectus urbi* (*Chron. Min.* I p. 65). He was the only officer to reach this elevated post until the reign of Diocletian; see Chastagnol (1960, 224–7); Christol (1997, 144–5). Aurelius Theodotus (*PLRE* Theodotus 4, p.906) was Prefect of Egypt from 14 August 262 to 8 November 263 (*P. Strassb.* 1.5.21; *P. Oxy.* 2107; 1467). See also *HA* (Gallienus 4.2). Marcianus was the general left by Gallienus to contain the situation on the Danube when Aureolus rebelled (Zosimus 1.40.1); he defended Athens, and may have been implicated in the plot against Gallienus; see *HA* (Gallienus 6.1; 13.10; 14.1.7; Claudius 6.1; 18.1). See also Paschoud (1971, 158 n.68). While the Emperor and the bulk of his army fought battles in one part of the Empire, the people living in neglected areas felt that they were being sacrificed for the benefit of a few favoured provinces, because nothing was done to alleviate the destruction and potential threats (Petit 1974, 187–8). The relationship between the army and the people degenerated in the third century, since the army had pay and provisions when the people had to make do. Gallienus tried to weld the different elements together but succeeded only in promoting the myth. He celebrated the alleged harmony between the army and the populace on his coinage; towards the end of his reign he issued coins with the legend *Concordia Populi Romani et Militum*. Examples are rare (Christol 1997, 149).

27 The Alamanni were defeated in northern Italy in 260 and gave no further trouble until 269 (Christol 1997, 145; de Blois 1976, 6). The chronology of events is inextricably

muddled, so it is impossible to say whether the revolts of Regalianus, Aemilianus and Macrianus occurred successively or contemporaneously; see Christol (1975; 1997, 141); Göbl (1951; 1953). On Regalianus see Fitz (1966a); Göbl (1970). The mint at Antioch coined for Gallienus from 262 onwards (Christol 1997, 145).

28 After 262 Gallienus launched a propaganda campaign promoting peace and prosperity, adopting the epithet used to describe Trajan, *optimus princeps* (de Blois 1976, 135). He celebrated his Decennalia in high style in Rome (*HA* Gallienus 7.2; Merten 1968; Christol 1997, 151). He identified himself with the highest Greek and Roman gods, Jupiter and Zeus (de Blois 1976, 155ff), and Hercules (de Blois 1976, 149–50); he claimed that he was under the special protection of Apollo and Diana (de Blois 1976, 163–4). Another of the gods that he promoted and identified with was Sol or Sol Invictus (de Blois 1976, 157 n.138; 159–60; 165–9). Eleven portraits of Gallienus are known, five from his joint rule with Valerian, and six from his sole reign; they took on a more abstract, spiritual aspect as his reign progressed, accentuating his majesty (Christol 1997, 149; de Blois 1976, 170–3; Haarlov 1976). Epithets such as Invictus and Magnus also appear in the Emperor's titulature towards the end of Gallienus' reign (*CIL* V 586; IX 80; XIV 4058; Christol 1997, 151; de Blois 1976, 148–9); he portrayed himself as saviour of the state (*CIL* XIV 5334).

29 Plotinus was reputedly favoured by Gallienus who wished to allot lands in Campania to the Platonists to found a school (de Blois 1976, 191 n.67; Porphyry V Plotinus 12). It is commonly assumed that Gallienus was initiated into the Eleusinian mysteries when he visited Athens, but there is debate as to the evidence for this; there is nothing in the sources that proves beyond doubt that the initiation ever took place (de Blois 1976, 185–6). Gallienus did not ultimately deliver the Empire from all its problems, so he was considered to have reneged on his promises; from then onwards he was the stereotype of the unsuccessful Emperor, accused as Macrinus was of enjoying leisure while the Empire suffered (Whittaker 1970, 27 n.1). Cities and communities had to fend for themselves; Aquileia received walls as early as 238, and walls were built round other northern Italian cities, such as Verona in 265 (*CIL* V 3329). According to literary sources most of the cities of Moesia were walled in the reign of Gallienus (*HA* Gallienus 13.6); see also Cizek (1994, 101); Loriot and Nony (1997, 89 no 44). Appeals to the Emperor for assistance are documented by Herrmann (1990). The Augsburg inscription records the defeat of the Semnones or Juthungi by the soldiers of Raetia and the German provinces, and also the civilians (*a militibus provinciae raetiae sed et Germanicianis itemque popularibus*); see Bakker (1993); Lavagne (1994); König (1997); Le Roux (1997). Dexippus' account of the defence of Athens is discussed by Millar (1969). Gallienus' campaign against the Goths is not well documented, but the opening of the mint at Siscia indicates impending military activity (Christol 1997, 150) and archaeology confirms the wide-ranging movements of the army in Illyricum (Loriot and Nony 1997, 87–9 no. 43). Although Zosimus notes the campaign (1.39–40) he does not mention any victory for Gallienus at all, ascribing it to Claudius Gothicus (1.43.2); see Ridley (1982, 144 n.79) and Paschoud (1971, 157 n.67) on Gallienus' successes. See also *HA* (Gallienus 13; Claudius 9).

30 Marcianus, an experienced general, was left in command of the army when Gallienus marched to Italy (Zosimus 1.40.1); see also *HA* (Gallienus 6.1; 13.10; 14.1.7; 15.2; Claudius 6.1; 18.1). The date of the assassination of Gallienus is disputed, varying from March 268 (Lafaurie 1965) to September 268; Besnier (1937, 185; 226) opts for July or August, basing his conclusion on papyrological evidence (*P. Oxy.* 1119). There are two versions of what actually happened, both of which are described by Zonaras (12.25); Heraclianus was the most probable instigator of the plot; see Paschoud (1971, 158 n.68). Cecropius was *dux Dalmatarum* according to *HA* (Gallienus 14.4–9). Claudius was probably implicated in the plot (*HA* Gallienus 14.1–2; Claudius 1.3; Aurelius Victor *de Caes.* 33.28); see Damerau (1934, 11–14).

31 On Claudius II Gothicus in general see *PLRE* (1, 209); Damerau (1934). The Emperor

was born 8 May 219, according to *HA* (Claudius 11.9). The sources may have invented a career for him to glorify his achievements; he is said to have been in command of all the forces in the Balkans under Gallienus (*HA* Claudius 14.16; Aurelius Victor *de Caes.* 33.28). At the time of the murder of Gallienus he was in command of the reserve forces at Ticinum (Cizek 1994, 80). He may have been implicated in the assassination of Gallienus (see above n.30; Zosimus 1.40.2), and may have rewarded Cecropius, the commander of the Dalmatian cavalry, who appears as *clarissimus* on an inscription (*CIL* VI 836). Claudius did not change any of Gallienus' policies (Cizek 1994, 82) and left equites in command of provinces where Gallienus had installed them (*CIL* III 3424). He had no time to reform the coinage, and was forced to put all the emphasis on military matters; coins were issued with the legends *Concordia Exercitus*, *Fides Militum* and *Pax Exercitus* (Cizek 1994, 83; Christol 1997, 157).

32 Claudius gave donatives to the soldiers when he was made Emperor, which calmed those who threatened to riot on the news of the death of Gallienus (*HA* Gallienus 15.2; Zosimus 1.41.1); see also Bird (1971). According to *HA* (Claudius 4.2) the new Emperor was hailed in May 268, but this depends upon the date of the death of Gallienus and the subsequent (or even prior) events leading to the choice of Claudius by the army. Cizek (1994, 81 n.67) dates the acclamation to September 268. The Senate ratified the army's choice and granted Claudius the name Augustus (*HA* Claudius 4; Eutropius 9.11.3). The new Emperor adopted a conciliatory policy towards the Senate, issuing coins with the legend *Genius Senatus* (*RIC* V.1 Claudius pp. 211–37; Christol 1997, 157; Cizek 1997, 82–3). The sources offer a brilliant portrait of Claudius (Aurelius Victor *de Caes.* 34.1.2; *HA* Claudius 13–18; Ammianus 31.5.17; Zosimus 1.46; Zonaras 12.26), but this may arise from the fact that Constantine adopted him retrospectively as one of his ancestors (Paschoud 1971, 158 n.68; Damerau 1934, 81–3). Aureolus tried to surrender to Claudius but was killed; where, when, and how are not elucidated. Aurelian may have been the instigator of the murder, or the tool of Claudius (*HA* Aurelian 16.2–3). Cizek (1994, 24) says that it is difficult to believe that Claudius was not implicated in the despatch of Aureolus, especially since Aurelian was immediately given the command of the cavalry (*HA* Aurelian 18.1); if he had murdered Aureolus contrary to Claudius' wishes or express command he obviously did not suffer for it. Zosimus (1.41.1) blames no one personally, but says that the soldiers killed Aureolus, a story that is also included in the life of Claudius (*HA* Claudius 5.2–3).

33 Zonaras (12.26) affirms that Claudius would have restored the unity of the Empire, but he had to spend all his time and energies fighting the barbarians. Preoccupied with the Goths and the Danube, Claudius did not try to win back the west; he sent the prefect of the *vigiles* Julius Placidianus to Narbonensis, where the latter had some success (*CIL* XII 2228 = *ILS* 569; Lafaurie 1964, 99; König 1981, 149–52; and see below note 51). Cizek (1994, 81–2) considers that this operation was to protect the west from attack while Claudius marched to the Danube. Spain also came over to Claudius (*CIL* II 3833; 3834; 4505) but Britain held out (*RIB* 1885; 2224–6). The chronology of Claudius' campaigns is confused, allowing for two completely different interpretations of his movements; Cizek (1994, 81) puts the battles against the Alamanni first, then the Goths; Christol (1997, 157) puts the first campaign against the Goths first, followed by the Alamanni, then another against the Goths during the course of which the Emperor died of plague. The Gothic menace is exaggerated in the sources, with widely divergent numbers for the ships they use and the numbers of men they could field; in the life of Claudius (*HA* Claudius 6.4) the Goths are said to have used 3,000 ships and mustered 320,000 men; Ammianus (31.5.15) reduces the ships from 3,000 to 2,000; this figure becomes 900 in *Suda*, and Syncellus (I p. 717.9 Bonn) has a more realistic figure of 500 ships; see Paschoud (1971, 159 n.70) who describes the invasions of the Goths at this epoch the most significant movement of the German peoples of the third century. See also Damerau (1934, 62–75) and Besnier (1937, 228). The Palmyrene extension of power into Egypt is documented by

Schwartz (1953; 1976). The full name of Tenagino Probus is given in an inscription (*AE* 1936, 58). In 268 he was *praeses* of Numidia (*AE* 1941, 33; *CIL* VIII 2571) and by 269 he was Prefect of Egypt (*SEG* 9.19; *HA* Probus 9). He was commissioned by Claudius to clear the seas of the Goths (Zosimus 1.44.2; Zonaras 12.27). He was killed or committed suicide in 270 (*HA* Claudius 11.2); see Paschoud (1971, 161 n.72).

34 According to Aurelius Victor (*de Caes.* 34.3–4) Claudius consulted the Sybilline Books before he set off on his campaign against the Goths. He put an end temporarily to the incursions of the Goths (Aurelius Victor *de Caes.* 34.3–8; Eutropius 9.11.2; *HA* Claudius 1.3; 3.6; 6–8; 11.4; Zosimus 1.43–45; Zonaras 12.26; Syncellus I, pp. 717–720 Bonn), and was rewarded with the title Gothicus (*RIC* V.1 nos. 247–52; 263–5). The victory at Naissus (*CIL* VIII 4876) was really Gallienus' victory purloined by the authors who wished to glorify Claudius' exploits; see *HA* (Gallienus 13; Claudius 9); Zosimus (1.43.2; 45.1); Paschoud (1971, 160 n.71; 161 n.73); Ridley (1982, 144 n.79). Some of the Goths who survived Claudius' campaigns settled as coloni in the Balkans, or were sold as slaves (*HA* Claudius 9.4–6).

35 Aurelian refused to pay subsidies to the barbarians (Petit 1974, 211 n.122). Claudius was preparing a campaign against the Juthungi in Raetia, and the Vandals in Pannonia (Cizek 1994, 82–3), when he died of the plague (Aurelius Victor *de Caes.* 34.5; *HA* Claudius 12.1–2; Zosimus 1.46.1; Zonaras 12.26). Quintillus reigned for only a short time, 17 days according to Eutropius (9.12), 77 days according to *Chron. Min.* (1.148); and a few months according to Zosimus (1.47). His coin issues indicate that he must have reigned long enough to organise and execute the design and minting, which suggests that Zosimus was correct; see Paschoud (1971, 162 n.75).

36 On the reign of Aurelian see Homo (1904); Cizek (1994). Aurelian (*PLRE* 1, 129) was born at Sirmium according to *HA* (Aurelian 3.1); according to Eutropius (9.13.1) the Emperor was born in the area that later became Dacia Ripensis. Aurelius Victor (*de Caes.* 35.1) felt obliged to point out that Aurelian was of low birth. See Cizek (1994, 11–12); Estiot (1995).

37 The date of Aurelian's proclamation was probably November 270 (Cizek 1994, 89). The sources indicate that he reigned for a little less than six years, but he was in his seventh year of tribunician power when he was killed; Cizek (1994, 90) following Lafaurie (1965) suggests that he backdated the first *trib. pot.* to November–December 269. Eutropius (9.14) calls Aurelian savage and bloodthirsty. On the Juthungi see Cizek (1994, 94–6); Dexippus frg. 6–7 *FHG* Müller III p. 682); Aurelius Victor (*de Caes.* 35.2). On the Vandals see Dexippus (frg. 24 *FHG* Müller III p. 685); Zosimus (1.48.2; 49.1); Cizek (1994, 359 n.8). See also note 40 (below).

38 For chronology in general see Lafaurie (1964; 1965). The revolt of the mint workers is not securely dated; see *HA* (Aurelian 38.2–3). Cizek (1994, 167–72) dates it to 274 on the grounds that Aurelius Victor (*de Caes.* 35.5–6) places his account of it after the triumph of 274, and the ancient authors who describe the troubles at the outset of Aurelian's reign make no specific mention of the moneyers. Felicissimus, the ringleader, was killed during the troubles (Eutropius 9.14). Homo (1904, 163) dates the revolt of the moneyers to 270, and the closure of the Rome mint to the same year; thus he is able to date the revolt and then the death of Felicissimus, who had been made redundant and removed from his profitable frauds, to the period just after the defeat of Aurelian at Placentia. None of these dates are, as it were, written in stone, both from the point of view of non-permanence and from the sadder point of view that no inscriptions have turned up to help fix the chronology. On the revolt in general see Turcan (1969); Cizek (1994, 169–72); for possible senatorial involvement see Callu (1969, 140).

39 The three attempted usurpations by Septiminus, Domitianus, and Urbanus are very little illuminated in the sources; see Zosimus (1.49.2). Urbanus appears in no other account except Zosimus (Paschoud 1971, 164 n.77). Septiminus appears in *Epit. de Caes.* (35.3). For Domitianus see *HA* (Gallienus 2.6; Thirty Tyrants 12.14; 13.3) and for his coinage

see *RIC* (V.2 590); Ridley (1982, 145 n.93). Aurelian gave 500 denarii per head to the populace of Rome (*HA* Aurelian 48.5). Under Aurelian the Senate's power and privileges, already weakened, were further eroded; the right to issue bronze coins was withdrawn; see Kent (1978, 43–4). Legislative powers were lost as the Emperor himself became the sole source of law; see Robinson (1997).

40 Paschoud (1971, 163 n.76) and Saunders (1992) outline the various discrepancies in the sources as to which tribes Aurelian fought against, and the order in which the battles and marching to and fro are described. *HA* (Aurelian 18.2) describes a victory over the Suebi and Sarmatians; then (18.3.6) the Marcomanni reaching Milan and the defeat of Aurelian at Placentia, followed of course by his ultimate victory (21.1–4). Zosimus (1.48.1–2) describes an invasion of Pannonia by the Scythians, followed by (1.49.1) an invasion of Italy by the Alamanni. The case for two Juthungian wars derives from Dexippus (frg. 6–7 *FGrH* Jacoby), who tells of a battle with the Juthungi after which they asked for peace, but Aurelian ignored them, and then a war against the Vandals which had to be quickly broken off because the Juthungi had invaded Italy. It is the order of these two fragments which is the crucial point; Saunders (1992, 311–27) recently re-examined the theory that Aurelian fought two Juthungian wars, which had been challenged by Alföldi (1950, 21–4 = 1967, 427–30) who in the course of his study tidied up the multiplicity of tribes, equating the Suebi and the Sarmatians with the Scythians of Zosimus, and the Marcomanni with the Alamanni, concluding that there was only one Juthungian war. Saunders concludes that the old theory that there were two wars was in fact correct; acceptance of Alföldi's theory that there was only one battle against the Juthungi involves reversing the order of the Dexippus fragments. On the chronology of the three battles see Petit (1974, 204 n.105); Fanum Fortunae is commemorated epigraphically (*CIL* XI 6308; 6309); *HA* (Aurelian 25) records the ultimate victory; *RIC* V.1 (Aurelian 305 no. 355) celebrates a German victory.

41 On the walls of Rome generally and their subsequent history see Homo (1904, 214–308); Richmond (1930); Todd (1978). Aurelian called a meeting of the Senate to discuss the building of the walls (*HA* Aurelian 21.9). The date of the commencement of the work is given in some sources (Zosimus 1.49.2; *HA* Aurelian 21.9; Eutropius 9.15.1) but not mentioned in others (Aurelius Victor *de Caes.* 35.7; Orosius 7.23.6). Paschoud (1971, 163 n.77) says that the date is most likely to be after the tribesmen appeared in Italy in the two Juthungian wars; see Cizek (1994, 98–102). Parts of the Fourteen Regions of Augustan Rome were excluded when the circuit was erected; sections of the 1st, 5th and 7th and much of the 14th regions were not enclosed (Cizek 1994, 99). *HA* (Aurelian 39.2) exaggerates the length of the circuit, giving the figure of 50 miles.

42 Civilian workers were employed to build the walls (Cizek 1994, 101). Loriot and Nony (1997, 271–2) provide a useful plan and synopsis of dimensions; see also note 41 (above). The building work was completed during the reign of Probus (Zosimus 1.49.2).

43 On Zenobia and Vaballathus see Schneider (1993); Dodgeon and Lieu (1991, 83–101). Milestones and coins document the progress of Vaballathus from Palmyrene ruler of the east to self-styled Emperor of Rome. *Rex regum* or king of kings was a customary eastern title, and is attested for Vaballathus on a milestone from the road from Palmyra to Emesa with Greek and Palmyrene text (*CIS* II.3 3971 = *OGIS* II 649 = *IGR* III 1028). At first Zenobia and her son honoured the legitimate Emperor Aurelian and confined themselves to emulating Odenathus and his honorary titles; an antoninianus from the Antioch mint (*RIC* V.1 Aurelian 308 no. 381) displays Aurelian on the obverse, and Vaballathus on the reverse with his titles (in expanded form) *Vir Clarissimus, Rex, Imperator, Dux Romanorum*; see Loriot and Nony (1997, 93 no. 47A). *P. Oxy.* 1264 dated March 272 records the Emperor Aurelian in his second year and Vaballathus in his fifth, reckoning from 29 August in the Egyptian fashion. Eventually Zenobia and Vaballathus showed their hands, purloining the titles Caesar Augustus and declaring victories over traditional Roman enemies; *RIC* V.2 (Vaballathus 585 no. 6) has the legend *Imp. Caes. Vhabalathus Aug.* on

the obverse and *Victoria Aug.* on the reverse; see Loriot and Nony (1997, 94 no. 47C). The text of a milestone (*AE* 1904, 60 = *ILS* 8924) from the road from Bostra to Philadelphia runs *Imp. Caesari L. Iulio Aurelio Septimio Vaballatho Athenodoro Persico Maximo Arabico Maximo Adiabenico Maximo Pio Felici invicto Aug.*

44 Aurelian fought the Goths under Cannobaudes on his way to the east (*HA* Aurelian 22.2; Eutropius 9.13.1; Orosius 7.23.4; Jordanes *Rom.* 290); see also below ch. 5 note 81. He took the title *Gothicus Maximus*; a Gothic victory was proclaimed on coins (*RIC* V.1 Aurelian 303 no. 339). See also Cizek (1994, 106). On the Palmyrene take-over of Egypt see Dodgeon and Lieu (1991, 87–8). *HA* (Probus 9.3) insists that it was the future Emperor Probus who retook Egypt and ousted the Palmyrenes, but the identity of the general responsible is disputed; whoever it was, the Antioch mint was coining for Aurelian alone by 271; quoting Vitucci (1952, 14), Paschoud suggests that Marcellinus reconquered Egypt (1971, 164 n.78; 172 n.93). Zosimus does not mention the reconquest of Egypt at all, but he is nonetheless the principal source for the Palmyrene campaign apart from *HA* (Aurelian 25); Paschoud (1971, 164 n.78) points out that the chronology of Zosimus is wrong, in that Aurelian did not arrive in the east until 271 and the campaign belongs to 272. Homo (1904, 84–107) dates it to the end of 271 and the beginning of 272. For the siege of Tyana see *HA* (Aurelian 22.5 to 24.6). Cizek (1994, 106–7) suggests that Aurelian wintered in Byzantium and marched towards Palmyra in the spring of 272. For the battle at Immae see Downey (1950). Aurelian ordered his troops to withdraw before the Palmyrene heavy cavalry and then to attack (Zosimus 1.50.3–4). Zenobia fled when she knew that Aurelian was the victor (*HA* Aurelian 25.1; Zosimus 1.50.1–2; Eutropius 9.13.2; Jordanes *Rom.* 290). The fort at Daphne was situated in a suburb of Antioch on the road to Emesa; it has been equated with Immae, but this is in error (Paschoud 1971, 165 n.80).

45 The Palmyrenes were defeated at Emesa (*HA* Aurelian 26.1; Cizek 1994, 111), where Aurelian perhaps tried to use the same stratagem that he had used at Immae (Paschoud 1971, 165–6 n.81). The siege of Palmyra followed; Aurelian was wounded by an arrow, but not seriously (*HA* Aurelian 26.2–6). He came to an arrangement with the desert tribes not to harass his supply columns, persuading them to betray their loyalty to Zenobia (*HA* Aurelian 28.2). The city of Palmyra ran out of food; starvation threatened and the Palmyrenes surrendered in 272 (Zosimus 1.55.1; Dodgeon and Lieu 1991, 96–9). Zenobia fled towards Persia on a camel; the female of the species, says Zosimus (1.55.2–3), are very fast. Likewise, according to *HA* (Aurelian 28.3) Zenobia escaped by camel '*camelis, quod dromedas vocant*'.

46 Zosimus (1.59) tells the fantastic tale that Zenobia died en route to Rome, either by refusing to eat or from an unnamed illness, and that almost all the Palmyrene prisoners were drowned except Zenobia's son. Ridley (1982, 146 n.106) suggests that this was a deliberate attempt to equate Zenobia with her heroine Cleopatra. The army wanted Zenobia killed (*HA* Aurelian 30.1), but she lived to walk in Aurelian's triumph and beyond (*HA* Thirty Tyrants 30.27; Aurelian 30.2l; 33.2; 34.3). She lived in a villa near Tivoli, married to a Roman senator, and there were descendants of hers still surviving in the fourth century (Eutropius 9.13.2). See Merten (1968, 131–4); Paschoud (1971, 168 n.87).

47 Marcellinus was put in command of the reduced province of Mesopotamia as *rector Orientis* (Cizek 1994, 185; Christol 1986, 113–14). He was *consul ordinarius* in 275 (*CIL* VI 10060; Zosimus 1.60.1) and was with Aurelian when he was killed; he persuaded the soldiers to go to the Senate for a decision on who should be Emperor (Homo 1904, 143). Paschoud (1971, 169 n.88) suggests that he was an eques who had been adlected to the Senate. Aurelian took the title *Carpicus Maximus* (*ILS* 581; 582; 8925; *CIL* VI 1112) at an unknown date, discussed by Kettenhofen (1987). Apsaeus (Dodgeon and Lieu 1991, 101–3) is mentioned on an inscription (*IGR* III 1049); in the *Historia Augusta* (Aurelian 31.2) Antiochus becomes Achillus; see also Paschoud (1971, 169 n.88). On Firmus see

Dodgeon and Lieu (1991, 103–5). He presumably acted in Egypt in concert with Apsaeus and Antiochus (Cizek 1994, 114–15; Paschoud 1971, 169 n.89). He appropriated the exports intended for Rome (*HA* Aurelian 32.2); this, it goes without saying, was the first item on the agenda of any self-respecting anti-Roman magnate who had managed to take control of Egypt.

48 Aurelian's sudden descent on Palmyra shocked the rebels (Zosimus 1.61.1). For the second Palmyrene campaign see Homo (1904, 108–15); Cizek (1994, 114–17). Palmyra never recovered from its almost total obliteration by Aurelian (Paschoud 1971, 169 n.89; Cizek 1994, 116).

49 Ammianus Marcellinus (22.16.15) comments on Aurelian's severe treatment of Alexandria; he pulled the walls down, and raised taxes on Egyptian goods such as glass, papyrus and linen (Cizek 1994, 172) which brought extra revenue for Rome (*HA* Aurelian 45.1). He raised two new legions which he placed in Syria and Arabia to control the territories occupied by the Palmyrenes (Cizek 1994, 116–17). Coins proclaimed Aurelian *Restitutor Orientis* (*RIC* V.1 Aurelian pp. 267–307). *HA* (Aurelian 28.4) makes the grand claim that he possessed the whole of the east (*totiusque iam orientis possessor*), and an inscription refers to him as *Imperator Orientis* (*AE* 1936, 129). Aurelian took the title *Palmyrenicus Maximus* (*CIL* V 4319); see Christol (1997, 162).

50 Postumus reigned for ten years, a point about which the sources are confused; Eutropius (9.9.1) gets it right, while *HA* (Gallienus 4.5) is mistaken. Postumus established government on Roman lines (Drinkwater 1987, 28–34). His coinage was good, and there is a clear break and a distinct decline after his death (Drinkwater 1987, 175; Cizek 1994, 75). He established himself in power on the basis that he would defend the Rhine provinces (Drinkwater 1987, 28; König 1981, 56), but he soon dropped the pretence of defending the whole of the Rhine frontier, limiting himself more realistically to Gaul (Drinkwater 1987, 89). Ulpius Cornelius Laelianus has rightly been described as a shadowy figure (Drinkwater 1987, 34). Judging from his name, Ulpius, he may have hailed from Spain, or had strong connections with the province (Drinkwater 1987, 176). It used to be thought that he was governor of Lower Germany at the time of his revolt, but since all the sources insist that the rebellion occurred at Mainz in Upper Germany, it is more likely that he was governor of the Upper province and was already using Mainz as his main base (König 1981, 133; Drinkwater 1987, 177). The date of the rebellion is disputed, but it occurred some short time after Postumus took up his fifth consulship on 1 January 269 (König 1981, 132–6). Laelianus' full name appears on his coinage, of which there were only three emissions (König 1981, 133 n.7), but among the ancient authors only Aurelius Victor (*de Caes*. 33.8) has the correct version; in the *Epit. de Caes*. (32.4) he becomes Aelianus; otherwise the variants L. Aelianus, A. Lollianus, and simply Lollianus occur in other sources (Eutropius 9.9.1; *HA* Gallienus 21.5; Thirty Tyrants 3.7; 4.1; 5.1; 5.4; 5.5; 5.8; 6.3; 8.1; 31.2; Claudius 7.4). On the defeat of Laelianus and the subsequent death of Postumus and his son see Aurelius Victor (*de Caes*. 33.8); Eutropius (9.9.1); *HA* (Thirty Tyrants 3.7); Orosius (7.22.11); König (1981, 132–6). Marius' reign was short, but not as short as the few days allowed him in the sources (Aurelius Victor *de Caes*. 33.9–11; Eutropius 9.9.2; *HA* Thirty Tyrants 8.1–12; Orosius 7.22.11). Drinkwater (1987, 35) suggests that he may have reigned for about twelve weeks, since he survived long enough to issue coins, which are superior to Laelianus' coins (Cizek 1994, 75; *RIC* V.2 pp. 376–8). Drinkwater (1987, 35; 90; 160; 177) says that Marius was a stop-gap army figure hastily chosen to fill the void after the failure of the revolt by Laelianus and the death of Postumus; with his close-cropped hair on his coin portraits he is closer to the Illyrian Emperors than to those of the Gallic regime.

51 M. Piavonius Victorinus was consul as colleague of Postumus in 268 (Christol 1997, 156; *CIL* II 5736 which König 1981, 143 dates to 267). See also *CIL* XIII 9040; XIII 8959 = *ILS* 564; *PIR2* III 38. Victorinus became Emperor in the late autumn 269, before 9 December of that year; this is established by working backwards from his third

year of tribunician power dated from 10 December 270 to 9 December 271, so the first was dated from whenever he came to the throne until 9 December 269; see König (1981, 143). Placidianus was successively prefect of the *vigiles*, Praetorian Prefect, and consul in 273 with Tacitus, possibly in absentia; see Howe (1942, 82 n.54); König (1981, 149–52). He was sent by Claudius II to guard the Alpine passes, to ensure the peace of Italy during the Danube campaign against the Goths. The inhabitants of the city of Autun, the capital of the Aedui, perhaps mistook the initial success of Placidianus in gaining control of part of Narbonensis as a sign that reintegration with the Empire was about to take place (Drinkwater 1987, 37). They revolted against Victorinus and were put under siege and severely punished. Their loyalty to the Roman Empire was not forgotten by the later panegyrists, one of whom spoke of the *fraternitas Aeduorum* (*Pan. Lat.* 8.4.3). At the end of the fourth century the poet Ausonius (*Parentalia* 4.1–16) related with pride that members of his family were proscribed by Victorinus and Tetricus (Loriot and Nony 1997, 79–80 no. 39).

52 Victorinus seems to have been killed in a simple hasty act of revenge, and his murderers made no plans for any successor (Drinkwater 1987, 38). When Victorinus died his mother Victoria held the Gallic Empire together until her chosen candidate P. Esuvius Tetricus, governor of Aquitania, became Emperor (Drinkwater 1987, 37–44; König 1981, 158–67); the exact date is not recorded, but it was in spring 271 (König 1981, 161). Tetricus' titles appear on *CIL* XIII 8927: *Imp. Caes. C. Pius Esuvius Tetricus Pius Felix Invictus Augustus Pontifex Maximus*. See also *PIR2* 88 no. 99; *PLRE* 1, 885. He made his son Caesar, indicating that he intended the boy to succeed him (Aurelius Victor *de Caes.* 33.14; Drinkwater 1987, 40–1). Spain rejoined the Emperor Claudius, as did Strasbourg (Cizek 1994, 117; 261 n.10). Britain remained loyal to Tetricus, as shown by *RIB* 605 = *ILS* 2548 from Lancaster, *RIB* 2241 from Lincoln, and *RIB* 1885 from Birdoswald, where the cohort is named for him; see also Loriot and Nony (1997, 79 no. 38 C–E). As his grip on his Gallic Empire weakened the propaganda messages on Tetricus' coins increased in tenor (Drinkwater 1987, 40; 185). The coins also proclaim a German victory, recording the fighting as Tetricus journeyed from Aquitania to Trier, where he set up his headquarters. The story that there was no battle at Chalôns-sur-Marne is probably a fabrication (König 1981, 177; Drinkwater 1987, 42). Aurelius Victor (*de Caes.* 35.4) says that Tetricus wrote to Aurelian to ask him to rescue him, quoting Virgil (*Aeneid* 6.365); other authors relay the same tale (Eutropius 9.13.2; *HA* Thirty Tyrants 24.3; Orosius 7.23). Up to February 274 the Lyons mint coined for Tetricus, but by March 274 it was coining for Aurelian (Cizek 1994, 121).

53 On Aurelian's triumph see Cizek (1994, 153–5). Zosimus (1.61.1) says that Aurelian was welcomed enthusiastically by the people and Senate, but he puts the triumph before the fall of the Gallic Empire, which is chronologically impossible, since Eutropius (9.12.2) and *HA* (Thirty Tyrants 30.27) both affirm that Tetricus marched with Zenobia in the triumphal procession. *HA* (Aurelian 33.2) describes the magnificence of the triumph. Tetricus retained his position and privileges and was appointed *corrector Lucaniae* (Cizek 1994, 156; Aurelius Victor *de Caes.* 35.5; Eutropius 9.13.2; *HA* Thirty Tyrants 24–5). Britain returned to the fold voluntarily, but an inscription refers to Aurelian as *Britannicus Maximus* (Cizek 1994, 120; *CIL* Suppl. 12333). The army was split up in Gaul so that there could be no collusion and rebellion, and Probus was put in charge of reconstituting the frontiers (Aurelius Victor *de Caes.* 35.3; *Epit. de Caes.* 35.7; *HA* Thirty Tyrants 24.4; *HA* Probus 12.3–4; Orosius 7.23.5). Aurelian had reunified the Empire and earned his title *Restitutor Orbis* emblazoned on inscriptions all over the Empire; see Loriot and Nony (1997, 113 nos. 66–7; *CIL* VI 1112ff; XII 5561 = XVII 172; VIII 10217).

54 On the evacuation of Dacia in general see Homo (1904, 313–21) who dates it to 275; Cizek (1994, 123–52). Five out of the six sources that mention the evacuation maintain that there was a partial abandonment under Gallienus; on the texts see Syme (1971a, 223); Cizek (1994, 264 n.20). Aurelius Victor (*de Caes.* 33.3) chooses his words with care,

insisting that the Romans left the province, and not that they lost it; Eutropius (9.8.2; 9.15.1) says that Aurelian could not defend Dacia so he brought the Romans out and settled them in Moesia; Jordanes (*Rom.* 217) blames Gallienus for leaving half of it, while Aurelian brought the troops out. *HA* (Aurelian 39.7) puts none of the blame onto Gallienus for an initial abandonment of Dacia. Modern authors have dated the evacuation to 270–1, early in Aurelian's reign when he was establishing himself in power and fighting the Goths (Cizek 1994, 262 n.5); Mattingly (*CAH* XII, 301) follows this dating. There is more support now for 274–5, not least because the ancient sources discuss the evacuation towards the end of Aurelian's reign (Cizek 1994, 125; 262 n.6; Homo 1904, 314), but since chronology is not a strong point nor the most important concern among the ancient sources, the argument cannot be sustained on these grounds alone. The middle date of 272 has more credibility, combined with the war against the Carpi and the need to go back to the east. Aurelian took the title *Carpicus Maximus* in 272, the most likely context for the sudden ending of the war and the surrender of Dacian territory to the Carpi and the Goths (Cizek 1994, 127); Christol (1997, 159) thinks that the evacuation was completed before Aurelian went back to the east in 273. For the coin hoard from Visoara see Cizek (1994, 125–7; 262 n.7 for references). *HA* (Aurelian 39.7) says that the new province divided the two Moesias. At some time after Aurelian's reign but before 285, the new Dacia was divided into two provinces (Christol 1997, 150). Coins of Aurelian carry the legend *Dacia Felix* (*RIC* V.1 Aurelian 253 no. 108).

55 The inhabitants of the old province of Dacia displayed no awareness of impending disaster; there were no sudden flights and destruction of property (Cizek 1994, 123–5). It was a purely military decision to withdraw the troops to defend the Danube; Aurelian strengthened the fortresses of Ratiaria and Oescus (Christol 1997, 151). The capital was at Serdica (modern Sofia) on the road from Viminacium to Byzantium (Christol 1994, 150). Though it has been postulated that there was a treaty with the Goths, who said that Aurelian had called upon them to fight in the east, Cizek (1994, 145–6) doubts that there was any such formal agreement.

56 It is not possible to discern how many civilians followed the army out of Dacia; it is clear that there was no mass emigration, since there is evidence of continuity of settlement in Dacian villages and farms; the evacuation may not at first have been intended to be a permanent measure (Cizek 1994, 142–5). There may be a slight bias in interpretation since connections with the Roman past are strongly emphasised in Romania, as the very name of the country suggests. The pagan religion survived longer than in other parts of the Empire; Christianity made little headway in Dacia until the fifth century (Cizek 1994, 143).

57 On Aurelian's titles as evidenced by epigraphy see Sotgiu (1961). Epithets like *Victoriosissimus* and *Gloriosissimus, Fortissimus*, and *Indulgentissimus* appear in inscriptions e.g.: *ILS* 578; 579. The Emperor is eternal, undefeated (*CIL* XI 6308 = *ILS* 583; *CIL* XI 6309). He is restorer of the world (*Restitutor Orbis*) (*CIL* XII 5456 = *ILS* 577; *CIL* XII 5561 = *CIL* XVII, 172; *CIL* VIII, 10217 = *ILS* 578; Christol 1997, 161; Loriot and Nony 1997, 113 no. 66). He is equated with Hercules (*CIL* XI 6308), divine (*CIL* VIII 25820) and a living god (*CIL* II 3832; VIII 4877 = *ILS* 585; *AE* 1938, 24). These inscriptions date from Aurelian's lifetime; *ILS* 5687 dates from the reign of Probus or Carus, so cannot be added to the list of inscriptions proclaiming Aurelian's divinity while he still lived. Contemporary coins proclaim that Aurelian was born a god *Deo et Domino Nato* (*RIC* V.1 Aurelian 299 nos. 305–6). Aurelian wore a diadem (Cizek 1994, 186) and cloth of gold (*Epit. de Caes.* 35.5).

58 On the reform of the coinage see Callu (1969, 274–305; 1975, 608–11); Christol (1997, 177–8); Cizek (1994, 172–5); Harl (1996, 143–8); Homo (1904, 155–75). The reform coincided with a rise in prices, whether cause or effect is debatable; it is possible that the numbers on the silver coinage, XX, XXI, etc., could be connected to this price rise in an attempt to establish an overestimated value for the coins (Christol 1997, 177); see Lo

Cascio (1993) and Carrié (1993) for the reforms and the price rises. Zosimus (1.61.3) says there was only a limited effect on commercial transactions. Revenues increased once Aurelian had defeated Palmyra (Cizek 1994, 172; *HA* Aurelian 39.6; Aurelius Victor *de Caes.* 35.7; Eutropius 9.15.1), and new taxes were raised (*HA* Aurelian 45.1).

59 Aurelian took care to provide food for the urban plebs. Homo (1904, 182–3) considered that Aurelian's schemes probably represented the greatest effort that was ever made to feed the Roman populace. The system was modelled on Trajan's alimentary scheme; Postumius Varus who had been city prefect in 271 is attested as *curator alimentorum* (*CIL* VI 1419). Aurelian stopped the distribution of grain, which had been irregular since the days of Severus Alexander (Pavis d'Escurac 1976, 35) and substituted the distribution of bread (*HA* Aurelian 47.1), using the wheat levied as part of Egyptian taxes. Special functionaries were engaged to oversee the distribution, and bakers were responsible to and directly supervised by the *praefectus annonae* (Pavis d'Escurac 1976, 266) who was himself supervised by the city prefect (Rickman 1980, 199). The free distribution of oil had been started by Severus (*HA* Septimius Severus 18.3), but it had lapsed so Aurelian reintroduced it. He added pork to the rations (Aurelius Victor *de Caes.* 35.7; *Epit. de Caes.* 35.6; *HA* Aurelian 35.2; 48.1), and tried to introduce free wine as part of his scheme to encourage vine growing in Italy and the provinces; it would have been a brilliant idea if it had succeeded, combining as it did the recultivation of abandoned lands and the supply of wine at no cost to the Treasury (Homo 1904, 180). In the end Aurelian compromised and sold the wine at a reduced price. The reforms went further than the provision and distribution of food, since Aurelian made arrangements for collection, transport and delivery to Rome as well as distribution in Rome; he created new posts for officials on the Nile and the Tiber to oversee operations (Homo 1904, 180; Pavis d'Escurac 1976, 228; Cizek 1994, 166). On the *annona* in general see Sirks (1991, esp. ch. 1 on transport and the *navicularii*), and on the corn supply of Rome in the late Empire see Rickman (1980, 198–209 esp. 187 and 197 on Aurelian's reforms).

60 On the cult of the Sun god in general see Halsberghe (1972); see also Cumont (1909); Nock (1947); Turcan (1978). For the religious developments in Aurelian's reign see Homo (1904, 184–97); Cizek (1994, 175–82). There were precedents for the elevation of the Sun god under Claudius and Quintillus, who honoured the god on their coinage (Cizek 1994, 177). Aurelian drew the priests of the cult of Sol Invictus from the aristocracy (*HA* Aurelian 35.3); though this is the only ancient source to mention it, inscriptions confirm that the senators functioned as priests (Cizek 1994, 181–2; *CIL* VI 1397; 1418; 1673; 1739; 1740; 2151; *CIL* X 5061). Aurelian's coinage honoured Sol with various titles; *Sol Invictus* and *Sol Conservator* (*RIC* V.1 Aurelian 309 no. 390); *Sol Dominus Imperii Romani* (*RIC* V.1 Aurelian 258; 264; 301 nos. 319 and 322). Cizek (1994, 179) says that there was no official form to the cult before 274; the first stage was to associate himself and his reign with the protective power of the Sun god, then the second stage began in 274 when the temple was consecrated. Building of the temple probably began in about 271. It is mentioned by most of the sources, situated in the Seventh Region of Rome on the *Campus Agrippae* (Chronographer 354; Aurelius Victor *de Caes.* 35.7; Eutropius 9.15.1; *HA* Aurelian 1.3; 25.6; 28.5; 35.3; 39.2; Zosimus 1.61.2).

61 The Persian regime was in difficulties in 274–5, so it was a favourable time to make war (Homo 1904, 322–3; Cizek 1994, 195). See Christol (1997, 181–2) on the persistent dangers from the east. On the Persian wars of the third century see Kettenhofen (1982).

62 Aurelian was a great admirer of Trajan, and may have already conducted a campaign against the Persians after the fall of Palmyra; coins display the legend *Victoria Parthica* (*RIC* V.1 292 no. 240; Cizek 1994, 193–4). *HA* (Aurelian 35.4) says that Aurelian assembled his army in Illyricum and declared war on the Persians (*Persis ... bellum indixit*). The assassination of the Emperor at Caenophrurium is described in several sources (*HA* Aurelian 35.4; Aurelius Victor 35.8; Eutropius 9.15.2; Zosimus 1.62.1; Lactantius *de Mort. Pers.* 6.2; Orosius 7.23.6). Not all the sources agree as to the precise

details; Zosimus (1.61.1–2) relays the story of Eros who forged the list of names of those on Aurelian's list; Aurelius Victor (*de Caes.* 35.8; 36.2) blames the plot on a secretary (*officium secretorum*); *HA* (Aurelian 35.5) says that a *notarius* hatched the plot and the man who killed Aurelian was called Mucapor. Cizek (1994, 197) speculates that the murderer may have been a Thracian; he also asks why the conspirators believed so readily that they were to be killed when Eros produced the list of names (1994, 198). Paschoud (1971, 171 n.91) speculates that the murderers used the event as the excuse they had been looking for all along, or even that they invented the story of Eros in order to provide themselves with a reason for the assassination.

63 Christol (1997, 182) opts for September 275 for the date when Aurelian was killed; Chastagnol (1980b, 76–7; 1994b, 1027–9) prefers October 275. In Egypt it was thought that Aurelian was still alive on 10 October 275 (*P. Oxy.* 1455). Cizek (1994, 196) follows Chastagnol's dating. Tacitus deified Aurelian, allegedly proposing the move immediately after the news reached Rome that Aurelian was dead, and before he was made Emperor himself (*HA* Aurelian 41.13); see also *HA* (Aurelian 37.2–4; 42.4); Eutropius (9.15). Some inscriptions survive naming Aurelian *Divus* (*CIL* VIII 10.961; 11.318); the law codes also name him *Divus* (*CJ* 4.12.63; 11.58.1; Cizek 1994, 201). On some inscriptions Aurelian's name is obliterated (*CIL* V 4319; III suppl. 12.736). Diocletian censured Aurelian for cruelty, but it is probable that the roles of previous Emperors were played down in Diocletian's rewriting of his arrival at the summit, and his need to portray himself as the saviour of the state. In assessing Aurelian's contribution to the revival of Rome at the end of the third century, it is not easy to escape the predominant influence of Diocletian and Constantine. Crees (1911) considered that Aurelian 'must be regarded as Rome's saviour', and Cizek (1994, 239–45) concludes that whilst Aurelian could have chosen an alternative path he did nothing to soften the growing despotism that his reign brought to the Roman world; his authoritarianism is undeniable, but he achieved reunification of the Empire and he strengthened it, enabling it to survive for another two centuries.

64 The soldiers were very unhappy about Aurelian's death and made it clear that they were not willing to accept any of the generals as Emperor (*HA* Aurelian 40.2; Tacitus 2.5). Marcus Claudius Tacitus (*PIR2* C 1036; *PLRE* Tacitus 3) may have been a native of one of the Danube provinces and was possibly one of Gallienus' generals, according to Syme (1971, 245–7), but this is disputed; see Chastagnol (1994b, 1030–1); Christol (1997, 182) thinks that Tacitus did not hail from the Danube regions, and may have been an equestrian who had been adlected to the Senate. There are those who disagree with the story that Tacitus was chosen by the Senate; Zonaras (12.28) admits that there was a military influence in the choice, by which he probably means the Praetorians (Cizek 1994, 208). *HA* (Probus 6.2–7) insists that Probus was the designated successor of Aurelian, but this is false because no one had been marked out during the reign (Cizek 1994, 202). The situation after Aurelian's death was probably quite complex, with embassies being sent back and forth between the Senate and the army; the sources indicate that the Senate was reluctant to appoint an Emperor and kept referring back to the soldiers (Aurelius Victor *de Caes.* 35.10; *HA* Aurelian 40.3; 41.3; Tacitus 2.6; Homo 1904, 325; Cizek 1994, 204). Without doubt there will have been a short period of time without an Emperor, and this interregnum of indeterminate length has caused much dispute among modern authors who try to interpret what the ancient sources mean when they describe such a period. Aurelius Victor (*de Caes.* 35.12) and *Epit. de Caes.* (35.10) describe a 'sort (*species*) of interregnum' while *HA* (Aurelian 40.4; Tacitus 1.1; 2.1; 2.6) says that it lasted for six months. Adding further confusion *HA* (Tacitus 14.5) says that the short reigns of Tacitus and Florian made it seem as though they were merely *interreges* between Aurelian and Probus; these two statements, that the interregnum lasted for six months and that Tacitus and Florian were like *interreges*, allow modern scholars to equate the six-month reign of Tacitus with the interregnum itself (Christol 1997, 182; Cizek 1994, 203–6).

65 Tacitus punished the conspirators who had murdered Aurelian (*HA* Aurelian 37.1; Tacitus 13.1; Aurelius Victor 36.2), but he presumably did not complete the task, since Probus is also credited with punishment of Aurelian's murderers (*HA* Probus 13.2; Zosimus 1.65.1–2). The supposed revival of senatorial influence when Tacitus became Emperor is not much in evidence; despite the fact that *ius proconsulare* was restored and the right of hearing appeals was granted to the city prefect, there was no resurgence of senatorial privileges (*CAH* XII, 311). Paschoud points out (1971, 172 n.92) that although Zosimus does not mention any such revival of senatorial influence it was nonetheless very real, although much exaggerated by such authors as Aurelius Victor (*de Caes.* 35.9–12), who thought that the senators allowed a great opportunity to pass them by, and by the *HA* where Tacitus is credited with much more than he achieved. Tacitus achieved some successes against the Goths as evidenced by Zonaras (12.28) and by the title *Gothicus Maximus* (*CIL* XII 5563; XVII 17 = *ILS* 591; Loriot and Nony 1997, 112 no. 65A). The choice of his kinsmen Florianus as Praetorian Prefect and Maximinus as governor of Syria Coele was unwise in the case of the former and disastrous in the case of the latter, on account of Maximinus' cruelty (Zosimus 1.63.2; Zonaras 12.28; Cizek 1994, 214; 216). Neither the place, Tarsus or Tyana, nor the cause of Tacitus' death is clear in the sources (*HA* Tacitus 13.2; *Epit. de Caes.* 36.2; Eutropius 9.16), leaving room for speculation about disease, accident, or murder. Zosimus (1.63.1) says that the Emperor was killed on his way back from the Black Sea campaign; he relates the murder to the cruelty and harsh rule of Maximinus, who was also killed, by some of the men who had murdered Aurelian. The last recorded document of Tacitus is dated 12 July 276 (Christol 1997, 182).

66 Marcus Annius Florianus (*PIR2* A 649; *PLRE* Florianus 6) is accused of seizing the throne as though it were his hereditary right (*HA* Tacitus 14.1; Probus 10.1.8; 11.3.4) without waiting for approval from the Senate. Aurelius Victor (*de Caes.* 36.2) is also sure that Florian was a usurper rather than the legitimate Emperor. Zonaras (12.29) and Zosimus (1.64.1) both say that the Senate appointed Florian. Paschoud (1971, 172–3 n.93) dates the acclamation of Florian and Probus to almost the same time, in June 276. In Egypt the regnal years of Probus are reckoned from summer 276; the earliest papyrus (*P. Strassb.* 30) to mention him dates from 7 September 276, when he is in his second year, beginning 29 August 276 in accordance with Egyptian reckoning. There is no mention of Florian in Egyptian coinage or papyri, which leads to the conclusion that Egypt declared for Probus immediately (Cizek 1994, 220–1; Christol 1997, 183–4). The war between Probus and Florian is described in most detail by Zosimus (1.64). The length of Florian's short reign is disputed. Zonaras (12.29) says that it lasted only 2–3 months; see also Eutropius (9.16); *HA* (Tacitus 14.2). *Epit de Caes.* (36.2) says that Florian committed suicide after 60 days; see also *HA* (Probus 10.1); Zosimus (1.64.2–4). Lafaurie (1965), followed by Paschoud (1971, 173 n.93) and Cizek (1994, 220), dates Florian's death to 5 September 276. On the reign of Florian and the remaining monuments to him see Sauer (1998).

67 Probus (*PIR2* A 1583; *PLRE* Probus 3; Crees 1911; Vitucci 1952) was in command of troops in the east when Tacitus died and Florian was declared Emperor, according to Zosimus (1.64.1–3). Zosimus is 'a source of first rate importance' (Crees 1911, 20), but the unfortunate lacunae at the end of Book I and the beginning of Book II make it very difficult to attempt any reconstruction of the reign of Probus, and the problem is compounded by the fact that the little information that survives is no longer based on the work of Dexippus, and Zosimus' continuator Eunapius did not regard the establishment of a strict chronology as his main purpose (Loriot and Nony 1997, 100). The coinage does nothing to establish a chronology either (Crees 1911, 17–18; Christol 1997, 184–5). From the works of Aurelius Victor and Eutropius it is clear that they both used a common source, but although they both overlap they do not retain the same details (Loriot and Nony 1997, 100–4). Crees (1911, 59–65) tabulated the main events in each

of the sources touching on the reign of Probus, a process which serves to highlight the similarities in the sources as well as their sometimes quite wide divergences.

68 The number of campaigns that Probus conducted on the Rhine frontier and in Gaul are not crystal clear, nor is it properly established which tribes he fought or in which order he fought them. Zosimus (1.67–8) describes two campaigns, one in which the Emperor took part personally and another where he was represented by a lieutenant; he then goes on to describe 'other wars'. First he defeated the Longiones and the Lugii; secondly he and his generals fought against the Franks, perhaps simultaneously in two theatres of war, and thirdly he fought a separate campaign against the Burgundians and Vandals; see Paschoud (1971, 173–5 n.96); Vitucci (1952, 40–5); Crees (1911, 101–2). Ridley (1982, 147 n.125) says that the tribal name Lugii is a collective term for all the south Germans including the Vandals; they were known to the Romans in the first century when the Lugii asked Domitian for assistance (Tacitus *Annals* 12.29–30; Dio 67.5.2). For Franks, Vandals and Burgundians see Zosimus (1.68.1–3); for Alamanni see *HA* (Probus 12.3). Paschoud (1971, 174 n.96) considers that Semno of the Longiones ought to be one of the nine kings who submitted to Probus, as recorded in the *HA* (Probus 13.5). According to Zosimus (1.67.1) Probus was compelled to assist the German cities, by which he presumably means Gallic cities, since his geographical knowledge of the west is never precise (Ridley 1982, 147 n.124). This ties in well with the assertion in *HA* (Probus 13.5–8) that Probus restored 60 towns in Gaul; by the time of the Emperor Julian this had increased to 70 towns (Crees 1911, 104). In Zosimus' account there is emphasis on the return of booty and prisoners, to which Semno agreed (Zosimus 1.67.3) but a chieftain called Igillus did not; Probus sent Igillus and the other captives to Britain where they helped to suppress a rebellion later on (1.68.3); in an earlier passage (1.66.2) where he groups all the revolts against Probus under one heading, Zosimus describes a revolt in Britain which was put down by Victorinus the Moor. Victorinus was rewarded with the consulship in 282 (Paschoud 1971, 173 n.65).

69 On the settlement of tribemen see Demougeot (1969, 535–50); Probus settled 100,000 Bastarnae in Thrace (*HA* Probus 18.1; Zosimus 171.1); this exercise was a successful one (Crees 1911, 140; Christol 1997, 247 n.12). Gepids and Vandals were settled inside the Empire (*HA* Probus 18.2–3), but this was not such a success since the Vandals profited from the distractions elsewhere in the Empire, and the Franks seized ships and returned home (Paschoud 1971, 177 n.100). The revolt of Palfurius or Palfuerius is described by *HA* (Probus 16–17), and that of Lydius by Zosimus (1.69.1–70.5). Ridley (1982, 148 n.127) disagrees with the theory that they are one and the same person, because among other reasons their deaths are quite different; see Paschoud (1971, 175–6 n.98; Rougé 1966a).

70 The revolt of Ptolemais (Zosimus 1.71.1) is dated to 280 by Paschoud (1971, 177 n.100). The Blemmyes are recorded by both Zosimus (1.7.1.) and *HA* (Probus 17.2) where it is said that the captured tribesmen featured in Probus' triumph. They had taken Coptos and Ptolemais, and though defeated by Probus they were troublesome once again under Diocletian (Crees 1911, 109). The revolt of Saturninus is described at some length in *HA* (Forty Tyrants 7–11), and briefly by Aurelius Victor (*de Caes*. 37.2–4); *HA* (Probus 18.4–5), and Zosimus (1.66.1). An aureus gives his name as Julius Saturninus (Paschoud 1971, 173 n.95). He was killed by the eastern troops before Probus had to wage war. In the *HA* the revolt is listed before that of Proculus (Eutropius 9.17) and Bonosus (Aurelius Victor *de Caes*. 37.2–4); Vitucci (1952, 58–61) dates the Saturninus revolt to 280–1.

71 Zosimus does not mention the triumph of Probus in 281 (Paschoud 1971, 177 n.101). *HA* (Probus 19) says that the triumph was celebrated over the Germans and the Blemmyes; see Vitucci (1952, 115–22) on this and the preparations for the Persian campaign. On vine growing in the provinces, *HA* (Probus 18.1) says that he permitted Gaul, Spain and Britain to have vines; Eutropius (9.17) mentions Gaul and Pannonia and says that the Emperor used soldiers to plant vines on the hills in Moesia. Aurelius Victor (*de Caes*.

37.2–4) also documents the use of soldiers on civilian projects, in this case draining the marshes near Sirmium; he also says that Probus boasted that soon there would be peace and no need for an armed force in the Empire. See Crees (1911, 125; 138) on Probus' treatment of the army.

72 When he was preoccupied with the Rhine frontier and other wars, Probus made peace with the Persians (*HA Probus* 18); see Dodgeon and Lieu (1991, 111–12). There was no Persian provocation when Probus decided to attack. The internal troubles in the Persian Empire are mentioned in the life of the Emperor Carus (*HA Carus* 8), but there is nothing about such problems in the *HA* concerning Probus (Crees 1911, 124). Probus held the title *Parthicus Adiabenicus* (*AE* 1975, 765; Winter 1988, 111). All the sources agree on the death of Probus, who was killed by his own soldiers at Sirmium after taking refuge in the 'iron tower' (*HA Probus* 21.2; Aurelius Victor *de Caes.* 37.4; Eutropius 9.17).

73 Marcus Aurelius Carus, or perhaps Marcus Aurelius Numerius Carus (*PIR2* A 1475; *PLRE* Carus). On the life of Carus in the *HA* Chastagnol has produced several studies (1970; 1976; 1980a; 1994a; 1994b). He was a native of Narbonne in Gaul, not an Illyrian soldier as some authorities (Syme 1971a, 247) would have it (Chastagnol 1980a, 50–9; Loriot and Nony 1997, 104–6 nos. 56–9; Christol 1997, 185). He probably revolted before the death of Probus, who was killed between September and December 282. Aurelius Victor (*de Caes.* 37.5) complains that the army took away from the Senate the right to appoint the Emperor; Chastagnol (1980a, 49–50) agrees with this statement, because the reality of the situation was that the Senate merely acquiesced in the army's choice, instead of taking the initiative. Zonaras (12.20) says that Carus always intended to go to Rome, but in fact he never did. Carinus (*PIR2* A 1473; *PLRE* Carinus) went there instead (Christol 1997, 187; 248 n.21) when he married Magnia Urbica (*ILS* 610; Christol 1997, 249 n.22). The poet Nemesianus (or Olympias as he is sometimes known) devotes several lines of his *Cynegeticon* (64–85) to a description of the glories of the Persian campaign, and to an imaginary scene where Carinus and Numerianus are welcomed back to Rome.

74 According to the *HA* (*Carus* 5.4) and Zonaras (12.30) Carus is said to have had a military and civilian career, but these statements should be treated with a healthy scepticism (Christol 1997, 248 n.20; Barnes 1972, 152–3). Carus was never consul (Christol 1997, 185). The dates when Carinus and Numerianus were made Augusti is not clear; the debate is outlined by Christol (1997, 187–8).When Carus went to the east and Carinus to the west the ancient sources imply that there was a division of territory on the lines of the later division of the Empire (*HA Carus* 7.1; 16.2) but this is not the case (Christol 1997, 249 n.22; Chastagnol 1980b, 79; 1976 84–90; 1983a, 99–113). Carus celebrated his eastern campaign with the adoption of the title *Parthicus Maximus* (Zonaras 12.30; Aurelius Victor *de Caes.* 38; Eutropius 9.18), harking back to the Parthian regime rather than the Persian Empire. See also *CIL* VIII 12522 = *ILS* 600; *IGR* I.114.

75 Carus' victory held long-lasting importance, and it enabled Diocletian to come to a diplomatic understanding with the Persians; Winter (1988, 141) says that there was an agreement in 288. The death of Carus earned more fame in the fourth century than it did in the third; Sidonius Apollinaris (*Poems* 23, 88–96) addresses Consentius of Narbonne, reminding him of the hero Carus, a native of the same city; see also Synesius (*de Reg.* 18); Loriot and Nony (1997, 104–6 nos. 56–9); *HA* (*Carus* 8.2; 8.7). Carus' younger son Marcus Aurelius Numerius Numerianus (*PIR2* A 1564; *PLRE* Numerianus) was probably killed by the Praetorian Prefect Aper, who is variously named Lucius or Arrius Aper (Christol 1997, 190).

4 A WORLD GEARED FOR WAR: 284–324

1 Eutropius (9.19.2) says that Diocles was born in Dalmatia, into a low-class family, but beyond these details virtually nothing is known of his origins. The date of his birth is not established except that it must have been some time after 230. His early career is also

obscure; Zonaras (12.31) mentions a command in Moesia, and then there is nothing to fill the gap in knowledge until Aurelius Victor (*de Caes*. 39.1) affirms that Diocles was the commander of the *protectores domestici* of Numerianus. *P. Oxy.* 47 shows that Diocletian was still known in Egypt as Diocles as late as March 285 (Williams 1985, 240 n.37). Diocletian's full name was Gaius Aurelius Valerius Diocletianus (*CIL* III 22); for his name and titles see Barnes (1982, 4; 18). Diocletian killed Aper with his own hand in front of all the soldiers (*HA* Carus 13).

2 The soldiers declared Diocles Emperor 20 November 284 (Barnes 1982, 4 n.4 quoting *P. Beatty Panopolis* 2.162–4; 170; 187–8; 199; 260–1). The new Emperor made himself consul with Caesonius Bassus, who is identified with L. Caesonius Ovinius Manlius Rufinianus Bassus, who became *praefectus urbi* in 285, probably after the defeat of Carinus (*AE* 1964 223; *PIR2* C 212; *PLRE* Bassus 18). Marcus Aurelius Julianus (*PIR2* A 1538; *PLRE* Julianus 24 and 38) is described as Sabinus Julianus by Zosimus (1.73.1) and *Epit. de Caes*. (38.6). He was responsible as *corrector* for the whole of northern Italy; from there he extended his power over Pannonia and began to issue coins from the mint at Siscia (*RIC* V.2, 593–4). The revolt is to be dated after the death of Numerianus and the accession of Diocletian, though the sources make it seem that it occurred anterior to the death of Carus. The battle between Carinus and Diocletian is not securely located because of the confusion in the sources (*HA* Carus 18; Aurelius Victor *de Caes*. 39.1; Eutropius 9.20). Williams (1985, 38) settles for Margus near Belgrade, but admits that there may have been more than one battle (Seston 1946, 53). Tiberius Claudius Aurelius Aristobulus (*PIR2* C 806; *PLRE* Aristobulus) was confirmed in his office as Praetorian Prefect and consul by Diocletian (Aurelius Victor *de Caes*. 39.15). He was proconsul of Africa 290 to 294 and *praefectus urbi* from January 295 to February 296 (Barnes 1982, 97).

3 Williams (1985, 41) maintains that Diocletian did not go to Rome because he was committed to his policy of removing the seat of government and of divorcing senators from any share in it, but it is unlikely that he had crystallised such a policy at this early date. Chastagnol (1982, 93–4) also affirms that Diocletian did not visit Rome; Barnes (1982, 50; 1996, 537) suggests that Diocletian may have visited northern Italy, and Christol (1997, 192; 250 n.3) points out that the series of coins minted at about this time could be an *adventus* series celebrating the arrival of the Emperor.

4 Maximian (*PLRE* Maximianus 8) added Valerius to his name when he was made Caesar, 21 July 285 (Barnes 1982, 4 n.5; 57); see Aurelius Victor (*de Caes*. 39.1). Eutropius is the only source for Maximian as Caesar, and since there are no confirmatory coins or papyri, modern authors have postulated that Maximian may never have been Caesar, but was Augustus from the beginning, or at least as a reward for suppressing the Bagaudae, perhaps without having been Caesar (Nixon and Rodgers 1994, 47). For those who accept that Maximian was made Caesar, the exact date is disputed; see Kolb (1987, 22–67) for discussion and synopsis of theories; see also Christol (1997, 195; 250 n.4); Barnes (1976, 175; 1996, 537–8); Chastagnol (1967, 55–6). Kolb (1987, 44–5), followed by Nixon and Rodgers (1994, 45), points out that the papyrological evidence (*P. Lond.* 710) used by Seston to prove that Maximian was *filius Augusti* is suspect. When Diocletian and Maximian were both Augusti they were described as brothers (*Pan. Lat.* 10 (2).1.5; 4.1; 9.1; 9.3; 10.6). Jovius and Herculius are strictly adjectival names meaning of Jupiter and of Hercules, and could be applied to military units (Nixon and Rodgers 1994, 44–5; Kolb 1987, 58 n.262). The use of these titles and the association with the gods probably began quite early. Aurelius Victor (*de Caes*. 39.18) says that it all began after Maximian defeated the Bagaudae; Nixon and Rodgers (1994, 49–50) point out that coins issued by Diocletian alone do not bear the name Jovius but that as soon as the coinage appears for the two Augusti together the titles are included, so there is every reason to suppose that the religious associations and the titles are closely bound up with the elevation of Maximian to Augustus.

5 On Maximian's campaign against the Bagaudae see Seston (1946, 57–81). On Amandus

and Aelianus see Barnes (1982, 10). Gallétier (1949, 14) in *Pan. Lut.* points out that nowhere in the panegyric to Maximian are the Bagaudae mentioned by name, but are called giants or monsters; quite appropriate, given that Maximian was equated with Hercules, as a comparison with the monsters that Hercules defeated (see *Pan. Lat.* 10(2).4). If the supposition that Maximian was made Augustus after the suppression of the Bagaudae (see note 81 below), then the whole campaign may have been over by the spring of 286, perhaps even at the end of 285.

6 On the Franks and Saxon pirates see Demougeot (1969, 25–30); Seston (1946, 69–73). Carausius may have been appointed by Carus or Carinus (Christol 1997, 193), but the consensus of opinion is that Maximian commissioned him (Barnes 1982, 10–11). Aurelius Victor (*de Caes.* 39.19) and Eutropius (9.21) say that Carausius was ordered by Maximian to build a fleet and to operate against the pirates, but instead he rebelled against him. The date is not attested and can be given only as sometime in 286, associated by some authors with the elevation of Maximian to Augustus, which could have come about because Carausius had already rebelled and Diocletian needed a counterweight of his own choosing (see note 9 below), or alternatively it was the elevation of Maximian that prompted Carausius to raise himself to Augustus to put him on an equal plane; the argument is somewhat circular to say the least; see Nixon and Rodgers (1994, 50). Carausius' full name is not known for certain; on inscriptions it is given in abbreviated form as Maus. (*RIB* 2291 = *ILS* 8928), usually expanded to Mausaeus. Salway (1991, 287) equates Diocletian's title *Britannicus Maximus* with exploits of Carausius in defending Britain; Diocletian took the title before 301, since it is attested on the currency edict and the price edict of that year (Barnes 1982, 18–19). Maximian was made Augustus 1 April 286, after the suppression of the Bagaudae (Salway 1991, 287; Christol 1997, 195). The earliest attested source for Maximian as Augustus derives from *BGU* 922 = 24 May 286; *P. Oxy.* 1260 = 12 June 286 (Barnes 1982, 4 n.6; 1996, 538). Kolb (1987, 33–4; 49) disagrees with the date 1 April. Some scholars suggest that the rebellion of Carausius had a direct influence on the elevation of Maximian and the Tetrarchic system that evolved later (Seston 1946, 57–81 esp. 74–6; Williams 1985, 48; 241 n.5; Christol 1997, 195; 250 n.7). Carausius is equated with the pirates in contemporary literature (*Pan. Lat.* 11 (3).5.3; 7.1–2); see Nixon and Rodgers (1994, 79; 107–8) where it is suggested that Carausius could have been the last prefect of the *Classis Britannica* or the first *dux tractus Armoricani et Nervicani*.

7 For Carausius see Shiel (1977); Elbern (1984, 9–11; 38); Casey (1994). Most of the evidence for Carausius derives from his coinage which was of good quality (Salway 1991, 299); he minted at London and Colchester, probably at Rouen (*RIC* V.2 Carausius 516) and possibly at Boulogne (*RIC* V.2 523 nos. 702–5) (Barnes 1982, 11). The coins list the legions over which Carausius had some control, but it is not known if he commanded whole legions or just parts of them, and there is a puzzling omission in that *VI Victrix* from York is missing (Salway 1991, 297). Carausius styled himself the restorer of Britain (*Resitutor Britanniae*) and gave out via quotations from Virgil (*Aeneid* 2.282.3) that he was the one for whom everyone had been waiting (*Expectate Veni*) (*RIC* V.2, 554; Kent 1978, p. 322 no. 566). He also advertised himself as the brother of the Emperors, putting Maximian and Diocletian in second place after himself (*Carausius et fratres sui*) and on the reverse proclaiming *Pax Auggg.* to indicate that there were three Emperors (*RIC* V.2, 550; Kent 1978, p. 322 no. 570); see also Salway (1991, 297–9); Barnes (1982, 10–11). Maximian was preparing for a campaign against Carausius for which the panegyricist of 289 held out great hopes (*Pan. Lat.* 10 (2).12.1ff), but there is no mention of any campaign, successful or otherwise in the panegyric to Maximian in 291 (Nixon and Rodgers 1994, 107). The panegyric to Constantius (8 (5).12.2) dated to 297 refers to the bad weather as a cause of the failure of Maximian's attempt (see Nixon and Rodgers 1994, 107; Gallétier 1949, 43).

8 The Saxon Shore forts have been studied by several scholars. Johnson (1976, 94–113) puts five of the forts into the narrow date range from 276 to 285, which places them anterior

to the insurrection of Carausius; he suggests that Reculver and Brancaster were the earliest forts in the chain, then Burgh Castle and Dover followed, with Richborough, Lympne and Portchester added sometime later; see also Lander (1984, 173). In another work Johnson (1989, 43) dates all the forts to the broad range between 250 and 300. Mann (1989, 2; 10–11) emphasises the fact that the forts were oriented to naval operations, but that does not necessarily mean that they were all originally built with a unified plan or purpose in mind. Johnson (1989, 30) investigates the most likely contexts when the forts were amalgamated into a unified command.

9 Williams (1985, 48; 241 n.5) following Seston (1946, 57–81) assumes that the actions of Carausius influenced Diocletian's decision to elevate Maximian, who was made Augustus on 1 April 286 (Barnes 1982, 4 n.5). See also Barnes (1982, 10–11) for discussion of the date when Carausius declared himself Augustus, which is worked out by extrapolating backwards from the date of Carausius' death; he was killed after Constantius was made Caesar 1 March 293, so subtracting the six or seven years of his rule in Britain attested respectively by Aurelius Victor (*de Caes.* 39.40) and Eutropius (9.22.2), the conclusion is that at some point during 286 Carausius withdrew to Britain and made himself Augustus. Salway (1991, 289) suggests that the army officers in Britain were already compromised and so decided to go along with Carausius. Elbern (1984, 47) discounts Seston's theory that the merchant class in Britain had the power to influence Carausius to declare himself Augustus.

10 In the panegyrics there is reference to an alliance between Maximian and Gennobaudes (*Pan. Lat.* 10 (2).3), the latter being equated with the Frankish king referred to in another speech (*Pan. Lat.* 11 (3).5.4). Both Maximian and Constantius are credited with the settlement of Franks, Chamavi and Friesians between the Rhine and the Waal from Nijmegen to Utrecht, and on vacant lands in Gaul (Williams 1985, 51; 73). The insecurity of the provinces is emphasised in the contemporary sources (*Pan. Lat.* 10 (2).6). Maximian adopted a scorched-earth policy in dealing with the Alamanni, whose lands were wasted (*Pan. Lat.* 8 (5).2; 10; Williams 1985, 45–51).

11 On the failure of Maximian's expedition against Carausius see Christol (1997, 193–5), Williams (1985, 55–6; 242 n.21) and note 7 above.

12 The fact that Diocletian fought the Sarmatians in 285 is deduced from the number of Sarmatian victory titles that he took. Barnes (1982, 50 n.23) explains that the discovery of the inscription from Aphrodisias of Diocletian's edict on prices made it clear that Maximian held the title *Sarmaticus Maximus* for only the third time in 301, while Diocletian was *Sarmaticus Maximus IV*. This means that Maximian was one step behind Diocletian, as he was in the case of the German victory titles, so working back from the Sarmatian titles of 294 and 289, when Maximian would be *Sarmaticus Maximus II* and *I*, there is one more to account for in Diocletian's titles, which must be projected back to 285. See also Barnes (1982, 27; 255 table 5) and Williams (1985, 52; 242 n.15).

13 On the eastern settlement with Persia see Winter (1988, 137–9), who points out that the references in the panegyric of 289 (*Pan. Lat.* 10 (2).7.5; 9.2; 10.6) to *dona Persica* and the voluntary submission of the Persians most probably indicate that the Persians made some kind of offering to Diocletian and that there was an informal agreement after protracted negotiation, probably in 288. See also Barnes (1982, 51) who dates this to 287. By 298 Diocletian took the title *Persicus Maximus* (*ILS* 618); see Chaumont (1969, 93ff). Winter (1988, 150–1) says that although Diocletian did not follow up Carus' victory with an aggressive attack, he took the earliest opportunity to strengthen Rome's position in the east. While Vahram II was occupied with his internal problems, Diocletian installed Tiridates in Armenia. He fortified Circesium on the Euphrates (Ammianus Marcellinus 23.5.2). On Diocletian's Sarmatian victory titles see Barnes (1982, 17–29; 255 table 5).

14 Barnes (1982, 51) dates the Saracen war to summer 290, specifically May or June; see *Pan. Lat.* (11 (3).4.2; 7.1 and 8 (5).3.3). The celebrations in Milan are described by Williams (1985, 56–8); see also Barnes (1982, 52) and *Pan. Lat.* (11 (3).8.1).

15 König (1974; 1986) suggested that it was Maximian's ambitious plans for himself and Constantius that forced Diocletian to promote Galerius to balance the situation. Seston (1946, 353) thought that Diocletian promoted Maximian only because he was faced with war in the eastern half of the Empire and also the rebellion of Carausius, and then in 293 he needed further help so he promoted Constantius and Galerius, but he did so 'de mauvaise grâce'. See also Nixon and Rodgers (1994, 44) who discuss the circumstances and point out that there was nothing in Maximian's track record so far to suggest that he was disruptive or disloyal.

16 Seston (1946, 353) thought that the Caesars were created at different dates, according to circumstances pertaining in the east and west, so there was no co-ordinated plan formulated at the beginning and steadily unfolded as time went on; according to Seston, Galerius was invested 21 May at Nicomedia. Barnes (1982, 52; 62 n.73) dates the event to 1 March, the investiture taking place simultaneously at Milan and Sirmium, the latter deduced from the movements of Diocletian, and the date because the *dies imperii* of Galerius was 1 March. The *Chronicon Pascale* (*Chron. Min.* 1.229) gives the date 21 May that Seston used; Barnes suggests that it was the date when the laurelled portrait of the Emperor arrived in Alexandria. The marriages of the Caesars are sometimes dated to 293 as though their investiture and their marriages were simultaneous and related events. Barnes (1982, 37) points out that Constantius married Theodora before 21 April 289, and though the date of Galerius' marriage is not known the tradition that he divorced his first wife in 293 to marry Valeria is not valid (Barnes 1982, 38 n.47).

17 All the Emperors shared the same victory titles; Constantius for instance took the title *Persicus Maximus* though he had not campaigned in the east (Barnes 1982, 17–29; 254–7 tables 4–7). Despite the apparent equality with regard to titles, Constantius was senior to Galerius; on inscriptions his name always took precedence; see Christol (1997, 196); Chastagnol (1967, 57–9; 1982, 99–100); Nixon and Rodgers (1994, 50–1). Territorial boundaries were not strictly drawn between the four main areas where the Tetrarchs operated. Aurelius Victor (*de Caes.* 39) indicates the headquarters and the regions that they controlled; according to his description, Constantius was based at Trier and took charge of the territory beyond the Gallic Alps; Maximian ruled Africa and Italy from Milan; Galerius was based at Thessalonika and controlled Greece and the Danube provinces; Diocletian at Nicomedia controlled Asia, Egypt and the east. Lactantius (*de Mort. Pers.* 7) accused Diocletian of multiplying the civil and military personnel in each of the four areas where the Tetrarchs governed. Neither Aurelius Victor nor Lactantius were correct; there was no division of the Empire into four separate units and though there was probably an increase in personnel because each of the Tetrarchs required their own entourage and staff, a fourfold multiplication of the armies and administrators would have been impossible; Cameron (1993, 33) says that Lactantius' statement was 'more a jibe than a sober estimate'. Diocletian remained the senior partner, and could override decisions of the other Tetrarchs (Barnes 1982, 3), but it is not known how far the other Tetrarchs could interfere in the zones not under their control (Barnes 1982, 42). See also Williams (1985, 67; 243 n.12).

18 On the abdication of Diocletian in general, the proclamation of the Caesars and the reliability of Lactantius, see Rougé (1992). Nixon and Rodgers (1994, 46–7) question whether Diocletian had a blueprint for the Tetrarchy and for his abdication as early as 284 or even as late as 293. At some time between then and the actual abdication, he started to build the palace at Split, which would have been a lengthy enough undertaking, so Diocletian presumably had it in mind, before he reached the watershed of 305, to retire there (Williams 1985, 65). Nixon and Rodgers (1994, 46; 188–90) acknowledge that the building of the palace will have taken a long time, but suggest that work could have continued after the abdication, and they accept Lactantius' statement (*de Mort. Pers.* 18) that Diocletian fell ill. Lactantius also says that it was the pressure from the ambitious Galerius that finally decided Diocletian, because Galerius threatened to make war on Maximian.

19 The lack of reliable sources makes it very difficult to establish a firm chronology for the major events of the Tetrarchy; see Barnes (1982); Kienast (1990, 262ff).

20 Constantius captured Boulogne by building a mole across the harbour (*Pan. Lat.* 8 (5).6–7; Williams 1985, 71; Barnes 1982, 60). Probably as a result of the loss of the Gallic harbour and town, Carausius was murdered by Allectus, his finance minister according to Aurelius Victor (*de Caes.* 39.41) or his ally (*socius*) according to Eutropius (9.22); see also Casey (1994); Salway (1991, 305); Williams (1985, 72). Constantius did not invade Britain immediately, but was occupied in Italy and Gaul (*Pan. Lat.* 6 (7).5.3; 7 (6).4.2; 8 (5).8–9; 9 (4).14.1; Barnes 1982, 60). Galerius was in Egypt probably from 293 to 295 (Barnes 1982, 62 nn.74–5 on the evidence of *P. Grenfell* 2.110 and *P. Oxy.* 43). On the forts in Sarmatian territory see *Chron. Min.* (1 p. 230) which mentions *castra facta in Sarmatia contra Acinco et Bononia*; Mócsy (1974, 269) equated these forts with the entries in the *Notitia Dignitatum*, listing a unit in one of the forts under the command of the *dux Pannonia Secundae*, namely *auxilia Augustensia contra Bononia in barbarico in castello Onagrino* (*Not. Dig. Oc.* XXXII 41), and another unit in a fort *contra Acinco in barbarico* under the command of the *dux Provinciae Valeriae* (*Not. Dig. Oc.* XXXIII 48).

21 For the aggressive actions of Narses see Williams (1985, 80). Galerius was probably still in Egypt in 295 (*P. Oxy.* 43). His Persian expedition met with defeat between Carrhae and the Euphrates (Aurelius Victor *de Caes.* 39.34; Eutropius 9.25; Ammianus 14.11.10; see also Christol 1997, 251 n.12; Schwartz 1974; Castritius 1971; Zuckerman 1994). In order to release Constantius for the British campaign Maximian took charge of the Rhine (*Pan. Lat.* 8 (5).13.3). The panegyric addressed to Constantius in 297 (*Pan. Lat.* 8 (5)) is the only detailed source for the reconquest of Britain (Nixon and Rodgers 1994, 106–8; see also Gallétier 1949, 76). On Allectus see Eutropius (9.22), who calls him an ally (*socius*) of Carausius; see also Seston (1946, 101–3); Salway (1991, 305–12); Casey (1994); Christol (1997, 197). On Constantius' campaign in Britain see Eichholz (1953); Salway (1991, 307–10). The medallion proclaiming that Constantius had returned the eternal light to Britain (*Redditor lucis aeternae*) was minted at Trier (*RIC* VI, 34); see Christol (1997, plate p. 198); Kent (1978, p. 324 no. 585).

22 Eutropius (9.22–3) describes the long siege of Alexandria after the revolt; on Domitianus and Achilleus see Barnes (1982, 54); Williams (1985, 81; 244–5 n.1). Maximian took troops from Germany and the Rhine to Mauretania, as witnessed by the presence in north Africa of a soldier from *Legio VIII Augusta* from Strasbourg, and German units at Tangier; see Christol (1997, 200); Speidel (1979; 1982; 1984, 406 quoting inscriptions of *II* and *III Italica* and *II Herculia* from Sétif, *AE* 1972, 709; 710; *CIL* VIII 8440, which Speidel associates with Maximian's campaign). See also Drew-Bear (1981); Warmington (1954); Zuckerman (1994, 67). Aurelius Victor (*de Caes.* 39.34) and Eutropius (9.24) describe Galerius' assembly of a new army.

23 Alexandria capitulated early in 298; administration of Egypt tightened, and Alexandria lost the right to issue coinage (Williams 1985, 81–2). Diocletian travelled up the Nile after the disturbances were over (*P. Oxy.* 1416; *IGR* 1.1291; Procopius *History of the Wars* 1.19.27). For Maximianus' Mauretanian campaigns see Christol (1997, 200; 251 n.15); *Pan. Lat.* (9 (4).21.2) for a reference to the defeat of the Moors by Maximian; *Pan. Lat.* (7 (6).8.6) for the campaign around Sirta and one against the mountain tribes; see also Seston (1946, 115–28); Rebuffat (1992); Benabou (1975); Barnes (1996, 542). For the source material for Galerius' and Diocletian's Persian campaign see Dodgeon and Lieu (1991, 125–39). For the history of the war see Winter (1988, 152–215); see also Christol (1997, 251 n.13); Seston (1946, 172–7). Lactantius (*de Mort. Pers.* 9.6) accuses Diocletian of cowardice, skulking in the background while Galerius did the fighting. On the treaty between Narses and Diocletian see Winter who dates it to 298 (1988, 169–70; 1989); the principal account of the negotiations and the treaty is to be found in *Petr. Patr.* (frgs. 13 and 14); see Dodgeon and Lieu (1991, 131–4). Aurelius Victor (*de Caes.* 39.34–6) describes the campaign and says that Galerius was keen to continue the war to annex

Persian territory, but was restrained by Diocletian; see also Eutropius (9.25) and Zonaras (12.31). Diocletian strengthened the eastern frontier after the war (Dodgeon and Lieu 1991, 136–8; Winter 1989; Williams 1985, 85).

24 Galerius received a hero's welcome in Antioch (Williams 1985, 86), then shortly afterwards he was called to the Danube to fight the Marcomanni (*Chron. Min.* 1.230; Lactantius 13.2). On the arch of Galerius at Thessalonika see Ramage and Ramage (1995, 274–5; figs 11.11; 11.12). Constantius fought against the Franks on the Rhine; see Barnes (1996). A victory over the Germans in the territory of the Lingones is recorded (*Pan. Lat.* 6 (7).6.2; *CIL* X 3343) and another near Vindonissa (*Pan. Lat.* 6 (7).6.3). In 303 Diocletian and Maximian celebrated their *vicennalia* in Rome (Williams 1985, 186ff; Christol 1997, 211–13 and pl 211 for coins; 252 n.9; Chastagnol 1983b, 14–17). There are some indications that Maximian promised that he would abdicate along with Diocletian in a ceremony in the Temple of Jupiter (*Pan. Lat.* 7 (6).15.16; Lactantius *de Mort. Pers.* 20.4).

25 Lactantius (*de Mort. Pers.* 17.3) describes Diocletian's exit from Rome; in a later passage (18.1) he records that Maximian and Galerius met at an unknown location; no one knows what they discussed; see Barnes (1982, 60; 64). On Diocletian's illness see Williams (1985, 188–9), and on the abdication and its consequences see Williams (1985, 186–200). Lacantius (*de Mort. Pers.* 18) says that Galerius forced Diocletian to abdicate, but at the same time he is certain that an arrangement was made between Maximian and Diocletian in 303 (*de Mort. Pers.* 20.4). On the abdication see (Nixon and Rodgers 1994, 188). Maximian was said to be reluctant to renounce power (Eutropius 9.27.1; Aurelius Victor *de Caes.* 39.48); Nixon and Rodgers (1994, 44–6) describe the emphasis in the sources on the harmonious relationship between Maximian and Diocletian, and question whether there was ever a long-term plan in Diocletian's mind for an eventual abdication. Williams (1985, 148–9; 192–4) and Nixon and Rodgers (1994, 189–90) point out that the palace at Split was not built on a sudden whim in 305, but had been planned long before; it was not a private retreat, but an Imperial palace built on the lines of a fortress. For an alternative interpretation that the palace was a indeed a private retreat, where Diocletian was a *privatus*, see Duval (1997, 143–7). On the palace itself see Wilkes (1993).

26 The new Caesars were both Galerius' men; Maximinus Daia was the son of Galerius' sister. His date of birth is sometimes given as 285, the date of Diocletian's accession, but it is more probable that this date was when he enrolled in the army, so he was probably born *c.*270 (Barnes 1982, 39); see also Aurelius Victor (*de Caes.* 40.1; 40.8); Zosimus (2.8.1); Lactantius (*de Mort. Pers.* 18.13–14). Lactantius describes Maximinus, career as *scutarius* in the Imperial guard, then Protector, tribune, and from there he was promoted directly to Caesar (*de Mort. Pers.* 19.16). Severus married Galerius' daughter (Williams 1985, 191; Barnes 1982, 39). He hailed from Illyricum (Aurelius Victor *de Caes.* 40.1) and was a friend of Galerius (Lactantius *de Mort. Pers.* 18.12). He may have been Galerius' Praetorian Prefect (Barnes 1982, 39). On Constantius' campaigns in Britain see *Pan. Lat.* (6 (7).7.1; *AE* 1961, 240). The tribes are named as Caledonians, and the first mention of the Picts appears (*Pan. Lat.* 6 (7).8.2). See also Salway (1991, 315–19).

27 See Seston (1946, 211–30) on the Emperors as Jove and Hercules. On Diocletian's reforms in general see Seston (1946, 261–352); Christol (1997, 208–9); Williams (1985).

28 Zosimus (2.34) praises Diocletian for securing the frontiers and protecting the Empire, contrasting the disastrous policy of Constantine whom he accuses of taking troops away from the frontiers and placing them in cities which did not need protection. On the army reforms see Seston (1946, 295ff); Williams (1985, 91–101); Southern and Dixon (1996, 23–33 for frontier armies and 15–17 for field armies). On the Rhine–Iller–Danube *limes* see Drack (1980); Drack and Fellmann (1988); Southern and Dixon (1996, 43 fig. 7). For the *Strata Diocletiana* see the study by van Berchem (1952); see also Isaac (1992, 164); Southern and Dixon (1996, 28–9 and fig. 3). The earthworks east of the Danube are described by Mócsy (1974, 269); see also Southern and Dixon (1996, 26, fig. 1).

29 On the change of shape in late Roman forts see Johnson (1983, 253); Southern and Dixon (1996, 24). Lander (1980) discussed the Diocletianic forts.

30 The responsibility for building city walls rested with the civil population; MacMullen (1976, 154) mentions corvées drawn from civilians for wall building. However, in some cases, like that of Grenoble, Imperial assistance is recorded (Johnson 1983, 62–3 n.45; *CIL* XII 2229), and there are instances of the army helping to build walls (Johnson 1983, 63). See also Liebeschuetz (1992, 4; 6). The major effect of the building of walls resulted in reduced perimeters of the cities, especially in Gaul (Liebeschuetz 1992, 8; 10; Duval 1959; Février 1973; Duby 1980). See Wightman (1985, 223–33) on the cities in Gaul, and Keay (1988, 178–81) for Spain. It has been argued that at least in some cities the areas that were walled functioned as citadels and a suburban population survived outside the walls; thus the reduced perimeters did not necessarily denote a corresponding reduction in population (Roblin 1951; 1965).

31 On Diocletian's army see Southern and Dixon (1996, 15–17; 23–33). Duncan-Jones (1978, 549) suggested that auxiliary units were possibly divided up and stationed in more than one fort, and that the cavalry vexillations on the frontiers were probably 500 strong.

32 Seston (1946, 298) suggests that the number of legions rose to about sixty in the period from 284 to 305. Jones (1964, 59–60) says that most of the 34 pre-Diocletianic legions survived. The fourth-century author Vegetius (*Epit. Rei Milt.* 2.3) complains of the difficulty of keeping the legions up to strength, and in other passages (1.7; 2.2) he says that Diocletian's legions were 6,000 strong; see Duncan-Jones (1978, 553). Mommsen (1889, 229; 254) thought that Diocletianic legions were only 1,000 strong; Jones (1964, 56; 68) and Seston (1946, 299) suggested that old legions remained at 6,000 but the new ones raised by Diocletian were 1,000 strong. For the legionary fortress at El Lejjun see Parker (1987); Kennedy and Riley (1990, 131). The fortress was the headquarters of the prefect of *Legio Quarta Martia* (*Notitia Dignitatum Or.* XXXVII 22). The *Notitia Dignitatum* (*Occ.* XXXV 17–19; 21–22) records *Legio II Italica* at several different forts, which could mean that there were detachments of about a thousand men at each location, and one of the same size in the field army, giving a total of 6,000 like the old legions; see Filtzinger *et al.* (1986, 99). Duncan-Jones (1978, 552) says that the legions listed in the *Notitia* are parts of units rather than whole ones.

33 The cavalry of Gallienus was described by George Cedrenus (*Compendium Historiarum* 454 in Migné vol. 121, 495) as the first mobile cavalry army, but he wrote at a time when the field armies were normal features of military defence. Seston (1946, 305–7) says that Carinus or Diocletian deprived it of its single commander because such a man was too powerful and therefore a potential rival for the throne. See also van Berchem (1952, 106–8; 1977a, 542). The existence of Diocletian's *comitatus* is not in doubt (Southern and Dixon 1996, 15–17; Jones 1964, 54), but it is not certain how it functioned. Nischer (1923, 10–12) thought that Diocletian's *comitatus* was made up of the Emperor's friends and advisers, as it always had been; he suggested that Diocletian introduced a system of reserves, but it was left to Constantine to create the mobile field army; Baynes (1925) and Parker (1935, 272–3) disagreed, arguing that it was Diocletian who introduced the mobile field armies. The cavalry, the vexillations and the *comites* of Diocletian are attested in 295 in Egypt, mentioned on a papyrus (*P. Oxy.* 43 col. 2, 24–8). *CIL* III 6196 = *ILS* 2781 records a soldier of *Legio XI Claudia* in the Imperial guard (*lectus in sacro comitatu lanciarius*); see Casey (1991, 10–12). *CIL* III 5565 = *ILS* 664 causes problems because of the abbreviated Latin of the inscription, which records the building of a temple by the *praepositus* of a Dalmatian cavalry unit. The unit is described collectively as *comit[es]* or *comit[atenses]*; either interpretation is possible. Hoffman (1969–70, 257–8) thinks that it should be interpreted as *comitatenses*, and that therefore Diocletian was responsible for the first mobile field army. Williams (1985, 93) disputed the existence of a central reserve, since each of the Tetrarchs had their own *comitatus*, and there was no central mobile army.

34 Assessment of Diocletian's achievements is bedevilled by the lack of reliable sources; most of the evidence is Constantinian or later in date (Jones 1964, 56). The division of the army into *limitanei* and *comitatenses* most probably took place under Constantine, and any description of frontier troops as *limitanei* before this date is anachronistic; for instance, the mention of *limitanei* in the army of Severus Alexander (*HA* Severus Alexander 58) is not to be taken as evidence that such troops had been established in the mid-third century. Van Berchem (1952, 21) suggests that Diocletian did put troops on the frontiers who were tied to the land, like the later *limitanei*, but not yet called by that name; the Byzantine chronicler John Malalas (*Chron.* 12.308) attributes such troops to Diocletian. Warmington (1953, 173–4) disagrees, because the *alae* and *cohortes* are still found in expeditionary armies in Diocletian's reign; see Southern and Dixon (1996, 35). The concept of defence in depth was described by Luttwak (1976); see also Williams (1985, 91–101).

35 Williams (1985, 52; 94; 108–9) describes the separation of military and civil commands; the collection of the taxes became the responsibility of the *praeses*, which reduced the military pressure on tax collection; Williams suggests that the possibilities for armed rebellion were also reduced because the *dux* would have to form so many alliances with both military and civilian colleagues; this leaves out of the equation any deep-seated and/or widespread discontent that might have motivated a group effort at rebellion. The date when the changes were made in each part of the Empire is not known, but as early as 289 the contemporary sources speak of *duces* and *iudices* (*Pan. Lat.* (10 (2).3.3) indicating that the military *duces* were accepted as the norm by then and that the provincial governors whose main tasks were judicial were already installed in most provinces. There were still some small provinces such as Mauretania Caesariensis and Isaurica where the governor and the military commander were one and the same person; the *Notitia Dignitatum* (*Oc.* XXX) lists one commander as *dux et praeses* The equestrian *duces* took command of the troops even in the province where there was a senatorial governor (*CAH* XII 395). The political and social careers of senators between the accession of Diocletian and the death of Theodosius I were examined by Arnheim (1972) who showed that though the role of senators declined there was no total expulsion of senators from government.

36 Williams (1985, 117–19) describes how the collection of the *annona* degenerated into arbitrary requisitioning. Jones (1964, 131; 626) says that collection took place three times per year. See also Southern and Dixon (1996, 62; 79–81) on rations for the soldiers.

37 For the clearest and most concise explanation of the new Diocletianic taxation system see *CAH* XII 399–403. Evidence for the assessments derives from *The Syro-Roman Law Book* CXXI = *FIRA* II 796; see Lewis and Rheinhold (vol. 2 1966, 128); Cameron (1993, 36–8); Christol (1997, 208–9). Piganiol (1935) studied the *capitatio* and the sources for it.

38 The sources for the taxation system are very uneven; hardly anything survives for the west, while the evidence from Syria and Egypt predominates; see Cameron (1993, 36–7) on the lack of sources and the difficulties of carrying out the census and the assessments of tax payments. On the census see Seston (1946, 261–94); Williams (1985, 118–19). The Edict of the Prefect of Egypt of 297 was interpreted as the date of inauguration of the taxation system, but Piganiol (1935, 34) showed that this document represented only a stage in the whole process which probably began in 287; see Seston (1946, 279–80; 289), who also dates the beginning of the scheme to 287; Christol (1997, 209); Cameron (1993, 37); Carrié (1993, 292–3).

39 The separation of civil and military office did not immediately affect the role of the Praetorian Prefects, whose military skills were still necessary, but from the beginning of the fourth century, as the Praetorian Guard receded into the background and the administrative duties of the Prefects increased, the military functions were shed; the Prefects were indispensable, in effect second in command to the Emperor; see *CAH* (XII 379; 381 on financial duties); Williams (1985, 110). Knowledge of the Prefects of the Tetrarchy is

338

scant, but much of the work of reform hinged on them (Williams 1985, 249 n.20). See Howe (1942). Once the apportionment had been made by the Praetorian Prefects, the municipal councils were responsible for collecting the taxes and making up the shortfall in their areas. The crippling expenses of the decurionate were pressing, and in fact there had been a noticeable decline both in their numbers and their wealth since the second century (see Garnsey 1974). Avoidance tactics to escape the office became common; to counteract these and to spread the net wider Diocletian lowered the qualification to serve on the councils to 25 *iugera* of land (Williams 1985, 133). On the burdens of the decurions see Williams (1985, 133–4; 251 n.8); MacMullen (1976, 166–7). The members of the decurionate, once nominated, could not hope to escape, and men with as little as 10 or 15 *iugera*, or even under-age minors could be found on municipal councils, even in the mid-third century (*CJ* 4.13.3; 4.26.1; 10.39.3; MacMullen 1976, 288–9 nn.54–9).

40 Diocletian's currency edict (*AE* 1973, 526a; Erim and Reynolds 1970; Erim *et al.* 1971) was issued in 301, sometime before September of that year (Barnes 1982, 17–18). Mac-Mullen (1976, 113–15) says that the price rises ought to have ended after the three-metal currency was restored, especially since the mints all issued coins of uniform types as local mints were brought into line, but, as MacMullen himself points out (1976, 114), there is no information as to how the Diocletianic coins related to each other, so it is not known how many of a smaller denomination made one of a higher denomination, and so on; MacMullen assumes that the values will have varied in different parts of the Empire. On the monetary reforms see Callu (1975, 608–11); Harl (1996, 148–57). The price edict is better known than the currency edict, since more copies or fragments have survived; it was written on wood, on papyrus and inscribed on stone; see Erim and Reynolds (1973); Lauffer (1971) (but see Barnes (1982, 18) who points out that the heading of the edict in this work is now known to belong to the currency edict); for discussion see Corcoran (1996, 205–33). The edict was issued probably at the end of November or the beginning of December 301 (Barnes 1982, 18–19; Corcoran 1996, 206). The text is translated into English in Frank (1940, Appendix I); see also Williams (1985, 128–32; 224–7). Lactantius (*de Mort. Pers.* 7.5–7) waxes lyrical about the edict's ineffectiveness.

41 There was no total or universal lapse into a natural economy when taxes began to be collected in kind, and money payments did not die out altogether (Callu 1969, 295–7; *CAH* XII, 402). On the state control of the factories and their operation see Williams (1985, 136ff); MacMullen (1976, 158–89). All the evidence for compulsion to remain in hereditary employment is Constantinian (MacMullen 1976, 163).

42 For evidence of peasants abandoning the farms and efforts to put them back on the land see MacMullen (1976, 173–3). Lactantius (*de Mort. Pers.* 7.3) says that it was the oppressive taxes that caused the flight from the land in the first place, but it must be remembered that he was at pains to find fault with Diocletian. The Roman colonate and taxation system has been studied by Goffart (1974); for the view that the late Roman colonate is a modern myth see *OCD* refs p. 365. The *coloni* were not tied to their farms until the reign of Constantine (MacMullen 1976, 179–80); the evidence comes from a law of 332 (*Cod. Th.* 5.17.1), in which it is stated that anyone who shelters a *colonus* belonging to someone else must return him and pay the taxes he had avoided. As MacMullen points out (1976, 180), this law was aimed at rent-paying farmers who held no property, since there is also evidence of *coloni* who held estates of their own in the early fourth century (*Cod. Th.* 5.19.1; 11.1.4; 12.1.33).

43 The earliest reference for the term *scrinia* used of departments is dated to 313 (*Cod. Th.* 6.35.1); see Williams (1985, 110). The argument about Diocletian's *consilium/consistorium* cannot be settled since the earliest attested use of the latter term is post-Tetrarchic (*CJ* 9.47.12; Kunkel 1974, 429). In the reign of Constantine one man is described as *a consiliis sacris* (*CIL* VI 1704); another inscription in honour of Vulcacius Rufus, consul in 347, describes him as *comes intra consistorium*.

44 On the orientalising of the Diocletianic and Tetrarchic courts and the ritualised forms of

address see Aurelius Victor (*de Caes.* 39.1–8) who ascribes all the pomp and ceremony to Diocletian's humble origins, for which he overcompensated by having everyone make obeisance to him. See also Ammianus (16.10); Eutropius (9.26). *Pan. Lat.* (11 (3).2) compares the ceremonial *adoratio* to that performed in the holy of holies. See Williams (1985, 111); Seston (1946, 185–8; 45).

45 The dioceses were formed before the division of the provinces (Christol 1997, 209); the traditional date is 297 (Seston 1946, 334–7), but in part this derives from Mommsen's dating of the *Laterculus Veronensis* to that year; see Barnes (1982, 203–5) where it is argued that the information concerning the western half of the Empire dates from 303 and 314, and that for the eastern half is dated 314 to 324. Williams (1985, 105) provides a list of the 12 dioceses; Barnes (1982, 140–7) lists the dioceses in the same order as the *Laterculus Veronensis*, with the *vicarii* where they are known; he also lists the various editions of the *Laterculus Veronensis*, based on the surviving seventh-century manuscript from Verona (1982, 201–2). The legal decisions of the *vicarii* could not be overturned by anyone except the Emperor (Williams 1985, 106). See also Chastagnol (1994c).

46 Lactantius (*de Mort. Pers.* 7.4) accused Diocletian of splitting the provinces into smaller units in order to increase terror and make it easier to supervise the population. See Barnes (1982, 147–74) for a list of the provincial governors under Diocletian and Constantine. Williams (1985, 104–5) recounts the theory that the provinces were split to make it more difficult to foment rebellion with reduced resources and outlines the military necessity for dividing frontier provinces, but also points out that the senatorial provinces such as Africa and Asia, where there were no large armies, were subdivided into three and six smaller provinces respectively.

47 Even Eusebius, no supporter of Diocletian, admits that he was lenient during the first part of his reign (*History of the Church* 8.1.1–6). Lactantius (*de Mort. Pers.* 11) says that Diocletian asked his advisers what he should do about the Christians, but they were too afraid of Galerius and therefore advocated persecution. The fact that an ancient source partly exonerates Diocletian allows modern authors to follow suit and throw the blame onto Galerius; see *CAH* (XII, 668). Williams (1985, 173) says that Diocletian was too ill to put a stop to Galerius' insistent demands for persecution. On the Manichaeans see Christol (1997, 210–12); for the text of the edict against them see Chastagnol (1991, 149–50). Seston (1940) thought that it was to be dated to 297; Barnes (1976, 181) redates it to 302; see Christol (1997, 252 n.7).

48 For the martyrs to the Christian cause, Maximilian and Marcellus, see Williams (1985, 170; 254 nn.10–11); Campbell (1994, 237–8); Christol (1997, 210–11; 252 n.6); Siniscalco (1974) for Maximilian; Lanata (1972) for Marcellus. At first the Tetrarchs seemed willing to make it easier for Christians to serve as soldiers, exempting them from pagan worship (*CAH* XII, 661), but eventually the army was purged of Christians (Williams 1985, 173–4; Drew-Bear 1981; *AE* 1981, 777). Galerius forced officers to sacrifice or to leave the army (Eusebius *History of the Church* 8.4).

49 The texts of the edicts against the Christians are not known, since none of the ancient authors, even those who wrote of the martyrs, preserved the actual wording (*CAH* XII, 665). Lactantius (*de Mort. Pers.* 10–11) blamed Galerius for setting the mysterious fires in the palace at Nicomedia, in order to be able to accuse the Christians, and that he influenced Diocletian greatly. Eusebius (*History of the Church* 8.1.7) describes how Diocletian exhorted the army and the Imperial administrative staff to sacrifice to the gods; then in summer of 303 the order came to arrest the clergy (*History of the Church* 8.6.8–9). The third edict made sacrifice compulsory, but the letter of the law was applied very unevenly (Williams 1985, 179). In the west, Constantius did not pursue the Christians, except to close churches; as Christol points out (1997, 212) the west was not Christianised to the same degree as the east, so there was not the same pressing need to eradicate the potential dissidents. Williams (1985, 183) considers that Diocletian tried to put into effect a bloodless purge, but that it got out of hand.

50 For Constantine's career before 306 see Barnes (1982, 39–42 esp. 41) where a chronology is worked out from the various sources. The date of Constantine's birth is not known and the sources are not certain about his age at death, which is listed anywhere between 60 and 65; see Barnes (1982, 40). The life of Constantine is beset by the problem that even contemporaries were polarised with regard to his achievements and character, and modern scholars are no less divided. Cameron (1993, 47–9) sums up the one-sided nature of the sources, either wholly favourable or totally antagonistic towards Constantine, with the result that it is impossible to ignore the arguments. In order to assess Constantine it is necessary to evaluate his biographer Eusebius, and Lactantius, both contemporaries, and the panegyrics. For Eusebius see Barnes (1981) and Stevenson (1987); on Lactantius see Barnes (1973); on the Panegyrics see Gallétier (1941–55); and Nixon and Rodgers (1994).

51 According to Lactantius (de Mort. Pers. 18.10; 19.1) Constantine was at Nicomedia in April/May 305; see also Barnes (1982, 42). For his flight from Galerius see Lactantius (de Mort. Pers. 24); Eusebius (Life of Constantine 1.21); Aurelius Victor (de Caes. 40.2–4). Zosimus (2.8.3) recounts the gruesome story of killing all the horses at relay stations, and interprets the action as a pre-emptive measure by Constantine who thought he would be followed because it was already clear to everyone how much he wanted to be Emperor. Cameron (1993, 48) points out that though some of the sources say that Constantine reached his father Constantius in Britain, he actually joined him at Boulogne before the campaign had started.

52 On the campaign in Britain see Salway (1991, 318–9); Pan. Lat. (6 (7).7.1ff) mentions the usual features of marshes and woods, and Caledonians, 'other tribes' and Picts, without giving any useful information as to where Constantius and Constantine may have operated; Salway (1991, 318 n.3) draws comparisons with Dio (76.13) and Herodian (3.14.5). When Constantius died the soldiers declared Constantine Emperor on 25 July 306, which he always celebrated as his *dies imperii*, though this question is disputed; see Barnes (1982, 69); Nixon and Rodgers (1994, 179–80; 215 n.8). Zosimus (2.9.1) says that the troops conferred the rank of Caesar on him, but this conflates the proclamation by the British troops and Galerius' recognition of Constantine as Caesar; see Lactantius (de Mort. Pers. 25.3–5). Salway (1991, 322–3) suggests that Constantine favoured Germanic troops during his reign because the man responsible for his elevation as Emperor was allegedly the Alamannic king, Crocus, who was in charge of his own men as part of the expeditionary army in Britain; he also suggests that the Tetrarchic principle of non-hereditary succession would have broken down sooner or later because the hereditary factors were too entrenched with the soldiers.

53 Maxentius (*vir clarissimus: ILS* 666) was declared Emperor at Rome in October 306; Zosimus (2.9.2) says that he saw the images of Constantine when they arrived in the city and was incensed because the son of a harlot had been made Emperor, while he was over-looked, yet he was the son of Maximian. He avoided the title Augustus at first, calling himself *princeps invictus* (*RIC* VI 367–70), but declared himself Augustus in 307 (Barnes 1982, 12–13). He controlled southern Italy, Sicily, Sardinia and Africa, but not Spain which was in Constantine's hands (Barnes 1982, 13; 197–8). Lactantius (de Mort. Pers. 26.7) says that Maxentius recalled Maximian, inviting him to become Emperor again; Zosimus (2.10.2) has a different version, that Maximian feared for his son's safety and proceeded to Ravenna where Severus was besieged; Paschoud (1971, 195 n.15) considers that Zosimus' version is the correct one. See also Christol (1997, 217). Severus' expedition to oust Maxentius from Italy ended in failure and ultimately his death (Lactantius de Mort. Pers. 26.5–8). Zosimus (2.10.1) says that Maxentius bribed Severus' troops, which is entirely possible since many of them had been Maximian's soldiers (Paschoud 1971, 195 n.15). According to Zosimus (2.10.1–3) it is Maximian who is blamed for the death of Severus, since he lured him out of Ravenna with false promises and hanged him. In the second half of 307 (see Paschoud 1971, 196 n.17; Lactantius de Mort. Pers. 27.2–7)

Galerius also entered Italy to make war on Maxentius but distrusted the loyalty of his troops and went back to the east (Zosimus 2.10.3).

54 Nixon and Rodgers (1994, 187) point out that Maximian was technically a usurper, and Constantine's power depended upon him; not an ideal situation, and Constantine detached himself after Maximian's so-called plot against him. At the beginning of their alliance, Constantine married Maximian's daughter Fausta (Barnes 1982, 69–70 n.103; Lactantius *de Mort. Pers.* 27.1). Zosimus (2.10.6–7) implies that Maximian attached strings to the arrangement; he had promised his daughter to Constantine some time before and Maximian honoured the agreement, but then tried to persuade his son-in-law to attack Galerius as he left Italy. When this proposal failed, he tried to implicate Constantine in a plot against Maxentius. Zosimus places these events after the conference at Carnuntum, but Paschoud (1971, 197 n.18) suggests that to restore the correct order of events, paragraphs 4 and 5 of Zosimus 2.10, describing the conference, should be placed after paragraphs 6 and 7 describing the machinations of Maximian. Constantine was active on the Rhine in 308, raiding the territory of the Bructeri and building a bridge across the river (Barnes 1982, 70; *Pan. Lat.* 6 (7).12.1ff; 4 (10).18.1).

55 Zosimus (2.10.4) places the conference at Carnutum (in Gaul), instead of Carnuntum, but this is most likely a copyist's error; see Paschoud (1971, 197 n.18). An inscription from the Mithraeum at Carnuntum records the meeting of the Emperors, and the attempt to reassert the Iovian–Herculean partnership (*CIL* III 4413; Christol 1997, 219; Bruun 1979; Arnaldi 1975). Constantine did not attend the conference, being fully engaged on the Rhine frontier; see note 54 above. After the conference Galerius named as Augustus his colleague Licinius, and then according to Zosimus (2.11) he died of an old incurable wound; Paschoud (1971, 198 n.19) points out the mistaken chronology and the confusion with the death of Maximinus Daia; see note 57 below. Both Maximinus and Constantine were made Caesars, and given the added distinction of *filius Augustorum* (Lactantius *de Mort. Pers.* 32.1). Both accepted at first; coins from Alexandria show Constantine as Caesar but he and Maximinus soon adopted the title of Augustus (Grant 1993, 25) which Galerius finally condoned (Nixon and Rodgers 1994, 216 n.9).

56 Fausta proved loyal to Constantine by revealing to him the plotting of Maximian (Zosimus 2.11). The panegyric addressed to Constantine probably in 310 has to deal with the delicate situation of Maximian's revolt and the fact that there was little certainty as to how he had died (Nixon and Rodgers 1994, 215–16). For a chronology of events from the elevation of Constantine to the death of Maximian see Nixon and Rodgers (1994, 214), differing from the chronology of Sydenham reproduced in Gallétier (vol. 2 p. 50). Sydenham (1934) examined the varied fortunes of Maximian from his abdication in 305 to his death in 310. Constantine looked for another lineage and attached himself to Claudius Gothicus (*Pan. Lat.* 6 (7).2.1–3; *RIC* VII p. 180). Licinius attached himself to Philip the Arab (Grant 1993, 26–7). Constantine began to display Sol on his coinage at the same time as he sought a new ancestry (Christol 1997, 221; *RIC* VI London 101–2; 113–15; Trier 826; 865–876; Lyons 307–12).

57 On the death of Galerius see Lactantius (*de Mort. Pers.* 35.3), who delights in the Emperor's suffering; Zosimus' chronology and description of Galerius' demise are confused; see note 55 above. Lactantius (*de Mort. Pers.* 24) and Eusebius (*History of the Church* 8.17) document the edict of toleration that Galerius issued just before his death. Maximinus refused to end the persecution of the Christians in his territories (Mitchell 1988). There are two versions of the outbreak of the war against Maxentius, one blaming Maxentius for the hostilities and the other crediting Constantine with liberating Rome from the tyrant, which is a later interpretation put about after Constantine had won (Grant 1993, 33). Zosimus (2.14.1–2) accuses Maxentius of overweening ambition, which made him search for excuses to make war on Constantine.

58 Speidel (1986; 1988) examined the last days of Maxentius. See also Barnes (1982, 12–13). Zosimus (2.15–17) is one of the main sources for the battle; he relays the story that Max-

entius destroyed the bridge and erected a new one that was designed to be easily pulled down from under the feet of Constantine's troops should they approach the city, but in fact it was Maxentius who fell from it and drowned. It is dubious in the extreme and sounds more like a little parable of ironic divine retribution, exonerating anyone except himself for his death. For Constantine's progress through Italy and into Rome see *Pan. Lat.* (12 (9).5.1; 16.2; 19.1). The Christian symbols that Constantine saw before the battle are variously described. Even contemporaries could not agree; Lactantius (*de Mort. Pers.* 44) is confident that Constantine witnessed the chi-rho. Eusebius (*History of the Church* 9.9) describes the battle without mentioning divine symbols, but in the *Life of Constantine* (1.27) written later he tells of a cross of light in the sky, seen some weeks before the battle. The panegyric of 313 to Constantine takes a pagan view of the affair.

59 Constantine wrote to Maximinus the day after his entry into Rome (Lactantius *de Mort. Pers.* 37.1; Eusebius *History of the Church* 9.9.12). The marriage of Licinius to Constantine's half-sister Constantia took place at Milan in 313 (Lactantius *de Mort. Pers.* 45.1; Eusebius *History of the Church* 10.5.4; Zosimus 2.17). Paschoud (1971, 207 n.27) points out that the alliance between Licinius and Constantine was aimed directly at Maximinus. The edict of Milan was to promote religious toleration over the whole Empire; Lactantius saw the text at Nicomedia and reported it in *de Mort. Pers.* (48); Eusebius reported on the text he saw at Caesarea in Palestine (*History of the Church* 10.5.2–14).

60 Coins proclaim Constantine as Maximus Augustus; Kent (1978, plate 159, p. 328 no. 629); the obverse shows Constantine paired with the god Sol, and on the reverse only two Emperors are mentioned, acknowledging Licinius but ignoring Maximinus; see also Christol (1997, 226); Grant (1993, 239); *RIC* VII 305 no. 67. The Senate voted the title Maximus Augustus to Constantine, despite the fact that Licinius was the senior Emperor. Lactantius (*de Mort. Pers.* 45–9) is the main source, very detailed, for the campaign of Licinius against Maximinus; see Barnes (1982, 66–7; 81). Maximinus committed suicide at Tarsus (Lactantius *de Mort. Pers.* 49.1); see also Barnes (1982, 67); *P. Oxy.* (3144). Licinius removed all of Maximinus' circle (Grant 1993, 40); there is no mention of this in Zosimus (Paschoud 1971, 208 n.28). Barnes (1982, 9) dates the execution of Valeria to September 314; see Lactantius (*de Mort. Pers.* 39.5; 41.1; 51).

61 On Bassianus see Grant (1993, 41); Christol (1997, 240). On Bassianus' marriage to Anastasia, Constantine's half-sister, see Barnes (1982, 37). Valens was *dux limitis* in Dacia when Licinius made him Augustus, which event took place after the battle at Cibalae (Barnes 1982, 15). Zosimus (2.19.2) calls him Caesar, but coins name him as Augustus; see *RIC* VII 644; there were also many forgeries in the name of Valens. See Barnes (1982, 73; 81) for the sources for the war, and Paschoud (1971, 208 n.28) for the traditional date of 314 and the establishment of the date of 316 for the final battle; see Bruun (1953, 17–21). Licinius ceded territories to Constantine; Barnes (1982, 198; 313–24) for the division of the Empire; Paschoud (1971, 210 n.30). Three Caesars were created in 317, which accords well with the revised date of 316 for the war (Paschoud 1971, 210 n.30); see Barnes (1982, 83–5). On Crispus see Pohlsander (1984).

62 The consulships were judiciously shared between the Augusti and the Caesars for a while (Christol 1997, 241–2; Barnes 1982, 95). For Crispus' expedition to the Rhine see Barnes (1982, 74; 83); *Pan. Lat.* (4 (10).17.2). In 323 tribes invaded Roman territory and Constantine pushed them back; they are variously described as Goths or Sarmatians; see Barnes (1982, 75); Christol (1997, 241–2). Zosimus confuses campaigns of 322 and 323 (Paschoud 1971, 213 n.31); he describes Constantine's preparations for war (2.22.1).

63 For Adrianople see Barnes (1982, 75); Grant (1993, 46–7). The siege of Byzantium is described by Zosimus (2.23.1; 25.1), and Zosimus is the best source for Crispus' command of the fleet and the approach to Byzantium which is discussed by Paschoud (1971, 215 nn.33–4). Licinius surrendered on the advice of Constantia (Zosimus 2.28.1; Barnes 1982, 76; Grant 1993, 47–8). On the execution of Licinius and his son see Barnes (1982, 44); Zosimus (2.28.1); Eutropius (10.6.1–3); Jordanes (*Getica* 111); Aurelius

Victor (*de Caes.* 41.8–9). Licinius was accused of conspiring with the Goths as the excuse for putting him to death; it was probably untrue but would perhaps have been credible because Licinius had asked the Goths to help him in the war against Constantine (Grant 1993, 47). After the demise of Licinius Eusebius' attitude was changed; in Book 9 Licinius was acceptable, even good; in Book 10 he was the villain (Grant 1993, 48; Cameron 1993, 52).

64 For a full analysis of the reign of Constantine and the sources see Barnes (1981; 1982), and for an introductory synopsis see Cameron (1993). Whether or not Constantine was a confirmed Christian or whether he used Christianity as a political tool will always be the subject of debate; Pohlsander (1996, 23–4) is sure that Constantine chose Christianity from religious conviction; Williams (1985, 206) considers that he used the Christian God as Diocletian used Jupiter. Hopkins (1999, 86) considers that Constantine wanted to promote at least the idea of unity, even though the Church was rent by heresies, and that there was nothing but political expediency behind the so-called conversion of Constantine. Arnheim (1972, 73 n.1) disagrees with the theory of political expediency, quoting Baynes (1929) who argued that the Church was still very weak in the early fourth century and gained in strength only because Constantine promoted it. This does not wholly answer the question of whether or not Constantine was an ardent convert to Christianity or whether he thought purely in political terms; MacMullen (1984, 43) thinks that he was moved only by politics, adopting Christianity when he needed support for his regime. The debate has been ongoing for some time; see Cameron (1993, 213–14) for an up-to-date bibliography. See also notes 43–7 in ch. 7; Alföldi (1948); Jones (1948); Frend (1984).

65 Clergy were exempted from service on town councils (Eusebius *History of the Church* 10.7; Cameron 1993, 55) and the Church was granted privileges, such as the right to hold property; the ecclesiastical courts were given equal validity with Imperial courts and litigants could be tried in either (Hyde 1970, 193). New senators were created by Constantine (see Eusebius *History of the Church* 6.1). Arnheim (1972, 73 n.1) suggested that because Constantine favoured the Christians and the Church authorities, he needed to placate the pagan Senate of Rome, and that was why he created new senators. For senatorial careers under Constantine see Arnheim (1972, 49–73); senators never regained access to military commands. Diocletian's arrangements for provincial government were not changed by Constantine (Cameron 1993, 53) and for those people entrenched in heritable professions there was no relief (Williams 1985, 204).

66 Zosimus (2.34) accused Constantine of weakening the frontiers that Diocletian had strengthened by removing troops to the cities. On the army in the later Roman Empire see Campbell (1994); on the *comitatenses* and *limitanei* see Southern and Dixon (1996, 17–20; 33–7).

67 On the *scholae* see Williams (1985, 207); Grant (1993, 84); Campbell (1994, 233); Southern and Dixon (1996, 56; 60). The Praetorian Prefects lost their military functions under Constantine (Grant 1993, 83–4).

68 Emperors had been peripatetic since the days of Marcus Aurelius; writing in the early third century Herodian (1.6.5) said that Rome was where the Emperor was. Byzantium was known as *altera Roma* by 324 according to Grant (1993, 121), who quotes Socrates Scholasticus *Historia Ecclesiastica* (1.16). The city of Constantinople has a large bibliography; Krautheimer (1983) gives a concise description, but Cameron (1993, 213) says that he attributes much more to Constantine than the sources can support. See also Dagron (1974).

5 BEYOND THE NORTHERN FRONTIERS

1 The choice of suitable terminology for the so-called barbarians is fraught with difficulties. Vogt (1967, 61–2) pointed out that the Romans themselves had a two-faced attitude towards the peoples that they called barbarians, treating them as robbers and aggressors

while continually calling upon them to serve in the army and support Rome. He suggested that it would be preferable to dispense with the word 'barbarian' altogether since its modern connotations place the peoples so described as 'beyond the moral pale', but even he was unable to suggest anything better than aliens, which is almost as derogatory a term as barbarians. Braund (1989, 16) has a useful summary of Roman attitudes to 'us and them'. The Romans did not distinguish between the northern tribes and any other peoples who were foreign to them. Sophisticated civilisation, culture, art and literature counted for nothing if it was not Roman in origin. The Parthians were barbarians as far as Rome was concerned; see Dio (75.8.3) where he says that after Pescennius Niger was defeated by Septimius Severus he fled towards the Euphrates, planning to make his escape to the 'barbarians', by which Dio means the Parthians. He also described the Arabian horsemen as barbarians (Dio 76.11.2).

2 Dauge (1981, intro) suggests that the elevation of the barbarians is admirable but it has been achieved at the expense of the Romans. He examines the Roman perception of the tribes surrounding the Empire at all periods of Rome's history; for the third century he proclaims a turning point, when the barbarian world represented for Rome the 'dechainement universel du mal sous toutes les formes' with the consequence that Rome had to restructure herself to meet the threat.

3 Todd (1992, 30–1) points out that the tribe 'was not a fixed and indissoluble unit'. The idea is expressed more fully in Wenskus (1961). Tacitus (*Germ.* 26) says that the Germans shifted their tilled lands from time to time, which Delbrück (1990, 26) found more readily acceptable than the annual changes described by Caesar. See also Demougeot (1969, 305). Wolfram (1997, 7) describes the poor agricultural techniques and the inability to preserve surplus production, which necessitated the constant search for new lands.

4 Wolfram (1988, 11; 379 n.45) quotes Synesius of Cyrene (*Oratio de regno ad Arcadium Imperatorem* ch. 15) who explained the changes of tribal names and their shifting allegiances, in a speech to Arcadius, to try to demonstrate that there were no new tribes, only realignments of old ones. The altar from Augsburg records a two-day battle against the barbarians, described as Semnones or Iouthungi, in April 260 (Bakker, 1993; Lavagne 1994; Kellner 1995, 342–4; Loriot and Nony 1997, 76–7 no. 36; Christol 1997, 171 n.6).

5 There is some uncertainty as to where exactly the Romans placed *barbaricum*. Barford (1994, 166) limits the description to the lands beyond the Danube. An inscription from Preslav mentions an expedition undertaken on account of danger in barbarian lands, *periculis in barbarico* (Sarnowski 1991). On the *topoi* used to describe the barbarians see Kremer (1994) and Dauge (1981).

6 Polybius (2.27.31) described the barbarians as plunderers.

7 Dio (56.18.2) thought that the barbarians were adaptable, but elsewhere (75.2.6) he deplored the appearance of the German soldiers in Rome; among other things he described them as boorish in conversation, which suggests that at least he had tried to talk to them. On Franks in the Roman army see James (1988, 37–8); in the army of Carausius and Allectus see Casey (1994, 109; 134).

8 Demougeot (1969) surveys the development of Europe from the Roman Empire and the migration period onwards; Krüger (1983) documents the Germanic tribes north of the Rhine and Danube; see also Christlein (1979); Grünert and Dölle (1975); Günther and Köpstein (1978); Hachmann (1971); Hedeager (1992); James (1988); Todd (1992); Wolfram (1988). This list is by no means exhaustive.

9 Dauge (1981) surveys the Greek and Latin literature on the barbarians. The later histories were designed to impose a unity on tribal development which did not exist; Jordanes wrote in the mid-sixth century, using several earlier sources, especially Cassiodorus, a Roman senator in the secretarial service of Theodoric the Great. Cassiodorus advocated the need to assimilate Roman and Gothic traditions, and set out to write a history of the Goths that would place them on a level with the Romans. Jordanes wrote the *Romana* and

the *Getica* in the same spirit (Mierow 1915, 12–16). Towards the end of the sixth century, Gregory, bishop of Tours, chronicled the history of the Franks, with much the same result if not for the same reasons; his work documents the amalgamation of Roman and Frankish customs. The reliability of Jordanes for the early history of the Goths and of Gregory for the history of the Franks is debatable.

10 Kremer (1994, 330–1) and Wolfram (1988, 3) both detect a change in the Roman attitude to the barbarians when Caesar wrote his account of the Germans across the Rhine. He was the first to treat them as people, rejecting the myth and hyperbole for what he saw. On the Marcomannic wars see Birley (1987, 159–83); Thompson (1982, 13); Rémondon (1964, 75) Dio records how Marcus would not let the natives migrate or settle, and stationed 20,000 troops among them so they could do nothing in safety; thus he wore them down until they sued for peace (72.20).

11 Braund (1984) surveys client kingship in general. Intelligence gathering on the frontiers and the specific duties of the *beneficiarii consularis* are examined by Austin and Rankov (1995, 196; 203–4). Traders could also provide information; the best-known example is Quintus Atilius Primus, of the late second and early third century, whose tombstone (*AE* 1978, 635) found in Slovakia describes him as a legionary centurion and also as a merchant and interpreter among the Quadi (Elton 1996, 79–80; Todd 1992, 89).

12 Pius celebrated bestowal of kings upon the Quadi and the Armenians, proclaiming the facts on his coinage: *Rex Quadis datus* and *Rex Armeniis datus* (Kent, 1978, 296 no. 306; *BMC* IV Pius 1273; 1274). See also Birley (1987, 61; 272 n.19); *HA* (Pius 5.4); Syme (*JRS* 52, 1962, 87f).

13 Tacitus noted that the Germans chose their kings from among the nobles and their warriors from those of proven valour (*Germ.* 7). On *reges* and *reguli* see Bursche (1996a, 39; Krüger 1983, 12 n.2). Nine *reguli* of the Alamanni submitted to Probus (*HA* Probus 14.1). Wolfram (1997, 15–18) challenges the idea of simultaneous existence of kings and *duces* in favour of the view that the two types of kingship supplemented and succeeded each other. Burns (1974, 123) suggests that the king was the ruler of the *gens* or people, and the *dux* was the warrior leader, and that the Roman diplomats would not confuse the two (1974, 127). It was not usual for one man to extend rule over large numbers of people from different tribes, so Maroboduus and his domination of a large group of people was an exception (Todd 1992, 35–6); but it foreshadowed the growth of the federations of tribesmen in the third century. Maroboduus entered into a treaty with Rome (Tacitus *Ann.* 2.46.2) and after his defeat he settled in Ravenna for the last 18 years of his life (*Ann.* 2.63.1–5). Vannius was installed as leader of the remnants of his followers (Tacitus *Ann.* 12.29); on Catvalda see Tacitus (*Ann.* 2.63). See also Velleius Paterculus (2.108.2; 109.2–4); J. Dobias (*Klio* 38, 1960, 155–66); Millar (1981, 296–8; 311–12).

14 It was important to foster friendly kings so that they could maintain their positions against less Roman-oriented rivals (Heather and Matthews 1991, 24). Tacitus recognised that the German war leaders could maintain their following only by dint of constant warfare (*Germ.* 14).

15 On gift exchange in general see Mauss (1927). On prestige goods and their value to the tribal chiefs see Hedeager (1992, 88; 243–4) and Krüger (1983, 14) On subsidies see Klose (1934, 138); Birley (1976, 271 n.4); Braund (1984, 62); Austin and Rankov (1995, 149). Todd (1992, 87) describes how the subsidies could comprise coins, food supplies or general assistance. Dio (67.7.4; 5.2) records that Domitian sent engineers to Decebalus, and 100 cavalry to help the Lugii against their enemies.

16 Bursche (1996b, 110) prefers the phrase *annua munera* to describe subsidies. See Braund (1989, 18) on gift exchange in Germanic tribal customs. He distinguishes the reputation of good and bad Emperors and how that influenced the attitude towards their subsidy payments. Caracalla's payments were cast in a very dubious light by Dio himself (78.14.3), because he drained gold from the Empire and used debased currency at home, and by the Emperor Macrinus, because he paid more to the barbarians than he did to the

soldiers (Dio 79.17.3). Themistius (*Oration* 10) says that the payments to the Goths were not called tributes, but ought to be so labelled because they were paid to buy peace, which the Romans usually bestowed instead of purchasing; see also Daly (1972, 362–3); Heather and Matthews (1991, 43). Klose (1934) distinguished between payments made as grants to enable a king to sustain himself and those made to buy peace. Bursche (1996b, 106–10) lists examples of tributes and ransoms, especially to the Germans in the reign of Severus Alexander, and to the Persians. Pertinax chose to stop subsidies and was highly regarded for it (Dio 74.6.1). The Goths were paid subsidies after the treaty of 238 (Petrus Patricius frg. 8; *FHG* vol. 4, 186–7 Müller, possibly derived from Dexippus' *Scythica*; see also Demougeot 1969, 395; Bursche 1996b, 111–12 nn.78–83). The Emperor Philip stopped payments in the 240s (Jordanes *Getica* 89; Demougeot 1969, 398; Bursche 1996b, 112), after securing the Danube frontier by sending Decius to command the forces there (Wolfram 1988, 45). Instead of securing the frontier, Decius rebelled after his troops hailed him as Emperor (Zosimus 1.21), so the Gothic leader Cniva invaded Moesia (Wolfram 1988, 397–8 n.61) 'taking advantage of the neglect of the Emperors' to defend the area (Jordanes *Getica* 101). After the death of Decius at the battle of Abrittus, Cniva came to terms with Trebonianus Gallus who reinstated subsidies in 253 (Demougeot 1969, 413–14). Aemilianus stopped the subsidies and was proclaimed Emperor by his troops after defeating Cniva (Jordanes *Getica* 105–6; Eutropius 9.5; Zosimus 1.28–9); Paschoud (1971, 150 n.55) discusses the problems of dating these episodes; see also Wolfram (1988, 44–6); Alföldi (1967, 316; 319–21)

17 See Braund (1989, 17–19) on subsidies and their uses. The payments were not necessarily kept by the king or leader to whom they were given; everyone among the people under the rule of the king could benefit; thus Kazansky (1991, 58) links the finds of coins, the growth of larger houses and the development of crafts in the Cherniakov culture directly to the subsidy policy of Constantine. (Cherniakov is a village near Kiev which has given its name to the Gothic culture associated with it.) See Le Bihan (1993, 10–14) on acculturation and merging of Roman and barbarian customs. Dio (73. 2) describes the peace treaty of Commodus with the Quadi and Marcomanni, when he asked for troops but relieved them of an annual levy. Herodian (1.6.9) is much more dismissive of Commodus' arrangements, insisting that he simply bought peace for an exorbitant amount of money. On Goths in the army in the 240s see Todd (1992, 150); Wolfram (1988, 44; 384 n.13; 397 n.59). Corroborative evidence can be found in the tri-lingual inscription recording the exploits of Shapur I, king of Persia (*Res Gestae Divi Saporis* 1.6.7), referring to Gordian III levying troops from the Goths and the Germans for his expedition to the east; see Maricq (1958); Loriot (1975, 758–9 nn.54–62) for full references.

18 See Heather and Matthews (1991, 23–4) on the need to furnish friendly kings with the means to sustain a following and keep out rivals and enemies. The role of subsidies in the defence of the Empire is the special study of C.D. Gordon (1949). Zosimus (1.32.2) says that the Bosporans were paid annual subsidies as a fee for defending their lands against the Scythians; the arrangements broke down when dynastic squabbles weakened the Bosporan kingdom (Ridley 1982, 141 n.60). The Borani broke through the Bosporan defences and were actually helped to cross into Asia. This probably dates to 254 (Paschoud 1971, 152 n.59). Procopius (*Bell.* 2.10.23) records that the Romans (that is, the Romans of the Eastern Empire) paid annual subsidies in gold to the Huns and Saracens as a fee for guarding their lands at all times; see also Isaac (1992, 245).

19 On the actual methods of payment of subsidies see Austin and Rankov (1995, 147–8).

20 For Roman imports into Germania, see Eggers (1951); Hedeager (1978); for the Baltic see Kaul (1993a). On trade and the frontiers see Middleton (1983); Whittaker (1983b; 1989); Hedeager (1987); Elton (1996, 78–81) lists references on frontiers and trade. Tacitus divided the Germans into two groups: the frontier tribes who traded with Rome and were used to money, and those further away who had a natural economy (*Germ.* 5.17.23); he also documented trade with Maroboduus in Bohemia (*Ann.* 2.6.2.3). On

coins in barbaricum see Harl (1996, 290–314). The Roman coin finds bear out Tacitus' assertion that the Germans preferred silver to gold (Harl 1996, 295; Todd 1992, 101), while the coins found in the Ukraine may have been connected to the slave trade (Todd 1992, 101). The Romans installed Vannius of the Quadi as king of the followers of Maroboduus, and he soon established taxes on goods crossing his territory, which he presumably collected in coin (Harl 1996, 296). Low denomination coins could have arrived in *barbaricum* via theft or booty, but in general the presence of bronze coinage can be construed as evidence of trading activities (Lee 1993, 73). Todd (1992, 102) suggests that the tribes distant from the frontiers did in fact use coins in a primitive economic system; Hedeager (1992, 236 fig. 5.4) illustrates the uses of coins as 'the medium of exchange between the Roman market economy and the Germanic prestige goods system'. In the third century Scandinavia was cut off from coin supplies and the supply to the Ukraine diminished (Harl 1996, 296; Todd 1992, 100).

21 Barford (1994) and Bursche (1996a; 1996b) review the contacts of all kinds between Rome and the more distant tribes. Charpy (1993, 36–41) assesses the two-way contacts between the Mediterranean and the barbarians, from the Etruscan period onwards. Bursche (1996a, 33) considers that trade accounts for most of the items found in *barbaricum*. The late-second-century trader in the territory of the Quadi, Quintus Atilius Primus, has already been mentioned (above, n.11). Pliny (*NH* 6.15) noted that Roman traders reached the Baltic area, and he knew of the amber routes (*NH* 37.43). Harl (1996, 295) says that amber was the principal precious commodity, but Todd (1992, 97–8) thinks that the trade could have been only a minor one. On the major routes, see Charlesworth (1926, 175–6); Demougeot (1969, 262; 272) Lee (1993, 74); Todd (1992, 97–8).

22 Braund (1989, 14; 18) argues that trade was vitally important to the tribes outside the Empire, and Burns (1974, 154–5) says that the Goths in the later Empire were dependent on food supplies coming up the Danube, but this is not strictly reliant upon trade and falls more readily into the category of subsidies. Whittaker (1983b; 1989) emphasises the importance of trade to the natives. Hedeager (1992, 121; 243–4) describes the importance to the leading families of controlling trading activities; see also Todd (1992, 103).

23 Fulford (1985; 1989, 87) denies that trade had any importance at all and suggests that the frontiers were impermeable barriers, behind which the Romans were self-sufficient and had no need to trade. Lee (1993, 74) says that the natives did not supply anything especially valuable to the Romans. Loan-words from Germanic/Gothic to Latin/Greek and vice versa mostly derived from trade: see Lee (1993, 67 n.89); Thompson (1966, 39); Wild (1976, 60–1). On Feddersen Wierde see Haarnagel (1979a; 1979b); Todd (1992, 64–6) For Wijster and Bennekom see Todd (1992, 68–9); van Es (1965). Kolendo (1981, 459) points out that there will have been fluctuations in the volume and extent of trade, and he suggests that after the Marcomannic wars trade fell off dramatically, so everything found in *barbaricum* that post-dates the wars must be booty. Sakar (1970, 69) found that trade in Bohemia did fall off after the Marcomannic wars, but Bursche (1996a) attests that trade increased after this time in the area north of the Carpathians. See also Todd (1992, 84; 95–104).

24 Dio (72.11.3) records that Marcus Aurelius designated the places where the Marcomanni and Quadi could trade. Diocletian's treaty stipulating Nisibis as the sole place of trade is recorded by a fragment of the work of Petrus Patricius (*FHG* vol. 4, 188–9 Müller; Blockley 1992, 6–7). The treaty with the Goths allowed them to trade at any point on the frontier, and was on that account very unusual (Todd, 1992, 152; Heather and Matthews 1991, 91–3). The Vandals were not treated so liberally; having contributed 2,000 horsemen to the Roman army, they established a market place where trade could be conducted; see Millar (1969, 25).

25 A law of the late Empire establishes that goods were taxed at their exit points, supervised by the *comites commerciorum* (*CJ* IV 40.2; Whittaker 1983a, 167; Elton 1996, 80). See also Hopkins (1980).

26 Thompson (1982, 10) accepts the ban on the export of metals and weapons, and Braund (1989, 19) accentuates the special privileged position of Maroboduus and the Hermunduri. Rankov collects together the references on the supposed ban on the export of weapons (ROMEC XI conference, 10–13 September 1998, Mainz); the laws are aimed at enemies of the state: see *Digest* 39.4.11; 48.4.4; *CJ* 4.41.2. Among those who opt for a legal trade in weapons are Dabrowski and Kolendo (1972); Kunow (1986); Lonstrup (1986); others have decided that the presence of such a large number of Roman weapons in *barbaricum* must represent an illegal trade, the product of raiding expeditions, or theft: see Erdrich (1994); Rald (1994). The appearance of Roman or Roman-style swords in Germany begins in the third century (Todd 1992, 37–40). Hedeager (1992, 179 n.12) says that the swords found in Germanic territory should be regarded as imports.

27 Caesar settled the Usipetes and Tencteri to protect them from their neighbours (*BG* 4.1). Agrippa brought in the Ubii (Hachmann 1971, 70). Pressure from more distant tribes may have precipitated the Marcomannic wars (*HA* Marcus 14.1; Kolendo 1981, 454). MacMullen (1963a, 553–4 nn.4–6) collects references to settlement of tribesmen: Augustus and 50,000 Getae (Strabo 7.303); Tiberius and 40,000 Germans (Eutropius 7.9); Nero and tribes settled in Moesia (*ILS* 986); Marcus and the Naristae (Dio 72.21); Probus and the Bastarnae (*HA* Probus 18.1).

28 Hadrian's law concerning land tenure (Birley 1997, 208; 343 n.10) was still in force when Pertinax tried to attract people to farm wastelands (Herodian 2.4.6; Whittaker in his Loeb translation of Herodian adds a footnote that the law may have needed restating by the reign of Severus). Aurelian tried to make city councils responsible for the provision of landlords or the payment of the taxes on deserted lands (Millar 1981, 94–5). Marcus Aurelius had some trouble with barbarians settled in Ravenna and banished all of them (Dio 72.11.5; see also *HA* Marcus 22.2).

29 See MacMullen (1963a, 555–60) on the archaeological and documentary traces of the tribes settled within the Empire. Lee (1993, 67–8) points out that the settlements were well within the Empire, not on frontiers, and agrees with MacMullen that the tribesmen were probably never fully integrated into the Empire. The earliest mention of the *laeti* dates from 297 (*Pan. Lat.* 4 (8).21); the *praefecti laetorum* are listed in the *Notitia Dignitatum* (*Oc.* XLII 33–44); *terrae laeticae* are mentioned in the *Codex Theodosianus* (13.11.10). See also Doorselaev (1975, 235–40) on *laeti* in Belgium; Zollner (1970, 13 n.8) on *laeti* in Gaul and Günther (1975, 225–34) for northern Gaul; Günther and Köpstein (1978, 344–52) on the settlements and terms of the treaties; see also James (1988, 45); Liebeschuetz (1990, 12); MacMullen (1963a, 557–8); Périn and Feffer (1987, 42–4); Simpson (1977a; 1977b); Southern and Dixon (1996, 48; 61; 70). Zosimus (2.54) thought the *laeti* were Gauls; Jordanes (*Getica* 191) called them Liticiani. Drew (1991, 4) traces the later history of the *laeti* who expanded their territory very gradually, without causing an outcry from landowners or displaced peasants, so presumably vacant lands were always available.

30 Constantine settled barbarians in Roman territory (MacMullen 1963a, 553–4). Themistius (*Oration* 16) said that it was better to fill Thrace with farmer-soldiers than with corpses.

31 On Ariovistus see Caesar (*BG* 1.30–54); Dio (38.34–50). On warriors serving in the Roman army see Todd (1992, 59–61).

32 On Arminius see Tacitus (*Ann.* 2.10.3) and Velleius Paterculus (2.118.2). On Civilis see Tacitus (*Hist.* 4.13.1).

33 Roman coins in *barbaricum*: Bursche (1996a, 39) discusses coins in the graves of the Luboszyce and Wielbark cultures, pointing out that many of these are female graves. Barbarians were attracted to military service in Roman armies (Thompson 1982, 6; Todd 1992, 59). On interpreters see Lee (1993, 66 n.83), who lists the reference; see also note 21 above. MacMullen (1976, 297 n.10) says that there were adequate numbers of men to satisfy Roman recruitment needs until the third century, and then conscription was necessary.

34 On the Britons in Germany see Southern (1989, 94–8). Marcus Aurelius sent 5,500 Sarmatians to Britain (Dio 72.16). Commodus raised 13,000 Quadi for the army and a lesser number of Marcomanni (Dio 73.2.3).

35 Recruitment of tribesmen did not cease after the invasions of the third century; there were Goths in the army after their defeat by Claudius Gothicus, and indeed the employment of tribesmen increased during the course of the third century (Todd 1992, 59; 150; 152). See also Liebeschuetz (1990, 7–25); MacMullen (1976, 183) emphasises the importance of the barbarians as a source of manpower for the army. The Gallic Emperors used Frankish troops (James 1988, 37–8); there were Alamannic and Frankish officers in the army at the end of the third century (James 1988, 43). The *Notitia Dignitatum* lists several cohorts of Alamanni and Franks. The decisive influence in use of tribesmen in the army was that of Constantine (Todd 1992, 59).

36 The Germans knew of the weaknesses of the Romans (Todd 1992, 34–5). The men who had served in the Roman army brought back new ideas to their tribes (Hedeager 1992, 249).

37 Thompson (1982, 3–6) argues that the Roman Empire was a kind of El Dorado for the tribesmen.

38 On state formation in general see Runciman (1982). Hedeager (1992, 83–93) describes state formation among the Iron Age societies of northern Europe; see also Lee (1993, 27) and Demougeot (1969, 284) where it is argued that the tribes of the Elbe were the first to show signs of state formation whereas the tribes nearest to the frontiers of the Empire, hemmed in and not allowed to expand, were constantly in turmoil and therefore restricted in their opportunities to create settled states.

39 Migrations were often precipitated by pressure from other tribes; it has been argued that the Marcomannic wars were caused by pressure from other tribes forcing the Quadi and Marcomanni to move (Kolendo 1981, 454). At a later date Ermenaric the Gothic leader resisted the Huns for a long time (*diu*) but eventually gave in (Ammianus 31.3.1–2). Planned invasions with the purpose of conquest were not part of tribal ideology, and it required long-term planning to carry out invasions of this kind (Hedeager 1992, 91–2). When the Goths moved towards the Empire, there was no royal-led migration, centrally planned (Wolfram 1988, 44). The Alamanni did not settle in the *agri decumates* immediately after overrunning the area (Todd 1992, 58), and the Goths chose not to settle in the territories that they had overrun in the Greek east (Wolfram 1997, 46).

40 On climate change at the beginning of the third century see Demougeot (1969, 468–9), who associates the flooding of the coastal areas with the abrupt disappearance of coins from the low-lying settlements of Flanders around or just after 260. The panegyric to Constantius Chlorus, dated to 297, mentions the inundations (*Pan. Lat.* 4 (8).8; Périn and Feffer 1987, 30). Bloemers (1989, 192) enumerates the evidence for withdrawal from the coast and for the raising up of inland settlements to avoid the encroachment of rising water levels.

41 Weapon deposits begin to appear on a large scale at the beginning of the third century in northern Europe (Pearson 1989, 212–14; Kaul 1993a; 1993b). Hedeager (1992, 247) suggests that the weapon finds indicate warfare undertaken to gain control of strategic resources.

42 In tribal society war was regarded as normal (Wolfram 1997, 8). The princely graves (Fürstengräber) are indicative of elite groups which were able to monopolise Roman imports and other sources of wealth, using direct personal contacts and connections (Hedeager 1992, 143; 148; 157; 160); see also Hedeager (1992, figs. 3.39 and 3.40) for the early scatter of princely graves and the later centralised clusters; for the classification of types see Gebühr (1974). For the Baltic see also Kaul (1993a).

43 Different kinds of leaders were supported by Rome, who ruled via the nobility, via chiefs, or via kings, according to the arrangements that best suited her purpose (Demougeot 1969, 295). In the third century a new type of kingship emerged (Wolfram 1988, 13).

44 War and hardship combined to produce the circumstances for leading families to seize lands and gain control over production and trade (Wolfram 1988, 6–7; 1997, 54). Warfare and food shortages also created groups of landless men who gravitated towards a strong leader, who was able to impose control over land ownership (Hedeager 1992, 248).

45 Warrior bands were a normal part of tribal life, as described by Caesar (*BG* 3.22.1–3); see Tacitus (*Germ.* 13.2–3) on the *comitatus*, a title which the Romans used to describe the military following of a chieftain or king (Todd 1992, 31); see also Anderson (1938, 91; 94). The warbands could be formed from men from different tribes (Todd 1992, 31). During the third century a new type of warband developed, supported by their control of agricultural production, and free of tribal ties (Hedeager 1992, 248–9; Krüger 1983, 12–14; Lee 1993, 27). Leagues of tribesmen could be formed for different purposes (Demougeot 1969, 341–2). They were more fitted for hit-and-run raids than for open warfare, and raided their neighbours as well as the Empire (Demougeot 1969, 311; Zonaras 12.14). MacMullen (1966, 214–15) points out that the tribesmen had only narrowly focused, short-term interests, usually restricted to immediate personal gain.

46 Lee (1993, 27 n.63) argues that the federations of tribesmen of the Marcomannic wars foreshadowed the third-century coalitions, and Kolendo (1981, 463–4) points out that the federations existed long before the third century, possibly under different names. They were primarily occupied with fighting each other.

47 The attacks of the new federations coincided with internal anarchy in the Roman Empire (Todd 1992, 57). See also note 55 below.

48 On the Alamanni in general see Christlein (1979); Nuber (1993); Schmidt (1983); Todd (1992, 207–10); Wolfram (1997, 45–8), and on the probable ethnic origins see Radnoti (1967) and Werner (1973). On tribal names see Wolfram (1997, 4–6). The name Seubi or Suevi was known in the first century BC, and was applied generally to the Germanic tribes (Wolfram 1988, 19; 1997, 9). The name Suebi means 'people of one law' or 'us' (Junghans 1986, 11). Gregory of Tours knew that the Alamanni derived from the Suebi '*Suebi id est Alamanni*' (*History of the Franks* 7.2). The Greek and Latin authors applied the label 'Scythians' to most of the tribes north of the Danube (Shaw 1982, 9) until it was replaced by the term 'Goths' (Wolfram 1988, 19–20; 1997, 39). Opinion varies on the Franks; they were the Free Men (Zollner 1970, 1) or their name derived from *Frekkr*, fierce or courageous (Périn and Feffer 1987, 18). James (1988, 6–9) prefers not to attach too much fixed meaning to the origin of the Frankish name, which could have changed over long periods of time. Alamanni means 'all men' (Schmidt 1983, 336–7; Demougeot 1969, 335).

49 The choice of a descriptive name like 'all men' was a political act (Christlein 1979, 22).

50 Dio (77. 13.4–6; 14.2; 15.2–3) refers to Alamanni, but the passages in question could probably be later interpolations (Nuber 1993, 104). Wolfram (1997, 39) doubts the authenticity of Dio's text, quoting Castritius' article (1990) in support of his argument. Caracalla took the title 'Alamannicus' according to the *HA* (Caracalla 16.6), but the authenticity of this work is doubtful and it dates from a much later period than the early third century. The Arval Brethren in Rome prayed for the safety and success of the emperor, and on 6 October 213 they gave thanks for the victory, referring to Caracalla as *Germanicus Maximus* (*CIL* VI 2086). On Caracalla's campaign and the military movements associated with it see Schönberger (1985, 414–18).

51 The first truly authentic reference to the Alamanni is in the panegyric extolling Maximian's victory in 286 (*Pan. Lat.* 2 (10).5.1). The date of the formation of the league of the Alamanni is disputed. Demougeot (1969, 335; 479) suggests that it occurred prior to 213, and projects the possible origins back to the reign of Severus. Christol (1997, 133) places the federation and the choice of the name Alamanni much later, in 256. The Alamanni probably absorbed the Hermunduri and Naristi (Demougeot 1969, 243). The earliest known reference to the Juthungi is on the inscription from Augsburg dating to 260 (Bakker 1993; Kellner 1995, 341–4; König 1997; Loriot and Nony 1997, 76–7 no. 36)

Agathias (1.6.3) writing in the sixth century knew that the Alamanni were a mixed group of people. He used the work of the third-century author Asinius Quadratus (the remains of whose work are preserved in *FGrH* 97 ed. F. Jacoby). See also Krüger (1983, 16); Nuber (1993, 105 nn.53 and 54).

52 The Alamanni were ruled by independent kings and princes (Schmidt 1983, 337–8). The land where they settled prevented easy communications and was not conducive to unity (Todd 1992, 207), and their lack of unity under one strong king contrasts with the history of the Goths, whose cohesion was greater (Wolfram 1997, 47).

53 The purpose of the raids was not to find new lands or to settle but to plunder (Krüger 1983, 11–12; Wolfram 1997, 45).

54 Destruction layers at many Raetian towns and forts have been interpreted as evidence of the passage of the Alamanni (Schmidt 1983, 338; Kellner 1995, 315–54). Coin hoards have been added to the evidence to produce an overall picture of devastation. For the invasion of 233, see Kellner (1995, 321–7). On the destruction of the fort at Pfünz see Okamura (1996); Kellner (1995, 323; 500–1; 564 nn.36–7); Winkelmann (1926, 54–6); for an alternative view see Baatz (1986, 78–89). In Upper Germany rebuilding of the shrine at Öhringen and the baths at Walldürn are attested by inscriptions (*CIL* III 6541; 6592); see also Filtzinger *et al.* (1986, 88; 464–5; 606). Sites where the latest coins date from the reign of Severus Alexander include the villa at Treuchtlingen, and the fort baths at Weissenburg; in general these sites are confined to the western half of southern Bavaria (Kellner 1995, 325–7). For maps of coin finds associated with the invasion of 233 see Drack and Fellmann (1988, 73 fig. 38; Filtzinger *et al.* 1986, 89 fig. 22; 93 fig. 23). There seems to have been more trouble in the 240s while Gordian III and his army was in the east (Kellner 1995, 330–5). The daggers and iron and metal hoards at Künzing were dated by an As of Gordian III (Kellner 1995, 330 fig. 89). Whilst it cannot be said with any certainty that it was the Alamanni who caused the destruction during any of the invasions, and it is not possible to apply fixed dates to the events, there is no doubt that dire things were happening in the mid-third century. The burning, the gruesome deaths, and the burials of coins and treasure, cannot have come about accidentally. Some of the evidence is fairly graphic, as seen in the two smashed skulls found in a well at the villa at Regensburg-Harting (Kellner 1995, 329). For coin and treasure hoards associated with the invasions of 260 see Drack and Fellmann (1988, 77 fig. 39); Filtzinger *et al.* (1986, 93 fig. 23; 95 fig. 24).

55 Lee (1993, 132–4) investigates the intelligence-gathering capacities of the tribesmen who attacked the frontiers at moments when the Romans were weakened by other wars or internal problems. Demougeot (1969, 466) lists the occasions when the attacks coincided with such problems. Wightman (1985, 193) also highlights the talent of the northern tribesmen for crossing the frontiers when they were least well defended. Eadie (1980, 1048) disagrees with the conclusion that the tribesmen knew of weaknesses, and in particular does not think that the Alamanni knew of the problems facing the Empire in 259–60. The news of Valerian's capture reached Egypt in the early autumn, at some time between 29 August and 29 September (Drack and Fellmann 1988, 75; 587 n.89). The regnal years of Valerian, Gallienus and Saloninus break off at the end of August 260 (Christol 1997, 139; *P. Oxy.* 2186). On the chronology of the year 260 in general see Christol (1975; 1997, 139–41).

56 The abandonment of the Raetian frontier is generally attributed to Gallienus in the ancient sources. The territory opposite Mainz was occupied by the barbarians under Gallienus '*sub Gallieno imperatore a barbaris occupatae sunt*' (*Laterculus Veronensis* 15). Another source (*Pan. Lat.* 4 (8).10) states that under Gallienus Raetia was lost '*sub principe Gallieno ... Raetia amissa*'. Nuber (1993, 104) concludes that the frontier was given up during the reign of Gallienus, somewhere between 260 and 268. Kellner (1995, 338–46) reassesses the problem in the light of the new inscription found at Augsburg, revealing that the Raetian frontier was for a short time under the command of the Gallic Empire; see also

Bakker (1993); Lavagne (1994); Loriot and Nony (1997, 76–7 no. 36). Gallienus reoccupied and refortified Vindonissa (Windisch) probably before the invasions and not as a response to them, and he installed garrisons in Augusta Raurica, Castrum Rauracense and Basilia (Drack and Fellmann 1988, 74–6); Bernhard (1990, 119) suggests that Vindonissa was refortified after a smaller invasion in 259, not after the major one in 260. The full reparation after the invasions of the Alamanni could only begin under Probus, who is credited with the establishment of the new frontier along the Danube–Iller–Rhine line, leaving the *agri decumates* to the Alamanni (Kellner 1995, 351–4). On the Danube–Iller–Rhine frontier in general see Filtzinger *et al.* (1986, 97–8 fig. 25); Drack and Fellmann (1988, 278, fig. 276).

57 The *agri decumates* remained a poor area, with little or no Roman imports (Demougeot 1969, 279).

58 Insecurity of the inhabitants is reflected in the flight to hilltop refuges. For a catalogue of known hilltop refuge sites in the Empire see Johnson (1983, 280–90; figs. 85–8). Raetia was seemingly worse afflicted than Gaul (Johnson 1983, 116). Some of these refuges have been associated with the invasion of 233, as for instance those in the Jura mountains; some of these refuges were occupied for a considerable time, especially Wittnauer Horn (Drack and Fellmann 1988, 82–7). On Aurelian's walls of Rome see Richmond (1930); Todd (1978); Cizek (1994, 98–102; 259 nn.10–12).

59 Probus defeated the Alamanni and brought them to terms. Nine kings submitted to him, and the terms of the treaty exacted the contribution of 16,000 troops (*HA Probus* 13–14). Junghans (1986, 131–2) finds the 16,000 recruits credible but doubts the story that Probus settled 400,000 tribesmen. The units of Alamanni and Juthungi are attested much later in the *Notitia* (Schmidt 1983, 339), though Radnoti (1967) prefers to think that the Juthungi were not fighting with the Alamanni but against them as allies of the Romans.

60 The panegyric to Maximian refers to his victory over the Burgundiones and Alamanni in 286 (*Pan. Lat.* 2 (10).5.1). In 290 Diocletian is named on an inscription as *fundator pacis aeternae* (Kellner 1995, 355–7); the fact that it is located at Augsburg makes the connection with the Alamanni more definite. A panegyric of 291 (*Pan. Lat.* 3 (11).17.4) mentions a victory over the Burgundiones and Alamanni again. Six years later, the place name Alamannia appears (*Pan. Lat.* 4 (8).2.1), and in 298 a victory monument of Constantius Chlorus at Nicaea also attests to 'Alamania' [*sic*] (Nuber 1993, 108; Bittel 1954). The place-name appears on coins from the early third century onwards (Nuber 1993, 103; 105 n.51; 108; Christ 1960, 154–66).

61 Frangones are mentioned in one of Cicero's letters (*ad Att.* 14.10), but these have nothing to do with the later Franks (Zollner 1970, 2 n.2). James (1988, 6–9) discusses the theories about the Frankish name, and whether it derives from adjectives meaning 'fierce' or 'free'. He concludes that there is no single source for the name and that its meaning changed over time; see also Zollner (1970, 2–3) and Wenskus (1961, 512–18). Gregory of Tours, writing in the sixth century, thought that the Franks came from Pannonia (*History of the Franks* 2.9). On the increasingly fabulous stories about the Franks, especially the Trojan origins, see Zollner (1970, 5) and Périn and Feffer (1987, 12–13).

62 The smaller tribes who made up the Frankish league are listed by Zollner (1970, 2–3 nn.3–9) and James (1988, 35). The Chamavi are equated with the Franks in the *Tabularia Peutingeriana*. The Bructeri are described as Frankish by Gregory of Tours (*History of the Franks* 2.9), but in the same passage he includes the Chatti, by which he perhaps meant Chattuarii, who are described as Franks by Ammianus (20.10.2); the Salii appear as Frankish in the works of Zosimus (3.6) and Ammianus (17.8.3). Périn and Feffer (1987, 27) point out that the only sure means of survival for these small groups of people lay in combining forces. The composition of the warrior bands was multi-ethnic, not even confined to members of those tribes who formed the Frankish league (Krüger 1983, 381).

63 It was considered that the raids across the frontier in 253–4 were probably associated

with the withdrawal of troops by Valerian from the Rhine to fight the usurper Aemilianus, but this is now discredited. By 254 Gallienus was calling himself *Germanicus Maximus* (Zollner 1970, 8), but these victories may be associated with the Germans of the Danube, possibly Pannonia. Soon after establishing himself as Emperor with Gallienus as his colleague, Valerian went to the east. The mint at Antioch reopened after a cessation of coin production in 253, probably caused by the capture of the city by Shapur; see Paschoud (1971, 149–50 n.54) on the chronology and the number of times that Antioch fell into the hands of the Persians; see also Ridley (1982, 140 n.52) and Christol (1997, 132–5; 169–70 nn.4–6). Ancient sources for the Frankish invasion of 257 include Aurelius Victor (*de Caes.* 33.3); Eutropius (9.8.2); Orosius (7.22.8; 7.41.2), who says that the Franks remained in Spain for 12 years; see also Zollner (1970, 8) and Périn and Feffer (1987, 30). On the mid-third-century inscription from Tamuda see Zollner (1970, 8 n.5, quoting Thouvenot *Revue des Études Latines* 16, 1938, 266f and Fiebiger *Germania* 28, 1940, 145f).

64 The mint was transferred from Viminacium to Cologne in 257 (Zollner 1970, 8 n.5). Postumus was highly regarded by Gallienus and was left in command on the German frontier, but it is not certain whether he was actually governor of Lower Germany (Drinkwater 1987, 25–6; 88).

65 Postumus proclaimed himself Emperor probably in the summer of 260 (Périn and Feffer 1987, 31; Drinkwater 1987, 24), though the date is disputed (Zollner 1970, 8–9). He celebrated his achievements in clearing the Franks out of Gaul as *restitutor Galliarum* (Périn and Feffer 1987, 34). He may have recruited Franks to fight in his army (Aurelius Victor *de Caes.* 33.8; Krüger 1983, 380–1).

66 Tetricus issued coins proclaiming a German victory (Zollner 1970, 10 n.1; Drinkwater 1987, 40; 186; Aurelius Victor *Epit. de Caes.* 35.3). The invasions of 274–5 were the most serious of all, supposedly involving the destruction of 70 cities which Probus repaired (*HA* Probus 13.5). Coin hoards on the Cologne–Tongres–Bavai route have been interpreted as evidence of Frankish raids (Krüger 1983, 381); see also Bernhard (1990, 120–2, esp. 121 fig. 60).

67 Probus brought the war to an end in 278 (Zosimus 1.68; 69). He fortified the Rhine frontier and built bridgehead forts on the right bank of the Rhine (*HA* Probus 13.8; 14.7; 18.5). The Franks whom he settled around the mouth of the Danube sailed back home again (Zollner 1970, 11; Zosimus 1.71.2; *HA* Probus 18.2). Kunow (1987, 88–9) suggests that after the lower Rhine frontier was abandoned the Franks changed their policy from one of swift raids to a new ideal of settlement within the Empire.

68 The German victories of Carus and Carinus could have been over the Franks, but it is known that Carus fought the Quadi as well (Zollner 1970, 11 n.5; *CIL* XII 12522). Maximian captured Gennobaudes and brought the Franks to terms (*Pan. Lat.* 2 (10).10.3–5). Some Franks were settled as *laeti* around Amiens, Beauvais, Troyes and Langres (Krüger 1983, 382–3 and fig. 94; *Pan. Lat.* 4 (8).21).

69 On Carausius and Allectus in general see Casey (1994). Périn and Feffer (1987, 39) claim that Carausius was not aiming at rule of the whole Roman world, but only equality with the Augusti. See also Aurelius Victor (*Epit. de Caes.* 39.20.21); *Pan. Lat.* (4 (8).17; 18); Orosius (7.25.2); Eutropius (9.21). On the brutality of the war against the Franks see Krüger (1983, 383 n.34); Eutropius (10.3.2); Eusebius (*de Vita Constantini* 1.25.1); *Pan. Lat.* (4 (8).16; 6 (7).4; 7 (6).11).

70 Constantine recruited large numbers of Germans for the army, including many Franks (Todd 1992, 59). Many of the units of Franks in the *Notitia Dignitatum*, or those tribes such as the Chamavi, Ampsivarii, Bructeri and Salii which made up the Frankish league (*Not. Dig. Occ.* 5; *Or.* 31) were probably recruited by Constantine (Zollner 1970, 15–16). The Frank Bonitus became an officer in the Roman army (Ammianus 15.5.33); on Frankish officers in the Roman army in general see Zollner (1970, 164).

71 The Imperial family maintained a presence at Trier despite the threat to the eastern half

of the Empire from the Goths (Périn and Feffer 1987, 447). After the death of Constantine the Franks invaded in 341 (Zollner 1970, 16–17) and were eventually settled in Toxandria in the Brabant (Périn and Feffer 1987, 48).

72 Ptolemy mentions the Gutones (*Geog.* 3.5.8). It is not certain whether the Guti are the same tribe as the Gutones; see also Ptolemy (*Geog.* 2.11.33; 34; 35); Tacitus (*Germ.* 43) Pliny (*NH* 4.100; 37.35); Pomponius Mela (3.3.31). See Wolfram (1988, 19–35) on the Gothic tribal names and their history.

73 See Mierow (1915, 15–16) on Cassiodorus and his aims in writing the history of the Goths. Wolfram (1988, 30) supposes that Cassiodorus read some historical sources, and integrated songs and folk tales into his narrative, but is sceptical about the existence of Ablabius (*ibid.* 386, n.36 where Wolfram summarises the latest arguments about Ablabius as a historical source). Hachmann (1970, 452) accepts that Ablabius was a real personality and traces his work in that of Cassiodorus. See also Heather (1996, 10). Jordanes (*Getica* 16–24) links the Goths with Scandinavia (Scandza), quoting Ptolemy and Pomponius Mela as corroborative sources. The German scholar Kossina accepted the origins of the Goths in Scandinavia (Heather 1996, 13), but Hachmann (1970) dismissed the Scandinavian stories as myths. Among those who accept the Scandinavian origins of the Goths, or who do not reject the idea totally, most scholars prefer the theory of small-scale progressive movements of the tribesmen rather than the idea of a mass migration (Wolfram 1988, 39; 395 n.21 quoting Wenskus [1961] 2nd edn 1977). Heather (1996, 14–18) points out that it is too simplistic to try to compare the Scandinavian and the later Gothic evidence, hoping to find recognisable points of contact in chronological order; instead he opts for a combination of the migration theory and the processual approach, because it is probable that both elements were at work.

74 Kazansky (1991, 14–15) proposes a sensible solution to the problem that does not go against any of the sources and positively agrees with most of them.

75 See Heather (1996, 43) on the mixed nature of the Wielbark culture. See Wolfram (1988, 12; 38–40; 385 n.24), and for an archaeological overview of settlements and artefacts see Kazansky (1991, 18–28; 30).

76 The Goths began to move at the end of the second and beginning of the third century (Demougeot 1969, 344–94; Kazansky 1991, 28; Jordanes *Getica* 26–7). On the Cherniakhov culture see Wolfram (1988, 42); Kazansky (1991, 39–59). The passage in the *Historia Augusta* (Marcus Aurelius 14.1) shows that the Romans knew of the presence of another large tribe to the north of the Danube, who pressured the Marcomanni and Quadi, but there may be an analogy with the fourth-century situation when the Huns were beginning to make their presence felt (Heather 1996, 35). Early Roman contacts with the Goths may have extended as far back as the reign of Severus (Heather 1996, 39, quoting Speidel 1977, 716–18, on Guththa, son of Erminarius, *praepositus* of the *gentiles* in the Roman army in Arabia in 202).

77 The Goths were accustomed to Roman goods before they began to raid across the frontiers; they were especially interested in luxury goods, oil and wine (Kazansky 1991, 32). The Empire was attractive to the developing Gothic society (Heather 1996, 31). Gothic kings possessed greater authority than many other tribal kings, and were often at the head of multi-racial groups (Wolfram 1988, 12).

78 The attack in 238 is attested by Dexippus (frg. 14 *FGrH* II Jacoby). The Carpi were still pre-eminent at this time (Wolfram 1988, 44–5). On the attack on Olbia and Tyras and the disappearance of the coinage see Christol (1997, 94; 121). On the subsidies to the Goths and the probable treaty exacting service in the Roman army see Wolfram (1988, 44–5). See also Demougeot (1969, 395); Bursche (1996b, 111–12 nn.78–83).

79 The decade between 238 and 248 saw more trouble from the Carpi than the Goths (Wolfram 1988, 44). Philip stopped the payment of subsidies (Christol 1997, 121; Jordanes *Getica* 89). Decius cleared Dacia of the Goths in 250 and was hailed as *restitutor Daciarum* (*CIL* III 1176 = *ILS* 514). Trebonianus Gallus was powerless to stop the Goths

from proceeding to their homes with their booty and prisoners (Christol 1997, 127; Wolfram 1988, 46). Paschoud (1971, 147–8 n.51) says that Trebonianus concluded a disastrous peace.

80 Zosimus (1.27–31) puts the first appearance of the Goths on the Black Sea in 254–6, although it could be interpreted that he meant 255–7 (Heather and Matthews 1991, 3). Paschoud (1971, 152, n.59) discusses the theories of dating but prefers 254, while Ridley (1982, 141 n.61) says that the Goths first appeared anywhere between 255 and 259. On Aemilianus see Zosimus (1.28–9); Aurelius Victor (*de Caes.* 31.1–2); Eutropius (9.5); Jordanes (*Getica* 105–6). On the first sea raids see Wolfram (1988, 48); Heather (1996, 40). It is possible that the Goths resorted to raids from the sea because the land routes had been well-guarded and access by those entry points was denied (Heather 1996, 42). Wolfram (1988, 53) dates the effective protection of the Danube and Dacia to a later time, by about 268. On sieges by the Goths see Zosimus (1.32–3; 43; 70); Jordanes (*Getica* 92; 102–3; 113); Ammianus (17.6.1; 29.6.12). Dexippus defended Athens against the Heruli during the Gothic invasions (Dexippus frg. 25, *FGrH* II, 466; 470–2; 474 Jacoby; Millar 1969, 12–29).

81 The Canonical Letter of Gregory Thaumaturgus is not precisely dated, but it illustrates the general situation and the breakdown of law and order that accompanied the invasions (Heather and Matthews 1991, 4–5). The raids of 268 were of unprecedented size (Wolfram 1988, 54). On the victories of Gallienus and Claudius Gothicus see Heather (1996, 41); Wolfram (1988, 53); Demougeot (1969, 425–8). On Claudius II Gothicus in general see Damerau (1934); he was the first to adopt the title *Gothicus Maximus* (Wolfram 1988, 55; Christol 1997, 157). There is great variation in the sources as to the statistics concerning the numbers of Gothic ships and men; Zosimus (1.48) gives preposterous figures of 6,000 ships and 320,000 men; *HA* (Claudius 8.2) halves the ships but agrees with the number of men; Ammianus (31.5.15) says 2,000 ships; the *Suda* gives 900 ships, and Syncellus (I. p. 717, 9 Bonn) gives a more realistic 500; see Paschoud (1971, 159 n.70). Aurelian's victory over the Goths was total (Cizek 1994, 105–6); Aurelian see *HA* (Aurelian 22.2); Eutropius (9.13); Orosius (7.23.4). Cizek (1994, 105) suggests that Cannobaudes might be Cniva under another name.

82 The date of the evacuation of Dacia is disputed. Cizek (1994, 125–6) suggests that it occurred in 273, before the second Palmyrene campaign. Wolfram (1988, 56–7) points out that the move was a success for Rome, since the Goths were occupied for years in fighting other tribes for possession of it. Ammianus (31.5.17) says that the Goths remained peaceful for 'centuries'.

6 BEYOND THE EASTERN FRONTIERS

1 Millar (1993, 141–7) documents the Romano-Persian wars to the reign of Philip, and points out (1993, 142–3) the overriding predominance of the east in Roman affairs in the early third century under the Severans. All Rome's efforts were concentrated on the east, save for the campaigns in Britain in 208–11 and in Germany in 213, and this was before the seizure of power by the Persians in 224. For a brief outline of Roman–Persian relations see Dodgeon and Lieu (1991, 1–4), and for fuller discussion see Kettenhofen (1982). Isaac (1992, 31; 52) points out that there are no concrete reasons why Rome and Parthia and then Rome and Persia constantly went to war, and that Rome was more often the aggressor. Whenever there was an internal or external problem in either the Parthian/Persian Empire or the Roman Empire the other power chose that moment to attack (Lee 1993, 121; 125). Ardashir attacked when Maximinus Thrax was occupied on the Rhine (Dio 80.4.1–2); conversely Gordian III chose the moment when Shapur had to deal with problems on his own eastern frontier, and Carus invaded when Vahram II was faced with a rebellion instigated by his brother Hormizd (*Pan. Lat.* 3 (11).17.2; Eutropius 9.18.1; *HA* Carus 8.1). The source material for the third-century Roman wars

with the Persians is gathered together and translated into English by Dodgeon and Lieu (1991) and the sources for the Sassanids are assembled by Felix (1985). In their relations with the foreign enemy the Romans were not gracious, routinely referring to the Parthians and the Persians as barbarians; see the narrative of Herodian.

2 Control of Armenia either indirectly via a friendly king or directly by armed intervention was a constant theme in Romano-Parthian and Romano-Persian relations; see Isaac (1992, 249–50). There were occasional attempts by the Romans to annex Armenia; Mark Antony briefly took it over in 34 by capturing its king Artavasdes and sending him as a prisoner to Alexandria; Trajan also annexed the kingdom when he campaigned in the east, but Hadrian rapidly restored the status quo, probably because he anticipated that in order to retain it he would have to go to war against the Parthians. Similarly, Severus' creation of the province of Mesopotamia altered the balance of power and caused endless trouble thereafter (Millar 1993, 141–2); Dio (75.3.2–3) explained that it brought Rome into closer contact with the allies of Persia and nearer to the king of kings, while lengthening communications with Rome.

3 On the demise of the Arsacid Parthians and rise of the Sassanid Persians see Christensen (1944, 84–96); Debevoise (1938, 240ff). See Loriot (1975, 755 n.766) on the variants of the name of Ardashir = Ataxerxes. The lineage of Ardashir is convoluted and perhaps mythical; the sources are laudatory to the point of disbelief. Agathias 3.27.1–5 and Syncellus (translated in Dodgeon and Lieu 1991, 9–10) both repeat with slightly different elaborations the story that Pabag received into his house a guest called Sasan, and with his gifts as a seer he realised that any offspring of Sasan would rise to unrivalled fame, so he allowed the honoured guest to sleep with his wife, and the result of the union was a son, Ardashir, who was brought up as the son of Pabag. Later, when Ardashir was on the road to kingship, both Sasan and Pabag each claimed him as his own son. Roman sources take no notice of the origins of Ardashir, but document his sudden arrival on the scene as he conquered the Parthians in three battles, killed Artabanus (Dio 80.3.1–2), overran all the barbarian kingdoms on the borders of his own territory, and then turned against the Romans (Herodian 6.2.1–2; 6–7). See Dodgeon and Lieu (1991, 10; 349 n.3 on the possible locations of the battles).

4 It is assumed without question in the narrative of Herodian (6.2.1–2; 2.6–7) that Ardashir set out from the beginning to reconstitute the ancient Empire of the Persians, but it is more likely that Ardashir was an opportunist with ability and great ambition, but no such clearly defined aims. His conquests were not so routine as Herodian implies; he was unsuccessful in trying to take Hatra and met with resistance in Armenia (Dio 80.3.2–3; Dodgeon and Lieu 1991, 14–16). As Dodgeon and Lieu point out (1991, 350 n.4) Artabanus V was not the only Parthian ruler, since he controlled only the eastern Parthian Empire, and his brother Vologaeses V had ruled the Parthian sectors of Mesopotamia, and Babylonia, from c.208 onwards; see also Debevoise (1938, 268ff). Zoroastrianism was established as a state religion by the Sassanids, who assembled the sacred texts of the Avesta and brought the priests and magi out of hiding, elevating them on a par with the nobility (Christensen 1944, 141–205; Gagé 1964a, 107–13). Kartir is generally regarded as the founder of the Zoroastrian religion as established by the Sassanids; Shapur gave him the task of organising the new cult, and from the very beginning Kartir assumed an important place at the Royal court, blending political and religious influence; see Winter (1988, 123). Kartir appears on the relief carvings of the Sassanid kings, and gained considerably in influence under Vahram II; he is depicted on five reliefs of this king (Vanden Berghe 1984, 76–7).

5 Herodian (6.5.3; 7.1–6) describes the Parthian army in terms bordering on contempt, because 'the barbarians' as he calls the Parthians did not have a standing, paid army like the Romans and did not leave permanent garrisons in strong points. He also suggests that the soldiers disliked leaving their homes and families. Herodian does however accede that the Parthians were skilled bowmen, born in the saddle and never putting their bows

down, because unlike the Romans they hunted with them all the time. Whittaker (1970, 110 n.1) explains that the king summoned the army for each campaign, and the soldiers served on feudal terms under their lords. The aristocrats provided the cavalry arm. The Sassanid military organisation was not very different in that there was never a standing army; weapons and stores were kept in great magazines, issued to the soldiers when they were called up for campaigns, and returned when the campaigns were concluded, though there were some garrisoned places on the Persian borders (Christensen 1944, 97ff; 206ff).

6 Millar (1993, 141) points out that police work and military functions were closely interwoven on the Roman eastern frontier, and that a complex security problem can still exist even without the constant threat of armed invasion by a foreign power. He also notes (1993, 130–1) that military personnel were frequently asked to mediate in local disputes and sometimes did so, with varying degrees of success. In particular, the official position of the army officers as police is highlighted by the inscription mentioning a centurion in charge of public order at Sphoracene; see also Feissel and Gascou (1995). The term 'Saracens' began to be used in the late third century to describe disruptive elements no matter what their origin, and does not necessarily denote a particular tribe. The first known reference to Saracens occurs on the panegyric to Maximian in 291 (*Pan. Lat.* 2 (3).5.4), but as Eadie (1996, 76–7) points out, Maximian as the western Augustus is unlikely to have fought against the Saracens. By the fourth century the term was in regular use; in 334 an inscription attests the building of a reservoir so that the local people could get water without being harassed by the 'Saracens' (Millar 1993, 435–6); on Rome and the Saracens generally see Parker (1986; 1987), who consistently claims that the Roman frontier was geared to this type of threat from semi-nomadic, unsettled peoples where policing rather than full-scale military action was called for; see also Bowersock (1983, 73). The eastern frontier was not a strongly defended line designed to stop movement across it; the main function of the small posts strung out along the frontier line was more likely to protect traffic moving along the border routes (Millar 1993, 138–9). On the eastern Roman frontier, its function, and its installations see French and Lightfoot (1989); Kennedy and Riley (1991); Isaac (1992).

7 The presence of the Roman Emperor on campaign was mandatory in the third century, especially in the east (Millar 1993, 141). New Persian attacks began in the 230s when Ardashir overran Cappadocia and laid siege to Nisibis (Zonaras 12.15; Dodgeon and Lieu 1991, 17); see also Winter (1988, 45ff); Loriot (1975, 717 n.471; 760 nn.767–8); Gilliam (1950, 220; 249–50); Fink (1971, 192–7). Herodian (6.2.5–6) affirms that the Persians looted Roman provinces and invaded Mesopotamia with their infantry and cavalry; they besieged the forts on the banks of the river Euphrates. The eastern governors then demanded the presence of the Roman Emperor (Herodian 6.3.1).

8 Herodian (6.3.1–4) documents the preparations for war and the three-pronged attack of Severus Alexander; see Dodgeon and Lieu (1991, 18). See Loriot (1975, 760–1) on the outbreak of the war; see also Maricq (1957). Both Millar (1993, 150) and Whittaker (1970, 108–9) outline the possible routes taken by the Romans. Herodian (6.7.1–6) mentions a truce at the end of the war, which Severus Alexander thought would check the activities of the Persian king, but it seems that there was no formal treaty; see Winter (1988, 45–79) on the war and its conclusion.

9 Agathias (4.24.2) describes the death of Ardashir and the accession of Shapur (Dodgeon and Lieu 1991, 34). Shapur recorded his accession by means of rock carvings at Naqs-i Rajab near Persepolis, in which he is depicted at his investiture by Ahuramazda himself, thus firmly establishing his rule as god-given. In the *RGDS* he lists his possessions at the time of his accession (lines 1–6 in the Greek version; Dodgeon and Lieu 1991, 34–5). On the inscription see Carratelli (1947); Chaumont (1969; 39–46); Ensslin (1949); Guey (1955); Maricq and Honigman (1953); Maricq (1958); Mazzarino (1971); Olmstead (1942; 251–6); Sprengling (1953; 79–84). See Vanden Berghe (1984) on the rock carvings. On the battle at Meshike see *RGDS* (lines 6–9 in the Greek version; Dodgeon and

Lieu 1991, 35); for discussion see Kettenhofen (1982, 31–6). No Roman source mentions this battle at Meshike. All the ancient versions of the death of Gordian III are listed in Dodgeon and Lieu (1991, 36–45; 355–6 n.9); see also Hartmann (1982, 76–8); Kettenhofen (1982, 31ff); Winter (1988, 83–97). Zosimus (3.32) says that Philip made a dishonourable peace with the enemy; only the *RGDS* says that the Roman Emperor paid 500,000 denarii and became a tributary of the Persians; Dodgeon and Lieu (1991, 358 n.25) agree that it is possible that besides the sum just mentioned, Philip probably paid a regular tribute as well. See Winter (1988, 80–123, esp. 100ff) on the war and its outcome, and the payments to the Persians. Armenia was lost but since the coinage of Edessa, Rhesaena, and Nisibis continued without a break it is likely that the Romans did not lose control of these cities, and it is possible that Philip kept most of Mesopotamia except for the fringe areas bordering on Persian territory (Winter 1988, 83–97; Christol 1997, 98). Winter (1988, 105–6; 119) detects no territorial changes after the peace of 244; see also Guey and Pékary (1961).

10 Philip issued coins proclaiming *pax fundata cum Persis* (*RIC* IV.3 p. 79 no. 69) and took the victory titles *Parthicus Maximus* (*CIL* III 4634; 10619 = *ILS* 507) and *Persicus Maximus* (*CIL* VI 1097 = *ILS* 506; *AE* 1953, 27). Julius Priscus was made prefect of Mesopotamia according to Zosimus (1.19.2), and his rule over the east was too harsh (Zosimus 1.20.2). The title bestowed on him, *rector orientis*, is attested on an inscription (*CIL* III 141495.5 = *ILS* 9005) dedicated to Priscus by the *primus pilus* Trebonius Sossianus. It is the first attested use of the term, and may even be the very first time that it appeared (Millar 1993, 156). The precise functions and the extent of the powers of this post are not elucidated, but it is closely paralleled by the office bestowed on Vaballathus of Palmyra, and possibly Odenathus before him, by Gallienus, as *corrector orientis* or *restitutor orientis* (Dodgeon and Lieu 1991, 47–8; 359 n.35). See also Christol (1997, 99–100).

11 According to the *RGDS* (lines 10–19 in the Greek version) the Persians defeated 60,000 Romans at Barbalissos, but the Roman sources uniformly neglect to mention this; see Dodgeon and Lieu (1991, 50) and Kettenhofen (1982, 53–4). Shapur follows up his claim with a list of the cities taken from the Romans, proud of the fact that he devastated Syria; he also captured Nisibis (Dodgeon and Lieu 1991, 49–50; 361–3 nn.7–19). Millar (1993, 159) says that Shapur was not interested in Mesopotamia but aimed directly for Syria. The main struggle was over control of Armenia. In the *RGDS*, just before the claim that 60,000 Romans were killed, Shapur says that the Roman Caesar lied again, and did wrong over Armenia. There is debate about which Emperor is meant; some scholars assume it must be Philip, others that it must be Trebonianus Gallus, which puts the date at some point between 251 and 253; Dodgeon and Lieu (1991, 360 n.3) opt for Gallus; Zosimus places the invasion of Syria in the reign of Gallus (Dodgeon and Lieu 1991, 363 n.20); see Felix (1985, 56). The chronology of the attacks on Armenia and Syria is not clearly elucidated and allows for more than one interpretation; Kettenhofen (1982) says that Armenia was a Sassanid province from 252 and Antioch was captured in 253.

12 Shapur lists all the cities that he took on his third campaign (*RGDS* lines 19–37; Dodgeon and Lieu 1991, 57; 365–7 nn.36–45). Dura-Europos fell, and Shapur may have captured Antioch again, though the number of times that Antioch was captured and the exact dates are disputed; Dodgeon and Lieu (1991, 53–4; 363 n.23) point out that Antioch may have been the Persian objective during the second campaign noted in *RGDS*, as it would have provided the most easily accessible booty and captives, so it may have fallen in 257 after Dura-Europos, which could not have been taken before 256. Whether Antioch was taken by the Persian again in 260 is debatable; see Paschoud (1971, 149–50 n.54; 153 n.60); Ridley (1982, 141 n.57) The coinage from Carrhae and Nisibis continues unbroken, strongly implying that the Romans retained control of these cities (Winter 1988, 100–3). Odenathus was *vir consularis* before 258 according to *IGR* III 103, and Kettenhofen (1982, 133) postulates that he may have been active on Rome's behalf as early as 253. Millar (1993, 164–5) denies that Odenathus had any special

position at this time, but presumes (1993, 334) that he was governor of Syria Phoenice and stepped into the vacuum created by the Persian invasions.

13 The date of the capture of Valerian is much discussed, ranging from 258 to 260. Périn and Feffer (1987 vol. 1, p. 31) link the defeat and capture of the Emperor to the first invasion of the German tribes from across the Rhine, and therefore have to date the capture to 258. De Blois (1975, 10–11; 1976, 2–3) opts for 259, but Christol (1997, 139; 179 nn.4 and 7) points to papyrus evidence from Egypt which indicates that the date must be 260 since *P. Oxy.* 2186, dated to August 260, mentions Valerian, Gallienus, and Saloninus, while *P. Oxy.* 1476, dated to October 260, acknowledges the two sons of Macrianus as Emperors. See Lopuszanski (1951) for discussion of the events, and Dodgeon and Lieu (1991, 57–65) for the ancient references, including Zosimus (1.36.2), Zonaras (12.73), *HA* (Valerian 4.2); Aurelius Victor (*de Caes.* 32.5). On the reliefs at Bishapur, Naqs-i Rustem and Daragbird see Vanden Berghe (1984, 68–74); Grishman (1962, 137ff esp. 142–3). One ancient source (Petrus Patricius frg. 10, *FHG* 4; Dodgeon and Lieu 1991, 68) implies that Odenathus may have tried to forge an alliance with Shapur, to whom he sent gifts, but they were rejected. Dodgeon and Lieu (1991, 369 n.3) accept the story, pointing out that protection of the trade routes, vitally important to Palmyra, will have been the main motive for trying to promote good relations with Shapur. Though the friendly overtures are traditionally dated to the period after the capture of Valerian, the insecure period of 253 is just as likely. The ancient sources claim great victories for Odenathus. According to *HA* (Valerian 4.2–4) he restored Roman power, though the story that he captured the treasury and the Royal harem is too similar to the victory of Galerius nearly four decades later. It is unlikely that Odenathus' main aim was to free Valerian, as claimed by *HA* (Gallienus 10.8). Eutropius (9.10), Jerome (*Chronicon*: see Dodgeon and Lieu 1991, 72) and Zosimus (1.39.2) all say that Odenathus reached Ctesiphon, but only Zosimus claims that he did so on two separate occasions. The activities of Odenathus are not to be construed as rebellion against Rome, since he acted in a Roman capacity on behalf of Rome; the rebellion came later after his death, when Zenobia and Vaballathus tried to gain control of Egypt (Millar 1993, 221).

14 The provinces of Mesopotamia and Osroene remained outside Rome's control, despite the claim in the ancient sources (*HA* Thirty Tyrants 15.3; Gallienus 12) that Odenathus reconquered them. Winter (1988, 128) points out that although Zosimus (1.60.1) says that Aurelius Marcellinus was *praefectus Mesopotamiae* the province seems to have been under Sassanid influence. Eadie (1996, 72) does not believe that Odenathus succeeded in recovering the provinces, whereas Kettenhofen (1982, 125) says he did, in 262, and as a consequence Gallienus took the title *Persicus Maximus* (*CIL* VIII 22765 = *ILS* 8293). Aurelian won a victory over the Palmyrenes Zenobia and Vaballathus, but he did not go on to campaign against the Persians (Eadie 1996, 73). When he had dealt with the troubles of the western half of the Empire he was ready to deal with Persia but was killed before he had begun (*HA* Aurelian 34.4–5). Probus had some diplomatic contact with the Persians, reported in bombastic terms but naming the wrong Persian king as Narses, but in reality it must have been Vahram II (*HA* Probus 17.5); see Felix (1985, 97). When he was ready Probus embarked on a campaign but was killed en route (*HA* Probus 20.1). Dodgeon and Lieu (1991, 373 n.1) speculate that the aim may have been to install Tiridates on the throne of Armenia. Carus' expedition is described by Aurelius Victor (*de Caes.* 38.2–4) as a pre-emptive strike because after the death of Probus all the barbarians, which includes the Persians, invaded Roman territory, and the east was particularly vulnerable to attacks. Other sources emphasise the internal problems that faced the Persians (*HA* Carus 8.1; Eutropius 9.18.1; *Pan. Lat.* 11 (3).17.2); see Winter (1988, 130–2); Dodgeon and Lieu (1991, 112) on the expedition.

15 Winter (1988, 134) doubts that there was a treaty between the Romans and Persians in 283 when the army withdrew under Numerianus and the Praetorian Prefect Aper. The arrangements made in 287 were more formal, involving some kind of submission from

Persia (Millar 1993, 17–6) including the installation of Tiridates on the throne of Armenia, which was beneficial to Rome; Diocletian was honoured as the founder of eternal peace (Eadie 1996, 73). Barnes (1982, 51) dates the event to 287, Winter (1988, 137–151) dates it to 288 and discusses the arrangements. See also Dodgeon and Lieu (1991, 121–2) on the sources.

16 Hostilities resumed when Vahram III was ousted by Narses, one of the sons of Shapur (Dodgeon and Lieu 1991, 124). Narses was cast as the arch-villain in the Roman sources; Lactantius (de Mort. Pers. 9.5) accuses him of wishing to take over the whole Roman east. Narses invaded Armenia and removed Tiridates, probably in 293. Diocletian appointed Constantius and Galerius as Caesars in 293 (Barnes 1982, 37–8), so it is assumed that he did so in order to be better able to deal with the eastern crisis; Eutropius (9.22.1) relates all the ills of the Empire together, the rebellion of Carausius in Britain, of Achilleus in Egypt, and the warlike activities of Narses, and links them with the elevation of Maximian as Augustus and Constantius and Galerius as the two Caesars; see also Eadie (1996, 73). König (1974; 1986) is of the opinion that Galerius was promoted to balance the potentially overambitious activities of Maximian.

17 On Galerius' campaigns see Dodgeon and Lieu (1991, 125); Christol (1997, 251 n.12); Schwartz (1974); Castritius (1971). Between the campaigns after his initial defeat Galerius raised a new army (Aurelius Victor de Caes. 39.34; Eutropius 9.24). On the treaty of 298 or 299 see Petrus Patricius (frg. 13–14 FGH IV pp. 188–9); Dodgeon and Lieu (1991, 131–3). Winter (1988, 169–70; 1989) dates it to 298; Blockley (1992, 5–7) dates it to 299, lists the terms of the treaty and discusses them from the point of view of Narses. See also Eadie (1996, 75) who links the treaty to the establishment of the *Strata Diocletiana*. On this frontier road see van Berchem (1952); Eadie (1996, 75–81) includes a discussion of its function; Kennedy and Riley (1991, 40); Dodgeon and Lieu (1991, 378 nn.61–4). In 354 Ammianus Marcellinus (14.3.2) noted fortifications and road posts in Mesopotamia, but there is no evidence of Diocletianic fortifications in the area; Eadie (1996) considers that the *Strata Diocletiana* represents the finished frontier arrangements after the treaty of 298.

18 For sources on the reign of Narses and his failure to overpower the Romans see Felix (1985, 110ff); Dodgeon and Lieu (1991, 136); Blockley (1992, 6–7); Winter (1988, 208ff). Maximin Daia and Licinius undertook eastern campaigns, but few details are known (Millar 1993, 179; 207; Blockley 1992, 7; Barnes 1982, 81). Hormizd fled to the Romans and was received by Licinius (Dodgeon and Lieu 1991, 147ff), but no war ensued to put Hormizd on the throne of Persia. According to *Epit. de Caes.* (41.20) Constantine placed his kinsman Hannibalianus on the throne of Armenia; see Dodgeon and Lieu (1991, 155). Diplomatic relations between Shapur II and Constantine prevented war for the time being (Eusebius *Life of Constantine* 4.8–13; Dodgeon and Lieu 1991, 150–2), but by 337 Constantine was preparing for war (Eusebius *Life of Constantine* 4.56; Aurelius Victor de Caes. 41.16). The main focus shifted from Armenia to Mesopotamia, which Shapur laid waste before going on to besiege Nsisbi; he departed after two months without taking the city (Eutropius 10.8.2; Dodgeon and Lieu 1991, 155–62). See Blockley (1992, 9–10) for a brief account of Shapur's activities, and Dodgeon and Lieu (1991, 161) for the sources for the later wars with Shapur.

7 THE EMPIRE TRANSFORMED

1 Williams (1985, 203–10) describes Constantine's 'completion' of Diocletian's work, but points out that all Constantine's references to his predecessor were derogatory (1985, 204) and that he distanced himself from the Tetrarchy. Only the legions with the titles Jovian and Herculean remained to bear witness to Diocletian's reforms, and in all other respects such titles disappeared. Though he completed most of Diocletian's reforms, Constantine reversed religious policy, abandoned the price control and the currency reforms, and

re-opened posts to senators (Williams 1985, 207). Arnheim (1972, 5) describes the transition between Diocletian and Constantine not as a continuation but as a sharp break. Grant (1993, 81–5) describes Constantine's continuation of Diocletian's reforms and his innovations which departed from them.

2 Chastagnol (1992, 203) emphasises the senatorial background of Emperors until the accession of Maximinus Thrax, and lists the senatorial and non-senatorial Emperors (1992, 207). Brauer (1975) dates the 'age of the soldier Emperors' from the reign of Philip the Arab to Diocletian. Elbern (1984, 43) ascribes some of the usurpations to invasions by the tribes from beyond the frontiers, and some to political and economic problems (1984, 46).

3 On accessibility to the Emperors see Millar (1977, 465–8); he draws a comparison between Nicolaus of Damascus' description of the affability and approachability of Octavian–Augustus and the panegyric addressed to Constantine (*Pan. Lat.* 6 (7).5.1) praising him for accepting and helping all who come to him for refuge or with petitions. On Imperial rescripts in general see Honoré (1979). MacMullen (1988, 110) says that all such Imperial activity in attending to the appeals of ordinary people began to tail off in the reign of Diocletian and finally disappeared.

4 MacMullen (1988, 104–18, esp. 109) ascribes the remoteness and growing isolation of the Emperor to the selfish ambitions of the courtiers who surrounded the ruler. Various Emperors were described as *sanctissimus* on inscriptions (Severus Alexander: *ILS* 485; 2494; Gallienus: *ILS* 544). Aurelian became a god (*ILS* 585; 5687); Diocletian and Maximian were themselves gods and creators of gods: *dii geniti et deorum creatores* (*ILS* 629). Turcan (1978, 1080ff) concludes that the Imperial cult began to fade in importance after 260, specifically after the reign of Claudius Gothicus when information dries up, but this corresponds exactly with the phase when Emperors began to call themselves gods and to be accepted as divine while living.

5 The autocratic tendencies of later Roman Emperors were probably inevitable; Chambers (1966, 43) says that absolutism was necessary in the grim circumstances of the third and fourth centuries, and that since the Emperors possessed Imperium it was reasoned that they could also legislate, and so Emperors became the fount of law. Jurisconsults survived until the early third century, and then compilers took over (MacMullen 1988, 5). The legal experts survived as the teachers in law schools and advisers to the Emperor, but the only legal authority was the Emperor himself (Robinson 1997, 19). Contact between the Emperor and the Senate was broken when the invasions began and the Imperial entourage and the Emperor himself remained absent and often distant from Rome (Chastagnol 1992, 234).

6 On the problems of the succession of the soldier-Emperors in the third century see Hartmann (1982), who examines the careers of the successful Emperors and the unsuccessful usurpers, and every variety of Imperial demise from death through illness to assassination, and the politics and economics behind every type of accession from self-promotion to military acclamation.

7 Birley (1988, 107) points out that continuity with the previous regime was facilitated for Severus, who took over intact most of the *familia Caesaris* from Commodus and Pertinax. Other Emperors could not always avail themselves of the opportunity, but it is likely that new Emperors who were elevated far away from Rome took over the previous Emperor's staff in the same way that they took over the soldiers, by promises, gifts and cash payments.

8 Discussing usurpers of the fourth century, Wardman (1984, 236) says that usurpation was built into the fabric of Roman society as a method of holding onto power when an Emperor died; the point is just as valid for the third century. In some cases, the so-called usurpers had no intention of taking over the whole Empire, because their interests were narrowly focused (MacMullen 1966, 214–15). Vogt (1967, 63) points out that the armies were mostly made up of local men who were more interested in defending their own areas

and did not wish to supplant Rome; he contends that Postumus did not set up a national-ist state, but organised a regional administration. Usurpers who were not successful were usually labelled as brigands (*latrones*) or tyrants by the men who were successful (Wardman 1984, 224).

9 Defence of an area often did depend upon local initiative; Ingenuus defeated the Sarma-tians with the help of peasants and urban inhabitants in his army (Lengyel and Radan 1980, 105). Decius wrote to the city of Philippopolis, anxious that the inhabitants taking to arms might cause rebellion (Millar 1969, 25). As Millar points out, very often the Greeks fought the invading tribesmen alone, without any sign of the Roman army. In Lycia the *praepositus vexillationum* Castus may have welded together an army of civilians; he denied the barbarians land or water, so he may have been dealing with pirates (*ILS* 8870 = *IGR* 481; Saxer 1967, 54–5 no. 100). Postumus had civilians in his army when he fought the Semnones or Iuthungi, according to the inscription found at Augsburg (Christol 1997, 140; Bakker 1993; Lavagne 1994; Le Roux 1997). The inscription men-tioning *defensor provinciae suae* comes from Auzia (modern Aumale) in the province of Mauretania (*CIL* VIII 9045 = *ILS* 2766; Saxer 1967, 53 no. 98). MacMullen (1966, 213) comments on the readiness of the population to do for themselves what Rome could not do for them. But as Wolfram points out (1988, 47–8), a greater degree of self-help could lead to the formation of a power base that could threaten Rome; hence Decius' worries mentioned above (see pp. 74–5, 307 n.93).

10 The building of city walls was obviously a psychological boost (Johnson 1983, 246); for example in the case of Gaul, where the number of cities that built walls and the unifor-mity of the building work suggest that there was a regional plan of Imperial design and also Imperial financial assistance, since the costs would have been too great for the decuri-ons to bear. The programme perhaps began with Probus and may have been continued by Diocletian (Johnson 1983, 114). Though the decurions probably did not bear the costs of the initial building work, they were responsible for maintenance of the walls once they were built (Johnson 1983, 64–5). Wightman (1985, 223) also attributes the fortification work in Gallic cities to Probus, who is said to have restored 60 Gallic cities – as Wight-man points out, that comprises all the major cities in Gaul. Athens was damaged by the Heruli, but little repair was carried out; instead the citizens fortified the Acropolis, where coin evidence also links the building with Probus (Walker 1981, 192). The cities where the Emperors resided benefited greatly from the Imperial presence; for a survey of Imper-ial residences see Duval (1997). Hilltop refuges were set up in the third century in the western provinces; for a list of refuges of all dates see Johnson (1983, 280–90); for Gallia Belgica see Wightman (1985, 246–7). Fortified villas were not very widespread, though examples are known (Johnson 1983, 243). Ausonius mentions fortified villas in the fourth century in the Moselle valley (*Mosella* 9). In Upper Pannonia and Moesia, large defended villas grew up in the second half of the third century (MacMullen 1988, 19–20); Mócsy (1974, 230–5) suggests that large landowners swallowed up villages. Civilians may have taken refuge in forts, or gone to live inside them in some areas: Strasbourg sheltered civil-ians from Brucomagus (modern Brumath) (Cüppers 1990, 139); traces of civilian occupa-tion have been found at Eining and Regensburg (Czysz 1995, 368–9; 434–5; 507). Lauriacum and Virunum on the Danube never received walls, even though they were in the path of invaders, and the walls of Aguntum were never completed (Poulter 1992, 104), At Adraha in Syria, it took fifteen years to complete the circuit (Johnson 1983, 65). In Britain where there was no direct threat of invasion, walls were still built around cities (Johnson 1983, 131).

11 Greene (1986, 117) says that no generalisations can be made about Empire-wide economy since all regions differed. Local cultures were not stamped out by Rome, but regional social traditions, art forms and religions did not give rise to political national uprisings (Vogt 1967, 63). It was possible to be loyal to Rome and a locality at the same time. Reece (1981a, 36) says that in the west the outward form remained Roman, but the social

structure of each cultural area dominated. Fentress (1979, 205–6) concludes that in Auzia in north Africa identification with Rome was only superficial, and that threats to security may have made this identification a little stronger but was more likely to strengthen the sense of identity as Auzians. For the common use of titles such as *restitutor* see MacMullen (1963b, 177; 1976, 33).

12 The influence of the Senate waned in the third century; for studies see Chastagnol (1992); Christol (1982; 1986). Severus was the first to rely so overtly on the army (Chastagnol 1992, 204).

13 Maximinus did not go to Rome to have power bestowed on him by the Senate (*HA* Maximinus 12.9; Eutropius 9.1.1), and by ignoring the proper forms he diminished the influence of the Senate (Chastagnol 1992, 205; 210–11). Florian took over the Empire after the death of his brother Tacitus, and caused a problem even for the ancient historians as to the legality of his actions. Some authors considered it scandalous that he did not wait for the sanction of the Senate (*HA* Tacitus 14.1; Probus 10.1.8; 11.3.4); other considered him a usurper (Aurelius Victor *de Caes.* 36.2); others insist that the Senate did bestow power on him (Zonaras 12.29; Zosimus 1.64.1).

14 The senatorial career changed dramatically in the mid-third century, after the reforms of Gallienus; see Christol (1982; 1986); Pflaum (1976). The junior magistracies of the early Empire disappeared (Chastagnol 1992, 214; Pflaum 1976, 109), but the higher echelons of the senatorial career remained untouched (Chastagnol 1992, 214); on the city prefects see Chastagnol (1960). Senators retained their privileged positions and their wealth, and were sometimes sent on special missions by the Emperors (Chastagnol 1992, 213–15). On the *correctores* see Chastagnol (1992, 219–20); Arnheim (1972, 54) analysed the postholders and concluded that aristocratic *correctores* outnumbered non-aristocratic ones. Usually the *correctores* governed a region of Italy, such as Campania, Tuscany, or Umbria (*ILS* 1217 = *CIL* X 5061) but *ILS* 1211 = *CIL* VI 1673 = 31901a records L. Aelius Helvius Dionysius, *corrector utriusque Italiae.*

15 Whereas Diocletian stifled the senatorial career, Constantine remodelled and revitalised it (Arnheim 1972, 5; 49). He reduced the power and importance of the offices of quaestor and praetor, which were henceforth held by the sons of senators; the praetors lost all the legal functions that they used to exercise (Chastagnol 1992, 242–3). Sons of senators as young as sixteen became quaestors (*Cod. Th.* 6.4.1). The consulship underwent 'an enormous mutation' (Chastagnol 1992, 246ff); see also Bagnall (1987). On Constantine's reform of the Senate in general see Chastagnol (1992, 236–48; 427–9 nn.12–57).

16 Petit (1974, 233–4) writes of the triumph of the equestrian class, pointing out that they were recruited almost exclusively from the army and occupied almost all the administrative posts. On the equites generally see Saller (1980); Brunt (1983); for their rise in the third century see Keyes (1915); on the equestrians as military commanders see Osier (1974; 1977); Devijver (1989), and on Gallienus' reforms see Pflaum (1976).

17 The Praetorian Prefects rose to prominence during the third century, and became almost second in command to the Emperor. The career of Plautianus was exceptional, in that he was already *eminentissimus* when he entered office (Chastagnol 1992, 221; 227). Comazon was another exception; see Howe (1942, 97–100); Chastagnol (1992, 223); Pflaum (1960, 752–6 no. 290). Chastagnol (1992, 223–4) examined those Prefects who received *ornamenta consularia* and their subsequent careers. Laetus was awarded *ornamenta consularia* in 205, and called himself *cos. II* when he became consul (Chastagnol 1992, 221; 424 n.64; Pflaum 1960, 581–3 no. 219; *ILS* 2187 = *CIL* V 228). Volusianus was consul in 261 while still Prefect, and went on to become *praefectus urbi* in 267–8 (Chastagnol 1992, 227; 426 n.94). Aristobulus and Asclepiodotus both reached the consulship and went on to become city prefect (Chastagnol 1992, 235).

18 Reece (1981a, 36) comments on the lack of contemporary sources to explain what happened in the third century, and the inability of the few pieces of evidence that survive to help; people were concerned with day-to-day detail, whereas historians want broad

general analysis. MacMullen (1988, 3) shows in tabular form that while the output of Greek authors remained fairly stable from the first to the third centuries, Latin authorship declined to vanishing point in the third century; similarly Latin inscriptions tail off dramatically (MacMullen 1988, 4–5). Millar (1981, 243) considers that the lack of evidence for building work in cities is the most compelling evidence for third-century decline.

19 Italian industry was in decline in the second century as manufacturing and trade migrated to the new western provinces (Boak 1955, 62, quoting Frank 1940, 249; Mac-Mullen 1988, 15). In north-western Gaul the evidence for third-century destruction is too strong to refute (Wightman 1985, 200). Galliou (1981) describes worsening conditions and then total collapse in the north-west. MacMullen (1988, 22–3) puts it more dramatically by saying that the area that is now modern Brittany entered the Dark Ages a few hundred years ahead of the rest of Gaul. Resettlement of Gallic sites did occur, not perhaps by the original inhabitants, but it is not known by whom; it could have been by *foederati*, or by refugees (Wightman 1981, 239–40). A late-third-century upsurge has been detected in Pannonian and Moesia, probably connected with the army, who provided security and a means of attaining wealth; large villas grew up, many of them new foundations (MacMullen 1988, 19–20). In Spain the once-flourishing ports disappeared from view, as long-distance and maritime trade collapsed (Rougé 1966b, 476; 486). Blazquez (1982, 567; 580; 594) detects agricultural decline, a contraction of commerce and the concentration of lands under the ownership of fewer people. Africa stagnated towards the end of the third century (MacMullen 1988, 29), but there was no contraction of cities as in Gaul (Millar 1981, 181). The African provinces flourished in the fourth century (Lactantius *de Mort. Pers.* 8.3; Whittaker 1983a, 175–6). See Lepelley (1981) on the cities of north Africa.

20 Antioch suffered some destruction at the hands of the Persians, but flourished in the fourth century (Millar 1981, 241; MacMullen 1988, 32; 228 nn.115–16). Palestine likewise enjoyed prosperity in the fourth century; Ammianus Marcellinus (14.8.11) comments on the rich fields in the province. Millar (1993, 147–8) argues that the Persians were interested only in destructive raids when they attacked in the 250s and in 260, but also mentions that according to Dio (80.3.4) the Romans perceived Ardashir as a threat because he was apparently bent on reconstituting the Persian Empire of old.

21 On the apparent shrinkage of cities in the west see Salmon (1974, 142–4). For the theory that the walls enclosed only a citadel with the population living outside see Roblin (1951; 1965); Salmon (1974, 144–5); Johnson (1983, 115). Reece (1981a, 28–9), quoting evidence from French excavations, points out that the topography of Tours and Tournai makes it unlikely that any of the populace lived outside the walls. The problem is not limited to Gaul; in Raetia, Kempten and Augsburg also shrank and withdrew into a circuit of walls on higher ground (Johnson 1983, 121–2). A downturn in city fortunes can be seen in excavations; Wightman (1985, 221) points out that in Gallia Belgica, cemeteries are sometimes found encroaching on the streets. See also Lewit (1991, 63).

22 The interdependence of the cities and the surrounding agricultural lands is emphasised by Boak (1955, 15–18) who ascribes the decline of cities to the decline of the rural population and the destruction of the land (Boak 1955, 56; 62; see also Salmon 1974, 143). The cities and towns required a regular surplus in production, which seems to have been much reduced in the second half of the third century, but the problem may not have been caused solely by a reduction in the rural population. It has been shown that the land was still cultivated even when the small farms had been deserted (Whittaker 1983a, 175; see note 25 below), so it is probable that actual production did not decline but was diverted, especially when tax payments began to be collected in kind; see note 29 below. The decline of the population is very difficult to prove and causes disagreement among scholars; Salmon (1974, 140–50) discusses the evidence and concludes that there was a definite decline after plagues in the late second and mid-third centuries, the civil wars, and the tribal invasions.

23 The hereditary tendencies of the decurial class were already in evidence before the end of the third century, but the shortage of suitable recruits for urban councils meant that the rules had to be changed, for instance candidates no longer had to have held a magistracy before entering the council (Garnsey 1974a, 242). When the shortage was acute underage minors were recruited, and men who held as little as 25 *iugera* of land (Boak 1955, 78–81). Despite these problems, traders and businessmen were only rarely elected to councils, as Jones (1974a, 41) points out, quoting Callistratus who thought it degrading to have lower-class men in office, especially if there were respectable citizens still available in the cities. Reluctance to serve on councils is illustrated by the fact that men were willing to give up property so that they would not qualify (*P. Ryl.* ii 75); see MacMullen (1988, 47–8). Decurions as oppressors were a feature of the fourth century; see Lepelley (1983).

24 See Salmon (1974, 140–50) on the various causes of depopulation, and note 21 above. St Cyprian (*Ad Demetrianum* 2–3), writing in the mid-third century, complained of the lack of agricultural workers, sailors and soldiers.

25 Vacant lands were never absent from the Roman Empire; MacMullen (1990, 49–50) lists the most famous or notorious cases where Emperors settled large numbers of tribesmen: 50,000 Getae in Moesia under Augustus; 40,000 Germans in Gaul and the Rhineland under Tiberius; Marcus Aurelius admitted 3,000 Naristae and Probus brought in 100,000 Bastarnae; Constantine settled 300,000 Sarmatians in Thrace, Italy, and Macedonia. Attempting to attract Roman or provincial farmers, Pertinax offered tax relief for settlers (Herodian 2.4.6) and Aurelian tried to make the city councils responsible for finding cultivators or making up the shortfall in taxes (Millar 1981, 94). Sometimes tribesmen were settled on lands that they had wasted, according to the contemporary authors (*Pan. Lat.* 8 (5).8); see also MacMullen (1976, 174–5); Salmon (1974, 147); Demougeot (1969, 540) on tribesmen settled in Thrace. The *laeti* were settled on the land by the end of the third century (Jones 1964, 2; 620); Probus may have begun the settlements, and Constantius Chlorus settled Franks as *laeti* in Gaul after defeating them in battle, specifically in the regions around Trier, Amiens and Langres (Southern and Dixon 1996, 48). Grosse (1920, 208–9) suggested that the term *laeti* derived from Germanic roots, meaning people who were only half free. In the mid-fourth century laws refer to *praepositi laetorum*, and the *Notitia Dignitatum* (*Oc.* XLII 33–44) lists several of these officials in Gaul (James 1988, 45; Grosse 1920, 208; Southern and Dixon 1996, 48). At the end of the fourth century some lands were designated *terrae laeticae* (*Cod. Th.* 13.11.10). When lands were resettled it is not possible to say who the new occupants were; see note 19 above. For the continued cultivation of lands in Gaul even though the farms were deserted see Whittaker (1983a, 175). Though the invasions may have caused some flight from the land, as evidenced by the lack of attention to drainage in parts of Gaul and the consequent ruin of the agricultural potential (Demougeot 1969, 533–4), there are other factors to take into account, such as climate and soil exhaustion; see Greene (1986, 86–7; 116–17). The next most serious problem that caused desertion involved the harsh taxation schemes of the late third century. The panegyric addressed to Constantine in 311 lays emphasis on this feature of life around the city of Autun (*Pan. Lat.* 5 (8).6.2; 11.4; 14.3). The difficulties faced by Autun were not isolated examples, and applied to the whole Empire (Nixon and Rodgers 1994, 263). Lactantius (*de Mort. Pers.* 23; 26.2) makes mileage out of the harshness of the census that was the basis of the taxation system in Gaul and the rest of the Empire. See MacMullen (1976, 173) on peasants leaving the land because they could not meet the taxes levied on them. On the supply of the army on the frontiers and in the late Empire see Whittaker (1994, 98–131; 165, 183–4). MacMullen (1976, 129–52) discusses how the Diocletianic taxation system worked. For the army as consumer see Lewit (1991, 87), who argues that when a regular tax system replaced arbitrary requisitioning the farmers may have found the new scheme beneficial.

26 Decline of agricultural production is difficult to prove, but it is assumed that at least in

the west where there is evidence of destruction, agricultural produce must have diminished. There is some evidence that cereal production did decline in times of war (Groenmann-van Waateringe 1989, 98). Apart from the effects of the invasions, climatic changes affected production in the north western province (Bloemers 1989, 192), and soil exhaustion possibly resulted from the cultivation of wheat, which exhausts the soil faster than barley (Groenmann-van Waateringe 1989, 99–100). For other provinces, such as Spain, Africa and the east, production was probably not so seriously affected. Lewit (1991) challenges the idea that production declined, and makes a case for the survival of the peasant farmer. For the stimulation of agriculture by the presence of the army see Jones (1974a, 127); Whittaker (1978). For the economic effects of frontier policy in general see Birley (1981b). For supply of the frontier armies see Whittaker (1989), contradicted in part by Fulford (1989).

27 Inflation gained momentum after the 260s (Crawford 1975, 571). Wheat prices are listed by Rémondon (1964, 111) who shows that there was a slow rise up to 269, then staggering increases from then until 301. Army pay was the largest outflow of cash in the Empire (MacMullen 1988, 39) and is another indication of the rate of inflation (Greene 1986, 58; Duncan-Jones 1974, 10). Short-term measures to ease the payments to the army included calling in the old coinage and reissuing it with debased metal content (Greene 1986, 61). Harl (1996, 126) suggests that the debasement under the Severans was intended to provide between one-third and one-half more coinage. See Callu (1975, 602–6) on the antoninianus; Tyler (1975, 5) says that antoniniani of different alloy standards circulated in the Empire. The drain of precious metals in subsidy payments was detrimental because it did not circulate; nothing came back into the Empire. Philip paid gold to the Persians, who melted it down and issued dinars (Harl 1996, 129).

28 For the adverse effect on the gold coinage after the debasement of the silver coinage see Harl (1996, 132–4), who says that there was 'a baffling array of aurei of different values' in circulation. The problem of coins of different values is illustrated by the closure of the Egyptian banking houses, and their refusal to accept the coins of one of the short-lived Emperors; the banks were ordered to reopen and accept all coins except counterfeit ones (*P. Oxy.* 141). On the reforms of Aurelian and Diocletian see Crawford (1975, 575–7; 577–8). The coinage did not recover until the mid-fourth century; see Greene (1986, 61–2).

29 On the dearth of coinage in Gaul and Britain see King (1981); Reece (1973). A high percentage of imitations were in circulation in northern Gaul which King (1981, 97) supposes were made to supply the local market; imitations are also found in Britain and on the Rhine, but not in southern Gaul, Italy or Spain. The people of Skaptopara made a plea for help against the depredations of the soldiers, whose anti-social activities were forcing the inhabitants to leave their village (*CIL* III 12336 = *IGR* 1674; Loriot and Nony 1997, 49–50 no. 20; Herrmann 1990, 18–27). The date is 238.

30 On the decline of the urban markets see Hopkins (1978; 1980; 1983b); the new tax payments in kind meant that the money economy changed, and the urban markets were no longer necessary to the farmers to convert their produce into cash. As long-distance trade fell away and urban markets declined, markets in the rural areas concentrated on the local produce; third-century sites yield fewer imported objects, but instead local artefacts of a lower artistic and technical standard are more common (Miller 1981, 246).

31 Herodian (2.6.14) recognised the dependence of the Emperor on the army and thought that in the process the army had been corrupted by the donatives and cash payments, so that they lost their respect for Emperors. MacMullen (1963b, 116) comments on the difficulties of recruiting sufficient numbers of soldiers from the end of the second century, a problem that Severus tried to rectify by making service more attractive. Smith (1972a, 499) points out that the recruitment of Illyrians at the beginning of the third century was a response to the lack of interest of other candidates in joining the army. Goths were drafted into the expeditionary army that Gordian III took to the east, and Claudius

Gothicus also recruited them (Todd 1992, 150; 152). The presence of Goths and Germans in Gordian's army is noted in Shapur's *Res Gestae Divi Saporis* (Maricq 1958, 295; Millar 1993, 154). Both Postumus and Carausius recruited Franks (James 1988, 37–8). MacMullen (1976, 183; 296 n.7; 297 n.10) says that settlement of tribesmen within the Empire was usually undertaken with the agreement that the tribes would provide recruits, and that reception of barbarians was a cause for 'courtly congratulation'. When Constantine was preparing to march against Maxentius he recruited Germans; Todd (1992, 59) and Thompson (1982, 6) both consider that life in the army was very attractive to tribesmen. See also Liebeschuetz (1990, 7–25).

32 Herodian (2.11.5) complained of the decline of Italians in the army; from his point of view there was an estrangement of the Roman populace from the army; see Whittaker (1970, 216 n.1). Alienation of the Praetorians from the population also featured at the beginning of the third century (Herodian 2.4.4; 5.1–3; 5.6); see also Durry (1938, 56; 382). Isaac (1992, 24–6) comments that the upper classes feared the soldiery, approving of Emperors who kept them in check; Isaac lists examples of the army causing trouble in peacetime or whenever the soldiers were under lax discipline. For the army as a springboard for careers see the references on the rise of the equites (above, note 16).

33 On the *duces* see Jones (1964, 1; 44; 2; 608–10); Williams (1985, 26; 52; 108); Southern and Dixon (1996, 58–60). The early *duces* were not permanent commanders in charge of specific units; the title did not denote a rank, like that of *praepositus*; see Smith (1972b). The title *dux limitum*, attested in the sources of the later Empire, indicates that the *duces* were primarily responsible for the defence of the frontiers (*Cod. Th.* 7.22.5; see also *Cod. Th.* 7.1.9 dating from 367 in the reign of Valens and Valentinian; *Notitia Dignitatum Oc.* I.38; 39).

34 The Byzantine chronicler George Cedrenus states that Gallienus was the founder of the first mobile cavalry army (*Compendium Historiarum* 454 in Migné vol. 121, 495). The occasion most suited to the amalgamation of the various cavalry troops would most likely be the period after Postumus seized power in Gaul, but de Blois (1976, 26) prefers the date of 255 when Gallienus was fighting on the Rhine. Whether the cavalry army was intended to be a permanent arm is disputed; Ferrill (1986, 32) thinks that Gallienus had no long-term Imperial policy in mind when he formed the cavalry. According to Zosimus (1.40.1) the mounted troops under their commander Aureolus were based at Milan to prevent Postumus from descending on Italy. In another passage Zosimus says that Aurelian used the cavalry to good effect against the Palmyrene heavy-armoured horsemen (1.50.3–4; 52.3–4), but there is no evidence of the presence of the cavalry army in northern Italy after 285 (de Blois 1976, 28); see also Southern and Dixon (1996, 11–14).

35 According to a papyrus (*P. Oxy.* 1.43 col. 2 lines 24–8) Diocletian's expeditionary army included *vexillationes*, cavalry, and another body of cavalry, distinct from the other horsemen, listed as *comites*. Seston (1946, 305–7) and van Berchem (1952, 106–8; 1977a, 542) object to the continued existence of a central cavalry force on the grounds that anyone who commanded it would be in a favourable position to usurp, and Diocletian's aim was to avoid this. They therefore argue that although Diocletian definitely had a *comitatus*, it was not a mobile cavalry army at this stage but only a bodyguard. Two inscriptions reinforce the opposite argument that Diocletian founded the *comitatenses*: *CIL* III 5565 = *ILS* 664 records the *praepositus* of a Dalmatian cavalry unit building a temple; the unit is collectively styled *comit(es)* or *comit(atenses)*. The abbreviation makes it impossible to decide which restoration is correct. Hoffman (1969–70, 257–8) prefers the reading *comitatenses*. Another inscription (*CIL* III 6196 = *ILS* 2781) found at Troesmis documents a soldier of *Legio XI Claudia* who was chosen to enter the Imperial guard (*lectus in comitatu lanciarius*). The *lanciarii* were later an important element in the *comitatus* of Constantine. See Southern and Dixon (1996, 15–16). Van Berchem (1952, 87) dated the separation of the army into mobile field units and frontier troops to a period between 311 and 325 (see below, note 36).

36 Jones (1964, 54) traces the origins of the *scholae* back to the Tetrarchy, even though the earliest evidence dates from the reign of Constantine. Hoffman (1969–70, 281) acknowledges that the *scholae* could date to the reign of Diocletian, but considers that they were formed by Constantine.

37 Zosimus (2.34) complains that after Diocletian had secured all the frontiers by placing the troops in forts to defend them, Constantine took them away again and put them into cities that did not need them. Isaac (1992, 163) points out that this is not a valid criticism for the eastern frontier, where troops had been stationed in cities before Diocletian's reign. MacMullen considers that although soldiers were sometimes billeted in cities temporarily at all periods of the Empire, there was a discernible increase after 300; he lists the evidence for soldiers in cities in an appendix (1988, 209–27) and draws the conclusions in the text (1988, 145ff). There is some evidence that in 311 the usual division of the army into legions and auxiliary troops still persisted, but by 325 there had been a change. A law of that year (*Cod. Th.* 7.20.4) lists three classes of troops, the *comitatenses* the *ripenses*, and the *alares* and *cohortales*. The last two categories were less privileged than the first, in the law of 325 just cited and in another 50 years later (*Cod. Th.* 7.13.7.3). See Southern and Dixon (1996, 35–6). The *ripenses* comprised the units along the frontier whether they were legions, or cavalry. The uses of the term *limitanei* are discussed by van Berchem (1952, 100–1). Troops called *limitanei* are mentioned anachronistically in *HA* (Severus Alexander 58). By the sixth century they had become a sort of militia who were tied to the soil; according to the *Codex Justinianus* (1.27.2.8) they were obliged to defend the cities of the frontiers and to cultivate the fields. The Byzantine scholar John Malalas (*Chron.* 12.308) says that Diocletian established such *limitanei* on the eastern frontier, and van Berchem (1952, 21) accepts the theory; Warmington (1953, 173–4) disagrees on two counts, because even if it were true for parts of the east, it is not necessarily true of other frontiers; secondly some of the frontier troops contributed men to the field armies, so they were not yet tied to their lands. The frontier troops that were taken into the field army were sometimes known as *pseudo-comitatenses*.

38 On Roman frontiers in general see Whittaker (1994); on intelligence and information-gathering see Austin and Rankov (1995); Lee (1993). See also Millar (1982).

39 On occasion the tribesmen who invaded the Empire were in search of food, and especially on the Rhine there were tempting fertile lands where encroachment gradually took place; see Johnson (1983, 69), who acknowledges the search for food theory but points out that this does not explain why the Franks, for instance, travelled so far into Gaul and Spain. Schönberger (1985, 401–24) documents the invasions across the northern frontier of the provinces of Germany from Marcus Aurelius to Gallienus, many of the forts showing signs of destruction in *c.*233 are clustered in the fertile Taunus–Wetterau region, where the frontier encloses rich corn lands on easily drained soil, as opposed to the clay lands that lie beyond. This might suggest that the motive for invasion was to take advantage of the food supply. Not all the signs of destruction are necessarily attributable to tribal activities; Okamura (1996, 13–15) suggests that the forts at Pfünz and Niederbieber were attacked and destroyed by rival Roman troops during the civil wars, and that from the 230s onwards troops were steadily withdrawn from the northern frontier. Probus may have been responsible for establishing the Danube–Iller–Rhine frontier; building was undertaken by Diocletian and the Tetrarchs, as shown by an inscription from Burg bei Stein am Rhein (*CIL* XIII 5256), and much later under Valentinian (Drack and Fellman 1988, 279; Southern and Dixon 1996, 25). Legionary strength before and after Diocletian is fraught with difficulty and debate. Diocletian inherited about thirty-four legions and added several new ones, probably about thirty-five in total. Theories abound. Some authors think that all legions, including the new Diocletianic ones, were 6,000 strong, which would strain manpower resources considerably; others suggest that although the new legions were 6,000 strong they were reduced by Diocletian's successors (Jones 1964, 56; 68); yet others follow Mommsen (1889, 229; 254) who thought that the old legions

remained at 6,000 but the new late-third-century legions were only 1,000 strong (Seston 1946, 299); van Berchem (1952, 110–11); Some of the legions may have been split up into detachments of a thousand men and stationed in different forts (Southern and Dixon 1996, 30–2). On Diocletian's efforts to refortify the Rhine and Danube see von Petrikovits (1971, 181–2), and on the Danube forts with U-shaped towers enclosing the gates, and fan-shaped corner towers, see Johnson (1983, 253); Southern and Dixon (1996, 23–33; 133–9). Von Petrikovits (1971, 184) attributes these forts to Constantine. Blockley (1992, 9) points out that defence behind the scenes was criticised and that Constantine and his successors used the mobile army as an attack force.

40 As Isaac (1992, 31) points out no ancient source elucidates the reasons why Rome and Parthia or Persia went to war against each other. Rome was more often the aggressor than Persia (1992, 52). Lee (1993, 121; 125) notes that the Persians took advantage of the problems on the Rhine that kept the Romans occupied. For instance, in the late 230s Ardashir adopted an aggressive policy when Maximinus Thrax was fully committed on the northern frontier; according to Dio (80.4.1–2) he captured Nisibis and Carrhae in 238. Similarly the Romans took advantage of Persian difficulties; Gordian III opened a campaign when Shapur was occupied on his own eastern frontier; Carus invaded in 283 when Vahram II had to protect himself against the revolt of his brother Hormizd (*Pan. Lat.* 3 (11).17.2; Eutropius 9.18.1; *HA* Carus 8.1).

41 Isaac (1992, 29–30) documents Persian attacks on Syria, and Millar (1993, 141–7) describes the Roman–Persian wars to the reign of Philip.

42 Dio (75.3.2–3) disapproved of Severus' conquest and annexation of Osroene and Mesopotamia because the new provinces brought Rome into contact with Persian allies and lengthened communications for the Romans while shortening them for the Persians. Armenia was also a bone of contention; the Persians would never tolerate a Roman presence or preponderant influence in Armenia or east of the Euphrates; see Isaac (1992, 32; 249–50). The Diocletianic frontier, the *Strata Diocletiana*, was studied by van Berchem (1952). Most of the forts along the stretches of the frontier that have been studied can be dated epigraphically to Diocletian or the Tetrarchy (Isaac 1992, 164), and there are many Tetrarchic milestones along the route, but see also Kennedy and Riley (1990, 70; 140) who point out that rebuilding at some of the forts on the eastern frontier makes it difficult to pinpoint their foundation dates.

43 Hyde (1970, 196) attributes Constantine's conversion, if indeed there was one, to political motives. Hopkins (1999, 79; 346 n.7) says that conversion in a blinding flash is romantic, but in reality it happened over a much longer period than Eusebius (*Life of Constantine* 1.27ff) allows; Lactantius (*de Mort. Pers.* 44) tells a different story from Eusebius. MacMullen (1984, 43) strips away the romance: 'at a sticky point in his [Constantine's] career, he had a dream that could be interpreted in the light of his necessities'. Constantine issued coins in honour of the Sun god until 322; pagan cults were finally outlawed in 391 (*Cod. Th.* 16.10.11; Hopkins 1999, 79; 346 n.8).

44 The Christian community was in the minority, but was powerful and wealthy (Grant 1993, 130). No other cult was ever as successful as the Christians were in gaining new adherents (MacMullen 1984, 109–10). Frend (1974, 268) points out that the cult was mostly urban based and had not spread to the rural areas, so the power and influence of the bishops was nucleated in urban centres. The authority of the bishops rivalled that of the Emperors (Chadwick 1981, 6; Grant 1993, 125–6).

45 The persecution of the Christians under Diocletian and Galerius was very uneven, the excesses of Galerius himself leading to the accusation that it was all his fault rather than Diocletian's personal predilection (Grant 1993, 130). Williams (1985, 184) says that many pagans thought it was wrong to persecute Christians because they themselves had no quarrel with them; MacMullen (1984, 104) describes the lack of interest of most pagans about their Christian neighbours, and the general lack of support among the populace for the persecutions. Frend (1974, 268–9) considers that Decius' persecution almost

succeeded, and that there was in fact popular support for it. Ultimately the persecution of Diocletian failed, but some authors consider that the edict of toleration came about purely from cold political motives and not from any retraction of opinion about Christianity (Williams 1985, 198–9; Grant 1993, 130; 136–7). The text of the edict is reported by Eusebius (*History of the Church* 8.17.6–10); Galerius still insisted that the Christians were in error, and disapproved of their assemblies and the fact that they were a law unto themselves; see Grant (1993, 136–7).

46 The pagan gods disappeared from the coinage during the early years of Constantine's reign, even before he finally defeated Licinius; by 317 most of the gods ceased to be honoured on the coinage, except for Apollo and the Sun who remained until *c.*320 and 322 (Grant 1993, 134). The idea that the whole Empire became Christian when Constantine embraced the religion in 312 is erroneous; the conversion of the Empire depended on how Constantine's successors viewed the matter, and it happened very slowly (Hopkins 1999, 1; 79). The effect on the majority of people over the whole Empire in 312 and the following years was absolutely nil (MacMullen 1984, 44). Constantine and successive Emperors did not withdraw support from the state cults (Hyde 1970, 193), and practising Christians could still combine pagan priestly functions with their beliefs: a Church council at the end of the third century investigated the matter and decided that any Christian who was also a *flamen* of the Imperial cult was not necessarily compromised (Chadwick 1981, 12–13). Without Imperial support the Christians could not have flourished, but gained rapid supremacy once the Emperor awarded special patronage to the Church (MacMullen 1984, 43; Hopkins 1999, 79).

47 On the *labarum* see Eusebius (*Life of Constantine* 1.28; Grant 1993, 142–5). The chi-rho symbol had been used in papyri as the abbreviation for *chreston*, meaning 'good' (Grant 1993, 142; 246 n.48). Hyde (1970, 193) outlines the privileges granted to the Church: the clergy were exempted from military service, the Church courts were given equal validity with the Imperial courts, and the Church was granted the right to hold property, so it gained great wealth. To the end, Constantine maintained an ambiguous stance as to his own beliefs (Grant 1993, 143; Hyde 1970, 195); though he favoured the Church, he wanted it firmly under his control, and he chose the bishops himself (Grant 1993, 152; Hopkins 1999, 86).

BIBLIOGRAPHY

ANCIENT SOURCES

Ammianus Marcellinus, Loeb

Aurelius Victor *de Caesaribus Epitome de Caesaribus*

Caesar, *Gallic War*, Loeb

Cedrenus, *Compendium Historiarum*, in Migné vol. 121

Chronographer of 354, ed. Th. Mommsen, *MGH: Auctores Antiquissimi* IX, Berlin

Cyprian, Ep

Dexippus, *FGrH* II 100 pp. 452–80; commentary pp. 304–11, ed. F. Jacoby

Digest, trans, A. Watson, 1985, University of Pennsylvania Press

Dio, *Roman History*, Loeb

Eusebius, *History of the Church*, trans. G.A. Williamson, Penguin Classics, rev. edn 1989

Eutropius

Gregory of Tours, *History of the Franks*, Penguin

Herodian, *History of the Empire*, Loeb

Hieronymus, *Chronicon*

Jordanes, *Getica = The Gothic History of Jordanes*, with intro and commentary by C.C. Mierow, Princeton University Press 1915, (2nd edn), reprinted Cambridge 1966

Jordanes, *Romana*

Lactantius, *De Mortibus Persecutorum*

Livy

Orosius

Panégyriques Latins, ed. P. Gallétier, Paris 1949–55, 3 vols

Petrus Patricius, *FGH* vol. 4, ed. K. Müller

Pliny, *Natural History*, Loeb

Scriptores Historiae Augustae, Loeb

St Cyprian = Saint Cyprien, *Correspondence*, trans. Le Chanoine Bayard, Paris: Les Belles Lettres, 2 vols, 1925

Strabo, *Geography*, Loeb

Suetonius, Loeb

Synesius

Synesius, Rep

Tacitus, *Annals*, Loeb

Tacitus, *Histories*, Loeb

Tacitus, *Germania*

Tertullian, *Apologeticus*
Themistius, *Orations*
Ulpian, *Digest*
Velleius Paterculus, *Compendium of Roman History*, Loeb
Zonaras
Zosime, *Histoire Nouvelle*, trans. F. Paschoud, Paris: Les Belles Lettres, 1971–9, 3 vols
Zosimus, *New History*, trans. and with commentary by R.T. Ridley, Australian Association
  for Byzantine Studies, 1982

MODERN SOURCES

Agache, R. 1978, *La Somme Préromaine et Romaine*. Amiens.
Alföldi, A. 1927, 'Zur Kenntnus des Zeit des römisohen Soldatenkaiser I: der Usurpator
  Aureolus und die Kavalleriereform des Gallienus,' *Zeitschrift für Numismatik* 37, 197–212.
—— 1929, 'The numbering of the victories of the Emperor Gallienus and the loyalty of his
  legions', *NC* 5th series 9, 218–79 = Alföldi 1967, 73–119.
—— 1938, 'La grande crise du monde romain au IIIe siècle', *Antiquité Classique* 7, 5–18.
—— 1948, *The Conversion of Constantine and Pagan Rome*. Oxford.
—— 1950, 'Über die Juthungeneinfälle unter Aurelian', *Bulletin de l'Institut Archiologique
  Bulgare* 16, 21–4.
—— 1967, *Studien zur Geschichte der Weltkrise des dritten Jahrhunderts nach Christi*. Darmstadt:
  Wissenschaftliche Buchgesellschaft.
Alföldi, M.R. 1959, 'Zu den Militärreformen des Kaisers Gallienus', *Limes-Studien; Vorträge des
  3. Internationalen Limes-Kongresses in Rheinfelden/Basel 1957*. Basel, 13–18.
Alföldy, G. 1969, 'Ein praefectus der cohors VI Nerviorum in Britannia', *Hommages M.
  Renard II* Collection Latomus 102. Brussels, 3–6 = Alföldy, G. 1987, 223–7.
—— 1970, 'Eine Proskriptionsliste in der Historia Augusta', *Bonner Historia-Augusta Colloquium 1968–1969*. Bonn, 1–11 = Alföldy 1989b, 174–8.
—— 1971a, 'Cassius Dio und Herodian über die Anfänge des Neupersischen Reiches',
  Rhienisches Museum für Philologie 114, 360–6 = Alföldy 1989b, 229–37.
—— 1971b, 'Zeitgeschichte und Krisenempfindung bei Herodian', *Hermes* 99,
  429–49 = Alföldy 1989b, 273–94.
—— 1973, 'Der Heilige Cyprian und die Krise des römischen Reiches: die Bedeutung
  Cyprians für die Darstellung seiner Zeit', *Historia* 22, 479–501 = Alföldy 1989b,
  295–318.
—— 1974a, 'The crisis of the third century as seen by contemporaries', *Greek Roman and
  Byzantine History* 15, 89–111 = Alföldy 1989b, 319–42.
—— 1974b, *Noricum*. London: Routledge.
—— 1976, 'Bemerkungen zu Ramsay MacMullen: *Roman Government's Response to Crisis A.D.
  235–337*', *Hispania Antiqua* 6, 341–6.
—— 1978, 'Die Alamannen in der *Historia Augusta*', *JRGZM* 25, 196–207.
—— 1987, *Römische Heeresgeschichte*. Amsterdam.
—— 1989a, 'Die Krise des Imperium Romanum und die Religion Roms', *Religion und
  Gesellschaft in der römischen Kaiserzeit: Kolloquium zu Ehren von Friedrich Vittinghof*. Cologne,
  53–102.
—— 1989b, *Die Krise des Römischen Reiches*. Wiesbaden: Franz Steiner Verlag.
Alston, R. 1994, 'Roman military pay from Caesar to Diocletian', *JRS* 84, 111–23.

Anderson, J.G.C. 1938, *Tacitus: Germania*. Oxford.

Armstrong, D. 1987a, 'Tribunician dates of the joint and separate reigns of Valerianus and Gallienus: a plea for the August–September theory', *ZPE* 67, 215–23.

—— 1987b, 'Gallienus in Athens', *ZPE* 70, 235–58.

Arnaldi, A. 1975. 'Osservazione sul convegno di Carnuntum', *Mem. Isituto Lombardo (Lett.)* 35, 217–38.

Arnheim, M.T.W. 1972, *The Senatorial Aristocracy in the Later Roman Empire*. Oxford: Clarendon Press.

Austin, N.J.E. and Rankov, N.B. 1995, *Exploratio: military and political intelligence in the Roman world from the Second Punic War to the battle of Adrianople*. London: Routledge.

Baatz, D. 1986, 'Ein Beitrag der Mathematischen Statistik zum Ende der Rätischen Limes', in Unz 1986, 78–89.

Baatz, D. *et al.* (eds) 1982, *Die Römer in Hessen*. Stuttgart: Theiss.

Bagnall, R.S. 1987, *Consuls of the Later Roman Empire*. Atlanta.

Bakker, L. 1993, 'Raetien unter Postumus – das Siegesdenkmal einer Juthungenschlacht im Jahre 260 n. Chr. aus Augsburg', *Germania* 71.2, 370–86.

Balty, J.-C. 1988, 'Apamea in Syria in the second and third centuries AD', *JRS* 78, 91–104.

Barbieri, G. 1952, *L'albo senatorio da Settimio Severo a Carino (193–285)*. Rome.

Barford, P. 1994, 'Roma and Barbaricum: recent work on the Roman period in Poland', *Antiquity* 68, 165–72.

Barnes, T.D. 1967, 'The family and career of Septimius Severus', *Historia* 16, 87–107.

—— 1973, 'Lactantius and Constantine', *JRS* 63, 29–46.

—— 1976, 'Imperial campaigns, AD 285–311', *Phoenix* 30, 174–93.

—— 1978, *The Sources of the Historia Augusta*. Collection Latomus vol. 155. Brussels.

—— 1981, *Constantine and Eusebius*. Cambridge, Mass. and London.

—— 1982, *The New Empire of Diocletian and Constantine*. Cambridge, Mass: Harvard University Press.

—— 1984, 'The composition of Cassius Dio's Roman History', *Phoenix* 38, 240–55.

—— 1996, 'Emperors, panegyrics, prefects, provinces and palaces (284–317)', *JRA* 9, 532–52.

Barrett, J.C. *et al.* (eds) 1989, *Barbarians and Romans in North-West Europe from the later Republic to late Antiquity*. Oxford: BAR S471.

Bayard, le Chanoine 1925, see under St Cyprian in ancient sources.

Baynes, N.H. 1925, 'Three notes on the reforms of Diocletian and Constantine', *JRS* 15, 195–208.

—— 1926, *The Historia Augusta: its date and purpose*. Oxford.

—— 1929, Constantine the Great and the Christian Church. *Procs of the British Academy* vol. 15.

Bechert, T. 1969, 'Ein Alemanneneinfall am Obergermanischen Limes unter Elagabal', *Ep. Stud.* 8, 53–62.

Bellezza, A. 1964, *Massimino il Trace*. Geneva.

Bellinger, A.R. 1940, *The Syrian Tetradrachms of Caracalla and Macrinus*. Numismatic Studies 3. New York.

Benabou, M. 1975, *La Résistance Africaine à la Romanisation*. Paris.

Benario, H.W. 1972, 'Albano and the Second Parthian Legion', *Archaeology* 25, 257–63.

Bernhard, H. 1990, 'Die römische Geschichte in Rheinland-Pfalz', in Cüppers 1990, 39–168.

Bersanetti, G.M. 1940, *Studi sull'Imperatore Massimino il Trace*. Rome; reprinted 1965.

—— 1942, 'Eracliano, prefetto del praetorio di Gallieno', *Epigraphica* 4, 169–76.

Besnier, M. 1937, *L'Empire Romain et L'Avènement des Sévères au Concile de Nicée.* Histoire Ancienne II; Histoire Rome IV.1. Paris.

Bird, H.W. 1971, 'Aurelius Victor and the accession of Claudius II', *CJ* 1970–1, 242–54.

Birley, A.R. 1969, 'Coups d'état of the year 193', *BJ* 169, 247–80.

—— 1972, 'Virius Lupus', *Archaeologia Aeliana* 4th series, 50, 179–89.

—— 1974a, 'Roman frontiers and Roman frontier policy', *Trans. Architectural and Archaeological Society of Durham and Northumberland* 3, 13–25.

—— 1974b, 'Septimius Severus, *propagator imperii*', *Actes du IXe Congrès Internationale d'Études sur les Frontières Romaines, Mamaia 1972.* Bucharest, 297–9.

—— 1976, 'The third century crisis in the Roman Empire', *Bulletin of the John Rylands Library* 58, 253–81.

—— 1981a, *The Fasti of Roman Britain.* Oxford University Press.

—— 1981b, 'The economic effects of Roman frontier policy', in King and Henig 1981, 39–54.

—— 1987, *Marcus Aurelius.* London: Batsford.

—— 1988, *The African Emperor: Septimius Severus.* 2nd edn. London: Batsford.

—— 1990, 'Decius reconsidered', in Frézouls and Jouffroy 1990, 57–80.

—— 1997, *Hadrian: the restless Emperor.* London: Routledge.

Birley, E. 1953, 'Senators in the Emperor's service', *PBA* 39, 197ff.

—— 1969, 'Septimius Severus and the Roman army', *Ep. Stud.* 8, 63–82.

Birley, R.E. 1962, 'Excavation of the Roman fortress at Carpow 1961–2', *PSAS* 96 (1962–3), 184–207.

—— 1963, 'The Roman legionary fortress at Carpow', *Scottish Historical Review* 42, 126–34.

Bittel, K. 1954, 'Das Alamannia Relief in Nicaea (Bithynia)', *Festschrift für Peter Goessler.* Stuttgart, 11–22.

Blazquez, J.M. 1982, 'La economia de la Hispania Romana', in *Espana Roman (218 a. de J.C. – 414 de J.C.). La Conquista y la exploitacion economica.* Madrid. 293–607.

Blockley, R.C. 1992, *East Roman Foreign Policy: formation and conduct from Diocletian to Anastasius.* Liverpool: Francis Cairns.

Bloemers, T. 1989, 'Acculturation in the Rhine/Meuse basin in the Roman period: demographic considerations', in Barrett *et al.* 1989, 175–97.

Boak, A.E.R. 1955, *Manpower Shortage and the Fall of the Roman Empire in the West.* Connecticut: Greenwood Press.

Bowersock, G.W. 1983, *Roman Arabia.* London and Cambridge, Massachusetts.

Brauer, G.C. 1975, *The Age of the Soldier Emperors: Imperial Rome 244–284.* New Jersey: Noyes Press.

Braund, D.C. 1984, *Rome and the Friendly King; the character of client kingship.* London: Croom Helm.

—— 1989, 'Ideology, subsidies and trade: the king on the northern frontier revisited', in Barrett *et al.* 1989, 14–26.

Breeze, D. and Dobson, B. 1970, 'The development of the mural frontier from Hadrian to Caracalla', *PSAS* 102, 109–21.

Brilliant, R. 1967, *The Arch of Septimius Severus in the Roman Forum. MAAR* 29. Rome.

Brunt, P.A. 1983, 'Princeps and equites', *JRS* 73, 42–75.

Bruun, P. 1953, 'The Constantinian Coinage of Arelate', *Finska Fornminnesföremingens Tidskrift.* Helsinki, 52.2.

—— 1960, 'The battle of the Milvian Bridge: the date reconsidered', *Hermes* 88, 361–70.

—— 1975, 'Constantine's change of *dies imperii*', *Arctos* 9, 11–29.

—— 1979, 'The Negotiations of the Conference at Carmuntum', Numismatica e Antichitè Classiche 8, 255–78.

Buckley, B. 1981, 'The Aeduan area in the third century', in King and Henig 1981, 287–315.

Burian, J. 1963, 'Zur historischen Glaubwürdigkeit der Gordiani tres in der Historia Augusta', Atti del Colloquio Patavino sulla HA, Univ. Padua, Pubbl. Istit. Stor. Ant. 4, 41–66.

Burns, T.S. 1974, 'Transformations in Ostrogothic Social Structure', Diss Ph.D. University of Michigan 1974, published 1984 by University Microfilms. Ann Arbor: University of Michigan.

—— 1984, History of the Ostrogoths. Bloomington: Indiana University Press.

Bursche, A. 1996a, 'Contacts between the late Roman Empire and north–central Europe', Ant. J. 76, 31–50.

—— 1996b, Later Roman–Barbarian Contacts in Central Europe: numismatic evidence. Studien zu Fundmunzen der Antike Band II. Berlin: Gebr. Mann Verlag.

Butler, R.M. 1959, 'Late Roman town walls in Gaul', AJ 116, 25ff.

Calderini, A. 1949, I Severi: la crisi dell'impero nel III secolo. Bologna.

Callu, J.P. 1969, La Politique Monétaire des Empereurs Romains de 238 à 311. Paris.

—— 1975, 'Approches numismatiques de l'histoire du 3e siècle (238–311)', ANRW II.2, 594–613.

Cameron, A. 1993, The Later Roman Empire. London: Fontana.

Campbell, B. 1994, The Roman Army 31 BC–AD 337. London: Routledge.

Campbell, J.B. 1984, The Emperor and the Roman Army 31 BC–AD 235. Oxford: Clarendon Press.

Carlsen, J. et al. (eds) 1994, Landuse in the Roman Empire. Rome: Bretschneider.

Carratelli, G. Pugliese 1947, 'Res Gestae Divi Saporis', Parola del Passato 2, 209–39.

Carrié, J.-M. 1993, 'Le riforme economiche da Aureliano a Costantino', in Storia di Roma III pt 1: L'eta tardoantica: Crisi e trasformazione. Turin, 284–322.

Casey, J. 1991, The Legions in the Later Roman Empire. Fourth Annual Caerleon Lecture. National Museum of Wales.

—— 1994, Carausius and Allectus: the British Usurpers. London: Batsford.

Castritius, H. 1969, Studien zu Maximinus Daia. Kallmünz.

—— 1971, 'Zum höfischen Protokoll in der Tetrarchie: Introitus (Adventus) Augusti et Caesares', Chiron 1, 365–76.

—— 1990. 'Von politischer Vielfalt zur Einheit: die Ethnogenesen der Alamannen', in Wolfram and Pohl 1990, 71ff.

Chadwick, H. 1981, 'The Church of the third century in the west', in King and Henig 1981, 5–13.

Chambers, M. 1966, 'The crisis of the third century', in White, 1966, 1–29.

—— (ed.) 1970, The Fall of Rome: can it be explained? 2nd edn. New York: Holt, Rinehart and Winston.

Champion, T.C. and Megaw, J.V.S. (eds) 1985, Settlement and Society: aspects of west European prehistory in the first millennium BC. Leicester.

Charlesworth, M.P. 1926, Trade Routes and Commerce of the Roman Empire. 2nd edn. Chicago: Ares Publishers Inc.

Charpy, J.J. 1993, 'Barbarian Europe and the Mediterranean world', in Rome Faces the Barbarian, 36–44.

Chastagnol, A. 1960, La Préfecture Urbaine à Rome sous le Bas-Empire. Paris: Presses Universities de France.

—— 1967, 'Les années regnalesde Maximin Hercule en Egypte et les fêtes vicennalesde 20 Novembre 303', *RN* 6th series 9, 54–81.

—— 1970, *Recherches sur l'Histoire Auguste*. Bonn.

—— 1976, 'Trois études sur la *vita Cari*', *HAC 1972–4*, Bonn, 75–90.

—— 1980a, 'Quatres études sur la *vita Cari*', *HAC 1977–8*, Bonn, 45–71.

—— 1980b, 'Sur la chronologie des années 275–285', *Mélanges de numismatique, d'archéologie et d'histoire offerts à Jean Lafaurie*. Paris, 75–82.

—— 1982, *L'Evolution Politique, Sociale et Economique du Monde Romain 284–363*. Paris.

—— 1983a, 'Étude sur la *Vita Cari*', *HAC1979–81*, Bonn 1983, 99–113.

—— 1983b, 'Les jubilés impériaux de 260 à 337', in Frézouls 1983, 11–25.

—— 1984a, 'La signification géographique et ethnique des mots *Germani* et *Germania* dans les sources latins', *Ktéma* 9, 97–101.

—— 1984b, Les fêtes décennales de Septime Sévère', *BSNAF*, 91–107.

—— 1991, *Le Bas-Empire*. Paris.

—— 1992, *Le Senat Romain à l'Époque Impériale*. Paris: Les Belles Lettres.

—— 1994a, 'Etudes sur la vita Cari', *HAC Genevense (Atti dei convegno sulla Historia Augusta II)*. Bari, 18–99.

—— 1994b, *Histoire Auguste: les Empereurs romaines des IIe et IIIe siècles*. Paris.

—— 1994c, 'L'evolution politique du règne de Dioclétien', *AT* 2, 23–31.

Chaumont, M.L. 1969, *Recherches sur l'Histoire d'Arménie*. Paris.

Christ, K. 1960, *Antike Munzfunde Südwestdeutschlands*. Heidelberg.

Christensen, A. 1944, *L'Iran sous les Sassanides*. 2nd edn. Copenhagen.

Christlein, R. 1979, *Die Alamannen: Archäologie eines lebendigen Volkes*. Stuttgart: Theiss.

Christol, M. 1971, 'Un écho des jeux séculaires de 204 après J.C. en Arabie sous le gouverne- ment de Q. Aiacius Modestus', *REA* 73, 124–40.

Christol, M. 1972, 'Le trésor de Turin, le dernière émission de Gallien à Milan et la révolte d'Auréolus', *BSFN* 17, 250–4.

—— 1975, 'Les règnes de Valérien et Gallien (253–68): travaux d'ensemble, questions chronologiques', *ANRW* II.2, 803–27.

—— 1977, 'La carrière de Traianus Mucianus et l'origine des *protectores*', *Chiron* 7, 393–408.

—— 1981, 'L'État Romain et la Crise de l'Empire sous le Règne des Empereurs Valérien et Gallien'. Doctoral thesis, Paris.

—— 1982, 'l'État romain et la crise de l'Empire (253–268)', *L'Information Historique* 44, 156–63.

—— 1986, *Essai sur l'Evolution des Carrières Sénatoriales dans la 2e moitié du IIIe Siècle après J.-C.* Paris.

—— 1988, 'Armée et société politique dans l'Empire romain au IIIe siècle apr. J.-C.' *Civilta Classica e Cristiana* 9, 169–204.

—— 1992, 'L'oeuvre de C. Octavius Pudens Caesius Honoratus en Maurétanie Césarienne', in *L'Africa Romana: Atti del X convegno di studio, Oristano 11–13 dicembre 1992, Sassari 1994*, 1141–52.

—— 1997, *L'Empire Romain du IIIe Siècle: histoire politique 192–325 après J.-C.* Paris: Editions Errance.

Cizek, E. 1994, *L'Empereur Aurélien et son Temps*. Paris: Les Belles Lettres.

Clarke, G.W. 1965, 'The secular profession of St Cyprian of Carthage', *Latomus* 24, 633–8.

Clausing, R. 1925, *The Roman Colonate*. Diss. University of Columbia.

Clavel, M. and Levêque, P. 1971, *Villes et Structures Urbaines dans l'Occident Romain*. Paris: Armand Colin.

Cope, L.H. 1969, 'The nadir of the Imperial *Antoniniani* in the reign of Claudius II Gothicus', *NC* 9, 145–61.

Corcoran, S. 1996, *The Empire of the Tetrarchs: Imperial pronouncements and government AD 284–324*. Oxford: Clarendon Press.

Coriat, J.-P. 1997, *Le Prince Législateur: la technique législative des Sévères et les méthodes de création du droit impériale à la fin du Principat*. Ecole Française de Rome.

Crawford, M. 1975, 'Finance, coinage and money from the Severans to Constantine', *ANRW* II.2, 560–93.

Crees, J.H.E. 1911, *The Reign of the Emperor Probus*. University of London Press.

Crook, J. 1955, *Consilium Principis: Imperial councils and counsellors from Augustus to Diocletian*. Cambridge University Press.

Cumont, F. 1909, 'La théologie solaire du paganisme romain', *Mémoires présentés par divers savants. à l'Académie des Inscriptions et Belles-Lettres*, 12.2, 449–79.

Cüppers, H. 1990, *Die Römer in Rheinland-Pfalz*. Stuttgart: Theiss.

Czysz, W. *et al.* (eds) 1995, *Die Römer in Bayern*. Stuttgart: Theiss.

Dabrowski, K. and Kolendo, J. 1972, 'Les epées romaines decouvertes en Europe centrale et septentrionale', *Archaeologia Polona* 13, 59–109.

Dagron, G. 1974, *Naissance d'une Capitale: Constantinople et ses institutions de 330 à 451*. Paris.

Daly, L.J. 1972, 'The Mandarin and the Barbarian: the response of Themistius to the Gothic challenge', *Historia* 21, 351–78.

Damerau, P. 1934, 'Kaiser Claudius II Gothicus', *Klio* Beiheft 33. Leipzig.

Daniels, C. 1987, 'The frontiers of Roman Africa', in Wacher 1987, vol. 1, 223–65.

Dauge, Y.A. 1981, *Le Barbare; recherches sur la conception romaine de la barbare et de la civilisation*. Collection Latomus vol. 176. Brussels.

de Blois, L. 1975, 'Odaenathus and the Roman–Persian wars of 252–64', *Talanta* 6, 7–23.

——— 1976, *The Policy of the Emperor Gallienus*. Nederlands Instituut te Rome.

——— 1979, 'The reign of the Emperor Philip the Arabian', *Talanta* 10–11, 1978–1979, 11–43.

de Neeve, P. 1984, *Colonus: private farm tenancy in Roman Italy during the Republic*. Amsterdam.

Debevoise, N.C. 1938, *A Political History of Parthia*. University of Chicago Press; reprinted 1968 by Greenwood Press.

Delbrück, H. 1990, *The Barbarian Invasions. History of the Art of War* vol. 2. University of Nebraska Press; reprint of 1921 edn.

Demougeot, E. 1969, *La Formation de l'Europe et les Invasions Barbares des Origines Germaniques a l'Avénement de Dioclétien*. Paris: Aubier.

Develin, R. 1971, 'The army pay rises under Severus and Caracalla and the question of *annona militaris*', *Latomus* 30, 687–95.

Devijver, H. 1989, 'Veränderungen in der Zusammensetzung der Ritterlichen Offiziere von Septimius Severus bis Gallienus (193–268)', in H. Devijver, *Equestrian Officers in the Roman Imperial Army*. Amsterdam: Gieben, 316–38.

Dietz, K.H. 1985, 'Zwei neue Meilensteine Caracallas aus Gundelfingen', *Germania* 63, 75–86.

——— 1986, 'Zum Feldzug Caracallas gegen die Germanen', *Studien zu den Militägrenzen Roms III: Vorträge des 13 Internationaler Limeskongresses Aalen 1983*. Stuttgart.

Dodgeon, M.H. and Lieu, S.N.C. 1991, *The Roman Eastern Frontier and the Persian Wars (AD 226–363): a documentary history*. London: Routledge.

Doorselaev, A. van 1975, 'Diskussionsbemerkungen zum Stand der Laetenforschung in Belgien', in Grünert and Dölle 1975, 235–40.

Dore, J. and Gillam, J.P. 1979, *The Roman Fort at South Shields*. Newcastle upon Tyne.

Downey, G. 1950, 'Aurelian's victory over Zenobia at Immae, AD 272', *TAPhA* 81, 57–68.

—— 1961, *A History of Antioch in Syria*. Princeton University Press, Princeton.

Drack, W. 1980, *Die Spätrömische Grenzwehr am Hochrhein*. Archäologische Führer der Schweiz 13. Zurich.

Drack, W. and Fellmann, R. 1988, *Die Römer in der Schweiz*. Stuttgart: Theiss.

Drew, K.F. 1991, *The Laws of the Salian Franks*. Philadelphia: University of Pennsylvania.

Drew-Bear, Th. 1981, 'Les voyages d'Aurelius Gaius, soldat de Dioclétien', in *La Géographie Administrative et Politique d'Alexandre à Mahomet: Actes du Colloque de Strasbourg 14–16 juin 1979*, Leyde 1981, 93–141.

Drinkwater, J.F. 1971, 'A new inscription and the legionary issues of Gallienus and Victorinus', *NC* 11, 325f.

—— 1987, *The Gallic Empire: separatism and continuity in the north-west provinces of the Roman Empire AD 260–274*. Stuttgart.

Duby, G. (ed.) 1980, *Histoire de la France Urbaine I: la ville antique des origines au IXe siècle*. Paris.

Duncan-Jones, R. 1974, *Economy of the Roman Empire: quantitative studies*. Cambridge.

—— 1978, 'Pay and numbers in Diocletian's army', *Chiron* 8, 541–60.

Durry, M. 1938, *Les Cohortes Prétoriennes*. Paris: de Boccard.

Dusanic, S. 1976, 'The end of the Philippi', *Chiron* 6, 427–39.

Duval, P.-M. 1959, 'Une enquête sur les enceintes gauloises', *Gallia* 17, 37–62.

—— 1997, 'Les résidences Impériales: leur rapport avec les problèmes de légitimité, les partages de l'empire et la chronologie des combinaisons dynastiques', in Paschoud and Szidat 1997, 127–53.

Eadie, J.W. 1980, 'Barbarian invasions and frontier politics in the reign of Gallienus', in Hanson and Keppie 1980, vol. 3, 1045–50.

—— 1996, 'The transformation of the eastern frontier, 260–305', in Mathisen and Sivan 1996, 72–81.

Eggers, H.J. 1951, *Der Römischen Import im Freien Germanien*. Hamburg.

Eichholz, D. 1953, 'Constantius Chlorus' invasion of Britain', *JRS* 43, 41–6.

Elbern, S. 1984, *Usurpationen im Spätrömischen Reich*. Bonn: Habelt.

Ellis, L. 1996, 'Dacians, Sarmatians and Goths on the Roman Carpathian frontier: second–fourth centuries', in Mathisen and Sivan 1996, 105–25.

Elmer, G. 1941, 'Die Münzprägung der gallischen Kaiser in Köln, Trier und Mailand', *BJ* 146, 1–106.

Elton, H. 1996, *Frontiers of the Roman Empire*. London: Batsford.

Enmann, A. 1884, 'Eine verlorene Geschichte der römischen Kaiser', *Philologus* supplement band 4, 337–50.

Ensslin, W. 1939, 'The reforms of Diocletian', Chapter 11 in *Cambridge Ancient History* XII, 383–408.

—— 1949, 'Zu den Kriegen des Sassaniden Schapur I', *Sitzungsbericht der Bayersichen Akademie der Wissenschaft, Ph. Hist Klasse*, fasc. 5, 1–17.

Erdrich, M. 1994, 'Waffen in mitteleuropäischen Barbaricum: Handel oder Politik' *JRMES* 5, 199–209.

Erim, K.T. and Reynolds, J. 1970, 'The copy of Diocletian's edict on maximum prices from Aphrodisias in Caria', *JRS* 60, 120–41.

—— 1973, 'The Aphrodisias copy of Diocletian's edict on maximum prices', *JRS* 63, 99–110.

Erim, K.T., Reynolds, J. and Crawford, M. 1971, 'Diocletian's currency reform: a new inscription', *JRS* 61, 171–7.

Estiot, S. 1995, 'Aureliana', *RN*, 51–94.

Faro, S. 1980, 'La coscienza della crisi in un anonimoretore del III secolo', *Athenaeum* 58, 406–28.

Feissel, D. and Gascou, J. 1995, 'Documents d'archives romaines inédits du Moyen Euphrate (IIIe s. ap. J.-C.), *JS*, 65–119.

Felix, W. 1985, *Antike Literarische Quellen zur Aussenpolitik des Sasanienstaates (Erster Band 224 309)*. Vienna: Verlag der österreichischen Akademie der Wissenschaften.

Fentress, E.W.B. 1979, *Numidia and the Roman Army: social, military and economic aspects of the frontier zone*. Oxford: BAR S53.

Ferrill, A. 1986, *The Fall of the Roman Empire: the military explanation*. London: Thames and Hudson.

Février, P.A. 1973, 'Origin and growth of cities in southern Gaul to the third century AD', *JRS* 63, 1–28.

Filtzinger, P. *et al.* 1986, *Die Römer in Baden-Württemberg*. Stuttgart: Theiss.

Fink, R.O. 1971, *Roman Military Records on Papyrus*. American Philological Association Monograph 26.

Finley, M.I. (ed.) 1974, *Studies in Ancient Society*. London: Routledge and Kegan Paul.

Fischer, T. and Spindler, K. 1984, *Das Römische Grenzkastell Abusina-Eining*. Stuttgart.

Fitz, J. 1961, 'Massnahmen zur militärischen Sicherheit von Pannonia Inferior unter Commodus', *Klio* 39, 199–214.

—— 1966a, *Ingenuus et Régalien*. Collection Latomus vol. 81. Brussels.

—— 1966b, 'Les antoniniani des légions de Gallien', *Mélanges d'épigraphie, d'archéologie et d'histoire offerts à J. Carcopino*. Paris, 353–65.

—— 1976, *Der Römische Limes in Ungarn*, Taschenbuch für die Teilnehmer XI Limekongresses. Székesfehévár.

Foot, M.R.D. 1973, *War and Society: essays in memory of J. Western*. London.

Frank, T. 1940, *An Economic Survey of Ancient Rome*. Vol. 5. New York.

Freeman, P. and Kennedy, D. (eds) 1986, *The Defence of the Roman and Byzantine East*. Oxford: BAR S297, 2 vols.

French, D.H. and Lightfoot, C.S. (eds) 1989, *The Eastern Frontier of the Roman Empire*. Oxford: BAR S553, 2 vols.

Frend, W.H.C. 1974, 'The failure of the persecutions in the Roman Empire', in Finley 1974, 263–87.

—— 1984, *The Rise of Christianity*. Philadelphia.

Frere, S.S. 1987, *Britannia*. London: Routledge.

Frézouls, E. (ed.) 1983, *Crise et Redressement dans les Provinces Européenes de l'Empire: milieu du IIIe siècle – milieu du IVe siècle ap. J.-C.* Actes du Colloque de Strasbourg, décembre 1981.

Frézouls, E. and Jouffroy, H. (eds) 1990, *Les Empereurs Illyriens: Actes du Colloque de Strasbourg (11–13 octobre 1990)*. Université des Sciences Humaines de Strasbourg: Contributions et Travaux de l'Institut d'Historie Romaine VIII.

Fulford, M. 1985, 'Roman material in barbarian society, c.200 BC–c.AD 200', in Champion and Megaw 1985, 91–108.

—— 1989, 'Roman and barbarian: the economy of Roman frontier systems', in Barrett *et al.* 1989, 81–95.

Gagé, J. 1934a, *Recherches sur les Jeux Séculaires*. Paris.

—— 1934b, 'Les jeux séculaires de 204 ap. J.-C. et la dynastie des Sévères', *MEFRA* 51, 33–78.

—— 1964a, *La Montée des Sassanides et l'Heure de Palmyre*. Paris.

—— 1964b, *Les Classes Sociales dans l'Empire Romain*. Paris.

Galliou, P. 1981, 'Western Gaul in the third century', in King and Henig 1981, 259–85.

Garnsey, P. 1970, *Social Status and Legal Privilege*. Oxford.

—— 1974, 'Decline of the urban aristocracy in the Empire', *ANRW* II.1, 229–52.

Garnsey, P. and Whittaker, C.R. (eds) 1983, *Trade and Famine in Classical Antiquity*. Cambridge.

Garnsey, P. *et al.* (eds) 1983, *Trade in the Ancient Economy*. London: Chatto and Windus.

Gawlikowski, M. 1985, 'Les princes de Palmyre', *Syria* 62, 251–61.

Gebühr, M. 1974, 'Zur Definition altkaiserzeitlicher Fürstengräber vom Lubsow-Typ', *Praehistorische Zeitschrift* 49, 82–128.

Gilliam, J.F. 1950, 'Some Latin military papyri from Dura', *Yale Classical Studies* 11, 169–209.

—— 1961, 'The plague under Marcus Aurelius', *American Journal of Philology* 82, 225–51.

Göbl, R. 1951, 'Der Aufbau der römischen Münzprägung in der Kaiserzeit. V.1 Valerianus und Gallienus', *Mz. Num. Zeitschrift* 74, 8–45.

Göbl, R. 1953, 'Der Aufbau der römischen Münzprägung in der Kaiserzeit. V.2 Gallienus als Alleinherrscher', *Mz. Num. Zeitschrift* 75, 5–35.

Göbl, R. 1970, *Regalianus und Dryantilla*. Vienna: Österreichische Akademie der Wissenschaften.

Goffart, W. 1974, *Caput and Colonate: towards a history of late Roman taxation. Phoenix* suppl. vol.

Gordon, C.D. 1949, 'Subsidies in Roman imperial defence', *Phoenix* 3, 60–9.

Graham, A.J. 1973, 'Septimius Severus and his generals AD 193–7', in Foot 1973, 255–75.

Grant, M. 1993, *The Emperor Constantine*. London: Weidenfeld and Nicolson.

Greene, K. 1986, *The Archaeology of the Roman Economy*. London: Batsford.

Grishman, R. 1962, *Iran Parthians and Sassanians*. London: Thames and Hudson.

Groenmann-van Waateringe, W. 1989, 'Food for soldiers, food for thought', in Barrett *et al.* 1989, 96–103.

Grosse, R. 1920, *Römische Militärgeschichte von Gallienus bis zum Beginn der Byzantinschen Themenverfassung*. Berlin: Wiedmannsche Buchhandlung; reprinted New York, 1975.

Grünert, H. and Dölle, H.-J. 1975, *Römer und Germanen in Mitteleuropa*. Berlin: Akademie-Verlag.

Guey, J. 1955, 'Les *Res Gestae Divi Saporis*', *REA* 57, 113–22.

Guey, J. and Pékary, Th. 1961, 'Autour des Res Gestae Divi Saporis', *Syria* 38, 261–83.

Günther, R. 1975, 'Germanische Laeten, Foederaten und Gentilen im nördlichen und nordöstliche Gallien in der Spatantike', in Grünert and Dölle 1975, 225–34.

Günther, R. and Köpstein, H. 1978, *Die Römer an Rhein und Donau: zur politischen, wirtschaftlichen und sozialen Entwicklung in den römischen Provinzen an Rhein, Mosel und oberer Donau im 3. und 4. Jahrhundert*. Vienna: Hermann Bohlaus.

Haarlov, B. 1976, 'A contribution to the iconography of the Emperor Gallienus', in *Studia Romana in Honorem Petri Krarrup Septuagenarii*. Odense University Press, 113–21.

Haarnagel, W. 1979a, 'Das eisenzeitliche Dorf "Feddersen Wierde", seine siedlungsgeschichtliche Entwicklung, seine wirtschaftliche Funktion und Wandlung seiner Sozialstruktur', in Jankuhn and Wenskus 1979.

—— 1979b, *Die Grabung Feddersen Wierde vol. 2: Methode, Hausbau, Siedlungs- und Wirtschaftsformen, sowie Sozialstruktur*. Wiesbaden.

Hachmann, R. 1970, *Die Goten und Skandinavien*. Berlin: De Gruyter.

—— 1971, *The Germanic Peoples*. London: Barrie and Jenkins.

Halsberghe, G.H. 1972, *The Cult of Sol Invictus*. EPRO 23. Leiden.

Hannestad, H. 1986, *Roman Art and Imperial Policy*. Aarhus.

Hanson, W.S. and Keppie, L.J.F. (eds) 1980, *Roman Frontier Studies 1979*. Oxford: BAR S71, 3 vols.

Harl, K.W. 1996, *Coinage in the Roman Economy 300 BC to AD 700*. Johns Hopkins University Press.

Hartmann, F. 1982, *Herrscherwechsel und Reichskrise: Untersuchungen zu den Ursachen und Konsequenzen der Herrscherwechsel im Imperium Romanum der Soldaten Kaiserzeit*. Frankfurt am Main: Peter Lang.

Heather, P. 1995, 'The Huns and the end of the Roman Empire in Western Europe', *EHR* 110, 4–41.

—— 1996, *The Goths*. Blackwell.

Heather, P. and Matthews, J. 1991, *The Goths in the Fourth Century*. Liverpool University Press: Translated Texts for Historians, 11.

Hedeager, L. 1978, 'A quantitative analysis of Roman imports in Europe north of the Limes, and the question of Roman–Germanic exchange', in Kristiansen and Paluden-Muller 1978, 191–216.

—— 1987, 'Empire, frontier and barbarian hinterland: Rome and northern Europe from AD 1–400', in Rowlands *et al.* 1987,.

—— 1992, *Iron Age Societies: from tribe to state in northern Europe 500 BC–AD 700*. Blackwell.

Herrmann, P. 1990, *Hilferufe aus Römischen Provinzen: ein Aspekt der Krise des römischen Reiches im 3. Jhdt. n. Chr.* Hamburg.

Hirschfeld, O. 1913, *Zur Geschichte der Römischen Kaiserzeit in den ersten drei Jarhhunderten*. Kleine Schriften, Berlin.

Hoffmann, D. 1969–70, *Die Spätrömische Bewegungsheer und die Notitia Dignitatum. Epigraphische Studien 7*. Düsseldorf.

Homo, L. 1904, *Essai sur le Règne de l'Empereur Aurélien*. Paris.

Honoré, A.M. 1962, 'The Severan lawyers; a preliminary survey', *SDHI* 28, 162–231.

—— 1979, 'Imperial rescripts AD 193–305: authorship and authenticity, *JRS* 69, 51–64.

Honoré, T. 1982, *Ulpian*. Oxford: Clarendon.

Hopkins, K. 1978, *Conquerors and Slaves*. Cambridge.

—— 1980, 'Taxes and trade in the Roman Empire (200 BC–AD 400)', *JRS* 70, 101–125.

—— 1983a, Introduction, in Garnsey *et al.* 1983, ix–xxv.

—— 1983b, 'Models, ships and staples', in Garnsey *et al.* 1983, 84–109.

—— 1999, *A World Full of God: Pagans, Jews and Christians in the Roman Empire*. London: Weidenfeld and Nicolson.

Horn, H.G. 1987, *Die Römer in Nordrhein-Westfalen*. Stuttgart: Theiss.

Howe, L.L. 1942, *The Praetorian Prefect from Commodus to Diocletian*. Chicago; reprinted Rome: Bretschneider 1966.

Hyde, W.W. 1970, *Paganism and Christianity in the Roman Empire*. New York: Octagon Books.

Isaac, B. 1992, *Limits of Empire*. 2nd edn. Oxford.

Jacques, Fr. 1992. ' Les *nobiles* exécutés par Septime Sévère selon l'*Histoire Auguste*: liste de proscription ou énumération fantaisiste?', *Latomus* 51, 121–44.

James, E. 1988, *The Franks*. Blackwell.

Jankuhn, H. and Wenskus, R. (eds) 1979, *Geschichtswissenschaft und Archäologie*. Sigmaringen.

Jardé, A. 1925, *Etudes Critiques sur la Vie et le Règne de Sévère Alexandre*. Paris.

Jarrett, M. 1972, 'An album of equestrians from North Africa in the Emperor's service', *Ep. Stud.* 9, 146–232.

Johne, K.-P. 1993, *Gesellschaft und Wirtschaft des Römischen Reiches im 3. Jahrhundert.* Akademie Verlag.

Johnson, S. 1976, *Roman Forts of the Saxon Shore.* 2nd edn. London: Elek.

—— 1983, *Late Roman Fortifications.* Batsford.

—— 1989, 'Architecture of the Saxon Shore forts', in Maxfield 1989, 30–44.

Jones, A.H.M. 1948, *Constantine and the Conversion of Europe.* London: English University Press; reprinted 1962.

—— 1964, *The Later Roman Empire 284–602.* Oxford: Blackwell, 2 vols.

—— 1966, *The Decline of the Ancient World.* Harlow: Longman.

—— 1974a, *The Roman Economy: studies in ancient economic and administrative history.* Oxford (ed. by P.A. Brunt).

—— 1974b, 'The Roman colonate', in Finley 1974, 288–303.

Jones, R.F.J. 1981, 'Change on the frontier: northern Britain in the third century', in King and Henig 1981, 393–414.

Junghans, S. 1986, *Sweben-Alamannen und Rom: die Anfange der Schwäbisch-alamannischen Geschichte.* Stuttgart: Theiss.

Kaul, F. 1993a, 'Roman imports in the Baltic area', in *Rome Faces the Barbarian*, 122–30.

Kaul, F. 1993b, 'Weapon sacrifices in northern Europe', in *Rome Faces the Barbarian*, 138–44.

Kazansky, M. 1991, *Les Goths Ier–VIIe après J.-C.* Paris: Editions Errance.

Keay, S.T. 1988, *Roman Spain.* London.

Keil, B. 1898, *Aelii Aristidis Smyrnaei Quae Supersunt Omnia.* Berlin.

Kellner, H.-G. 1953, 'Eine neue Münzschatz bei Kastell Gunzenhausen und der Fall des rätischen Limes', *Germania* 31, 168–77.

—— 1995, 'Die grosse Krise im 3. Jahrhundert', in Czysz *et al.* 1995, 309–57.

Kennedy, D. and Riley, D. 1990, *Rome's Desert Frontier from the Air.* London: Batsford.

Kennedy, D.L. 1977, 'Parthian regiments in the Roman Army', *Limes; Akten des XI Internationalen Limeskongresses Székésferhervar 30.8–6.9.1976.* ed. J Fitz. Budapest: Akademiai Kiado, 521–31.

—— 1979, 'Ti. Claudius Subatianus Aquila, first prefect of Mesopotamia', *ZPE* 36, 225–61.

—— 1980, 'The frontier policy of Septimius Severus', in Hanson and Keppie 1980, 879–88.

—— 1982, *Archaeological Explorations on the Roman Frontier in North East Jordan.* Oxford: BAR S134.

Kent, J.P.C. 1978, *Roman Coins.* London: Thames and Hudson.

Keppie, L. 1991, *Understanding Roman Inscriptions.* London: Batsford.

Kettenhofen, E. 1982, *Die Römisch-persischen Kriege des 3. Jahrhunderts n.Chr nach der Inschrift Sahpurs I an der Ka 'be-ye Zartost.* Wiesbaden: Dr Ludwig Reichert Verlag.

—— 1987, 'Aurelianus Carpicus Maximus', *Studii Classici* 25, 63–9.

Keyes, C.W. 1915, *The Rise of the Equites in the Third Century of the Roman Empire.* Princeton University Press, Princeton.

Kienast, D. 1990, *Römische Kaisertabelle: Grundzüge einer römischen Kaiserchronologie.* Darmstadt.

King, A. and Henig, M. (eds) 1981, *The Roman West in the Third Century.* Oxford: BAR S109, 2 vols.

King, C.E. 1981, 'The circulation of coin into the western provinces', in King and Henig 1981, 89–126.

—— 1984, 'The legionary *antoniniani* of Gallienus from Milan', *La zecca di Milano: Atti del convegno internazionale di studio 9–14 May 1983.* Milan, 103–31.

Klose, J. 1934, *Roms Klientelstaaten am Rhein und an der Donau: Beiträge zu ihrer Geschichte und rechtlichen Stellung im 1. und 2. Jahrhundert n.Chr.* Breslau.

Kolb, F. 1987, *Diokletian und die erste Tetrarchie*. Berlin.

Kolendo, J. 1981, 'Les influences de Rome sur les peuples de l'Europe centrale habitant loin des frontières de l'Empire', *Klio* 63, 453–72.

Kolnik, T. 1978, 'Q. Atilius Primus, interprex, centurio, and negotiator', *Acta. Arch. Hung.* 30, 61ff.

König, I. 1974, 'Die Berufung des Constantius Chlorus und des Galerius zu Caesaren: Gedanken zur Enstehung der ersten Tetrarchie', *Chiron* 4, 567–76.

—— 1981, *Die Gallischen Usurpatoren von Postumus bis Tetricus*. Munich: Beck'sche Verlag.

—— 1986, 'Lactanz und das "System" der Tetrarchie', *Labeo* 32, 180–93.

—— 1997, 'Die Postumus Inschrift aus Augsburg', *Historia* 46, 341–54.

Kotula, T. 1960, 'L'insurrection des Gordiens et l'Afrique romaine', *Eos* 51, 1959–60, 197–211.

Krautheimer, R. 1983, *Three Christian Capitals: topography and politics*. Berkeley: University of California Press.

Kremer, B. 1994, *Das Bild der Kelten bis in Augustische Zeit*. Historia Einzelschriften 88. Stuttgart: Franz Steiner Verlag.

Kristiansen, K. and Paludan-Muller, C. (eds) 1978, *New Directions in Scandinavian Archaeology*. Copenhagen.

Krüger, B. (ed.) 1983, *Die Germanen: ein Handbuch in zwei Bänden*. Band II: *Die Stämme und Stammesverbande in der Zeit vom 3. Jahrhundert bis zur Herausbildung der politischen Vorherrschaft der Franken*. Berlin: Akademie-Verlag.

Kubitschek, W. 1915, 'Deus et Dominus als Titel der Kaiser', *Numismatische Zeitschrift* 1915, 167–8.

Kunkel, W. 1974, *Kleine Schriften*. Weimar: Hermann Böhlaus.

Kunow, J. 1983, *Der Römische Import in der Germania Libera bis zu den Marcomannerkriegen*. Neumunster.

—— 1986, 'Bemerkungen zum Export römischer Waffen in das Barbaricum', *Studien zu den Militärgrenzen Roms III*, 740–6.

—— 1987, 'Die Militärgeschichte Niedergermaniens', in Horn 1987, 27–109.

Lafaurie, J. 1964, 'La chronologie des Empereurs gaulois'. *RN* 6th series, 91ff.

—— 1965, 'Chronologie impériale de 249 à 285', *Bulletin de la Société des Antiquaires de France* 1965, 139ff.

—— 1975a, 'L'Empire gaulois: apport de la numismatique', *ANRW* II.2, 853–1012.

—— 1975b, 'Réformes monétaires d'Aurélien et de Dioclétien', *RN* 1975, 73–138.

Lambrechts, P. 1937, *La Composition du Sénat Romain de Septime Sévère à Dioclétien 193–284*. Budapest.

Lanata, G. 1972, 'Gli atti del processo contro il centutione Marcello', *Byzantion* 41, 509–22.

Lander, J. 1980, 'Typology and late Roman fortification: the case of the "Diocletianic type" ', in Hanson and Keppie 1980, 105–60.

—— 1984, *Roman Stone Fortifications: variation and change from the first century AD to the fourth*. Oxford: BAR S206.

Latouche, R. 1947, 'Aspect démographique de la crise des grands invasions', *Population* 2, 681–90.

—— 1961, *Birth of the Western Economy*. London.

Lauffer, S. 1971, *Diokletians Preisedikt: Texte und Kommentare*. Berlin.

Lavagne, H. 1994, 'Une nouvelle inscription d'Augsbourg et les causes de l'usurpation de Postume', *CRAI* 1994, 431–46.

Le Bihan, J.P. 1993, 'Barbarian Europe and the Mediterranean World – the protagonists', in *Rome Faces the Barbarian*, 16–25.

Le Bohec, Y. 1989, *La Troisième Légion Auguste*. Paris.

Le Roux, P. 1997, 'Armées, rhétorique, et politique dans l'Empire gallo-romain: à propos de l'inscription d'Augsbourg', *ZPE* 115, 281–90.

Lee, A.D. 1993, *Information and Frontiers*. Cambridge University Press.

Lengyel, A. and Radan, G.T.B. 1980, *The Archaeology of Roman Pannonia*. University Press of Kentucky/Akadémiai Kiado.

Lepelley, C. 1981, *Les Cités de l'Afrique Romaine au Bas-Empire*. Paris, 2 vols.

—— 1983, 'Quot curiales, tot tyranni: l'image du décurion oppresseur au Bas-Empire', in Frézouls 1983, 153–6.

Lewis, N. 1996, 'The humane legislation of Septimius Severus', *Historia* 45, 104–13.

Lewis, N. and Rheinhold, M. 1966, *Roman Civilization: Sourcebook II: The Empire*. New York: Harper and Row (rev. edn).

Lewit, T. 1991, *Agricultural Production in the Roman Economy, AD 200–400*. Oxford: BAR S568.

Liebenam, W. 1900, *Städteverwaltung im Römischen Kaiserreiches*. Leipzig.

Liebeschuetz, W. 1990, *Barbarians and Bishops*. Oxford: Clarendon Press.

Liebeschuetz, W. 1992, 'The end of the ancient city', in Rich 1992, 1–49.

Lippold, A. 1968, 'Der Kaiser Maximinus Thrax und der römische Senat', *HAC 1966–1967*, 73–89.

Lo Cascio, E. 1993, 'Dinamiche economiche e politiche fiscali fra i Severi e Aureliano', *Storia di Roma III pt 1'età tardoantica: Crisi e trasfomazione*. Turin, 247–82.

Long, J. 1996, 'Two sides of a coin: Aurelian, Vaballathus and eastern frontiers in the early 270s', in Mathisen and Sivan 1996, 59–71.

Lonstrup, J. 1986, 'Das zweischneidige Schwert aus der jungeren römischen Kaiserzeit im freien Germanien und im Römischen Imperium', *Studien zu den Militärgrenzen Roms III*, 747–9.

Lopuszanski, G. 1951, *La Date de la Capture de Valérian et la Chronologie des Empereurs Gaulois. Cahiers de l'Institut d'Etudes Polonaise en Belgique 9*. Brussels.

L'Orange, H.P. 1984, *Die Spätantike Herrscherbild von Diokletian bis zu den Konstantin-Söhnen 284–361 n.Chr*. Berlin.

Loriot, X. 1975, 'Les premières années de la grande crise du IIIe siècle: de l'avènement de Maximin le Thrace (235) à la mort de Gordien III (244),' *ANRW* II.2, 657–787.

Loriot, X. and Nony, D. 1997, *La Crise de l'Empire Romain 235–285*. Paris: Armand Colin.

Luttwak, E.M. 1976, *The Grand Strategy of the Roman Empire*. Baltimore: Johns Hopkins University Press.

Macdermott, B.C. 1954, 'Roman Emperors in the Sassanian reliefs', *JRS* 44, 78ff.

MacMullen, R. 1963a, 'Barbarian enclaves in the northern Roman Empire', *Antiquité Classique* 32, 552–61.

—— 1963b, *Soldier and Civilian in the Later Roman Empire*. Harvard University Press.

—— 1966, *Enemies of the Roman Order: treason, unrest and alienation in the Empire*. Cambridge, Mass.: Harvard University Press.

—— 1969, *Constantine*. New York.

—— 1976, *The Roman Government's Response to Crisis AD 235–337*. New Haven: Yale University Press.

—— 1980, 'How big was the Roman army', *Klio* 62, 451–60.

—— 1984, *Christianizing the Roman Empire*. New Haven: Yale University Press.

—— 1988, *Corruption and the Decline of Rome*. New Haven: Yale University Press.

—— 1990, *Changes in the Roman Empire*. Princeton: Princeton University Press.

MacMullen, R. and Lane, E.N. (eds) 1992, *Paganism and Christianity 100–425 CE: a sourcebook*. Minneapolis: Fortress Press.

Malcus, B. 1969, 'Notes sur le révolution du système administratif romain au III siècle', *Opuscula Romana* 7, 213–37.

Mann, J.C. 1953, ' "Honesta Missio" and the Brigetio table', *Hermes* 81, 496–500.

—— 1974, 'The frontiers of the Principate', *ANRW* II.1, 508–31.

—— 1989, 'Historical development of the Saxon Shore', in Maxfield 1989, 1–11.

Manni, E. 1947, 'Note di epigrafia Gallieniana', *Epigraphica* 9, 137–52.

—— 1949, *L'Impero di Gallieno*. Rome.

Marelli, U. 1984, 'L'epigrafe di Decio a Cosa e l'epiteto "restitutor sacrorum" ', *Aevum* 58, 52–6.

Maricq, A. 1957, 'Les dernières années de Hatra: l'alliance romaine', *Syria* 34, 288–96.

—— 1958, 'Res Gestae Divi Saporis', *Syria* 35, 295–360.

Maricq, A. and Honigmann, E. 1953, 'Recherches sur les RGDS', *Mémoires Acad. Roy. Belg. Classe des Lettres* 47.4, ch. 3, 111–22.

Mathisen, R.W. and Sivan, H.S. 1996, *Shifting Frontiers in Late Antiquity*. Aldershot: Variorum.

Mauss, M. 1927, *The Gift: form and function of exchange in archaic societies*, trans. by R. Cunnison 1954. London.

Maxfield, V. 1987, 'The Danube frontier', in Wacher 1987, vol. I, 171–93.

—— (ed.) 1989, *The Saxon Shore: a handbook*. University of Exeter Press for 15th International Congress of Roman Frontier Studies 1989.

Maxfield, V. and Dobson, M.J. (eds) 1991, *Roman Frontier Studies 1989: Proceedings of the XV International Congress of Roman Frontier Studies*. University of Exeter.

Mazzarino, S. 1971, 'La tradizione sulle guerre tra Shabuhr I e l'Impero romano', *Acta Ant. Acad. Sc. Hung.* 19, 59–82.

Merten, E. 1968, *Zwei Herrscherfeste in der Historia Augusta*. Bonn.

—— 1985–6, *Stellenbibliographie zur Historia Augusta*. Bonn, 3 vols.

Middleton, P. 1983, 'The Roman army and long distance trade', in Garnsey and Whittaker 1983, 75–83.

Mierow, C.C. 1915, see Jordanes in ancient sources.

Millar, F, 1962, 'The date of the *Constitutio Antoniniana*', *JEA* 48, 124–31.

—— 1964, *A Study of Cassius Dio*. Oxford.

—— 1969, 'P. Herennius Dexippus: the Greek world and the third century invasions', *JRS* 59, 12–30.

—— 1977, *The Emperor in the Roman World*. Duckworth.

—— 1981, *The Roman Empire and its Neighbours*. 2nd edn. London: Duckworth.

—— 1982, 'Emperors, frontiers and foreign relations, 31 B.C. to A.D. 378', *Britannia* 13, 1–23.

—— 1993, *The Roman Near East 31 BC to AD 337*. Cambridge, Mass.: Harvard University Press.

Millett, M. 1981, 'Whose crisis? the archaeology of the third century: a warning', in King and Henig 1981, 525–30.

Mitchell, S. 1983 (ed.) *Armies and Frontiers in Roman and Byzantine Anatolia: proceedings of a conference held at University College Swansea, April 1981*. Oxford: BAR S156.

—— 1988, 'Maximinus and the Christians in AD 312: a new Latin inscription', *JRS* 78, 105–24.

Mócsy, A. 1974, *Pannonia and Upper Moesia*. London: Routledge.

Mommsen, Th. 1989, 'Das römische Militärwesen seit Diocletian', *Hermes* 24.

Moreau, J. 1956, *La Persécution du Christianisme dans l'Empire Romain*. Paris.

Musset, L. 1975, *The Germanic Invasions: the making of Europe A.D. 400–600*. London: Elek.

Nischer, E.C. 1923, 'The army reforms of Diocletian and Constantine and their modifications up to the time of the Notitia Dignitatum', *JRS* 13, 1–55.

Nixon, C.E.V. and Rodgers, B.S. 1994, *In Praise of Later Roman Emperors: the Panegyrici Latini*. Berkeley: University of California Press.

Nock, O.S. 1947, 'The Emperor's divine *comes*', *JRS* 37, 102–16.

Nuber, H.U 1993, 'Der Verlust der obergermanisch-raetischen Limesgebiete und die Grenzsicherung bis zum Ende des 3. Jahrhunderts', in Vallet and Kazansky 1993, 101–8.

Okamura, L. 1991, 'The flying columns of Emperor Gallienus: "legionary" coins and their hoards', in.

Maxfield and Dobson 1991, 387–91.

Okamura, L. 1996, 'Roman withdrawals from three transfluvial frontiers', in Mathisen and Sivan 1996, 11–19.

Oliva, P. 1962, *Pannonia and the Onset of Crisis in the Roman Empire*. Prague.

Oliver, J.H. 1978, 'The piety of Commodus and Caracalla and the Eis Basileia', *Greek, Roman and Byzantine Studies* 19, 375–88.

Olmstead, A.T. 1942, 'The mid-third century of the Christian era', *Classical Philology* 37, 241–62; 398–420.

Osier, J.F. 1974, *The Rise of the Ordo Equester in the Third Century of the Roman Empire*. Ann Arbor: University of Michigan Press.

—— 1977, 'The emergence of third century equestrian military commanders', *Latomus* 36, 676–87.

Parker, H.M.D. 1933, 'The legions of Diocletian and Constantine', *JRS* 23, 175–89.

—— 1935, *History of the Roman World AD 138–337*. London: Methuen.

Parker, S.T. 1986, *Romans and Saracens*. Winona Lake.

—— (ed.) 1987, *The Roman Frontier in Central Jordan: interim report on the Limes Arabicus project 1980–1985*. Oxford: BAR S340, 2 vols.

Paschoud, F. 1971, see under Zosime in ancient sources.

Paschoud, F. and Szidat, J. (eds) 1997, *Usurpationen in der Spätantike*. Historia Einzelschriften 111. Bonn.

Pavis d'Escurac, H. 1976, *La Préfecture de l'Annone: service administratif impérial d'Auguste à Constantin*. Ecole Française de Rome.

Peachin, M. 1990, *Roman Titulature and Chronology AD 235–284*. Amsterdam.

Pearson, M. Parker. 1989, 'Beyond the Pale: barbarian social dynamics in Western Europe', in Barrett *et al.* 1989, 198–226.

Périn, P. and Feffer, L.-C. 1987, *Les Francs: tome 1: à la Conquête de la Gaule*. Paris: Armand Colin.

Petit, P. 1974, *La Crise de l'Empire: des derniers Antonins à Dioclétien*. (*Histoire générale de l'Empire romain*). Paris: Editions du Seuil.

Petrikovits, H. von 1971, 'Fortifications in the north-western Roman Empire from the third to the fifth centuries A.D.', *JRS* 61, 178–218.

Pflaum, H.-G. 1948, *Le Marbre de Thorigny*. Paris.

—— 1952, 'La fortification de la ville de Adrata d'Arabie (259–60 à 274–5)', *Syria* 29, 307–30.

—— 1955, 'Deux carrières équestres de Lambése et de Zama', *Libyca* 3, 123–54.

—— 1960, *Les Carrières Procuratoriennes Équestres sous le Haut-Empire*. Paris.

—— 1966, 'P. Licinius Gallienus nobilissimus Caesar et Imp. M. Aurelius Numerianus, à la lumière de deux nouveaux milliaires d'Oum-el-Bouaghi', *Bulletin d'Archéologie Algérienne* 2, 175–82.

—— 1969, 'Inscriptions impériales de Sala', *Ant. Afr.* 3, 133–44.

—— 1976, 'Zur Reform des Kaisers Gallienus', *Historia* 25, 109–17.

—— 1982, *Supplément: Les Carrières Procuratoriennes Équestres sous le Haut-Empire*. Paris.

Piganiol, A. 1935, 'La capitation de Dioclétien', *RH* 176, 1–13.

Pohlsander, H.A. 1984, 'Crispus: brilliant career and tragic end', *Historia* 33, 79–106.

—— 1996, *The Emperor Constantine*. London: Routledge.

Potter, D.S. 1996, 'Palmyra and Rome: Odenathus' titulature and the use of the Imperium Maius', *ZPE* 113, 271–85.

Poulter, A. 1992, 'Use and abuse of urbanism in the Danubian provinces during the later Roman Empire', in Rich 1992, 99–135.

Radnoti, A. 1967. *Die Germanischen Verbündeten der Römer*. Frankfurt am Main.

Rald, U. 1994, 'The Roman swords from Danish bog finds', *JRMES* 5, 227–41.

Ramage, N.H. and Ramage, A. 1995, *Roman Art*. 2nd edn. London.

Raven, S. 1993, *Rome in Africa*. 3rd edn. Routledge.

Rea, J. 1984, *The Oxyrhyncus Papyri, LI*. Oxford.

Rebuffat, R. 1992, 'Maximien en Afrique', *Klio* 74, 371–9.

Reece, R. 1973, 'Roman coinage in the western Roman Empire', *Britannia* 4, 227–92.

—— 1981a, 'The third century: crisis or change?' in King and Henig 1981, 27–38.

—— 1981b, 'Coinage and currency in the third century', in King and Henig 1981, 79–125.

Rémondon, R. 1964, *La Crise de l'Empire Romain de Marc-Aurèle a Dioclétien*, Paris: Presses Universitaires de France.

Reynolds, P.K.B. 1926, *The Vigiles of Imperial Rome*. Oxford University Press.

Rich, J. (ed.) 1992, *The City in Late Antiquity*. London: Routledge.

Richmond, I.A.R. 1930, *The City Wall of Imperial Rome*. Oxford.

Rickman, G. 1980, *The Corn Supply of Ancient Rome*. Oxford: Clarendon Press.

Ridley, R.T. see under Zosimus in ancient sources.

Rilinger, R. 1988, *Humiliores–Honestiores: zu einer sozialen Dichotomie im Strafrecht der römischen Kaiserzeit*. Munich: R. Oldenburg Verlag.

Rivet, A.L.F. 1988, *Gallia Narbonensis*. London: Batsford.

Robert, L. 1977, 'La titulature de Nicée et de Nicomédie: la gloire et la haine', *HSCPh* 87, 1–39.

Robinson, O.F. 1997, *Sources of Roman Law: problems and methods for ancient historians*. London: Routledge.

Roblin, M. 1951, 'Cités ou citadelles: les enceintes romaines du Bas-Empire d'aprés l'example de Paris', *REA* 53, 300–11.

—— 1965, 'Cités ou citadelles: les enceintes romaines du Bas-Empire d'aprés l'example de Senlis', *REA* 67, 368–91.

Rome Faces the Barbarian: 1000 years to create an Empire. Exhibition at the Abbaye of Daoulas, 19 June to 26 September 1993.

Rostovtzeff, M.I. 1943, 'Res Gestae Divi Saporis and Dura', *Berytus* 8, 17–60.

—— 1957, *Social and Economic History of the Roman Empire*. 2nd edn. Oxford: Clarendon Press.

Roueché, Ch. 1989, *Aphrodisias in Late Antiquity*. London.

Rougé, J. 1966a, 'L'Histoire Auguste et l'Isaurie au IVe siècle', *REA* 68, 282–315.

—— 1966b, *Recherches sur l'Organisation du Commerce Maritime en Méditérannée*. Paris.

—— 1992, 'L'abdication de Dioclétien et la proclamation des Césars; degré de fiabilité du récit de Lactance', in *Institutions, Société et Vie Politique dans l'Empire Romain au IVe Siècle ap. J.C.* Rome, 76–89.

Rowlands, M. *et al.* (eds) 1987, *Centre and Periphery in the Ancient World*. Cambridge.

Rubin, Z. 1975, 'Dio, Herodian and Severus' second Parthian war', *Chiron* 5, 419–41.

—— 1980, *Civil War, Propaganda and Historiography*. Collection Latomus 173. Brussels.

Runciman, W.G. 1982, 'Origins of states', *Comparative Studies in Society and History* 24, 351–77.

Sablayrolles, R. 1996, *Libertinus Miles: Les Cohortes de Vigiles*. Ecole Française de Rome.

Sakar, V. 1970, *Roman Imports in Bohemia*. Fontes Archeologici Pragenses vol. 14. Prague.

Salama, P. 1953, 'Nouveaux témoignages de l'oeuvre des Sévères en Maurétanie Césarienne (première partie)', *Libyca* 1, 231–61.

—— 1955, 'Nouveaux témoignages de l'oeuvre des Sévères en Maurétanie Césarienne (deuxième partie)', *Libyca* 3, 329–67.

—— 1977, 'Les déplacements successifs du limes en Maurétanie Césarienne (essai de synthèse)', *Limes: Akten des XI Internationalen Limeskongresses, Budapest 1976*. Budapest, 577–97.

Salamon, M. 1971, 'The chronology of the Gothic incursions into Asia Minor in the third century AD', *Eos* 59, 110–39.

Saller, P. 1980, 'Promotion and personal patronage in equestrian careers', *JRS* 70, 44–59.

Salmon, P. 1974, *Population et Dépopulation dans l'Empire Romain*. Collection Latomus Vol. 137. Brussels.

Salway, P. 1991, *Roman Britain*. Oxford University Press.

—— 1993, *Oxford Illustrated Roman Britain*. Oxford University Press.

Sarnowski, T. 1991, 'Barbaricum und ein Bellum Bosporanum in einer Inschrift aus Preslav', *ZPE* 87, 137–44.

Sasel, J. 1983, 'Dolichenus Heiligtum in praetorium Latobicorum (Caracalla, Caesar, Imperator destinatus)', *ZPE* 50, 203–8.

Sasse, Chr. 1958, *Die Constitutio Antoniniana: eine Untersuchung über den Umfang der Bürgerrechtsverleihung auf Grund der P. Giss. 40,1*. Wiesbaden.

Sauer, E. 1998, 'M. Annius Florianus: ein Drei-Monate-Kaiser und die ihm zu Ehren aufgestellten Steinmonumente (276 n. Chr.)', *Historia* 47, 174–203.

Saumagne, Ch. 1962, 'La persécution de Dèce en Afrique d'après la correspondance de S. Cyprien', *Byzantion* 1962, 1–9.

Saunders, R.T. 1992, 'Aurelian's two Juthungian wars', *Historia* 41, 311–27.

Saxer, R. 1967, 'Untersuchungen zu den Vexillationen des römischen Kaiserheeres von Augustus bis Diokletian', *Ep. Stud.* 1.

Scardigli, B. 1976, 'Die gotisch-römischen Beziehungen im 3. und 4. Jahrhundert n. Chr.: ein Forschungsbericht 1950–1970', *ANRW* II.5.1, 200–85.

Schlumberger, D. 1943, 'Les gentilices romains des Palmyréniens', *Bulletin d'Etudes Orientales* 9 (1942–3), 53–82.

Schmidt, B. 1983, 'Die Alamannen', in Krüger 1983, 336–60.

Schneider, E. 1993, *Septimia Zenobia Sebaste*. Berlin.

Schönberger, H. von, 1964, 'Die Römerkastell Künzing Grabung 1962', *Saalburg Jahrbuch* 21, 1963–4, 46–8.

Schönberger, H. von, 1969, 'The Roman Frontier in Germany: an archaeological survey', *JRS* 59, 144–97.

Schönberger, H. von, 1985, 'Die römische Truppenlager der frühen und mittleren Kaiserzeit zwischen Nordsee und Inn', *BRGK* 66, 321–497.

Schwartz, J. 1953, 'Les Palmyréniens et l'Egypte', *Bulletin de la Société archéologique d'Alexandrie* 40, 63–81.

—— 1966, 'L'Histoire Auguste et Palmyre', *HAC 1964–1965*, 185–95.

—— 1974, 'Autour de l'humiliation de Galère', in *Mélanges d'Histoire Ancienne offerts à William Seston*. Paris, 463–6.

—— 1976, 'Palmyre et l'opposition à Rome en Egypte', in *Palmyre: Bilan et Perspectives*. Strasbourg, 139–51.

—— 1983, 'De bon usage des Historiographes', in Frézouls 1983, 2–3.

Seston, W. 1940, 'De l'authenticité et de la date de l'édit de Dioclétien contre les Manichéens', in *Mélanges de Philologie, de Littérature et d'Histoire Anciennes Offerts à Alfred Ernout*. Paris, 345–54.

—— 1946, *Dioclétien et le Tétrarchie: guerres et réformes*. Paris: Boccard.

Shaw, B.D. 1982, 'Eaters of flesh, drinkers of milk: ancient Mediterranean ideology of the pastoral nomad', *Ancient Society* 13, 5–31.

—— 1984, 'Bandits in the Roman Empire', *Past and Present* 105, 3–52.

Sherwin-White, A.N. 1973a, *The Roman Citizenship*. 2nd edn. Oxford.

—— 1973b, 'The *Tabula* of Banasa and the *Constitutio Antoniniana*', *JRS* 63, 86–98.

Shiel, N. 1977, *The Episode of Carausius and Allectus*. Oxford: BAR 40.

Shotter, D. 1996, *The Roman Frontier in Britain: Hadrian's Wall, the Antonine Wall, and Roman policy in the north*. Preston: Carnegie Publishing.

Simpson, C.J. 1977a, '*Laeti* in northern Gaul: a note on *Pan. Lat.* VIII, 21', *Latomus* 36, 169–70.

—— 1977b, 'Julian and the *laeti*: a note on Ammianus Marcellinus XX, 8,13', *Latomus* 36, 519–21.

Siniscalco, P. 1974, *Massimiliano: un obiettore di coscienza nel tardo impero*. Turin.

Sirks, B. 1991. *Food for Rome*. Amsterdam: J.C. Gieben.

Smith, R.E. 1972a, 'The army reforms of Septimius Severus', *Historia* 21, 481–99.

—— 1972b, '*Dux, praepositus*', *ZPE* 36, 263–78.

Sotgiu, G. 1961, *Studi sull'epigrafia di Aureliano*. Palermo.

Southern, P. 1989, 'The Numeri of the Roman Imperial army', *Britannia* 20, 81–140.

Southern, P. and Dixon, K.R. 1996, *The Late Roman Army*. London.

Speidel, M. 1977, The Roman army in Arabia', *ANRW* II.8, 687–730.

—— 1979, '*Agens sacro comitatu*', *ZPE* 33, 183–4 = 1984, 397–8.

—— 1982, 'Legionary cohorts in Mauretania: the role of legionary cohorts in expeditionary armies', *ANRW* II.10.2, 850–60 = 1984, 65–75.

—— 1984, *Roman Army Studies I*. Amsterdam.

—— 1986, 'Maxentius and his Equites Singulares in the battle of the Milvian Bridge', *Classical Antiquity* 5, 253–62.

—— 1988, 'Les prétoriens de Maxence. Les cohortes palatines romaines', *MEFRA* 100, 183–6 = 1992, 385–9.

—— 1992, *Roman Army Studies II*. Stuttgart.

—— 1993, 'Commodus the God-Emperor and the army', *JRS* 83, 109–14.

Sprengling, M. 1953, *Third Century Iran*. Chicago.

Stehlin, K. 1957, *Die Spätrömischen Wachttürme am Rhein von Basel bis zum Bodensee*. I: *Untere Strecke von Basel bis Zurzach*. Basel.

Sterzl, A. 1978, *Der Untergang Roms an Rhein und Mosel*. Cologne: Greven Verlag.

Stevenson, J. 1987, *A New Eusebius: documents illustrating the history of the Church to AD 337*. London: SPCK (rev. edn).

Strobel, K. 1993, *Das Imperium Romanum im 3. Jahrhundert: Modell eine historische Krise?* Stuttgart: Franz Steiner Verlag.

Swift, L.J. 1966, 'The Anonymous Ancomium of Philip the Arab', *Greek, Roman and Byzantine Studies* 7, 268–89.

Sydenham, E.A. 1934, 'The vicissitudes of Maximian after his abdication', *NC* 5th series 14, 237–53.

Syme, R. 1968, *Ammianus and the Historia Augusta*. Oxford.

—— 1970, 'Three jurists', *Historia Augusta Colloquium 1969–70*. Bonn, 309–23.

—— 1971a, *Emperors and Biography*. Oxford.

—— 1971b, *The Historia Augusta: a call for clarity*. Bonn.

—— 1980, 'Fictions about jurists', *ZSS* 97, 78–104.

—— 1983, *Historia Augusta Papers*. Oxford.

Theodoridès, A. 1947, 'Les XXviri consulares ex S.C. reipublicae curandae en 238 de notre ère', *Latomus* 6, 31–43.

Thomasson, B. 1960, *Die Statthalter der römischen Provinzen Nordafrikas von Augustus bis Diocletianus*. Lund.

—— 1984, *Laterculi Praesidium* I. Göteborg.

Thompson, E.A. 1966, *The Visigoths in the Time of Wulfila*. Oxford.

—— 1982, *Romans and Barbarians: the decline of the Western Empire*. Madison: University of Wisconsin Press.

Thylander, H. 1973, '*Senatus militia vetuit et adire exercitum*', *Opuscula Romana* 8, 67–71.

Todd, M. 1978, *The Walls of Rome*. London: Elek.

—— 1992, *The Early Germans*. Blackwell.

Tomlin, R. 1987, 'The army of the late Empire', in Wacher 1987, 107–35.

Trousset, P. 1974, *Recherches sur le 'limes Tripolitanus' du chott el-Djerid à la frontière tuniso-libyenne*. Paris.

Trout, D.E. 1989, 'Victoria Redux and the first year of the reign of Philip the Arab', *Chiron* 19, 221–33.

Turcan, R. 1969, 'Le délit des monétaires rebellés contre Aurélien', *Latomus* 28, 948ff.

—— 1978, 'La culte impériale au IIIe siècle', *ANRW* II.16.2, 996–1084.

Tyler, P. 1975, *The Persian War of the Third Century AD and Roman Imperial Monetary Policy*. Historia Einzelschriften Heft 23. Wiesbaden.

Unz, C. (ed.) 1986, *Studien zu den Militärgrenzen Roms III*. Stuttgart: Theiss.

Vallet, F. and Kazansky, M. (eds) 1993, *L'Armée Romaine et les Barbares du IIIe au VIIe siècle*. Association Française d'Archéologie Merovingienne et Musée des Antiquités Nationales.

van Berchem, D. 1937, 'L'annone militaire', *Mémoires de la Société Nationale des Antiquaires de France* X, 117–201.

—— 1952, *L'Armée de Dioclétien et la Réforme Constantinienne*. Paris: Imprimerie Nationale.

—— 1977a, 'Armée de frontière et armée de manoeuvre: alternative stratégique ou politique?', *Studien zu den Militärgrenzen Roms II: Vorträge des 10 Int. Limeskongresses in der Germania Inferior*. Cologne: Rheinland-Verlag, 541–3.

—— 1977b, 'L'annone militaire est-ell un mythe?', in *Armées et Fiscalité dans le Monde Antique. Paris 14–16.10.1976*. CNRS, 331–9.

van Es, W.A. 1965, 'Wijster: a native village beyond the Imperial frontier', *Palaeohistoria* 11, 29ff.

Vanden Berghe, L. 1984, *Reliefs Rupestres de l'Iran Ancien ver 2000av. J.C.–7e siècle après J.C.* Brussels: Musées Royaux d'Art et d'Histoire.

Visy, Z. 1977, *Intercisa: Dunaujváros in the Roman period*. Corvina.

Vitucci, G. 1952. *L'Imperatore Probo*. Rome.

Vogt, J. 1967, *The Decline of Rome: the metamorphosis of ancient civilization*. London: Weidenfeld and Nicolson; reprinted 1993.

Wacher, J. 1987, *The Roman World*. London: Routledge, 2 vols.

Wagner, J. 1983, 'Provinciae Osrhoenae: new archaeological finds illustrating the military organisation under the Severan dynasty', in Mitchell 1983, 103–29.

Walbank, F.W. 1969, *The Awful Revolution: the decline of the Roman Empire in the West*. Liverpool University Press.

Walker, S. 1981, 'The burden of Roman grandeur; aspects of public building in cities of Asia and Achaea', in King and Henig 1981, 189–97.

Walser, G. and Pekáry, T. 1962, *Die Krise des Römischen Reiches: Bericht über die Forschung zur Geschichte des 3. Jahrhunderts (193–284 n. Chr.) von 1939 bis 1959*. Berlin: de Gruyter.

Wardman, A. 1984, 'Usurpers and internal conflicts in the fourth century AD', *Historia* 33, 220–37.

Warmington, B.H. 1953, Review of van Berchem 1952, *JRS* 43, 173–5.

—— 1954, *The North African Provinces from Diocletian to the Vandal Conquest*. Cambridge.

Watson, G.R. 1969, *The Roman Soldier*. London: Thames and Hudson.

Welles, C.B. 1941, 'The epitaph of Julius Terentius', *Harvard Theol. Review* 34, 79–102.

—— 1959, *Excavations at Dura-Europos: final report V part I: the parchments and papyri*. New Haven: Yale University Press.

Wenskus, R. 1961, *Stammesbildung und Verfassung*. Cologne (2nd edn 1977).

Werner, J. 1973, 'Bemerkungen zur mitteldeutschen Skelettgräbergruppe Hassleben-Leuna', *Mitteldeutsche Forschungen* 74.1, 1–30.

White, L. 1966, *The Transformation of the Roman World*. Berkeley: University of California Press.

White, P. 1967, 'The authorship of the Historia Augusta', *JRS* 57, 115–33.

Whittaker, C.R. 1969, *Herodian* Books I–IV (trans. and notes). Cambridge, Mass.: Harvard University Press.

—— 1970, *Herodian* Books V–VIII (trans. and notes). Cambridge, Mass.: Harvard University Press.

—— 1978, 'Land and labour in North Africa', *Klio* 60, 331–62.

—— 1982, 'Labour supply in the later Roman Empire', *Opus* 1, 161–70.

—— 1983a, 'Late Roman trade and traders', in Garnsey *et al.* 1983, 163–80.

—— 1983b, Trade and frontiers of the Roman Empire', in Garnsey and Whittaker 1983, 110–25.

—— 1989, 'Supplying the system: frontiers and beyond', in Barrett *et al.* 1989, 64–80.

—— 1994, *Frontiers of the Roman Empire*. Baltimore: Johns Hopkins University Press.

—— 1981 'The fate of Gallo-Roman villages in the third century', in King and Henig 1981, 235–44.

Wightman, E. 1981, 'The fate of Galio-Roman villages in the third century', in King and Henig 1981, 235–44.

—— 1985, *Gallia Belgica*. London: Batsford.

Wild, J.P. 1976, 'Loanwords and Roman expansion in north-west Europe', *World Archaeology* 8, 57–64.

Wilkes, J. 1969, *Dalmatia*. London: Routledge.

—— 1993, *Diocletian's Palace, Split*. Oxford new edn. Originally published Sheffield, 1986.

Will, E. 1992, *Les Palmyréniens: la Venise des sables*. Paris.

Williams, S. 1985, *Diocletian and the Roman Recovery*. London: Batsford; reprinted 1997 by Routledge.

Williamson, G.A. 1989, see under Eusebius in ancient sources.

Winkelmann, F. 1926, *Katalogue West- und Süd-deutscher Altertumssammlungen IV*. Berlin.

Winter, E. 1988, *Die Sasanidischen-römischen Friedensverträge des 3. Jahrhundertsn.Chr.: ein Beitrag zum Verständnis der aussenpolitischen Beziehungen zwischen den beiden Grossmächten.* Frankfurt am Main: Peter Lang.

—— 1989, 'On the regulation of the eastern frontier of the Roman Empire in 298', in French and Lightfoot 1989, 555–71.

Wolff, H. 1978, *Die Constitutio Antoniniana und Papyrus Gissensis 40, 1.* Cologne.

Wolfram, H. 1988, *History of the Goths.* Berkeley, University of California Press.

—— 1997, *The Roman Empire and its Germanic Peoples.* Berkeley: University of California Press.

Wolfram, H. and Pohl, W. (eds) 1990, *Typen der Ethnogenese.* DsÖAW 201, Vienna.

Zollner, E. 1970, *Geschichte der Franken bis zur Mitte des sechsten Jahrhunderts.* Munich: Verlag C.H. Beck.

Zuckerman, C. 1994, 'Les campaigns des Tetrarches 296–298: note de chronologie', *AT* 2, 65–70.

—— 1998, 'Sur le dispositif frontalier en Arménie, le limes et son évolution, sous le Bas-Empire', *Historia* 47, 108–28.

INDEX